HEAVEN ON EARTH

HEAVEN ON EARTH

TEMPLES, RITUAL, AND COSMIC SYMBOLISM IN THE ANCIENT WORLD

edited by

DEENA RAGAVAN

with contributions by

Claus Ambos, John Baines, Gary Beckman, Matthew Canepa,
Davíd Carrasco, Elizabeth Frood, Uri Gabbay, Susanne Görke,
Ömür Harmanşah, Julia A. B. Hegewald, Clemente Marconi,
Michael W. Meister, Tracy Miller, Richard Neer, Deena Ragavan,
Betsey A. Robinson, Yorke M. Rowan, and Karl Taube

Papers from the Oriental Institute Seminar

Heaven on Earth

Held at the Oriental Institute of the University of Chicago

2–3 March 2012

THE ORIENTAL INSTITUTE OF THE UNIVERSITY OF CHICAGO
ORIENTAL INSTITUTE SEMINARS • NUMBER 9
CHICAGO, ILLINOIS

Library of Congress Control Number: 2013938227
ISBN-13: 978-1-885923-96-7
ISBN-10: 1-885923-96-1
ISSN: 1559-2944

The Oriental Institute, Chicago

THE UNIVERSITY OF CHICAGO
ORIENTAL INSTITUTE SEMINARS • NUMBER 9

Series Editors

Leslie Schramer

and

Thomas G. Urban

with the assistance of

Rebecca Cain, Zuhal Kuru, and Tate Paulette

Publication of this volume was made possible through generous funding
from the Arthur and Lee Herbst Research and Education Fund

Cover Illustration:
Tablet of Shamash (detail). Gray schist. Sippar, southern Iraq. Babylonian,
early 9th century B.C.E. British Museum BM 91000–04

Printed by McNaughton & Gunn, Saline, Michigan

The paper used in this publication meets the minimum requirements of
American National Standard for Information Services — Permanence of
Paper for Printed Library Materials, ANSI Z39.48-1984.

∞

TABLE OF CONTENTS

PREFACE

The present volume is the result of the eighth annual University of Chicago Oriental Institute Seminar, held in Breasted Hall on Friday, March 2, and Saturday, March 3, 2012. Over the course of the two days, seventeen speakers, from both the United States and abroad, examined the interconnections among temples, ritual, and cosmology from a variety of regional specializations and theoretical perspectives. Our eighteenth participant, Julia Hegewald, was absent due to unforeseen circumstances, but fortunately her contribution still appears as part of this volume.

The 2012 seminar aimed to revisit a classic topic, one with a long history among scholars of the ancient world: the cosmic symbolism of sacred architecture. Bringing together archaeologists, art historians, and philologists working not only in the ancient Near East, but also Mesoamerica, Greece, South Asia, and China, we hoped to re-evaluate the significance of this topic across the ancient world. The program comprised six sessions, each of which focused on the different ways the main themes of the seminar could interact. The program was organized thematically, to encourage scholars of different regional or methodological specializations to communicate and compare their work. The two-day seminar was divided into two halves, each half culminating in a response to the preceding papers. This format, with some slight rearrangement, is followed in the present work.

Our goal was to share ideas and introduce new perspectives in order to equip scholars with new questions or theoretical and methodological tools. The topic generated considerable interest and enthusiasm in the academic community, both at the Oriental Institute and more broadly across the University of Chicago, as well as among members of the general public. The free exchange of ideas and, more importantly, the wide range of perspectives offered left each of us with potential avenues of research and new ideas, as well as a fresh outlook on our old ones.

I'd like to express my gratitude to all those who have contributed so much of their time and energy to ensuring this seminar and volume came together. In particular, I'd like to thank Gil Stein, the Director of the Oriental Institute, for this wonderful opportunity, and Chris Woods, for his guidance through the whole process. Thanks also to Theo van den Hout, Andrea Seri, Christopher Faraone, Walter Farber, Bruce Lincoln, and Janet Johnson, for chairing the individual sessions of the conference. I'd like to thank all the staff of the Oriental Institute, including Steve Camp, D'Ann Condes, Kristin Derby, Emma Harper, Anna Hill, and Anna Ressman; particular thanks to John Sanders, for the technical support, and Meghan Winston, for coordinating the catering. A special mention must go to Mariana Perlinac, without whom the organization and ultimate success of this seminar would have been impossible. I do not think I can be grateful enough to Tom Urban, Leslie Schramer, and everyone else in the publications office, not only for the beautiful poster and program, but also for all the work they have put into editing and producing this book. Most of all, my thanks go out to all of the participants, whose hard work, insight, and convivial discussion made this meeting and process such a pleasure, both intellectually and personally.

Deena Ragavan

Seminar participants, from left to right: Top row: John Baines, Davíd Carrasco, Susanne Görke;
Middle row: Matthew Canepa, Uri Gabbay, Gary Beckman, Elizabeth Frood, Claus Ambos;
Bottom row: Yorke Rowan, Ömür Harmanşah, Betsey Robinson, Michael Meister, Tracy Miller, Karl
Taube, Clemente Marconi; Front: Deena Ragavan. Not pictured: Julia Hegewald and Richard Neer

HEAVEN ON EARTH:
TEMPLES, RITUAL, AND COSMIC SYMBOLISM
IN THE ANCIENT WORLD

Deena Ragavan, The Oriental Institute

> Just think of religions like those of Egypt, India, or classical antiquity: an impenetrable tangle of many cults that vary with localities, temples, generations, dynasties, invasions, and so on.
>
> — Émile Durkheim, *The Elementary Forms of Religious Life*[1]

Introduction

The image on the cover of this volume is from the sun-god tablet of Nabu-apla-iddina;[2] it depicts in relief the presentation of the king before a cultic statue, a sun disc, the symbol of the god Šamaš. The disc is central to the composition, but to its right, within his shrine, sits the sun god portrayed in archaic fashion. The temple itself is reduced to an abstraction, to its most salient elements: its canopy, a human-headed snake god, perhaps representing the Euphrates River, supported on a date-palm column; below lie the cosmic subterranean waters of the Apsû, punctuated by stars; the major celestial bodies, the sun, moon, and Venus, representations of the gods themselves, mark the space in between. His throne is the gate of sunrise in the eastern mountains, doors held apart by two bison men.

The idea that sacred architecture held cosmic symbolism has a long history in the study of the ancient Near East. From the excavations of the mid-nineteenth century to the scholars of the early twentieth century, we see repeated the notion that the Mesopotamian ziggurat reflected the form of the cosmos. Inevitably, the question of ritual was drawn in. The cult centers of the ancient world were the prime location and focus of ritual activity. Temples and shrines were not constructed in isolation, but existed as part of what may be termed a ritual landscape, where ritualized movement within individual buildings, temple complexes, and the city as a whole shaped their function and meaning. Together, ritual practice and temple topography provide evidence for the conception of the temple as a reflection, or embodiment, of the cosmos. Even among the earlier works on sacred architecture, the topic encouraged a comparative perspective. In the light of substantial research across fields

---

[1] Durkheim 1912 (abridged and translated 2001), p. 7.
[2] The interpretation of the relief that follows is based largely on Christopher Woods's comprehensive article, "The Sun-God Tablet of Nabû-apla-iddina Revisited" (2004).

and regional specializations, this volume is an attempt to revitalize this conversation. This seminar series is, I feel, based on a desire to re-open the often too self-contained field of ancient Near Eastern studies to external and comparative perspectives. In keeping with this motivation, I hope that this book will contribute to galvanizing this avenue of research in both directions, encouraging Near Eastern scholars to look outward, as well as encouraging scholars of all regions of the ancient world to once again consider the "Cradle of Civilization" with respect to their own field.

In this Introduction, I would like to first sketch an outline of this particular idea's path through the history of my own discipline, Assyriology,[3] before assessing the framework on which this volume rests.

History: Out of Babylon

In 1861, after excavations at Birs Nimrud, ancient Borsippa, a site in central Mesopotamia a little to the south of Babylon, Henry Rawlinson connected the painted colors on the staged tower he had found with the colors assigned to the different planets in the Sabaean system.[4] He announced:

> we have, in the ruin at the Birs, an existing illustration of the seven-walled and seven-coloured Ecbatana of Herodotus, or what we may term a quadrangular representation of the old circular Chaldaean planisphere ... Nebuchadnezzar, towards the close of his reign, must have rebuilt seven distinct stages, one upon the other, symbolical of the concentric circles of the seven spheres, and each coloured with the peculiar tint which belonged to the ruling planet.[5]

Although Rawlinson's interpretation of the ziggurat at Borsippa has been shown to be quite flawed,[6] the idea that sacred buildings might represent parts of the cosmos persisted.

Following the decipherment of cuneiform, the study of Mesopotamia became increasingly a philological venture, making it possible to offer new interpretations of excavated sites and materials based on the words of the inhabitants. Writing at the end of the nineteenth century, Morris Jastrow understood the Babylonian ziggurat as "an attempt to reproduce the shape of the earth" which, together with a basin representing the underground fresh waters (*abzu*, *apsû*), became "living symbols of the current cosmological conceptions."[7] His view rested upon the idea that the Mesopotamian cosmos took the form of a mountain, a possibility raised just a few years earlier by another scholar, Peter Jensen, who had observed the correlation between mountains and temples in Mesopotamia and compared it with the existence of the "world-mountain" (Mount Meru) of Indian mythology.[8]

---

[3] This path has been mapped before; in particular, the abbreviated story of Eliade and his predecessors presented here owes a great deal to Frank J. Korom's "Of Navels and Mountains: A Further Inquiry into the History of an Idea" (1992), as well as the writings of Jonathan Z. Smith, as cited throughout.

[4] The connection between the colors and the planets had already been posited by Rawlinson twenty years earlier (Rawlinson 1840, pp. 127–28; James and van der Sluijs 2008, pp. 57–58).

[5] Rawlinson 1861, p. 18.

[6] James and van der Sluijs 2008.

[7] Jastrow 1898, p. 653.

[8] Jensen 1890, pp. 208–11. On Jensen as the originator of this comparison, see Korom 1992, p. 109. Despite the similar timing and subject matter of their work, Jensen was simply a contemporary, rather than a member of the pan-Babylonian school (Parpola 2004, p. 238).

Another deeply flawed theory was this idea of the Mesopotamian world-mountain, or *Weltberg*, the German term by which it was more popularly known.[9] Still, it became widespread among a small, but prolific, group of scholars through the early years of the twentieth century. These scholars, the so-called pan-Babylonians, motivated by Friedrich Delitzsch's lectures on *Bibel und Babel* and the overt influence of Mesopotamian culture on ancient Israel, extended his conclusions and in so doing sought Mesopotamian influence everywhere. Spearheaded by one Alfred Jeremias, these scholars took it upon themselves to draw comparisons between Mesopotamian mythology, and especially cosmology, and those of many other cultures, from Egypt to India. The pan-Babylonian movement soon encountered considerable resistance from within the field of Assyriology, which opted, in the early twentieth century, to turn its gaze largely inward, maintaining its distance from interdisciplinary endeavors in the study of Mesopotamian religion.[10]

Although the precedence of the comparative approach receded from Assyriology, the challenge was taken up by another discipline. It is from this group that we come to a scholar whose reputation endures at the University of Chicago, and whose influential work continues to overshadow any discussion of the cosmic symbolism of sacred architecture: Mircea Eliade.

In 1937, heavily influenced by the pan-Babylonians, and linking Near Eastern sources with Indian traditions, Eliade began to develop his notion of the *axis mundi* — a cosmic axis — communicating with different levels of the universe and located at the center of the world.[11] It is this axis, and various related symbols, such as trees, pillars, and mountains, that in his view temples represent. Closely related, however, and at the heart of the seminar published here, is his concept of *imago mundi*: the idea that architectural forms at any scale can be images, replicas, of the greater cosmos — microcosms of the macrocosm. It is with Eliade's writings, too, that the element of ritual is drawn into the mix, through his correlation between the construction and consecration of sacred places and the creation of the world: rites that construct, demarcate, and enable the occupation of sacred spaces are ritualized cosmogonies, integral to the meaning of places and structures, binding the microcosm to the macrocosm. Like the pan-Babylonians before him, Eliade's concern is mythology, and through it cosmology, using these sources to build an understanding of space and time. Architecture itself is secondary; when it is considered at all it is in conceptual terms, as something constructed, symbolic. But it is in Eliade's writings that we see for the first time united the three overarching themes of this seminar: temple, ritual, and cosmos.

Eliade's theories have since been heavily criticized for their attempts to universalize principles that are specific to certain regions and for his misunderstanding of the various traditions he described. Jonathan Z. Smith, notably, observed his "questionable interpretations"[12] of the Babylonian material in particular and in his subsequent work took more focused aim at Eliade.[13] Eliade's approach has been often viewed as fundamentally lacking

---

[9] For its flaws see Korom 1992; Smith 1987; and Clifford 1972.

[10] Parpola lays a large part of the responsibility for "effectively paralys[ing] interdisciplinary study of Mesopotamian religion" at the door of Benno Landsberger (2004, p. 240) and his enormously influential 1926 essay, "Die Eigenbegrifflichkeit der babylonischen Welt" (translated in 1976 as "The Conceptual Autonomy of the Babylonian World").

[11] Eliade reiterated and elaborated on these notions across several of his works, beginning in 1937 with *Cosmologie și alchimie babiloniană*; they reached their clearest expression in *The Sacred and the Profane* (1959, esp. pp. 37–39).

[12] Smith 1972, p. 144.

[13] On the Near Eastern material, see especially Smith 1987, pp. 13–23.

in historical context or key theoretical underpinnings.[14] A recent, severe critique, by Daniel Dubuisson, emerging from a conference held at the University of Chicago on the legacies of Wach and Eliade, condemned the latter's writings as empty rhetoric, unscientific, indistinguishable from a pastiche.[15] Nevertheless, Eliade's ideas linger on in the academic consciousness. The *axis mundi*, *imago mundi*, and symbolism of the center: these Eliade coined, codifying their form and creating shorthand that is familiar to any student of religion.[16]

Given this motley timeline of misunderstandings, careless errors, and dubious comparisons, one might wonder what further merit lies in this topic. Despite these criticisms, some measures have been taken to redeem Eliade's work, with supporters arguing that elements may yet be valuable.[17] Even Dubuisson relents somewhat, observing that Eliade "was bold enough to build bridges between academic culture, the Orient, the primitives, and prehistory."[18] Indeed, Eliade explicitly expressed fears that "the History of Religions will be endlessly fragmented and the fragments reabsorbed in the different philologies."[19]

And to some extent, he was right. If a tendency to generalization and a desire to find common origins was characteristic of the early part of the twentieth century, then the latter half can certainly be said to be governed by increasing academic specialization. The trend among scholars of the ancient world, particularly those concerned with philology, has often tended toward a narrow field of vision.[20] And, due perhaps to an early desire to establish independence and a degree of separation from the study of the biblical world, Assyriology, in this respect, is far from unique.

Fortunately, recent decades have seen both the symbolism of sacred architecture as well as the comparative perspective regaining interest often informed by the questions of spatiality raised in contemporary sociocultural disciplines. The conception and construction of space and place has been a fundamental preoccupation of twentieth century scholarship.[21] Space may be understood through a variety models: from the mathematical spaces described by Euclid or Newton, to the symbolic conceptualization of sacred topographies and cosmic models, to physical space as it is inhabited by and relates to the human body.[22] A key work in this regard is Henri Lefebvre's *The Production of Space* (1991), which demonstrated the dynamic nature of space, producing and produced by the social order.

With regard to the ancient world, by adopting and adapting phenomenological and sociocultural approaches to space, the post-processualist archaeologists have been eager to embrace the question of the subjective experience of architecture, landscape, and space, emphasizing qualities such as memory, power, and ritual.[23] Working in the ancient Near

---

[14] Allen (1988) and Jones (2000, vol. 2, p. 349 n. 36) provide a useful summary of many the arguments of Eliade's detractors.

[15] Dubuisson 2010, p. 138.

[16] In addition, see Davíd Carrasco's essay in this volume.

[17] Allen 1988; Studstill 2000.

[18] Dubuisson 2010, p. 145.

[19] Eliade 1965, p. 17. See Alles 1988, p. 109, and Smith 2001, pp. 139–40, for further comment on this line of thinking.

[20] Smith's more recent work reflects an acute consciousness of these concerns, noting that "[t]o a de-

gree, this has occurred, and has brought with it a new ethos of particularism that challenges the global ambitions which, from time to time, have animated the field. But, more can be said" (2001, p. 140).

[21] As observed notably by Michel Foucault in a 1967 lecture (Foucault 2002).

[22] In general, see Gehlen 1998.

[23] Wilkinson (2003, pp. 4ff.) provides a useful review of post-processualism as a reaction to positivism and its impact on landscape archaeology specifically.

East, Wilkinson highlights the need for an integration of phenomenological and functionalist approaches to archaeological landscapes, emphasizing the accumulated features, layers, and meanings of a place.[24] Such an integrated approach is increasingly evident in recent comparative enquiries into the relationship between architecture and the social order,[25] and the experience of sacred architecture in particular.[26] Nor has the correlation between cultic topography and cosmic order been neglected in the ancient Near East, with a contribution in this regard by Beate Pongratz-Leisten, who marks a distinction between mythologized and ritualized space in Mesopotamia.[27] Most useful of all, Lindsay Jones, mustering an array of methodological approaches in his *Hermeneutics of Sacred Architecture* (2000), appeals for the consideration of sacred architecture in terms of "ritual-architectural events."

This volume, then, seeks to be part of this conversation, asking broadly how ritual mediates between two types of space: the physical, inhabited space defined through architecture, archaeological remains, or visual or textual descriptions; and the symbolic space of the cosmos, sacred topographies conceptualized in myths, narratives, and art.

Themes: Temples — Ritual — Cosmos

The fundamental basis of this volume is the interaction among three intertwining themes: sacred architecture (which by its nature shapes and delimits sacred space), ritual practice, and cosmology. While each of these subjects is worthy of study by itself, I would argue that they are best approached together, rather than independently. The diversity of the disciplines represented here has resulted in considerable disparity among theoretical and methodological approaches. In order to mitigate this somewhat, I would like to first introduce the papers themselves by looking briefly at the variation in how they address these three main themes.

Temples: Architecture and Space

One inevitable problem is the identification and definition of sacred architecture and space: what is a temple? Each paper offers diverging examples — some dramatically different, others only subtly so: from the monumental architecture of classic "temples" (Hegewald, Taube), often homes to divinities, to open-air settings for ritual activities (Canepa, Robinson). Permanent structures of lasting materials, brick and stone — some shrines even hewn from the mountainside itself (Beckman, Meister) — inevitably dominate given the antiquity of the sources, but evidence of transitory forms and perishable materials still emerges (Baines, Ambos). In many cases, the approach to the whole is mediated through smaller structural elements, such as gates (Ragavan), and often decorative features, such as relief, painting, or

---

[24] Wilkinson 2003, p. 6. Especially relevant is the example he gives of the ritual sacrifice of an animal prior to the first use of a well, which "does not imply that the monument itself was 'ritual', rather that it was deemed necessary to enact a ritual before such a feature was inaugurated."

[25] For example, Parker, Pearson, and Richards 1994; Maran et al. 2009.

[26] Wescoat and Ousterhout 2012.

[27] For Pongratz-Leisten, mythologized space describes the cosmological and mythological associations of features of the urban and natural landscape, while ritualized space is that made sacred through the performance of rituals and processions (1994, pp. 13–16). The other major work on cultic topography in Mesopotamia is George 1992.

sculpture (Frood, Marconi). Architectures are present in every form and at every scale. Tracy Miller's paper, notably, features a free-standing architectural form, a pillar, which incorporates a sculpture of a ritual building. The range of forms at issue here attests to the multi-layered accumulation of meaning that must be addressed before we are able to incorporate questions of ritual and cosmos.

Many of the papers are less concerned with the physical structures themselves than with the space to which they relate, that contained within them, and often around them. Some contributions trace topographies around and through large-scale complexes (Görke) and beyond into the urban and surrounding environment (Gabbay). The expansion beyond designated sacred areas into the architectonics of the city itself is also considered (Harmanşah). It is Yorke Rowan's paper, however, that really emphasizes the critical nature of ritual in regard to space. In contrast with many of the other essays, Rowan, working in a prehistoric context with only the archaeological record, and without the indicators that explicit textual evidence can provide, is concerned with the more fundamental question of how to identify and define sacred space. For Rowan, sacred space is space in which ritual is performed. The papers highlight the lack of clear distinction between sacred and profane space, as many of the spaces and buildings have multiple values, both functional and subjective, and through the focus on ritual we create a lens for one particular subjective experience of space.

Ritual: Religion and Performance

At this point, the importance of ritual to this topic should be evident — the inseparability of ritual and place. Smith argued that "[r]itual is ... a mode of paying attention" and "as a fundamental component of ritual: place directs attention."[28] Just as place is fundamental to ritual, so is ritual fundamental to our conception of sacred space. It is unclear that one may see a building as possessing any inherent significance — one, or many, meanings that may be extrapolated if one makes the correct calculations. Rather, the meaning of a space or structure is dependent on its context: how it was formed, used, and re-used. Above all, the significance, or experience, of a place as sacred is mediated through ritual activity. As Kathleen Ashley put it in her introduction to a volume on art and ritual,[29]

> ritual is performance that often directs the gaze of its participants toward focal artworks that are constituted through ritual action for ritual performance in that context. The relation between them is not unidirectional (art *used in* ritual) but reciprocal; ritual creates its artworks while the art or architecture also enables ritual activity.

Performance theory as a theory of ritual is somewhat flawed, due, in part at least, to the presumption that it is intended to affect and be interpreted by an audience.[30] Catherine Bell avoids postulating another theory of ritual, but instead prefers the term "ritualization," as "a way of acting that is designed and orchestrated to distinguish and privilege what is being done in comparison to other, usually more quotidian, activities" (Bell 1992, p. 74). Nevertheless, this performative aspect of ritual is central to many of the papers in this volume. Given

---

[28] Smith 1987, p. 103.
[29] Ashley 1992, p. 10.

[30] For a more complete overview of the critiques, see Bell 1992, p. 42–46.

the vast distance in time between the studies and their subjects,[31] direct observation is mostly impossible. The character and form of ritual acts must be inferred, typically in conjunction with other sources, in addition to the structures and spaces under discussion. Some contributors are fortunate to have detailed, prescriptive documents, describing ritual participants, words, and actions (Ambos, Görke); others focus on the words and liturgies, mindful of their use in historical context (Gabbay). The often laconic, but abundant, administrative records can provide remarkable insight into offerings and sacrifices, through the practical accounting of religion: rites and festivals reduced to expenditures of sheep and oil (Canepa, Ragavan). Images allow us to look at the performers of rites (Baines, Marconi), while artifacts suggest the acts and activities performed (Baines, Rowan).

If ritual is a type of performance, what, then, of religion? The bias of the sources is evident: the narrative most provide is the dominant one, that of the state religion, the official cult.[32] This is emphasized in many cases by the figure of the central ritual performer: the king (Ambos, Baines, Canepa). Just a few, however, hint at the question of personal or domestic religion (Frood, Rowan).

For Durkheim, religion was the combination of belief and ritual. Rappaport took ritual as "the ground from which religious conceptions spring."[33] The Myth and Ritual school of the late nineteenth and early twentieth centuries, notably Sir James Frazer and S. H. Hooke, were strong proponents of the idea that myth emerged from, or provided justification for, ritual activities. By contrast, competing and more current schools of thought see ritual as stemming from myth, or as independent, and that myth is not synonymous with belief. Nevertheless, mythology represents an integral part of any consideration of ancient ritual. Moreover, myths are often fundamental for understanding cosmology (Beckman, Meister, Ragavan).

Cosmos: Universe and Order

Cosmology in the modern, scientific sense is the study of the origin, form, and laws of the universe, commonly used now in the context of astrophysics. The term has its origins in the ancient Greek, describing "order," a well-regulated or harmonious arrangement. By the late Classical period, the term came to be used to mean "world," and thence, "universe, everything." While this semantic shift has been attributed to the idea of everything in its place — meaning the systematic ordering of its parts, the different cosmic regions, celestial, terrestrial, or further adjoining areas — it is in fact extended from a secondary meaning of cosmos as "heaven";[34] nevertheless, this conception of an ordered system of different parts is present in several of the cosmological systems described: from the extraordinarily detailed and complex cosmos of the Jainas (Hegewald), to simpler two- or three-part arrangements (Ambos, Görke, Miller). Incorporated within this sense of cosmology are the elements, forces, and bodies that move through the cosmos, as well as the patterns and paths that they follow

---

[31] With the particular exception being Julia Hegewald's paper, as she is able to draw on more contemporary sources for Jaina practices.

[32] Smith makes the distinction between domestic and national religion or, as he terms them, "here" and "there" (Smith 2004, pp. 325–29), which offers a useful parallel to the dichotomy between state-

sponsored monumental architecture and private dwellings.

[33] Rappaport 1999, p. 3.

[34] For the idea of cosmos as world order, see, e.g., Wright 1995, pp. 3-6; for cosmos as "heaven," see Finkelberg 1998, esp. p. 130; see also Richard Neer's contribution to this volume.

(Ragavan, Gabbay). These include natural phenomena, as well as the observable physical environment: the topography of the earth and features of the landscape (Beckman, Robinson).

Ancient cosmologies explain not only the organization of the universe, but also man's place in it, reiterating, justifying, and establishing the social order (Baines, Harmanşah). In many ways, then, the idea of cosmos as the ordered universe brings us back full circle to conceptions of architecture, which would see the construction of the built environment and the production of space as a means of representing the social order. Both construction and cosmology can be understood as sharing the same purpose, as imposing order.

Interactions

One of the greatest challenges in approaching this topic is the remarkable diversity of fields and disciplines represented. Each paper focuses on its own unique evidentiary traditions — from sculpture to literary text, from building plan to ritual prescription. Nevertheless, we are united in some basic questions: Is there a correspondence between sacred architecture and cosmic geography? Do we find importance attached to replicas of the universe as a whole, or of its parts — the natural world or mythical locations? How do sacred space and ritual practice interact? — That is, how does ritual movement transform and give meaning to space and structures, and how then is that ritual affected by the space it inhabits?

Below, I use these questions to trace one possible path through this volume, outlining a few of the ways in which the three conference themes interact. The organization of the papers could be understood to follow loosely the historical trajectory of the topic mapped out above, beginning with the broad relation between sacred architecture and the cosmos, before foregrounding the importance of ritual and moving to a broader interpretation of space. Although the conference format encouraged a division into short, apparently rigidly categorized sections, the boundaries between them should be understood (and hopefully can be shown) to be rather more permeable.

I. Architecture and Cosmology

As noted above, the cosmic symbolism of sacred architecture has been a productive focus of research across the years and across a range of fields, and it remains so today. This approach would interpret an architectural form, be it a pillar, a room, a building, or a city, as an imitation of all or part of the cosmos. From the broadest perspective, do we find any value in the Eliadean model of the *imago mundi*? Do we see a correspondence between architecture and cosmology?

Each of the first three papers in the volume approaches this question differently. In the first, Tracy Miller investigates the embedded meaning of a Chinese monument, a memorial known as the Yicihui Pillar. From the pillar's axial form to the sculpted Chinese-style Buddhist worship hall at its top, carved with abstract, geometrical representations of the cosmos, the monument certainly recalls Eliade's categories of the *axis mundi* and *imago mundi*. This pillar, she argues, demonstrates the adaptation of South Asian cosmic geometries to generate Chinese architectural forms. The resulting combination serves to amplify existing Chinese architectural and cosmological traditions in the Yicihui Pillar. And while the themes of architecture and cosmos are brought to the fore, the pillar's role as a memorial imbued with hope of reincarnation is not forgotten.

In contrast to the harmonious integration presented above, Susanne Görke suggests that the incursion of foreign cosmologies into Hittite Anatolia had a different transformational effect. Using Hittite ritual texts as her focus, she investigates the relationship between the shape of the Hittites' cosmos and the topography of their temples. In doing so she raises deeper questions about the social order and its expression in ritual tradition, as well as the impact of foreign cosmologies on local traditions. The form of the cosmos represented here is not the abstract geometries of the South and East Asian cosmologies, or the landscapes, real or imagined, described further below, but rather a simple division of the cosmos into two or three parts. She argues that the older traditions reflected a more open, publicly accessible topography, while later foreign-influenced ones required restricted sacred spaces. She suggests that these restrictions, or the lack thereof, were matched by their conception of the universe, in which movement between cosmic realms was either freely permitted or equally constrained.

Julia Hegewald also raises questions of access and entrance. For the Jainas, cosmographic representations are present at every level and in every aspect of temple design and construction. With a more recent perspective than the other papers, Hegewald describes the complex cosmography of the Jaina religion, its imagined continents and mountains. Most striking is the necessity of these images for adherents of the religion: above all, these representations are meant to be seen, contemplated, and ultimately understood, in order to achieve enlightenment. From abstract, hourglass-shaped representations of the cosmos positioned at entrances, to temples containing models, or themselves fashioned or named in the image of cosmic mountains and continents, the reciprocity of the relationship between the devotee and the object of veneration is manifest.

II. Built Space and Natural Forms

The naming of structures with regard to specific mythical or cosmic locations, together with their construction as deliberate replicas of such places, is evident in the monumental temples of the ancient Maya, as Karl Taube demonstrates. Noting a previous perception in Maya studies of temples as ceremonial centers, he asks what these architectural forms meant to them. Drawing on archaeological, textual, and ethnographic data, Taube locates the Mayan temple tradition firmly within the bounds of Eliadean conceptions of sacred space. Geometrical forms recur here, with four-cornered and four-sided temples, houses, and fields that are representative of the four-sided earth. Through a variety of symbolic imagery, from the Mayan paradise of Flower Mountain to zoomorphic caves, Taube argues for the temple's embodiment of natural features of the landscape, caves, and mountains.

Both Hegewald and Taube's contributions show, in particular, a tendency not only to represent the cosmos as a whole, but specifically toward imitating natural forms through artificial means: the temple designed, or imagined, as a mountain, an example also familiar from the writings of the pan-Babylonians. But what, then, of the inverse? What further correlation between the natural and built environments? Are natural features held to be intrinsically important locations, transformed through ritual practice or other means into sacred areas?

Michael Meister reiterates the relationship between the temple and the natural world by tracing the evolution of Indian temple architecture through two key images, the seed and the mountain. Mapping a transition from rock-cut and free-standing shrines embedded in the mountainside to the later, elaborate constructed temples with mountain-like peaks, Meister shows how the temples materialize South Asian cosmogony and cosmology. He provides an elegant illustration of the transformational power of construction, as the mountain becomes a temple, which becomes a mountain.

Even if places must undergo transformation to become sacred, there may be a belief in their sacredness as an intrinsic property. Gary Beckman explores this complex interdependency by drawing attention to the Hittite belief in immanent cosmic forces, from the storm god at the head of the pantheon to the gods of mountains, rivers, and other natural features. He argues not for a simple dichotomy between constructed and natural spaces, but for a continuum, with prominent natural features of the landscape marked by ritual, modified through carving or installation, or even realized in fully artificial constructions.

III. Myth and Movement

For Betsey Robinson, the mountains and landscapes of ancient Greece are invested with meaning through mythic narratives related to their function as the settings of festivals and rites. Investigating the mountains Helicon and Parnassus through a comparison of the sites themselves with their representations in Greek and Roman reliefs and poetry, Robinson reveals the persistent inspirational value of these mountains. Sacred architecture and space are not simply objects to be studied, but settings and focal points of experiences that affect the viewer, the worshipper, and the ritual practitioner, just as they themselves are affected.

Robinson elaborates on the idea, touched on above, that the movement of the gods through the cosmos, as represented in myth, is matched by ritual movement in a cultic context. The question of ritual movement reminds us that we are not necessarily dealing with single, isolated structures, but a dynamic environment, where different spaces and types of space (natural, social, mythic) interweave.

My own paper deals with this very intersection by investigating the symbolism of gates as the meeting point between worlds and their further transformation through ritual practice. I argue that gates appear as symbols of cosmic boundaries in Sumerian mythology; they serve to separate and allow access between different worlds: the human, visible, and mundane realm, on the one hand, and the divine, hidden, imagined, on the other. Gates mark stopping points on divine itineraries, especially those leading to the netherworld, providing the setting for significant encounters. This meaning correlates with their usage in ritual practice, where sacrifices and offerings at gates are necessary as part of lengthier ritual processions, conspicuously so in funerary rites. I contend that the performance of rituals at gates serves to emphasize the liminal status of the rites, in turn affecting (and affected by) the monumental and sculptural program of the gates themselves, as well as their own liminal position.

IV. Sacred Space and Ritual Practice

From a focus on single stops and settings as stages in longer itineraries and rites, we move to a more extensive analysis of the cultic topography of ritual procession. Uri Gabbay goes a long way toward answering questions raised in my paper with his detailed description of the sacred topography delineated by Mesopotamian literary lamentations. He argues that these prayers, which lament an angry god's abandonment of his city, correlate the god's cosmic movement, leaving the earthly realm, with the cultic movement of the divine statue, leaving the temple. Through the ritual performance of the prayers, the urban landscape is imbued with multiple layers of meaning. Gabbay, reminding us of the need to place ritual in its appropriate historical context, draws a contrast between the performance of these prayers in the third and first millennia B.C.E. In the earlier period, he suggests, the topographical content of the prayers mirrored the accompanying processional movement, but by the later period, the recitation of the laments occurred outside of a ritual procession, only in the sanctuary of the god.

Thus far, most of the papers have examined large-scale urban topographies, distinctive natural features, or monumental architecture, but an excessive focus on obvious surviving forms may mask the importance of more transitory structures. Claus Ambos's paper provides an important counterpoint with a focus on the ephemeral structures built only for specific rituals, whose existence has left no trace outside the cuneiform record. Examining the detailed Mesopotamian ritual texts, he analyzes the architectural forms and the topography of the space they describe. Reed structures and areas demarcated with flour mark the path of ritual purification procedures, not part of the temple cults but rather of the royal cult. These structures replicate a miniaturized cosmic landscape, through which ritual movement may be linked to the movement of the sun(god) through the cosmos. Situated beyond the temple and beyond the city itself, these rites synthesize symbolic forms with space and ritual to accentuate the liminal status of their performer, the king.

Rather than looking at how ritual movement defines sacred space, Yorke Rowan uses evidence of ritual paraphernalia, together with indications of specially marked spaces and structures, to suggest the identification of performative — sacred — space. Supplying an archaeological perspective, Rowan looks at a diverse range of ritual spaces from late prehistory to the Early Bronze Age in the southern Levant. Concentrating on three sites from the Chalcolithic period, he establishes the increasingly pronounced distinction of formal ritual spaces from domestic areas, but notes the tension between ritual spaces within settlements and those in extramural locations. Rowan suggests that the path to resolving this tension lies in a better understanding of the complexity of mortuary process and ritual surrounding burial and domestic religious practices.

V. Architecture, Power, and the State

Where the challenge of separating ritual and domestic space is evident for the prehistoric period, the focus on monumental structures and official mythologies often hides the existence of less formal practices. Elizabeth Frood's paper reminds us of this fact, just as she demonstrates the inadequacy of previous arguments that Egyptian temple graffiti are indicative of popular or personal religious practices. Frood shows how graffiti inscribed in Egyptian temple complexes could reconfigure these spaces and adapt them to different social needs. Performed by members of priesthood, she argues, these secondary markings are nonetheless institutional rather than personal productions, marking the processional movements and the daily devotions of the religious elite. Frood's paper highlights the tendency to view the longevity of monumental architecture as evidence of static traditions. But a structure may stand for generations, while its meaning and purpose are subject to development and evolution as the culture around and within it changes.

While the evolution of sacred architecture in a region may manifest in the continual use, re-use, and recycling of architectural forms, transmitted and transformed across time, the desire to see continuity can lead scholars to ignore disjunctions in architectural traditions. With this in mind, Matthew Canepa challenges a long-standing and pervasive misunderstanding of Iranian sacred structures. Marshalling a formidable range of archaeological, textual, and visual sources, Canepa demonstrates that it is necessary to reassess the identification of pre-Sasanian temples and sacred structures in ancient Iran as fire temples. Rather than a single linear temple tradition, he shows instead the wide variation among the Elamite, Achaemenid, and Seleukid traditions, such as adaptations, innovations, and discontinued forms. Canepa emphasizes the royal cult and the central figure of the king as ritual performer among the Achaemenids, in contrast to the later Zoroastrian religion.

As Ambos and Canepa show, the ruler is often the primary focus of the official cult. So we might ask: how does royal ideology affect conceptions of space? Ömür Harmanşah argues that the Mesopotamian political ideology of early second-millennium B.C.E. rulers was translated into literature through metaphors describing the ancient Mesopotamian city as cattlepen and sheepfold. Calling on Foucault's idea of pastoral power, he explores the use of pastoral imagery, from nostalgic representations of the major urban centers in literary texts describing the semi-mythical past, to the visual manifestation of these metaphors in temple decoration. Harmanşah suggests that this presentation of urban space was a conscious reminiscence of the rural past in order to reinforce the conception of the king as shepherd, caring for his urban flock.

VI. Images of Ritual

Continuing the focus on the figure of the ruler, John Baines describes the impact of kingship and state formation on Egyptian temple architecture and decoration at the turn of the third millennium B.C.E. He maps transformations in ritual, architectural, and visual forms: from small-scale perishable structures to the massive, monumental temples of the Egyptian state; from portable decorated artifacts to immovable structures with conventionalized pictorial imagery. Baines shows the development of iconographic practices around the beginning of the dynastic period and the increasingly central depiction of the king as ritual performer.

Just as the implication of Baines's paper is that the iconographic imagery displays the social order, with the king as the prominent intermediary between the human and divine, Clemente Marconi argues that Greek temple sculpture holds a mirror to the social organization of the ancient Greek world. Taking an anthropological perspective on the role of ritual as an intermediary between the human and the numinous, Marconi re-evaluates several well-known examples of Greek sculptural imagery, revealing them to be representations of ritual. He contends that these images, often of processions and dances, provide settings for ritual movement. Reflecting and enhancing the content and meaning of the cult practices taking place alongside them, they serve to reinforce and commemorate the social order, as well as the relation between the human and the divine.

VII. Responses

The final section brings the volume to a conclusion with responses, from Davíd Carrasco and Richard Neer, which draw together the disparate civilizations and approaches developed in the first and second halves of this volume respectively. Carrasco, dealing with the first eight essays, locates them firmly in the context of the history of religions and, in so doing, reaffirms the applicability of Eliade's approach to this topic. In particular, he reminds us of Eliade's concept of "archetype and repetition" and shows how this theme is itself repeated throughout the volume. Ultimately, Carrasco suggests that we might question which, in the case of cosmos and architecture, is the archetype, and which the repetition.

While considering the second group of essays, Richard Neer reaches a similar conclusion from a quite different perspective. Observing how our conceptions of space are constrained by the limits of our fields and our modes of research, Neer challenges one of the fundamental assumptions of this seminar: the idea of sacred architecture as a reflection of the cosmos. Rather, he makes explicit the reversal that Carrasco touches on in his response, suggesting instead that, in some instances, architecture might be the model on which the conception of the cosmos is based.

Conclusions

The integration of philological data, visual imagery, and archaeological evidence is necessary not only to enable our understanding of architecture and ritual long since partly (or fully) lost, but also to create a coherent framework with which to analyze their interaction. Through close textual analysis, art-historical approaches to the experience of architecture, and anthropological perspectives on ritual, we may advance our knowledge of ancient religious practices.

Despite the extensive critiques leveled at the pan-Babylonians and Eliade, for their often inadequate usage of comparative data, scholars have continued to argue strongly for the utility, indeed the necessity, of comparison with regard to religion in general and sacred architecture in particular.[35] Comparison and the understanding of patterns are vital tools in the interpretation of cultures, and especially ancient religion. It is important to do so with as full as possible understanding of the historical context, or, as Smith notes, we must develop "the integration of a complex notion of pattern and system with an equally complex notion of history."[36] This volume then brings together specialists from different fields and disciplines as part of this process, in order to contribute to the discussion of these complex themes, while providing a more firmly grounded basis for comparison.

---

[35] Smith 1982; Jones 2000, vol. 1, p. 152; see in addition the essays in Patton and Ray 2000.

[36] Smith 1982, p. 34.

Bibliography

Allen, Douglas
    1988   "Eliade and History." *Journal of Religion* 68: 545–65.

Alles, Gregory D.
    1988   "Wach, Eliade, and the Critique from Totality." *Numen* 35: 108–38.

Ashley, Kathleen
    1992   "Art in Ritual Context: Introduction." *Journal of Ritual Studies* 6: 1–11.

Bell, Catherine M.
    1992   *Ritual Theory, Ritual Practice.* New York: Oxford University Press.

Broadbent, Geoffrey; Richard Bunt; and Charles Jencks
    1980   *Signs, Symbols, and Architecture.* New York: Wiley.

Clifford, Richard J.
    1972   *The Cosmic Mountain in Canaan and the Old Testament.* Harvard Semitic Monographs 4. Cambridge: Harvard University Press.

Dubuisson, Daniel
    2010   "The Poetical and Rhetorical Structure of the Eliadean Text: A Contribution to Critical Theory and Discourses on Religions." In *Hermeneutics, Politics, and the History of Religions: The Contested Legacies of Joachim Wach and Mircea Eliade,* edited by Christian K. Wedemeyer and Wendy Doniger, pp. 133–46. New York: Oxford University Press.

Durkheim, Émile
    1912   *The Elementary Forms of Religious Life.* Translated by Carol Cosman; abridged with an introduction and notes by Mark S. Cladis (2001). New York: Oxford University Press.

Eliade, M.
    1937   *Cosmologie şi alchimie babiloniană.* Bucharest: Editura Vremea.
    1959   *The Sacred and the Profane: The Nature of Religion.* Translated from the French by Willard R. Trask. 1st American edition. New York: Harcourt, Brace.
    1965   "Crisis and Renewal in History of Religions." Translated from the French by Harry B. Partin. *History of Religions* 5: 1–17.

Finkelberg, Aryeh
    1998   "On the History of the Greek κόσμος." *Harvard Studies in Classical Philology* 98: 103–36.

Foucault, Michel
    2002   "Of Other Spaces." In *The Visual Culture Reader,* edited by Nicholas Mirzoeff. 2nd ed. New York: Routledge.

Gehlen, Rolf
    1998   "Raum." In *Handbuch religionswissenschaftlicher Grundbegriffe,* volume 4, pp. 377–98. Stuttgart: Kohlhammer.

George, Andrew R.
    1992   *Babylonian Topographical Texts.* Orientalia Lovaniensia Analecta 40. Leuven: Departement Oriëntalistiek.

James, P., and M. A. van der Sluijs
    2008   "Ziggurats, Colors, and Planets: Rawlinson Revisited." *Journal of Cuneiform Studies* 60: 57–79.

Jastrow, Morris
    1898   *The Religion of Babylonia and Assyria.* Handbooks of the History of Religions 2. Boston: Ginn.

Jensen, P.
    1890   *Die Kosmologie der Babylonier.* Strassburg: Verlag von Karl J. Trübner.

Jones, Lindsay
    2000   *Hermeneutics of Sacred Architecture: Experience, Interpretation, Comparison.* 2 volumes. Cambridge: Harvard University Center for the Study of World Religions.

Korom, Frank J.
    1992   "Of Navels and Mountains: A Further Inquiry into the History of an Idea." *Asian Folklore Studies* 51: 103–25.

Landsberger, Benno
    1926   "Die Eigenbegrifflichkeit der babylonischen Welt. Ein Vortrag." *Islamica* 2: 355–72.
    1976   *The Conceptual Autonomy of the Babylonian World.* Translated by T. Jacobsen, B. Foster, and H. von Siebenthal. Sources and Monographs on the Ancient Near East 1:4. Malibu: Undena.

Lefebvre, Henri
    1991   *The Production of Space.* Translated by Donald Nicholson-Smith. Oxford: Blackwell.

Maran, Joseph, et al., editors
    2009   *Constructing Power: Architecture, Ideology and Social Practice — Konstruktion der Macht: Architektur, Ideologie und soziales Handeln.* Hamburg: LIT Verlag.

Parker Pearson, Michael, and Colin Richards, editors
    1994   *Architecture and Order: Approaches to Social Space.* London: Routledge.

Parpola, Simo
    2004   "Back to Delitzsch and Jeremias: The Relevance of the Pan-Babylonian School to the Melammu Project." In *Schools of Oriental Studies and the Development of Modern Historiography* (Proceedings of the Fourth Annual Symposium of the Assyrian and Babylonian Intellectual Heritage Project, held in Ravenna, Italy, October 13–17, 2001), edited by A. Panaino and A. Piras, pp. 237–47. Melammu Symposia 4. Milan: Università di Bologna and IsIAO.

Patton, Kimberley C., and Benjamin C. Ray, editors
    2000   *A Magic Still Dwells: Comparative Religion in the Postmodern Age.* Berkeley: University of California Press.

Pongratz-Leisten, Beate
    1994   Ina šulmi īrub: *Die kulttopographische und ideologische Programmatik der* akitu-*Prozession in Babylonien und Assyrien im 1. Jahrtausend v. Chr.* Baghdader Forschungen 16. Mainz am Rhein: Philipp von Zabern.

Rappaport, Roy A.
    1999   *Ritual and Religion in the Making of Humanity.* Cambridge Studies in Social and Cultural Anthropology 110. Cambridge: Cambridge University Press.

Rawlinson, H. C.
    1840   "Memoir on the Site of the Atropatenian Ecbatana." *Journal of the Royal Geographical Society of London* 10: 65–158.
    1861   "On the Birs Nimrud." *Journal of the Royal Asiatic Society* 18: 1–34.

Smith, Jonathan Z.

1972   "The Wobbling Pivot." *Journal of Religion* 52: 134–49.

1982   "In Comparison a Magic Dwells." In *Imagining Religion: From Babylon to Jonestown,* by Jonathan Z. Smith, pp. 19–35. Chicago: University of Chicago Press.

1987   *To Take Place: Toward Theory in Ritual.* Chicago: University of Chicago Press.

2001   "A Twice-told Tale: The History of the History of Religions." *Numen* 48: 131–46.

2004   *Relating Religion: Essays in the Study of Religion.* Chicago: University of Chicago Press.

Studstill, Randall

2000   "Eliade, Phenomenology, and the Sacred." *Religious Studies* 36: 177–94.

Wedemeyer, Christian K., and Wendy Doniger, editors

2010   *Hermeneutics, Politics, and the History of Religions: The Contested Legacies of Joachim Wach and Mircea Eliade.* New York: Oxford University Press.

Wescoat, Bonna D., and Robert G. Ousterhout, editors

2012   *Architecture of the Sacred: Space, Ritual, and Experience from Classical Greece to Byzantium.* New York: Cambridge University Press.

Wilkinson, T. J.

2003   *Archaeological Landscapes of the Near East.* Tucson: University of Arizona Press.

Woods, Christopher E.

2004   "The Sun-god Tablet of Nabû-apla-iddina Revisited." *Journal of Cuneiform Studies* 56: 23–103.

Wright, M. R.

1995   *Cosmology in Antiquity.* London: Routledge.

NATURALIZING BUDDHIST COSMOLOGY IN THE TEMPLE ARCHITECTURE OF CHINA: THE CASE OF THE YICIHUI PILLAR

Tracy Miller, Vanderbilt University

Temples, ritual, and cosmic symbolism have long been central to the study of pre-modern China. Yet, the discourse on connections between the visual culture of the sacred in China and the rest of the Eurasian continent is as fraught as that of the Mesopotamian tradition described in Deena Ragavan's introduction to this volume. Indeed even the term "religion," or its corollary, the dichotomy between the "sacred and the profane," have their own complex histories inextricably tied to Western societal constructs. Thus, as has been detailed recently by Robert Campany, the use of the term "religion" to discuss the "religious landscape" of Early Medieval China (ca. first–ninth centuries C.E.) is highly problematic.[1] Yet, in the Early Medieval period a new belief system, Buddhism, was introduced from South Asia and did become widespread in East Asia. Although always identified as having "foreign" roots, Buddhist concepts of the cosmos and the place of life within it became an important part of the Chinese cultural landscape. The concern of this paper is to examine how these concepts were expressed visually and to question the role of visual arts in transmitting both the concepts of Buddhism as well as its spiritual power, without reducing the regional complexity of Asia, or even Early Medieval China, to essentializing categories. By inquiring into the impact of new, or newly understood, architectural forms in north China during the Early Medieval period, I hope also to contribute to our knowledge of the potential of sacred architecture to help people achieve their spiritual goals in at least one time and place.

In the following essay, I explore how cosmology embodied in the Buddhist monuments of South Asia was mapped onto the indigenous architectural traditions of the Yellow River Valley. When Buddhism traveled east, the symbolically charged forms of the South Asian altar and temple were not directly transplanted into this new cultural context. Rather, they were translated into a visual language that could be "read" by a new population unfamiliar with South Asian architectural forms.[2] To illustrate this process, I focus on one example, the Yicihui Stone pillar (The Benevolent [Society's] Stone Pillar of Kindness and Compassion 義慈惠石柱) of Dingxing, Hebei province. By comparing elements of this structure with the sacred architecture of South Asia, I show how Chinese Buddhist monuments could embody South Asian concepts of time and space through the formal language of Chinese architecture.

---

[1] Campany 2011.

[2] Deitrich Seckel discussed the concept of "translating" the architecture of Buddhism into the Chinese visual language in his early article on the pagoda: "Stūpa Elements Surviving in East Asian Pagodas" (1980, p. 250).

A Benevolent Society's Pillar of Compassion and Kindness

The Yicihui Pillar is a unique monument composed of completely familiar parts (figs. 2.1–4). The structure consists of five elements: a foundation stone (2 m square; 30 cm high), a pillar base (1.23 × 1.18 × 0.54 m) carved with a twelve-petal lotus, the octagonal pillar tapered from bottom to top (two sections totaling 4.54 m in height), and a rectangular stone abacus placed horizontally across the top of the pillar (1.26 × 1.05 × 0.28 m) on top of which sits a 3 × 2 bay temple hall (0.79 × 0.69 m; the roof is a separate piece of stone). All elements were made out of limestone.[3] Intriguingly, the pillar itself was said to have been originally made of wood, but was replaced with stone between 567 and 570 C.E. Unfortunately, we have no evidence regarding its original shape.

The overall form of the Yicihui Pillar has long been associated with the funerary pillars marking entry to the spirit path of tombs dedicated to emperors in the Southern Dynasties (fig. 2.5).[4] The Yicihui Pillar is similar in its overall composition: both types of pillars are made of stone; consist of base, shaft, and capital; have a built-in rectilinear plaque below the abacus providing information about the monument; and incorporate the lotus blossom as part of the central pillar. But it departs from this type in significant ways. Rather than being elliptical in plan, the Yicihui Pillar is an irregular octagon slightly wider in the east–west direction than north–south and with the same maximum width at its base as the hall above (fig. 2.2).[5] Instead of fluting, the surface of the Yicihui Pillar is carved with a text of more than 3,400 characters telling the history of its founding and providing the names of more than 200 members of the devotional society with which the monument was associated (Liu Shufen 1994).[6] The lotus form of the base in the Yicihui Pillar is used at the top of the funerary pillar.[7] And rather than a leonine animal atop this ripe lotus blossom,[8] we find a seemingly undecorated stone platform supporting a Buddhist worship hall in the Chinese style.

The worship hall is rectangular with four columns across the front and three in depth creating a 3 × 2 bay building (figs. 2.2–3). The building is oriented facing southwest, and the front and back facades contain a seated figure in the central bays and windows in each of the side bays. Both south and north figures appear to be Buddhist icons with idiosyncratic

---

[3] Fu 2009, pp. 153–54. Based on a comparison between my photographs and those of Liu Dunzhen's team in the early 1930s, the foundation stone has been replaced. I am not certain whether Fu Xinian is using old or new measurements of this element. The stone has now been covered by the foundation to a pavilion constructed to protect the monument.

[4] Liu Dunzhen 劉敦楨 made the connection between the two monuments in his detailed 1934 article on the monument, "Dingxingxian Bei Qi shi zhu 定興縣 北齊石柱" (reprinted in Liu Dunzhen 劉敦楨 2007, p. 177).

[5] Fu (2009, p. 146) provides a concise overview of the use of stone pillars (referred to as either "stone pillar/column" 石柱 or "tomb memorials" 墓表) in funerary settings from the Han period.

[6] Liu Shufen (1994, p. 41) argues that this monument is the precursor to *dharani* pillars used in Buddhist

ritual practice, yet functionally it has a stronger relationship to the steles commissioned by devotional societies across north China during this period. See also Wong 2004, and below. Thanks to Robert Campany for emphasizing this point.

[7] The pillar base carved as a lotus blossom is a common element in the architecture of China and can be traced back to stone carvings as early as 501 C.E. but likely has earlier precedents, e.g., Mogao 254, dated to 465.

[8] The creature is very similar to the monumental animals that also frame the spirit paths leading to the tombs of the Southern Dynasty rulers. They are often called *bixie* 辟邪 because they were thought to guard the tomb. A variety of different stone animals could be used, from lions to magical *qilin*, and variation may have been an indication of status; see Wu 1994, p. 58.

hand positions (*mudrā*), pronounced uṣṇīṣa on top of the head, as well as a pointed *mandorla* reminiscent of a *chaitya* arch behind the head. The figures are damaged, but their hands were originally positioned in different *mudrās*. The figure on the southern side holds the right hand up on the chest, and the left hand is across and above the belly in what is likely a position of teaching (either the *dharma-chakra-pravartana mudrā* or *vitarka mudrā*). The obtuse angle between the left wrist and hand is typical of figures holding their hands with the palm up, a position seen in paintings of the Buddha teaching on the east walls of Cave 285 at the Mogao grottoes in Dunhuang (dated ca. 538 C.E.) as well as the left hand in the image of "Preaching in a Pure Land" from the Northern Qi caves at South Xiangtangshan, Hebei province, presently preserved in the Freer Gallery of Art (fig. 2.6). This relief, carved at a site only 336 kilometers (209 miles) southwest of the Yicihui Pillar, is thought to date to 565–577.[9] The figure on the northern side is much more difficult to identify, but is distinguished by the locations of the arms to the side and both hands either in the lap or over the knees. It is too damaged, however, to be certain of the original *mudrā*.

Liu Dunzhen's analysis of the shrine's architecture reveals nothing inconsistent with the date of the stone column that supports it. On the contrary, the work is taken as a representative example of traditional Chinese architecture of the period used for audience halls in imperial palaces as well as Buddhist worship halls. The timber-frame column grid structure of the temple/palace hall in China developed in the regional context of the Yellow River Valley, which was rich in timber and loessial soil. From as early as the first millennium B.C.E., ritual structures in the Yellow River Valley employed a full grid of timber columns for primary roof support placed on an elevated platform of pounded earth, which, because interior walls could be non-structural, allow for maximum flexibility of use for a single building type. Even at this formative stage, fired ceramic tiles were already being employed, to a limited extent, for roofing. Pictorial and archaeological evidence from the Han Dynasty (206 B.C.E.–220 C.E.) shows that earthen foundations, ceramic roof tiles, and timber-frame construction continued to be used during the early imperial period for palatial architecture as well as for buildings specifically designed to satisfy ritual functions.[10] Representations of gatehouses and palace halls seen in funerary art from the Early Medieval period attest to the widespread use of this "classical" timber-frame form for the architecture of the imperial court.[11]

As is well known, from as early as the fourth century, we have evidence that the timber-frame buildings used for audience halls as well as worship space in the imperial courts of China were also employed within Buddhist settings.[12] Wall paintings dating to the fifth to sixth centuries found in cave temples of the Mogao grottoes employ Central Plains-style architecture in their representations of the palaces and cities discussed in traditional South Asian Buddhist narrative tales (Sun Ruxian 孫儒僴 and Sun Yihua 孫毅華 2001). The worship hall for the Buddha within the imperially sponsored Yongningsi 永寧寺, constructed in the

---

[9] Here I follow the identification of Angela Howard (1996, pp. 14–17).

[10] For an overview of developments in the timber-frame tradition of palatial and religious architecture during the early imperial period, see Liu Xujie 2009, pp. 458–500. For a discussion of the use of geometry and the ritual Bright Hall during the Han period and before, see Tseng 2011, pp. 37–88.

[11] For more on images of palatial architecture in Tang Dynasty funerary art, see Fu Xinian 1998.

[12] The word "*tang* 堂," a term commonly denoting timber-frame audience and ritual halls in the Chinese style, was used to describe a hall to house the Buddha in the Tanxi Monastery 檀溪寺 of Dao'an 道安 (312–385); see "Dao'an *zhuan* 道安傳" in Taishō 2059 (Takakusu and Watanabe 1983–1987, vol. 50, p. 352b)

Northern Wei capital in 516 C.E., was described as having the shape of the Taiji Hall 太極殿, the primary audience hall in the imperial palace.[13]

Though constructed more than two centuries after the Yicihui Pillar, our earliest extant timber-frame hall in China is consistent with this shared style of palatial and religious architecture. The main hall of Nanchansi, dated to 782 C.E., shares a number of characteristics with the building crowning the Yicihui Pillar (fig. 2.7). It has a similar three-bay front facade with four columns supporting the deeply overhanging eaves, a centrally placed entry door, and windows in each of the subsidiary bays.[14] Details of the timberwork, such as the shuttle shape (or entasis) of the columns, and large bearing block joined directly into the top of the eaves columns, are also shared by the Tang example.[15] Where the architecture of the Yicihui stone hall departs from the main hall at Nanchansi, specifically in the lack of corbelled bracketing and the use of square eaves rafters that run perpendicular to the facade all the way to the corner hip rafters, parallels can be found in earlier buildings such as stone shrine architecture from the eastern Han Dynasty (25–220 C.E.) and timber Buddhist architecture from the seventh century still preserved in Japan.[16]

Yet, what might be thought of as "decoration" distinguishes this structure from extant ritual halls. Carving on the walls of the side facades and the bottom of the abacus suggest that the building does more than house the Buddha in a Chinese palace; it embodies Buddhist cosmology (figs. 2.2, 8–9). Examination of the underside of the stone, the portion most visible to a viewer looking at the column, reveals detailed carving of lotus blossoms, lotus buds, stylized disks (or Chinese coins), and a complex figure composed of seven interconnected circles.[17] These figures are, in fact, the plan of the Buddha hall surmounting the pillar. Four of

---

[13] Not only was the main worship hall constructed in the manner of the main audience hall in the imperial palace, but the walls were also covered with short timber rafters and ceramic tiles, as were palace walls (寺院墙皆施短椽, 以瓦, 覆之, 若今宫墙也). Yang Xuanzhi 楊衒之 (d. 555?) 2006, p. 12. See also the English translation by Yang Hsüan-chih (1984, p. 16).

[14] It should be noted, however, that the Yicihui hall is two bays in depth, while the main hall of Nanchansi is three bays in depth.

[15] Liu Dunzhen notes that the Yicihui Pillar may be the earliest known example of the shuttle-shaped column. The proportions are different from other examples known to him, including the seventh-century timber-frame Middle Gate of Hōryūji and that described in the Northern Song Dynasty *Yingzaofashi* (published 1103), and appear to be of an earlier style (Liu Dunzhen 2007, p. 180). Based on her study of the Xiangtangshan grottoes, Angela Howard (2008) argues that sculptural style of the Northern Qi reflects a strong influence from the artistic culture of the Southern Dynasties, which may have been directly influenced by southeastern India through maritime routes. The newly "Indianized" style may have contributed to the development of more naturalistic representations of the body characteristic of the Tang Dynasty. The architectural style of the miniature columns in the Yicihui Pillar may be further

evidence to support her argument of southeastern Chinese influence on Northern Qi and eventually Tang art.

[16] Liu Dunzhen made detailed comparisons with Japanese examples, in particular the Tamamushi Shrine preserved at Hōryūji. This is an interesting comparison, for it is a timber Buddha hall on a pillar and may resemble the original timber structure after which this stone replacement was made. The lack of eaves bracketing is also noticeable here, but Liu compares this to small funerary shrines made of stone from the eastern Han period and in so doing helps to confirm an early date for the architecture. See Liu Dunzhen 2007, p. 181.

[17] General descriptions of the underside of the base often describe the disks as Chinese coins; close examination does not reveal a coin shape. The description of the objects as coins may have been influenced by possible associations of the object with Han-period "money trees," which combine the worship of indigenous deities such as Xiwangmu (西王母 Queen Mother of the West or Western Spirit Mother) with early Buddha-like images. For more on indigenous use of the circle to symbolize heaven in the Han period and before, see Tseng 2011. For an extensive discussion regarding the influence of Buddhist art in these objects, see Abe 2002, esp. pp. 28–51. The coins are in combinations of twos and threes and exist in

these interconnected circles are incised into each of the four corners of the foundation. Two lotus blossoms, each with eight petals, appear on the north and south sides of the foundation. Similarly, one lotus blossom, also of eight petals, is placed on each of the narrower east and west sides. Combined, the ten forms match the number of columns in the building above.[18] In order to understand the purpose of these drawings, it is useful to know something about the history and purpose of the monument itself.

History of the Monument

The Yicihui Pillar was erected in central Hebei province during the Northern Qi Dynasty (550–577 C.E.) as a memorial for the burial of rebels fighting against the Northern Wei government between 525 and 528 C.E. — as well as other meritorious acts. After the rebellion was put down, locals gathered the remains of the deceased in the area and buried them in a mass grave. A Benevolent Society Hall (義堂) was erected next to the burial location to feed the hungry. Additionally, a Buddhist ward (僧坊) was built next to the site to recruit monks for meritorious service. In 546 the government road (官路) was moved to the west, and the offering hall and monastic residences were relocated to a site nearer the new road. In 555 and 557, members of this developing Buddhist devotional society provided relief for suffering individuals who were pressed into corvée labor and who suffered from famine (Fu 2009).[19] In 559 the local government sent a memorial for official court recognition of the deeds of this community. Based on this document, in 562 the Department of State Affairs (尚書省) officially authorized (and provided funds for) the establishment of a memorial pillar. A wooden pillar was erected in 563 and was replaced in 567–570 with a stone version (Fu 2009; Liu Shufen 1994). According to Liu Shufen 劉淑芬 (1994), important Buddhist monks of the period had spent some time in residence within the Buddhist ward, but never planned to remain there permanently. Thus, the Benevolent Society Hall and Buddhist Ward functioned primarily as a charity to aid the suffering of the lay Buddhist community.

The mid-sixth century was also an important time for the followers of Buddhism in north China, as many believed that they were entering the age of the "final dharma" or "age of decline" (*mofa* 末法). The doctrine of the *mofa* posited three different periods in the future of Buddhism based on the passage of a certain amount of time from the *Parinirvāṇa* of the historical Buddha. Different dating systems were used (the first may be 500 years, second 1,000, and final 3,000–10,000 years), after which Maitreya would descend from Tushita heaven and restore order.[20] Depending somewhat on the date of the Buddha's entry into *Parinirvāṇa*, a topic of significant debate, the widespread belief in sixth-century north China was that the first two phases would be complete in the between the mid-fifth and sixth centuries (Howard

---

two versions either with or without what appear to be petals surrounding the perimeter. Additionally, some have traces of what appears to be Sanskrit text in the center. Although full discussion is beyond the scope of this paper, preliminary investigation suggests that these may be symbols of the sun and moon in rotation, reinforcing the cosmic symbolism of the monument.

[18] My thanks to Jinah Kim for making this observation.

[19] Yi communities of lay Buddhists were frequent sponsors of stone steles in north China from the last decades of the fifth century. These usually took the shape of the traditional commemorative stele known from Qin-Han times (Wong 2004).

[20] For more on the different dating systems of the *mofa*, see Nattier 1991.

1996). What has been described as a "pervasive apocalyptic attitude" developed in response to several factors, including actions taken against the Buddhist establishment in northwest India in the early sixth century (McNair 2007, p. 89). The wars in north China during the same period would have confirmed notions that the *mofa* was soon approaching and that something must be done. As discussed in *Sutra of Resolving Doubts During the Age of the Semblance Dharma* (Xiangfa jueyi jing 像法決疑經), an "indigenous Chinese scripture" likely composed during the sixth century, sincere assistance to the poor, orphans, elderly, and hungry was the best way to attain karmic merit for self and society (Liu Shufen 1994; Tokuno 1995, p. 257). The large number of devotional societies, like the one that sponsored the Yicihui Pillar, may have been founded as a constructive response to this feeling of crisis.[21]

Meaning in "Decoration"?

As Fu Xinian's team points out, the horizontal stone abacus at the top of the column serves as the foundation for the miniature building above it. If these forms had something to do with the building above, in what way could the combinations of circles be related to temple design?

Altars and Symbolic Time

In his discussion of the Śiva temple at Muṇḍeśvarī, Michael Meister has explained the way in which complex building plans were derived from simple, yet symbolically charged, geometries: the circle and the square (fig. 2.10). From as early as the early seventh century, most Hindu temples relied on the *Vāstupuruṣa maṇḍala* for their plans, physically manifesting the moment of creation (and thus the potential for re-creation) within the towering superstructure of the mountainous temple form. This is accomplished through a layering of symbolism formally tied to the square base of the altar. Thought to have had its origins in the Vedic fire altars constructed of individual square bricks, the *Vāstupuruṣa maṇḍala* is a *yantra,* a magical diagram that, when used as a building plan, enables a structure to embody the Puruṣa, the supernal man (Kramrisch 1980, vol. 1, pp. 11 and 67). Norman Brown notes that an important characteristic of Puruṣa (ultimately derived from the deity Agni) is that he represents the generative principle, entering plants and waters and becoming the "embryo within them." Additionally, "Puruṣa alone is this entire world, both past and future .... From him was born Virāj (the primordial waters), and from Virāj was born Puruṣa. When born he overpassed the earth both in the west and in the east" (Rig Veda 10.91, translated in Brown 1931). Extending out in all directions, the newly created earth takes the form of a square, which can be fixed in time and space through orientation to the cardinal directions. Significantly, the square is also the shape of the foundation of the cosmic Mount Meru (Kramrisch 1980, vol. 1, p. 42). A temple constructed on the basis of the *Vāstupuruṣa maṇḍala* allows for the "relation of the Supreme Principle (Brahman) and of manifestation [to be] seen as coterminous" (Kramrisch 1980, vol. 1, p. 67). As Kramrisch notes in a quotation from Varāhamihir's (505–587) *Brihat*

---

[21] Howard also suggests that the violence that took place in war-torn north China during the sixth century contributed to belief in *mofa* doctrine (Howard 1996). Although the *Sutra of Resolving Doubts During* the *Age of the Semblance Dharma* was written in the sixth century, it is set at the time of the Buddha's *Parinirvāṇa* and modeled on Indian and central Asian sūtras; see Tokuno 1995, pp. 257–71.

Samhitā, "the form of the *Vāstupuruṣa maṇḍala* is square .... It can be converted into a triangle, hexagon, octagon and circle of equal area and retain its symbolism" (quoted in Kramrisch 1980, vol. 1, p. 21).

The lines and squares of the *Vāstupuruṣa maṇḍala* also become the physical body of an anthropomorphic conception of the primal creative force. As suggested by Kramrisch, the understanding of the Supreme Principle as an anthropomorphic deity whose traces, in the form of drawings or plan, could uphold the cosmic order was part of the religious substrata of South Asia and is evident in both Brahmanism and Buddhism (Kramrisch 1980). As Kramrisch explains elsewhere in her *The Hindu Temple*, the altar from which the *maṇḍala* derives was also a means of representing and controlling time. The altar was built by individual square bricks, which together were a symbolic measure of the seasons, year, and time as a whole. To subdivide this microcosm, the square is divided first by marking the rising and setting sun to the east and west, then by marking north and south and dividing the line, and then,

> so that by a geometrically progressive series the original two points engender four and eight, sixteen and thirty-two. These stations are marked along the outline of the square diagram .... They encompass all manifestation, in terms of space, as it is beheld on the level of the earth. This initial translation of the rhythm of time into the pattern in space forms the basis of larger cycles than that of the day; they also are supported by the square drawn on the ground. (Kramrisch 1980, vol. 1, p. 30)

When rendered into a building plan, the border is divided into thirty-two units, representing the regents of the four planets who rule over the points represented by the cardinal directions (as the equinoxial and solstitial points) and the regents of the twenty-eight Nakshatras, or the lunar mansions of the course of the moon (fig. 2.11). The central space of the *Vāstumaṇḍala,* either a point or square based on the layout of the grid, was the space of Brahman, the force of creation. Thus the *Vāstumaṇḍala* embodies the power of creation, and through the monthly revolutions of the moon, and the solar cycle of days and years, and the power of recreation and rebirth (Kramrisch 1980).

Critical to the implementation of the *Vāstumaṇḍala* is orientation toward the cardinal directions and protection of the corners, weak points that must be reinforced to eliminate the possible introduction of evil influences. Michael Meister suggests that the circle may have been employed to determine the orientation of the *Vāstumaṇḍala* partially because of the strength of its geometry, and that the octagon of Muṇḍeśvarī's plan might have been thought to be better able to withstand negative forces than the square, while still retaining its spiritual power. The *Śulba Sūtras* describe how a gnomon and cord were used to determine the square of the *Vāstumaṇḍala* and orient it toward the cardinal directions. The technique of using circles to create the square may also have allowed for the incorporation of alternative concepts of cosmological time related to the rotation of the planets and the Zodiac introduced from west Asia during the first centuries C.E. This was not, as Meister emphasizes, presented as a means to replace the local cosmology. The *Śulba Sūtras* were coordinated with the structure of the *Vāstumaṇḍala* to create powerful architectural forms able to accommodate different conceptions of the universe. In this way "the Vedic universe, in the Hindu temple as in later cosmology, makes some concessions to a circular world view" (Meister 1981, p. 86). If the *Vāstumaṇḍala* was employed by the temple builders to gain access to divine forces and harness the cycles of time, then incorporating a new cosmology into the process of its construction might broaden the reach of that power and increase its potency.

Indian Buddhist monuments shared in an architecture culture that was part of the larger ritual landscape of South Asia. Much of the symbolism employed to construct the towering temples dedicated to the deities of the Hindu pantheon was marshaled for Buddhist purposes when desired. As Debala Mitra, Pramod Chandra, and others have discussed, a multitude of architectural types, including the stūpa, cave shrine, and towering temple, were employed in South Asia for religious purposes by Buddhists as well as members of other religious communities.[22] Could Northern Qi builders have known the constructive methods of the *Śulba Sūtras* and *Brihat Samhitā*? As if to answer our question, the craftsmen have gone to great effort to show us that the diagram is the generative force between the lotus and the Chinese-style Buddha hall.

In the case of timber-frame buildings within the Chinese tradition, one of the most important aspects is the location of the columns within the structural frame.[23] Knowing this we can see that the diagram of six circles around a center results in a ground plan for a rectangular building with two of the sides divided into three parts, and two into two parts. Thus, the diagrams of interconnected circles work to indicate the location of the corner columns as well as the spacing of the columns between the corners (fig. 2.12). The four corner columns located at the corners of the rectangle drawn around the diagram (rather than by the intersection of the circles themselves) are reflected in the four diagrams at the corner of the abacus and are oriented in the direction of the building on top of the abacus. The plan of a Chinese temple and the plan of a South Asian temple could be generated through a single method.

Pillars and the Vertical Axis of Progression

The craftsmen also wanted us to see clearly that the columns located by this diagram were cognate with the lotus as the Buddhist symbol of rebirth. Two images of the diagram appear on the walls of the side facades. These are matched with lotus buds with a prominent circular center on either side of a larger lotus on the foundation stone. Each of the six columns located by the intersection of the circles is matched by an eight-petal lotus on the bottom of the foundation. Finally, the central circle of the diagram itself is used to generate the eight-petal lotus. Again the three objects — lotus, pillar, and diagram — are generated from the one circle, thereby retaining the circle's symbolic potency.

As is well known, the lotus embodies regeneration, the potential for rebirth in a Buddhist paradise, while following the bodhisattva path toward ultimate personal extinction or nirvana. A natural metaphor for rebirth, the root system of the lotus grows along the bottom of lake or pond. Consequently, stem and bud emerge each spring directly from the water. And when the blossom matures, the petals fold back, and the ripe seeds of the calyx are fully exposed, thereby emphasizing the plant's generative (and regenerative) potential. Yet, like other monuments known from their Buddhist associations, its full symbolic potential is only

---

[22] Although some stūpa shrines appear to have been specifically Buddhist, the same craftsmen were likely employed to build religious structures regardless of sectarian affiliation (Mitra 1971). See also Chandra 1983. Although Mitra and Chandra do not specifically mention caves in their discussions of this issue, inscriptions from Mauryan caves in the Barābar hills

indicate that at least one of them was dedicated for Ājīvika, not Buddhist, use (Huntington 1974/1975).

[23] There is evidence to suggest that the spacing of columns in imperial palace buildings of Chinese empires was considered important enough for foreign visitors to replicate in their own palaces (Coaldrake 1996).

realized through an examination of the pre-Buddhist context from which it developed. As John Irwin detailed in the 1970s, votive pillars with lotus "bell" capitals long associated with King Aśoka (ca. 304–232 B.C.E.) were often erected at the sites of Buddhist stūpas and could be engraved with edicts, though not always (Irwin 1973).[24] Interestingly, although made of stone, they were originally erected in wood (Irwin 1974). Irwin argues that the column was a pre-Buddhist symbol of cosmic parturition, the device used to separate the earth from the heavens and connect man with the divine abode of the gods. The cosmogonic act not only caused the creation of the square earth, seen in the form of the *Vāstumaṇḍala* discussed above, but also released the sun, thereby bringing about the creation of time as well as space (Irwin 1976).[25] The bell shape of the capital embodies both cosmogony and reincarnation in its basic form as ripe lotus blossom.

In his series of articles on the pillar, Irwin argues that the symbolism of lotus and pillar was fundamental to South Asian cosmology and was absorbed into the religious monuments of Buddhism at their inception. Stūpas, such as the Great Stūpa at Sanchi, layered the symbolism of both pillar and altar into the pre-Buddhist funerary mound to create a rich religious architecture. Emerging through the square form of the *harmikā*, marked as sacred by the *vedikā* railing around it, the pillar (*yaṣṭi*) extends through three round *chhatras,* which shelter the sacred remains with a symbol of royalty. The symbol of square (*Vāstumaṇḍala* and base of the cosmic Mount Meru) is combined with the pillar to form a monument embodying the idea of the Buddha as the source of enlightenment.[26] The eight-petal lotus so prominently displayed on the Yicihui Pillar abacus may function in a similar manner, reworked for an audience unfamiliar with the formal language of South Asian religious spaces. The divisions of the eight petals are suggestive of the eight directions surrounding a generative center adding the cosmogonic significance of the *Vāstumaṇḍala* to Buddhist monuments through the presence of the Buddha (symbolically or through relics) in the central squares occupied by the generative force of Brahman in the Hindu context.[27] The rite of circumambulation around the body of the Buddha also acts as a means to "turn the wheel of the *dharma,*" the teachings of the Buddha that are cognate with the Buddha himself.

The numerous parallels between the cosmology embodied in the *Vāstumaṇḍala* and Aśokan pillars with that documented the Han Dynasty (206 B.C.E.–220 C.E.) likely facilitated the reception of Buddhism in this new context. As detailed by Lillian Lan-ying Tseng, by the third century B.C.E., the use of the circle to represent heaven and square to represent earth already had a long history in China (Tseng 2011). The nine-square grid was developed in pre-Buddhist China as a means to express the divisions of the earth into nine by Yu the Great.[28]

[24] For a discussion of the interpretation of lotus symbolism and lotus capitals, see Meister 1992.

[25] Although verifying his evidence in a close reading of the Rig Veda, Irwin describes the pillars as an "*axis mundi*" following ideas developed by Mircea Eliade. For more on Eliade and his influence on our understanding of Asian cosmology, see Korom 1992 and Deena Ragavan's *Introduction* to this volume.

[26] Although the stūpa form itself was pre-Buddhist, the earliest datable Buddhist stūpas are from the Mauryan period (Mitra 1971).

[27] Thanks to Tony Stewart for emphasizing this point.

[28] According to Edward Shaughnessy (1993) in his essay on the *Shangshu* 尚書, the "Yu gong 禹貢" section may date as late as the Qin Dynasty (221–206 B.C.E.). According to Lewis (2005), Sima Qian 司馬遷 attributes the organization of nine provinces of Yu into a geometric grid to Zou Yan 鄒衍 (ca. 305–240 B.C.E.). Also Sima Qian 1999, vol. 74, p. 2344. Lewis emphasizes that the earliest descriptions of the nine provinces were not organized into a grid. I doubt that this would have made the similarities of division any less important; on the contrary, if we conceive of the grid as a type of "science," cross-cultural similarities may have added to its believability. See also the Zong Bing quote below.

The *Kaogongji* 考工記, dating from the late Warring States period (ca. 481–221 B.C.E.), suggests that the square form of the carriage box and circular form of the umbrella mounted above it were selected because of their formal relationship to the heaven and earth (Tseng 2011).[29] Furthermore, Han Dynasty devices used for divination were constructed out of squares and circles separated by a pin. The square bases were marked with calendric symbols and the round tops with diagrams of Ursa Major, allowing the diviner to "bring the power of the cosmos into the divination to improve its efficacy" (Tseng 2011, p. 49).

We see this at a larger scale in the earliest excavated *Mingtang* (明堂, Bright Hall or Hall of Light) located in the Western Han capital of Chang'an. Here the circle and square, heaven and earth, monthly progression, and the cycle of the seasons were incorporated into a single, multi-storied building organized around a central axis. The building enabled the emperor to perform his intermediary role as the source of communication between heaven and earth and display his heavenly mandate (*tianming* 天命) to rule (Tseng 2011).[30] As in South Asia, the consolidation of multiple systems of knowledge about the cosmos (ancestral worship and the imperial academy were also included in this version) made the monument that much more powerful.

The teachings of Buddhism allowed the larger population to create similar multi-valent monuments with the ability to harness divine power. The Northern Qi patrons of the Yicihui Pillar, those who had seen entire villages destroyed by war, were likely motivated by fear of losing their access to security, if not in this life then in the next. Now firm believers in reincarnation, the population of the sixth-century Hebei region created structures that incorporated methods used to create South Asian religious architecture in order to magically charge their own monuments in familiar ways. Like the temple at Muṇḍeśvarī, an effort appears to have been made to protect the corners of the pillar and hall: the pillar's irregular octagonal in plan is the rectangular plan of the hall with chamfered corners, the abacus has the seven-circle structural diagram on each of the four corners, and small strongmen (*lishi* 力士) support and turn up the corners of the eaves (fig. 2.13). The circle used to generate both building plan and eight-petal lotus may also be used to embody the movement of time through rotating the circular diagram. The lotus leaves between the petals are located by rotating the construction circles of the eight-petal lotus (fig. 2.14), expressing both the cycle of reincarnation and the turning of the wheel of the law that enables one to escape that cycle.[31] The stone foundation of the pillar itself expresses a rotation of the diagram used to generate the plan of the hall at its apex, as a doubling of the six circles results in a twelve-petal lotus at the base of the monument. Perhaps as an expression of the twelve constellations in the Zodiac, or the twelvefold chain of dependent origination discussed in the *Sūtra of Resolving Doubts Concerning the Semblance Dharma*, the twelve leaves are folded back to reveal the circular calyx of ripe lotus that holds the pillar (Tokuno 1995). By unwinding the circle of the seven-circle diagram, the lotus pillar of cosmic time is able to resolve itself into the space of the Chinese palace that houses the eternal form of the Mahāyāna Buddha.

---

[29] For more on the date of the *Kaogongji*, see Boltz's 1993 essay on the dating of the *Zhouli* 周禮.

[30] Tseng details the numerous cosmologies ultimately incorporated into different "bright halls" constructed in the Han period. The *Mingtang* of Wang Mang

王莽 (9–23 C.E.), which also included aspects of the Imperial Academy and ancestor worship, was only one of three in this period.

[31] For more on representations of the Wheel of the Law in Chinese Buddhism, see Teiser 2006.

Conclusion

The introduction of the South Asian *maṇḍala* as a cosmological symbol allowed pre-existing architectural forms to be subsumed into a new organizational scheme that naturalized the concept of reincarnation. This process, replicated in the form of the Yicihui Pillar, provided a Buddhist devotional society in war-torn north China the means to express their hopes for the rebirth of their loved ones in a better place. The pillar was at once a lotus, tree (original wood), and (now in stone) mountain, providing an elevated view, "diminishing worldly attachments and le[ading] to an appreciation of limitless space and time."[32] Finally, by time and the concept of reincarnation reached the familiar rectilinear ritual halls through the South Asian methods of temple construction, the lay Buddhist communities in China could have access to their own sages of the past, present, and future. As Zong Bing (375–443) said,

> [when the sage rulers of the past were] roaming in sublime freedom, how do we know that they did not follow the Way of Tathāgata (the Buddha)?[33]

Of course, the sages of the Chinese past would have been housed in the Chinese-style palace — one made more powerful (and potentially more "divine") by employing the constructive diagrams of South Asia used to generate the universe to derive its plan.

---

[32] Bush 1983, p. 136.

[33] Translation is after Zürcher 2007, p. 270. Cited also in Bush 1983, p. 136.

Figure 2.1. Yicihui Pillar (567–570 C.E.), stone, view from south (photo by the author)

Figure 2.2. Yicihui Pillar, angle view of Buddha hall (photo by the author)

Figure 2.3. Yicihui Pillar, detail of upper Buddha hall, (*top*) present front (south) facade and (*bottom*) present back (north) facade (photos by the author)

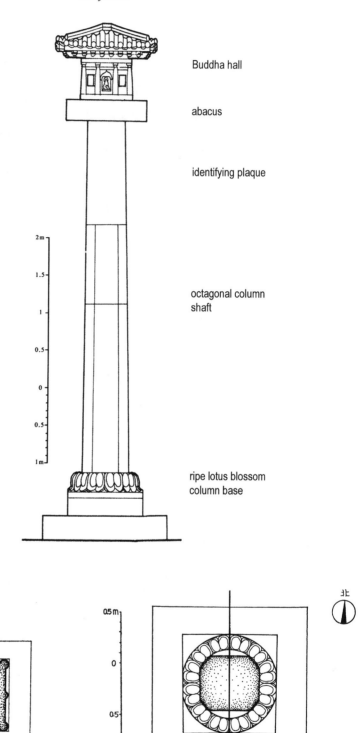

Figure 2.4. Yicihui Pillar, (*top*) elevation drawing and section drawings cut at (*bottom left*) base of upper Buddha hall and (*bottom right*) above lotus pedestal (after Liu Dunzhen 2007, p. 171)

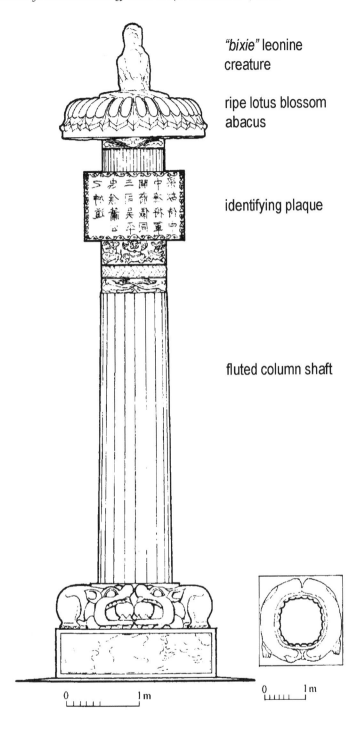

"bixie" leonine creature

ripe lotus blossom abacus

identifying plaque

fluted column shaft

Figure 2.5. Funerary pillar from the tomb of Liang Xiao Jing 蕭景 (477–523 C.E.) (after Fu Xinian 2009, p. 146)

Figure 2.6. "Preaching in a Pure Land" from the Northern Qi caves at South Xiangtangshan, Hebei province, presently held in the Freer Gallery of Art (photo: Freer Gallery of Art, reproduced with permission)

Figure 2.7. Main hall of Nanchansi, 782 C.E., front facade (photo by the author)

Figure 2.8. Yicihui Pillar, detail of underside of abacus (photo by the author)

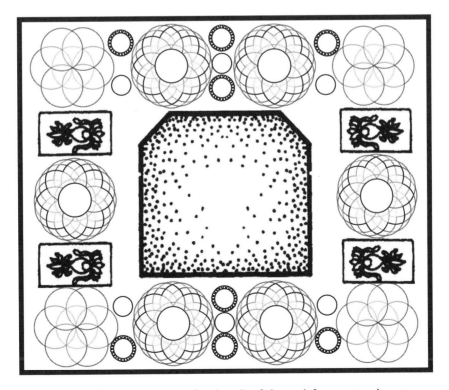

Figure 2.9. Yicihui Pillar, line drawing of underside of abacus (after Liu Dunzhen 2007, p. 171, redrawn to show how construction circles were used to generate the shape of the lotus blossoms)

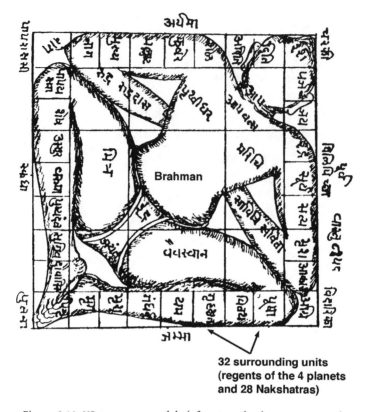

Figure 2.10. *Vāstupuruṣa maṇḍala* (after A. Volwahsen 1969, p. 44)

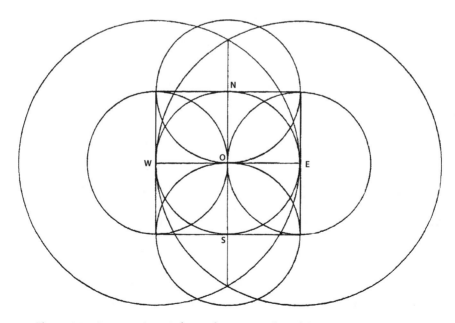

Figure 2.11. Construction circles to determine plan of the Muṇḍeśvarī Temple
(drawing after Meister 1981, p. 83)

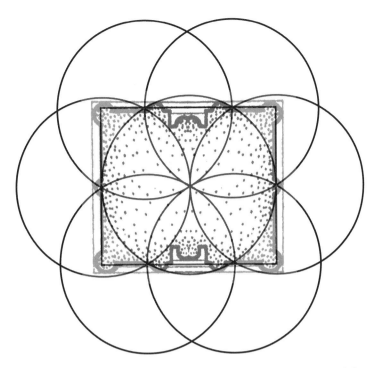

Figure 2.12. Diagram on Yicihui Pillar superimposed on the section drawing of the Buddha hall
(drawing by the author)

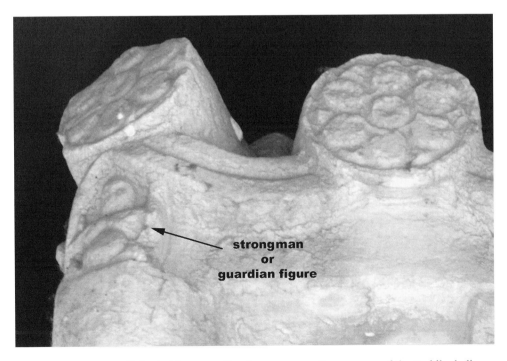

Figure 2.13. Strongmen (*lishi* 力士) or guardian figures supporting corners of the Buddha hall eaves
(photo by the author)

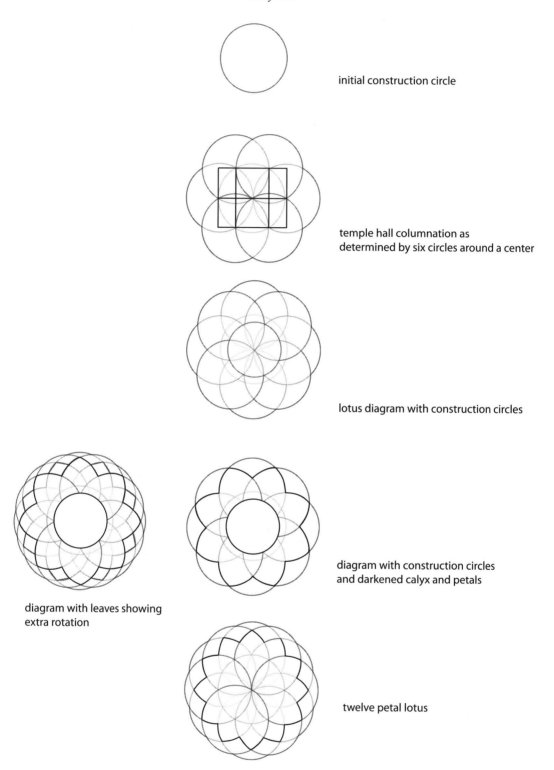

initial construction circle

temple hall columnation as
determined by six circles around a center

lotus diagram with construction circles

diagram with construction circles
and darkened calyx and petals

diagram with leaves showing
extra rotation

twelve petal lotus

Figure 2.14. Use of construction circle to derive seven-circle diagram, eight-petal lotus,
and twelve-petal lotus (drawings by the author)

Bibliography

Abe, Stanley K.

2002   *Ordinary Images.* Chicago: University of Chicago Press.

Boltz, William G.

1993   "Chou Li 周禮." In *Early Chinese Texts: A Bibliographical Guide*, edited by Michael Loewe, pp. 24–32. Early China Special Monograph Series 2. Berkeley: Society for the Study of Early China and the Institute for East Asian Studies, University of California.

Brown, W. Norman

1931   "The Sources and Nature of Puruṣa in the Puruṣasūkta (Rig Veda 10.91)." *Journal of the American Oriental Society* 51: 108–18.

Bush, Susan

1983   "Tsung Ping's Essay on Landscape and the 'Landscape Buddhism' of Mt. Lu." In *Theories of the Arts in China*, edited by Susan Bush and Christian F. Murck, pp. 132–64. Princeton: Princeton University Press.

Campany, Robert

2011   "Chinese History and Writing about Religion(s): Reflections at a Crossroads." In *Dynamics in the History of Religions between Asia and Europe: Encounters, Notions, and Comparative Perspectives*, edited by Marion Steinicke and Volkhard Krech, pp. 273–94. Leiden: E. J. Brill.

Chandra, Pramod

1983   *On the Study of Indian Art.* Cambridge: Harvard University Press.

Coaldrake, William H.

1996   *Architecture and Authority in Japan.* London: Routledge.

Fu Xinian 傅熹年

1998   "Tangdai suidao xing mu de xingzhi gouzao he suo fanying de dishang gong-shi 唐代隧道型墓的形制構造和所反映出的地上宮室." In *Fu Xinian jianzhushi lunwenji*, pp. 245–63. Beijing: Wenwu chubanshe.

Fu Xinian 傅熹年, chief editor

2009   *Zhongguo gudai jianzhu shi, di er juan, Sanguo Liang Jin, Nan-Bei chao, Sui-Tang, Wudai jianzhu* 中國古代建築史, 第二卷, 三國, 兩晉, 南北朝, 隋唐, 五代建築. 2nd edition. Beijing: Zhongguo jianzhu gongye chubanshe.

Howard, Angela

1996   "Buddhist Cave Sculpture of the Northern Qi Dynasty: Shaping a New Style, Formulating New Iconographies." *Archives of Asian Art* 49: 6–25.

2008   "Pluralism of Styles in Sixth-century China: A Reaffirmation of Indian Models." *Ars Orientalis* 35: 67–94.

Huntington, John C.

1974/1975   "The Lomās Ṛṣi: Another Look." *Archives of Asian Art* 28: 34–56.

Irwin, John

1973   "'Aśokan' Pillars: A Reassessment of the Evidence." *The Burlington Magazine* 115 (848): 706–20.

1974   "'Aśokan' Pillars: A Reassessment of the Evidence — II: Structure." *The Burlington Magazine* 116 (861): 725–26.

1976   "'Aśokan' Pillars: A Reassessment of the Evidence —V: Symbolism." *The Burlington Magazine* 118 (884): 740–41.

Korom, Frank J.
1992   "Of Navels and Mountains: A Further Inquiry into the History of an Idea." *Asian Folklore Studies* 531/1: 103–25.

Kramrisch, Stella
1980   *The Hindu Temple.* 2 volumes. Reprint. Delhi: Shri Jainendra Press.

Lewis, Mark Edward
2005   *The Construction of Space in Early China.* Albany: SUNY Press.

Liu Dunzhen 劉敦楨
2007   "Dingxingxian Bei Qi shi zhu 定興縣北齊石柱." In *Liu Dunzhen quanji*, vol. 2, pp. 170–90. Beijing: Zhongguo jianzhu gongye chubanshe.

Liu Shufen 劉淑芬
1994   "Bei Qi Biaoyixiang Yicihui shizhu—zhonggu Fojiao shuhui jiuji de ge'an yanjiu 北齊標異鄉義慈惠石柱 — 中古佛教社會救濟的個案研究." *Xinshixue* 4/5: 1–47.

Liu Xujie 劉叙杰, editor
2009   *Zhongguo gudai jianzhu shi, di yi juan, Yuanshi shehui, Xia, Shang, Zhou, Qin Han jianzhu* 中國古代建築史, 第 一 卷, 原始社會, 夏商周秦漢建築. 2nd edition. Beijing: Jianzhu gongye chubanshe.

McNair, Amy
2007   *The Donors of Longmen: Faith, Politics, and Patronage in Medieval Chinese Buddhist Sculpture.* Honolulu: University of Hawaii Press.

Meister, Michael W.
1981   "Muṇḍeśvarī: Ambiguity and Certainty in the Analysis of a Temple Plan." In *Kalādarśana = Kalādarśana: American Studies in the Art of India*, edited by Joanna G. Williams, pp. 77–90. New Delhi: Oxford and IBH in collaboration with American Institute of Indian Studies.

1992   "Introduction: The Language and Process of Early Indian Architecture." In *Essays in Early Indian Architecture*, by Ananda K. Coomaraswamy, edited by Michael W. Meister, pp. xvii–xxviii. Delhi: Oxford University Press.

Mitra, Debala
1971   *Buddhist Monuments.* Calcutta: Sahitya Samsad.

Nattier, Jan
1991   *Once Upon a Future Time: Studies in a Buddhist Prophecy of Decline.* Berkeley: Asian Humanities Press.

Seckel, Deitrich
1980   "Stūpa Elements Surviving in East Asian Pagodas." In *The Stūpa: Its Religious, Historical and Architectural Significance*, edited by Anna Libera Dallapiccola in collaboration with Stephanie Zingel-Ave Lallemant, pp. 249–59. Wiesbaden: Franz Steiner Verlag.

Shaughnessy, Edward L.
1993   "Shang shu 尚書 (Shujing 書經)." In *Early Chinese Texts: A Bibliographic Guide*, edited by Michael Loewe, pp. 379–89. Berkeley: Society for the Study of Early China and the Institute of East Asian Studies, University of California.

Sima Qian 司馬遷
1999   *Shiji* 史記. Reprint edition. Taipei: Dingwen shuju.

Sun Ruxian 孫儒僩 and Sun Yihua 孫毅華, chief editors
2001   *Dunhuang shiku quanji 21: Jianzhu huajuan* 敦煌石窟全集 21 建築畫卷. Hong Kong: Shangwu yinshuguan.

Takakusu Junjirō 高楠順次郎, and Watanabe Kaigyoku 渡边海旭, editors

1983–1987   *Taishō Shinshū Daizōkyō* 大正新脩大藏經. 100 volumes. Taibei: Xinwenfeng. Reprint of Tokyo: Taishō issaikyō kankōkai, 1924–1934.

Teiser, Steven F.

2006   *Reinventing the Wheel: Paintings of Rebirth in Medieval Buddhist Temples.* Seattle: University of Washington Press.

Tokuno, Kyoko

1995   "The Book of Resolving Doubts Concerning the Semblance Dharma." In *Buddhism in Practice*, edited by Donald S. Lopez, Jr., pp. 257–71. Princeton: Princeton University Press.

Tseng, Lillian Lan-ying

2011   *Picturing Heaven in Early China.* Harvard East Asian Monographs 336. Cambridge: Harvard University Asian Center.

Wong, Dorothy C.

2004   *Chinese Steles: Pre-Buddhist and Buddhist Use of a Symbolic Form.* Honolulu: University of Hawaii Press.

Wu Hung

1994   "The Transparent Stone: Inverted Vision and Binary Imagery in Medieval Chinese Art." *Representations* 46: 58–86.

Yang Hsüan-chih

1984   *A Record of Buddhist Monasteries in Lo-yang.* Translated by Yi-t'ung Wang. Princeton: Princeton University Press.

Yang Xuanzhi 楊衒之

2006   *Luoyang qielanji xiaojian* 洛陽伽藍記校箋. 2nd edition. Beijing: Zhonghua shuju.

Zürcher, Eric

2007   *The Buddhist Conquest of China.* 3rd edition. Leiden: Brill.

3

HINTS AT TEMPLE TOPOGRAPHY AND COSMIC GEOGRAPHY FROM HITTITE SOURCES

Susanne Görke, Mainz University*

Excavations in the Hittite capital Ḫattuša have lasted for more than 100 years at present and have brought to light archaeological remains, artifacts, and thousands of cuneiform tablets. These allow contemporary researchers to gain insight into a civilization living in Anatolia between around 1600 and 1200 B.C. During the past few decades, several archaeological excavations have revealed further Hittite villages and cities, like Maşat Höyük (Tapikka), Kuşaklı (Šarišša), Ortaköy (Šapinuwa), Kayalıpınar (Šamuḫa?), and Oymaağaç (Nerik?), to mention just some recently discovered sites in the heartland of Hittite settlement. In almost all cases, archaeological activities have concentrated on exposed positions like hills or centers of the *höyük*s, where big buildings were found that were often immediately described as a "palace" or "temple." From an archaeological point of view, those can be distinguished by various features.[1] In fact, Hittite texts employ the expressions É.GAL "big house," commonly interpreted as "palace" (Hitt. *ḫalentuwa-*),[2] and É.DINGIR-*LIM* "house of the god," for "temple" (Hitt. *karimmi-*).[3] Nevertheless, due to the absence of significant numbers of administrative Hittite texts, the whole economic system is not yet fully understood, and differences between temple and palace, and their significance at all, are not clear.[4] Theo van den Hout, for example, has observed that despite the apparent archaeological evidence for a "palace" in Maşat Höyük,[5] there is no evidence for a major administrative role for this building like the É ^{URU}*Tapigga* "palace of the town Tapigga" in textual sources.[6]

This paper tries to analyze examples of Hittite ritual practice, hinting at temple topography and cosmology visible in Hittite cuneiform texts in order to examine the extent of a possible interpretation of temples and festivals as an image of cosmic concepts.

* I would like to thank Gary Beckman for correcting my English. Abbreviations are according to the Chicago Hittite Dictionary (CHD).

[1] See Mielke 2011, pp. 161–67.

[2] See Mielke 2011, p. 161 with n. 15 and further literature on the discussion of this term. Mielke also notes the difference between "palace" as building and as institution; the Hittite word seems to refer only to the building, not the institution. See also van den Hout 2003–05.

[3] See Beckman 2010, p. 71; Zimmer-Vorhaus 2011, p. 205. Cf. HED 4, pp. 83–85.

[4] See Mielke 2011, p. 161 with n. 17 and further literature.

[5] Cf. Mielke 2011, p. 165, but see ibid., p. 169, where he points out arguments for an interpretation as a temple.

[6] Van den Hout 2007, p. 397. Cf. van den Hout 2003–05.

Ritual Practice

The major body of Hittite texts belongs to the religious sphere, namely, rituals and festivals that provide information about venerated gods, religious beliefs, and offering practice. Moreover, they allow the reconstruction of the development and changes in religious thought. One can therefore differentiate between older Hattian-Anatolian traditions and younger concepts that show influences of Mesopotamian, south Anatolian, and northern Syrian ideas that came to central Anatolia due to political and territorial changes.

The religious ideology of the Hittites, at least in the old Hattian-Anatolian tradition, shows the king as the administrator appointed by the main gods of the country, the Storm-god and Sun-god: "The land belongs only to the Storm-god. ... He made the Labarna, the king, (his) deputy/administrator. ... Let the Labarna keep administering the whole land with his hand."[7] Therefore, the king states in a building ritual, "To me, the king, the gods, (namely) Sun-god and Storm-god, handed over the land and my house. And I, the king, will protect my land and my house."[8] The king's duty, among others, was to worship all gods. Correct worship guaranteed prosperity, wealth, and strength to the king, his family, and the whole country. This reverence for the gods is extensively documented in Hittite festival texts, where it is normally described in a rather stereotyped way: "The king comes out of the palace. [The chief of the palace servants] <hands> a stick to the king. Two palace servants (and) one bodyguard run before [the king]. § The king enters the temple of the Storm-god and steps in front of the altar. ... The king makes offerings in a round to the two gods."[9] Other texts provide information about the sequence of worship for the gods and details about people attending the ceremony or the precise things that are to be offered: "[King (and) qu]een drink the Storm-god of Ḫ[att]i three times while standing. He breaks three thick breads. The Hattian singer sings. § [King (and)] queen drink Ḫebat *mušni*, Ḫebat Šarruma three times. He breaks x thick breads. The Hurrian singer sings."[10]

Besides festival texts, descriptions of the worship of gods can also be found in the so-called inventory texts. Here, the god is often taken to an outdoor sanctuary, where offerings and entertainment take place (see below for examples). In contrast with festival texts, it is rarely the king who celebrates those offerings, but priests or the impersonal "they."

Temple Topography

Hittite festival texts concentrate on the portrayal of offerings and therefore do not provide extensive descriptions of the location or appearance of Hittite temples. Dirk Mielke recently stated, "Larger temples — in Boğazköy (especially Temples 1–7, 30 and 31) as well as in Kuşaklı — were erected in prominent positions on artificially constructed or enlarged natural terraces, whereas Hittite architecture otherwise tended to be integrated into natural topography."[11] The following textual examples give rudimentary hints about temple locations within

---

[7] IBoT 1.30 3–6; CHD L–N 169a.

[8] KUB 29.1 obv. i 17–19, CTH 414.1 §5; S. Görke (ed.), hethiter.net/: CTH 414.1 (TX 25.08.2011, TRde 11.05.2011). See an English translation of the text in Beckman 2010, p. 72–75.

[9] KUB 58.6 + KUB 28.91 rev. vi 7–15; Popko 1994, pp. 246f. Cf. García Trabazo and Groddek 2005, pp. 19f.

[10] KBo 11.28 rev. v 22′–28′; Lebrun 1976, pp. 157, 163.

[11] Mielke 2011, p. 170.

towns that seem to support Mielke's idea: "On the next day the helmeted (?) SANGA-priest, the *tazzelli*-priest, the ḫamena-man, the GUDU₁₂-priest and all temple personnel come **up** to the temple."[12] The next example describes the king's arrival at a town named Taḫurpa: "The king goes into Taḫurpa in a coach. As soon as he reaches the gate in town, the ALAM.ZU₉-man shouts *aḫa* in front of the door. § ... § Then he (i.e., the king) drives **up** by coach to the gate house. The men of the ritual run before (him). The king goes into the palace."[13] Even if this case does mention a palace, the next sample text implies the proximity of temple and palace: "King (and) queen go [again from] the palace to the temple of the Storm-god."[14] Scanty hints in Hittite texts therefore seem to confirm the evidence of archaeological features that palace and temple were both situated in a prominent place in a town.

A bit more can be said concerning the appearance of Hittite temples.[15] The well-known example of a major state festival called the "festival of the AN.TAḪ.ŠUM-plant" provides the following information: "King (and) queen go into the temple of the god Zababa. The king is standing in the gatehouse ... King (and) queen step within the temple of Zababa into the courtyard. ... Afterwards, king (and) queen enter the temple of Zababa. They bow again once to the god. ... The king steps to the throne, the queen goes into the inner chamber."[16] Besides these hints about a courtyard, gatehouse, and inner chamber, one also finds allusions to parts of the inner décor: "The supervisor of the cooks makes a libation in front of the throne three times. ... The supervisor of the cooks libates once at the hearth, once at the throne, once at the window, once at the door bolt, and furthermore once next to the hearth. And for the statue of Ḫattušili he makes a libation one time."[17] In a cult inventory one can read, "Formerly the god was (standing) [at the rea]r of the inner room and the community did not see him. Now he is standing at the alta[r]."[18] Moreover, one can find hints as to the decoration of the altar in cult inventory texts.[19] The mention of temple parts is not restricted to festival texts, as the following example of a mythological text shows:[20] "The house (i.e., the house of the god Telipinu) shall release (?) them (i.e., wrath and anger of Telipinu). The central pillar (?) shall let them go, the window shall let them go, the door hinge, the inner courtyard shall let them go, the door shall let them go, the gatehouse shall let them go."[21]

---

[12] KUB 41.30(+) obv. iii 10′–15′; cf. Popko 1994, pp. 270f. (listed as obv. iii 17′–22′ due to text reconstruction).

[13] KBo 11.73+ obv. iii 12′–25′ with complements of KUB 58.22 obv. ii 1′–11′; see Nakamura 2002, pp. 151, 153.

[14] KUB 11.34+ rev. vi 40–41; see Nakamura 2002, pp. 236, 238. The text describes the situation in Ḫattuša; see the colophon.

[15] See Görke in press; for archaeological evidence of the architecture with hints concerning Hittite expressions, see Zimmer-Vorhaus 2011, pp. 205–09.

[16] KBo 4.9 obv. ii 7–43; compared to the autography, the photo shows lacunae (hethiter.net/: PhotArch BoFN00966); for a translation, see Klinger 2008, p. 199; Görke 2010, p. 53.

[17] KBo 4.9 obv. iii 1–12; Klinger 2008, pp. 199f.; Görke in press.

[18] KUB 42.100+ rev. iii 36′–38′; Hazenbos 2003, pp. 19, 23.

[19] KUB 42.91 obv. ii 9f.; see Hazenbos 2003, pp. 112, 114.

[20] See VBoT 58 rev. iv 25–35 (CTH 323 §15″–17″ ff.) mentioning two tables being set up in the temple. Other texts reveal parts of the temple (ᴱ*karimmi-*), like walls, nails, windows, doors (KBo 26.94 rev. iii 4′–10′ – CTH 348.I.26 §5″; KBo 26.83 3′–12′ – CTH 348.I.27 §1′). For those texts, see the online publication on hethiter.net (E. Rieken et al., eds., hethiter.net/).

[21] KUB 17.10 rev. iv 9–11 – CTH 324.1 §30″ (E. Rieken et al., eds., hethiter.net/: CTH 324.1, TX 2009-08-26, TRde 2009-08-26); Hoffner 1998, p. 17 (§26), with a thematic introduction.

Besides information on temples, cult inventories provide an idea of outdoor sanctuaries:

> The [n]ext day they carry the deity down to the w[e]ll. They hold thick bread (and) a ḫarši-(vessel) up before [...] The ḫazgara(-women) go behind [...] They wash the deity in front of the well. Before the altar they take up the garment [from the deity]. They offer 1 sheep. ... They entertain the deity. [At the time of] sunset they carry [the deity] home (and) pl[ace] (him) on the altar.[22]

For the question of where a temple was built, Hittite texts provide only sparse information. From a cult inventory, it becomes evident that places of worship — at least outdoor sanctuaries — might be chosen according to political situations:

> The next day the SANGA-priests, the GUDU$_{12}$-priests, the lords, the noblemen [...] arrive. They carry (Mount) Halwannaš up to the mountain. When (the region) is being oppressed by the enemy, they carry him to the mountain and [place] him [in front of the ḫuwaši] – and the ḫuwaši stands under the poplar. They break 3 loaves of bread of an UPNU(-measure) and they offer beer. When (the region) is not being oppressed by the enemy, they place him at the ḫuwaši under the poplar next to the river and they offer [...] ... 1 ox (and) 8 sheep; the lord of the district delivers (them).[23]

Unfortunately, hints as to why a place was chosen or a temple was built on its particular site are extremely rare. In contrast with other ancient Near Eastern civilizations, (almost) no building inscriptions of Hittite rulers have come down to us.[24] Within the few Hittite building rituals, one finds the following information: "If one builds a new temple or new houses at an untouched place."[25] This ritual starts with the laying of foundation stones in connection with a sacrifice; the following ritual actions are intended to stabilize, consolidate, and strengthen the foundations of that house that is said to be "on the dark earth" — the netherworld.[26] According to the text, the temple is built for a god by the gods — but the choice of place is not explained. Nor does a second building ritual, CTH 414.1, provide information on the choice of place — unfortunately the text is broken. The first paragraph might mention an oracular inquiry to the Sun-god and Storm-god, and one wonders if this includes the question of

---

[22] KBo 26.182 obv. i 7–17; Hazenbos 2003, pp. 68–71. See Ökse 2011 for an overview of Hittite open-air sanctuaries; she stresses their proximity to natural water sources. Cf. Beckman in this volume.

[23] KUB 25.23(+) obv i 10′–16′; cf. Hazenbos 2003, pp. 30–40. The text continues with a rather vivid description of the god's worship: KUB 25.23(+) obv. i 17′–25′: "They set down meat, from the raw (and) from the [c]ooked. (There are) thick breads of the ḫarši-vessel (and) 1 vessel of beer on the altar. (There are) 30 loaves of bread (and) 4 vessels of beer for provisions. And what towns (are situated) around the mountain, they together bring bread (and) beer. They break bread. They fill the rhytons. They eat. They drink. They fill the cups. Before the deity they begin boxing (and) wrestling. They entertain (the deity). When the leafy branches seize the Sun-god of <Heaven>, they carry the deity home to the town,

and they place him inside the temple. They set down meat in front (of him). They break thick bread, and they offer beer." See Hazenbos 2003, pp. 31f., 36.

[24] An exception is the hieroglyphic inscription of Chamber 2, the so-called Südburg Inscription in Ḫattuša; see Hawkins 1995 and Melchert 2002 (for a slightly different interpretation). Building inscriptions are quite common among the hieroglyphic Luwian inscriptions of the Iron Age; see Hawkins 2000. Cf. Beckman in this volume.

[25] KBo 4.1+ obv. 1 – CTH 413.1 §1 (S. Görke, ed., hethiter.net/: CTH 413, TX 25.08.2011, TRde 06.05.2011). See an English translation in Beckman 2010, pp. 85–87.

[26] KBo 4.1+ obv. 9f. – CTH 413.1 §2: "This temple shall be constant and it shall be eternal on the dark earth" (S. Görke, ed., hethiter.net/: CTH 413, TX 25.08.2011, TRde 06.05.2011).

place.[27] This indifference to place also is found in a third building ritual, CTH 726.1, where a king builds new houses "somewhere."[28] Therefore, according to Hittite building rituals, there was normally no need to mention the reason for building a temple at a particular place. One might think that the place where a temple was built was either clear to everyone or was of no importance. This impression seems to be strengthened by other text examples. In mythological texts, one reads, "The goddess Inara built herself a house on a rock in the country of the town Tarukki."[29] This supports the above-mentioned preference in regard to temples and palaces for prominent places, but gives no further concrete reason.

Cosmic Geography

The last examples showed how difficult it is to retrieve information from Hittite texts on temple topography. The same applies to cosmology and cosmic geography.

Knowledge of Hittite cosmology is mainly based on a few mythological texts. From the Song of Kumarbi (CTH 344), for example, we learn that gods fought for kingship in heaven and that the defeated god fled down to the dark earth (i.e., netherworld).[30] Various gods are living in the dark earth, among them the ancient or former gods, who were driven there by the Storm-god, or Allani, the mistress of the underworld, who lived there in a palace, as told in the Song of Release.[31] Moreover, evil things are locked in large vessels made of bronze, their lids made of lead; they stand down in the dark earth, and whatever goes into them does not come up again.[32] The formation or emergence of the world is only briefly mentioned in mythological texts found in Hittite Anatolia.[33] Within the Hurrian Ullikummi myth, one reads, for example, "When it happened that one cut heaven and earth with a copper knife."[34] Already in 1970, Otten and Siegelová published a Hittite fragment that mentions a distribution of heaven and earth among the gods: "When they too[k] heaven and earth, the gods separated. The upper [gods] took heaven, but the inferior gods took [e]arth (and) underground land. Everybody took [h]is (part)."[35] Just as Güterbock associated the Ullikummi statement

---

[27] KUB 29.1 obv. i 3f. – CTH 414.1 §1: "[If the king] builds [a new palace somewhere and one covers it] with wood [one speaks as follows: Concerning the palace] that you built, one has asked [Sun-god] and Storm-god" (S. Görke, ed., hethiter.net/: CTH 414.1, TX 25.08.2011, TRde 11.05.2011). This translation applies to a reading *a-a-ra-i-e-er* in KUB 29.1 obv. i 4, even if the correct form of *ariya-/arai-* should be *ariyaer* or *arier* (see HED 1, 137; HW² A 290). Beckman 2010, p. 72, translates "they have worshipped [the Sun-goddess] and the Storm-god properly" (likewise Cohen 2002, p. 35, with a reading *a-a-ra i-e-er*). The photo reveals no gap.

[28] KBo 37.1 obv. 1f. – CTH 726.1 §1: "If the king builds new houses somewhere […], if one lays the foundations, the *akuttara*-man conducts the ritual and speaks these words" (G. Torri, ed., hethiter.net/: CTH 726.1, TX 04.03.2011, TRit 04.03.2011). See an English translation in Beckman 2010, pp. 77f.

[29] KUB 17.5 obv. i 19′ f. – CTH 321 §11 (E. Rieken et al., eds., hethiter.net/: CTH 321, TX 2010-11-23, TRde 2010-11-23); see Hoffner 1998, p. 12 (§13), with a thematic introduction.

[30] See Hoffner 1998, pp. 40–45, for a translation and thematic introduction; Beckman 2011.

[31] See Haas 1994, pp. 127–31.

[32] As one learns from a passage of the Telipinu myth: KUB 17.10 rev. iv 15–17 – CTH 324.1 §31″ (E. Rieken et al., eds., hethiter.net/: CTH 324.1, TX 2009-08-26, TRde 2009-08-26); Hoffner 1998, p. 17 (§27), also with an thematic introduction.

[33] See also Güterbock 1946, p. 108.

[34] KUB 33.106+ Rs. III 42′, 52′ f. – CTH 345.I.3.1 §§22 and 24; E. Rieken et al., eds., hethiter.net/: CTH 345.I.3.1 (TX 2009-08-31, TRde 2009-08-30); Hoffner 1998, p. 64 (§§61, 63), also with a thematic introduction.

[35] Bo 3617 obv. i 8′–12′; Bo 3078+ obv. ii 7′–11′; Otten and Siegelová 1970, pp. 32f.

with Sumerian mythology,[36] Otten and Siegelová linked this passage to the Sumerian myth of Gilgameš, Enkidu, and the netherworld:[37] "... when the heavens had been separated from the earth, when the earth had been delimited from the heavens, (when the fame of mankind had been established,) when An had taken the heavens for himself, when Enlil had taken the earth for himself, when the nether world had been given to Ereškigala as a gift, ..."[38] Otten and Siegelová already noted that, in contrast with the Sumerian passage with its separation into heaven, earth, and netherworld, the Hittite text obviously only knows a separation into celestial and chthonic realms (1970, pp. 37f.). Itamar Singer elaborated this approach in his treatment of one of Muwatalli's prayers, where he faced the following discrepancies in two versions of the text:

A. (KUB 6.45+ rev. iii 9–10 – CTH 381):
DINGIR.LÚ^{MEŠ} DINGIR.MUNUS^{MEŠ} [A]N-*aš* **GE$_6$-*iš*** KI-*aš ne-pí-iš te-kán*
"male gods (and) female gods of heaven, dark earth, (and) heaven (and) earth"

B. (KUB 6.46 rev. iii 47–49):
DINGIR.LÚ^{MEŠ} [DINGIR.MUNUS^{ME}]^Š [*ne-p*]*í-aš* **da-an-ku-ia-aš** *da-ga-zi-pa-aš ne-*[*p*]*i-*[*i*]*š te-kán*
"male gods (and) female gods of heaven (and) of dark earth, heaven (and) earth"

Singer stated in 1996 (pp. 62f.),

> The "dark netherworld" is treated differently in the two manuscripts. B takes it as a genitive, providing a twofold division of the pantheon into "male gods and female gods of [hea]ven (and) of the dark earth." I assume that this was the original meaning, followed by a similar bipartition of the universe into "heaven (and) earth." On the other hand, A takes the "dark netherworld" as a nominative (GE$_6$-*iš* for *dankuiš*), which may reflect a different cosmological perception — a tripartition of the universe into the dark netherworld, the (surface of the) earth, and heaven. A threefold division of the cosmos, with gods dwelling in heaven and in the netherworld and men inhabiting the earth, is typical for the Mesopotamian cosmogony.

Also the Hurrian-influenced Song of Ullikummi (CTH 345) and the so-called Theogony (CTH 344) as part of the Kumarbi myths[39] show a division of the world into three vertical zones: heaven, earth, and underworld. Therefore, different cosmological concepts seem to have existed among the Hittites: an older Hattian-Anatolian twofold world (heaven – earth/netherworld),[40] and a younger Mesopotamian-influenced tripartition (heaven – earth – netherworld).

---

[36] Güterbock 1946, p. 108.

[37] Otten and Siegelová 1970, p. 37b.

[38] ETCSL translation: t.1.8.1.4–2.1.2012 (http://etcsl.orinst.ox.ac.uk).

[39] See Hoffner 1998, pp. 40–42, for the context of the Kumarbi Cycle; Beckman 2011.

[40] Within a "myth and invocation of fire," CTH 457.1, the goddess Kamrušepa recites a spell of fire that clearly shows a separation into two: "Up above, let heaven overcome it (i.e., illness). Below, let the Dark Earth overcome it" KUB 17.8 rev. iv 9–10; see Hoffner 1998, p. 33 (§3); F. Fuscagni, ed., hethiter.net/: CTH 457.1 (TX 09.05.2012, TRde 20.01.2012).

I. Tatišvili has elaborated on these hints. She traced elements of Hattian-Hittite cosmology by examining the deities of heaven and earth, their functions, and their interrelationships. One can discern between celestial or upper gods and gods of earth or lower gods. Based on the observation that the Hittite expressions "Sun deity of heaven" and "Sun deity of earth" do not refer to two different Sun deities, "but to two essential functions of the same deity, the two hypostases of the Sun,"[41] Tatišvili stated that the Anatolian Storm-god also functions as ruler of rain and of chthonic waters.[42] Therefore, he obviously succeeds in crossing the boundaries between heaven and underworld and vice versa, like other gods hiding in the underworld and able to return without harm.[43] The two old Anatolian-Hattian spheres — heaven and earth/underworld — do not seem to belong to a particular deity or group of deities. Tatišvili (2007, p. 190) considers it a peculiarity of the Hattian-Hittite cosmology that various sections of the world do not seem to be strictly delimited from one another. Therefore she suggests understanding the gods not as those of heaven and those of earth, "but as the unity of the deities each being the deity of heaven as well of the earth."[44]

Already in 1994 Haas stated that the netherworld — according to "Hittite perception" (Haas 1994, p. 127) — lies directly beneath the inhabited land, accessible through caves, pits, or wells. The Storm-god of Nerik, for example, descended to the netherworld through a cave and was able to return afterward.[45] Moreover, the netherworld appears as the reflection of the inhabited land (Haas 1994, pp. 127f.). The close proximity of earth and netherworld is also clear in the above-mentioned expression concerning the erection of a new temple: "This temple shall be constant and it shall be eternal on the dark earth."[46]

To support the assumption of two different cosmological concepts in Hittite Anatolia and to combine it with temple topography, it is worth taking a look at participants in Hittite festivals. Concentrating on passages that describe offering scenes in temples, one can state that large parts of the Hittite population seem to take part in offering scenes, sometimes assisting the king. Within the major state AN.TAH.ŠUM[SAR] festival, for example, which partly reflects older traditions, the following persons are mentioned as taking part in offering scenes at the temple of the god Zababa and its courtyard on the sixteenth day of the festival:[47]

> Courtyard (KBo 4.9 obv. ii 11–36): royal couple, supervisor of bodyguards, SANGA-priest of [D]LAMMA, palace servants, supervisor of palace servants
>
> Temple of Zababa (KBo 4.9 obv. ii 37–rev. v 17): royal couple, <u>musicians</u>: ALAM.ZU₉-man, *kita*-man, *halliyari*-singer, *palwatalla*-man, singer; <u>palace officials</u>: supervisor of cooks, supervisor of "table"-men, "table"-men, supervisor of palace servants, palace servants, supervisor of bodyguards, bodyguards, herald; <u>other</u>: barber
>
> Courtyard (KBo 4.9 rev. v 18–39): herald, princes, cooks, "holy" priest, lord of Hattuša, Godmother-priestess, singers

---

[41] Tatišvili 2007, p. 188.

[42] Tatišvili 2007, p. 187.

[43] See Hoffner 1998, pp. 14–33, for myths relating the disappearance of various gods. Mesopotamian celestial gods seem to lose their power when entering the netherworld, as told, for example, in the Mesopotamian myth Ištar's Descent to the Netherworld.

[44] Tatišvili 2007, p. 190.

[45] KUB 36.89 obv. 12: "The Storm-god of Nerik was angry and went down into a pit"; see Haas 1970, pp. 144f., and Haas 1994, p. 127.

[46] KBo 4.1+ obv. 9f. – CTH 413.1 §2 (S. Görke, ed., hethiter.net/: CTH 413, TX 25.08.2011, TRde 06.05.2011).

[47] KBo 4.9 obv. ii 11–rev. vi 32; see translation and remarks on the contents by Klinger 2008, pp. 199–202; cf. Görke in press. All persons mentioned are listed here, irrespective of their active or passive role.

> Temple of Zababa (KBo 4.9 rev. v 40–vi 32): royal couple, <u>palace officials</u>: supervisor of bodyguards, bodyguards, palace servants, cooks, "table"-men, herald, cupbearer; <u>musicians</u>: singers, *ḫalliyari*-singers, ALAM.ZU₉-men, *palwatalla*-man, *kita*-man, <u>others</u>: *UBĀRŪ*-foreigners, lord of *zaḫurti*, dignitaries of inner room, assembly, barbers

A second example is the Hittite KI.LAM festival, also part of the old Hattian-Anatolian tradition. This short festival was celebrated only in the Hittite capital and contains unique descriptions of a procession of animal images taking place in the palace's courtyard and a "great assembly" with offerings to various gods at the *ḫuwaši*-stones. Also during this festival, many people are mentioned:[48]

> Palace / inner rooms, throne room: king, palace servants
> Palace / courtyard: king, palace servants, bodyguards; priests, singers, musicians, dancers, shepherds, military people, people of the towns of Anunuwa and Ḫariyaša
> Palace / entrance hall: king, palace servants
> Journey to temple: king in a coach, musicians
> Temple / entrance hall: king, palace servants, administrators of cities of the Lower Land, the Upper Land, and Land of Ḫattuša
> *ašuša* city gate: royal couple, bodyguards, runners, priests
> Great Assembly at the *ḫuwaši*-stones: royal couple, king's family, palace servants, bodyguards, singers, musicians, dancers, priests, craftsmen, people of Anatolian cities, foreigners

The old Anatolian festivals therefore seem to include many persons besides cultic and palatial personnel in acts of worship of the god that took place within temple precincts.[49] On the other hand, taking a look at participants in younger festivals influenced by Hurrians and Mesopotamians and their threefold vision of the world, one can recognize some differences. With regard to the *ḫišuwa* festival, one can state that the following participants are mentioned at the end of the first day and the beginning of the second:[50] priest of the Storm-god *manuzi*, "one," king, *palwatalla*-man. Even if one does not know who exactly is meant by "one," it seems likely that it is a member of the cultic personnel.

Concerning the festival for the gods Teššub and Ḫebat of Lawazantiya, about which the third tablet with descriptions of the fifth day is preserved, the persons mentioned seem also to be restricted to priests and musicians.[51] The protagonist, often only impersonally mentioned as "he," seems to be a SANGA-priest, as the following passage suggests:

> Moreover, the SANGA-priest sprinkles fine oil three times in front of the Storm-god and three times in front of the gods of the father. Afterwards, the king sprinkles (fine oil) three times to the Storm-god and in front of the gods of the father three times. They also take up the birds of *puri(ya)* and the *ḫuprušḫi*-vessel out of the basket into which (the foodstuffs) have been poured.[52]

---

[48] For a synopsis of the festival and the "great assembly," see Singer 1983, pp. 58–64, 71–80; cf. Görke 2008, pp. 51–57; Görke in press.

[49] For participants of the *nuntarriyašḫa* festival, see Görke in press. Due to the often fragmentary state of the texts, it is sometimes difficult to say whether offering scenes really took place in temples or in some other kind of cultic place.

[50] CTH 628; for a recent translation and text assemblage, see Klinger 2008, pp. 202–06. For a treatment of the festival, see Wegner and Salvini 1991.

[51] KBo 21.34 + IBoT 1.7 – CTH 699; see Lebrun 1977, pp. 116–42.

[52] KBo 21.34 obv. ii 61–66; Lebrun 1977, pp. 121, 130; see CHD P 387b–388a, which notes *puri(ya)-*, *wuri(ya)*-n. as a Hurrian offering term.

Who exactly is indicated by "they" remains unclear, but again cultic personnel is likely.

For the only partially preserved winter festival for Ištar of Nineveh, the following persons are mentioned:[53] queen, HAL-priest, AZU-priest, *kireštenna*-man, *katra*-women, BURRITIM-women, [LÚ.MEŠ]EN.DINGIR[MEŠ], singer.

The last example presented here is part of the above-mentioned AN.TAH.ŠUM[SAR] festival. This spring festival was probably compiled under the Hittite king Šuppiluliuma I and combines formerly independent and partly old Hittite rites and festivals with younger traditions.[54] Contrary to the above-mentioned activity in the temple of the god Zababa, the ritual actions of the twenty-ninth day take place in and in front of the temple of the god Ea. As the worship of the Mesopotamian god Ea is known in Hittite Anatolia only from the early Empire period on, these rites therefore belong to younger traditions.[55] According to the text reconstruction by Popko and Taracha, texts belonging to the first tablet of the twenty-ninth day of the AN.TAH.ŠUM[SAR] festival mention the ALAM.ZU$_9$-man, the supervisor of cooks, a palace servant, "table"-men, and the HAL-priest.[56]

Remarkable is the reference to a scribe who reads a tablet on which the offerings for the gods are listed: "He (i.e., either king or a priest) invokes all the gods in sequence. But offerings he prepared for those gods to whom the scribe (assigned) sheep on a tablet."[57] On the second tablet, singer, cupbearer, AZU-priest, and *halliyari*-men are mentioned besides the royal couple.[58]

The persons mentioned in festivals that show influences from Hurrian and Mesopotamian thought are on the whole rather small in number. This seems to be comparable to services to gods in other cultures. S. Roth was, for example, able to prove that the house of the temple and its inner sanctum were restricted to god, pharaoh, and cultic personnel during the ancient Egyptian Opet festival. The royal family and Egyptian and alien dignitaries were allowed access only to the temple court and halls. Only outside the temple area, along the processional roads, Egyptian people or military contingents were permitted contact.[59] J. Smith analyzed the biblical book Ezekiel 40–48 according to different hierarchies and was thereby able to map various parts of the temple area and to populate them with different people. In this case too the sanctum was restricted to only a few priests, and attendance grew gradually with an increasing distance.[60]

In contrast with these schemes, the inner sacred part of a Hittite temple seems not to have been restricted to cultic personal, at least not in old Hattian-Anatolian festivals like the AN.TAH.ŠUM[SAR] or KI.LAM. Coming back to Tatišvili's opinion that in the old Hattian-Anatolian vision of the world with a twofold partition there was no strict limitation between

---

[53] CTH 715 only consists of two texts: KBo 33.138 with duplicate(?) KBo 49.287 and KUB 10.63; see Wegner 1995, pp. 164–71 (nos. 38 and 39). The BURRITIM-women are only mentioned in KBo 33.163 rev. 5.

[54] Haas 1994, p. 772; Klinger 2008, p. 196.

[55] See Archi 1993.

[56] See Popko and Taracha 1988, pp. 87–99, with explanations for assigning the texts presented in transliteration and translation to the first tablet of day 29. KBo 9.140, which likely does not belong to the AN.TAH.ŠUM[SAR] festival, moreover mentions *hapiya*-men(?) and singers.

[57] KUB 20.59 rev. v 2–6; see Popko and Taracha 1988, pp. 90f. and 94; Groddek 2004, p. 106, and HEG Š 1059 with a new reading *ši-pa-an-z[a-a]š-ta*.

[58] For the texts belonging to the second tablet of the twenty-ninth day of the AN.TAH.ŠUM[SAR] festival, see Popko and Taracha 1988, pp. 99–110.

[59] See Roth 2008, pp. 137–45, and especially the schematic drawing on p. 139.

[60] See Smith 1987, pp. 47–73, with different schematic drawings.

the two and therefore no reason to separate "normal human beings" from "cultic personnel," the observations concerning the number of people entering temples seem to strengthen her argument. Temples were accessible to a broader part of the population, and offerings to gods were not open only to priests and closed to the majority of the people. This intimacy of temple and population may also be reflected in the above-mentioned phrase from a cult inventory text: "Formerly the god was (standing) [at the rea]r of the inner room and the community did not see him. Now he is standing at the alta[r]."[61]

Summary

This paper, even though presenting only some preliminary thoughts and results, comes to the conclusion that the public attending Hittite festivals of different religious backgrounds is divergent: texts describing old Hattian-Anatolian rites seem to offer the possibility of a large audience and many non-cultic people attending the offering scenes in the inner temple room. Texts influenced by a Hurrian or Mesopotamian cultural background, on the other hand, seem to describe offering scenes with only cultic personnel and an inner circle of court dignitaries[62] and musicians participating.[63] It is tempting to combine this new observation with already known different cosmological ideas: on the one hand, a division of the world into two (heaven – earth/netherworld) without strict borders and with the possibility for gods to move back and forth between the realms, temples without strict rules of access, and no barring of the public; on the other hand, a division of the world into three (heaven, earth, underworld) with strict borders and perhaps no possibility for crossing them, restricted access to inner temple rooms only for cult personnel, and a select audience.

In sum, this paper suggests that Hittite temples might to a certain extent be an image of Hittite society. Hittite mythological texts reveal different ideas of the cosmos influenced by divergent cultural traditions. These also seem to have influenced the manner of celebrating festivals, at least in regard to the incorporation of smaller or greater portions of Hittite society.

---

[61] KUB 42.100+ rev. iii 36′–38′; Hazenbos 2003, pp. 19, 23. See note 18 above.

[62] See already Alp 1940 for the identification of different circles surrounding the king.

[63] One nevertheless has to bear in mind that there is still a lack of detailed research on Hittite festivals. The festival texts influenced by Hurrian or Mesopotamian thought are younger than some of the "older" Hattian-Anatolian ones, and detailed studies on the changes in texts or forms are absent. The above-mentioned differences might therefore partly be due to changes in form or scribal habits.

Abbreviations

Bo	Inventory numbers of Boğazköy tablets excavated 1906–1912
CHD	*The Hittite Dictionary of the Oriental Institute of the University of Chicago.* Chicago, 1980–
CTH	Emmanuel Laroche, *Catalogue des textes hittites*, 2nd ed. Études et commentaires 75. Paris: Klincksieck, 1971
HED	Jaan Puhvel, *Hittite Etymological Dictionary.* Berlin: Mouton, 1984–
HEG	Johann Tischler and Günter Neumann, *Hethitisches etymologisches Glossar.* Innsbruck: Institut für Sprachwissenschaft der Universität Innsbruck, 1983–
HW²	Johannes Friedrich and Annelies Kammenhuber, *Hethitisches Wörterbuch*, 2nd ed. Heidelberg: C. Winter, 1975–
IBoT	İstanbul Arkeoloji Müzelerinde Bulunan Boğazköy Tabletleri(nden Seçme Metinler). Istanbul, 1944, 1947, 1954; Ankara, 1988
KBo	*Keilschrifttexte aus Boghazköi* (vols. 1–22 are a subseries of WVDOG = Wissenschaftliche Veröffentlichungen der Deutschen Orient-Gesellschaft). Leipzig, Berlin
KUB	*Keilschrifturkunden aus Boghazköi.* Berlin
VBoT	Albrecht Götze, *Verstreute Boghazköi-Texte.* Marburg: Lahn, 1930

Bibliography

Alp, Sedat
>   1940   *Untersuchungen zu den Beamtennamen im hethitischen Festzeremoniell.* Gräfenhainichen: C. Schulze.

Archi, Alfonso
>   1993   "The God Ea in Anatolia." In *Aspects of Art and Iconography: Anatolia and Its Neighbors; Studies in Honor of Nimet Özgüç,* edited by Machteld J. Mellink, Edith Porada, and Tahsin Özgüç, pp. 27–33. Ankara: Türk Tarih Kurumu Basımevi.

Beckman, Gary
>   2010   "Temple Building among the Hittites." In *From the Foundations to the Crenellations: Essays on Temple Building in the Ancient Near East and Hebrew Bible,* edited by Mark J. Boda and Jamie R. Novotny, pp. 71–89. Alter Orient und Altes Testament 366. Münster: Ugarit-Verlag.

>   2011   "The Song of Emergence." In *Hethitische Literatur: Überlieferungsprozesse, Textstrukturen, Ausdrucksformen und Nachwirkungen,* edited by Manfred Hutter and Sylvia Hutter-Braunsar, pp. 25–33. Alter Orient und Altes Testament 391. Münster: Ugarit-Verlag.

Cohen, Yoram
>   2002   *Taboos and Prohibitions in Hittite Society: A Study of the Hittite Expression* natta āra *("Not Permitted").* Texte der Hethiter 24. Heidelberg: Universitätsverlag C. Winter.

García Trabazo, José Virgilio, and Detlev Groddek
>   2005   *Hethitische Texte in Transkription: KUB 58.* Dresdner Beiträge zur Hethitologie 18. Wiesbaden: Harrassowitz.

Görke, Susanne
>   2008   "Prozessionen in hethitischen Festritualen als Ausdruck königlicher Herrschaft." In *Fest und Eid: Instrumente der Herrschaftssicherung im Alten Orient,* edited by Doris

                    Prechel, pp. 49–72. Kulturelle und sprachliche Kontakte 3. Würzburg: Ergon-
                    Verlag.

2010   "Die Darstellung von Orten nach den 'Reisefesten' des hethitischen Königs." In
                    *Ort und Bedeutung: Beiträge zum Symposion Die Darstellung von Orten, von der Antike
                    bis in die Moderne, am 20. und 21. Juni 2008 in Heidelberg*, edited by Jan Christian
                    Gertz and Detlef Jericke, pp. 49–68. Kleine Arbeiten zum Alten und Neuen Testa-
                    ment 10. Kamen: Hartmut Spenner.

In press   "Hethitische Rituale im Tempel." In *Akten des siebten internationalen Colloquiums
                    der DOG München*, edited by W. Sallaberger.

Groddek, Detlev
2004   *Hethitische Texte in Transkription: KUB 20.* Dresdner Beiträge zur Hethitologie 13.
                    Wiesbaden: Harrassowitz.

Güterbock, Hans G.
1946   *Kumarbi: Mythen vom churritischen Kronos aus den hethitischen Fragmenten zusam-
                    mengestellt, übersetzt und erklärt.* Istanbuler Schriften 16. New York: Europaverlag.

Haas, Volkert
1970   *Der Kult von Nerik: Ein Beitrag zur hethitischen Religionsgeschichte.* Studia Pohl 4.
                    Rome: Päpstliches Bibelinstitut.

1994   *Geschichte der hethitischen Religion.* Handbuch der Orientalistik, Erste Abteilung:
                    Der Nahe und Mittlere Osten 15. Leiden: Brill.

Hawkins, John David
1995   *The Hieroglyphic Inscription of the Sacred Pool Complex at Hattusa (SÜDBURG).* Studien
                    zu den Boğazköy-Texten, Beiheft 3. Wiesbaden: Harrassowitz.

2000   *Corpus of Hieroglyphic Luwian Inscriptions*, Volume 1: *Inscriptions of the Iron Age*. 3
                    volumes. Untersuchungen zur indogermanischen Sprach- und Kulturwissen-
                    schaft, neue Folge 8.1. New York: W. de Gruyter.

Hazenbos, Joost
2003   *The Organization of the Anatolian Local Cults during the Thirteenth Century B.C.: An
                    Appraisal of the Hittite Cult Inventories.* Cuneiform Monographs 21. Leiden: Brill;
                    Boston: Styx.

Hoffner, Harry A., Jr.
1998   *Hittite Myths.* 2nd edition. Writings from the Ancient World 2. Atlanta: Scholars
                    Press.

Klinger, Jörg
2008   "Texte der Hethiter: Rituale." In *Omina, Orakel, Rituale und Beschwörungen*, edited
                    by Bernd Janowski and Gernot Wilhelm, pp. 187–206. Texte aus der Umwelt des
                    Alten Testaments, neue Folge 4. Gütersloh: Gütersloher Verlagshaus.

Lebrun, René
1976   *Samuha: foyer religieux de l'empire hittite.* Publications de l'Institut orientaliste
                    de Louvain 11. Louvain-la-Neuve: Institut orientaliste, Université catholique
                    de Louvain.

1977   "Textes religieux Hittites de la fin de l'empire." *Hethitica* 2: 93–153.

Melchert, H. Craig
2002   "Tarḫuntašša in the SÜDBURG Hieroglyphic Inscription." In *Recent Developments
                    in Hittite Archaeology and History: Papers in Memory of Hans G. Güterbock*, edited by
                    K. Aslıhan Yener and Harry A. Hoffner Jr., pp. 137–43. Winona Lake: Eisenbrauns.

Mielke, Dirk Paul

    2011   "Hittite Cities: Looking for a Concept." In *Insights into Hittite History and Archae-ology*, edited by Hermann Genz and Dirk Paul Mielke, pp. 153–94. Colloquia Antiqua 2. Leuven: Peeters.

Nakamura, Mitsuo

    2002   *Das hethitische* nuntarriyašḫa-*Fest*. Publications de l'Institut historique-archéolo-gique néerlandais de Stamboul 94. Leiden: Nederlands Instituut voor het Nabije Oosten.

Ökse, A. Tuba

    2011   "Open-air Sanctuaries of the Hittites." In *Insights into Hittite History and Archae-ology*, edited by Hermann Genz and Dirk Paul Mielke, pp. 219–40. Colloquia Antiqua 2. Leuven: Peeters.

Otten, H., and J. Siegelová

    1970   "Die hethitischen Gulš-Gottheiten und die Erschaffung der Menschen." *Archiv für Orientforschung* 23: 32–38.

Popko, Maciej

    1994   *Zippalanda: Ein Kultzentrum im hethitischen Kleinasien*. Texte der Hethiter 21. Hei-delberg: Universitätsverlag C. Winter.

Popko, Maciej, and Piotr Taracha

    1988   "Der 28. und der 29. Tag des hethitischen AN.TAḪ.ŠUM-Festes." *Altorientalische Forschungen* 15: 82–113.

Roth, Silke

    2008   "Angesichts des ganzen Landes: Zu Partizipationsstruktur und Affirmationsme-chanismen von Festen des altägyptischen Königtums." In *Fest und Eid: Instrumente der Herrschaftssicherung im Alten Orient*, edited by Doris Prechel, pp. 135–58. Kul-turelle und sprachliche Kontakte 3. Würzburg: Ergon-Verlag.

Singer, Itamar

    1983   *The Hittite KI.LAM-Festival*, Volume 1. Studien zu den Boğazköy-Texten 27. Wies-baden: Harrassowitz.

    1996   *Muwatalli's Prayer to the Assembly of Gods through the Storm-god of Lightning (CTH 381)*. Atlanta: Scholars Press.

Smith, Jonathan Z.

    1987   *To Take Place: Toward Theory in Ritual*. Chicago Studies in the History of Judaism. Chicago: University of Chicago Press.

Tatišvili, I.

    2007   "Aietes – Son of Helios (For the Study of Hittite–Georgian Religious Parallels)." *Phasis* 10/1: 182–91.

van den Hout, Theo

    2003–2005   "Palast. A. VII. Bei den Hethitern." *Reallexikon der Assyriologie* 10: 227–29.

    2007   "Some Observations on the Tablet Collection from Maşat Höyük." *Studi Micenei ed Egeo-Anatolici* 49: 387–98.

Wegner, Ilse

    1995   *Hurritische Opferlisten aus hethitischen Festbeschreibungen*, Volume 1: *Texte für Ištar-Ša(w)uška*. Corpus der hurritischen Sprachdenkmäler I, Abteilung, Die Texte aus Bogazköy 3. Rome: Bonsignori.

Wegner, Ilse, and Mirjo Salvini

    1991   *Die hethitisch-hurritischen Ritualtafeln des* (ḫ)išuwa-*Festes.* Corpus der hurritischen Sprachdenkmäler I, Abteilung, Die Texte aus Bogazköy 4. Rome: Multigrafica editrice.

Zimmer-Vorhaus, Caroline

    2011   "Hittite Temples: Palaces of the Gods." In *Insights into Hittite History and Archaeology*, edited by Hermann Genz and Dirk Paul Mielke, pp. 195–218. Colloquia Antiqua 2. Leuven: Peeters.

4

IMAGES OF THE COSMOS:
SACRED AND RITUAL SPACE IN
JAINA TEMPLE ARCHITECTURE IN INDIA

*Julia A. B. Hegewald, University of Bonn**

The Jainas, a relatively small but ancient religious group in India,[1] have developed a remarkably complex picture of their religious cosmos. Jaina devotees consider a correct and detailed understanding of the nature of the universe necessary to enable the practitioner to attain enlightenment and to break out of the continuous circle of rebirths by departing from the human regions of the cosmos. Due to the high status that cosmography enjoys in a Jaina context, their temples regularly house depictions of cosmic elements for veneration, and in many instances the architecture itself re-creates cosmographic formations.

The sculptural and architectural reproductions translate highly intricate and convoluted textual descriptions of the Jaina universe into a visual and concrete physical shape in order to make them easier to comprehend. Wall and cloth paintings, carved stone panels, three-dimensional sculpted representations, architectural models, and full-scale temples illustrate various aspects or views of the universe. Small replicas are displayed in shrines as educational tools and objects of veneration. Sacred architecture molded on the cosmos enables worshippers, mendicants, and priests to reenact cosmic and mythical happenings. Particularly widespread are temples inspired by the shape of sacred mountains and certain cosmic continents, to which human beings in reality have no access. The temples offer believers the opportunity to enter extraterrestrial space, to participate in cosmic events, and to anticipate their own enlightenment.

However, ritual practices carried out in Jaina temples, which have no immediate visual connection with celestial structures, also relate to and reenact mythical and cosmic events by transforming the area around ritual objects and ceremonial activities into cosmic and mythical space and time.

This chapter examines correspondences between the cosmic geography and the sacred architecture of the Jainas. It highlights the interaction between sacred and ritual space and the association between mythical events and ritual practices. At the start, a short paragraph introduces the reader to the most crucial Jaina cosmological items. This is followed by a

* I would like to express my gratitude to the German Research Foundation (DFG), who have continuously funded and supported my research on Jaina art and architecture in South Asia since 2002.

[1] The Jainas make up less than half of 1 percent of the total Indian population. Mahāvīra, the last of the twenty-four enlightened Jaina teachers of this world era, lived in about the fifth or sixth century B.C.E. His teachings, however, appear to have been a codified and standardized version of the wisdom of earlier reformers, and Jainas themselves argue for the existence of Jainism at the time of the Indus civilization in about the third millennium B.C.E. (Hegewald 2009a, pp. 216, 314).

section that illustrates the translation of these concepts into architecture. In addition, myths and legends that describe events that occurred in distant quarters of the universe have led to the creation of ritual implements and venerated objects. These play an important role in Jaina ritual, which has molded the architecture enshrining sacred ceremonial activities.

Jaina Cosmology: Texts and Meanings

Jaina cosmology and cosmography are not about the physical shape and geography of the external world of matter. They are primarily concerned with providing an understanding of the path to enlightenment, and as such their main incentive is soteriological.[2] The soul's journey toward omniscience is compared to a pilgrimage through the universe (Babb 1998, pp. 49–52). Because of the considerable religious significance of a detailed knowledge of the cosmos as a means to reaching liberation, the Jainas have dedicated a substantial amount of attention to the study of cosmology and cosmography.

The beginnings of Jaina cosmography appear to date back to the fifth or sixth century B.C.E., even though the earliest surviving texts dealing with the subject date from about the first century C.E.[3] The canonical literature, the *Āgamas*, just like selected philosophical, scientific, and technical treatises, provide minute descriptions of the geography of the Jaina universe.[4] Despite the fact that Jaina perceptions of the cosmos are related to Buddhist, Vedic, and above all *Purāṇic* ideas of the world, Jaina cosmography is distinct.[5] The most pronounced points of difference are the Jaina belief that the universe, although it goes through cycles, has no beginning and no end, and secondly, that it has not been created by a god or divine being.

It is noteworthy that we have a variety of different and at times contradictory Jaina accounts of the cosmos. This is partly due to the fact that terminologies changed and measurements were standardized only after the formulation of texts.[6] In addition, there is a certain amount of variation between Digambara and Śvetāmbara descriptions.[7] Further essential aspects are that Indian cosmologies in general developed over a long period of time and in

---

[2] For instance, this is evident from the drawings of the cosmos and the transit of the souls that accompany and illustrate the discussion of the various ways of transit through the universe that lead to liberation, which have been included in the English translation of the *Tattvārtha-sūtra* and its combined commentaries edited by Kerry Brown and Sima Sharma (1994, p. 49).

[3] According to Richard F. Gombrich, this may be partly due to earlier texts having been lost (1975, p. 118).

[4] Among the canonical scriptures, the third *Upāṅga*, called the *Jīvājīvābhigama*, is one of the principal texts dealing with Jaina cosmography. This was further elaborated upon in the *Jambūdvīpaprajñapati*. The *Sūryaprajñapati* and the *Candraprajñapati* primarily deal with Jaina astronomy, an area closely related to cosmography (Bose, Sen, and Subbarayappa 1971, pp. 42–45). Also Kundakunda's *Tattvārthādhigamasūtra* deals with the structure of the universe and with cosmography. For an analysis of additional texts on Jaina cosmology, particularly from a Digambara background, see S. S. Lishk 1998, p. 9.

[5] For similarities with the *Vedas*, see Surender K. Jain 1997, p. 59, and for those issues relating to the *Purāṇas* and Buddhist perceptions of the cosmos, see D. C. Sircar 1967, pp. 56–57. The most detailed comparison of all three world systems, Hindu, Buddhist, and Jaina, can be found in Richard F. Gombrich's article on ancient Indian cosmologies (1975, pp. 119–20).

[6] We find a comparable situation in the West. S. S. Lishk reminds us that it was as late as 1878 C.E. that the length of the British mile became standardized (1998, p. 9).

[7] Above all, these differences relate to the form of the inner cosmos (Schubring 1995, p. 205), the breadth of the space of the world (von Glasenapp 1999, p. 250), and the number of heavens in the upper part of the universe (Coomaraswamy 1994, p. 26; Brown and Sharma 1994, pp. 92–93, figs. 10–11). Digambaras and Śvetāmbaras make up the two largest groups of Jainas in India.

a vast geographical area by absorbing new cultural elements without necessarily discarding earlier, often conflicting, accounts (Gombrich 1975, pp. 111, 131).

Somewhat confusing to start with are the gigantic numbers and dimensions one is confronted with when dealing with the measurements of the universe and its constituent components.[8] Belonging to a religious world system, however, they too have to be viewed from a soteriological viewpoint. In this context, the incomprehensibility of the dimensions express in a striking way the extreme difficulty of attaining omniscience in such a vast and superhuman system (Babb 1998, p. 38).

A large number of detailed accounts of Jaina cosmology and cosmography survive, and these have been analyzed by a number of scholars.[9] The aim of this chapter is to introduce the reader to examples where Jaina cosmological ideas have been translated into three-dimensional visual form, especially architecture. Because of the gigantic size and the complexity of the Jaina cosmos, only certain aspects or elements have been given visual shape. It is fascinating to observe which continents and sacred mountains were chosen for representation and veneration in temple complexes and where and when such commissions were made. The following is a brief overview of the basic composition of the Jaina cosmos and of those segments within it that have been translated into Jaina art and architecture.

The Shape of the Jaina Universe

Consistent with the Jaina view of the cosmos, time and the structure of the universe are eternal and self-created. Therefore, Jainism does not have a creation story or cosmogony. Jaina cosmology can be studied on a variety of levels. In Jaina cosmographical texts, the universe as a whole, as if viewed from outside the system, is described. It is explained as consisting of superimposed layers of heavens and hells and a middle world, which is partly inhabited by human beings. This central area accommodates a number of cosmic continents, mountains, rivers, and trees, bringing a superhuman world system down to a more human level.

The Hourglass and the Cosmic Person

The Jaina universe is believed to be vast yet finite and to consist of two major elements, the world of existence (*loka, lokākāśa*) and that of non-existence (*aloka, alokākāśa*), alternatively referred to as non-universe space or non-world. The world of existence forms the inner core of this cosmic system and is surrounded on all sides by the hollow sphere of non-existence.[10]

---

[8] These enormous numbers apply to both cosmic time and space. The Jaina universe is measured in terms of a standard unit called a "rope" (*rajju*). A *rajju* is said to be the equivalent of ten million *joyanas*, and a *joyana* equals about eight miles (Gombrich 1975, p. 130). Based on this conversion, Mount Meru, which is minute when considered within the larger cosmic framework, measures 800,000 miles in height (Babb 1998, p. 38).

[9] For meticulous descriptions of the nature and shape of the Jaina cosmos, see Collette Caillat 1981; Willibald Kirfel 1990; Walther Schubring 1995, pp. 204–46; S. S. Lishk 1998; and Helmuth von Glasenapp 1999, pp. 241–70.

[10] The key difference between these two areas is that matter and motion are absent from the outer universe. For additional information, see D. M. Bose, S. N. Sen, and B. V. Subbarayappa 1971, pp. 472–75; G. R. Jain 1985, pp. 8, 12–14; Nagin J. Shah 1998, p. 12; and Hegewald 2000, 37 n. 12).

The central nucleus of the Jaina cosmos, which is portrayed as firm and unchanging, is represented by the outline of an hourglass. A second, closely related form, which is slightly more common than the previous one, depicts the structure of the universe as a triangle topped by a diamond shape (fig. 4.1). In paintings and carvings illustrating the Jaina cosmos, either model is frequently compared to the shape of a human being, standing upright with legs apart and arms either raised above the head or akimbo, resting on both sides of the waist with elbows stretched out (fig. 4.2). This conception of the Jaina universe is related to the idea of the cosmic man (*loka-puruṣa*), though representations portraying the cosmic person as a woman too are widespread.[11]

It is significant that the various descriptions outlined above all create a tripartite division of the cosmos (*tri-loka*), consisting of a lower world (*adho-loka*), a middle world (*madhya-loka*), and an upper world (*ūrdhva-loka, uḍḍha-loka*). The central element, which takes the form of a thin disc, coincides with the narrow waist of the cosmic being. Broadly speaking, the lower section of the Jaina universe contains various levels of hells (*naraka*),[12] the middle portion consists of the human world and a series of zones inhabited by divine beings, whereas the upper segment of the inner cosmos comprises numerous heavens (*deva-loka*).

At the apex of the upper world is a small, clearly delineated area, the region of the so-called liberated perfected souls or blissful beings. This inverted umbrella-shaped section at the crown of the universe is known as the *siddha-loka* or *siddha-śilā*.[13] Running like a vertical shaft throughout the entire cosmos is a channel known as the *trasa-nāḍī*, the sphere of the mobile beings (*trasa-jīvas*). It is striking how small the disc of the terrestrial world is in comparison to the enormity of the heavens and hells located below and above it.

Two-dimensional artistic representations of the abstract hourglass version as well as of the anthropomorphic human-shaped Jaina cosmos are habitually exhibited at the entrance points to shrines and monastic establishments (*dharmaśālās*) throughout India. Most cosmic depictions have been painted on cloth or paper, carved out of stone, or cast in metal. Positioned at the doors of access to sacred Jaina complexes, cosmic imagery is used as a marker and powerful symbol of Jaina identity (fig. 4.3).

The Middle World

More frequent than portrayals of the entire universe are paintings, sculptures, and architectural structures relating exclusively to the middle world (*madhya-loka*). The central segment of the Jaina cosmos is described as a thin disc, consisting of innumerable concentric

---

[11] A painting of the cosmic woman has been reproduced in Collette Caillat 1981, p. 53. The idea of the cosmic man is not unique to Jainism. Cosmogonies relating to the *puruṣa* are equally common in a Hindu context. With respect to the correlation of cosmos and human beings in Jainism, it is fascinating to note that Vasunandi in his *Śrāvakācāra* describes a meditation in which practitioners imagine their own body as the cosmos, with Mount Meru in the navel, the hells below, the heavenly spheres around the shoulders and the neck portion, and, finally, the place of the liberated souls (*siddha-śila*) located on the forehead (Jain 1977, p. 38).

[12] The lower world is supposed to be inhabited by infernal beings (*nāraki*). Nevertheless, the uppermost levels of the netherworld, known as *rayaṇappabhā*, are occupied by demi-gods and divinities. These divine beings can move about freely and also reside in the middle world (Schubring 1995, p. 213; Jaini 1990, p. 128).

[13] The space at the very tip of the universe is alternatively referred to as the *īṣatpragbhāra* or the paradise of the perfected. It is located outside the sphere of *saṃsāra*, in which all living beings are subject to the cycle of rebirths (Coomaraswamy 1994, p. 26).

islands separated by rings of oceans (*samudra*).[14] At the core of the flat disc is a solid circular island called Jambū-dvīpa (the rose-apple-tree island). The entrance porches of Jaina temples regularly display carved panels and painted representations depicting the large circular disc of the entire middle world or of a representation of just the innermost island of Jambū-dvīpa (fig. 4.4). This island is regarded as particularly vital as it lies at the center of the universe and is the place where human beings are born and where escape from the cycle of rebirth can be achieved.

In the middle of Jambū-dvīpa rises the world mountain. This peak is known by a number of different names, often listed as sixteen (Caillat 1981, p. 30). Among the most prevalent names are Meru, Sumeru, Sudarśana Meru, Mandara, and Aṣṭāpada.[15] The mountain is located on the central continent or world region (*varṣa*) of the island of Jambū, called Mahāvideha or Videha, and denotes the axis of the universe (*axis mundi*) (fig. 4.5). This sacred area, the Mahāvideha-kṣetra, is further subdivided into four countries. Purva-Videha lies to the east, Avara-Videha to the west, Devakurā to the south, and Uttarakurā to the north.

In each of the latter two continents grows a large cosmic tree. The tree found in Devakurā (*kurā* of the gods) is called the Śālmalī or Kūḍasāmalī (Lishk 1998, p. 21; Schubring 1995, p. 217), and that in Uttarakurā (northern *kurā*) is referred to as the Jambū tree (Jambū Vṛkṣa). This is the tree after which the entire central world island has been named. The two trees are wish-granting trees (*kalpa-vṛkṣas*, *kalpa-drumas*), which are characteristic of the so-called realms of enjoyment (*bhoga-bhūmi*). In the *bhoga-bhūmi*s, life is effortless, but enlightened teachers of the Jaina religion, the Jinas (conquerors, spiritual victors) or Tīrthaṅkaras (builders of the ford, fordmakers), cannot be born, and liberation cannot be attained.[16] Both continents together are said to contain ten types of *kalpa-vṛkṣas*.

A fascinating artistic delineation of a wish-fulfilling tree, dating from the seventeenth century, has been assembled inside the compound of the Pārśvanātha Temple at Lodruva (Ludravā) near Jaisalmer in Rajasthan (fig. 4.6). The original sacred edifice was erected in 1152 C.E. but destroyed and rebuilt in 1615 C.E. The tree is made of metal and has been raised on a three-tiered square structure with gateways facing the four directions. According to local legend, it is an artificial replacement of a natural tree that once grew at the site.[17] Many contemporary Jaina temples have similar representations of celestial trees set atop three-tiered

---

[14] The number of concentric island continents is said to be innumerable or uncountable (*asaṅkhyāt*). However, they do not extend forever in space, and there is a limit beyond which there is only empty space (Babb 1998, p. 40).

[15] Meru and Sumeru are the most recurring terms. Meru is Sanskrit, and Sumeru (or Sineru) derives from Pali (Gombrich 1975, p. 119). According to S. S. Lishk, there are textual passages referring to the central world mountain as Sudarśana Meru (1998, p. 20) and Mount Mandara (ibid., p. 27). For further usages of these names, see U. P. Shah 1955, p. 117, and Walther Schubring 1995, p. 217. The use of the term "Aṣṭāpada" is attested to by Harihar Singh (1982, p. 154).

[16] In the *bhoga-bhūmi*s, the regions of enjoyment, human life is full of happiness, and all desires are

granted by the *kalpa-vṛkṣas*, wish-fulfilling trees. However, as such an environment is not conducive to asceticism, Tīrthaṅkaras cannot be born in these areas of the cosmos. On this topic, see G. Amar 1975, p. 518; Surender K. Jain 1997, p. 61; and Lawrence A. Babb 1998, p. 40. Outside the *bhoga-bhūmi*s lie the *karma-bhūmi*s, which are discussed below.

[17] Jaina temples all over India have natural trees growing inside their walled compounds, which are venerated as sacred objects because of their mythical or cosmic associations. Examples of such revered trees are found in the Ādinātha Temple at Ranakpur (Rāṇakapura) in Rajasthan, behind the Ādīśvara Temple on Mount Śatruñjaya near Palitana (Pālitānā) in Gujarat, and in the complex of the Candraprabha Temple at Phalghat (Palakkad) in Kerala.

pedestals, as may be seen inside the cosmological hall in the pilgrimage complex at Mandu (Māndū) in Madhya Pradesh and next to the Candraprabha Temple at Arrah (Ārā) in Bihar.

The innermost area of Jambū-dvīpa is surrounded by six zones that are separated from each other by long chains of mountains (*vāsadhara-pavvaya*) stretching from east to west.[18] The mountain ridges contain lakes (*mahā-ddaha*), which accommodate floating islands in lotus form. Their descriptions appear to have inspired lotus-shaped temples constructed by the Jainas at pilgrimage sites such as Mangi Tungi (Mangī Tungī) in Maharashtra and Hastinapur (Hastināpur) in Haryana (fig. 4.7).

Issuing from the mountain lakes are rivers, eventually flowing into the Lavaṇa Samudra, the Sea of Salt, which surrounds the island of Jambū on all sides.[19] Beyond this circle of water are innumerable concentric rings of land, separated by further bands of oceans. Human beings are said to inhabit Jambū-dvīpa, the next island ring of Dhātakīkhaṇḍa, and the inner half of Puṣkaravara-dvīpa, the third island continent from the center.[20] These are referred to as the two-and-a-half islands, the Aḍhāī-dvīpa, or more generally as the *manuṣya-loka*, the human universe (fig. 4.8). The two-and-a-half islands are regions of labor (*karma-bhūmis*) where one has to work for one's living but where escape (*mokṣa*) from the cycle of rebirth can be attained. Due to their significant position in the Jaina world system, the Aḍhāī-dvīpa have regularly been depicted in Jaina art, and many representations adorn the walls and entrance halls of temple structures.

Mount Meru is not the only named and significant hill of the Jaina cosmos. Particularly interesting is a cluster of four peaks, surrounding the central world mountain and creating a group of five, known as the *pañca-meru*.[21] Mount Meru or Sumeru is located at the center of Jambū-dvīpa. Mount Vijaya and Mount Acala are situated on the second island continent called Dhātakīkhaṇḍa, to the east and west, respectively. Hills number four and five, called Mandara (a term also used for the central world mountain) and Vidyunmāli, respectively, are located in the eastern and western sections of the inner half of Puṣkaravara-dvīpa, the next concentric island ring, creating an east–west line of five revered hills. There are ample illustrations of the *pañca-meru* in Jaina art (fig. 4.9). Metal sculptures dating from the thirteenth and fifteenths centuries, respectively, that display all five mountains stacked to create one tall pillar-like peak are housed in the Śvetāmbara Hastiśālā of the Lūṇ-vasahī at Mount Abu (Ābū Parvata, Delvāṛa), Rajasthan, and in the Digambara Jaina Temple at Surat (Sūrat), Gujarat.[22] Even more typical are such conical metal representations, measuring about one

---

[18] Based on different textual traditions, Jaina scholars have provided different names for the seven world regions of Jambū-dvīpa. While Walther Schubring refers to them as Mahāvideha, Bharata, Hemavaya, Harivāsa, Eravaya, Hiraṇṇavaya, and Rammaga (1995, p. 217), it is more common for them to be named as Bharata, Haimavata, Hari, Videha, Ramyaka, Hairaṇyaka (or Hairanyavata), and Airāvata (Jain 1997, p. 61; Lishk 1998, p. 20; Brown and Sharma 1994, p. 77). It is noteworthy that all versions contain an area referred to as Bhārata-kṣetra or Bhārata-varṣa, the land of India as we know it from our modern perception of world geography. This is the place where the twenty-four Jinas of the present age have all been born (Jindal 1987, p. 224; Gombrich 1975, p. 131).

[19] Walther Schubring provides the names of the rivers originating at the apex of the mountains and the directions into which they flow (1995, pp. 218–19).

[20] Halfway through the island of Puṣkaravara is said to be an impassable mountain ring. This is called Mānuṣottara Parvata, and Jainas believe that beyond this only so-called *tiryañcas* (sub-humans or animals) reside, and no human being can survive there.

[21] Occasionally the *pañca-meru* are referred to as *sudarśana* (Amar 1975, p. 521). Yet this term is more regularly applied to Mount Sumeru, the central peak of the assembly of five.

[22] For a reproduction of the latter example, see U. P. Shah 1955, pl. 29, fig. 78G). Gopilal Amar disagrees with this identification and considers it to be a rep-

meter in height, of Digambara shrines in Tamil Nadu and Kerala. In central India, the shape of the statues is usually more straight sided (fig. 4.10).

There is an infinite number of concentric island rings that surround the central island of Jambū-dvīpa. Most texts on Jaina cosmography provide the names for at least the sixteen innermost and the sixteen outermost concentric island rings (Lishk 1998, pp. 16–18). The only other island, apart from Jambū-dvīpa, that has frequently been portrayed in Jaina art is the eighth island from the center, called Nandīśvara-dvīpa. On this island too there are a large number of mountains and shrines (*garbha-gṛha*s) dedicated to the Tīrthaṅkaras. There are four Añjana Parvatas, mountains of black color, which are located in the cardinal directions. Each of these four peaks is surrounded by four crystal- or curd-colored mountains, the Dadhimukha Giris, and by another eight golden mountains, the Ratikara Giris. All together, they create four groups of thirteen mountain peaks each, which are located in the cardinal directions.[23] According to the descriptions, there is a natural, self-created Jaina temple at the summit of each of the hills, creating a total of fifty-two sacred mountains and shrines of the Jainas on the island of Nandīśvara.[24]

Many Jaina temples in the north of India contain stylized diagrammatic representations of the eighth island that have been carved on circular stone plaques. These are referred to as *citra-paṭa*s, and most show a central mountain hub, surrounded by four lozenge- or diamond-shaped groups of thirteen pavilions (fig. 4.11). Unlike Jaina texts, which describe the island of Nandīśvara as a ring, sculptural and architectural reproductions portray it as a solid disc or as a round or staggered temple space, respectively.[25] Nandīśvara-dvīpa depictions from the south of India follow a different tradition. The Digambara examples are made of metal and have representations of the fifty-two mountains arranged in a three-dimensional pyramidal form (fig. 4.12).[26]

Each continent of the Jaina universe is described as having an elaborate system of rivers and lakes, as well as innumerable mountains, forests, gardens, and sanctums dedicated to the fordmakers. The account of the middle world provided here is only a brief and simplified description. However, many of the components delineated above have been translated into architecture in the form of Jaina temple structures. Sacred architecture, as a stage for the performance of cosmic and mythical actions, is the focus of the following paragraph.

---

resentation of just a single *meru* (1975, p. 525 n. 1). For a discussion of this issue, see Hegewald 2000, p. 39 n. 28). However, as the same kind of sculptural arrangement is very typical of South Indian Jaina art, where it is regarded as a depiction of the *pañca-meru* and is called by this name, I agree with the identification by U. P. Shah.

[23] This brief account is based on the relevant text passages in the *Triṣaṣṭiśalākāpuruṣacarita*, the *Harivaṃśa* of Jinasena, the *Trilokasāra* of Nemicandra, the *Sthānāṅga Sūtra*, and the *Āvaśyaka Cūrṇi* as summarized by U. P. Shah (1955, pp. 119–20) as well as on the descriptions by Willibald Kirfel (1990, pp. 253–57), S. S. Lishk (1998, pp. 54–57), and Gopilal Amar (1975, pp. 525–29). There is a certain amount of variation among these accounts.

[24] The shrines positioned on the peaks of these hills are all said to have one hundred and eight *garbha-gṛha*s or platforms, each housing or supporting a statue of one of the Tīrthaṅkaras. Based on this concept, Jaina temples throughout India regularly have large numbers of sanctums, and those in northwestern India in particular often have fifty-two shrines (*devakulikā*s), making such complexes representative of Nandīśvara-dvīpa.

[25] For a detailed examination of this unusual feature and possible explanations for it, see Hegewald 2000, pp. 26–27.

[26] Further illustrations can be found in Jyotindra Jain and Eberhard Fischer 1978, p. 19, and in U. P. Shah 1955, pl. 24, fig. 63.

The Cosmos in Jaina Architecture

Particularly fascinating is the close connection between descriptions of the universe and Jaina temple architecture. Many Jaina sacred structures are direct microcosmic illustrations of macrocosmic items outlined in the literature. It is remarkable how closely cosmological texts and architectural compositions are related and that the temples directly bear the names of cosmic elements. Especially widespread are shrines that house sizeable models or that themselves re-create certain extraterrestrial continents and sacred mountains. In the following, I discuss the most prevalent forms of Jaina cosmic architecture.

Jambū-dvīpa Temples

The innermost island of the Jaina universe, Jambū-dvīpa, has frequently been displayed as a symbol of Jaina identity in the entrance porches of sacred structures. In addition, there are three-dimensional representations of this continent. In the shape of sculptural and large-scale architectural replicas, the complex geography of the cosmic island, including its mountain ranges and rivers, could be modeled more accurately than in small paintings or relief carvings. Walkways and galleries allow visitors in some shrines to study the cosmic reproductions from various levels and viewpoints.

Large sculptural models of the central world continent have regularly been accommodated inside Jaina temples. In the so-called Cosmological Temple at the pilgrimage site of Bahubali (Bāhubalī) at Kumbhoj in Maharashtra, a sizable replica is found in the principal sanctum on the ground floor (fig. 4.13). In other sacred edifices, the representations are housed on a raised story, usually located above a figural image enshrined below. This is the case in the Ādinātha Temple on the sanctified Jaina hill known as Pisanhari-ki Maria (Pisanhārī-kī Maṛhiyā) near Jabalpur in Madhya Pradesh. Both constructions date largely from the twentieth century.

One of the most detailed monumental reproductions of Jambū-dvīpa is venerated at Ajmer (Ajmīr) in Rajasthan. Behind the main temple, known as the Śrī Siddhkut Caityālaya, the Nasiyan or Soni Jaina Temple (1864) is a large multi-storied hall. The Svarna Nagarī Hall displays a huge architectural model of the central world continent with a tall central mountain reproduction, locally referred to as Sumeru Parvata (fig. 4.14). Immediately above the summit of the mountain are the heavenly realms. In Ajmer, these are symbolized by representations of the *vaimānika-devas*, gods in their celestial vehicles or airships, which have been suspended from the ceiling on long ropes. Devotees can view the entire assemblage from galleries on various levels. Believers meditate on the nature of the universe and reflect on the path to enlightenment.

The *vaimānika-devas* circulating around the top of the sacred hill are related to the *jyotiṣk* or *jyotiṣa* deities, which are divinities of light, equated with the planets. The Jainas venerate nine planets, the *nava-grahas*.[27] These have been depicted at the foot of the pedestals supporting Jina statues (Nagar 1999, pp. 33, 76) and adorn door lintels as, for instance, in the Pārśvanātha Temple at Khajuraho (Khajurāho), Madhya Pradesh (Hegewald 2006, p. 407). In the south of India, especially in Tamil Nadu, three-dimensional sculptural illustrations of the

---

[27] In Jainism, the nine planets are the sun, the moon, Mars, Mercury, Jupiter, Venus, Saturn, Rāhu, and Ketu (Nagar 1999, p. 367). Initially, Rāhu and Ketu were treated as one (ibid., p. 373).

group of nine planets are commonly displayed for veneration in the halls providing access to Jaina shrines (fig. 4.15).

Besides models of Jambū-dvīpa contained within temple edifices or large halls as discussed so far, there are freestanding architectural conceptions illustrating this theme. An open-air representation of the central world island has been raised in the western corner of the Śvetāmbara temple complex in the fort of Mandu in Madhya Pradesh (fig. 4.16). In Mandu, the tall mountain rising at the center of the Jambū-dvīpa reproduction is embodied by a tall pillar, surrounded by the world regions located to the north and south of Mahāvideha. The sacred depiction is used as a pedagogical tool by monks and saintly teachers and as an object of religious contemplation.

The probably largest and most complex reconstruction of the geography of Jambū-dvīpa was fashioned at Hastinapur in Haryana in the twentieth century (fig. 4.17).[28] The enormous reproduction of the central world disc measures about thirty-five meters in diameter and has been furnished with simplified mountain chains and water channels. The latter signify the cosmic rivers on Jambū-dvīpa and bear clear labels precisely identifying and naming them. The Lavaṇa Samudra, the Sea of Salt, surrounding the island of Jambū, is represented by a circular water channel enclosing the cosmological monument (fig. 4.18). A small boat allows visitors to travel around the Sea of Salt and to examine the geography of the innermost world continent. At the center of the assembly rises the tall Sumeru Parvata in the shape of a lofty tower. This measures about sixty meters in height, and an internal staircase provides believers and visitors with the opportunity to climb the cosmic mountain and to gaze down from various stories and directions onto a miniature adaptation of the world we live in. On this microcosmic scale, the structure of the universe becomes more comprehensible. The devotees seem to partake in a view down onto the world of man, which is offered only to the liberated souls, who have floated to the apex of the universe. Through this act, believers figuratively forestall their own enlightenment.

Meru Temples

As described in the previous paragraph, depictions of the central world mountain, Mount Meru, regularly constitute an element of larger cosmic re-creations. Nevertheless, mountain representations can exist independently. When forming the sole focus of a sculptural or architectural model, more attention has generally been paid to the various constituent segments and superimposed levels of the sacred hill. Mount Meru is described as having three receding tiers and to be crowned by a self-created or natural Jaina shrine (*cūlikā*) (fig. 4.19). In three-dimensional reproductions that have regularly been accommodated in Jaina temples throughout India, the structure at the summit of the mountain is usually represented by either a single or a four-faced statue of a Jina (*caturmukha*, *caumukha*), sometimes seated beneath a canopy or inside a small pavilion.[29] Although Digambara and Śvetāmbara Jainas both venerate *meru*s, they appear to be more widespread in a Digambara environment.

---

[28] The construction of the Jambū-dvīpa Rachanā was inspired by Śrī Jñānamatī Mātā Jī, an influential Jaina nun, prolific writer on Jaina cosmology, and founder of the Digambara Jaina Institute of Cosmographic Research at Hastinapur, north of Delhi.

[29] A relatively rare case of a *meru* sculpture with four standing statues on the apex is enshrined inside the Digambara Candraprabha Temple in Arrah.

Small versions of *meru* sculptures in metal and larger ones in stone are revered inside the *garbha-gṛhas* of Jaina temples all over India. While bronze replicas are particularly typical of the south of India, stone versions are more common in the north. In most instances, these form the primary focus of veneration. They are referred to by the generic term *meru*, combined with the name of the fordmaker or the main representative of a group of four Tīrthaṅkaras, placed at the apex (fig. 4.20).[30] The latter examples illustrate that not all *meru* temples explicitly house depictions of Mount Meru, the central world peak. There are other sacred hills and mountain chains located on Jambū-dvīpa and on adjacent island rings, and these have similarly been given visual shape. Other peaks are simply referred to as *merus* or *parvatas* as generic terms without a specific denomination.

Even clearer than the sculpted versions discussed above in the section on Jaina cosmology are architectural reproductions of the five sacred mountains, the *pañca-meru* of the Jaina universe. At Taranga (Tāraṅgā) in Gujarat, large stone representations of the five *merus*, dating from about the fifteenth to sixteenth century, have been enshrined in a freestanding pavilion located in the southeastern corner of the Ajitanātha Temple complex. Others are housed in larger temple structures. It is fascinating that the group of five holy mountains has often been accommodated on raised floor levels. Two examples are those venerated on the first story of a shrine inside the Tuṅk of Lālcand Modī Premcand on Mount Śatruñjaya at Palitana (Pālitānā), Gujarat, and in the so-called Cosmological Temple at the pilgrimage site of Bahubali, at Kumbhoj.

There are other cosmic and mythical mountains whose sculptural reproductions are revered inside shrines or that have been transformed into Jaina temple structures themselves. Most prominent among these are Aṣṭāpada, Sameta Śikhara, and Mount Kailāśa. The Mallinātha Temple, alternatively known as the Vastupāla Vihāra or the Vastupāla-Tejapāla Temple, on Mount Girnār near Junagadh (Junagaṛh) in Gujarat, has three major sanctuaries connected to a central hall (*maṇḍapa*). The eastern *garbha-gṛha* is dedicated to Pārśvanātha and contains a figural representation. The chapels on the other sides contain large-scale reproductions of cosmic mountains. The shrine to the north houses a sizeable model of Mount Aṣṭāpada and that to the south a large replica of Sameta Śikhara. Both mountain representations fill almost the entire space of the dark and unlit sanctums.

Sameta Śikhara, the mountain worshipped in the south shrine on Mount Girnār, is a model-like portrayal of the actual Mount Paraśnātha, a popular hill and pilgrimage destination in Bihar.[31] Such miniature reproductions of holy pilgrimage sites are referred to as "manifestations" of the real sites, *avatāras* or *uddhāras* (Shah 1955, p. 117). Twenty of the twenty-four Tīrthaṅkaras are supposed to have attained enlightenment at the summit of Mount Paraśnātha.

Mount Aṣṭāpada, the second mountain *avatāra* on Mount Girnār, is famous as the place of liberation (*nirvāṇa-sthān, mokṣa-bhūmi*) of the first Jina Ṛṣabhanātha.[32] This is attested to

---

[30] *Meru* representations of this type are discussed in Hegewald 2005, pp. 491–93; 2007, pp. 133–34; 2011, pp. 212–13).

[31] The pilgrimage site near Madhuban in Bihar is known by a number of names. In addition to "Mount Paraśnātha," the following are frequently used: Śrī Sameta Śikhara, Śikharjī, and Sametagiri.

[32] The name "Aṣṭāpada" derives from a narrative according to which Bharata erected a shrine for his

deceased father Ṛṣabhdeva. He then created eight steps (*aṣṭa pada*) in the form of vast and insurmountable terraces around the sacred mountain so as to protect it against intruders. According to the account in Jinaprabha Sūri's *Aṣṭāpada-giri-kalpa*, the shrine at the summit of Aṣṭāpada (*siṁhaniṣadyā*) has a *caturmukha* layout. It houses the statues of fourteen Tīrthaṅkaras. For information on the organization of the icons of the fordmakers inside the shrine, see

in the *Triṣaṣṭi* and the *Abhidhāna Cintāmaṇi*, according to which Aṣṭāpada Parvata is additionally known as Kailāśa, Harādri, or Sphaṭikādri Mountain (Shah 1955, p. 116). Following other religious interpretations, Kailāśa and Mount Meru are believed to be identical (Lishk 1987, p. 59), which suggests that Aṣṭāpada can be equated with Mount Meru too. Based on these accounts, it becomes clear that it is not so much a particular single named hill that is the focus of veneration, but the general idea of a sacred peak.

Shallow relief carvings of Aṣṭāpada are to be found at most sanctified sites in northwestern India and are typical of eastern and central India, especially in a Śvetāmbara context (fig. 4.21). The Aṣṭāpada Temple in Jaisalmer is particularly well known; however, it is closed to non-Jainas. The same theme is remarkably prevalent at Jalor (Jālor) in Rajasthan, where two temples, one in the fort and one in a twentieth-century complex at the foot of the hill, have been dedicated to the veneration of this specific cosmic mountain. The Aṣṭāpada Temple on the outskirts of the town consists of a large mountain formation contained inside a glass structure. Yet the revered hill practically takes up all the internal space. The carvings adorning the mountain monument with its eight terraces are incredibly detailed and represent legends associated with the hill.

There are other artistic models of cosmic and mythical mountain peaks. The Ādinātha Temple at Ayodhya (Ayodhyā) and the Barā Jaina Temple at Jabalpur contain small modern sculptural delineations of Mount Kailāśa. A temple in Campapuri (Campāpur, Campāpurī) in Bihar re-creates its shape in architecture (fig. 4.22), and a large arrangement at Sonagiri (Sonāgiri) in Madhya Pradesh, which represents Kailāśa, incorporates 108 miniature shrines into its layout. It is intriguing that Mount Sonāgiri itself, on which the latter reproduction was erected, is said to have the same number of temples, indirectly relating the local pilgrimage site to the cosmic and mythological mountain of the Jaina religion. An even larger reproduction of the sacred hill was under construction at Hastinapur in 2000.[33]

Nandīśvara-dvīpa Temples

Jaina shrines that re-create in architecture the characteristics of the island of Nandīśvara are especially close visual translations. The main features of the island are its four groups of thirteen mountain peaks located in the cardinal directions, with each peak topped by a small Jaina temple. There is a large number of temple edifices throughout India, which house fifty-two sacred mountain statues (fig. 4.23). Others, going by the same name, simply consist of fifty-two shrines accommodating Jaina icons.

It seems that the Nandīśvara-dvīpa pavilion in the compound of the Ajitanātha Temple at Taranga, dating from about the fifteenth to sixteenth century, is among the earliest surviving architectural examples (fig. 4.24). The Nandīśvara-dvīpa pavilion is located adjacent to the small building containing a model of the *pañca-meru*, mentioned above. Similar, though on a larger scale, is the Nandīśvara-dvīpa Temple (1840 C.E.) in the Tunk of Ujambi Hemabāī on the northern ridge of Mount Śatruñjaya. Whereas the structure at Taranga is a small pavilion, which remains closed on ordinary days, the cosmological temple on Mount Śatruñjaya is a large edifice, which is open to visitors on a regular basis. In both shrines, the cosmological reproduction forms the central object of veneration, and there are no additional chapels

---

the passages of the *Aṣṭāpada-giri-kalpa* in Shah 1955, pp. 116–17.

[33] Nearby, a truly monumental reproduction of Mount Aṣṭāpada was being raised at the same time.

housing figural or other representations. In the middle of the sanctum at both sites rises a single mountain sculpture, which is emblematic of Mount Meru. Following the same scheme, however, on an altogether larger scale, incorporating courtyards and side shrines, is the Nandīśvara-dvīpa Temple in the complex at Jalor.

Dating from the eighteenth or nineteenth century is a similar replica of the island of Nandīśvara in the sanctum on the first floor of the Digambara Meru Temple in Old Delhi (fig. 4.25). The *garbha-gṛha* below used to hold a figural representation but is now empty and not in use any longer. This might indicate that in this multi-shrined temple structure, the cosmological model was regarded as more important or sacred than the statue below. The inner walls of the upper sanctum, containing a reproduction of the fifty-two mountains and shrines on Nandīśvara-dvīpa, are elaborately painted. In the Delhi temple, we do not find just a single Sumeru Parvata at the center of the spatial conception. Instead, there is a line of five mountain sculptures, depicting the *pañca-meru*, portrayed in the same way as the surrounding cosmic mountain peaks.

In addition, there are many contemporary examples of Nandīśvara-dvīpa temples or subsidiary shrine rooms belonging to larger complexes. The Pañcāyatī Temple at Arrah has an early twentieth-century extension, which contains a large model of the eighth island continent (fig. 4.26). Here, the color of the mountain replicas reflects the black, white, and either golden or brown coloring of the peaks as described in the cosmic literature. While in this case, the *pañca-meru* group at the center consists of small pillar-like sculptures, those found in the center of the enormous twentieth-century Nandīśvara-dvīpa hall in the Digambara Jaina Prācīn Baṛā Mandir compound at Hastinapur are large towers dominating the entire cosmic reproduction (fig. 4.27). In recent years, substantial Nandīśvara models have regularly been created in the south of the subcontinent too. A particularly impressive example is venerated in a temple at the foot of Ponnūr Hill in Tamil Nadu.

Mythical Structures

So far we have concentrated only on cosmic edifices. In Jaina writings, however, there is a close relationship between cosmic and mythical structures and events, often with no clear differentiation between the two. Strictly speaking, cosmology deals with the shape and development of the universe in space and time, while Jaina mythology is primarily concerned with the lives of the twenty-four omniscient Jinas and their divine attendants who are supposed to inhabit various regions of the Jaina cosmos. Because certain events in the lives of the Tīrthaṅkaras are regarded as having taken place in distant quarters of the universe and to have involved spaces and structures not mentioned as such in cosmographical literature, the two exist in close correlation.[34]

A number of items that play a significant role in Jaina mythology and the lives of the fordmakers have been translated into art and architecture to enable devotees to participate

---

[34] In order to explain the close relationship between mythical and cosmological issues, Lawrence A. Babb refers to the *pañca-kalyāṇa-pūjā* of Pārśvanātha, which leads through various states of existence in different parts of the universe (1998, p. 38). For other examples, see Gopilal Amar 1975, p. 518. A further area expressing the interrelatedness between cosmic and mythical aspects is temple rituals. All ritual activities conducted within Jaina shrines are related to and symbolic of cosmic and mythical space (Jain 1977, p. 36).

in mythical events as part of temple rituals. The life stories of all twenty-four Jinas are closely related and follow a standardized scheme. All are said to have been born into a family belonging to the *kṣatriya* caste. After their birth, they are taken to Mount Meru, where they receive their birth ablutions from the god Indra (Hegewald 2011, p. 210) (fig. 4.28). We have seen that many statues of the Tīrthaṅkaras are seated on *meru* platforms, making direct reference to this story.[35] Besides, Jaina temples have ceremonial stands, known as *siṃhāsana*, that fulfill the function of a *meru* support during rituals. The ritual implements are made of metal or wood which has been covered with sheet metal. Small portable metal images are placed on the ritual supports and bathed with a number of purifying substances (fig. 4.29). The ablutions performed on the small metal icons are believed to apply themselves directly to the main sculpture (*mūla-nāyaka*) housed in the central *garbha-gṛha*.

After their childhood, the Jinas are awakened by the gods and made aware of their destiny as spiritual teachers. Consequently, they renounce the world to become wandering ascetics, and after strenuous austerities reach enlightenment.[36] Having attained omniscience (*kevala-jñāna*), the Tīrthaṅkaras deliver their first formalized teachings. For this purpose, the gods create an amphitheater-like open-air construction. This is referred to as a *samavasaraṇa*, or more colloquially as *samosaraṇa* or *samosaraṇ*, which literally means "assemblage." It is fascinating to note that representations of *merus* and *samavasaraṇas* are visually closely related and often difficult to tell apart (Hegewald 2011, pp. 213–14). Both consist of three terraces topped by a platform (*pīṭha*) accommodating a single or multiple Tīrthaṅkara statues.

Most descriptions of the *samavasaraṇa* mention a tree, usually referred to as a *caitya* tree (*caitya-vṛkṣa*), growing at the apex of the structure. The Jina who has attained enlightenment takes his seat on the platform beneath the sheltering canopy of the tree. Subsequently, the gods create three duplicates of the omniscient being, leading to a *caturmukha* or fourfold image facing the cardinal directions (Shah 1955, pp. 85, 88). If a *samavasaraṇa* is not available, a *siṃhāsana* stand can take its place and fulfill its function in rituals (Hegewald 2011, pp. 210, 222–24).

Samavasaraṇas have been depicted in a variety of media. We have paintings, carved panels, small metal sculptures, and larger stone versions, which are revered inside temple settings, as well as large-scale architectural representations. Carved versions appear already in early Orissan caves dating from the first century C.E. There are many stone panels and painted examples in Jaina temples throughout India, dating from the eleventh to thirteenth centuries. Architectural models generally date from later periods, such as the eighteenth to twenty-first centuries, and express an unbroken continuity of the *samavasaraṇa* theme.

In the village of Pavapuri (Pāvāpurī; ancient Pāpā) in Bihar, a modern *samavasaraṇa* marks what is believed to be the actual place of Mahāvīra's first sermon. However, mythical preaching auditoriums were raised at many sites throughout India as reminders of the goal of enlightenment and are not always linked to an actual historical or mythical event. Other demonstrative illustrations are the monumental *samavasaraṇas* at Papora (Paporā) in Madhya Pradesh and at Ramtek (Rāmṭek) in Maharashtra (fig. 4.30). Full-scale *samavasaraṇas* frequently incorporate portrayals of the sacred tree into their design, as can be seen in the temple at the foot of Mount Śatruñjaya (fig. 4.31). The latter structure illustrates another important aspect of *samavasaraṇa* temples, dating from the twentieth and twenty-first centuries.

---

[35] I have argued this elsewhere in much detail (Hegewald 2005, pp. 491–93).

[36] Paul Dundas has described and analyzed patterns in the life stories of the fordmakers (1992, pp. 18–19).

Contrasting with earlier reproductions, these recent monuments have been provided with an internal space. Traditionally, *samavasaraṇas* are solid symbolic formations that cannot be entered and as such are similar in concept to stupas (*stūpa*).[37]

Although the examples discussed above demonstrate very faithful re-creations of the *samavasaraṇa*, every Jaina temple, what ever shape it takes, is symbolically regarded as a replica of the mythical preaching auditorium (Dundas 1992, p. 31; Nagar 1999, p. 172).

Temple Ritual as Reenactment of Sacred Events

Jaina architecture has been molded by ritual practices and by a distinctive form of image veneration. Due to a pronounced ritual of giving (*dāna*), the significance of Jaina statues as models and ideals more than as holy beings one can personally address and communicate with,[38] Jaina temples accommodate large numbers of figural icons and abstract venerated symbols. These are held in usually complex multi-storied and multi-shrined sacred edifices, which in their spatial structuring are distinct from the temples of other religious groups on the subcontinent.[39] Many elements of Jaina ritual are directly linked to cosmic and mythical actions performed by gods and enlightened beings in distant regions of the universe, which are reenacted in present-day temple ritual throughout India. The rituals surrounding the *meru* as cosmic and mythical structure make direct reference to the birth ablutions the Tīrthaṅkara receives from the god Indra on Mount Meru. Temples in the shape of *samavasaraṇas* and any other Jaina shrine too symbolize the first formalized preaching of the Jina after his attainment of enlightenment. *Siṁhāsana* ritual stands can signify either of these two items in ritual practices.

Meru, *samavasaraṇa*, and *siṁhāsana* play a particularly vital role in the dedication rituals surrounding sacred sculptures. Jaina icons have to be formally installed and consecrated through the performance of specific ceremonies in order to function ritually and to be transformed into potent religious objects. In a Jaina context, these installation and consecration rituals are known as the *pañca-kalyāṇa-pratiṣṭhā-mahotsava* or the Jina-*bimba-pratiṣṭhā* (Babb 1998, p. 66; Jain 1983, p. 114; Fischer and Jain 1974, p. 35). The rituals aim at reenacting the five central events in the life of a fordmaker. At the end of the sequence, the Tīrthaṅkara has figuratively "re-lived" the five auspicious occasions of conception, birth, renunciation, omniscience, and release. Only in this fully enlightened and liberated state can the images be enshrined in the sanctums of temples. These consecration rites are usually conducted on a small replacement statue made of metal (Fischer and Jain 1974, p. 35). The two aspects of the rituals, birth (*janma-kalyāṇaka*) and enlightenment (*nirvāṇa-kalyāṇaka*), are reenacted on *meru* and *samavasaraṇa* supports or on a *siṁhāsana* stand.

The re-fashioning of the birth ablutions is a lengthy and costly endeavor. However, bathing ceremonies are not performed just as part of the celebrations of the *pañca-kalyāṇa pūjā*.

---

[37] For an in-depth analysis of this issue and other occurrences illustrating this modern tendency, see Hegewald 2011, pp. 218–19).

[38] This clearly differentiates Jaina ritual from Hindu image worship, in which through the ritual of *darśana* a direct encounter and visual exchange with the divinity are provoked. On the Hindu ritual of adoring statues, see Eck 1981, pp. 3–17, 33–38; and

Mallebrein and Lobo 1998. On Jaina figural veneration, see Jaini 1990, pp. 191–203; Hegewald 2009a, pp. 29–37; 2009c, pp. 91–93.

[39] On this topic, see the monograph by Hegewald (2009a) or one of the concise summaries of the subject by the author (Hegewald 2001, 2002, 2008, 2009c, pp. 94–101).

They should be performed every morning for all Jinas housed in a temple. Therefore, these ablutions form one aspect of the *pūjā* of eight substances (*aṣṭa-prakārī-pūjā*), but are similarly a preliminary to any major ritual or veneration in general (Babb 1998, p. 69). When the bathing ceremony is not performed as part of the sequence of the *pañca-kalyāṇa-pūjā*, it is more often referred to simply as *jala-pūjā* (water worship) or *abhiṣeka* (ibid., p. 85). Priests or devotees conducting a lustration ceremony are meant to imagine themselves as Indra, and any bathing ritual is symbolically regarded as representative of the birth of the Tīrthaṅkara.

Especially interesting are the rituals associated with Nandīśvara-dvīpa temples. According to Jaina mythology and cosmology, Nandīśvara-dvīpa is the island to which the gods retire after having celebrated the *pañca-kalyāṇa*, the five auspicious events in the life of a fordmaker. It is believed that the gods venerate the images at the summit of the fifty-two mountain peaks three times a year.[40] It is imperative that the island of Nandīśvara is inaccessible to humans and that the edifices, which re-create the topography of the eighth island continent in architecture, make extraterrestrial space accessible to human beings. The temples constructed in our world allow devotees to participate in ritual actions, which are reserved for the gods only.

During the festive periods in October, February, and June, Jainas all over India celebrate the *aṣṭāhnikā* festival (*aṣṭāhnikā-parva-pūjā*).[41] As part of the celebrations, believers observe a fast and worship the *citra-paṭas* of Nandīśvara-dvīpa displayed in Jaina shrines and visit Nandīśvara-dvīpa temples. The festival period is concluded with a chariot procession (*ratha-yātra*) during which the male members of the community visit all the Jaina temples of a village or town (Jain 1977, p. 40; Jain and Fischer 1978, p. 19; Lishk 1998, pp. 54–57), imitating and participating in the divine actions of the gods.

Conclusion: Temple Topography and Ritual Landscapes

The analysis in this chapter has interpreted Jaina temple topography as an embodiment of cosmic symbolism and Jaina ritual as a reenactment of mythical events. This has established a close link among the macrocosm, its microcosmic representation — temple architecture — and ritual practice. Jaina shrines were not built in isolation but exist as part of a larger ritual landscape.[42] There are sets of pilgrimage sites, which should be visited in sequence, and the environment surrounding sanctified sites was consciously shaped to reflect universal sacred standards.[43] As a consequence, temples not only contain *meru* sculptures but also have regularly been erected on natural mountain sites, which through layers of legends have been imbued with a particular sanctity.

---

[40] The gods are believed to venerate the statues from the eighth to the fifteenth day (which is the full-moon day, *pūrṇimā*) of the bright half of the months of *kārtika*, *phālguṇa*, and *aṣāḍha*, roughly corresponding to October, February, and June.

[41] The particular meaning that the *aṣṭāhnikā* festival holds for Jainas is clearly expressed by the fact that it is the only festival to which the older religious advisers to Jaina householders (*śrāvakācāras*) devote any attention (Jain and Fischer 1978, p. 19).

[42] The significance of the concept of landscape in Jaina art and architecture, as constructed, conceptualized, represented, cosmic, and ideological landscapes is analyzed in detail in Hegewald 2009b.

[43] The conscious re-structuring of the site of Pavapuri, as the place of enlightenment and the first sermon and death of Mahāvīra, is a particularly good example of this (Hegewald 2009b, pp. 424–27).

Cosmographical texts provide the Jaina community with detailed descriptions of large numbers of island continents, oceans, world regions, planets, heavens, and hells. A comparatively small number of these have been depicted in Jaina art and architecture. Most common are representations of the island of Jambū, of various cosmic mountains (merus), and of Nandīśvara-dvīpa, the eighth island continent. Indirectly at least, the second and the third island rings, Dhātakīkhaṇḍa and Puṣkaravara Dvīpa, are present in pañca-meru arrangements too.

These specific items of Jaina cosmology appear to have been chosen because of the particular relevance they have for members of the Jaina community. Jambū-dvīpa lies at the very center of their universe. India, as well as the rest of the physical world as we know it, is believed to be located on this central continent. The island of Jambū and the next concentric one-and-a-half island rings are the only places in the vast Jaina cosmos where human beings can be born, live, and attain enlightenment. The area of the Aḍhāī-dvīpa is also where most of the merus portrayed in Jaina art are situated. These sacred mountains play a crucial role in Jaina mythology and ritual. It is at the top of cosmic and mythical mountains that infant Jinas receive their first ceremonial bath from the god Indra, and where they reach liberation at the end of their life. As such, mountain peaks are symbolic markers of focal points of transition in a pure and religious life. For this reason and in order to partake in mythical and cosmic events, devotees conduct arduous pilgrimages to holy mountains at the summit of which Tīrthaṅkaras have attained omniscience.

Related but at the same time distinct is the island of Nandīśvara. According to Jaina belief, only the gods can reach the eighth island continent and venerate the images housed in the shrines at the summit of the fifty-two sacred mountains. Therefore, an elaborate Jaina festival, conducted three times a year, developed around the veneration of this island and gained great importance with the Jainas. Because humans cannot visit Nandīśvara-dvīpa, substitutes were created for the reenactment or the symbolic participation of humans in this auspicious cosmic act. The aṣṭāhnikā festival is unique to the Jainas.

This final point seems to have played a crucial role in the creation of the other cosmic temple types as well. While there are similarities with the cosmological literature of Hindus and Buddhists, the specific layout of the Jaina universe is distinct and so are its artistic representations. In contrast to the Jainas, Hindus and Buddhists do not appear to have conceived such literal translations of the cosmos into three-dimensional sculptural and architectural forms.[44]

Although examples from the early centuries c.e. have been preserved, cosmological depictions date largely from later periods. It was during the twelfth and thirteenth centuries that Jaina sacred architecture started to develop an individual language, differentiating itself more clearly from the edifices of other religions in India. Particularly during the rebuilding of many sites during the relatively peaceful period of the fifteenth century, distinct types of cosmological temples were developed and constructed more widely all over India. Cosmological and mythical architecture clearly gained in popularity during the fifteenth and sixteenth centuries and has continued to steadily gain in significance to the present day.

---

[44] The superstructures of Hindu temples are equated with Mount Kailāśa, while the domes of Buddhist stupas are believed to represent Mount Meru. Also certain architectural arrangements in Southeast Asia have been found to have cosmological mean-

ings. Most of these constellations, however, are quite abstract and less literal or immediate translations of cosmographic concepts than the cosmic Jaina sculptures and shrines examined in this chapter.

It appears that the primary aim for the creation of cosmological illustrations and shrines has been to visualize the complex nature of the Jaina universe. By making it more accessible and understandable to the laity, the representations aid them in their quest for enlightenment and final liberation. Additionally, the specific pictorial, sculptural, and architectural forms, reflecting ideas expressed in Jaina cosmology, provide the Jaina community with a discrete group of cosmic models in art and architecture and with a unique set of rituals and festival cycles. These relate exclusively to Jaina philosophical and soteriological concepts. Finally, the temple structures provide devotees with a stage for the reenactment of mythical proceedings and allow human beings to participate in divine and cosmic events and to anticipate their own enlightenment.

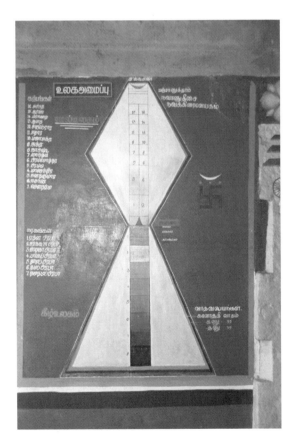

Figure 4.1. The Jaina cosmos as a whole is visualized in the shape of an hourglass, as can be seen in this mural from a Jaina temple in Ponnur, Tamil Nadu (all photographs are by the author)

Figure 4.2. The Jaina cosmos has often been represented in the shape of a cosmic person, as in this marble relief from a temple on Mount Śatruṭjaya in Gujarat

Figure 4.3. Simplified representations of the cosmos function as markers of Jaina identity, as here above the gateway of a Jaina temple at Arrah in Bihar

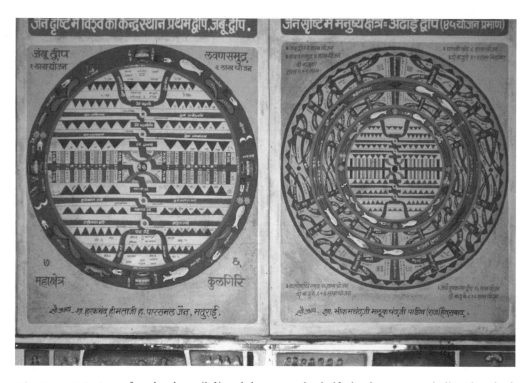

Figure 4.4. Paintings of Jambū-dvīpa (*left*) and the two-and-a-half island continents (Aḍhāī-dvīpa) of the middle world (*right*) from Mandu in Madhya Pradesh

Figure 4.5. Carved panel of the middle world, showing the central mountain as a tall pillar decorating a small shrine on Mount Śatruṭjaya in Gujarat

Figure 4.6. Large-scale model of a wish-fulfilling tree (*kalpa-vṛkṣa*), venerated in the temple complex at Lodruva in Rajasthan

Figure 4.7. The cosmic Lotus Temple or Kamal Mandir at Hastinapur in Haryana has been set inside a circular water basin

Figure 4.8. Large mural of the Aḍhāī-dvīpa adorning
the walls of the cosmic shrine in a Jaina temple at
Ponnur in Tamil Nadu

Figure 4.9. A line of metal representations of the five
sacred mountains (*pañca-meru*) arranged in a Jaina
shrine at Sanganer in Rajasthan

Figure 4.10. A central Indian metal statue in which the *pañca-meru* are shown one above the other in a tower-like shape from a Jaina temple in Seoni in Madhya Pradesh

Figure 4.11. Carved marble *citra-paṭa* illustrating the eighth cosmic island of Nandīśvara-dvīpa, from a temple at Kumbharia in Rajasthan

Figure 4.12. Three-dimensional Digambara representation of Nandīśvara-dvīpa in the shape of a metal pyramid, from Melsittamur in Tamil Nadu

Figure 4.13. Large Jambū-dvīpa model enshrined on the ground floor of the Cosmological Temple at Kumbhoj in Maharashtra

Figure 4.14. A vast model of the central world continent is
housed inside the Svarṇa Nagarī Hall in Ajmer in Rajasthan

Figure 4.15. Statues of the nine celestial gods, the *nava-graha*, displayed in the detached
hall of a Jaina temple in Venkundram in Tamil Nadu

Figure 4.16. Open-air representation of Jambū-dvīpa in a Śvetāmbara
temple complex in the fort of Mandu in Madhya Pradesh

Figure 4.17. The Sumeru Parvata tower at the center of this monumental Jambū-dvīpa
reconstruction at Hastinapur in Haryana measures about sixty meters in height

Figure 4.18. View from the mountain tower at Hastinapur onto the circular disc of the central island continent surrounded by the Sea of Salt

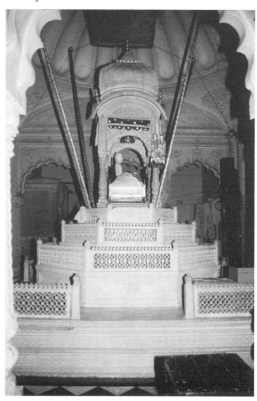

Figure 4.19. The *meru* has three tiers and is topped by a Jina temple, as shown in a contemporary wall painting from Mandu in Madhya Pradesh

Figure 4.20. The *meru* of Pārśvanātha is a white marble representation, housed in the main shrine of a Jaina temple in Allahabad in Uttar Pradesh

Figure 4.21. Painted relief carving in marble showing
Mount Aṣṭāpada in a Jaina temple at Varkanna in Rajasthan

Figure 4.22. The Kailāśa Temple in the sacred temple complex at Campapuri in Bihar
re-creates in architecture the mythical shape of this cosmic mountain

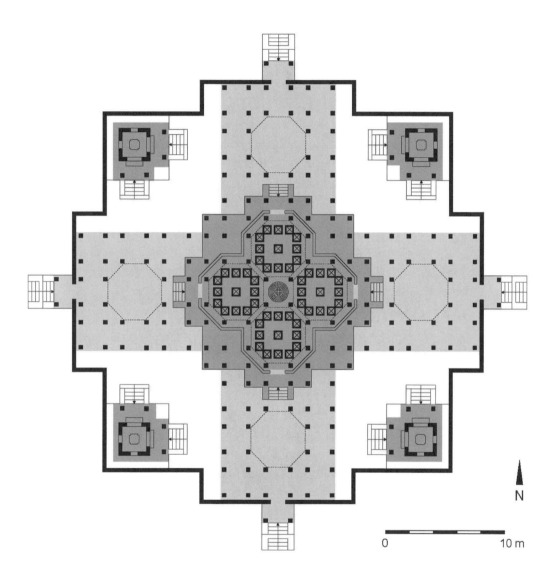

Figure 4.23. Spatial arrangement of the four groups of thirteen mountain statues inside Nandīśvara-dvīpa temples, based on the temple example from Jalor in Rajasthan

Figure 4.24. One group of thirteen mountain representations housed inside the cosmological pavilion at Taranga in Gujarat

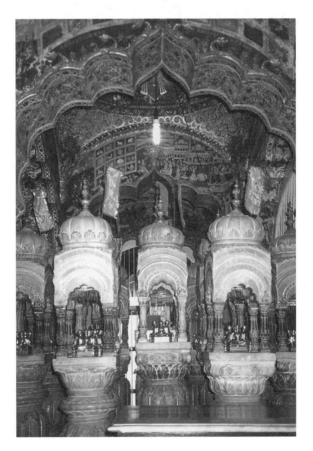

Figure 4.25. View into the Nandīśvara-dvīpa shrine on the first floor level of a Jaina temple in the old part of Delhi

Figure 4.26. In the Nandīśvara-dvīpa temple in Arrah in Bihar, the coloring of the mountain replicas reflects the textual descriptions of the cosmic peaks

Figure 4.27. The *pañca-meru* at the center of the Nandīśvara-dvīpa temple in Hastinapur are tall tower-like statues

Figure 4.28. Relief carving from Patan in Gujarat showing Indra and other gods performing the birth ablutions on the Jina at the summit of Mount Meru

Figure 4.29. A lay woman performing rituals on a Tīrthaṅkara statue placed on a *siṃhāsana* ritual stand in a temple in Vijayawada in Andhra Pradesh

Figure 4.30. Architectural representation of the mythical preaching
auditorium of the Jinas, the *samavasaraṇa*, from Ramtek in Maharashtra

Figure 4.31. Monumental *samavasaraṇa* structure in Palitana in Gujarat whose roof structure
imitates the canopy of a tree

Bibliography

Amar, Gopilal

    1975   "Cosmography and Architecture." In *Jaina Art and Architecture*, edited by A. Gosh, vol. 3, pp. 514–33. New Delhi: Bharatiya Jnanpith.

Babb, Lawrence A.

    1998   *Ascetics and Kings in a Jain Ritual Culture*. Lala Sunder Lal Jain Research Series 9. Delhi: Motilal Banarsidass Publishers.

Bose, D. M.; S. N. Sen; and B. V. Subbarayappa, editors

    1971   *A Concise History of Science in India*. New Delhi: Indian National Science Academy.

Brown, Kerry, and Sima Sharma, translators and editors

    1994   *Tattvārtha Sūtra: That Which Is*. London and San Francisco: HarperCollins and Pymble.

Caillat, Collette

    1981   *The Jain Cosmology*. New York: Ravi Kumar Publishers.

Coomaraswamy, Ananda K.

    1994   *Jaina Art*. New Delhi: Munshiram Manoharlal.

Dundas, Paul

    1992   *The Jains*. London: Routledge.

Eck, Diana L.

    1981   *Darśan: Seeing the Divine Image in India*. Chambersburg: Anima Books.

Fischer, Eberhard, and Jyotindra Jain

    1974   *Kunst und Religion in Indien: 2500 Jahre Jainismus*. Zurich: Vertrieb, Museum Rietberg.

Gombrich, Richard F.

    1975   "Ancient Indian Cosmology." In *Ancient Cosmologies*, edited by Carmen Blacker and Michael Loewe, pp. 110–42. London: Allen & Unwin.

Hegewald, Julia A. B.

    2000   "Oceans, Islands and Sacred Mountains: Representations of Cosmic Geography in Jaina Art and Architecture." *Cosmos: The Journal of the Traditional Cosmology Society* 16: 3–42.

    2001   "Multi-shrined Complexes: The Ordering of Space in Jaina Temple Architecture in North-Western India." *South Asian Studies* 17: 77–96.

    2002   "Aspects of Jaina Temple Architecture in Rajasthan and Gujarat." *South Asia Research* 22/2: 107–22.

    2005   "Representations of the Jina's Birth and Enlightenment in Jaina Art, Architecture and Ritual." In *South Asian Archaeology 2003* (proceedings of the Seventeenth International Conference of the European Association of South Asian Archaeologists, 7–11 July 2003, Bonn), edited by Ute Franke-Vogt and H.-J. Weisshaar, pp. 491–99. Forschung zur Archäologie Außereuropäischer Kulturen 1. Aachen: Linden Soft.

    2006   "Architectural, Sculptural and Religious Change: A New Interpretation of the Jaina Temples at Khajuraho." In *Studies in Jaina History and Culture: Disputes and Dialogues*, edited by Peter Flügel, pp. 401–18. Routledge Advances in Jaina Studies. New York: Routledge.

    2007   "*Meru*, *Samavasaraṇa* and *Siṁhāsana*: The Recurrence of Three-tiered Structures in Jaina Cosmology, Mythology and Ritual." In *Kalhār (White Water-lily): Studies in*

	Art, Iconography, Architecture, and Archaeology of India and Bangladesh (Professor Enamul Haque Felicitation Volume), edited by Gouriswar Bhattacharya, Gerd J. R. Mevissen, Mallar Mitra, and Sutapa Sinha, pp. 132–46 and pls. 17.1–20. New Delhi: Kaveri Books.
2008	"Jaina Temple Architecture: A Progression from Images to Shrines and Temple Cities." In *South Asian Archaeology 1999* (proceedings of the Fifteenth International Conference of the European Association of South Asian Archaeologists, held at the Universiteit Leiden, 5–9 July 1999), edited by Ellen M. Raven, pp. 427–37. Gonda Indological Studies 15. Groningen: Egbert Forsten.
2009a	*Jaina Temple Architecture in India: The Development of a Distinct Language in Space and Ritual.* Monographien zur Indischen Archäologie, Kunst und Philologie 19. Berlin: G+H Verlag.
2009b	"Jala Mandirs, Tīrtha Paṭas and Cosmic Islands: Creating, Replicating and Representing Landscape in Jaina Art and Architecture." In *Prajñādhara: Essays on Asian Art, History, Epigraphy and Culture in Honour of Gouriswar Bhattacharya*, edited by Gerd J. R. Mevissen and Arundhati Banerji, pp. 422–37 and pls. 43.1–20. New Delhi: Kaveri Books.
2009c	"Sacred Place and Structured Space: Temple Architecture and the Pilgrimage in Jainism." In *Victorious Ones: Jain Images of Perfection*, edited by Phyllis E. Granoff, pp. 90–110. New York: Rubin Museum of Art.
2010	"Visual and Conceptual Links between Jaina Cosmological, Mythological and Ritual Instruments." In *International Journal of Jaina Studies,* Volumes 4–6, 2008–2010, edited by Peter Flügel, pp. 209–27. Mumbai: Hindi Granth Karyalay. Available online at http://www.soas.ac.uk/research/publications/journals/ijjs/archive/

Jain, G. R.

| 1985 | "Space, Time and the Universe." In *Perspectives in Jaina Philosophy and Culture*, edited by Satish Kumar Jain and Kamal Chand Sogani, pp. 7–18. New Delhi: Ahimsa International. |

Jain, Jyotindra

| 1977 | "Jaina Ritual and Space: Cosmic, Mythical and Symbolic Space and Contemporary Jaina Ritual." *Art and Archaeology Research Papers* 11 (June): 36–41. |

Jain, Jyotindra, and Eberhard Fischer

| 1978 | *Jaina Iconography*, Volume 2: *Objects of Meditation and the Pantheon*. Leiden: Brill. |

Jain, Jyoti Prasad

| 1983 | *Religion and Culture of the Jains.* 3rd edition. Murtidevi Granthamala, English Series 6. New Delhi: Bharatiya Jnanpith Publications. |

Jain, Surender K., editor

| 1997 | *Glimpses of Jainism.* Delhi: Motilal Banarsidass. |

Jaini, Padmanabh S.

| 1990 | *The Jaina Path of Purification.* New Delhi: Motilal Banarsidass. First published 1979. |

Jindal K. B.

| 1987 | *An Epitome of Jainism.* New Delhi: Munshiram Manoharlal. |

Kirfel, Willibald

| 1990 | *Die Kosmographie der Inder: Nach den Quellen dargestellt.* Zurich and New York: Georg Olms Verlag, Hildesheim. First published 1920. |

Lishk, S. S.

| 1987 | *Jaina Astronomy.* Delhi: Vidya Sagar Publications. |

Lishk, S. S., translator

    1998   *Jaina Geography.* Original text by Pujya Ganini Pramukh Shri Jnanamati Mataji (*Jain Bhūgol).* Hastinapur: Digamber Jaina Institute of Cosmographic Research.

Mallebrein, Cornelia, and Wibke Lobo

    1998   "Darshan: Blickkontakte." In *Darshan: Blickkontakte mit indischen Göttern; Die ländliche und tribale Tradition,* edited by Cornelia Mallebrein, pp. 8–39. Veröffentlichungen des Museums für Völkerkunde Berlin, n.F., 67. Berlin: Museum für Völkerkunde.

Nagar, Shantilal

    1999   *Iconography of Jaina Deities.* 2 volumes. Delhi: B. R. Publishing Corporation.

Schubring, Walther

    1995   *The Doctrine of the Jainas: Described after the Old Sources.* Delhi: Motilal Banarsidass. First published 1962.

Shah, Nagin J., translator

    1998   *Jaina Philosophy and Religion.* Original text by Muni Shri Nyayavijayaji (*Jaina Darśana).* Delhi: Motilal Banarsidass.

Shah, U. P.

    1955   *Studies in Jaina Art.* Benares: Jaina Cultural Research Society.

Singh, Harihar

    1982   *Jaina Temples of Western India.* Parshvanath Vidyashram Series 26. Varanasi: Parshvanath Vidyashram Research Institute.

Sircar, D. C.

    1967   *Cosmography and Geography in Early Indian Literature.* Sir William Meyer Endowment Lectures in History 1965–66. Calcutta: Indian Studies, Past & Present.

von Glasenapp, Helmuth

    1999   *Jainism: An Indian Religion of Salvation.* Lala Sundar Lal Jain Research Series 14. Delhi: Motilal Banarsidass.

5

THE CLASSIC MAYA TEMPLE: CENTRALITY, COSMOLOGY, AND SACRED GEOGRAPHY IN ANCIENT MESOAMERICA

Karl Taube, University of California, Riverside

With their elaborate sculptural programs and often detailed texts, Classic Maya temples have dominated our understanding of the ancient Maya. Indeed, for too long we have described their communities as "ceremonial centers," as if the monumental structures were hollow edifices only used for occasional, calendrically timed events. Although during the past fifty years Maya archaeological field research generally has turned away from the monumental architecture in favor of daily human existence, still they remain. Oddly, few studies have investigated what the "pyramids" meant to the people who created and sustained them for centuries. In this study, I focus on some of their underlying meanings, including the basic symbolic significance of being humanly created, ordered structures replicating the four-cornered house and the maize field. From this basic model, temples also encapsulate the world center framed by the intercardinal points. As such, ancient Maya temples evoke imagery pertaining to the household hearth and the pivotal world tree as forms of the *axis mundi*. In addition, pyramid temples are also symbolic mountains often evoking Flower Mountain, a paradise realm of honored ancestors. As zoomorphic mountains, many have entrances as fanged maws, the dark interior being a symbolic cave. The sides of these doorways frequently exhale elaborate breath scrolls, denoting the temples as living entities providing vital soul essence, in ritual practice probably in the form of aromatic incense.

Thanks to sixteenth-century sources and the highly developed writing and iconography of the pre-Hispanic Maya, much can be said of the symbolic significance of ancient Maya temples. In addition, the Maya were by no means in isolation from other cultures of ancient Mesoamerica, and the well-documented contact period Aztec of central Mexico constitutes a major source of information concerning the function and meaning of Mesoamerican temples. Moreover, native forms of temple structures — quite independent of Christian churches — continue to the present among the Ch'orti Maya and other peoples of Mesoamerica, including the Huichol of west Mexico (Girard 1962; Schaefer 1996; Zingg 1938). Moreover, as symbolic domiciles of gods and honored ancestors, ancient Maya temples relate to both ancient and modern vernacular architecture, including construction and dedication ceremonies as well as architectural terminology of contemporary Maya houses.

Aside from being palatial domiciles for exulted gods, Maya masonry temples are also stony mountains, the dark interior chamber constituting a symbolic cave. In a watershed paper published some twenty years ago, linguist Jane Hill (1992) defined the concept of Flower World, a realm pertaining to ideas of the soul and the paradise afterworld among Uto-Aztecan peoples, pertaining largely to central and western Mexico and extending as far as into the O'odham (Pima and Papago) as well as the Hopi region of the American Southwest. However, Flower World is not limited to one great language family, but also appeared among the Classic Maya and still more ancient Olmec of southeastern Mesoamerica (Taube 2004a; 2006; 2010b). For the ancient Maya, this region was a blossoming mountain, flowers being a basic symbol of the soul. In this study, I will note that Maya temple pyramids often denoted this sacred place, or "Flower Mountain," with the attendant music and incense symbolizing the fragrant soul essence of the gods and ancestors contained within.

Temples as God Houses

In a broad, cross-cultural study of ancient monumental architecture in both the Old World and the Americas, Bruce Trigger (1990, p. 121) noted that temples were widely regarded as houses for divine beings:

> the temples of the early civilizations were usually designed to be the earthly dwellings of gods rather than assembly places for communal worship. Much of the cult was conducted in seclusion inside these buildings, which in many cultures were called literally "god houses."

This certainly is the case for ancient Mesoamerica, with the sixteenth-century Yukatek Maya referring to a temple as *k'u nah*, or "god house," with similar terms readily found in other Maya languages (see Taube 1998, p. 428). Similarly, Carl Lumholtz (1900, pp. 8–9) mentions that while the Huichol refer to houses as *ki* (related to the Hopi term *kiva*), their community temples "are called toki'pa, which means 'house of all.'" In an important discussion of Classic Maya texts concerning temples and other monumental architecture, David Stuart (1998, pp. 376–78) notes that such buildings are commonly referred to as *nah* or *otot*, both terms referring to both house and structure in Mayan languages (fig. 5.1a–d). Among the Aztec, the term for temple was *teocalli*, specifically meaning "god house," with *teo* meaning "divinity" and *calli* "house" (Molina 1977, p. 100).

Although the Classic Mayan terms of *nah* and *otot* refer to both house and structures in general, ancient Maya temples were very much domiciles, that is, places of rest and residence for divine beings. Dating to the Late Classic period (A.D. 600–900), a small monument from Copan, Honduras, depicts the embodiment of Maya divinity, or *k'uh* in Maya script, seated in the doorway of a "god house" (fig. 5.1f). The accompanying text describes it as *uwaybil k'uh*, or "sleeping place of the god," to denote a domicile. In addition, the roof corners have a pair of holes, indicating that a curtain hung over the entrance of the occupying deity. It is no coincidence that many entrances to Classic Maya temples have similar curtain holes at the sides of doorways to establish both privacy and the inert "sleeping" nature of those inside (Taube 1998, p. 429). In contrast to mosques and churches, ancient Maya temples are typically small to only house the deity image and its ritual regalia, rather than being places of public worship. Instead, the loci of public ceremonies were the temple stairways and adjacent plazas below.

Aside from being relatively small and private places, ancient Maya temple chambers were dark, with the only source of light from the doorway, probably often covered by a curtain. Maya temple doorways often appear as cave entrances with zoomorphic fanged maws both in art, and with actual structures at Copan, Honduras, and in the northern Maya lowlands of Campeche and Yucatan, Mexico. Among the Maya, darkness pertains directly to spiritual power. Stone (1995, p. 17) notes that the colonial K'iché of highland Guatemala sequestered idols in dark places to conserve their spiritual force, and it is likely that ancient Maya temples or "god-houses" functioned similarly. For contemporary Ch'orti, dimness protects sacred objects, the favored places to contact supernaturals being "dark rooms or in dark places in the forest" (Wisdom 1940, p. 431). According to Rafael Girard (1962, p. 194) — who participated in many Ch'orti temple ceremonies in highland eastern Guatemala during the mid-twentieth century — darkness (*condición de oscuridad*) is a basic, shared trait of Ch'orti temples.

The Aztec sign for the third day name of the 260-day calendar, Calli, meaning "house," is a masonry temple on a raised platform (fig. 5.1e). As Stuart (1987) notes, this day sign clearly relates to the Classic Maya *yotot* logograph, a temple in profile with a stepped platform and thatch roof (cf. fig. 5.1a–b). While Calli designates the third Aztec day name, its ancient Maya equivalent was Ak'bal, meaning "darkness," the same meaning also recorded for the Zapotec of Oaxaca (see Thompson 1971, p. 73). In addition, the Aztec patron of the day Calli was Tepeyollotl, or "heart of the mountain," the jaguar god of caves (Seler 1963, vol 1, p. 73).

As houses for gods and royal ancestors, ancient Maya temples are three-dimensional models of the cosmos. They had many metaphors for the earth, including a crocodile, the circular domed form of a turtle floating on the sea, or a square space with the central sides denoting the directions or its corners at the intercardinal points (Taube 1988). Although strikingly different and even contradictory concepts, the attendant imagery overlaps in many ways. Clearly enough, temples and houses correspond to the four-sided model, *constructions of concerted effort*, including also a basic element of Maya life, the maize field. As noted by Charles Wisdom (1940, p. 429) in his classic work on Ch'orti ethnography,

> Four is of greatest ritual significance for men, probably because it is the sum of the corners of the milpa. It is also applied to the altar and the world, as both are in the form of squares.

According to Maya sources, the cutting of the fields expresses the same making of the four-sided world. As a maize field or house, physically exacting and often dangerous acts of human labor create the four-sided world, including cutting jungle for fields or erecting the massive roof beams of a house. As with "barn raising," these conditions are difficult if not impossible without the concerted social effort of a "community" outside of the immediate family. For this reason, the large expanses of quadrangular fields also relate to four-sided houses and towns, all socially constructed human space (Taube 2003a).

The concept of humanly created things — whether a four-legged table, a field, or a house — concerns far broader concepts of ancient and modern Maya cosmogony. Thus in the following Yukatek Maya account recorded by Harriet de Jong (1999, p. 285), the ordered world is a divinely created place:

> In the sky, there is that thing that supports the earth above the sky above the earth.
> It is like a table with four corners and it is like a house with four poles. In this way,
> the sky is held above the earth this is the way that god has made it.

Among Yukatek Maya, "the world, the village and the milpa are thought of as squares with four corners lying in the four cardinal points of the compass and with defined central points" (Redfield and Villa Rojas 1934, p. 114). According to William Hanks (1990, p. 299), this four-sided plan relates closely to Yukatek conceptions of place: "In most socially significant spaces, including towns, homesteads, plazas, and traditional cornfields, the four corners plus the center define the space as a whole." Other sources note that the square plan is a basic Yukatek model of the world (Redfield and Villa Rojas 1934; de Jong 1999, p. 285). Evon Vogt (1976, p. 58) notes very similar concepts among the Tzotzil Maya of Zinacantan:

> Houses and fields are smale-scale models of the quincuncial cosmology. The universe was created by the VAXAK-MEN, gods who support it at its corners and who designated its center, the "navel of the world," in Zinacantan center. Houses have corresponding corner posts; fields emphasize the same critical places, with cross shrines at their corners and centers.

The nearby Tzotzil of Chenalhó also perceive a four-sided earth: "The world, osil balamil, is a square like the house and the fields. The sky rests on four pillars, just like those of a house" (Guiteras-Holmes 1961, p. 254). Similarly, the Ch'orti compare the world to four-cornered altars and maize plots (Wisdom 1940, pp. 429–30). The milpa earth metaphor is especially developed in the Quichean *Popol Vuh*, which describes the act of creation as the measuring of a four-sided maize field (D. Tedlock 1996, pp. 63–64, 220).

Although the four-cornered world is a basic Mesoamerican model embracing maize fields, houses, and by extension temples, the world directions are by no means limited to the intercardinal points, which conceptually relate to the furthest dawn and dusk points of the summer and winter solstices. However, the cardinal points are also clearly present. Whereas the earlier Olmec portrayed the maize god framed by directional celts at the four corners, their caches feature greenstone celts to the four cardinal points (see Taube 2005). An Early Classic royal burial at Rio Azul in the northern Peten of Guatemala, Tomb 1 features the glyphs of east, north, west, and south placed appropriately in the center — and not the corners — of all four walls (see Freidel, Schele, and Parker 1993, fig. 2.8d). For the Ch'orti, the four directional sky gods simultaneously correspond to both the cardinal and intercardinal points:

> The sky deities inhabit each of the four world-directions, but they also inhabit intermediate positions between the cardinal points, thus forming the universe into a square as well as into a diamond. (Wisdom 1940, p. 427)

Clearly, much of this ambiguity is because whereas the four-sided cosmic model is fundamental to Mesoamerican thought, the corners of maize fields and structures, including temples, are not at the cardinal directions but rather at the perceived point of the annual passage of the sun to the highest points of dawn and dusk to the summer and winter solstices, as is documented for the Ch'orti as well as for the Hopi of the American Southwest (see Girard 1962, p. 15; Hieb 1979, p. 577).

In ancient Maya thought, four aged gods support the sky at the world directions and simultaneously at the intercardinal points as well. Commonly referred to as God N in the Paul Schellhas (1904) system of Maya deity classification, he can appear architecturally at the corners of temples as the four cosmic corner posts. A Late Classic panel from La Corona, Guatemala, has four God N deities supporting the roof of a temple (fig. 5.2a). At Chichen Itza, Yucatan, God N figures with upraised arms often appear in the upper jamb area of doorways and columns, much as if they support the roof (fig. 5.2b; see Seler 1902–1923, vol. 5, pp. 291–301).

The Late Classic Temple 11 at Copan has two massive God N sculptures at the northeast and northwest corners of the building, recalling the La Corona scene (fig. 5.2d). William Fash

(1991, p. 168) notes that they constitute "the largest anthropomorphic figures ever carved in the Maya area," and these great stone beings probably concern another basic theme of God N — his relation to sacred mountains. The sides of the inner doorway of the virtually adjacent Temple 22 feature a pair of God N sculptures holding up a saurian sky monster bearing cloud scrolls at both sides (see Maudslay 1889–1902, vol. 1, pls. 12–15). Their backs morph into the heads of "Witz Monsters" — zoomorphic embodiments of mountains — *witz* being the term for mountain in both ancient texts and contemporary Mayan languages (fig. 5.2e; for Witz Monster identification, see Stuart 1987, pp. 17–18). Cylindrical columns from the North Colonnade at Early Postclassic Chichen Itza portray four God N figures in sky-bearer pose emerging out of cleft Witz heads, much as if they were the quadripartite personifications of directional sacred mountains (fig. 5.2c). Carved in roughly the fifth century A.D., Tikal Altar 4 depicts a much earlier version of this theme, with quadripartite aspects of this god emerging from caves in four Witz Monster heads (see Jones and Satterthwaite 1982, fig. 58). The quadripartite God N figures probably relate to the yearbearers, the four directional day names out of a series of twenty naming each of the fifty-two years of the 365-day Maya calendar (see Thompson 1971, pp. 124–26). Among contemporary K'iche' of Momostenango, they are the Mam, meaning "grandfather," each embodying a specific mountain (B. Tedlock 1982, pp. 99–100, 147–48). Similarly, the Mam Maya of Todos Santos associate the four directional yearbearer days with specific mountains, known as "the lords of the mountain" (*dueños del cerro*; Oakes 1951, p. 71).

Both the Late Postclassic Maya Codex Dresden (pp. 25–28) and the roughly coeval Codex Borgia (pp. 49–53) of highland Mexico feature passages concerning the directional yearbearer days, gods and their temples, and, in addition, cosmic trees. Along with directional mountains, world trees denote the cardinal or intercardinal points, with a central one constituting the pivotal *axis mundi*. In Maya thought, their quadripartite arrangement relates to the corner posts of a house as a basic world metaphor. The colonial Yukatek *Book of the Chilam Balam of Chumayel* account of world creation describes a directional world tree as a housepost (*horcon* in Spanish) sustaining the sky (*yokmal ka'an*; Roys 1933, pp. 32, 100). Similarly, contemporary Ch'orti refer to the four cosmic posts supporting the sky as *oi*, "tree trunks set into the ground to support the roof and walls of a house" (Fought 1972, pp. 377–79).

Classic Maya four-sided lidded vessels often symbolize houses or temples (Houston 1998, pp. 349–51; Taube 1994a). For one Late Classic vase, the Maya maize god presides, with the lid occupied by a pair of birds denoting both roof and sky as well as being probable supernatural messengers (fig. 5.3b–c). In addition, birds often perch atop world trees, again linking the concept of house or temple to cosmic tree symbolism. With its cross motif, the rectangular roof finial is notably similar to a temple incised on a Late Classic brick from Comalcalco, Tabasco, containing a censer in its chamber (fig. 5.3a). Ceramic cache vessels from the Motagua Valley region of eastern Guatemala can also appear as houses, with one even displaying the doorway (fig. 5.4c). At Copan, many cylindrical cache vessels are trees with cacao pods sprouting from the trunk and a lid with a capping water lily blossom (fig. 5.4a). For the illustrated example, it appears that there were four vents for the incense, clearly relating to directional symbolism and the four cacao pods placed on the lid and sides of the lower vessel chamber. One Late Classic Copan cache vessel incorporates both the four-sided temple or house with cacao pods growing from the corner beams and lid roof, again topped with a water lily flower (fig. 5.4b; see McNeil, Hurst, and Sharer 2006, p. 242).

Combinations of sacred house and tree also appear on Early Classic ceramic cache vessels from the Escuintla region of south coastal Guatemala. One example has cacao pods "growing" from the central four sides rather than the corners of the Copan vessel (fig. 5.5a–b). For another Early Classic piece, in this case in the collection of the Museo Nacional de Antropología of Guatemala, spiny elements protrude from both the box and lid (fig. 5.5c; see also Schmidt et al. 1998, no. 252). These spikes, also commonly found on incense burners, allude to the green trunks of ceiba trees, symbolizing the *axis mundi* among ancient and contemporary Maya.

Both vessels contain supine human figures with oddly outspread arms and legs, suggestive of human sacrifice (fig. 5.5b–c). Their pose recalls the later Aztec earth deity, Tlaltecuhtli, including the massive Tlaltecuhtli Stone recently discovered at the base of the Templo Mayor in Mexico City, which has a circular wound in its abdomen, strongly suggesting heart sacrifice (see Draper 2010, p. 113). Moroever, the second Escuintla cache vessel — evidently a woman due to the skirt and lack of a loincloth — displays a prominent hole in the center of her body, much like the Aztec Tlaltecuhtli Stone (fig. 5.5c). This orifice surely held or contained an offering, perhaps an upright ear of maize, as symbol of the "earth navel," or world center. The Aztec capital of Tenochtitlan often appears as a nopal cactus growing from the abdomen of a supine victim (e.g., Teocalli of Sacred Warfare, Codex Azcatitlan pl. XII). For the aforementioned Codex Borgia year-bearer pages, world trees grow from the abdomens of supine earth goddesses (see Codex Borgia pp. 49–53). For the fifth tree of the world center, two maize ears project from the body, along with a growing maize plant as the *axis mundi* (see Codex Borgia p. 53). Simon Martin (2006) has compared the Codex Borgia supine females to the famed Sarcophagus Lid of K'inich Janahb Pakal of Palenque, who also lies on his back with a cruciform tree rising above his abdomen (fig. 5.8f). In view of its box-like form and lid, Mary Miller (1992) noted that it resembles a huge cache vessel, and in fact four large jades were placed at his feet and hands with a fifth over his loins, clearly relating to ancient Mesoamerican practices of cached jade offerings (Taube 2005, p. 25).

Both Escuintla examples have jade earspools on the sides of the "roof" lids, relating to well-known monumental caching practices of the Classic Maya and still earlier Olmec with jades placed at the four cardinal or intercardinal points (Taube 2005). Dating to roughly 600 B.C., an Olmec-style cache from the center line of a pyramidal temple platform at San Isidro, Chiapas, had four jade earspools and accompanying celts framing a central bowl (Lowe 1981, figs. 6, 13). An Early Classic centerline cache in the foundations of Temple 26 at Copan contained four earspool blanks at the four directions and another two in the center, perhaps to denote the zenith and nadir along with a jade image of the maize god with his legs raised above his head, a pose adopted by the maize god to denote the central world tree — a theme discussed below in terms of temple architecture (see fig. 5.6a, c–d; Taube 2005, p. 25, fig. 2a). At the Classic-period site of Salitrón Viejo, Honduras, jade earspool fragments were placed at the four corners of a temple platform as a dedicatory cache (Hirth and Hirth 1993, pp. 176–77). Far to the west in the Valley of Mexico, early colonial Aztec descendants placed dedicatory ritual offerings of precious stones or idols to the four corners of a newly created house, along with a sacrificial chicken (Garibay 1979, p. 129).

Stacked Witz heads occupy the four corners of Copan Temple 22 to frame the structure by four cosmic mountains (see Fash 1991, pp. 122–23). Similarly, four shrines oriented to the intercardinal points surround contemporary, nearby Ch'orti temples. According to one Ch'orti informant, they are the four posts and directional gods at the world corners (Girard

1962, p. 196). For the Ch'orti temple at Cayur, a leaf-covered cross referred to as a "tree cross" (*árbol de la cruz*), as the world tree stands before the central altar with two pits at its base, one to the god of the world center and the other for his consort, the earth goddess. For other Ch'orti temples, there is only one pit at the base of the foliated cross (ibid., pp. 197–98). The community Huichol *tuki* temples have a hole in the center of the structure for blood, sea-water, and other offerings usually covered with a stone disk supporting the temple hearth (Schaefer 1996, p. 346; Zingg 1938, pp. 180–82). This hearth is to Tatewarí, Grandfather Fire, his main shrine at Teakata being the cosmic center of the Huichol world. He is the Huichol version the Aztec fire god Huehueteotl, inhabiting the world center of *tlalxicco*, meaning "earth navel" (see Sahagún 1950–1982, book 6, p. 88).

The strikingly similar temple pits of the contemporary Ch'orti and Huichol readily recall the *sipapu* holes within Pueblo kivas of the American Southwest. However, although a wide-spread feature of native sacred architecture, floor pits for receiving offerings are not known for ancient Maya masonry temples. In part, this may be because the primary elite place for sacrificial offerings was portable stone or ceramic censers, with much of the ritual focus concerning fire rather than libations to the earth (see Stuart 1998; Taube 1998). However, the lack of open floor pits in ancient Maya temples may also be because many temple chambers constituted symbolic caves, the doorway and stairs below being the symbolic entrance.

Given the importance of world trees in ancient and contemporary cosmology, one would expect to see tree imagery and symbolism present in Maya monumental architecture. Located in virtually the epicenter of the walled site of Becan, Building 2 in the south plaza of Temple X constitutes an excellent example (for map, see Campaña Valenzuela 2005, p. 49). An Early Classic stucco facade on the roof crest features a frontally facing image of the maize god in contortionist position as the world tree (fig. 5.6a; see Taube 2005, p. 25, fig. 2a). The serpent head and body remaining on the upper left portion of the trunk clearly were on the other side as well, with much of the curving body still present. Rather than two snakes, the Becan facade surely denotes a bicephalic serpent hanging from the tree, as is found in later art at Palenque (see fig. 5.8e–f). The maize god displays the quatrefoil motif on his "trunk," a basic symbol of caves from the Olmec to the early colonial descendants of the Aztec (see Taube 2010a). Although its branches extend into the heavens, the world tree also offers access to the dark underworld, as is also reflected in the foliated cross and offering pits in Ch'orti Maya temples.

Aside from Becan, other Classic Maya trees have quatrefoil cave signs, a convention first known for Late Preclassic Izapa (see Norman 1973, pls. 45–46). This probably relates to the large, natural cavities appearing inside massive ancient trees, such as the well-known Sequoia redwoods of the northwest United States. As "living caves," great Maya trees may have been treated with special reverence as oracular portals to the heavens and underworld. The fingers of the Becan maize deity are oddly extended, and as Stephen Houston (pers. comm. 1997) points out, they denote growing roots, as can also be seen on the finely incised Early Classic tripod vase commonly known as the "Death Vase" (fig. 5.6c). Here the maize deity appears as a cacao tree before a stepped pyramidal platform flanked by two other foliated figures in the same headstand pose. Behind the personified trees looms a zoomorphic Witz mountain, marked with blossoms and Ak'bal signs denoting darkness.

The Early Classic vessel combines the three themes of temple pyramid, tree, and mountain, and this is also the case with the Becan facade, as two outwardly facing Witz heads flank the maize god tree (fig. 5.6a). For the better-preserved example at viewer's left, a round element with a pendant tassel projects from the brow, this same device partly preserved on the other mountain. Although the interior paint and stucco details are effaced, the outline is consistent with Early Classic Maya portrayals of flowers. As with the incised vase, the Becan facade portrays a maize god tree growing out of Flower Mountain, a theme discussed below. However, the Becan figure has an extra detail — the pair of diagonal elements projecting from the better-preserved side of the headdress. The bands on the oval upper portions and pendant tassels readily identify these as gourd rattles, as can be seen being shaken by a deity in a roughly contemporaneous incised Early Classic vessel scene (fig. 5.6b). The same vase portrays another pair of rattles between the legs of the maize god in the same the world-tree contortionist position at Becan (fig. 5.6c). The meaning of the rattles with the Becan maize-god tree and Flower Mountain remains unknown, although it may concern the widespread Mesoamerican identification of music with flowers, with this building being a place of song and performance (see Hill 1992; Taube 2004a).

For the Early Classic Maya, the best-preserved temple is Rosalila, in the heart and center of the Copan Acropolis (Agurcia Fasquelle 2004; Agurcia Fasquelle and Fash 2005). Rosalia is one of a remarkable series of structures beginning with a building containing the probable tomb of the founder, K'inich Yax K'uk' Mo', and ending with Temple 16, which, although constructed in the late eighth century — some 450 years later — still evokes the founding king buried deep below (Agurcia Fasquelle and Fash 2005; Taube 2004c). Constructed in the late sixth century A.D., Rosalila is covered with an elaborate program of painted stucco sculpture, much of it referring to K'inich Yax K'uk' Mo' (fig. 5.7). The temple is a three-tiered building with the total height of the preserved portion being roughly 13 meters, not counting the supporting platform below (Agurcia Fasquelle 2004). However, this was probably not the total height, as the uppermost level is poorly preserved, with the complete form of the capping crest still unknown.

The frontally facing skull in the center of the uppermost tier of the principal, western side of Rosalila is a monumental version of the "Quadripartite Badge," a skeletal bowl containing three offerings, the central element being the stingray spine used in penitential bloodletting (fig. 5.8c–f). More specifically, this offering vessel is a censer, commonly shown with the aforementioned spikes as well as smoke rising from the burning offering (fig. 5.8c; Stuart 1998; Taube 1994a, 2009). In previous research (Taube 2004c), I suggested that the uppermost portion of Rosalila featured a pair of serpents emerging directly out of this censer, their heads appearing on the central lower tier of the temple (fig. 5.7). Although there are scenes of serpents rising from burning offerings, the uppermost region was more complex. For one, the sides of the probable censer bowl have the remains of downturned serpent snouts with feathers, clearly denoting the tips of "serpent wings," that is, wings with feathers extending from the faces of profile serpent heads (see Bardawil 1976). In fact, many Early Classic examples of "Quadripartite Badge" censers appear with a long-necked aquatic bird as the bowl (see Hellmuth 1987, figs. 75–82, 269). However, the feathered snouts of much larger serpent wings flank the uppermost portion of the great serpent bodies. Given the fact that these creatures have prominent scaly and taloned bird limbs below their heads, the wings were probably on their backs, making them dragon-like "avian serpents." Since only the snout tips of these massive wings are intact, the uppermost tier must have been much higher. Rather than a pair of serpents emerging from the censer bowl, it is more likely that the upper facade was a single bicephalic serpent hanging from a world tree.

Occupying the central axis of the Copan Acropolis, Rosalila may have supported a tower-like form portraying a cruciform world tree with a winged bicephalic serpent above a skeletal offering bowl, much like the cited examples from later Palenque (figs. 5.7, 5.8e–f). This would make the entire structure much taller than its intact state and might help explain the large window-like gaps separating the descending winged serpents from the central censer bowl. These would lighten the load of the upper crest while the southern and eastern walls would provide support for not only the bicephalic serpent but also the arms of a cruciform tree. In this regard, it is important to note that the final structure of the Copan Axis, Temple 16, had a temple superstructure in the form of a tower, having four massive piers and a stairway leading up to at least a second story (see Taube 2004c).

In terms of Rosalila, the central tier supporting the suggested censer and world tree is a frontally facing Witz head flanked by two others in profile, these largely obscured by the limbs and body of the bicephalic serpent. Of course, this composition recalls the Early Classic facade at Becan, where the maize-god world tree and bicephalic serpent grow out of flanking Witz mountain heads (fig. 5.6a). Although I am not aware of any floral symbolism on the facades of Rosalila, there is another interesting detail. As in the case of the Becan facade, pairs of rattles with bands on the gourd chambers appear on the brow of the mountain (fig. 5.7). As suggested for the Becan structure, this motif may denote Rosalila as a mountain temple of music and song.

Mention has been made of the world trees of Palenque with censer offerings bowls at the base. The Cross Group at Palenque is composed of three temples containing interior shrines with elaborately carved tablets. For the Temple of the Cross and the Temple of the Foliated Cross, the central portion of these tablets feature world trees resembling the form and dimensions of a Christian cross (see fig. 5.8e–f). However, it is also likely that a similar cross was on the eastern, frontal roof comb of the third structure, the Temple of the Sun. In a detailed rendering of the roof by Jean-Frédéric Waldeck, who resided in Palenque from 1832 to 1833, the central element of the roof comb appears to be a cruciform world tree, much like the aforementioned example from the Temple of the Cross (fig. 5.9c). Thus the same trefoil element appears at the top of the cross and a stingray spine at the base. The thin horizontal element crossing the tree appears to have been beads, as can be seen on the body of the bicephalic serpent hanging from the Temple of the Cross tree (fig. 5.8e). In addition, it is likely that the supporting skeletal censer was also present below, as can be seen in a relatively recent photograph by Merle Greene Robertson (1991, fig. 133).

In Waldeck's illustration, the central tree is flanked by two figures in the world-bearer pose commonly found with God N, and two others appear on the opposite, western side of the Temple of Cross (fig. 5.9c–d). This probably portrays the four skybearers framing the central world tree, and a similar composition appears at the outer edges of the roof comb. For the frontal, eastern side, two cartouches contain human figures backed by curving elements (fig. 5.9c). These devices denote the solar K'in sign, and it is likely that the figures are either the sun god or royal ancestors apotheosized as this deity. It should be noted that Waldeck's illustration is quite different from Robertson's reconstruction of the Temple of the Sun roof comb (see Robertson 1991, fig. 134), although her painstaking documentation does corroborate major portions of the much earlier image. In a photograph by Robertson (ibid., fig. 149) of the cartouche to the viewer's right, the head and arm of the skybearer can readily be discerned (fig. 5.9a). In addition, the corners of the cartouche rim bear the remains of skeletal heads. Now known to be centipedes, these heads are commonly found on the edges of solar disks, including other Palenque examples (fig. 5.9b).

Two more solar disks occupy the west side of the Temple of the Sun roof comb, and the central figure also was probably backed by a fifth. This composition would create four solar figures flanking a fifth on the western side. Although at first glance it would appear that this figure would embody a western sun, it is quite the opposite. This being would be the dawning eastern sun facing its diurnal path to the west, a convention also seen with K'inich Yax K'uk' Mo' as the rising sun on the western-facing stairway of Copan Temple 16 (Taube 2004c). This also holds true for the earlier underlying Rosalila temple, which features a massive winged sun god on its principal western side (fig. 5.7). In other words, such western-facing sculptures are not passive, inert objects awaiting the first solar rays but rather are living embodiments of the sun itself traveling from east to west.

Among the most basic symbols of the world center in ancient Maya thought is the humble three-stone hearth of Maya households, often referred to as *yoket* in a number of Maya languages and probably in Classic Maya inscriptions as well (Stuart 2011, p. 220). When Tzeltal Maya construct a house, the horizontal roof beams frame these stones in the center of the home, "over the center of the house floor where the hearth or cooking fire will be made" (Berlin, Breedlove, and Raven 1974, p. 143; see fig. 5.13). Linda Schele identified the glyphic sign for these hearthstones in Classic Maya texts describing the creation of the great Bak'tun cycle beginning on August 14, 3114 B.C., and ending on December 23 of A.D. 2012 (fig. 5.10a–b; see Freidel, Schele, and Parker 1993, pp. 65–71). In other words, the creation of the present Bak'tun cycle concerned the setting up of the central hearth and by extension the cosmic house or temple (see also Taube 1998, pp. 432–46; Looper 2003, pp. 158–85; Stuart 2011, pp. 216–24). A Late Classic ceramic vessel often referred to as the Vase of the Seven Gods features the old merchant deity known as God L with six other gods seated in darkness (see Coe 1973, no. 49). The accompanying text explicitly refers to the 4 Ajaw 8 Kumk'u date beginning the present Bak'tun cycle, and along with the seven gods, there are three bundles, surely relating to the hearthstones.

During the Early Classic period (A.D. 250–600), Witz mountain heads appear with the three stones in their mouths, and by symbolic extension, the interior of temple chambers as well (fig. 5.10d–e). Structure E5-5 at Tonina has a stairway shrine as a frontally facing Witz head with two stones at the corners of its mouth (fig. 5.10d). In its open maw, the shrine contains a third, actual stone sphere, or hearthstone, with considerable evidence of burning on the chamber walls and ceiling. An immediately adjacent stela, Tonina Monument 106 portrays a very similar Witz head with three oval stones in its mouth (fig. 5.10e), probably the very same Structure E5-5 shrine (Taube 1998, p. 438). As far as I am aware, the placement of an actual hearthstone in the mouth of the Tonina shrine is unique. For most Classic Maya temples, this hearth probably would be a stone or ceramic censer, and as I have stated, "incense burners are the kitchen hearths for the gods and ancestors" (Taube 1998, p. 446).

For Classic-period Seibal, the supreme title for rulers could be paraphrased as the "sacred king of the hearthstones," the same three-stone sign found in inscriptions describing the mythic event of 3114 B.C. (fig. 5.10c). One of the most striking temples at this site is Structure A-3, a Late Classic radial pyramid with four stairways, each with a stela and an altar at it base (see Smith 1982, pp. 12–19; Schele and Mathews 1998, pp. 179–82). In addition, a fifth stela occupies the center of the temple superstructure, creating a cosmic plan of the four directions and world center. Buried below this central stela was a cache of three jade boulders, clearly relating to the three hearthstones denoting the royal title of Seibal (see Smith 1982, figs. 18a, 187; Schele and Mathews 1998, p. 182; Taube 1998, p. 441). Another royal title pertaining to the three hearthstones appears on a Late Classic Maya vase featuring a supine jaguar floating or swimming in water (fig. 5.10f). The accompanying text states that he is the *way*, or spirit co-essence of the *yoket ajaw*, or "hearthstone king." His stomach spots form the house cosmogram, with four at the corners framing three smaller ones in the center (fig. 5.10g). As a terrestrial creature floating on water, this jaguar may allude to the earth itself, and the splayed position of the limbs recalls both Maya portrayals of the cosmic crocodile as well as the aforementioned Aztec Tlaltecuhtli.

In his study concerning glyphic texts pertaining to ancient Maya monumental architecture, David Stuart (1998) identified a number of verbs pertaining to temple dedication. One of these Stuart deciphered as *och k'ak'* or "fire enters," whereas another is based on the aforementioned K'in marked censer bowl emitting fire scrolls (fig. 5.8a–b). Stuart (ibid., pp. 394–95) relates these explicit fire references to house dedication rituals among contemporary Maya peoples, including the Tzotzil, Ch'ol, and Yukatek Maya. Evon Vogt (1976, p. 52) provides a detailed description of such a ceremony among the Tzotzil of Zinacantan:

> An assistant then hangs a rope from the peak of the house, the end of which marks the center of the floor, where a hole is subsequently dug. A number of roosters and hens corresponding to the number and sex of the family members are hung by their feet from the end of the rope, with the heads concealed inside the hole. With the exception of one black rooster saved for burial in the center hole, their heads are cut off with a knife and the blood is allowed to drain in the hole ... their heads and feathers are buried with the blood as an offering to the Earth Lord. The shaman then censes the remaining black rooster .... He then buries the entire bird in the center of the "grave"....

The nearby Tzeltal perform a very similar house dedication, beginning with setting up and firing the household hearth: "The three hearthstones (*yoket*) are brought in and placed and a fire is started." The ritual culminates in the sacrifice of a rooster suspended from the ceiling above the central hearth and parts of its body offered to the four corners of the structure:

> It is hung feet down from the center of the house until dead. In each corner of the house, a portion of the chicken is buried as an offering to the plants whose materials were used in construction, requesting that these plants do no harm to those who reside in the new house. (Berlin, Breedlove, and Raven 1974, p. 150)

This offering recalls the aforementioned early colonial Aztec dedication of the offering of "stones of good color" to the house center and corners, as well as the ritual killing of a chicken. In addition, Stuart (1998, pp. 393–94) cites similar ceremonies for Aztec temple and house dedications as well as among the contemporary Nahua of Veracruz.

Temples as Mountains

In this study of ancient Maya temple imagery and symbolism, I frequently mention mountains, including their appearance on corners of buildings as well as their central facades. Based on his ethnographic fieldwork in highland Chiapas, Evon Vogt (1969, pp. 595–96) suggested that lacking major mountains, the ancient lowland Maya created pyramids as symbolic mountains with their dark interiors being symbolic caves:

> there appears to be a significant conceptual parallel between the sacred mountains ... with their caves on their sides ... in highland Maya communities such as Zinacantan, on the one hand, and the steep-sided pyramids with their corbeled vault passageways in lowland Maya sites, on the other.

In a major work devoted to ancient Maya cave symbolism, Andrea Stone (1995, p. 35) subsequently argued that masonry temple interiors are indeed symbolic caves. In support, Stone illustrated a Late Classic vase portraying the rain god Chahk seated in an explicit mountain cave that is also his divine palace, or temple, much like ancient Maya renderings of such structures (fig. 5.11c). Located in the northern Peten of Guatemala, La Pailita Cave contained a large, stucco-covered image of Chahk seated as if he were on a throne, clearly denoting the cave as a shrine or temple (see Graham 1997). The sculptural style and associated ceramic sherds suggest that this Chahk was fashioned in the second or third century A.D. For the aforementioned Vase of the Seven Gods, God L sits in a clear merging of mountain and temple, having a thatched temple roof supported by a mountain of superimposed Witz heads (Coe 1973, p. 109). As in the case of the Chahk temple cave scene, this building profile resembles an inverted "L" and is notably similar to not only Maya portrayals of temples, but also the central Mexican day sign Calli, which, as has been mentioned, is also a temple (fig. 5.1e).

In the Maya area, the merging of temple chamber and cave is of great antiquity and appears in the North Wall mural from the Late Preclassic site of San Bartolo, located in the northern Peten of Guatemala (Saturno, Taube, and Stuart 2005, pp. 14–18, fig. 12a). Dating to the first century B.C., the scene features a zoomorphic mountain bearing an ancient and bent tree, flowering plants, and wild beasts (fig. 5.11b). The mountain's undulating canine is clearly a stalactite, thereby denoting caves as fanged mouths of stony mountains with their teeth as speleothems (ibid., p. 14). The mountain exhales a massive plumed serpent, a widespread symbol of breath and wind in ancient Mesoamerica (Taube 2001, 2003b; Saturno, Taube, and Stuart 2005). Along with bearing the maize god and other figures, it carries a yellow flower on its back and breathes two more from its snout, a theme discussed below. The scene probably constitutes a version of the emergence myth of Mesoamerica and the American Southwest, here with the maize god and humans conveying food and water out of the ancestral cave of origin (Saturno, Taube, and Stuart 2005).

Aside from the San Bartolo mural, the roughly contemporaneous Takalik Abaj Monument 15 from the south coastal region of Guatemala portrays a sacred mountain containing a human figure in its fanged open maw, in other words, a cave chamber (see Schieber de Lavarreda and Orrego Corzo 2010, fig. 8.3a). Although damaged, the back of this freestanding monument appears to depict a feline and a serpent atop the mountain, immediately recalling the San Bartolo scene. The massive Monument 2 from nearby Izapa, Chiapas, constitutes another Late Preclassic example of a figure in a mountain cave (fig. 5.12a). The maw contains not only a human figure but also jaguars and a pair undulating floral elements at the sides. Although the latter could be vines, they probably are serpents with blossoms on their backs. Although heavily eroded, the upper part of these elements strongly resembles early Maya renderings of serpent heads (fig. 5.12b–c). If indeed floral snakes, they would be entirely comparable to the example emerging from Flower Mountain at San Bartolo (fig. 5.11b).

Monument 2 stands in front of Mound 30i of Izapa Group B, suggesting that it denotes the symbolic cave interior of the earthen platform (see Lowe, Lee, and Martinez Espinosa 1982, pp. 196–99, figs. 9.1, 9.15, 9.17). A similar and probably still earlier sculpture at Tiltepec, Chiapas, constitutes an exceptionally early form of the Witz creature, again containing a human figure in its widely open mouth (fig. 5.12d). The curving back and very narrow base suggest that it also was placed against a mound rather than being a freestanding stela, in other words, a mountain offering symbolic access to the interior of a temple mound. Although it may seem unusual to have stone monuments against pyramids, a basic fact for coastal Chiapas and Guatemala is that alluvial cobbles constitute the sole source of stone construction, with no readily available limestone or sandstone for ashlar masonry blocks or even lime plaster. For that reason, masonry temple superstructures do not exist, meaning that any monumental allusion to a cave would be better put at the lower slope of a platform rather than above in a temple superstructure of wood and thatch. Considering the impressive size of the Izapa and Tiltepec carvings, they probably were the symbolic stony cave "temples" of earthen mounds. It could well be that the aforementioned Witz mountain facade at Tonina and the many other projecting stairway blocks of Classic-period basal platforms relate to this early southern piedmont tradition (see fig. 5.10d).

The cave maw temple theme of the Maya occurs still earlier with the Middle Formative Olmec (900–500 B.C.). Situated in highland Morelos, Mexico, the site of Chalcatzingo has a mountain on its east side portraying finely carved petroglyphs rendered in Olmec style, as one would find at the contemporaneous site of La Venta, Tabasco, in the southern Gulf Coast region. For Chalcatzingo Monument 1, a skirted woman sits in a zoomorphic cave maw rendered in profile, with elaborate breath scrolls emanating from its mouth (fig. 5.13a). On the opposite north side of the same mountain face, there is Chalcatzingo Monument 13, which features another mountain cave occupied by a deity that I consider as a foliated or growing aspect of the Olmec maize god, identified by the back-curving cranial foliage resembling a hammer claw (fig. 5.13b; see Taube 2004b, pp. 94–99). An adjacent fragment of this monument demonstrates that it also had the elaborate breath volutes found with Monument 1 (fig. 5.13b). The mouths of these Chalcatzingo creatures are halved quatrefoil cave signs, and a third example from the same site portrays this zoomorphic mountain facing frontally with its mouth not only as a full quatrefoil but also as an obvious entrance to an actual chamber (fig. 5.13c). As in the case of the later Izapa and Tiltepec monuments, it probably was placed against a platform, the interior temple chamber constituting the symbolic cave of a humanly constructed hill.

For all three Chalcatzingo monuments, flowering plants emerge from the corners of the quatrefoil mouths and thus probably constitute early versions of Flower Mountain. Roughly some five hundred years later, there is the exceptional Maya example from the North Wall mural at San Bartolo (fig. 5.11b). Portrayals of Flower Mountain are widespread in Classic Maya art, including the previously discussed Early Classic Death Vase and the Becan stucco facade, both also portraying the maize god as a central figure (figs. 5.6a, d, 5.13). The cave maw can exhale a pair of serpents from corners of the mouth when viewed frontally or as a single serpent when Flower Mountain is portrayed in profile (figs. 5.11c, 5.14a–b). The probable floral serpents flanking the maw of Izapa Monument 2 may well be breath emanations from the cave chamber (fig. 5.12a).

Although masonry temple chambers are not a Maya southern piedmont tradition, this is by no means the case where quarried stone was readily available, including Copan as well as the Maya lowlands to the north, recalling Evon Vogt's suggestion that lowland Maya pyramids and temples replicate natural features of the Maya highlands to the south. Dedicated in A.D. 715, Copan Temple 22 has stacked Witz heads at its four corners and a central doorway explicitly portrayed as a massive fanged maw. In a recent study devoted to this temple, Jennifer von Schwerin (2011, p. 283) notes that it concerns "the creation of maize and the emergence of humanity from Flower Mountain." According to von Schwerin (ibid., p. 281), "The structure's facades represented a fertile mountain, with flowers, maize and flowing water." In support of the Flower Mountain interpretation, von Schwerin (ibid., figs. 14, 17d) identifies a series of sculptural motifs roughly a meter high as flowers, which may have topped the first-story cornice. Moreover, she notes that on this first level there were twenty maize gods emerging from Witz heads with blossoms on their brows, in other words, Flower Mountain (ibid., p. 283, figs. 2, 12).

The sides of the fanged doorway maw have a pair of elements resembling beaded streams of falling water (see von Schwerin 2011, fig. 15). However, rather than being fluid, these devices probably denote the moist breath of the mountain cave. The bicephalic jade serpent on the Tablet of the Temple of the Cross exhales similar beaded forms from its nostrils (fig. 5.8e). Dating roughly a hundred years after Copan Temple 22, temple doorways as zoomorphic maws are widespread in the northwestern Maya lowlands, especially with Rio Bec and Chenes architecture in the states of Campeche and Yucatan. In many cases, breath scrolls emerge from the corners of the mouth (see fig. 5.15c). According to Baudez (1999), the long-snouted zoomorphic masks on Río Bec, Chenes, and Puuc facades are representations of the "Cauac Monster," the same being that Stuart (1987, pp. 17–18) epigraphically identified as the zoomorphic Witz head. For Río Bec and Chenes architecture, the fanged doorway is composed of a principal frontal head with flanking profile ones below, creating a form resembling an inverted "T," with a lower jaw often projecting out horizontally as the low platform for entry (fig. 5.15c). However, although an architectural necessity to physically walk into the building, the lower jaw conceptually forms the lower extension of the T-shaped doorway, thereby creating the quatrefoil cave motif found far earlier at Chalcatzingo.

Many Classic Maya "Witz Monsters" have a prominent blossom in the center of the brow, denoting them as Flower Mountain (fig. 5.14; Taube 2004a; Saturno, Taube, and Stuart 2005). Similarly, for both the Puuc region and Chichen Itza, the many Witz temple facades are actually Flower Mountain, again with one or more blossoms on the forehead (fig. 5.15a–c, e; Taube 2004a, pp. 85–86). Michael Coe (2005, pp. 172–73) notes that the Chenes-style stucco facade at Ek' Bahlam, Yucatan, is Flower Mountain, in this case with many round blossoms on the brow and cheeks and breath scrolls emerging from the corners of the mouth (see Vargas de la Peña and Castillo Borges 2001, pl. 14). The interior of this structure contained a royal tomb with a vault capstone depicting the deceased king as the maize god, again linking this being of life and resurrection to Flower Mountain (see ibid., pl. 18). In the Chenes area proper, temple doorways at El Tabasceño, Hochob, and Manos Rojas display prominent flowers on the brow of the upper, frontally facing Witz head to identify it as Flower Mountain (fig. 5.14a–c; for Manos Rojas, see Gendrop 1983, fig. 76).

For all three Chenes sites, the mountains also have feather-crested serpents running across their brows (see fig. 5.15a–c). While the central Mexican feathered serpent tends to be a rattlesnake with quetzal plumes covering its entire body, the ancient Maya preferred to depict it as a snake with simply feathers on its brow, much like the crest of the male quetzal (fig. 5.15a–d; see Taube 2010a, figs. 24c–h, 25). As in central Mexico, the Maya plumed serpent embodies the living force of breath and wind. Thus, whereas Witz Monster facades in the Yucatan typically have breath scrolls emerging from the corners of the mouth, the doorway at Hochob has feather-crested serpents with floral tails instead, although breath scrolls also emerge from their mouths (fig. 5.15d). Although in profile, the earlier plumed serpent emerging out of Flower Mountain at San Bartolo maw could translate into two serpents exiting the corners of the mouth if viewed frontally, as has been discussed for the breath elements on Witz facades in Yucatan as well as Early Classic Maya examples of zoomorphic mountains exhaling pairs of serpents (figs. 5.10d–e, 5.11b; see Taube 2004a; Saturno, Taube, and Stuart 2005, figs. 13a, 16c). The celebrated and roughly coeval EVII-sub pyramid at Uaxactun had plumed serpent balustrades on all four sides with their upturned throats displaying rows of feathers, much like the feathered-serpent scene at San Bartolo (ibid., fig. 17b). These sculptures constitute early forms of the later plumed serpent balustrades known from central Mexico and Postclassic Yucatan, including the famed northern stairway of the Castillo at Chichen Itza. Rather than being mere architectural ornaments, these beings serve as symbolic roads or vehicles for celebrants ascending or descending sacred architecture (Taube 2002).

Conclusions

Ancient Maya temples incorporated cosmic symbolism in terms of the four directions and world center, with the corners of both buildings and the periphery of the cosmos represented by such metaphors as standing old men, mountains, house posts, world trees, and precious stones, many of these themes overlapping in both subtle and jarring ways. But what does it all mean? Clearly enough, as in the case of contemporary Maya houses, ancient temples were replications and encapsulations of the world, or, as Stacy Schaefer (1996) noted in her excellent study of Huichol temples, the "cosmos contained." However, with the four directions — whether cardinal or intercardinal — temples frame the central world axis, the "pivot of the four quarters," linking the entire horizontal plane to the bright sky above and the dark realm below. A symbolic hearth commonly denotes this central place, often represented by the three hearthstones or a sacrificial censer. This central, fiery place probably symbolizes not only the heart of the structure but also the source of its breath as rising clouds of smoke. At times, a world tree grows from the censer, again denoting it as the pivotal *axis mundi*. As themes related to world creation, many aspects of temple symbolism embody concepts of antiquity, such as ancient world trees, aged men as sky supporters and great mountains, in other words, "as old as the hills." Indeed, the monumental scale of temple pyramids denotes permanence, with many of these in continued use for hundreds of years. However, although ancient, such thematic motifs as growing trees, old but still powerful world-sustaining gods, and breathing cave doorways exhaling breath scrolls and serpents also denote Maya temples as living entities providing a vital link between humans and the numinous realm of gods and ancestors.

Figure 5.1. Maya glyphs and related imagery pertaining to Mesomerican temples (aside from *f*, all drawings by author): (*a*) Early Classic *yotot* glyph of house or temple, detail of carved vessel from Tikal (after Culbert 1993, fig. 108d); (*b*) Late Classic *yotot* glyph, Palace Tablet, Palenque; (*c*) Late Classic glyph of temple possibly read as *wih teh nah*, Copan Altar Q; (*d*) Late Classic text referring to a temple as the *sak xok nah*, detail of painted capstone, Ek' Balam; (*e*) Late Postclassic highland Mexican day name House, or Calli, as temple in profile, Codex Borgia p. 19; (*f*) stone temple model with text labeling it as *uwaybil k'uh*, Late Classic Copan (drawing courtesy of Stephen Houston, from Houston 1998, fig. 17)

Figure 5.2. The aged Maya deity, God N, in temple architecture (drawings by author): (*a*) Late Classic portrayal of God N figures serving as corner supports for temple, detail of Late Classic altar, from La Corona, Guatemala (from Taube 1994b, fig. 1a); (*b*) God N as capital of column, Chichen Itza, Yucatan (after Seler 1902–1923, vol. 5, p. 301); (*c*) detail of four God N figures emerging out of cleft mountains on cylindrical column, Northwest Colonnade, Chichen Itza (from Taube 1994b, fig. 2a); (*d*) head of massive God N sculpture from northeast corner of Temple 11, Copan; (*e*) God N figure with mountain Witz head as his back, inner doorway of Copan Temple 22

a

b

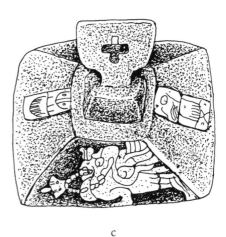

c

Figure 5.3. Classic Maya four-sided vessel as a temple palace: (*a*) Late Classic Maya graffito portraying three temples, Comalcalco (drawing courtesy of Stephen Houston); (*b*) Late Classic Maya vase with maize god enthroned in palace with the lid as the roof (drawing by author after Coe 1973, pp. 140–41); (*c*) detail of lid of *b* portraying supernatural bird on roof (drawing by author)

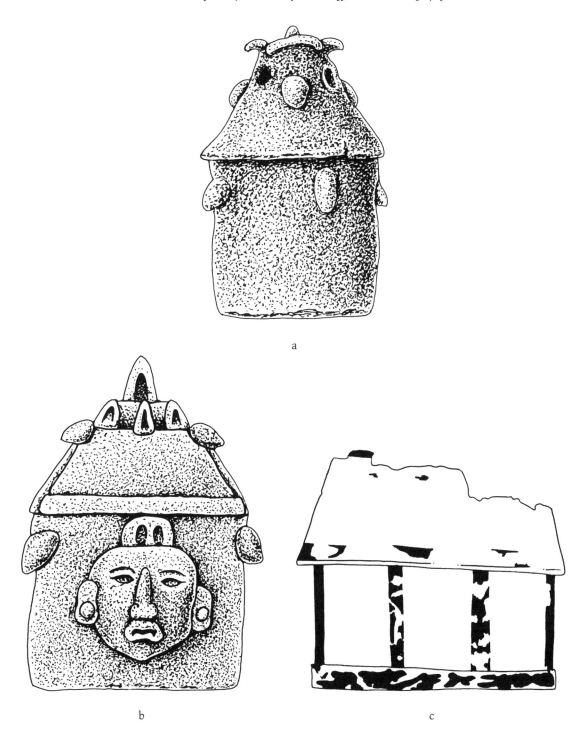

Figure 5.4. Late Classic Maya cache vessels as trees and houses: (*a*) Cylindrical cache vessel with cacao pods and blossom topping lid, Copan (drawing by author after Stromsvik 1941, fig. 20c); (*b*) Four-sided Copan cache vessel as structure with cacao pods and blossom on lid (drawing by author after McNeil, Hurst, and Sharer 2006, fig. 11.10); (*c*) Cache vessel as a house with painted doorway, Guaytan (drawing by Stephen Houston, from Houston 1998, fig. 14)

a

b

c

Figure 5.5. Early Classic cache vessels from the Escuintla region of southern Guatemala (drawings by author): (*a*) Cache vessel with cacao pods on sides and directional jade earspools on lid (after Sotheby's 1984, no. 183); (*b*) interior of vessel *a* portraying supine human figure (after Sotheby's 1984, no. 183); (*c*) cache vessel with spines of ceiba tree and interior portraying supine and apparently sacrificed female figure (after photograph by author)

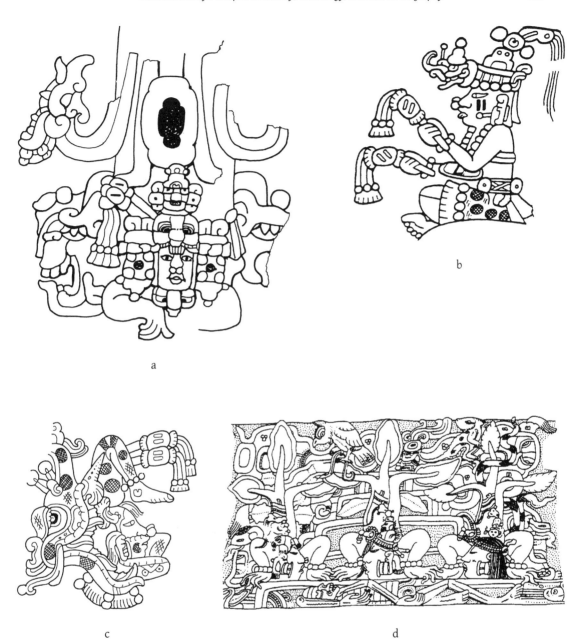

Figure 5.6. Early Classic imagery pertaining to music and maize god: (*a*) Maize god in contortionist position as world tree supporting serpents and flanked by zoomorphic mountains; note diagonal pair of gourd rattles on right side of headdress (drawing by author after Campaña Valenzuela 2005, p. 50); (*b*) Early Classic deity shaking pair of rattles, detail of incised ceramic vessel (drawing by author after Hellmuth 1988, fig. 4.2); (*c*) Maya maize god in contortionist position with pair of rattles between legs, detail of same vessel as *b* (drawing by author after Hellmuth 1988, fig. 4.2); (*d*) detail of Early Classic incised vessel with central figure as the maize god in contortionist position as a cacao tree backed by a stepped pyramid and a floral mountain (detail of drawing courtesy of Stephen Houston after Kerr and Kerr 2000, p. 972)

Figure 5.7. The Early Classic Rosalila Temple at Copan, Honduras
(drawing by author after Barbara Fash)

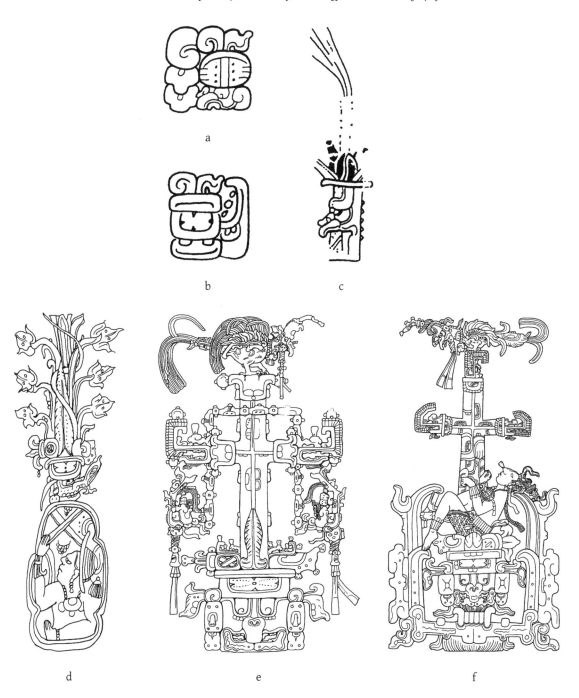

Figure 5.8. Classic Maya fire offerings, censers, and world trees: (*a*) Maya dedicatory verb, *och k'ak'*, or "fire enters" (drawing by author after Stuart 1998, fig. 8b); (*b*) Maya glyph read as *e'el nah*, or "house burning," detail of text from (drawing by author after Stuart 1998, fig. 11a); (*c*) Late Classic zoomorphic censer with solar K'in sign on brow (from Taube 1994a, fig. 8e); (*d*) censer with world tree above quatrefoil cave, detail of Late Classic vase (drawing by author after Coe 1978, no. 16); (*e*) world tree emerging from zoomorphic censer, detail of Tablet of the Temple of the Cross, Palenque (drawing by author); (*f*) world tree and ruler K'inich Janahb Pakal atop censer, detail of Sarcophagus Lid from the Temple of the Cross, Palenque (drawing courtesy of Simon Martin from Martin 2006, fig. 8.5a)

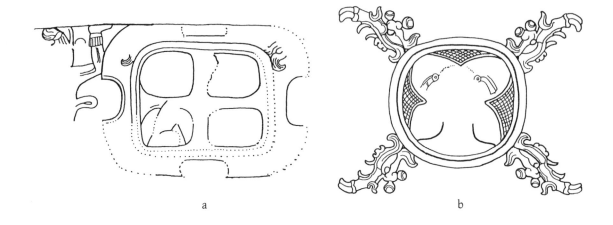

a   b

c

d

Figure 5.9. Roof crest facades from the Temple of the Sun, Palenque: (*a*) Intact portion of world bearer and solar disk from northern side of the eastern facade; note remains of centipede heads on upper portion of solar disk (drawing by author after Robertson 1991, fig. 140); (*b*) solar disk with four centipede heads, House A of Palenque Palace (drawing by author after Maudslay 1889–1902, vol. 4, pl. 6); (*c*) early rendering by Jean-Frédéric Waldeck of east facade of the Temple of the Sun roof crest (detail after Baudez 1993, pl. 25); (*d*) portrayal of west facade by Jean-Frédéric Waldeck (detail after Baudez 1993, pl. 26)

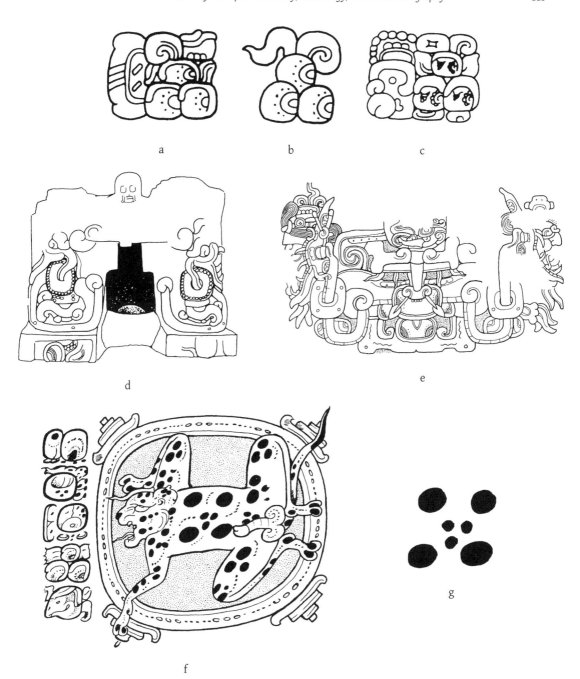

Figure 5.10. Hearthstone symbolism in Classic Maya epigraphy and art: (*a*) Glyph referring to the first (or green) hearthstone place concerning the beginning of the Bak'tun cycle beginning in 3114 B.C., Quirigua Stela C (from Taube 1988, fig. 3a); (*b*) hearthstones with fire sign, Tonina (from Taube 1988, fig. 3d); (*c*) emblem glyph for Seibal (from Taube 1988, fig. 3b); (*d*) Early Classic stairway shrine as Witz head with two hearthstones portrayed at base of stucco facade and actual stone in the interior maw, Structure E5-5, Tonina (from Taube 1988, fig. 4b); (*e*) Early Classic Witz head with three stone in mouth, compare pair of exhaled serpents to the examples appearing on the adjacent shrine of Structure E5-5, detail of Monument 106, Tonina (from Taube 1988, fig. 4c); (*f*) water jaguar described as the *way* spirit of the "hearthstone lord," detail of Late Classic vase (after Houston and Stuart 1989, fig. 3); (*g*) detail of central belly spotting on water jaguar

Karl Taube

a

b   c

Figure 5.11. Temples and caves in ancient Maya art: (*a*) Late Classic portrayal of temple in profile with roof and stepped platform, detail of Late Classic Maya vase (drawing by author after Kerr 1992, p. 443); (*b*) Late Preclassic Flower Mountain and cave resembling inverted "L," detail of North Wall mural, San Bartolo (detail of drawing by Heather Hurst, from Saturno, Taube, and Stuart 2005, fig. 5); (*c*) Chahk seated in cave temple, detail of Late Classic vase (drawing by author after Coe 1978, no. 11)

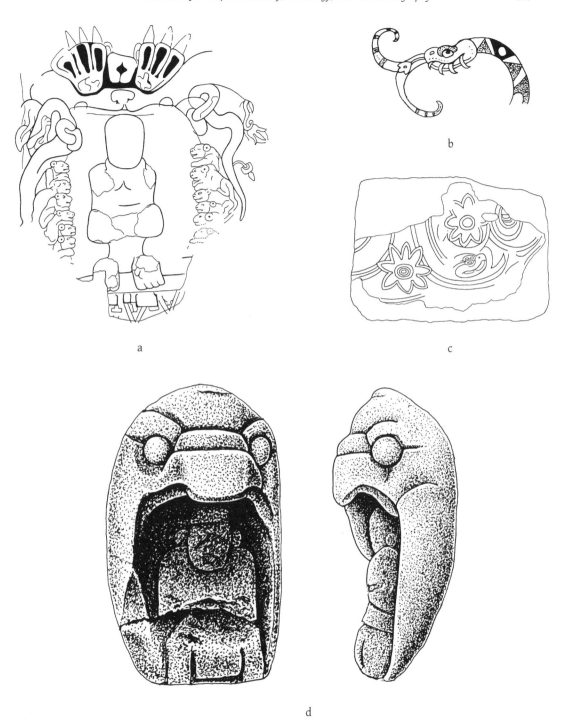

Figure 5.12. Preclassic imagery pertaining to mountains and caves (drawings by author): (*a*) Human figure seated in zoomorphic mountain cave flanked by felines and probable floral symbolism, Izapa Monument (drawing by Ayax Moreno, courtesy of the New World Archaeological Foundation); (*b*) Late Preclassic coral snake from West Wall mural, San Bartolo (after Taube et al. 2008, fig. 54a); (*c*) Late Preclassic mural fragment with serpent and flowers, Naranjo, Guatemala (drawing by author after Anonymous 2008); (*d*) stone monument with figure in cave maw, Tiltepec, Chiapas

a

b   c

Figure 5.13. Middle Formative Olmec cave iconography at Chalcatzingo, Morelos (drawings by author): (*a*) Woman seated in zoomorphic cave exhaling elaborate breath scrolls (from Taube 2010b, fig. 5.5c); (*b*) probable form of Olmec maize god in zoomorphic cave with breath scroll fragment (after Angulo 1987, fig. 10.12); (*c*) frontal view of Chalcatzingo cave as quatrefoil with passageway through mouth (from Taube 2010b, fig. 5.5b)

a

b

c

Figure 5.14. Classic Maya portrayals of Flower Mountain (all drawings by author): (*a*) Flower Mountain exhaling serpent with sun god in its maw, detail of Early Classic vase from Kaminaljuyu, Guatemala (from Taube 2004a, fig. 10d); (*b*) Early Classic Flower Mountain with large blossom on brow, note snakes exhaled from corners of mouth, Structure 5D-33-2nd, Tikal (from Taube 2004a, fig. 12b); (*c*) Flower Mountain with large cave maw, detail of Late Classic vase (from Taube 2004a, fig. 12d)

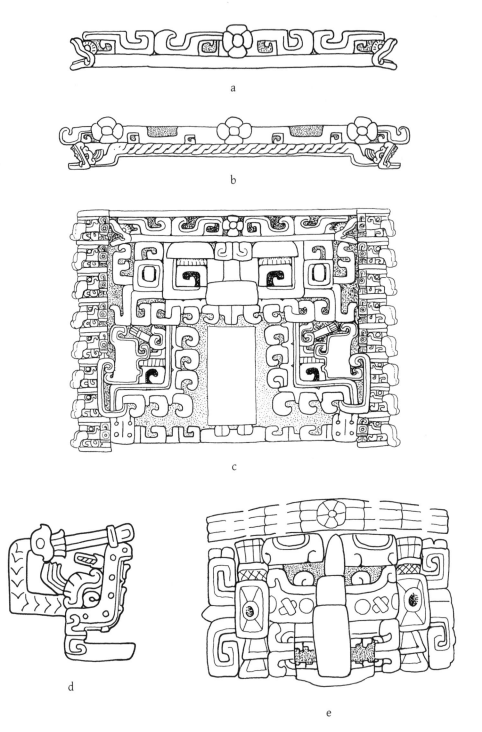

Figure 5.15. Flower Mountain iconography appearing in temple architecture from the northern Maya lowlands (all drawings by author): (*a*) Bicephalic plumed serpent with clouds and central blossom on back, El Tabascueño (see *c*); (*b*) bicephalic plumed serpent with clouds and blossoms on back, Hochob (after Seler 1916, fig. 20); (*c*) Flower Mountain facade, El Tabascueño (from Taube 2004a, fig. 13d); (*d*) plumed serpent with floral tail as breath of temple mountain maw, Hochob (from Taube 2010a, fig. 25c); (*e*) Puuc-style portrayal of Flower Mountain with blossom on brow, Osario platform, Chichen Itza (from Taube 2004a, fig. 14c)

Primary Sources

Codex Azcatitlan   Dominique Michelet, coordinating editor. *Codex Azcatitlan: Códice Azcatitlan.* Paris: Bibliothèque national de France, 1995.

Codex Borgia   Karl Anton Nowotny, commentator. *Codex Borgia: Biblioteca Apastolica Vaticana (Cod. Borg. Messicano 1).* Graz: Akademische Druck- und Verlagsanstalt, 1976.

Bibliography

Agurcia Fasquelle, Ricardo

2004   "Rosalila, Temple of the Sun King." In *Understanding Early Classic Copán*, edited by Ellen Bell, Marcello Canuto, and Robert Sharer, pp. 101–12. Philadelphia: University of Pennsylvania Museum of Archaeology and Anthropology.

Agurcia Fasquelle, Ricardo, and Barbara Fash

2005   "The Evolution of Structure 10L-16, Heart of the Copán Acropolis." In *Copán: The History of an Ancient Maya Kingdom*, edited by E. Wyllys Andrews and William L. Fash, pp. 201–37. Santa Fe: School of American Research Press.

Andrews, E. Wyllys V., and Barbara Fash

1992   "Continuity and Change in a Royal Maya Residential Complex at Copan." *Ancient Mesoamerica* 3/1: 63–89.

Angulo V., Jorge

1987   "The Chalcatzingo Reliefs: An Iconographic Analysis. In *Ancient Chalcatzingo*, edited by David. C. Grove, pp. 132–58. Austin: University of Texas Press.

Anonymous

2008   "El fragmento de mural del edificio B-15 de Naranjo, Petén." *Mexicon* 30/2: 33.

Bardawil, Laurence W.

1976   "The Principal Bird Deity in Maya Art – An Iconographic Study of Form and Meaning." In *The Art, Iconography and Dynastic History of Palenque*, Part 3: *The Proceedings of the Segunda Mesa Redonda de Palenque*, edited by Merle Greene Robertson, pp. 195–210. Pebble Beach: The Robert Louis Stevenson School.

Baudez, Claude François

1993   *Jean-Frédéric Waldeck, peintre: le premier explorateur des ruines mayas.* Fariglianos: Editions Hazan.

1999   "Los templos enmascarados de Yucatán." *Arqueología Mexicana* 7/37: 54–59.

Berlin, Brent; Dennis E. Breedlove; and Peter H. Raven

1974   *Principles of Tzeltal Plant Classification.* New York: Academic Press.

Campaña Valenzuela, Luz Evelia

2005   "Contribuciones a la historia de Becán." *Arqueología Mexicana* 13/75: 48–53.

Coe, Michael D.

1973   *The Maya Scribe and His World.* New York: The Grolier Club.

1978   *Lords of the Underworld: Masterpieces of Classic Maya Ceramics.* Princeton: Princeton University Press.

2005   *The Maya.* 7th edition. London: Thames & Hudson.

Culbert, T. Patrick

1993   *The Ceramics of Tikal: Vessels from the Burials, Caches and Problematical Deposits.* Tikal Report No. 25, Part A. Philadelphia: The University Museum, University of Pennsylvania.

de Jong, Harriet J.

1999   The Land of Corn and Honey: The Keeping of Stingless Bees (Meliponiculture) in the Ethno-ecological Environment of Yucatán (Mexico) and El Salvador. Ph.D. dissertation, Utrecht University.

Draper, Robert

2010   "Unburying the Aztec." *National Geographic* 218/5: 110–35.

Fash, William

1991   *Scribes, Warriors and Kings: The City of Copán and the Ancient Maya.* London: Thames & Hudson.

Fought, John

1972   *Chorti Mayan Texts.* Philadelphia: University of Pennsylvania Press.

Freidel, David; Linda Schele; and Joy Parker

1993   *Maya Cosmos: Three Thousand Years on the Shaman's Path.* New York: William Morrow.

Garibay, Angel Maria

1979   *Teogonia e historia de los Mexicanos: Tres opúsculos del siglo XVI.* 3rd edition. Mexico City: Editorial Porrua.

Gendrop, Paul

1983   *Los estilos Río Bec, Chenes y Puuc en la arquitectura Maya.* Mexico City: Universidad Nacional Autónoma de México.

Girard, Rafael

1962   *Los Mayas Eternos.* Mexico City: Libro Mex.

Graham, Ian

1997   "Discovery of a Maya Ritual Cave in Peten, Guatemala." *Symbols* (spring): 28–31.

Guernsey, Julia

2006   *Ritual and Power in Stone: The Performance of Rulership in Mesoamerican Izapan Style Art.* Austin: University of Texas Press.

Guiteras-Holmes, Calixta

1961   *Perils of the Soul: The World View of a Tzotzil Indian.* New York: Free Press of Glencoe.

Hanks, William F.

1990   *Referential Practice: Language and Lived Space among the Maya.* Chicago: University of Chicago Press.

Hellmuth, Nicholas M.

1987   *Monster und Menschen in der Maya-Kunst.* Graz: Akademische Druck, u. Verlagsanstalt.

1988   "Early Maya Iconography on an Incised Cylindrical Tripod." In *Maya Iconography,* edited by Elizabeth P. Benson and Gillett G. Griffin, pp. 152–74. Princeton: Princeton University Press.

Hieb, Louis A.

1979   "Hopi World View." In *Handbook of North American Indians,* general editor William Sturtevant, vol. 9, pp. 577–80. Washington, D.C.: Smithsonian Institution.

Hill, Jane H.
1992   "The Flower World of Old Uto-Aztecan." *Journal of Anthropological Research* 48: 117–44.

Hirth, Kenneth G., and Susan Grant Hirth
1993   "Ancient Currency: The Style and Use of Jade and Marble Carvings in Central Honduras." In *Pre-Colombian Jade: New Geological and Cultural Interpretations*, edited by Frederick W. Lange, pp. 173–90. Salt Lake City: University of Utah Press.

Houston, Stephen D.
1998   "Classic Maya Depictions of the Built Environment." In *Function and Meaning in Classic Maya Architecture*, edited by Stephen Houston, pp. 353–72. Washington, D.C.: Dumbarton Oaks.

Houston, Stephen, and David Stuart
1989   *The Way Glyph: Evidence for "Co-essences" among the Classic Maya*. Research Reports on Ancient Maya Writing 30. Washington, D.C.: Center for Maya Research.

Jones, Christopher, and Linton Satterthwaite
1982   *The Monuments and Inscriptions of Tikal: The Carved Monuments*. University Museum Monograph 44. Philadelphia: The University Museum, University of Pennsylvania.

Kerr, Justin, editor
1992   *The Maya Vase Book*, volume 3. New York: Kerr Associates.

Kerr, Barbara, and Justin Kerr, editors
2000   *The Maya Vase Book*, volume 6. New York: Kerr Associates.

Looper, Matthew
2003   *Lightning Warrior: Maya Art and Kinship at Quirigua*. Austin: University of Texas Press.

Lowe, Gareth W.
1981   "Olmec Horizons Defined in Mound 20, San Isidro, Chiapas." In *The Olmec and Their Neighbors: Essays in Memory of Matthew W. Stirling*, edited by Elizabeth P. Benson, pp. 231–55. Washington, D.C., Dumbarton Oaks.

Lowe, Gareth W.; Thomas A. Lee, Jr.; and Eduardo Martinez Espinosa
1982   *Izapa: An Introduction to the Ruins and Monuments*. Papers of the New World Archaeological Foundation 31. Provo: Brigham Young University.

Lumholtz, Carl
1900   *Symbolism of the Huichol Indians*. Memoirs of the American Museum of Natural History 3. New York: American Museum of Natural History.

Marquina, Ignacio
1951   *Arquitectura prehispánica*. Mexico City: Instituto Nacional de Antropología e Historia.

Martin, Simon
2006   "Cacao in Ancient Maya Religion: First Fruit from the Maize Tree and Other Tales from the Underworld." In *Chocolate in Mesoamerica: A Cultural History of Cacao*, edited by Cameron L. McNeil, pp. 154–83. Gainesville: University Press of Florida.

Maudslay, Alfred P.
1889–1902   *Biologia Centrali-Americana; Archaeology*. London: R. H. Porter and Dalau.

McNeil, Cameron L.; W. Jeffrey Hurst; and Robert J. Sharer
    2006   "The Use and Representation of Cacao During the Classic Period at Copan, Honduras." In *Chocolate in Mesoamerica: A Cultural History of Cacao*, edited by Cameron L. McNeil, pp. 224–52. Gainesville: University Press of Florida.

Miller, Mary Ellen
    1992   "The Image of People and Nature in Classic Maya Art and Architecture." In *The Ancient Americas: Art from Sacred Landscapes*, edited by Richard F. Townsend, pp. 158–69. Chicago: The Art Institute of Chicago.

Molina, Alonso de
    1977   *Vocabulario en lengua Castellana y Mexicana y Mexicana Castellana*. 2nd edition. Mexico City: Editorial Porrua.

Norman, V. Garth
    1973   *Izapa Sculpture*, Part 1: *Album*. Papers of the New World Archaeological Foundation 30. Provo: New World Archaeological Foundation, Brigham Young University.

Oakes, Maude
    1951   *The Two Crosses of Todos Santos: Survivals of Maya Religious Ritual*. Princeton: Princeton University Press.

Redfield, Robert, and Alfonso Villa Rojas
    1934   *Chan Kom: A Maya Village*. Carnegie Institution of Washington, Pub. 448. Washington, D.C.: Carnegie Institution of Washington.

Robertson, Merle Greene
    1991   *The Sculpture of Palenque*, Volume 4: *The Cross Group, the North Group, the Olvidado, and Other Pieces*. Princeton: Princeton University Press.

Roys, Ralph L.
    1933   *The Book of Chilam Balam of Chumayel*. Carnegie Institution of Washington, Publication 438. Washington, D.C.: Carnegie Institution of Washington.

Sahagún, Fray Bernardino
    1950–1982   *Florentine Codex: General History of the Things of New Spain*, translated by Arthur J. O. Anderson and Charles E. Dibble. Santa Fe: School of American Research.

Saturno, William; Karl Taube; and David Stuart
    2005   *The Murals of San Bartolo, El Peten, Guatemala*, Part 1: *The North Wall*. Ancient America 7. Barnardsville: Center for Ancient American Studies.

Schaefer, Stacy
    1996   "The Cosmos Contained: The Temple Where Sun and Moon Meet." In *People of the Peyote: Huichol Indian History, Religion and Survival*, edited by Peter Furst and Stacy Schaefer, pp. 330–76. Albuquerque: University of New Mexico Press.

Schele, Linda, and Peter Mathews
    1998   *The Code of Kings: The Language of Seven Sacred Maya Temples and Tombs*. New York: Scribner.

Schellhas, Paul
    1904   *Representation of Deities of the Maya Manuscripts*. Papers 4(1). Cambridge: Peabody Museum of American Archaeology and Ethnology, Harvard University.

Schieber de Lavarreda, Christa, and Miguel Orrego Corzo
    2010   "Preclassic Olmec and Maya Monuments and Architecture at Takalik Abaj." In *The Place of Stone Monuments: Context, Use, and Meaning in Mesoamerica's Preclas-*

sic Transition, edited by Julia Guernsey, John E. Clark, and Barbara Arroyo, pp. 177–230. Washington, D.C.: Dumbarton Oaks.

Schmidt, Peter; Mercedes de la Garza; and Enrique Nalda, editors

1998 *Maya*. New York: Rizzoli.

Seler, Eduard E.

1902–1923 *Gesammelte Abhandlungen zur Amerikanischen Sprach und Alterthumskunde*. 5 volumes. Berlin: Ascher.

1916 *Die Quetzalcoatl-Fassaden Yukatekischer Bauten*. Berlin: Der Königl. Akademie der Wissenschaften.

1963 *Comentarios al Códice Borgia*. Translated by M. Fenk. 3 volumes. Mexico City: Fondo de Cultura Económica.

Smith, A. Ledyard

1982 "Major Architecture and Caches." In *Excavations at Seibal*, general editor Gordon Willey. Memoirs of the Peabody Museum of Archaeology and Ethnology 15/1. Cambridge: Harvard University.

Sotheby's

1984 *Important Pre-Columbian Art, New York, November 27 and 28, 1984*. New York: Sotheby's.

Stone, Andrea J.

1995 *Images from the Underworld: Naj Tunich and the Tradition of Maya Cave Painting*. Austin: University of Texas Press.

Stromsvik, Gustav

1941 *Substela Caches and Stela Foundations at Copan and Quirigua*. Contributions to American Anthropology and History 37. Washington, D.C.: Carnegie Institution of Washington.

Stuart, David

1987 "Ten Phonetic Syllables." *Research Reports on Ancient Maya Writing*, No. 14.

1998 "'The Fire Enters His House': Architecture and Ritual in Classic Maya Texts." In *Function and Meaning in Classic Maya Architecture*, edited by Stephen Houston, pp. 373–425. Washington, D.C.: Dumbarton Oaks.

2011 *The Order of Days: The Maya World and the Truth About 2012*. New York: Harmony Books.

Stuart, David, and Stephen Houston

1994 *Classic Maya Place Names*. Studies in Pre-Columbian Art and Archaeology 33. Washington, D.C.: Dumbarton Oaks.

Taube, Karl

1988 "A Prehispanic Maya Katun Wheel." *Journal of Anthropological Research* 44/2: 183–203.

1989 *Itzam Cab Ain: Caimans, Cosmology and Calendrics in Postclassic Yucatan*. Research Reports on Ancient Maya Writing 26. Washington, D.C.: Center for Maya Research.

1992 *The Major Gods of Ancient Yucatan*. Studies in Pre-Columbian Art and Archaeology 32. Washington, D.C.: Dumbarton Oaks.

1994a "The Birth Vase: Natal Imagery in Ancient Maya Myth and Ritual." In *The Maya Vase Book*, volume 4, edited by Justin Kerr, pp. 650–85. New York: Kerr Associates.

1994b "The Iconography of Toltec Period Chichen Itza." In *Hidden in the Hills: Maya Archaeology of the Northwestern Yucatan Peninsula*, edited by Hanns J. Prem, pp. 212–46. Acta Mesoamericana 7. Möckmühl: Verlag von Flemming.

1998	"The Jade Hearth: Centrality, Rulership, and the Classic Maya Temple." In *Function and Meaning in Classic Maya Architecture*, edited by Stephen Houston, pp. 427–69. Washington, D.C.: Dumbarton Oaks.
2000	"The Turquoise Hearth: Fire, Self Sacrifice, and the Central Mexican Cult of War." In *Mesoamerica's Classic Heritage: From Teotihuacan to the Great Aztec Temple*, edited by Davíd Carrasco, Lindsay Jones, and Scott Sessions, pp. 269–340. Niwot: University Press of Colorado.
2001	"The Breath of Life: The Symbolism of Wind in Mesoamerica and the American Southwest." In *The Road to Aztlan: Art from a Mythic Homeland*, edited by Virginia M. Fields and Victor Zamudio-Taylor, pp. 102–23. Los Angeles: Los Angeles County Museum of Art.
2002	La serpiente emplumada de Teotihuacan. *Arqueología Mexicana* 53: 36–41.
2003a	"Ancient and Contemporary Maya Conceptions about the Field and Forest." In *The Lowland Maya Area: Three Millennia at the Human-Wildland Interface*, edited by Arturo Gómez-Pompa, Michael F. Allen, Scott Fedick, and J. Jiménez-Osornio, pp. 461–92. New York: Haworth Press.
2003b	"Maws of Heaven and Hell: The Symbolism of the Centipede and Serpent in Classic Maya Religion." In *Antropología de la eternidad: La muerte en la cultura Maya*, edited by Andrés Ciudad Ruíz, Mario Humberto Ruz Sosa, and María Josefa Iglesias Ponce de León, pp. 405–42. Madrid: Sociedad Española de Estudios Mayas and El Centro de la Cultura Maya.
2004a	"Flower Mountain: Concepts of Life, Beauty and Paradise Among the Classic Maya." *Res: Anthropology and Aesthetics* 45: 69–98.
2004b	*Olmec Art at Dumbarton Oaks*. Washington, D.C.: Dumbarton Oaks.
2004c	"The Stairway Sculptures of Structure 10L-16: Fire and the Evocation and Resurrection of K'inich Yax K'uk' Mo'." In *Understanding Early Classic Copán*, edited by Ellen Bell, Marcello Canuto, and Robert Sharer, pp. 265–96. Philadelphia: University of Pennsylvania Museum of Archaeology and Anthropology.
2005	"The Symbolism of Jade in Classic Maya Religion." *Ancient Mesoamerica* 16: 23–50.
2006	"Climbing Flower Mountain: Concepts of Resurrection and the Afterlife in Ancient Teotihuacan." In *Arqueología de historia del Centro de México: Homenaje a Eduardo Matos Moctezuma*, edited by Leonardo López Luján, Davíd Carrasco, and Lordes Cué, pp. 153–70. Mexico City: Instituto Nacional de Antropología e Historia.
2009	"The Womb of the World: The *Cuauhxicalli* and Other Offering Bowls in Ancient and Contemporary Mesoamerica." In *Maya Archaeology* 1, edited by Charles Golden, Stephen Houston, and Joel Skidmore, pp. 86–106. San Francisco: Precolumbia Mesoweb Press.
2010a	"At Dawn's Edge: Tulum, Santa Rita and Floral Symbolism of Late Postclassic Yucatan." In *Astronomers, Scribes, and Priests: Intellectual Interchange between the Northern Maya Lowlands and Highland Mexico in the Late Postclassic Period*, edited by Gabrielle Vail and Christine Hernandez, pp. 145–91. Washington, D.C.: Dumbarton Oaks.
2010b	"Gateways to Another World: The Symbolism of Flowers in Mesoamerica and the American Southwest." In *The Land Brightened with Flowers: The Hopi Iconography Project*, edited by Kelley Hays-Gilpin and Polly Schaafsma, pp. 73–120. Museum of Northern Arizona Bulletin 67, Museum of Northern Arizona. Flagstaff: Museum of Northern Arizona.

Taube, Karl; Heather Hurst; Edwin Román; William Saturno; and David Stuart

2008	"Actualización de los hallazgos arquitectónicos y pictóricos en la pirámide las Pinturas, San Bartolo." XXII Simposio de Investigaciones Arqueológicas en Guatemala, Guatemala City, July 25.

Tedlock, Barbara
 1982 *Time and the Highland Maya.* Albuquerque: University of New Mexico Press.

Tedlock, Dennis
 1996 *Popol Vuh: The Definitive Edition of the Mayan Book of the Dawn of Life and the Glories of Gods and Kings.* New York: Simon and Schuster.

Thompson, J. Eric S.
 1934 "Sky Bearers, Colors, and Directions in Maya and Mexican Religion." *Contributions to American Archaeology*, Pub. 436, No. 10: 209-242. Washington, D.C.: Carnegie Institution of Washington.
 1971 *Maya Hieroglyphic Writing: An Introduction.* Norman: University of Oklahoma Press.

Tozzer, Alfred M.
 1941 *Landa's Relación de las Cosas de Yucatan.* Papers of the Peabody Museum of American Archaeology and Ethnology 18. Cambridge: Harvard University Press.

Trigger, Bruce
 1990 "Monumental Architecture: A Thermodynamic Explanation of Symbolic Behavior." *World Archaeology* 22: 119–32.

Vargas de la Peña, Leticia, and Victor R. Castillo Borges
 2001 "La pintura mural prehispánica en Ek'balam, Yucatán." In *La pintura mural prehispánica en México: Area Maya, Estudios,* vol. 2, part 4, edited by Beatriz de la Fuente, pp. 403–18. Mexico City: Universidad Nacional Autónoma de México.

Vogt, Evon Z.
 1969 *Zinacantan: A Maya Community in the Highlands of Chiapas.* Cambridge: Harvard University Press.
 1976 *Tortillas for the Gods: A Symbolic Analysis of Zinacanteco Rituals.* Cambridge: Harvard University Press.

von Schwerin, Jennifer
 2011 "The Sacred Mountain in Social Context. Symbolism and History in Maya Architecture: Temple 22 at Copan, Honduras." *Ancient Mesoamerica* 22/2: 271–300.

Wisdom, Charles
 1940 *The Chorti Mayas of Guatemala.* Chicago: University of Chicago Press.

Zingg, R. M.
 1938 *The Huichols: Primitive Artists.* New York: G. Stechert.

6

SEEDS AND MOUNTAINS:
THE COSMOGONY OF TEMPLES IN SOUTH ASIA

Michael W. Meister, University of Pennsylvania

In the preface to his volume *The Golden Germ: An Introduction to Indian Symbolism*, F. D. K. Bosch (1960, p. 9) commented tartly that "the idea of a clear-cut whole is as incompatible with Indian symbolism as, for instance, the idea of a town enclosed within its ramparts is with that of a tropical primeval forest." Yet, in the body of South Asia's material remains, this rampart and forest might seem the same. His "golden germ" (the *hiraṇyagarbha*) is a widely shared origin myth in South Asia, commonly found in popular texts and imagery — the seed, egg, or womb opening out, like the calyx of the ripe lotus, to support deities or divine emblems (Maxwell 1982; Hayward Gallery 1982). The temple — as does the lotus — stands between water and sky.

This early cosmogony (Muir 1863, pp. 3–53) also referred to a *skambha* column that levered apart earth and heaven,[1] referenced architecturally as early as the Mauryan-dynasty freestanding pillars of the third century B.C.E. (Irwin 1973, 1974, 1975, 1976) that Coomaraswamy (1931; Meister 1992, pp. xvii–xviii) interpreted as scepters with insignia, their capitals in the form of a "ripe lotus" much more naturalistically represented bearing elephants or nature spirits on the railings of the Buddhist *stūpa* at Bharhut, around 100 B.C.E. (fig. 6.1). John Irwin (1973, 1974, 1975, 1976) less felicitously later described these capitals as "dying" lotuses, allying them with an Indian "water cosmology" (Coomaraswamy 1993) still referenced in popular imagery today.

Atharva-veda

Stella Kramrisch (1981, pp. 89–97) many years ago pointed to a "construction" within the cosmological speculation contained in the *Atharva-veda* (book 15) that, to her, foreshadowed the form of the Hindu temple a millennium and a half later.[2] As she (1983, pp. 89–97, passim) described,

---

[1] An influential early translation can be found in Muir (1863, p. 18): AV 10.8.35: "Skambha established both these [worlds] the earth and sky, Skambha established the wide atmosphere, Skambha established the six wide regions, Skambha pervaded this entire universe ..."; 41: "He who knows the golden reed standing in the water, is the mysterious Prajāpati"; see also Meister 2007.

[2] Griffith 1895–1896, vol. 2. AV 15.1.1: "The hyperbolical glorification of the Vrātya or Aryan Non-conformist"; AV 15.3.1–10: "For a whole year he stood erect. The Gods said unto him, Why standest thou, O Vrātya? He answered and said, Let them bring my couch. They brought the couch for that Vrātya. / Two of its feet were Summer and Spring, and two were Autumn and the Rains. / Brihat and Rathantara were the two long boards, Yajnāyajniya and Vāmadevya the two cross-boards. / Holy verses were the strings lengthwise, and Yajus formulas the cross-tapes. / Sacred lore was the blanket, Devotion the

The creation of the Sole Vrātya who is Mahādeva and the transfiguration of the Vrātya has three phases: the birth of a god, the vision of that god, and the building of his monument .... The sole Vrātya incorporates into his presence the four directions of the extended universe .... Time accompanied him on his way .... The sole Vrātya is a choreographed monument of deity built up by the words of hymns .... The sole Vratya now arises as the lord of the space-time universe, himself the central pillar of a four-sided pyramid.

Amala Fruit

The purpose of this paper is to question and problematize South Asia's material remains. By the first century B.C.E., in both Buddhist caves and Brahmanical columns, the lotus had been joined (and was later replaced) by the seed of the *amala* fruit (*emblic myrobalan* or Indian gooseberry) (fig. 6.2) continuing in the fifth century C.E. into the Gupta period as an emblem of cosmic parturition (fig. 6.3, right).

The *āmala*[*kī*] fruit, and its tree, however, was known and valued much earlier in Ayurvedic texts, such as the *Garika Saṁhitā*, for its rejuvenative properties: "the physician should consider the pulp (the fruit) of ... *āmalakī* as ambrosia" (Sharma 1976–2001, vol. 1, p. 14). This provided ground for a legend of King Aśoka's last gift (before his death) of half an *āmala*, then made into a tonic and distributed to the whole of the Buddhist community (Strong 1983, pp. 286–92).[3]

*Āmalaka*s were used to crown stone temples in the fifth century C.E. and later (Bhattacharyya 1963, p. 267);[4] and named by the Chinese pilgrim Xuanzang (1906) in the seventh century as crown for an "Āmalaka *stūpa*," the Bodh Gaya temple, and a shrine in honor of Aśoka's last gift.

Conceptually rising from the sanctum's center, through the sheath of the tower, above the upper *vedī* (*uttaravedī* "sky-altar"), a column held the *āmalaka*, as the lotus-calyx had once

---

coverlet. / The Sāman was the Cushion, and chanting the bolster. / The Vrātya ascended that couch. / The hosts of Gods were his attendants, solemn vows his messengers, and all creatures his worshippers. / All creatures become the worshippers of him who possesses this knowledge." AV 15.17.1–10: "His first diffused breath is this Earth. / His second diffused breath is that Firmament. / His third diffused breath is that Heaven. / His fourth diffused breath are those Constellations. / His fifth diffused breath are the Seasons. / His sixth diffused breath are the Season-groups. / His seventh diffused breath is the year. / With one and the same object the Gods go round the Year and the Seasons follow round the Vrātya. / When they surround the Sun on the day of New Moon, and that time of Full Moon. / That one immortality of theirs is just an oblation." AV 15.18.1–5: "Of that Vrātya. / The right eye is the Sun and the left eye is the Moon. / His right ear is Agni and his left ear is Pavamāna. / Day and Night are his nostrils. Diti and Aditi are his head and skull. / By day the Vrātya

is turned westward, by night he is turned eastward. Worship to the Vrātya!"

[3] Strong 1983, pp. 288–91: "Eventually, all Aśoka had left was a half of a myrobalan (*āmalaka*) fruit .... 'This today is my final offering; / my kingship and identity are gone. / Without good health, doctors, or medicinal herbs, / my only recourse is the assembly of noble ones.' ... Thereupon the myrobalan half was mashed, put in a soup and distributed to the community. ... 'I gave to the sangha this earth, / with its Mandara mountain, / and its dark blue blouse, the ocean, / and its face adorned with many jewel mines. / May the community enjoy the fruit.' ... The ministers therefore gave four koṭis of gold pieces ... in order to buy back the earth."

[4] Kramrisch 1946, p. 354: "Amala means without impurity, stainless; thus the name Amala-śilā 'pure stone' was given to it, especially by the Buddhists .... When, however, as generally in the Vāstu-śāstra, Āmalaka begins with a long 'a' it is the fruit of the Emblic Myrobalan, whose shape it remotely recalls."

opened to the sky (fig. 6.4).[5] Development of *āmalaka*-crowned temples in the fourth–fifth centuries C.E. is one of this paper's themes. Their significance ties them to themes of this symposium.

Terra-cotta models from the Gandhāra region of Pakistan (Nasim Khan 2009) include domed chapels as well as perforated incense covers with a crowning pot, corner *āmalaka*s on stems, and dormers between. These in function suggest the sheltering cottage roof of a rock-cut *caitya* cave at Guntupalli several centuries earlier, yet in form are radically different from *vihāra* chapel models from Gandhāra (fig. 6.5).[6] Yet their perforated form can even suggest the sheltering surround of perforated *stūpa*s on the upper levels of the Buddhist mountain-cosmogram at Borobudur, Java, centuries later (fig. 6.6).

Gupta-period Caves and Mountains

In India, the earliest Gupta-period stone temples cited (Cunningham 1880a) are rock-cut shrines at Udayagiri near Vidisha and Temple 17 at Sanchi in central India from early in the fifth century (fig. 6.7). Temple 1 at Udayagiri was built under an existing rock ledge, Cave 7 carved from a giant boulder, and others cut into the prepared rock face of the ridge. Temple 17, built on the top of the sacred Buddhist hill at Sanchi eight miles away, is, in my terms, a "constructed cave." The "flat-roofed" temple at Tigawa, probably a half century later, still follows a "flat-roofed" formula.

Of a similar flat-roofed lineage temple constructed under a rock ledge at Badami, Karnataka, Carol Bolon (1979, p. 255) observed, "The overhanging cliff was certainly the inducement for placing the temple here. It acts as a mountain-*śikhara* for the 'flat'-roofed temple." At Bilsar [Bilsaḍ], Uttar Pradesh (Cunningham 1880b, pp. 19–21; Williams 1982, pp. 73–76), however, in the reign of Kumāragupta, small models on uprights of a *pratōlī* gateway — associated in inscriptions on two freestanding columns dated 415 C.E. with a *svarga-sōpāna* or "flight of steps [leading] to heaven" (Bhandarkar 1981, p. 269) (fig. 6.13) — represent an altar platform crowned by corner and central *āmalaka*s (fig. 6.8).[7]

---

[5] Dhaky (1974) documents the presence of a "sky *liṅga*" above the crowning *āmalaka* of some temples in the seventh century.

[6] This model (IS.244-1960) in the form of a domed chapel was found at Pir Pai along with an *āmalaka*-crowned lid (Nasim Khan 2009). A similar "grey terracotta cover for an incense burner" in the Victoria and Albert Museum is identified (collections.vam. ac.uk/item/O479639/lid-unknown/) as a gift of M. Longworth Dames (1850–1922), "probably found in Banu District, Punjab" [Banu was founded in 1862; the NWFP district in 1901], and dated fifth–seventh century. "At the top is an upward-pointing aperture; three arched apertures are arranged around the lower part of the cover, with 3 birds supporting an 'amalaka'-shaped form at the top."

[7] Fleet 1888, pp. 44–45: "(L. 7.) — *at* this temple of the divine (*god*) Svâmi-Mahâsêna, whose wondrous

form is covered over with the accumulation of the lustre of the three worlds; who is the god Brahmanya; (*and*) who resides at ... ..., —this great work has been accomplished by Dhruvasharman, who follows the path of the customs of the Krita age, and of the true religion, (*and*) who is honoured by the assembly ... ... (L. 10.) — Having made a gateway, charming, (*and*) ... ... the abode of saints, (*and*) having the form of a staircase leading to heaven, (*and*) resembling a (*pearl*)-necklace of the kind called *kaubêrachchhanda*, (*and*) white with the radiance of pieces of crystalline gems; — (and *having made*), in a very proper manner, a [religious] almshouse (?), the abode of those who are eminent in respect of virtuous qualities; resembling in form the top part of a temple; — he, the virtuous-minded one, roams in a charming manner among the items of religious merit (*that he has thus accumulated*)...."

Even though these early chapels — freestanding or "rock cut" — seem not to have had constructed towers (Cunningham 1880a),[8] inscriptions early in the Gupta period compare their effect to "the lofty peak of the mountain Kailāsa"[9] and "as lofty as the peak of a hill and bearing the luster of the moon."[10] The important Gupta site of Udayagiri, Madhya Pradesh, paired such rock-carved and constructed cellas with reliefs of Vishnu sleeping the cosmos into existence and Varaha, his boar incarnation, lifting the earth up from the cosmic ocean (Willis 2009). In the sixth century, the Vaishnava "Gupta" Temple at Deogarh, Uttar Pradesh, narratively adorned its walls with reliefs of Vishnu saving an earthly king from a flood, Man and God-man (Vishnu and a sage — Nara-Nārāyana) discoursing in the Himalayas, and cosmic Vishnu awaking from his sleep on the cosmic ocean to a new day of creation (Lubotsky 1996).

Early *Āmalaka* Temples

Imminent parturition may also have been the symbolism of loose structural *āmalakas* early in the fifth century used as part of the construction of a temple in the Mukandara pass, Rajasthan (Meister 1981), with leaves elegantly carved within their bi-curved cusps (fig. 6.9, upper left). Surviving architectural pieces — a dormer fronton with musician and its backing, cornices, and a socketed crowning slab — suggest a superstructure with roll-cornice stories and corner and crowning *āmalakas* (fig. 6.9). The proliferation of foliage on this temple's architectural elements reinforces the perception of parturition, reflected also by the multiplying *āmalakas* of its superstructure.

Bilsar's "altar platform" can provide a mountain-like model for small "*āmalaka*" temples — the sign becoming its semantic substance — but is not yet a temple *śikhara*. Shrine-models on the sanctum doorframe of the early sixth-century "Gupta" temple at Deogarh offer possible models for an earlier shrine such as Temple 17 at Sanchi (fig. 6.10), and they stand in sequence with more nearly integrated "*latina*" shrine-models placed on the walls of Temple D at Bilot, Khyber Pakhtunkhwa, Pakistan, late in the sixth century (fig. 6.11, top right) (Meister 2010a, pp. 18–20; 2011). Reconstructed from fragmentary remains, Deogarh and Bilot's *śikharas* provide new evidence for fundamentals of the Nāgara temple marked by crowning

---

[8] Of Sanchi's Temple 17, Alexander Cunningham (1880a, pp. 60–62) wrote, "The flat roof, the square form, and the stern simplicity of this structural temple, all point to the rock-hewn cave as its prototype." For "Gupta-style" he proposed six characteristic features: flat-roofs, "T"-shaped doorframes, river goddesses marking the entrance, continuation of the portico's architrave as a molding around the temple, pillar capitals with addorsed lions, and "bosses of a *peculiar* form, like beehives with short side horns."

[9] Fleet 1888, pp. 76–78. "Gangdhar Stone Inscription of Vishvavarman (423–424 CE)": "(L. 22.) — He who has adorned (this) city on the banks of the Gargarâ with irrigation wells, tanks, and temples and halls of the gods, drinking-wells, and pleasure-gardens of various kinds, and causeways, and long pools, just as if (he were adorning his own) beloved wife with different sorts of ornaments; ... (L. 28.) — He, the illustrious Mayûrâkshaka, — who is sprung from a family

possessed of wisdom and prowess; whose heroism is renowned in every region; who holds himself under control; (and) who has accomplished, in his son Vishnubhata and also Haribhata, the duty of (continuing his) lineage, — caused to be built by his sons, the favourites of great good fortune, this shrine of the divine (god) Vishnu, which blocks up the path of sin —, seeing the aspect of which, **resembling the lofty peak of (the mountain) Kailâsa**, the Vidyâdharas, accompanied by their mistresses, come and gaze into it with happy faces that are like waterlilies, as if it were the very lustrous surface of a mirror ..." (emphasis added).

[10] Bhandarkar 1981, pp. 276–79, "Inscription of Kumāragupta I: The Year 116 [436 CE]": "... a settlement of merchants ... of the dignified name of Śridēva .... (Line 6), who constructed (a shrine of) the god (Pinākin), **as lofty as the peak of a hill and bearing the lustre of the moon**" (emphasis added).

and corner *āmalaka*s — both as precursors for Temple A at Kāfirkot (Meister 2010b, pp. 17–18) and a distant antecedent of the profligate "*āmalaka*"-bearing *śekharī* temples in North India of the tenth century and later (Hardy 2002).

For this architectural evolution, the emblematic *amala* fruit — like the stone *āmalaka* recently found buried at the Shahi site of Gumbatuna, Talash, Dir (fig. 6.12, bottom) (Meister 2010a) — provided the essential "seed," the luminous, pure source pouring radiance down the mountainous *śikhara* of the evolving temple. To quote the Mandasor inscription of 529 C.E. (Basham 1983), recording the replacement of a structure built earlier in the fifth century, "(The temple) which has broad and lofty towers [and] (thus) resembles a mountain, is pale-red like the mass of the rays of the moon just risen … charming to the eye … , the lovely crest jewel of the western ward (of the town)" (Bhandarkar 1981, p. 330).[11]

Mandasor: Architecture and Poetry

It is important to note that this Mandasor inscription is not, as Fleet (1888) and Bhandarkar (1981) treat it, an imperial Gupta inscription, despite its mention of Kumaragupta I, nor is the date suggested for the foundation of the silk-weavers' Sun temple (Kṛta 493 = 437–438 C.E.) that of the inscription itself, which records the temple's reconstruction in Kṛta Era 579 = 473–474 C.E.[12] Basham (1983, pp. 93–94) refers to the block of stone on which this inscription is written as "perhaps the finest relic of the Gupta age" but the inscription's author as a "hack poet … not a great poet — he used all the stock epithets and similes of the poetry of his time." The inscription is "one of the major sources for the social history of the period, and one of the main pieces of evidence for its high culture and urbanity," but "Our translation is rather free, for a close translation of Sanskrit poetry is impossible without sacrificing every bit of the poetic feeling of the original": "The silk weavers … with hoarded wealth had this incomparably noble temple made for the god with the burning rays" (ibid., p. 101).

Among translators of this inscription, Basham (1983, pp. 102–03) as a historian is perhaps the most sensitive to the chronological shift from the temple's construction to its commemoration: "The size of the original temple is not known, and it may have been comparatively modest, despite the hyperbole of the description …. This is not the end of the inscription, which commemorates not only the building of the temple, but also events which took place 37 years later":

> 37. This house of the sun has been again repaired … made altogether most noble ….
> 38. It is very high and white, as though touching the sky with its lovely pinnacles, a resting place for the first clear rays of the rising moon and sun.

---

[11] Fleet (1888, pp. 84–88) varied this slightly: "(L. 16.) — While he, the noble Bandhuvarman, the best of kings, the strong-shouldered one, was governing this city of Dashapura, which had been brought to a state of great prosperity — a noble (*and*) unequalled temple of the bright-rayed (*Sun*), was caused to be built by the silk-cloth weavers, as a guild, with the stores of wealth acquired by (*the exercise of their*) craft; — (a

temple) which, having broad and lofty spires, (*and*) resembling a mountain, (*and*) white as the mass of the rays of the risen moon, shines, charming to the eye, having the similarity of (*being*) the lovely crest-jewel, fixed (*in its proper place*), of (*this*) city of the west."

[12] For his analysis of the Kṛta Era, see Bhandarkar 1981, pp. 187–201.

Yet what may the poetry imply? Verse 30 describes the original temple with the phrasing "*Vistīrṇa-tuṅga-śikharaṁ śikharī-prakāśam=abhudgat-ēndv-amala-raśmi-kalāpa-gauraṁ ...*" — the temple's spire (*śikhara*) likened to those of a mountain range (*śikharī-prakāśam*); verse 38 describes the rebuilt temple with similar phrasing, "very lofty, burnished, as if it were touching the sky with (its) attractive spires" (*manōharaiḥ śikharaiḥ*), and as having "become the receptacle of spotless rays of the moon and the sun at (their) rise" (*amala-mayūkh-āyatana-bhūtaṁ*); verse 43 invokes Śiva's "tawny matted hair covered with the spotless digit of the moon" (*amalina-śaśi-lēkhā-daṁthuraṁ*) (Bhandarkar 1981, pp. 324–32).

A Tumain inscription, GE 116 = 436 C.E., records a shrine constructed "as lofty as the peak of a hill [*giri-śri(śṛṅ)ga-taṅgaṁ*] and having the luster of the moon"; yet between Tumain and the founding of the silk-weavers' temple at Mandasor and Mandasor's renovation, rhetoric and architecture had evolved. From *śṛṅga* to *śikhara* ("horn" to "top-knot") = tower, the temple became a receptacle for the pure light of the rising moon or sun (tawny, pale red, or white).[13] *Amala* as an adjective in these inscriptions refers to this purity, but may by this period be entangled with a synecdoche of the temple's crown — a "receptacle of spotless rays," *āmalaka*s marking every spire.

Archaeology versus Ideology

And yet temples constructed in the early fifth century have seemed to archaeologists to be only sheds, "flat-roofed" cave-like openings to a sacred world (Meister, Dhaky, and Deva 1988). From the "griddle"-topped natural boulder containing Cave 7, and the rock ledge sheltering Cave 1 at Udayagiri, to Temple 17's "constructed cave" on Sanchi hill nearby (fig. 6.7), these early Gupta temples need further social context. The temple — formulated in this period to mediate between earth and sky, cosmic waters and ultimate ether — was not a simple machine (Willis 2009).

Even before the reign of the Guptas, small shelters of impermanent materials had been placed on platforms — as at Pawaya (Williams 1982, pp. 18–22) — and then expanded, with societal implications (fig. 6.12, top). No shrine sanctum survives at Pawaya, but the scale of the site, the remains of a *toraṇa* gateway, and sculptures once crowning freestanding pillars link its political rulers to an Indic framework of cosmic and royal expansion (ibid., pp. 52–55; Garde 1940–1941).[14] Such early shrines were placed in contexts that served more than the ritual needs of the sects that first may have made them. As parts of larger complexes and political agendas, these may provide parallels we can discuss between South Asian temples and Mesopotamia and other parts of the world.

---

[13] Bhandarkar's shift to "pale red" from Fleet's "white" may well be based on the actual color of a rising harvest moon. Monier-Williams (1899, p. 81) gives as definitions of *amala* "spotless, stainless, clean, pure, shining."

[14] Of the preceding Nāgas, Williams (1982, pp. 18–19) wrote, "The chief site where a Nāga style might be expressed is Pawaya, the most established of the dynasty's centers. No sculpture from here, however, seems to belong to the third or fourth century. Even if some isolated fragments are assigned to this period, their paucity makes it difficult to think of Pawaya as a major artistic center where a new and non-Kushan style was formulated so early. In one way, however, the Hinduism of the Bhāraśiva Nāgas may have borne tangible fruit" referring to the "major architectural remain ... a brick pyramid originally of two terraces .... A similar terraced structure supporting a *liṅga* of Śiva was constructed at roughly the same time at Ahicchatrā."

At the site of Bilsar, Uttar Pradesh (Williams 1982, pp. 73–76), two inscriptions dated 415 C.E. on freestanding pillars record (Fleet 1888, pp. 44–45) that, "in the augmenting victorious reign of the Mahârâjâdhirâja, the glorious Kumâragupta [...] the restorer of the ashvamêdha-sacrifice, that had been long in abeyance," a *pratolī* gate, abode of saints, religious almshouse, and the two columns on which the inscriptions were written were donated in the compound of an existing temple (fig. 6.13) (Bhandarkar 1981, p. 270):

> At this temple of Lord Mahāsēna, the divine (one), whose wonderous body is produced out of the mass of the lustre of the three worlds; who is the god Brahmaṇya; (and) who resides at ... this magnificent work has been accomplished by Dhruvaśarman. Having constructed a gateway, charming (to the eye), (containing) abodes of sages, *having the appearance of a staircase leading to heaven* [emphasis mine], ... (and having constructed), in a very proper manner, a (religious) alms-house (?), a structure eminent in qualities, and as beautiful as the best of mansions; — he, of righteous intention, moves about piously among the pious. May Dhruva continue in bliss!

Of how these spaces were integrated or ritually used we have hardly any evidence. Cunningham (1880b, p. 18) suggested in the nineteenth century that a small cubical temple, on the model of Sanchi 17, with a cella and portico, once stood above a flight of stairs west of the surviving gate.[15] I might suggest an alternative — a platform more like the *āmalaka*-marked "altar" represented on the gateway (figs. 6.10, 6.13). If so, like the *aśvamedha* sacrifice itself — the sacrifice of a horse, whose perambulations for a year before indexically defined the expanding domain of the ruler — it may have represented an earlier ritual.

Through the fifth and sixth centuries, a significant series of such extended sites was created, intended to integrate royal ambitions with earlier cults and communities. At Garhwa [Gaḍhwa] (Williams 1982, pp. 152–55), for example, on the Gangetic plain, parts of a *pratolī* gateway also remain (fig. 6.14), as well as three inscriptions from Chandragupta and Kumāragupta's reigns (Bhandarkar 1981, pp. 244–47, 270–71, 293–94) — two dated 406–407 and 416–417 C.E. — that refer to gifts to "a Brāhmaṇa of the township of Sadāsattra" for maintenance of an almshouse (in a "place of perpetual almshouse[s]"). A gathering of Brāhmaṇas is represented on the *toraṇa* crossbeam, to the right of a central image of Viṣṇu Viśvarūpa (multi-formed cosmic progenitor), under worship as if in a shrine (Maxwell 1988, pp. 131–36); solar and lunar images are shown at either extremity, with processions that converge back toward the central Viśvarūpa (Meister, Dhaky, and Deva 1988, p. 32) (fig. 6.14).

Fleet (1888, pp. 268–69) published a fragmentary inscription from Garhwa dated 467–468 C.E. that he thought referred to building of a flat-roofed temple.[16] Of this inscription, Bhandarkar (1981, p. 84) only notes, "It is dated Gupta year 148 and records the setting up of an image of Anantasvāmin (Vishṇu) and the endowment of a grant."

---

[15] Cunningham also commented: "It is somewhat in favour of this view that there is a flight of steps leading upwards from the Toran pillars towards the West."

[16] "Having caused (a *temple having*) a flat roofs [sic] to be made, for the sake of increasing the religious merit of ... ... (*and*) having installed the feet of (the god) Anantasvâmin ... ... perfumes, incense, garlands ... ... for the purpose of repairing whatever may become ... ... torn, there have been given twelve ... ... belonging to the entrance of ... which belongs to the feet of the divine (god) Chitrakûtasvâmin."

A further terraced site, with a *toraṇa* gateway and inscription dated 520 C.E., is at Nagari near Chittorgarh (Bhandarkar 1920), although the present temple is from a later period. The upper cross-beam of the Nagari gateway had small altar platforms with single *āmalakas* set to either side of *phaṁsana*-pedimented roofs as part of its architectural representation (Meister 1976) (fig. 6.15).

Architecture's Semiotic Function

If a stone or rock-cut temple's sanctum was meant to be an opening in the cosmic strata — what Kramrisch (1983, p. 424) called the "uncreate" — acting as a 'womb' or *garbha-gr̥ha* (womb-house) for creation, the icon made visible within proliferates into the expanding world. This iconography is made explicit in sculpture (Buddhas, fig. 6.6; Viśvarūpa, fig. 6.14), and equally so in how temple architecture evolved (Meister 1985, 1986) (figs. 6.10–11).

A prototype for architecture's semiotic function can be found in the third century B.C.E., when the Mauryan royal family had caves excavated from a ridge of rock in wilderness Bihar to shelter Ājīvika ascetics — the Barabar caves, most prominently the Lomas R̥ṣi and Sudāma (Huntington 1974–1975), a sage's wattle-and-thatch cottage carved to one side in the interior gloom as a lithic emblem of ascetic power (Meister 2003).[17] A similar rock-cut cottage was used a century later to shelter a *stūpa* as *caitya* in a (Buddhist or Jain) cave at Guntupalle, Andhra Pradesh (Mitra 1971, pp. 44–46) (fig. 6.5, right).

Rock-cut Buddhist cathedral caves (Dehejia 1972) for many centuries after explored stone-carved architecture's semiotic function, the emblematic *stūpa* within representing cosmic Buddha, a construction most explicitly expressed in Southeast Asia in the *maṇḍala*-mountain at Borobudur, around the eighth–ninth centuries (Krom 1927; Dumarçay 1978) (fig. 6.6).

That the Indian temple could actuate the mountain of its earliest metaphors, building up forms and plans to materialize that image over centuries, becomes the detailed history of temple architecture in South Asia — perhaps most exceptionally made manifest in the rock-cut monument at Masrur, Himachal Pradesh, excavated in the seventh century, likely with royal patronage (fig. 6.16) (Meister 2006, 2008, 2009). Location of this complex was conditioned by a perpetual spring to fill the large excavated tank as well as by views of the Himalayan mountain range that the temple mirrored.

Beginning with a rock ridge facing the southern snow-covered Dhauladhar range, the temple's multiple spires were first carved out, then courts and a compound at a lower level facing the excavated rectangular tank. (The courts are partly filled by rubble from the destruction wreaked by earthquakes, most recently in 1905.[18]) Conceptually planned with cardinal halls leading to a central sanctum, the core of this temple was dedicated to Shiva, joined by Surya, Brahma, and Vishnu in an outer ring of shrines and entries, embedded in the mass of the temple or separated out (fig. 6.17) (Meister 2008, 2009) — cosmogony producing

---

[17] Meister 2003, p. 9: "The form of the hut has taken on a rhetorical use, emerging as a sacred shelter, striated as if straw, polished as if the golden germ of creation itself. The hut has become a sign, indexical of its vernacular source but iconic in its use." See also Renou 1998.

[18] Punjab Government 1926, p. 35, cites document no. 619, dated April 27, 1905, that gives extensive details of a major earthquake affecting this region in that year (Meister 2006, n. 1).

cosmology. As mountain range and palace of Shiva on Mount Kailasa, this temple complex was organized to make cosmic multiplicity and expansion manifest.

The typology of temple-mountain spread with Hinduism to Southeast Asia with cosmic and royal implications intact, the temple remaining both a source and model of the ordered world, most famously at Angkor Wat in Cambodia in the twelfth century, and later in the kingdom of Ayutthya in Thailand — seeds and mountains, the cosmogony of India, infusing and fulfilling temple architecture throughout.

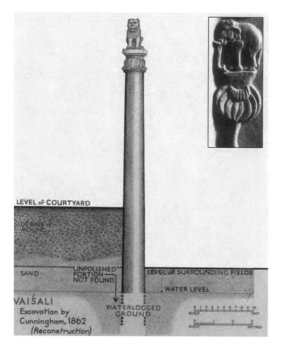

Figure 6.1. (*left*) Lion pillar, reconstruction of 1862 excavation, Vaishali, Bihar, second century B.C.E. (after Irwin, based on Cunningham 1871, pl. 22); (*inset*) *stūpa* decoration, with a ripe lotus supporting an elephant, Bharhut, Madhya Pradesh, ca. 100 B.C.E. (photo by author); (*right*) lion capital, Besnagar, Madhya Pradesh, first century B.C.E. (American Institute of Indian Studies, Center for Art and Archaeology, Gurgaon)

Figure 6.2. (*left*) Capital, portico pillar, caitya cave, Bedsa, Maharashtra, first century B.C.E. (photo by author); (*center*) drawing of *makara* pillar, Besnagar, Madhya Pradesh (Cunningham 1880a, pl. 14); (*right*) photomontage of Besnagar pillar capital and *makara* crown (American Institute of Indian Studies)

Figure 6.3. (*left*) Interior pillar, Karli, caitya cave, first century C.E. (K. Smith, Fischer Fine Arts Library Image Collection); (*center*) photomontage of *āmalaka* fruit (A. Sinha), Besnagar drawing (from fig. 6.2), and lotus (photo by author); (*right*) iron pillar, Delhi, Qutb Minar, early fifth century C.E. (Meister)

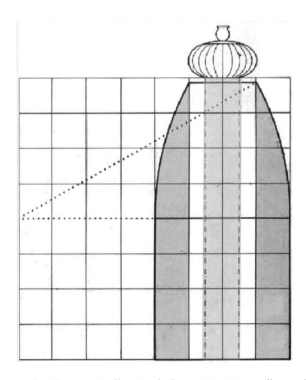

Figure 6.4. (*top left*) Garuda-Brahma Temple, Alampur, Andhra Pradesh, ca. 696–734 C.E.; (*bottom left*) Bhimgaja column, Badoh, Madhya Pradesh, 860 C.E.; (*right*) conceptual sketch of a formative *latina* Nāgara temple (photos and drawing by author)

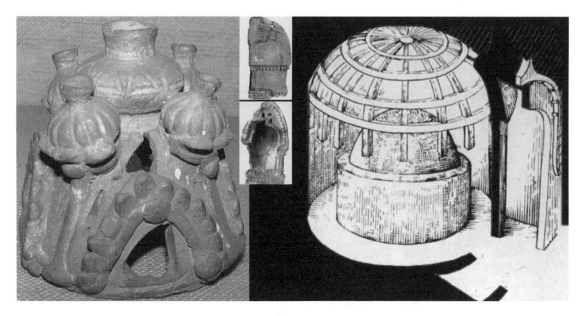

Figure 6.5. Gandhara, Pakistan: (*left*) Incense cover or shrine model, Shahji-ki-Dheri; Pir Pai, (*center, two views*) terra-cotta votive chapel, fifth century C.E. (after M. Nasim Khan 2009, figs. 18.1–2, 18.7); (*right*) *stūpa* in sheltering cottage, Guntupalli, Andhra Pradesh, caitya cave (after Mitra 1971, fig. 14)

Figure 6.6. Buddhist monument, Borobudur, Java, Indonesia, ninth century: (*left*) aerial plan (B. Richardson, American Council for South Asian Art); (*right*) circular upper terraces, perforated *stūpas* with interior Buddhas (photo by author)

Figure 6.7. Early Gupta rock-built shrines: (*top, left to right*) Temple 1, Udayagiri, Madhya Pradesh, and Temple 17, Sanchi, Madhya Pradesh (photos by author); Kankali Devi Temple, Tigowa, Madhya Pradesh; (*bottom*) Cave 7, Udayagiri (American Institute of Indian Studies)

Figure 6.8. (*left*) Representation of *āmalaka* platform, temple gate, Bilsar, Uttar Pradesh; (*right*) detail (after Williams 1982, pl. 81)

Figure 6.9. (*left*) Architectural remains, Śiva Temple, Darra, Rajasthan, early fifth century C.E., and (*right*) hypothetical photo reconstruction (Meister 2011)

Figure 6.10. (*top left*) Model, Bilsar, Uttar Pradesh; (*center, right*) Temple 17, Sanchi, Madhya Pradesh (American Institute of Indian Studies), superstructures superimposed from models on doorjambs, Deogarh, Uttar Pradesh, "Gupta" Temple, (Meister); (*bottom left, center*) Deogarh shrine models and (*right*) model from Bilot, Kyber Pakhtunkhwa, Pakistan, Temple D, south wall, sixth century C.E. (photos by author)

Figure 6.11. Reconstructed elevation drawings, Deogarh "Gupta" Temple and Bilot Temple D, sixth century C.E. (drawings by author); (*bottom left*) Temple A reconstruction, Kafirkot, Kyber Pakhtunkhwa, Pakistan, ca. 600 C.E. (by author); Kandariya-Mahadeva Temple, Khajuraho, Madhya Pradesh, ca. 1025 C.E. (photo by author)

Figure 6.12. Pawaya, Madhya Pradesh, fourth–fifth centuries C.E.: (*top*) site plan (modified from Williams 1982, figs. 2–3) with photos of two freestanding column sculptures (Vishnu and palm) (photos by author); (*center inset*) plinths (American Institute of Indian Studies); (*center*) parts of *toraṇa* crossbar (Meister/Williams); (*bottom*) *āmalaka* stone recently excavated at Ghumbat (District Dir), Kyber Pakhtunkhwa, Pakistan (L. Olivieri)

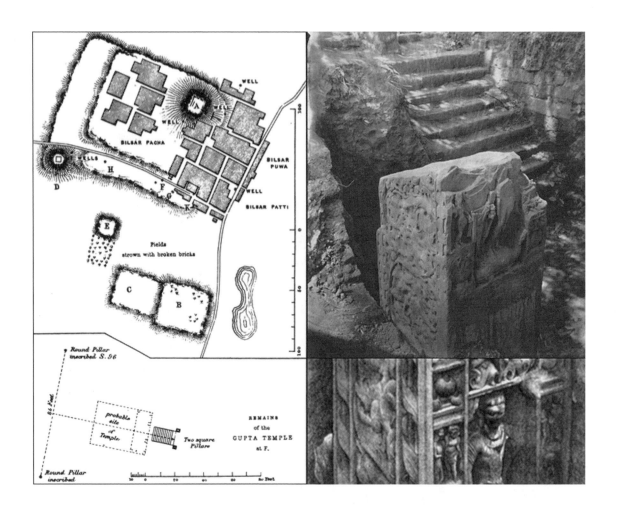

Figure 6.13. Bilsar, Uttar Pradesh: sketch plans of site (after Cunningham 1880a, pl. 5); upright of
gateway (Beglar 1871) (British Library); detail of *āmalaka* platform (after Cunningham 1880b, pl. 6),
early fifth century C.E.

Figure 6.14. Remains of *pratolī* gate, Garhwa, Uttar Pradesh, early fifth century C.E. (Beglar 1871) (British Library)

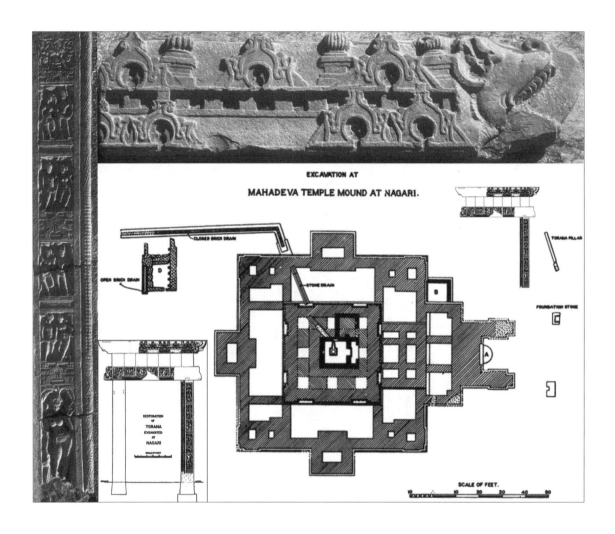

Figure 6.15. Nagari, Rajasthan, early sixth century C.E.: upright and crossbar of *toraṇa* gateway
(Meister); site plan and reconstruction of *toraṇa* (after Bhandarkar 1920, pls. 20, 23)

Figure 6.16. Masrur, Himachal Pradesh, rock-cut Śiva Temple, ca. 725–750 C.E.: from north (J.-H. Rice) and east-northeast (Meister); section and plan (after Meister 2006, fig. 24)

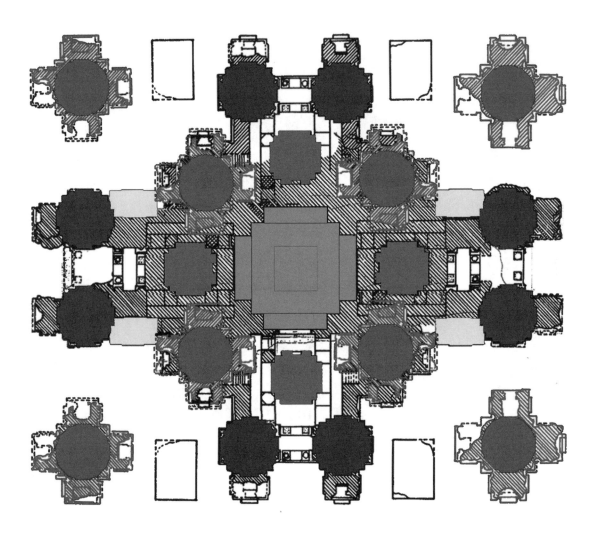

Figure 6.17. Conceptual plan, embedded and expanding shrines Masrur, Himachal Pradesh, Śiva Temple
(after Meister 2008, pl. 22.3)

Abbreviation

AV   *Atharva-veda*

Bibliography

Basham, A. L.
    1983   "The Mandasor Inscription of the Silk-Weavers." In *Essays on Gupta Culture*, edited
                    by Bardwell L. Smith, pp. 93–105. Delhi: Motilal Banarasidass.

Bhandarkar, Devadatta Ramakrishna
    1920   *The Archaeological Remains and Excavations at Nagari*. Memoirs of the Archaeologi-
                    cal Survey of India 4. Calcutta: Superintendent Government Printing.

    1981   *Inscriptions of the Early Guptas*. Corpus Inscriptionum Indicarum 3. Revised edi-
                    tion. Edited by Bahadurchand Chhabra and Govind Swamirao Gai. New Delhi:
                    Archaeological Survey of India.

Bhattacharyya, Tarapada
    1963   *The Canons of Indian Art* or *A Study on Vāstuvidyā*. 2nd edition. Calcutta: Firma
                    K. L. Mukhopadhyay.

Bolon, Carol Radcliffe
    1979   "The Mahākuṭa Pillar and Its Temples." *Artibus Asiae* 41: 253–68.

Bosch, Frederik David Kan
    1960   *The Golden Germ: An Introduction to Indian Symbolism*. Indo-Iranian Monographs
                    2. 'S-Gravenhage: Mouton.

Brown, Percy
    1942   *Indian Architecture: Buddhist and Hindu Periods*. Bombay: D. B. Taraporevala Sons.

Coomaraswamy, Ananda K.
    1931   "Origin of the Lotus- (so called Bell-) capital." *The Indian Historical Quarterly* 7:
                    747–50.

    1992   *Ananda K. Coomaraswamy: Essays in Early Indian Architecture*. Edited by Michael W.
                    Meister. New Delhi: Indira Gandhi National Centre for the Arts; Delhi: Oxford
                    University Press.

    1993   *Yakṣas: Essays in the Water Cosmology*. Edited by Paul Schroeder. New Delhi: Indira
                    Gandhi National Centre for the Arts; Delhi: Oxford University Press.

Cunningham, Alexander
    1871   *Archaeological Survey of India: Four Reports Made During the Years 1862-63-64-65*,
                    Volume 1. Simla: Government Central Press.

    1880a   *Archaeological Survey of India: Report of Tours in Bundelkhand and Malwa in 1874-75
                    and 1876 -77*, Volume 10. Calcutta: Office of the Superintendent of Government
                    Printing.

    1880b   *Archaeological Survey of India: Report on Tours in the Gangetic Provinces from Badaon
                    to Bihar, 1875-76 and 1877-78*, Volume 11. Calcutta: Office of the Superintendent
                    of Government Printing.

Dehejia, Vidya
    1972   *Early Buddhist Rock Temples: A Chronology*. Ithaca: Cornell University Press.

Dhaky, M. A.

    1974   "The 'Ākāsaliṅga' Finial." *Artibus Asiae* 36: 307–15.

Dumarçay, Jacques

    1978   *Borobudur.* Edited and translated by Michael Smithies. New York: Oxford University Press.

Fleet, John F.

    1888   *Inscriptions of the Early Guptas and Their Successors.* Corpus Inscriptionum Indicarum 3. Calcutta: Government of India, Central Publications Branch.

Garde, M. B.

    1940–1941   *Annual Report of the Archaeological Department Gwalior State for Samvat 1997.* Gwalior.

Griffith, Ralph T. H., translator

    1895–1896   *The Hymns of the Atharva-veda.* 2 volumes. Benares: E. J. Lazarus. Available online at www.sacred-texts.com/hin/av/index.htm

Hardy, Adam

    2002   "Śekharī Temples." *Artibus Asiae* 62: 81–137.

Hayward Gallery

    1982   *In the Image of Man: The Indian Perception of the Universe through 2000 years of Painting and Sculpture.* London: Hayward Gallery.

Huntington, John C.

    1974–1975   "The Lomās Ṛṣi: Another Look." *Archives of Asian Art* 28: 34–56.

Inden, Ronald

    2000   "Imperial Purāṇas: Kashmir as Vaiṣṇava Center of the World." In *Querying the Medieval: Texts and the History of Practices in South Asia*, edited by Ronald Inden, Jonathan Walters, and Daud Ali, pp. 29–98. New York: Oxford University Press.

Irwin, John

    1973   "'Aśokan' Pillars: A Reassessment of the Evidence." *The Burlington Magazine* 115: 706–20.

    1974   "'Aśokan' Pillars: A Reassessment of the Evidence — II: Structure." *The Burlington Magazine* 116: 712–27.

    1975   "'Aśokan' Pillars: A Re-Assessment of the Evidence — III: Capitals." *The Burlington Magazine* 117: 631–43.

    1976   "'Aśokan' Pillars: A Reassessment of the Evidence — IV: Symbolism." *The Burlington Magazine* 118: 734–53.

Kramrisch, Stella

    1946   *The Hindu Temple.* 2 volumes. Calcutta: University of Calcutta.

    1981   *The Presence of Śiva.* Princeton: Princeton University Press.

Krom, N. J.

    1927   *Barabuḍur: Archaeological Description.* The Hague: M. Nijhoff.

Lubotsky, Alexander

    1996   "The Iconography of the Viṣṇu Temple at Deogarh and the Viṣṇudharmottarapurāṇa." *Ars Orientalis* 26: 65–80.

Maxwell, T. S.

    1982   "The Image of Man: Tradition and Change Expressed in Indian Art." *History Today* 32/4: 27–32.

    1988   *Viśvarūpa.* New Delhi: Oxford University Press.

Meister, Michael W.

1976   "Phāṃsanā in Western India." *Artibus Asiae* 38: 167–88.

1981   "Dārra and the Early Gupta Tradition." In *Chhavi 2: Rai Krishnadasa Felicitation Volume*, edited by Anand Krishna, pp. 192–205. Banaras: Bharat Kala Bhavan.

1985   "Symbol and Surface: Masonic and Pillared Wall-Structures in North India." *Artibus Asiae* 46: 129–48.

1986   "On the Development of a Morphology for a Symbolic Architecture: India." *Res, Anthropology and Aesthetics* 12: 33–50.

1992   "The Language and Process of Early Indian Architecture." In *Ananda K. Coomaraswamy: Essays in Early Indian Architecture*, edited by Michael W. Meister, pp. xvii–xxviii. New Delhi: Indira Gandhi National Centre for the Arts; Delhi: Oxford University Press.

2003   "Vernacular Architecture and the Rhetoric of Re-making." In *Traditional and Vernacular Architecture*, coordinated by Michael W. Meister with D. Thiagarajan, edited by Subashree Krishnaswami, pp. 9–15. Madras: Madras Craft Foundation.

2006   "Mountain Temples and Temple-Mountains: Masrur." *Journal of the Society of Architectural Historians* 65: 26–49.

2007   "Iconopraxis and Iconoplasty in South Asia." *Res: Anthropology and Aesthetics* 51: 13–32.

2008   "Mapping Masrur's Iconography." In *Prajñādhara: Essays on Asian Art, History, Epigraphy and Culture in Honour of Gouriswar Bhattacharya*, edited by Gerd J. R. Mevissen and Arundhati Banerji, pp. 1–18. New Delhi: Kaveri Book Service.

2009   "India's Angkor: Śiva's Temple at Masrur." In *Kalādarpaṇa — The Mirror of Indian Art Essays in Memory of Shri Krishna Deva*, edited by A. Banerji and D. Desai, pp. 30–43. New Delhi: Aryan Books International.

2010a   "Gumbat, Tālāsh Valley, Dir: An Indus Temple in Greater Gandhāra." *Gandhāran Studies* 4: 245–54.

2010b   *Temples of the Indus: Studies in the Hindu Architecture of Ancient Pakistan*. Brill Indological Library 35. Leiden: Brill.

2011   "'Indo-Aryan' Temples: Noodling Seventh-Century Nāgara." *Journal of the Indian Society of Oriental Art*, new series, 27: 133–39.

Meister, Michael W.; M. A. Dhaky; and Krishna Deva, editors

1988   *Encyclopaedia of Indian Temple Architecture*, Volume 2/1: *North India: Foundations of North Indian Style*. Delhi: Oxford University Press.

Mitra, Debala

1971   *Buddhist Monuments*. Calcutta: Sahitya Samsad.

Monier-Williams, Monier

1899   *A Sanskrit-English Dictionary Etymologically and Philologically Arranged*. Oxford: Oxford University Press.

Muir, John

1863   *Original Sanskrit Texts on the Origin and History of the People of India, Their Religion and Institutions*, Volume 4. London: Trubner.

Nasim Khan, M.

2009   "Clay Models of Hindu Shrines from Ancient Gandhāra." In *Kalādarpaṇa: The Mirror of Indian Art, Essays in Memory of Shri Krishna Deva*, edited by Devangana Desai and Arundhati Banerji, pp. 160–70. New Delhi: Aryan Books International.

Punjab Government

1926   *Punjab District Gazetteers*, Volume 7, Part A: Kangra District 1924–25. Lahore: Punjab Government.

Renou, Louis

    1998   "The Vedic House." Edited by M. W. Meister, translated by Carrie LaPorte. *Res Anthropology and Aesthetics* 34: 141–61.

Sharma, Ram Karan

    1976–2001   *Agniveśa's Caraka Saṃhita.* 6 volumes. Text with English translation and critical exposition based on Cakrapāṇi Datta's Āyurveda dīpikā by Ram Karan Sharma and Bhagwan Dash. Chowkhamba Sanskrit Studies 94. Varanasi: Chowkhamba Sanskrit Series Office.

Strong, John S.

    1983   *The Legend of King Aśoka: A Study and Translation of the Aśokāvadāna.* Princeton: Princeton University Press.

Williams, Joanna Gottfried

    1982   *The Art of Gupta India: Empire and Province.* Princeton: Princeton University Press.

Willis, Michael

    2009   *The Archaeology of Hindu Ritual: Temples and the Establishment of the Gods.* Cambridge: Cambridge University Press.

Xuanzang

    1906   *Si-yu-ki: Buddhist Records of the Western World: Translated from the Chinese of Hiuen Tsiang (A.D. 629) by Samuel Beal.* 2 volumes. London: Kegan Paul, Trench, Trübner.

7

INTRINSIC AND CONSTRUCTED SACRED SPACE IN HITTITE ANATOLIA

Gary Beckman, University of Michigan

In this essay I discuss the venues at which reverence was shown by the Hittites to the para-human providers of life-sustaining water. Some of these loci were natural features of the landscape, whether situated in the countryside or within a town or city. Others had been fashioned by human hands, generally following a model presented by nature. In particular, a number of pools and reservoirs, imitative of natural ponds and lakes, served both as cultic sites and as sources of water for a settlement.

A well-known mythologeme featured in several rituals of the Hittite culture of Late Bronze Age Anatolia describes the consequences for the world when an angry god or goddess abandons his or her post:

> Mist seized the windows. Smoke seized the house. On the hearth the logs were stifled. [On the altars] the gods were stifled. In the fold the sheep were stifled. In the corral the cows were stifled. The sheep refused her lamb. The cow refused her calf.
>
> [The deity] went off and took away grain, the fertility of the herds, growth(?), plenty(?), and satiety into the wilderness, to the meadow and the moor. [The deity] proceeded to disappear into the moor. The ḫalenzu-plant spread over him. Barley and wheat no longer grew. Cows, sheep, and humans no longer conceived, and those who were (already) pregnant did not give birth in this time.
>
> The mountains dried up. The trees dried up, so that buds did not come forth. The pastures dried up. The springs dried up. Famine appeared in the land. Humans and gods perished from hunger.[1]

The sterility occasioned by the divinity's absence is here epitomized through the imagery of drought, for water was perceived by the Hittites as the most important among the elements that sustained the thriving of nature and humans.[2] This essential substance was provided by rivers and springs as well as by precipitation sent by the Storm-gods resident upon the numerous mountain peaks of the region.

To begin with water from above: the Storm-god of Ḫatti — or of heaven, personification of the rains — stood atop the Hittite pantheon, along with the Sun-goddess of the city of Arinna, who embodied the generative powers of the earth. In the central panel of the rock sanctuary of Yazılıkaya[3] located just outside the gates of the capital Ḫattuša (fig. 7.1), the two deities greet each other at the head of converging processions of gods and goddesses,

---

[1] KUB 17.10 (CTH 324.1.A) i 5′–18′. Translation slightly modified from my rendering in Hallo and Younger 1997, p. 151.

[2] For a survey of the place of this element in Hittite cult, see Erbil and Mouton 2012.

[3] The standard work on this shrine is Bittel et al. 1975; see also Seeher 2011.

respectively. Note that the Storm-god stands upon two heavily burdened mountain deities, identifiable by their scalloped skirts.[4] This iconographic feature, probably symbolic of a rocky hillside, is also visible in the anthropomorphic Anatolian Hieroglyphic sign (🗿) for divine mountain around which what we might call the "coat of arms" or *tuğra* of Hittite king Tudhaliya IV is assembled (fig. 7.2).

Among the "Thousand Gods of Ḫatti," the Storm-god was joined by innumerable local avatars, most connected with particular towns or mountains, as in the instance of Zaliyanu of the city of Kaštama, whose name might be written with either the cuneiform determinative for god or with that for mountain,[5] thus demonstrating the close association — or even identity — of deity and topographical component. Of course, this relationship is also expressed by the depiction of the Storm-god supported by mountains just mentioned. Zaliyanu's contribution to fertility is clearly stated in the following excerpt from an incantation: "Mount Zaliyanu is first (in rank) among all (the gods). When he has allotted rain in (the town of) Nerik, then the herald brings forth a loaf of thick bread from Nerik."[6]

Storm-gods were worshipped in most Hittite cities, as were mountains in various towns. In a long prayer of King Muwattalli II, many of the sections invoking the gods of particular localities conclude by calling upon their "mountains and rivers."[7] And for the sake of completeness, anonymous "mountains, rivers, springs, the great sea, heaven and earth, winds, and clouds"[8] might be included in the lists of deities summoned to witness treaties concluded by the Great King.

Within Ḫattuša, the Storm-god and the Sun-goddess were almost certainly the proprietors of the expansive Tempel I,[9] the only one of the more than thirty religious structures thus far excavated there to be provided with twin cellas. In the town of Zippalanda, cultic activity centered on the eponymous Storm-god and the nearby Mount Daḫa, the distinction between whom is not entirely clear.[10] This worship was conducted not only within the settlement but also at a stele[11] erected on Mount Daḫa itself, where a tent had previously been set up to accommodate the ritual preparations.[12] On the road between the capital and Zippalanda[13] was situated Mount Puškurunuwa, on whose slopes each year the king made offerings to a herd of sacred deer and a number of deities, including the mount itself,[14] during his spring progress known as the Festival of the Crocus (AN.TAḪ.ŠUM^SAR).[15] A portion of these ceremonies took place at the gate of an *ḫilamar*-building,[16] a substantial structure whose presence shows that the sacred site had been modified.

---

[4] For the iconography of this figure, see Danrey 2006.

[5] For attestations, see van Gessel 1998, pp. 571–72; and del Monte and Tischler 1978, p. 489.

[6] KBo 3.7 (CTH 321.A) ii 21′–24′, ed. Beckman 1982.

[7] KUB 6.45 + KUB 30.14 and duplicates (CTH 381), ed. Singer 2002, pp. 87–91.

[8] For instance, §20 of the treaty between Mursili II and Tuppi-Teššup of Amurru (CTH 62), translation in Beckman 1999, p. 63.

[9] Bittel 1976.

[10] Popko 1994, p. 32–39.

[11] Hittite *ḫuwaši-*; see Hutter 1993.

[12] Popko 1994, pp. 209–13; for mountains as sites of worship, see Popko 1999; Birchler 2006; and Mazoyer 2006, pp. 262–66.

[13] See del Monte and Tischler 1978, pp. 324–25.

[14] For a particularly generous offering to mountain, see KUB 29.1 and duplicates (CTH 414) iii 13–17 (§34): "When (the king) builds a palace in a town anywhere, whatever carpenter goes to the mountains to cut the beams takes from the palace one bull, three sheep, three jugs of wine, one jug of *marnuwa*, ten snack-loaves, twenty 'tooth'-loaves, and fifty ration-loaves." I have fully translated this text at Beckman 2010, pp. 72–75.

[15] KUB 25.18 (CTH 618) ii 1–11; see Mazoyer 2006, pp. 263–64.

[16] KUB 25.18 ii 4–5: ^É*ḫi-lam-na-aš* ^GIŠKÁ.GAL-*aš pí-ra-an*.

On the occasion of major festivals, distant mountains such as Mount Šarišša, Mount Tudḫaliya, and Mount Arnuwanda[17] could be summoned to Ḫattuša to participate in the ceremonies. For instance, note this invocation:

> Hey, Mt. Šarišša, get up! Hasten back to His Mighty Majesty and the Mighty Queen (Tawananna), the watchmen (of the land of Ḫatti), for the fattened oxen and rams! Let it come about that they are strong and protected! Let good news always find them, His Mighty Majesty and the Queen, on the throne of iron! Let it happen that only joy is present![18]

To the extent that this participation involved the actual physical presence of the mountains, this was undoubtedly achieved through the use of their cultic representations, which might be either anthropomorphic with various attributes or in the form of a mace.[19]

Furthermore, the numinous nature of mountains,[20] which after all constituted the most impressive features of the topography of the Hittite homeland, rendered them an appropriate location — that is, sacred space — for making contact with para-human elements of the cosmos beyond Storm-gods and the mounts themselves. "Stone Peaks" ([NA4]*ḫekur*)[21] were frequent sites for various religious activities, including the royal ancestor cult. As demonstrated by Theo van den Hout, mausolea constituted a subset of the "Peaks," themselves labeled "Stone Houses" (É.NA4). Cuneiform texts inform us that such royal structures could be endowed with extensive agricultural lands and personnel,[22] whose surplus would yield economic support for the continuing cult of the deceased ruler. Unfortunately, no *ḫekur* is so clearly described in the cuneiform records that we can with certainty identify it on the ground today, but we do know of a number of likely candidates for this designation.

The most well known of these prominences modified for religious purposes is Yazılıkaya (fig. 7.3), a shrine that incorporated and extended a large limestone outcropping.[23] Erosion and the carrying off of building stones by local villagers have made the recovery of the earlier stages of construction problematic, but it is clear that by the thirteenth century the massif had been complemented and indeed closed off from unauthorized entry by structures erected before it. The reconstruction in figure 7.4 indicates a melding of natural and man-made elements by which the products of human activity have been integrated into the natural environment. In the absence of any recognized ancient textual reference to Yazılıkaya, its particular religious function remains uncertain. Undoubtedly Chamber A, with its files of deities culminating in the meeting of the Storm-god and Sun-goddess (fig. 7.1), was the primary cult room of the complex and was perhaps the scene of the New Year's ceremonies of the Hittites.[24]

Chamber B, on the other hand, which has its own entrance, may well have served as the mausoleum of King Tudḫaliya IV, whose image in the embrace of his patron deity Šarruma graces one of its walls (fig. 7.5). Mortuary interpretation of the cleft is supported by carvings of an underworld deity in the shape of a dagger with an elaborate pommel composed

---

[17] The last two of these oronyms were adopted as personal names by several Hittite monarchs; see Freu 2006, pp. 239–41, and Lebrun 2006, pp. 253–54.

[18] KBo 21.67+ (CTH 591) iii 19′–27′, ed. Klinger 1996, pp. 320–21. The fattened animals here should be understood as the offering presented to attract the divine mountain.

[19] See Haas 1994, pp. 496–98.

[20] Note KUB 9.28 (CTH 442) i 10′f.: ḪUR.SAG-*i šu-up-pa-i pí-di ku-wa-pí-it* [*wa*]-*a-tar e-eš-zi* "on the mountain, in a pure place, wherever there is water."

[21] See van den Hout 2002 and Imparati 1977.

[22] KUB 13.8 (CTH 252), ed. Otten 1958, 106–07.

[23] For relevant literature, see note 3.

[24] See Otten 1956.

of four lions[25] (fig. 7.6) and a file of twelve chthonic gods[26] (fig. 7.7). Also lending support to this understanding of the passage's use are the artificial niches,[27] which could have accommodated the cremated remains[28] of the ruler and funerary gifts.

Another remarkable peak is that of Gavurkalesi, a massif situated 60 km southwest of Ankara bearing a large relief in which two gods approach a seated goddess (figs. 7.8–9). Recent renewed exploration[29] at the site has shown that in Hittite times the entire precinct was surrounded by a wall and that the prominent outcropping was incorporated within a cyclopean enclosure, cutting off view of the relief from the outside (fig. 7.10).[30] In addition, a small cell was cut into the rear of the rock. Although now empty, this space may well once have held the ashes of an important person; it is certainly too small for most other purposes. That is, Gavurkalesi might represent another "Stone House," although probably not the mausoleum of a Great King, given that its location is more than 250 km from the Hittite capital.

Within Ḫattuša itself, several outcroppings deserve our attention.[31] Nişantepe[32] (fig. 7.11), which bears the severely weathered Anatolian Hieroglyphic inscription referred to as Nişantaş[33] (fig. 7.12), is an alternate candidate for the mausoleum of Tudḫaliya IV. It may well be the "Eternal Peak" that the latter's son Šuppiluliuma II claims to have fashioned for him, since the cuneiform record in which he mentions this act of filial piety duplicates at least in part the content of the Hieroglyphic Nişantaş text.[34] Perhaps Tudḫaliya himself had intended Yazılıkaya to be his final resting place, but for some reason his heir decided that it was not well suited for this purpose and constructed a different "Stone House" for him.

It is also possible that Yenicekale[35] and Sarıkale,[36] yet other massifs within the walls of the capital, as well as Cihanpaşa in the wider vicinity of Ḫattuša[37] and Kızıldağ[38] farther afield, were *ḫekur*. All of these elevations feature human modifications to the natural topography to be dated to the Hittite period.

I turn now to earthly sources of water. The Hittites conceived of rivers and springs as minor goddesses and therefore as sacred spaces.[39] We saw earlier that they could be included within general enumerations of the *numina* of a particular locality, and they might also be the focus of reverent attention.[40] Thus when drawing water from a particularly hallowed source, it might be advisable to make an offering. For example, in a rite imported into Ḫatti from a southern province, we read,

> When Palliya, King of Kizzuwatna, set up the Storm-god of Kizzuwatna and worshipped him in fulfillment of a vow, from seven springs he took water of purification

[25] Seeher 2011, pp. 113–15.

[26] For a meditation on this group, see Masson 1989.

[27] For a photo of these cavities, see Seeher 2011, p. 107, fig. 115. According to Seeher (p. 106), these hollows had once been provided with doors or lids that allowed them to be closed securely.

[28] See the royal cremation rite described in Kassian, Korolev, and Sidel'tsev 2002, pp. 260–81.

[29] See Lumsden 2002 and cf. Kühne 2001. The site was already explored by von der Osten (1933, pp. 56–82).

[30] Thus the carvings were not intended for public view like so much Hittite rock art. On the socio-political function of ostentatious monumental display in ancient Anatolia, cf. Glatz and Plourde 2011 and Seeher 2012.

[31] See Schachner 2011, pp. 164–72.

[32] See van den Hout 2002, pp. 78–80.

[33] Laroche 1970.

[34] See Güterbock 1967.

[35] Schachner 2011, pp. 164–65.

[36] Naumann 1983.

[37] Strobel 2010.

[38] Bittel 1986.

[39] See Haas 1994, pp. 464–66, and Haas and Koch 2011, pp. 175–76. To judge from the number of texts mentioning their worship, it seems that springs were more important in cult than streams. On sacred space in Hittite religion, see Beckman 2004.

[40] See KBo 16.71+ and dupl. (CTH 635, ed. Popko 1994, p. 103) i 10′ for the sacrifice of oxen to a *luli-*, "pond."

of the city of Lawazantiya, and for the water of purification (in payment) he [took] these things: one shekel of silver, one blindfold, one woolen *kišri*, one bolt of [blue] woolen cloth, one bolt of red woolen cloth, one flask of fine oil, three unleavened breads of moist flour, and one jug of wine to the seven springs.[41]

Such activity obviously took place onsite, but springs could also be honored in ceremonies performed within a temple, although in one instance the spring Kuwannaniya receives her sacrificial loaves out through the window of the shrine, as befits a component of the landscape![42]

An essential component of Hittite urbanism was the storage of water for drinking, washing, industrial use, the extinguishing of fires, and so on. At present, more than twenty reservoirs have been identified at seven sites,[43] most of which were supplied through the damming of small streams. But aside from their obvious practical functions, several of these artificial bodies of water have yielded deposits of cultic vessels,[44] suggesting a sacred character. Particularly interesting is a small, tapered, quasi-trapezoidal basin (22.5–24.0 × 1.5–5.0 m) situated next to Gebäude J on the royal citadel Büyükkale,[45] which was apparently filled solely by rainwater. This sink was divided by a cross wall into two unequal parts, from the smaller of which were recovered numerous votive vessels recognizable by their miniature size and/or specialized shapes, as well as three of the ritual objects known as "libation arms."[46] This was definitely a site of worship.[47]

Of exclusively cultic use, as shown by its slight dimensions (5.19 × 1.40 m) and limited accessibility, is a grotto that Hittite builders excavated just south of the workshop annex of Tempel I in the capital in order to reach a small spring.[48] The capstone over the narrow entryway depicts a king in his priestly garb, while a stele set at the head of the stairway bears a worn Anatolian Hieroglyphic inscription that seemingly mentions "the divine spring Lurahu(ta)."[49]

Since it is situated on a mountain terrace too distant from any settlement to serve as its water supply, we may conclude that an artificial pond fed by springs about two and a half miles from the Hittite town of Kuşaklı/Šarišša (fig. 7.13)[50] was also solely a focus for worship. Together with its plastered skirt, the nearly round basin measures approximately 135 m in diameter. Nearby were excavated the remains of a structure that displays similarities to that of Hittite temples. Festival texts from both Ḫattuša[51] and Šarišša[52] describe ceremonies to be conducted at a stele (*ḫuwaši*) erected at the Šuppitaššu spring outside the latter town. Our complex is surely to be identified with this Šuppitaššu.

Another very impressive manmade sacred pond is to be found at Eflatun Pinar[53] (fig. 7.14) near Lake Beyşehir, which features a monumental facade presenting a schematic

[41] KUB 7.20 (CTH 475.A) i 1–9, ed. Beckman, forthcoming.

[42] KUB 2.8 (CTH 617.1) ii 27–28, translit. Groddek 2009, p. 63.

[43] Data collected in Hüser 2007, p. 144.

[44] For such finds in the ponds of the capital, see Ökse 2011, p. 226 with n. 36. Whether these accumulations are evidence for ritual practice at the reservoirs themselves or represent *favissae* for the disposal of sacred utensils employed elsewhere, their presence in any case indicates a religious significance.

[45] Neve 1971, pp. 13–16.

[46] On these cultic utensils, see Haas 1994, p. 538; for examples, see Fischer 1963, pp. 72–73, pls. 122–24.

[47] Additional major reservoirs from the Hittite era are Karakuyu (Hüser 2007, pp. 134–37), Köylütolu (Hüser 2007, p. 142), and Yalburt (Temizer apud Özgüç 1988, pp. xxv–xxvii; Hüser 2007, p. 145).

[48] Neve 1970.

[49] For the text, see Güterbock 1969, pp. 49–52.

[50] Hüser 2007, pp. 120–26.

[51] CTH 636. The attestations of Šuppitaššu are KUB 20.99 ii 14, 20, 22.

[52] Wilhelm 1997, pp. 18–19, no. 1.

[53] Bachmann and Özenir 2004; Hüser 2007, pp. 144–45.

representation of the Hittite cosmos (fig. 7.15). At its center are enthroned the rather worn images of a male and a female figure, presumably depicting the Storm-god and the Sun-goddess. Above them hover symbols of the sun, while below, supporting them, are five mountain gods. The installation beneath and in front of the deities was formed by the diversion of the waters of an adjacent natural spring around the periphery of an artificially shaped basin. An ingenious mechanism adjacent to the facade allowed the direction of the flow so that water would, if the operator so desired, issue into the pond from holes in the lower portion of the mountain deities rather than flow in directly from the main channel and seep in through vents on the lateral embankments. In the pool and next to the platform situated directly opposite the central facade (fig. 7.16) were recovered the remains of offerings and votive vessels. This constitutes another definite locus of cultic activity, although the reservoir might also have had secular purposes in connection with an unexcavated urban site not too far away.

Created entirely through human effort without the advantage of a natural spring was the Ostteich/Südburg[54] complex at Ḫattuša (fig. 7.17). Here a 6,000 sq. m rectangular hollow was excavated and buttressed with thick earthen banks, then filled with water piped in from the wooded slopes south of the city. In the sediments that collected in the pond thus constructed, archaeologists found many fragments of votive vessels. Subsequently, stone-built chambers were installed into both the western and northern corners of the pond's embankment. The western structure has been largely destroyed, but the northern one has survived almost intact, thanks to the protection afforded by the later Phrygian city wall constructed over it (fig. 7.18). Within this Chamber 2 were erected two relief slabs, one depicting the Sun-god and the other the building's patron, Šuppiluliuma II, the last attested Hittite Great King (fig. 7.19). The furnishings were completed by an Anatolian Hieroglyphic inscription (fig. 7.20) wherein this ruler sets forth his great martial deeds. He concludes this text with this statement: "Here … I constructed a 'Divine Earth Road'" (line 18), obviously referring to the chamber itself. This term (DEUS.🐟) corresponds to the cuneiform ideogram KASKAL.KUR, literally, "road to the underworld,"[55] which the Hittites employed to designate those openings in their karst landscape into which streams disappeared, only to emerge again at some distance.

For the ancient Anatolians, these dolines were sacred spaces, paths to the chthonic realm, and accordingly they received reverent attention.[56] At the Südburg, Šuppiluliuma has constructed a personal gateway to the netherworld, possibly in anticipation of his own funerary obsequies. Note that in his depiction within the shrine, he wears the horns of divinity, while traditionally Hittite monarchs were divinized only upon their deaths.[57]

In summation: I have shown that while the cosmic forces immanent in the world as experienced by Hittite men and women could be worshipped in urban temples and at unmodified natural features in the countryside, sacred space in which these powers might be honored and served was also constructed by this civilization through the modification of peaks and springs, both within and outside of settlements. At the extreme, as in the case of the Südberg at Ḫattuša, the Hittites created a sacred space *ex nihilo*, albeit in imitation of naturally occurring numinous places.[58]

---

[54] Neve apud Hawkins 1995, pp. 9–12; Hüser 2007, pp. 138–40.

[55] See the pioneering study by Gordon (1967).

[56] On Hittite conceptions of the netherworld, see Haas 1994, pp. 127–34; Hoffner 1988.

[57] On Hittite monarchs, their deaths, and their iconography, see van den Hout 2002.

[58] The role of the king as mediator between the human and divine spheres of the universe allowed him as patron of all official building activities to render a constructed space sacred. See the rite translated in Beckman 2010, pp. 77–78.

Figure 7.1. Central panel in Chamber A at Yazılıkaya (after Akurgal 1961, fig. 19)

Figure 7.2. Anatolian Hieroglyphic "arms" of Tudḫaliya IV in Chamber B at Yazılıkaya
(after Bittel et al. 1975, p. 183)

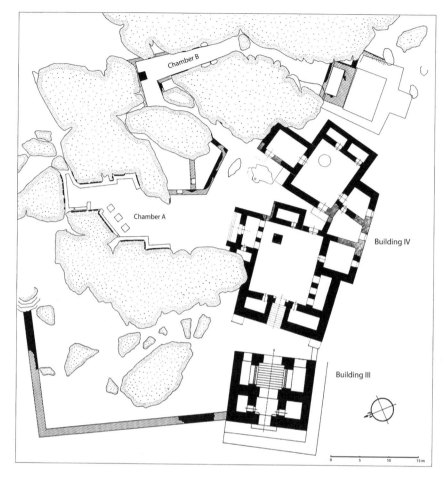

Figure 7.3. Plan of late thirteenth-century structures at Yazılıkaya (after Seeher 2011, fig. 142)

Figure 7.4. Reconstruction of late thirteenth-century structures at Yazılıkaya
(after Bittel et al. 1975, fig. 111)

Figure 7.5. Tudḫaliya IV in the embrace of his patron god Šarruma at Yazılıkaya
(photo by R. Tayfun Bilgin)

Figure 7.6. Sword-god in Chamber B at Yazılıkaya
(photo by R. Tayfun Bilgin)

Figure 7.7. File of chthonic deities in Chamber B at Yazılıkaya (photo by R. Tayfun Bilgin)

Figure 7.8. Portion of the reliefs at Gavurkalesi (photo by R. Tayfun Bilgin)

Figure 7.9. Reliefs at Gavurkalesi (after Kohlmeyer 1983, fig. 16)

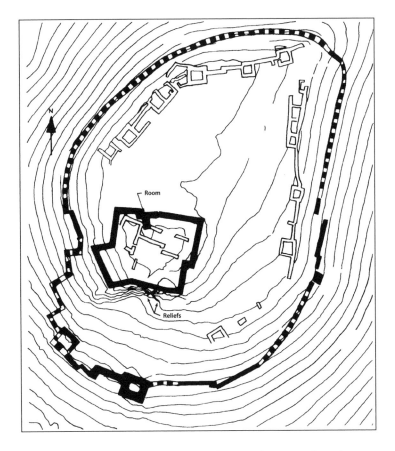

Figure 7.10. Plan of Gavurkalesi (after Kühne 2001, fig. 11)

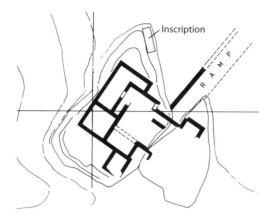

Figure 7.11. Plan of Nişantepe (Boğazköy) (after Neve 1993, fig. 122)

Figure 7.12. Anatolian Hieroglyphic inscription at Nişantepe (Boğazköy) (photo by the author)

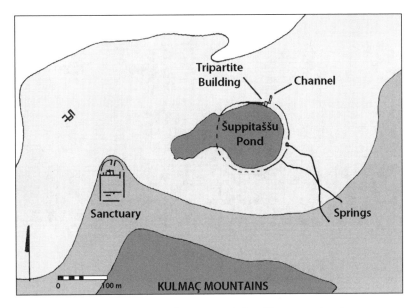

Figure 7.13. Plan of Šuppitaššu (after Ökse 2011, fig. 5)

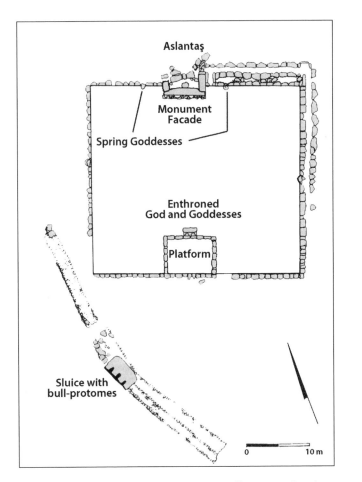

Figure 7.14. Plan of Eflatun Pınar (after Ökse 2011, fig. 2)

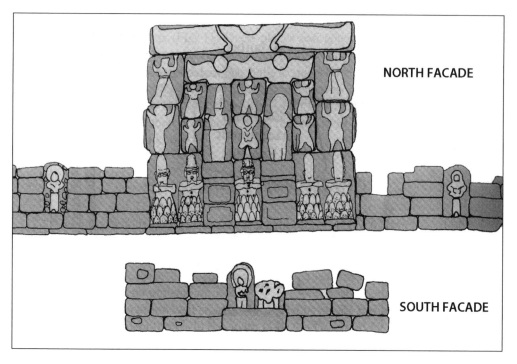

Figure 7.15. Eflatun Pınar facade (after Ökse 2011, fig. 3)

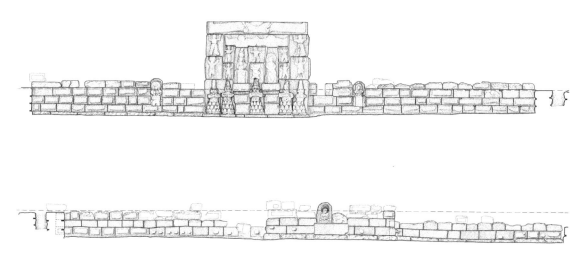

Figure 7.16. Constructions on the long sides of the pool at Eflatun Pınar
(after Bachman and Özenir 2004, fig. 32)

Figure 7.17. Südberg/Ostteich at Boğazköy (after Neve 1993, fig. 218)

Figure 7.18. Südberg Chamber 2 entrance (Boğazköy) (photo by R. Tayfun Bilgin)

Figure 7.19. Relief of Šuppiluliuma II in Südberg Chamber 2 (Boğazköy) (photo by R. Tayfun Bilgin)

Figure 7.20. Anatolian Hieroglyphic inscription in Südberg Chamber 2 (Boğazköy) (photo by R. Tayfun Bilgin)

Abbreviations

CTH   Emmanuel Laroche, *Catalogue des textes hittites*, 2nd ed. Études et commentaires 75. Paris: Klincksieck, 1971

KBo   *Keilschrifttexte aus Boghazköi* (vols. 1–22 are a subseries of WVDOG = Wissenschaftliche Veröffentlichungen der Deutschen Orient-Gesellschaft). Leipzig, Berlin

KUB   *Keilschrifturkunden aus Boghazköi*. Berlin

Bibliography

Akurgal, Ekrem

1961   *Die Kunst der Hethiter*. Munich: Hirmer.

Bachmann, Martin, and Sırrı Özenir

2004   "Das Quellheiligtum Eflatun Pınar." Special issue of *Archaeologischer Anzeiger* 2004/1: 85–122.

Beckman, Gary M.

1982   "The Anatolian Myth of Illuyanka." *Journal of the Ancient Near Eastern Society* 14: 11–25.

1999   *Hittite Diplomatic Texts*. 2nd edition. Society of Biblical Literature Writings from the Ancient World 7. Atlanta: Scholars Press.

2004   "Sacred Times and Spaces: Anatolia." In *Religions of the Ancient World: A Guide*, edited by Sarah Iles Johnston, pp. 259–64. Cambridge: Harvard University Press.

2010   "Temple Building among the Hittites." In *From the Foundations to the Crenellations: Essays on Temple Building in the Ancient Near East and Hebrew Bible*, edited by Mark J. Boda and Jamie R. Novotny, pp. 71–89. Münster: Ugarit-Verlag.

Forthcoming   "The Ritual of Palliya of Kizzuwatna (Catalogue des Textes Hittites 475)." *Journal of Ancient Near Eastern Religions*.

Birchler, Anne

2006   "Quelques réflexions sur la montagne comme lieu de culte des Hittites." *Res Antiquae* 3: 165–77.

Bittel, Kurt

1976   "The Great Temple of Hattusha-Boğazköy." *American Journal of Archaeology* 80/1: 66–73.

1986   "Hartapus and Kızıldağ." In *Ancient Anatolia: Aspects of Change and Cultural Development; Essays in Honor of Machteld J. Mellink*, edited by Jeanny Vorys Canby, Edith Porada, Brunilde S. Ridgway, and Tamara Stech, pp. 103–11. Madison: University of Wisconsin Press.

Bittel, Kurt; Joachim Boessneck; Bernhard Damm; Hans G. Güterbock; Harald Hauptmann; Rudolf Naumann; and Wulf Schirmer

1975   *Das hethitische Felsheiligtum Yazılıkaya*. Boğazköy-Ḫattuša Ergebnisse der Ausgrabungen 9. Berlin: Gebrüder Mann.

Danrey, Virginie

2006   "L'homme-montagne ou l'itinéraire d'un motif iconographique." *Res Antiquae* 3: 209–17.

del Monte, Giuseppe F., and Johann Tischler

1978   *Die Orts- und Gewässernamen der hethitischen Texte*. Répertoire Géographique des Textes Cunéiformes 6. Wiesbaden: Ludwig Reichert.

Ehringhaus, Horst

2005   *Götter, Herrscher, Inschriften: Die Felsreliefs der hethitischen Grossreichszeit in der Türkei*. Mainz: Philipp von Zabern.

Emre, Kutlu

1993   "The Hittite Dam of Karakuyu." In *Essays on Anatolian Archaeology*, edited by Mikasa no Miya Takahito, pp. 1–42. Wiesbaden: Harrassowitz.

Erbil, Yiğit, and Alice Mouton

2012   "Water in Ancient Anatolian Religions: An Archaeological and Philological Inquiry on the Hittite Evidence." *Journal of Near Eastern Studies* 71/1: 53–74.

Fischer Franz

1963   *Die hethitische Keramik von Boğazköy*. Wissenschaftliche Veröffentlichung der Deutschen Orient-Gesellschaft 75. Berlin: Gebrüder Mann.

Forrer, Emil

1937/1938   "Quelle und Brunnen in Alt-Vorderasien." *Glotta* 26: 178–202.

Freu, Jacques

2006   "Les montagnes dans l'historiographie et la géographie hittites." *Res Antiquae* 3: 219–43.

Glatz, Claudia, and Aimée M. Plourde

2011   "Landscape Monuments and Political Competition in Late Bronze Age Anatolia: An Investigation of Costly Signaling Theory." *Bulletin of the American Schools of Oriental Research* 361: 33–66.

Gonnet, Hatice

1968   "Les montagnes d'Asie Mineure d'après les textes hittites." *Revue hittite et asianique* 26: 93–170.

Gordon, Edmund I.

1967   "The Meaning of the Ideogram ^{d}KASKAL.KUR = 'Underground Water-course' and Its Significance for Bronze Age Historical Geography." *Journal of Cuneiform Studies* 21: 70–88.

Groddek, Detlev

2009   *Hethitische Texte in Transkription: KUB 2*. Dresdner Beiträge zur Hethitologie 30. Wiesbaden: Harrassowitz.

Güterbock, Hans G.

1967   "The Hittite Conquest of Cyprus Reconsidered." *Journal of Near Eastern Studies* 26: 73–81.

1969   "Hieroglyphische Inscriften." In *Boğazköy IV: Funde aus den Grabungen 1967 und 1968*, edited by Kurt Bittel et al., pp. 49–53. Abhandlungen der Deutschen Orientgesellschaft 14. Berlin: Gebrüder Mann.

Haas, Volkert

1994   *Geschichte der hethitischen Religion*. Handbuch der Orientalistik, Erste Abteilung, Der Nahe und Mittlere Osten 15. Leiden: Brill.

Haas, Volkert, and Heidemarie Koch

2011   *Religionen des Alten Orients: Hethiter und Iran*. Grundrisse zum Alten Testament 1.1. Göttingen: Vandenhoeck & Ruprecht.

Hallo, William W., and K. Lawson Younger, Jr., editors

1997　　*The Context of Scripture*, Volume 1: *Canonical Compositions from the Biblical World.* Leiden: Brill.

Hawkins, J. David

1995　　*The Hieroglyphic Inscription of the Sacred Pool Complex at Hattusa (SÜDBURG).* Studien zu den Boğazköy-Texten Beiheft 3. Wiesbaden: Harrassowitz.

Hoffner, Harry A.

1988　　"A Scene in the Realm of the Dead." In *A Scientific Humanist: Studies in Memory of Abraham Sachs*, edited by Erle Leichty, Maria deJ. Ellis, and Pamela Gerardi, pp. 191–99. Occasional Publications of the Samuel Noah Kramer Fund 9. Philadelphia: The University Museum.

Hüser, Andreas

2007　　*Hethitische Anlagen zur Wasserversorgung und Entsorgung.* Kuşaklı-Sarissa 3. Rahden: Verlag Marie Leidorf.

Hutter, Manfred

1993　　"Kultstelen und Baityloi: Die Ausstrahlung eines syrischen religiösen Phänomens nach Kleinasien und Israel." In *Religionsgeschichtliche Beziehungen zwischen Kleinasien, Nordsyrien und dem Alten Testament*, edited by Bernd Janowski, Klaus Koch, and Gernot Wilhelm, pp. 87–108. Freiburg: Universitätsverlag; Göttingen: Vandenhoeck & Ruprecht.

Imparati, Fiorella

1977　　"Le istituzioni cultuali del $^{na4}ḫekur$ e il potere centrale ittita." *Studi micenei ed egeo-anatolici* 18: 19–64.

Kassian, Alexei S.; Andrej Korolev; and Andrej Sidel'tsev

2002　　*Hittite Funerary Ritual: šalliš waštaiš.* Alter Orient und Altes Testament 288. Münster: Ugarit-Verlag.

Klinger, Jörg

1996　　*Untersuchungen zur Rekonstruktion der hattischen Kultschicht.* Studien zu den Boğazköy-Texten 37. Wiesbaden: Harrassowitz.

Kohlmeyer, Kay

1983　　"Felsbilder der hethitischen Großreichszeit." *Acta praehistoricae et archaeologicae* 15: 7–154.

Kühne, Hartmut

2001　　"Gavur Kalesi, ein Ort der Ahnenverehrung?" In *Kulturgeschichten: Altorientalische Studien für Volkert Haas zum 65. Geburtstag*, edited by Thomas Richter, Doris Prechel, and Jörg Klinger, pp. 227–43. Saarbrücken: Saarbrücker Verlag und Druckerei.

Laroche, Emmanuel

1970　　"Nişantaş." *Anatolica* 3: 93–98.

Lebrun, René

2006　　"La montagne dans le monde hittite." *Res Antiquae* 3: 253–60.

Lombardi, Alessandra

2000　　"Il culto delle montagne all'epoca di Tudḫaliya IV: Continuità e innovazione." In *Landscapes: Territories, Frontiers and Horizons in the Ancient Near East* (papers presented to the XLIV Rencontre Assyriologique Internationale, Venice, 7–11 July 1997), edited by Lucio Milano, S. de Martino, F. M. Fales, and G. B. Lanfranchi, pp. 83–88. Padua: Sargon.

Lumsden, Stephen

    2002   "Gavurkalesi: Investigations at a Hittite Sacred Place." In *Recent Developments in Hittite Archaeology and History: Papers in Memory of Hans G. Güterbock*, edited by K. Aslıhan Yener and Harry A. Hoffner, pp. 111–25. Winona Lake: Eisenbrauns.

Masson, Emilia

    1989   *Les douze dieux de l'immortalité: croyances indo-européennes à Yazılıkaya*. Paris: Les belles lettres.

Mazoyer, Michel

    2006   "Quand la montagne se rend à la ville." *Res Antiquae* 3: 261–70.

Naumann, Rudolf

    1983   "Sarıkale in Boğazköy." In *Beiträge zur Altertumskunde Kleinasiens: Festschrift für Kurt Bittel*, edited by R. M. Boehmer and Harald Hauptmann, pp. 383–90. Mainz: Philipp von Zabern.

Neve, Peter

    1970   "Eine hethitische Quellgrotte in Boğazköy." *Istanbuler Mitteilungen* 19–20: 97–107.

    1971   *Regenkult-Anlagen in Boğazköy-Hattuša*. Istanbuler Mitteilungen Beiheft 5. Tübingen: Ernst Wasmuth.

    1993   *Ḫattuša — Stadt der Götter und Tempel: Neue Ausgrabungen in der Hauptstadt der Hethiter*. Zaberns Bildbände zur Archäologie 8. Mainz: Philipp von Zabern.

Ökse, A. Tuba

    2011   "Open-air Sanctuaries of the Hittites." In *Insights into Hittite History and Archaeology*, edited by Hermann Genz and Dirk Paul Mielke, pp. 219–40. Colloquia Antiqua 2. Leuven: Peeters.

Otten, Heinrich

    1956   "Ein Text zum Neujahrsfest aus Boğazköy." *Orientalistische Literaturzeitung* 51: 101–05.

    1958   *Hethitische Totenrituale*. Deutsche Akademie der Wissenschaften zu Berlin, Institut für Orientforschung, Veröffentlichung 37. Berlin: Akademie-Verlag.

Özgüç, Tahsin

    1988   *İnandıktepe: An Important Cult Center in the Old Hittite Period*. Ankara: Türk Tarih Kurumu Basımevi.

Popko, Maciej

    1994   *Zippalanda: Ein Kultzentrum im hethitischen Kleinasien*. Texte der Hethiter 21. Heidelberg: C. Winter.

    1999   "Berg als Ritualschauplatz: Ein Beitrag zur Kenntnis der hethitischen Religion." *Hethitica* 14: 97–108.

Schachner, Andreas

    2011   *Hattuscha: Auf der Suche nach dem Großreich der Hethiter*. Munich: C. H. Beck.

Seeher, Jürgen

    2009   "Der Landschaft sein Siegel aufdrücken — hethitische Felsbilder und Hieroglypheninschriften als Ausdruck des herrscherlichen Macht- und Territorialanspruchs." *Altorientalische Forschungen* 36: 119–39.

    2011   *Gods Carved in Stone: The Hittite Rock Sanctuary of Yazılıkaya*. Istanbul: Ege Yayınları.

    2012   "Natürliche und künstliche, unbewusste und beabsichtigte Landmarken: Menschliche Wahrnehmung und herrscherliche Betonung der Besetzung von Landschaften und Territorien." In *Manifestationen von Macht und Hierarchien in*

Stadtraum und Landschaft, edited by Felix Pirson, pp. 25–42. Byzas 13. Istanbul: Ege Yayınları.

Singer, Itamar

    1996   *Muwatalli's Prayer to the Assembly of Gods through the Storm-god of Lightning (CTH 381)*. Atlanta: Scholars Press.

    2002   *Hittite Prayers*. Writings from the Ancient World 11. Atlanta: Society of Biblical Literature.

Strobel, K.

    2010   "Cihanpaşa: Ein monumentales Ḫekur vor den Toren von Ḫattuša." In *Acts of the VIIth International Congress of Hittitology*, edited by Aygül Süel, pp. 793–811. Ankara: T. C. Çorum Valiliği.

van den Hout, Theo J. P.

    1995   "Tutḫalija IV. und die Ikonographie hethitischer Großkönige des 13. Jhs." *Bibliotheca Orientalis* 52: 545–73.

    2002   "Tombs and Memorials: The (Divine) Stone-house and Ḫegur Reconsidered." In *Recent Developments in Hittite Archaeology and History: Papers in Memory of Hans G. Güterbock*, edited by K. Aslıhan Yener and Harry A. Hoffner, pp. 73–91. Winona Lake: Eisenbrauns.

van Gessel, Ben H. L.

    1998   *Onomasticon of the Hittite Pantheon*. Handbuch der Orientalistik, Erste Abteilung, Nahe und Mittlere Osten 33. Leiden: Brill.

von der Osten, Hans Henning

    1933   *Discoveries in Anatolia, 1930-31*. Oriental Institute Communications 14. Chicago: The Oriental Institute.

Wilhelm, Gernot

    1997   *Kuşaklı-Sarissa* I: *Keilschrifttexte aus Gebäude A*. Rahden: Verlag Marie Leidorf.

8

ON THE ROCKS:
GREEK MOUNTAINS AND SACRED
CONVERSATIONS

Betsey A. Robinson, Vanderbilt University*

> *... to converse with Orpheus and Museaus and Hesiod and*
> *Homer — how much would any of you give to do this?*
>
> — Plato, *Apology* 41a

The perceived places and perspectives of divine beings reflect complex realities of space, identity, and ideation in classical antiquity. Mountains were home to the gods, and it was in such places that humans might encounter deities and vestiges of their presence. Poetic imagery, from Olympian omniscience and Apollo's Parnassian gaze to the descent of the Heliconian Muses reified the sacred charisma of such mountains. For humans, mountains offered highly affective climbs and climactic revelations. Along the way, springs, streams, and caves marked the presence of gods and invited reverence and propitiation. In the creative arts, devotees explored new means of expressing the essences of places and summoning divine populations. Mountain prospects gave poets new metaphorical ranges for articulating the challenges of composition, the nature of inspiration, and initiation into the highest ranks of achievement. Indeed, they offered locations and means for conversing with gods and heroes.

This paper is part of a larger project exploring two Greek mountains, Helicon and Parnassus, and their most renowned sanctuaries, the Mouseion or "Vale of the Muses" and the Sanctuary of Apollo at Delphi. Given their proximity to each other and their intertwined traditions, the mountains and their sacred sites invite comparison, yet their "parallel lives" remain to be written.[1] My work engages with spatial, religious, and cultural discourses in classical antiquity, and considers real places, resident deities, and representations thereof. It is grounded in close looking and formal analysis, and it proceeds from the premise that

* I would like to express my thanks to Deena Raga-van, the Oriental Institute, and my fellow participants in the symposium "Heaven on Earth," particularly Clemente Marconi and Christopher Faraone, for helpful comments and enthusiastic discussion. For earlier and ongoing discussions of material in this paper, I am grateful to Daniel Berman, Emily Gangemi Campbell, Tracy Miller, David Petrain, Albert Schachter, and Barbara Tsakirgis, as well the Sacred Ecology Faculty Seminar at the Robert Penn Warren Center for the Humanities at Vanderbilt University. Any mistakes remain my own.

The translation of the lead epigram is by G. W. Most (2007).

[1] For earlier studies of Greek mountains, see especially Buxton 1992; and Langdon 2000. For overviews of Parnassus, its region, and the Delphic sanctuary, see McInerney 1999; Scott 2010; and Weir 2004. For the topography, traditions, and sacred ecology of Helicon, see Hurst and Schachter 1996; and Robinson 2012 (with further bibliography).

experiences and expressive media deserve, and reward, consideration together. My goal is not to provide simple explanations of complex phenomena but to stir the pot, to consider associations and suggest readings and responses by a knowledgeable and visually literate segment of society.

Here I shall begin on the slopes of Helicon and Parnassus and briefly consider the Vale of the Muses and the Sanctuary of Apollo in the last three centuries B.C.E., when Greece fell under the sway of powerful outsiders, first Hellenistic dynasts and, later, Romans. I will then turn from the mountains themselves to their representation on two carved relief panels. The first, showing Helicon personified, hereafter called the Euthycles stele after its dedicator, was found in 1889 in the Vale of the Muses. The other, the so-called Archelaos relief, portrays gods and poets in a mountainous setting; it was discovered near Rome around 1650. Enlivened with inscriptions, both reliefs speak to the significance of place and the nature of inspiration, but by means of different representational strategies. Seen against a backdrop of archaeological evidence, and understood by analogy to contemporary poetry, the panels' images and words can be read together to offer insight into perceptions and experiences of sacred landscapes, divine agency, and human institutions. Under the influence of new centers, particularly Ptolemaic Alexandria and Imperial Rome, where poets and artists adapted and inverted traditions for new audiences and purposes, Helicon and Parnassus evolved from well-traveled places into the symbols of creative inspiration and genius that they remain to this day.

Mountain Sanctuaries

Helicon and Parnassus, like other Greek mountains, were not themselves inherently sacred or objects of worship (fig. 8.1). Rather they were special because of their complements of sacred sites and religious festivals and other meaningful rituals that drew ever more diverse interests.[2] Mountains were believed by classical Greeks to be the habitats of gods, given their "divine predilection for heights."[3] The highest mountain in Greece, Olympus was known as the home of Zeus and the Olympian gods by the time of Homer (e.g., *Iliad* 15.21; *Odyssey* 24.351), but a variety of other deities also inspired reverence on other mountains. Lower in altitude, and with their east–west ranges permitting and channeling transit, Helicon and Parnassus were more geographically and culturally central. Their fame lay in their reputations as places of human contact with divinity.

The Muses were northern Greek divinities, born on Olympus in Pieria (Hesiod, *Theogonia* 53–62). They sang to Zeus, to "give pleasure to his great mind within Olympus," where they were born (*Theogonia* 36–37), and there they carried on for Homer (*Iliad* 2.484–485). But they also came to possess Helicon. Already in the Archaic period, common traditions and toponyms could be found, as the Muses, and eventually their cult, migrated south and were assimilated with traditions of local Nymphs.[4] On Helicon, the Muses were worshipped with Zeus, and on Parnassus, they preceded Apollo's arrival but were thereafter honored alongside him.[5] Thus, by the Hellenistic period, the Muses could be considered at home on Olympus,

---

[2] See Buxton 1992; Langdon 2000; I accept Langdon's contrast (esp. pp. 463–64) between Greek attitudes toward mountains and belief systems "where a broad cosmic view imbues the mountains themselves with divine power."

[3] Langdon 2000, p. 465.

[4] See Parke 1981; Schachter 1986, pp. 153–56; Larson 2001, pp. 138–39.

[5] Parke 1981, pp. 104–06.

Helicon, or Parnassus. In poetic invocations, they are rarely tied down to one place, and epithets like "Pierian" continue to recall their northern origins alongside their southern habitat. But when it came to meetings with the Muses, and poetic initiation more generally, Helicon developed a reputation as the primary point of contact.

The fertile piedmont of Helicon seems a fitting habitat of the Muses, particularly the upland valley near the ancient hill town of Askra. There, the Archaic poet Hesiod claimed that he was pasturing his lambs when those daughters of Zeus visited him, handed him a laurel wand, and inspired him to compose the *Theogony* (22–34). In his *Works and Days*, the poet added further personal details, his dislike for Askra (*Opera et Dies* 640), and that he dedicated a tripod, won in a victory at Chalcis, to the Muses on the site of his Heliconian visitation (650–659). The historicity of Hesiod and the integrity of his corpus have been debated since antiquity, but for the residents of the region and the nearby city of Thespiae, they became important traditions and sources of identity and honor.[6]

Centuries after Hesiod's lines were written, a Mouseion took shape in the valley between Askra and the flank of higher Helicon.[7] The history of the sanctuary is characterized by negotiations between locals and outsiders, from the Pergamene Attalids to the Alexandrian Ptolemies and, later, elite Romans.[8] All invested in Hesiod's historicity and the actuality of his inspiration at that locale. Musical competitions seem to have taken place in the valley by the mid-third century B.C.E., and by the early 220s, they became sacred games of the Muses managed by nearby Thespiai.[9] A crucial point in the development of the games came with their reorganization and elevation to crown competitions with the financial backing of Ptolemy IV (r. 221–205 B.C.E.) and Arsinoe III.[10]

Excavations in the Vale of the Muses have uncovered one of the boundary stones that marked the holy ground of "the Muses of Hesiod," as well as the remains of an altar, one or two stoas, and a theater, all dating to the period that followed; there appears to have been no temple.[11] The minimalist architecture subtly served the needs of the Muses' cult, neither detracting from, nor competing with, the sensory impact of the mountain, the valley, and its perennial water sources, including streams equated with Hesiod's Permessus and Olmeus (*Theogonia* 5–6). Far more conspicuous was the statuary that gradually came to animate the site.

A brief catalog will serve to characterize the collection. Some statues are known from the second-century C.E. traveler Pausanias's *Description of Greece* (9.29–31), which focuses on images of deities and heroes and largely excludes other works.[12] He counts multiple groups of Muses, and one statue of their nurse, Eupheme.[13] A sculptural group of Apollo struggling with Hermes for a lyre, and two statues of Dionysos, were also present. The poets included

---

[6] See Lamberton 1988a; 1988b; Most 2007.

[7] For the setting, see Roux 1954; Wallace 1974; Robinson 2012, esp. pp. 228–30.

[8] Schachter 1986; Robinson, in press. Pergamene interest in the Heliconian Muses is attested already under Philetaerus (d. 263 B.C.E.).

[9] See Manieri 2009, pp. 313–433; Schachter (2012) reconstructs the early history of the Mouseia, cataloging critical inscriptions reviewing earlier work.

[10] Schachter 2012, pp. 38–39.

[11] Boundary stone: *IThesp* 65; Schachter 1986, p. 160; Veneri (1996, p. 80) suggests that, more than followers of Hesiod, the association saw to the curation, study, and diffusion of Hesiod's works. For the architectural remains, see Roux 1954.

[12] See Moggi and Osanna 2010, pp. 376–91; Robinson 2012.

[13] See Robinson 2012, pp. 243–44. Although some were wrought by classical masters, they were likely assembled in the third century B.C.E. or later.

the shepherd Linus, Thamyris,[14] Arion, Sakadas, and Orpheus surrounded by bronze beasts. Finally, there was a statue of Hesiod. Among the prize tripods displayed, the oldest was *said to be* the very one that Hesiod won at Chalcis. Visitors were made to understand that it came specifically from his victory in a contest against Homer, a theme of great interest to Hellenistic and Roman partisans.[15]

Remains found in the valley include the bases of long-lost statues that once portrayed figures of a very different order. Most honor prominent Romans — would-be and actual benefactors. Lucius Cornelius Sulla received a statue, as did Julius Caesar.[16] Images of the wife and mother of a Republican official, Marcus Junius Silanus, were erected on a semicircular base in 34–30 B.C.E.; Silanus himself may have stood to their left on a block, now lost, calling to mind a poet with his Muses.[17] Between 30 and 27 B.C.E., the Thespians dedicated a statue of Octavian, son of the deified Caesar, to the Muses, recognizing him as savior and benefactor.[18] They added portraits of the emperor's closest kin about fifteen years later: on one base stood Agrippa (friend and son-in-law) and his family. Probably holding a baby daughter, Agrippa stood alongside his wife Julia and their boys, Gaius and Lucius (then heirs to the throne), as well as the empress Livia.[19] Another statue and inscription presented Livia as a companion to the Muses and savior of the world.[20] Her son, Tiberius, the second Roman emperor, was featured with a statue of his own.[21] Such dedications would slow in the early first century C.E., even as the games flourished.[22] In addition to festival attendance, other, more informal, visits are documented.[23]

The demographics of the reconstructed assemblage are striking: groups of Muses consorted with Apollo and Dionysos, accompanied by legendary poets and the heroized Hesiod but few, if any, historic counterparts — not Boetian Pindar or Corinna, and certainly not his greatest rival, Homer.[24] Elite Romans eventually joined them. Genealogy and family ties were emphasized: women were prominent, and, sometimes, children were included. The Muses and at least one poet, Linus, were honored with annual sacrifices (Pausanias 9.29.6–7).

---

[14] This is a unique case where Pausanias's account has been matched by an archaeological find. An inscribed base identifies the artist as Kaphisias and the donor Philetairos, the founder of the Attalid dynasty of Pergamum (*IThesp* 303). An epigram was added in the early Julio-Claudian period (*IThesp* 312), discussed in Robinson 2012, pp. 244–45.

[15] Pausanias (*Description of Greece* 9.31.3) is very specific; an anonymous, undated epigram (*Anthologia Palatina* 7.53) is inspired by this legend. For the rivalry between Homer and Hesiod and their followers, see below.

[16] Sulla: *IThesp* 397–98; Caesar: *IThesp* 420. For these and subsequently mentioned figures of the late Republic and early Empire, see Robinson 2012, pp. 237–42.

[17] *IThesp* 400/401/401*bis*; discussed in Plassart 1926, pp. 440–41, no. 76. Such a group would prefigure a theme that later became poplar on Roman relief

sarcophagi of the second and third centuries C.E., as discussed by Zanker (1995, pp. 267–89). His mother seems also to have received a second statue of her own: *IThesp* 402.

[18] Octavia (soon Augustus): 30–27 B.C.E.: *IThesp* 421.

[19] Family of Agrippa: *IThesp* 422–23; Rose 1997, pp. 13–14, 149–51.

[20] Livia (other candidates: Julia and Antonia Minor): *IThesp* 424.

[21] Early "emperor and son of an emperor": *IThesp* 428.

[22] Schachter 1986, pp. 173–79; Robinson 2012, pp. 240–42.

[23] For example, Plutarch (*Amatorius* 728–29), and presumably Pausanias.

[24] An epigram is preserved from a statue that Bacchiadas of Sicyon erected of himself at the Mouseion; Schachter 1986, p. 158, with bibliography.

Near the top of Helicon's eastern peak, some scholars recognize Hesiod's altar of Zeus (*Theogonia* 4) among ancient remains.[25] The spring of Hippocrene is found a little below, where it was reputedly struck by the divine horse Pegasos.[26] By the Hellenistic period, it probably appeared much as it does today, as a deep fissure in the bedrock, lined with irregular courses of stone. Although it was only one of the Muses' bathing spots in Hesiod's lines (*Theogonia* 1–7), its mountaintop setting excited imaginations above all. For Callimachus, the spring was also favored by Athena (*Hymn* 5.70–136), and the Latin poet Ovid imagined the goddess flying in to see it after its creation (*Metamorphoses* 5.262–263). The fame of Hippocrene, and Pausanias's itinerary, suggest that the climbing of Helicon to drink from the spring was a regular practice, if not certainly a formalized ritual.[27] Those who reached the top were also shown ancient lead tablets preserving Hesiod's *Works and Days* (Pausanias 9.31.4), which strengthened claims of Hesiod's historicity and the charisma of the place.

Archaic and Classical references to Helicon have a Hesiodic ring. For example, the Muses are simply Heliconiadae (Heliconian maidens) to Pindar (*Isthmian Odes* 2.34; 8.57; *Paean* 7b.16) and a fourth-century B.C.E. epigrammatist (*Anthologia Palatina* 7.709), and Euripides's mention of the "home of the Muses on Helicon" (*Hercules furens* 791) finds a parallel in the Achilles Painter's rendering of a Muse seated on Helicon on a white-ground lekythos of the mid-fifth century.[28] Mouseia proliferated in philosophical schools and libraries in the Hellenistic period, first among them the Alexandrian Mouseion, founded by Ptolemy I (r. 304–282 B.C.E.) and cultivated by his son, Ptolemy II.[29] While the pre-eminence of the Alexandrian institution is clear, its Heliconian counterpart benefitted from its reputation as "the real thing," the home of Hesiod's Muses. Homer, in contrast, was claimed by many Ionian cities and honored with shrines on Chios, Delos, at Smyrna, and in the Alexandrian Mouseion, where Ptolemy IV added a Homereion, perhaps best known for the image of Homer surrounded by personifications of all the cities who called him their own.[30] At the same time, Ptolemaic patronage of the Heliconian sanctuary of Hesiod's Muses ensured its success.

In Hellenistic intellectual circles, the interest in alternatives to epic form and content and attempts to validate increasingly diverse genres was paralleled by growing esteem for Hesiod and his works, spurring a rivalry between his followers and those of Homer.[31] The association of Helicon, the Muses, and Hesiod was sealed by the work of Callimachus of Cyrene, a scholar and poet active in Alexandria during the second quarter of the third century B.C.E. (under Ptolemy II and III). In a passage from the prologue to his first book of *Aetia* (or "causes," poems explaining the origins of local cults), Callimachus located Hesiod's visitation by the Muses on Helicon — though not on its flanks but at the summit, by Hippocrene (*Aetia* I,

---

[25] For more recent identifications of ancient remains as a watchtower, and summaries of earlier opinions, see Wallace 1974, pp. 23–24; Aravantinos 1996.

[26] The earliest attestation is in Aratus (*Phaenomena* 205–23), but it is likely an earlier tradition. See Robinson 2006.

[27] See Robinson 2012, pp. 247–51; *Anthologia Palatina* 9.230 for an epigram about the uphill struggle of making great art.

[28] For the date of the epigram, see Müller 1996, pp. 34–35. Lekythos: Munich, Staatliche Antikensamm-

lung inv. no. 80; *LIMC* 6.1, 660, s.v. Mousa, Mousai, no. 6 (A. Queyrel).

[29] See Hardie 1997; McKenzie 2007, p. 50, with bibliography.

[30] Clay 2004, pp. 74–76, 136–43 (testimonia, including Aelianus, *Varia Historia* 13.22, on poet and cities).

[31] See Argoud 1996, pp. 34–37; Calame 1996; Müller 1996; Gutzwiller 1998, p. 163; Most 2007, p. lxv. On the competition as explored in the second-century C.E. *Contest between Homer and Hesiod*, or *Certamen*, see Clay 2004, pp. 63, 74–76.

frag. 2.1–5 [Pfeiffer 1949/1953]).[32] It was there that Callimachus, too, claimed to have encountered the Muses, thus fashioning himself as a "new Hesiod," and his *Aetia* a sort of modernized sequel to the *Theogony*.[33] A major difference, however, was that Callimachus presented his meeting with the Muses as a dream, already a literary convention.[34] Most of his original lines have been lost, but the basic outline is reconstructed from poetic references and scholia. For Callimachus, the dream conceit offered an opportunity to recombine Heliconian, or Aonian, landmarks into an allusive, symbolic landscape.[35] In contrast to Hesiod's "actual" meeting, Callimachus's dream maintained a distance between human and divine spheres, leaving the poet license to elevate himself, from mere messenger to discussant, and to develop the *Aetia* as a lengthy conversation. As Hunter and Fantuzzi have noted, Callimachus's attention to the Heliconian Muses and the subsequent rise of Ptolemaic interest in the Heliconian Mouseion must be more than coincidental.[36] Together they secured the place of Helicon as the *locus classicus* of poetic inspiration. I return to Callimachus's Roman legacy below.

The Helicon range runs west into the higher Parnassus massif. On a southern exposure, the Delphic sanctuary of Apollo was one of the most hallowed Greek sites, and by the Hellenistic period, it was bursting at the seams. Established by about 800 B.C.E., it was the seat of a revered oracle and the site of sacred *agones*.[37] Musical competitions honoring Apollo might go back to the eighth century, and to the Pythian Games, traditionally founded in 583 B.C.E., the Soteria were added in the third century, in honor of Zeus the Savior as well as Apollo.[38] In contrast to the minimalism of the relatively new Heliconian sanctuary, ancient Delphi was jammed with buildings and statuary, and room had to be made for late installations by Hellenistic dynasties and leagues. Most prominent are the two stoas and terraces that break out of the precinct on either side. On the west, a stoa was built in honor of the Aetolian leadership against attacking Gauls in 279 B.C.E. Its pendant across the site was built by Attalus I of Pergamum toward the end of the century, in what ranged from "friendly emulation"[39] to fierce one-upmanship. Delphi and its games continued through the Roman imperial period, flourishing especially in the late first and second centuries C.E.[40]

The Temple of Apollo stood at the center of the sanctuary. It was the office of the oracle, the climax of any visit, and a physical point of intersection between Apollo and the Muses. Although they are "often mentioned together" in the literary record, Delphi offers the unique example of a cult of the Muses associated with an Apolline oracle.[41] Writing around the turn of the second century C.E., Plutarch (*De Pythiae oraculis* 402c) recalled the spot on the temple terrace, where the "fair-haired Muses' fount of holy water"[42] once rose, and where the Muses were established "as associates and guardians of the prophetic art ... beside the stream and the shrine to Earth, to whom it is said that the oracle used to belong ..." (402d)."[43] The spring coexisted with successive Archaic temples of Apollo, but the foundations of the late Classical

[32] Pfeiffer 1949/1953, vol. 1, p. 9; Harder 2012, pp. 99–105; echoed in frag. 112.5.

[33] Fantuzzi and Hunter 2004, pp. 51, 54; Harder 2012, p. 96

[34] Harder 2012, p. 94 (on dream convention).

[35] Descending from Callimachus (*Aetia* frag. 2a, esp. line 30 [Pfeiffer 1949/1953, vol. 2, pp. 102–03]; *Hymn* 4.75), Aonian reappears in Latin poetry (discussed below).

[36] Fantuzzi and Hunter 2004, pp. 51–52.

[37] Fontenrose 1988; Amandry 1990.

[38] Amandry 1990, p. 286.

[39] Thompson 1982, p. 175.

[40] Weir 2004, esp. pp. 140–75.

[41] Parke 1981, p. 105.

[42] Plutarch here quotes Simonides (Page 1962, frag. 72a), trans. Babbitt 1936 (Loeb).

[43] Trans. Babbitt 1936 (Loeb).

temple — the final instantiation, built during the third quarter of the fourth century B.C.E. — covered it completely.[44] Plutarch also preserves the tradition that the first Delphic Sibyl was said to have been reared by the Muses on Helicon (*De Pythiae oraculis* 398c), underscoring the proximity and cultural connections of Parnassus and Helicon.

Even when the Muses' spring disappeared, their representation in the eastern pediment of the new temple upheld their association with Apollo. The building that is seen in ruins today was visited in its prime by Pausanias (10.19.4), who described marble pedimental groups depicting Dionysos and the Thyiades on the west and, to the east, Apollo, Artemis, Leto, and the Muses. Excavations have produced corroborating, albeit fragmentary, evidence.[45] The dedication of the west pediment to Dionysos was a novelty, for although the god had long been a presence at Delphi, he was not previously featured in its monumental art.[46] Apollo's place over the main entrance, in contrast, was as familiar as it was appropriate, echoing his epiphany on the preceding temple's east pediment, a reference reinforced by the widely spaced, staid, non-narrative figures, which would have looked "stiff, old-fashioned, and conservative" in their time.[47] The kitharode Apollo sat upon a tripod at the center of his pediment, flanked by sister, mother, and a chorus of Muses, some seated on rocky bases. Centrally placed and long lived, the presentation on the temple was probably highly influential in bringing the Muses into the train of Apollo as patrons of poetry and music.[48] Thus even at Delphi, negotiations of cultic relationships were ongoing, and the prominence of the site ensured the impact of new traditions. Farther afield the distance between Parnassus and Helicon was gradually elided, as in a third-century epigram attributed to Theocritus: "The fresh roses and this thick creeping-thyme are a gift to the Heliconian Muses; the dark-leaved laurel branches are for thee, Pythian Paean [Apollo], since the rocks of Delphi gave thee this bright foliage to wear" (*Anthologia Palatina* 6.336).[49]

Mountains in Relief

Greek sanctuaries were always places where individuals and collectives promoted themselves even as they demonstrated piety. In the Vale of the Muses and at Delphi, we have seen how politics and patronage shaped sites and inflected traditions. In turning to the two reliefs, from real places to representations thereof, it is important to make a few points about

---

[44] Roux 1976, pp. 136–45; Parke 1981, p. 108. For the temple, see Croissant 2003; Ridgway 2001, pp. 17–21; Barringer 2008, pp. 144–61. Construction, perhaps driven by Athens, began before the middle of the century and had progressed to the roofline by 340/339 B.C.E., but the temple was completed only around 327/6, a decade after the Greeks' defeat at Chaironeia by Philip II of Macedonia. For a comparable, and nearly contemporary, group reconstructed in the pediment of the Temple of Apollo Patroos in Athens, see Thompson 1952, pp. 108–10; Ridgway 2001, pp. 19, 62 n. 7.

[45] See Ridgway 2001, pp. 17–21, 62 nn. 5–6; Barringer 2008, pp. 144–65.

[46] Barringer 2008, pp. 154–57.

[47] Barringer 2008, p. 152.

[48] Ridgway 2001, pp. 254–55. Representations of the Muses, sometimes with Apollo *Musagetes*, proliferated in the art and poetry of the Hellenistic age, as, for example, on the altar of Athena Polias at Priene, late third to mid-second century B.C.E. (Ridgway 2001, pp. 164–67, with bibliography), or in an unusual relief, probably part of a pediment, found at the Arcadian villa of Herodes Atticus, perhaps also late third or second century (Spyropoulos 1993, pp. 264–66, with thanks to A. Kuttner for drawing this to my attention). For a votive relief from Didyma, on which the Muses and Apollo occupy separate tiers, see below.

[49] Trans. Paton 1916 (Loeb).

Hellenistic art and culture. With the rise of royal capitals, cultural production was decentralized and diversified. Personification proliferated as a mode of expressing abstract concepts, including space and place. Features of the natural landscape also gained a more significant profile in art and literature.[50]

The Euthycles stele (fig. 8.2) is one of many offerings to the Muses to have been uncovered in the Heliconian Mouseion. There is strong agreement that it dates to the late third century B.C.E., based on letter style, which would put its dedication in the period in which the sanctuary was gaining international attention and fame.[51] Despite its local limestone and unpolished low-relief carving, the work is remarkably ambitious.[52] With its height originally about three times its width, the stele is divided into three parts, of which the middle is a recessed panel, a window framing a view of a male figure rising up between two eminences. It is especially the hair that makes the man. Locks radiate from the brow with lateral tufts falling from the temples in distinct strands, almost perfectly symmetrical. A full beard reaches the clavicles, long and full like the hair, and again, anything but unruly.[53] The face is damaged, leaving some details open to interpretation: where excavator Jamot saw great blind eyes, Deonna read wildness.[54] The figure's frontal torso shows well-developed, if flatly rendered, musculature; but from the abdomen down, he is "hidden" below the horizon. He drapes his right hand over one peak, palm down and fingers spread, while the back of his downturned left hand has fractured away, leaving only the fingers intact, clutching its peak.

The giant must be Helicon.[55] His form derives from the tradition of allegorizing natural features and phenomena with human figures. He shares a full beard and mature appearance with personifications of waterways and winds, and of the kinds of creatures that lived in the wilds, satyrs, centaurs, Pan, and the like. Mountains are never common among personifications, but there are examples, particularly in the Roman period.[56] Implied scale, pose, and abundant, truly leonine, hair communicate forceful character, and indeed, Helicon's appearance here would seem to suggest his association with a wild, uncivilized place.[57]

The figure's placement between the peaks locates him on his mountain. Such integration of figure and landscape again reflects late Classical and Hellenistic interest in depictions of

---

[50] For surveys, see Pollitt 1986; Smith 1991; Ridgway 2000; 2001.

[51] Athens, National Archaeological Museum inv. no. 1455; *IThesp* 274. The stele was found among the remains of a chapel on the site of the ancient altar in the Vale of the Muses. See Jamot 1890; Deonna 1907; Pottier 1908; Lechat 1908; Peek 1977; Schachter 1986, pp. 160–61; Hurst 1996; Veneri 1996; Kaltsas 2002, p. 305, cat. no. 640; Vottéro 2002, pp. 95–96, no. 34; *LIMC* 4.1, p. 573, s.v. Helicon I, no. 1 (O. Palagia).

[52] As Jamot (1890, pp. 549–50) writes, "sans doute, l'artiste qui a sculpté cette figure étrange n'était qu'un marbrier de petite ville. Cependant s'il n'était pas lui-même un maître, il appartenait à une époque où il y avait encore des maîtres."

[53] Jamot (1890, p. 550) likened it to seaweed; its resemblance to sculptured lions and lion-head spouts might suggest that the carver was a specialist in architectural sculpture.

[54] Jamot 1890, p. 550; Deonna 1907, p. 336.

[55] Despite early debate (with suggestions ranging from Hesiod himself to Boreas and Pan), this is now widely accepted, as per Kaltsas 2002, p. 305, cat. no. 640.

[56] See Foss 1982, esp. p. 184. Paralleling Ovid's portrayal of the Lydian mountain (or god) Tmolus as the judge of a contest between Apollo and Pan (*Metamorphoses* 11.173–79) are images of Mounts Tmolus and Sipylus on Roman provincial coins — as busts of bearded males resembling traditional river gods (*BMC* Sardis 78; *BMC* Magnesia ad Sipylum 25–23) or as a mature, heroic nude (*BMC* Tmolus Aureliopolis 1 and 5). I am grateful to Emily Gangemi for alerting me to this material.

[57] See Brilliant 1993, esp. p. 305 on the symbolism of hair.

divinities within their native habitats, generally distilled into their most characteristic features. Most common are reliefs of nymphs (and often Pan) within grottoes defined by "rocky" frames that, from the third quarter of the fourth century B.C.E., were dedicated in numinous caves in Greece, and later in southern Italy.[58] The rendering of cave canopies ranges from sharply faceted or doughy undulations on marble examples to the delicate shelly surfaces of later fictile art. In fact, a very similar figure appears on a relief found in the Cave of Pan on Mount Parnes, variously dated between the mid-fourth century and the first half of the first century B.C.E.[59] Indeed, the resemblance is strong enough to suggest a common model. The plaque from Mount Parnes depicts three female figures and a reclining male, Achelous, within a recess in a rocky landscape, with smaller figures posed around the frame, a nude youth and herm on one side and Pan on the other. At the very center, a male figure is rendered as if rising from behind the lip of a cave. His scale is greater than his neighbors, but only his left arm, shoulders, and (poorly preserved) head are exposed. On the Euthycles stele, however, the sculptor everted this norm and simplified the landscape to its essence, evoking the boundless space of mountain heights, and a giant towering over his peaks.

A slightly earlier document is also illuminating. That document, a fragment of poetry by Corinna, blurs the distinction between men and mountains in a way that would have delighted her Boeotian audience, probably mid- to late fourth century B.C.E.[60] She poses Helicon against neighbor(ing) Cithaeron, not as mountains per se but heroic contestants in a singing duel watched by the Muses and other deities. After Cithaeron is proclaimed victor, Helicon erupts from cultured competition to terrifying violence: "But, filled with harsh griefs, Helicon [ripped out] a bare rock ... and the mountain ... groaning pitifully he hurled it from on high into a myriad stones."[61]

A similar duality characterizes Helicon on the Euthycles stele: The formidable mountain speaks for himself through an inscription in hexameter verse. The lightly incised letters would have required a close look to be read, even if darkened with paint. Three lines across the upper frame identify the stele as a dedication to the Muses by an individual usually reconstructed as "Euthycles":

> Euthycles, son of Amphicritus, has made a dedication to the Muses,
> adorning it with epic verses. May their grace be everlasting,
> and keep safe the fulfillment of his family and his name.[62]

The image is directly below, and below that, there follows a direct invocation from Helicon himself, claiming oracular power, and sanctioning the authority of Hesiod and his *Works and Days*:

> Like this, facing you, very aged, like a mortal,
> I, Helicon, not ignorant of the Muses, proclaim an oracle:
> "For mortals who obey Hesiod's injunctions
> there will be good laws and the land will be full of fruits."

---

[58] On cave reliefs, see Edwards 1985; Larson 2001, p. 267; Robinson 2011, pp. 166–70.

[59] Athens, National Archaeological Museum inv. no. 1879. Edwards 1985, pp. 725–35, no. 76; Ridgway 2002, pp. 224, 247 n. 19 (favoring a date in the first half of the first century B.C.E.); Kaltsas 2002, p. 214, cat. no.

439 (mid-fourth century B.C.E.); *LIMC* 7.1, p. 190, s.v. Parnes, no. 1.

[60] Page 1962, frag. 654, col. 1; Pottier 1908; Berman 2010, pp. 42–43, 53–62; Larmour 2005, pp. 26–31.

[61] Trans. Larmour 2005, p. 27.

[62] Trans. Most 2007 (Loeb).

This kind of pronouncement would have been _lingua franca_ in Boetia, a land well endowed with oracles, but a unique one so far attested in the Vale of the Muses.[63] Finally, inscribed around a lightly carved laurel wreath is an homage to Hesiod, poet of Helicon and the Muses:

> Hesiod, son of Dius, the Muses and godly Helicon
> in most beautiful hymns [and the son of Amphicritus
> he makes homage to this illustrious] man.[64]

These last words reinforce Hesiod's connection to the place and its divine population. The "learned" reference to his father, Dius, and its homonymic allusion to Διός-Zeus, father of the Muses, as well as the likely renaming of Euthycles by his patronym, stress the importance of lineage.[65] The wreath suggests that Euthycles was himself a victorious poet in the sacred games of the Muses.[66]

The Euthycles stele is a precious document. Details and provenance allow us to reconstruct its original display context in the Mouseion and to imagine its function and reception. Image and words together functioned as an ephiphany. Although Helicon stands as if ready to wreak havoc, his metered words are those of a wise old man who knows the Muses' art. To read the inscription was to recite it aloud: every reading repeated the dedicatory ritual and uttered the oracle, renewing its promise, and reinforcing Hesiod's hold on the mountain.[67]

Very different devices — formal and epigraphic — are at work in the Archelaos relief, from Bovillae, Italy (fig. 8.3).[68] The marble plaque has two discrete parts. At the bottom is a conventional sacrifice scene, while the upper two-thirds map a mountain in three divinely populated registers. While both scenes are clearly outdoors, a striking contrast is set up between circumscribed ritual space and the unbounded mountain setting above. The pairing of scenes is not unique in ancient relief, but the particular subjects, the careful composition, and the delicate carving distinguish the work.[69]

Although most scholars recognize the relief as the image of a sacred mountain and an allegory of poetic inspiration, much else is still subject to interpretation, and the work has been the topic of continued debate since its discovery. There has been a tendency to identify

---

[63] For Boeotia's oracular reputation, Plutarch, _De defectu oraculorum_ 411f–412d; Larson 2001, pp. 7–8, 138–39; Veneri 1996, pp. 78–82 (eclipse by Delphi); Bonnechere 2007.

[64] Trans. adapted from Most 2007 (Loeb), merging that of Hurst 1996, p. 61, based on restoration by Peek 1977.

[65] See Hurst 1996, p. 61; Hesiod does not name his father in preserved poems; the name Dios "arose out of a misunderstanding of [_Works and Days_] 299" (Most 2007, p. lxiv) and was transmitted by the fourth-century B.C.E. historian Ephoros (_apud_ Strabo, _Geographia_ 13.3.6). This inscription is the earliest preserved primary source.

[66] Veneri 1996, p. 86; cf. Schachter 1986, p. 161.

[67] For ancient reading and effects, see Meyer 2007; Day 2010, pp. 224, 230.

[68] London: British Museum inv. no. 2191. The scholarship on this relief is extensive. See esp. Pinkwart 1965; Pollitt 1986, pp. 15–16; Stewart 1990, pp. 217–18; Smith 1991, p. 187; Ridgway 2000, pp. 207–08; 2001, pp. 263–64.

[69] Comparanda: Berlin, Staatliche Museen inv. no. Sc. 709 (Edwards 1985, no. 30; Newby 2007, pp. 158–59), fourth century B.C.E.: Hermes, Nymphs, and Pan (upper)/ worshiper approaching Demeter and Kore (lower); Istanbul, Archaeological Museum inv. no. 2192, from Didyma (Ridgway 2001, pp. 255–57; Newby 2007, pp. 159–60), mid-second century B.C.E., Apollo and other divinities (upper)/ Muses approached by worshipers (lower); Athens, National Archaeological Museum inv. no. 1485 (Kaltsas 2002, p. 304, cat. no. 639), late second century B.C.E., worshippers approaching Apollo and Cybele (upper)/ subdivided scene of banqueters in a row above or behind serving slaves, flautist, and dancing girl (lower).

historic persons among the figures on the plaque and to extrapolate specific contexts of production and dedication.[70] Proposed dates range from the third century B.C.E. to the mid-first century C.E., with the median the second half of the second century B.C.E.[71] The primary context of the work, and its relationship to a model or models, remain unresolved.

My approach is to proceed from provenance and stylistic dates — neither completely satisfying, but valid starting points — to interpretation. A marble relief signed by a Greek sculptor, Archelaos, son of Apollonios of Priene, the plaque was found among the remains of an ancient villa not far off the Appian Way in Bovillae, southeast of Rome.[72] The date can be bracketed between the second half of the second century B.C.E., suggested by letter style, and the second half of the next century, based on formal and iconographic parallels.[73] Even within this tighter frame, a variety of scenarios are possible. On one hand, it could have been commissioned by, or in honor of, a victor in sacred Greek *agones*, dedicated at a sanctuary or the victor's city, and later transferred to Italy.[74] On the other hand, it might have originated as an "educational pinax" appropriate to a cultural institution like a school or library, but equally at home in a Roman villa, such as the one in which it was found.[75] Ridgway has furthermore hypothesized that Archelaos carved the relief for a Roman patron as late as the first century B.C.E.[76] I believe that the particular assortment of subjects, characters, and motifs support this hypothesis. While I can only add my voice to the clamor of opinions about this famous work, my sense is that it finds its best fit in the cultural milieu of "Golden Age" Rome, of Catullus, Gallus, Virgil, and Propertius, of the Odyssey landscapes, and of the early *Tabulae Iliacae*, one of which was found in the same villa.[77]

Let us look closely at the plaque. At bottom left, a mature bearded male figure is enthroned and surrounded by devotees. They occupy a shallow space, backed by the smooth surface of a curtain, hung from a series of six Doric columns; only the abaci are visible above the subtly scalloped edge. That this godlike figure is Homer is indicated with a tiny inscription on the smooth band below. Other inscriptions name the figures that are gathered around him, revealing them to be not humans but personifications. At left, Time and the Inhabited World crown Homer. Genre figures (literally — a diminutive Myth, then History, Poetry, Tragedy, Comedy) gather at an altar, behind which a large humped bovid stands. History, a male figure, sprinkles incense on the altar; Poetry holds two torches aloft; Tragedy and

[70] Scholars have recognized Chronos and Oikoumene as portraits of an astounding range of Hellenistic dynasts, biasing them toward eastern production and earlier dates. As Ridgway notes (2000, p. 207; 2001, p. 262), the figures are small, and modern disagreement over their identifications is reason enough to doubt that likenesses were intended. She furthermore argues (2001, p. 265) against assumptions of production and dedication in the Hellenistic east, as well as explanations for its relocation to Italy as booty or by a proud owner.

[71] The latest estimate was offered in 1764 by Winckelmann (2006, p. 310), who believed that it was executed in the reign of Claudius (41–54 C.E.).

[72] See Ridgway 2001, pp. 263–64.

[73] For letter style, see Newby 2007, p. 174. Ridgway (2000, p. 208) finds similarities to neo-Attic reliefs of

the late second and early first centuries B.C.E., but notes that personifications align better with works of the later first century B.C.E.

[74] See, e.g., Pollitt 1986, p. 16; Newby 2007, p. 172.

[75] Ridgway 2000, pp. 207–08, developing an idea proposed by E. Voutiras.

[76] Ridgway 2000, p. 208.

[77] For provenance and the *Tabula Iliaca Capitolina* (Rome, Capitoline Museum inv. no. 316), see Ridgway 2001, pp. 265–66; Small 2003, pp. 93–96. For the Odyssey Landscapes, now in the Vatican Museums, see O'Sullivan 2011, pp. 116–49. If pressed, I would opt for a date in the middle or third quarter of the first century B.C.E., for, as Ridgway (2001, p. 266) notes, a "late first-century B.C. date for the Archelaos Relief may be stretching the evidence" (2001, p. 266).

Comedy raise arms in reverence. Behind them, four smaller female figures stand in a tight cluster, their postures signaling interest or apprehension; a small child tugs on a garment as if angling for attention. She personifies Nature, and they are virtues, Valor, Memory, Faith, and Knowledge. In reading each name, the viewer would enumerate the genres of literature and the benefits of learning.

This scene is related to votive plaques of a kind that became common in the late Classical and Hellenistic periods and was revived by neo-Attic workshops of the late Republic and early Empire.[78] Worshippers honor deities in conventional settings; the honorands are distinguished by their larger scale and were probably understood as the gods themselves. Perhaps such panels communicated greater pious effect than a simple statuette of similar cost, as Smith has suggested.[79] A viewer familiar with the type, when contemplating the Archelaos relief, would recognize the epiphany and empathize with worshippers, witnesses. A more textured understanding would come in reading and contemplating the richer, allegorical meanings. Certainly the godlike Homer is seen as a source for all literary production, eternally and everywhere, as well as cultural virtues and values. That it depicted Homer's apotheosis in the Alexandrian Homereion, as sometimes suggested, would be an unusually specific reading, but a valid interpretation then as now.[80]

If the lower frame suggests a quasi-narrative ritual, the upper reaches offer an expansive landscape populated by a divine assembly: Zeus and Mnemosyne, the Muses, and Apollo. Most of the figures are distributed across three parallel groundlines; however, several slight departures energize the composition. Zeus reclines in an exalted position just below the mountaintop — which coincides with the pointed top of the relief. His outcrop seat and the adjacent background are rendered as softly undulating "rocky" surfaces, a treatment that comes and goes throughout the upper tiers. The tilt of his head directs the viewer's eye down to Mnemosyne, the mother of the Muses, who stands on her own rocky ledge with hand on hip, returning Zeus's gaze. Also given her own ground at far right, one of their nine daughters dances downhill toward her sisters. The others are distributed across two frieze-like tiers, some standing, others sitting on rocky seats. In the lower level, right of center, one Muse stands with Apollo and the *omphalos* in a stylized grotto.[81] Its vault is rendered with a slight overhang that lifts up to press against the groundline above then descends as a wall on the right. In the narrow space beyond, a statue of a victorious poet stands in lively contrapposto on a square base; a prize tripod is rendered in low relief behind him. The poet is as tall as Apollo, but his segregation and slight vertical displacement, as well as his statuesque presentation, set him apart. He is a mortal, not quite intruding on the realm of the gods.

For our purposes, the plurality of the Muses, rather than their individual identities, matters most. Given the careful labeling of all figures in the lower panel, however, the lack of names above is striking. Most of the figures are based on well-known types, some known

---

[78] For examples, see Kaltsas 2002, pp. 224–26, cat. nos. 472–73, 475 (Athens, National Archaeological Museum inv. nos. 1332–33, 1841 — from the Athenian Asclepieion); pp. 304–05, cat. nos. 638–39 (inv. nos. 1453, 1485 — Hellenistic reliefs from Laconia and Bithynia). For the often-compared "Munich Relief" (Munich Glyptothek inv. no. 206), on which the sac-

rifice also takes place in a curtained-off space, see Smith 1991, pp. 186–87 (third century B.C.E.); Ridgway 2000, pp. 208–09 (late second century B.C.E.).

[79] Smith 1991, pp. 186–87.

[80] Cf. Stewart 1990, p. 217; Kuttner 1999, p. 106.

[81] For the *omphalos*, see Roux 1976, pp. 129–31.

in earlier examples, and it seems certain that they must have been recognizable, or meant to be.[82] Cohon's hypothesis, that they appear in Hesiodic order, is appealing.[83]

What can be said of place, so strongly evoked by topography and relief? The presence of Zeus could be taken to mean Olympus, but while that was his supreme abode, he was honored at altars on other peaks, including Helicon and Parnassus.[84] Likewise, Apollo's *omphalos* suggests Delphi, but serves equally as an attribute of the god. The cave in which he stands with a Muse is, however, more provocative. While no great cave has been uncovered in the excavations of Delphi, ancient sources refer to a variety of Parnassian grottoes and cavities — of the Python, of the Pythia, and, well above the sanctuary, the Corycian Cave.[85] Ancient references on the Delphic oracle, alone, include *stomion* (mouth), *muchos* (recess), and *antron* (cavern), but their meanings are often obscure; they seem alternatively to denote a natural or constructed feature, or to be purely figurative.[86] By the Hellenistic period, in any case, a numinous Delphic grotto cave was a well-known *topos*, to be echoed in a similar, conventionalized Heliconian or Aonian counterpart in imperial sources.[87] Based on figures and landmarks, scholars have tended to identify the mountain in the upper half of the relief as Parnassus or Helicon, or to identify the aspects of each as discrete reference points.[88] But as we have seen, their distinct iconographies were always evolving and sometimes converging, even at Delphi.

The figure at the right clearly represents a victorious poet who either commissioned the relief for himself or was honored with its dedication at home or at the site of his triumph; his event is debated: was it epic or lyric poetry?[89] It has also been identified as the statue of an esteemed forebear, such as Callimachus or Apollonius of Rhodes (unlikely indeed) or Hesiod and his tripod — more appealing, if unprovable.[90] The scene is sometimes likened to an invocation found in the prologue or opening lines of a poem.[91] I would amend this slightly. It is a visual counterpart to literary accounts that tell of — rather than asking for — inspiration and that describe confrontations with divinity that ultimately lead to immortality. Hesiod's meeting with the nine Muses at the beginning of the *Theogony* is the matrix composition. The Greek tradition culminates in Callimachus's "sacred conversation"; the distance maintained in his dream conceit is comparable to that imposed by the artist in his placement and handling of the poet's form. Roman poets would use similar scenes to play with genre, advertise accomplishments, and imagine their own initiation into legendary ranks.

---

[82] Ridgway 2001, pp. 257–61; Newby 2007, p. 160.

[83] Cohon 1991–1992, reading left to right, top to bottom; it is worth noting that his identifications are not unanimously accepted and debate continues; see Ridgway (2000, p. 207) for measured support, Small (2003, p. 92) for doubt.

[84] See Langdon 2000: Parnassus (Lucian, *Timon* 3; the scholiast on Pindar, *Olympian Odes* 9.70; Apollodorus, *Bibliotheca* 1.7.2), Helicon, Hymettus, Lycaeon, and Helicon in mainland Greece, with others on Crete and in Asia Minor.

[85] See McInerney 1997; Larson 2001, pp. 234–38.

[86] Ustinova 2009, pp. 121–53; cf. Fontenrose 1978, pp. 199–202.

[87] See Lycophron, *Alexandra* (207); in Latin, a passing place-reference in Ovid (*Metamorphoses* 3.14) can be compared to Lucan's more developed scene-setting

(*Pharsalia* 5.82–170). For a Heliconian cave, see Catullus 61; Propertius 2.30.26; 3.3.27–34 (see below); and cf. Virgil, *Georgics* 3.10–12.

[88] Parnassus: Smith 1991, p. 187. Helicon: Preuner 1920, pp. 419–23; Ferrari 1999, pp. 374–75; Clay 2004, pp. 91–92. Webster (1964, p. 146): "Olympos perhaps at the top ... but Parnassus at the bottom"; Pollitt (1986, p. 16): "Helikon or Parnassos"; Kuttner (1999, p. 106): the mountain "syncretizes" Olympus, Parnassus, and Helicon.

[89] Pollitt 1986, p. 16; Stewart 1990, p. 217; on genre, Clay 2004, p. 92.

[90] See Pollitt 1986, p. 16; for Hesiod, Preuner 1920, p. 420.

[91] Stewart 1990, p. 217; Ridgway 2001, pp. 262, 272 n. 26, citing Webster 1967, pp. 108–12.

How are we to understand the coupling of a thoroughly Hesiodic mountain of the Muses and the scene of Homer's worship below? Given what is known of the sophistication and the factionalism of Hellenistic scholarship, they would be strange bedfellows in that world. If we look to Rome, however, the themes and their combination find a better fit. Indeed, in what remains of this paper, I shall discuss how the plaque's composition might be explained in the context of Roman rethinking of the Greek heartland and its traditions, a process that involved "elements of domestication, usurpation, syncretism and continuing dialogue, which may not admit of being resolved into a single linear narrative."[92]

A Roman general might insert himself into the sacred landscape, as did Lucius Aemilius Paullus, Titus Quinctius Flamininus, and Lucius Mummius, with dedications at the Panhellenic centers.[93] Or, he might physically transfer traditions (and more famously, plundered works of art) as Marcus Fulvius Nobilior did in importing the cult of the Muses to Rome (to be worshipped with Hercules alongside their Roman counterparts, the Camenae) after his campaign against the Aetolian League in 189 B.C.E.[94] Poets and sculptors working for educated patrons, like their Hellenistic predecessors, further embraced and transformed received traditions. The observation that Roman artists reworked imagery and mixed metaphors in ways "that may make one wonder at times whether they were thinking clearly of the geographical position of the places which they named or merely throwing together evocative words borrowed from Greek poetry" applies as well to many Hellenistic Alexandrians.[95] In fact, from Ennius to Ovid, creative conflations alternate with references suggesting the firsthand experience of poets and patrons.[96] New values were attached to well-known *topoi*, and new associations were made, not through naiveté or confusion, but as a negotiation of genealogy and geography, at once subtle and significant.

The works of Callimachus were especially influential for Roman writers, but Helicon became "the mountain of all poets, not just of Callimacheans."[97] His dream conceit especially provided opportunities to explore genre, to exploit place and landscape as symbols, and to blur lines between human and divine realms.[98] Thus, Quintus Ennius, who had accompanied Nobilior in Greece, and probably visited Helicon and Parnassus, bragged that no Roman had before him climbed the "rough rocks of the Muses" (*Annales* 208–09 [Skutsch 1985]), and he began his *Annales* with a mountain vision that would soon rival those of his Greek predecessors in its iconic status. Once again, fragments and later references support a Heliconian setting (Lucretius, *De rerum natura* 1.117–119; Propertius 3.3.1–2). It appears that, after invoking the Muses, Ennius wrote of a dream and, in it, an encounter with the shade of Homer, who encouraged him to proceed with his grand designs.[99] A conversation with Homer on Helicon

---

[92] Hinds 1998, p. 63.

[93] See Tzifopoulos 1993; Yarrow 2006.

[94] *LTUR* III, s.v. Hercules Musarum, Aedes, 17–19 (Viscogliosi); Hardie 2007, pp. 560–64.

[95] Parke 1978, p. 206.

[96] See Schachter 1990; Robinson 2012, pp. 247–51. Even geographical points that appear distant on the map are often intervisible in reality — for example, Helicon, Parnassus, and Acrocorinth to the south — with transpositions of traditions often following sightlines (see Robinson 2006).

[97] Zetzel 1977, p. 251; see also Hinds 1998, p. 52; Tatum 2000; Hunter 2006.

[98] See above.

[99] Zetzel 1977, p. 251; 1983, pp. 95–96; Skutsch 1985, pp. 143–67. Given the piecemeal evidence, Skutsch argues that Ennius replaced a meeting with the Muses with the meeting of Homer" (p. 148). While internal evidence (Ennius, *Annales* 7) "makes it very probable that [Ennius] spoke of a mountain" (p. 150), and the Augustan poets clearly place his meeting on Helicon, Skutsch thinks it "certain that he did not name the mountain."

was unprecedented, but it might be expected for a figure who, like the legendary bard, would make a name in epic.

Poets of the first century B.C.E. further developed the imaginative mountainscapes of Callimachus and Ennius, populating them with an evolving cast of characters — divine, legendary, and now, increasingly, historical. An actual or imagined visit to Helicon by the poet Gallus is known from the sixth *Eclogue* (64–73) of Virgil. In his retelling, Gallus was met by a Muse and led uphill from the Permessus into the Aonian mountains to be greeted by her sisters — a so-called chorus of Apollo — and ultimately Linus, who presented him with a set of pipes, said to have belonged to Hesiod and to Orpheus before him.[100] Thus Gallus was initiated into the highest classes of poets — the heroic and legendary.

Still later in the first century B.C.E., Propertius claimed poetic descent along an "untrodden path from the Sisters' mount" (3.1.16–17), thus evoking Helicon and aligning himself with Ennius and Gallus while also touting his own originality. Elsewhere he asked Greek forebears — Callimachus and the generation-earlier Philetas — to allow his entry into their midst: into their grove (3.1.1–6).[101] In another poem (3.3), a Heliconian landscape takes shape in a dream. Propertius offers a detailed plot and rich visual and spatial impressions. Climbing Helicon, the poet is spotted by Apollo from Parnassus, then directed back downhill, where the Muse Calliope instructs him to abandon epic for elegy. He finds the Muses in their lovely home:

> Here was a green grotto lined with mosaics and from the hollow pumice timbrels hung, the mystic instruments of the Muses, a clay image of father Silenus, and the pipe of Arcadian Pan; and the birds of my lady Venus, the doves that I love, dip their red bills in the Gorgon's pool, while the nine Maidens, each allotted her own realm, busy their tender hands on their separate gifts .... (Propertius 3.3.27–34)[102]

Propertius's cave of the Muses is clearly an allusive feature rather than a "real" landmark, and so too, the "Gorgon's pool," a rebranding of Hippocrene. Such landmarks are evocative and symbolic, rather than imitative or mimetic, and they are paralleled in mythological and sacro-idyllic landscapes that gained interest in Roman wall paintings in the late first century B.C.E.[103] I believe that such imagery provides the keys to reading the Archelaos relief. In merging Heliconian and Parnassian themes, inserting set pieces, and posing Homer before them, it would have been well received in the intellectual milieu of Rome from the early second century forward, but especially in the mid-late first century B.C.E. It may be worth remembering that this would coincide with the period in which statues of Romans came to dominate the Heliconian Mouseion.

Thomas has emphasized that in the process of syncretism or transculturation, "identification of one god with another usually did not mean the eradication of one in favor of the other, but a situation in which two or more 'pictures' of the divinity were maintained in

---

[100] See Cairns 2006, pp. 120–25; Ross 2008; for my suggestion that the passage maybe influenced the actual experience of a visit to the Heliconian Mouseion, and a discussion of other interpretations, see Robinson 2012, pp. 249–50.

[101] Philetas of Cos was poet, scholar, and tutor of Ptolemy II Philadelphus; see Hardie 1997; Cairns 2006, pp. 127–28.

[102] Trans. G. P. Goold, 1999 (Loeb).

[103] Cairns 2006, pp. 131–40, on Propertian landmarks and wilderness; Bergmann 1992.

tension."[104] The same can be said of representations of divine places and phenomena. As I have argued, Helicon *was* inspiration for Hellenistic poets, and their Roman inheritors continued to employ that mountain to articulate the challenges of composition as well as the genealogy of genres.[105] The Archelaos relief graphically merges sacred geographies, bringing the realms of Hesiod and Homer together, yet maintaining a division. Homer is a mediator, functioning much as he does in Ennius's *Annales*, or as do Callimachus and Philetas for Propertius, and he is an example. But inspiration comes from "the rough rocks of the Muses" above.

Two sacred mountains and two sanctuaries, one ancient and bursting at the seams, the other, much newer, and for all its reputation, sparsely developed. Delphi was centered on an oracular temple and regularly enlivened by festivals. Also an important festival site, the Mouseion lacked even a temple but boasted a great art collection — highlighting gods, poets, and, increasingly, human lineages. In each case, settings and sacred topography inspired reverence, rituals and monuments amplified effects, and art and poetry captured the essences of the real places, and the places of humans. Through Roman ascendancy, lines were blurred from afar and traditions liberalized. By summoning divine inhabitants and human forbears, historic or legendary, and by juxtaposing familiar themes with innovations, poets and artists alike situated themselves in an honored tradition and set themselves apart. These developments maintained the centrality of Greek sanctuaries and their settings in ongoing negotiations of religion, culture, and power.

Figure 8.1. The mountain ranges of Parnassus and Helicon, view to the north across the Corinthian Gulf from Corinth, with the Perachora peninsula in the foreground. Parnassus looms in the distance to the west (left), while two peaks of Helicon stretch to the east (right) (photo by Betsey A. Robinson)

---

[104] Thomas 2004, p. 260.   [105] Lamberton 1988a, p. 146.

Figure 8.2. The Euthycles stele, from the Mouseion on Helicon. Late third century B.C.E.
Athens, National Archaeological Museum inv. no. 1455 (height: 1.19 m) (© Hellenic Ministry of
Culture and Tourism / Archaeological Receipts Fund)

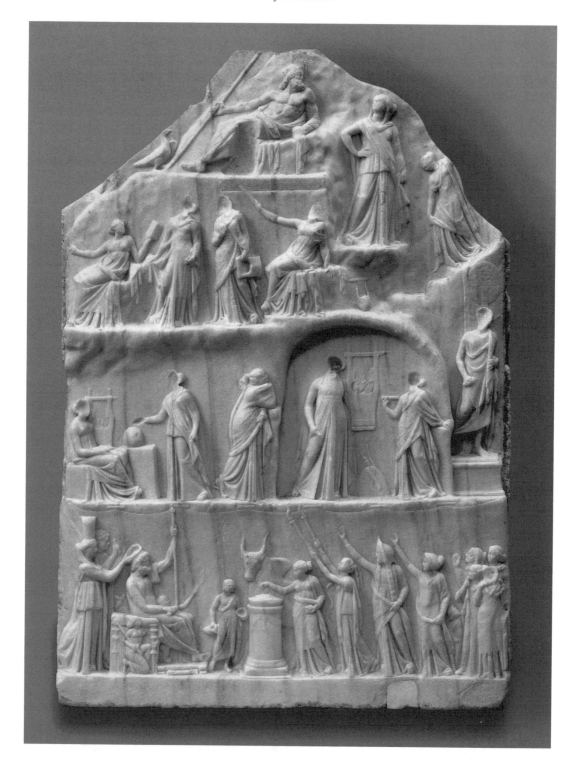

Figure 8.3. The Archelaos relief, from Bovillae, Italy. Second or first century B.C.E. London, British Museum inv. no. 2191 (height: 1.18 m) (© The Trustees of the British Museum)

Abbreviations

frag(s).	fragment(s)
BMC	British Museum Catalogue
IThesp	Paul Roesch, ed., *Les inscriptions de Thespies*. Online version edited by Gilbert Argoud, Albert Schachter, and Guy Vottéro; 2009 version available at http://www.hisoma.mom.fr/thespies.html
LIMC	*Lexicon iconographicum mythologiae classicae*. Zürich: Artemis, 1981–2009
LTUR	Eva Margareta Steinby, ed., *Lexicon topographicum urbis romae*, 6 volumes. Rome: Edizioni Quasar, 1993–2000

Bibliography

Amandry, Pierre
1990   "La fête des Pythia." *Praktika tês Akademias Athenôn* 65: 279–317.

Aravantinos, V. L.
1996   "Topographical and Archaeological Investigations on the Summit of Helicon." In *La montagne des muses*, edited by André Hurst and Albert Schachter, pp. 185–92. Recherches et rencontres 7. Geneva: Librairie Droz.

Argoud, G.
1996   "L'Helicon et la litterature grecque." In *La montagne des muses*, edited by André Hurst and Albert Schachter, pp. 27–42. Recherches et rencontres 7. Geneva: Librairie Droz.

Babbitt, Frank Cole, editor and translator
1936   *Plutarch's Moralia*, Volume 5: 351c–438e. Loeb Classical Library 306. London: Heinemann; New York: Harvard University Press.

Barringer, Judith M.
2008   *Art, Myth, and Ritual in Classical Greece*. Cambridge: Cambridge University Press.

Bergmann, B.
1992   "Exploring the Grove: Pastoral Space on Roman Walls." In *The Pastoral Landscape*, edited by John Dixon Hunt, pp. 20–46. Studies in the History of Art 36. Washington, D.C.: National Gallery of Art.

Berman, Daniel W.
2010   "The Landscape and Language of Korinna." *Greek, Roman and Byzantine Studies* 50: 41–62.

Bonnechere, Pierre
2007   "The Place of the Sacred Grove (*Alsos*) in the Mantic Rituals of Greece: The Example of the Alsos of Trophonios at Lebadeia (Boeotia)." In *Sacred Gardens and Landscapes: Ritual and Agency*, edited by Michel Conan, pp. 17–41. Dumbarton Oaks Colloquium on the History of Landscape Architecture 26. Washington, D.C.: Dumbarton Oaks.

Brilliant, Richard
1993   "Hairiness: A Matter of Style and Substance in Roman Portraits." In *Eius virtutis studiosi: Classical and Postclassical Studies in Memory of Frank Edward Brown (1908–*

1988), edited by Ann Reynolds Scott and Russell T. Scott, pp. 303–12. Studies in the History of Art 43. Washington, D.C.: National Gallery of Art.

Buxton, Richard

1992 "Imaginary Greek Mountains." *Journal of Hellenic Studies* 112: 1–15.

Cairns, Francis

2006 *Sextus Propertius: The Augustan Elegist.* Cambridge: Cambridge University Press.

Calame, Claude

1996 "Montagne des Muses et Mouséia: la consécration des *Travaux* et l'héroïsation d'Hésiode." In *La montagne des muses*, edited by André Hurst and Albert Schachter, pp. 43–56. Recherches et rencontres 7. Geneva: Librairie Droz.

Clay, Diskin

2004 *Archilochos Heros: The Cult of Poets in the Greek Polis.* Hellenic Studies 6. Washington, D.C.: Center for Hellenic Studies.

Cohon, Robert

1991–1992 "Hesiod and the Order and Naming of the Muses in Hellenistic Art." *Boreas* 14/15: 67–83.

Croissant, Francis

2003 *Fouilles de Delphes* IV: *monuments figurés, sculpture* VII: *les frontons du temple du IVᵉ siècle.* Athens: École francaise d'Athènes.

Day, Joseph W.

2010 *Archaic Greek Epigram and Dedication: Representation and Reperformance.* Cambridge: Cambridge University Press.

Deonna, W.

1907 "Borée?" *Revue des études anciennes* 9: 335–37.

Edwards, Charles M.

1985 Greek Votive Reliefs to Pan and the Nymphs. Ph.D. dissertation, New York University.

Fantuzzi, Marco, and Richard L. Hunter

2004 *Tradition and Innovation in Hellenistic Poetry.* Cambridge: Cambridge University Press.

Ferrari, Gloria

1999 "The Geography of Time: The Nile Mosaic and the Library at Praeneste." *Ostraka* 8/2: 359–86.

Fontenrose, Joseph E.

1978 *The Delphic Oracle.* Berkeley: University of California Press.

1988 "The Cult of Apollo and the Games at Delphi." In *The Archaeology of the Olympics: The Olympics and Other Festivals in Antiquity*, edited by Wendy J. Raschke, pp. 121–40. Madison: University of Wisconsin Press.

Foss, Clive

1982 "A Neighbor of Sardis: The City of Tmolus and Its Successors." *Classical Antiquity* 1/2: 178–201.

Goold, G. P., editor and translator

1999 *Propertius: Elegies.* Loeb Classical Library 18. Revised edition. Cambridge: Harvard University Press.

Gutzwiller, Kathryn J.

    1998   *Poetic Garlands: Hellenistic Epigrams in Context*. Hellenistic Culture and Society 28. Berkeley: University of California Press.

Harder, Annette, editor

    2012   *Callimachus:* Aetia: *Introduction, Text, Translation, and Commentary*. 2 volumes. Oxford: Oxford University Press.

Hardie, Alex

    1997   "Philitas and the Plane Tree." *Zeitschrift für Papyrologie und Epigraphik* 119: 21–36.

    2007   "Juno, Hercules, and the Muses at Rome." *American Journal of Philology* 128: 551–92.

Hinds, Stephen

    1998   *Allusion and Intertext: Dynamics of Appropriation in Roman Poetry*. Roman Literature and Its Contexts. Cambridge: Cambridge University Press.

Hunter, Richard L.

    2006   *The Shadow of Callimachus: Studies in the Reception of Hellenistic Poetry at Rome*. Roman Literature and Its Contexts. Cambridge: Cambridge University Press.

Hurst, André

    1996   "La stèle de l'Hélicon." In *La montagne des muses*, edited by André Hurst and Albert Schachter, pp. 57–71. Recherches et rencontres 7. Geneva: Librairie Droz.

Hurst, André, and Albert Schachter, editors

    1996   *La montagne des Muses*. Recherches et rencontres 7. Geneva: Libraire Droz.

Jamot, Paul

    1890   "Stèle votive trouvée dans l'hiéron des Muses." *Bulletin de correspondance hellénique* 14: 546–51.

Kaltsas, Nikos E.

    2002   *Sculpture in the National Archaeological Museum, Athens*. Translated by David Hardy. Los Angeles: J. Paul Getty Museum.

Kuttner, Anne

    1999   "Hellenistic Images of Spectacle, from Alexander to Augustus." In *The Art of Ancient Spectacle*, edited by Bettina A. Bergmann and Christine Kondoleon, pp. 97–123. Studies in the History of Art 56. Washington, D.C.: National Gallery of Art.

Lamberton, Robert

    1988a   *Hesiod*. New Haven: Yale University Press.

    1988b   "Plutarch, Hesiod, and the Mouseia of Thespiai." *Illinois Classical Studies* 13: 491–504.

Langdon, Merle K.

    2000   "Mountains in Greek Religion." *The Classical World* 93/5: 461–70.

Larmour, David H. J.

    2005   "Corinna's Poetic *Metis* and the Epinikian Tradition." In *Women Poets in Ancient Greece and Rome*, edited by Ellen Greene, pp. 25–58. Tulsa: University of Oklahoma Press.

Larson, Jennifer

    2001   *Greek Nymphs: Myth, Cult, Lore*. Oxford: Oxford University Press.

Lechat, Henri

    1908   "Borée ou Pan?" *Revue des études anciennes* 10: 33.

Manieri, Alessandra

 2009 *Agoni poetico-musicali nella Grecia antica*, Volume 1: *Beozia*. Testi e commenti 25, Certamina musica graeca 1. Pisa: F. Serra.

McInerney, Jeremy

 1997 "Parnassus, Delphi, and the Thyiades." *Greek Roman and Byzantine Studies* 38/3: 263–83.

 1999 *The Folds of Parnassos: Land and Ethnicity in Ancient Phokis*. Austin: University of Texas Press.

McKenzie, Judith

 2007 *The Architecture of Alexandria and Egypt, c. 300 B.C.–A.D. 700*. Yale University Press Pelican History of Art. New Haven: Yale University Press.

Meyer, Doris

 2007 "The Act of Reading and the Act of Writing in Hellenistic Epigram." In *Brill's Companion to Hellenistic Epigram*, edited by Peter Bing and Jon Steffen Bruss, pp. 187–210. Leiden: Brill.

Moggi, Mauro, and Massimo Osanna, editors

 2010 *Pausania: Guida della Grecia*, Libro IX: *La Beozia*. Scrittori greci e latini. Milan: Mondadori.

Most, Glenn W., editor and translator

 2007 *Hesiod: Theogony, Works and Days, Testimonia*. Loeb Classical Library 57, 503. Cambridge: Harvard University Press.

Müller, Christel

 1996 "L'Hélicon et la littérature grecque." In *La montagne des muses*, edited by André Hurst and Albert Schachter, pp. 27–42. Recherches et rencontres 7. Geneva: Librairie Droz.

Newby, Zahra

 2007 "Reading the Allegory of the Archesilaos Relief." In *Art and Inscriptions in the Ancient World*, edited by Zahra Newby and Ruth E. Leader-Newby, pp. 156–78. Cambridge: Cambridge University Press.

O'Sullivan, Timothy M.

 2011 *Walking in Roman Culture*. Cambridge: Cambridge University Press.

Page, Denys L.

 1962 *Poetae Melici Graeci*. Oxford: Oxford University Press.

Parke, Herbert W.

 1978 "Castalia." *Bulletin de correspondance hellénique* 102: 199–219.

 1981 "Apollo and the Muses, or Prophecy in Greek Verse." *Hermathena* 130/131: 99–112.

Paton, W. R., editor and translator

 1916 *The Greek Anthology*, Volume 1. Loeb Classical Library. London: Heinemann; New York: G. P. Putnam's Sons. Reprinted by Harvard University Press, 1999.

Peek, Werner

 1977 "Hesiod und der Helikon." *Philologus* 121: 173–75.

Pfeiffer, Rudolf

 1949/1953 *Callimachus*. 2 volumes. Oxford: Clarendon Press.

Pinkwart, Doris

 1965 *Das Relief des Archelaos von Priene und die "Musen des Philiskos."* Kallmünz: Lassleben.

Plassart, André
    1926   "Fouilles de Thespies et de l'hiéron des muses de l'Hélicon. Inscriptions: Dédicaces de caractère religieux ou honorifique, bornes de domaines sacrés." *Bulletin de correspondance hellénique* 50: 383–462.

Pollitt, J. J.
    1986   *Art in the Hellenistic Age*. Cambridge: Cambridge University Press.

Pottier, E.
    1908   "Borée? Pan? Hélicon?" *Revue des études anciennes* 10: 248–49.

Preuner, Erich
    1920   "Honestos." *Hermes* 55/4: 388–426.

Ridgway, Brunilde Sismondo
    2000   *Hellenistic Sculpture*, Volume 2: *The Styles of ca. 200-100 B.C.* Madison: University of Wisconsin Press.
    2001   *Hellenistic Sculpture*, Volume 1: *The Styles of ca. 331-200 B.C.* Madison: University of Wisconsin Press.
    2002   *Hellenistic Sculpture*, Volume 3: *The Styles of ca. 100-31 B.C.* Madison: University of Wisconsin Press.

Robinson, Betsey Ann
    2006   "Pegasos's Springs and Peaks of Inspiration." In *Common Ground: Archaeology, Art, Science, and Humanities* (Proceedings of the 16th International Congress of Classical Archaeology, Boston, August 23–26, 2003), edited by Carol C. Mattusch, A. A. Donohue, and Amy Brauer, pp. 102–04. Oxford: Oxbow.
    2011   *Histories of Peirene: A Corinthian Fountain in Three Millennia* (AAAC 2). Princeton: American School of Classical Studies.
    2012   "The Production of a Sacred Space: Mount Helikon and the Valley of the Muses." *Journal of Roman Archaeology* 25.

Rose, Charles Brian
    1997   *Dynastic Commemoration and Imperial Portraiture in the Julio-Claudian Period*. Cambridge Studies in Classical Art and Iconography. Cambridge: Cambridge University Press.

Ross, David O., Jr.
    2008   "The Sixth *Eclogue*: Virgil's Poetic Genealogy." In *Vergil's* Eclogues, edited by Katharina Volk, pp. 189–215. Oxford Readings in Classical Studies. Oxford: Oxford University Press.

Roux, Georges
    1954   "Le val des muses et les musées chez les auteurs anciens." *Bulletin de correspondance hellénique* 78: 22–48.
    1976   *Delphes: son oracle et ses dieux*. Confluents 2. Paris: Belles Lettres.

Schachter, Albert
    1986   *Cults of Boiotia 2: Herakles to Poseidon*. Institute of Classical Studies Bulletin supplement 38/2. London: Institute of Classical Studies.
    1990   "Ovid and Boiotia." In *Essays in the Topography, History and Culture of Boiotia*, edited by Albert Schachter, pp. 103–09. Teiresias supplement 3. Montreal: McGill University Department of Classics.
    2012   "The Mouseia of Thespiai: Organization and Development." In *Poesia, musica e agoni nella Grecia antica* (Atti del IV convegno internazionale di ΜΟΙΣΑ, Lecce, 28–30 ottobre 2010), edited by D. Castaldo, F. G. Giannachi, A. Manieri, pp. 31–61. Rudiae: Ricerche sul Mondo Classico 22–23 [2010–2011], tome 1. Lecce: Congedo.

Scott, Michael
    2010   *Delphi and Olympia: The Spatial Politics of Panhellenism in the Archaic and Classical Periods.* Cambridge: Cambridge University Press.

Skutsch, Otto, editor
    1985   *The* Annals *of Q. Ennius.* Oxford: Oxford University Press.

Small, Jocelyn Penny
    2003   *The Parallel Worlds of Classical Art and Text.* Cambridge: Cambridge University Press.

Smith, R. R. R.
    1991   *Hellenistic Sculpture: A Handbook.* London: Thames & Hudson.

Spyropoulos, T.
    1993   "Νέα γλυπτά αποκτήνματα του Αρχαιολογικού Μουσείου Τριπόλεως." In *Sculpture from Arcadia and Laconia* (Proceedings of an International Conference Held at the American School of Classical Studies at Athens, April 10–14, 1992), edited by Olga Palagia and William D. E. Coulson, pp. 257–67. Oxbow Monograph 30. Oxford: Oxbow Books.

Stewart, Andrew F.
    1990   *Greek Sculpture: An Exploration.* 2 volumes. New Haven: Yale University Press.

Tatum, W. Jeffrey
    2000   "Aspirations and Divagations: The Poetics of Place in Propertius 2.10." *Transactions of the American Philological Association* 130: 393–410.

Thomas, Christine M.
    2004   "The 'Mountain Mother': The Other Anatolian Goddess at Ephesos." In *Les cultes Locaux dans les mondes grec et romain* (actes du colloque de Lyon, 7–8 juin 2001), edited by Guy Labarre, pp. 249–62. Collection archéologie et d'histoire de l'antiquité, Université Lumière-Lyon 7. Lyon: Université Lumière-Lyon.

Thompson, Homer A.
    1952   "Excavations in the Athenian Agora: 1951." *Hesperia* 21/2: 83–113.
    1982   "Architecture as a Medium of Public Relations among the Successors of Alexander." In *Macedonia and Greece in Late Classical and Early Hellenistic Times,* edited by Beryl Barr-Sharrar and Eugene N. Borza, pp. 173–89. Studies in the History of Art 10. Washington, D.C.: National Gallery of Art.

Tzifopoulos, Yannis Z.
    1993   "Mummius' Dedications at Olympia and Pausanias' Attitude to the Romans." *Greek, Roman and Byzantine Studies* 34/1: 93–100.

Ustinova, Yulia
    2009   *Caves and the Ancient Greek Mind: Descending Underground in the Search for Ultimate Truth.* Oxford: Oxford University Press.

Veneri, Alina
    1996   "L'Elicona nella cultura tespiese intorno al III sec. a. C.: la stele di Euthy[kl]es." In *La montagne des muses,* edited by André Hurst and Albert Schachter, pp. 73–86. Recherches et rencontres 7. Geneva: Librairie Droz.

Vottéro, G.
    2002   "Boeotica Epigrammata." In *L'épigramme de l'Antiquité au XVIIe siècle, ou Du ciseau à la pointe,* edited by Jeanne Dion, pp. 69–122. Études anciennes 25. Nancy: A.D.R.A.

Wallace, Paul W.

    1974   "Hesiod and the Valley of the Muses." *Greek, Roman and Byzantine Studies* 15/1: 5–24.

Webster, T. B. L.

    1964   *Hellenistic Poetry and Art*. New York: Barnes & Noble.

    1967   *Hellenistic Art*. London: Methuen.

Weir, Robert George A.

    2004   *Roman Delphi and Its Pythian Games*. British Archaeological Reports, International Series 1306. Oxford: Archaeopress.

Winckelmann, Johann Joachim

    2006   *History of the Art of Antiquity*. Translated by Harry Francis Mallgrave. Los Angeles: Getty Research Institute.

Yarrow, Liv

    2006   "Lucius Mummius and the Spoils of Corinth." *Scripta Classica Israelica* 25: 57–70.

Zanker, Paul

    1995   *The Mask of Socrates: The Image of the Intellectual in Antiquity*. Translated by Alan Shapiro. Sather Classical Lectures 59. Berkeley: University of California Press.

Zetzel, J. E. G.

    1977   Review of *Backgrounds to Augustan Poetry: Gallus, Elegy, and Rome*, by David O. Ross. *Classical Philology* 72/3: 249–60.

Zetzel, James E. G.

    1983   "Re-Creating the Canon: Augustan Poetry and the Alexandrian Past." *Critical Inquiry* 10: 83–105.

9

ENTERING OTHER WORLDS:
GATES, RITUALS, AND COSMIC JOURNEYS
IN SUMERIAN SOURCES

*Deena Ragavan, The Oriental Institute**

Introduction

In 1909, Arnold van Gennep published his foundational work, *The Rites of Passage*, analyzing the patterns of the transitional rituals that punctuate human lives, including those surrounding birth, marriage, and death. In the course of this work, he correlated the shift in social status with the spatial movement that formed an integral part of many of these rituals, assessing the symbolism of doorways, which often featured prominently, thus:

> The door is the boundary between the foreign and the domestic worlds in the case
> of the ordinary dwelling, between the profane and the sacred worlds in the case of
> the temple. Therefore to cross the threshold is to unite oneself with a new world.
> (van Gennep [1909] 1960, p. xx)

Although his analysis may be dated, the symbolism of the gate remains a worthy, and to-date under-studied, topic for consideration in the context of Sumerian tradition.

The doors and gateways of Sumerian temples and cities were visually distinctive, monumental structures, marking and enabling the passage between one space and another. Their appearance in the mythology, especially as part of divine itineraries, and their occurrence in cult practice suggest that movement through the gate may symbolize the transition from one part of the cosmos to another. This paper addresses the function and meaning of gates, with a particular focus on the Sumerian tradition in the literary and administrative texts from the late third and early second millennium B.C.E.[1] Through close examination of these

---

* Some of the ideas presented here are greatly expanded and revised from a small section of my dissertation (Ragavan 2011, pp. 206–12). I am very grateful to John Brinkman, Gertrud Farber, Andrea Seri, Piotr Steinkeller, Irene Winter, and Chris Woods for commenting on various drafts of this paper. Assessment of the Ur III sources was considerably facilitated by the use of the Database of Neo-Sumerian Texts (http://bdts.filol.csic.es/) and the Cuneiform Digital Library Initiative (http://www.cdli.ucla.edu/). Unless otherwise noted, translations generally follow, or are modified from, the standard text editions. The names and full bibliographic details for
the Sumerian literary sources generally follow Cunningham 2007. Any errors, naturally, are my own.

[1] The bulk of the Sumerian literary material discussed here comes to us from copies made in the Old Babylonian period (ca. 1900–1600 B.C.E.), whereas the administrative documents on which I focus date to the preceding Ur III period (ca. 2112–2004 B.C.E.). The idea that some of this literary material does reflect or reproduce earlier traditions relies in part on the few surviving manuscripts that do date to the late third millennium, as well as the cumulative evidence that Mesopotamian religion showed remarkable continuity over time in many respects. Nevertheless, the

various sources, I aim to question the extent to which these mythological journeys may correlate with ritual movement, similarly punctuated by stops at the actual gates that permitted
access through city, precinct, and temple walls.

Gates in Cosmology and Mythology

The Sumerian cosmos comprised heaven (*an*) above and earth (*ki*) below. Below the surface of the earth lay the *abzu*, the underground waters and the netherworld, Sumerian *kur*,
also meaning mountain. Mesopotamian cosmology postulated the existence of cosmic gates,
situated in the mountains visible on the horizon to the east and to the west.[2] These were the
gates of heaven, used primarily by the sun god Utu (Akkadian Šamaš), but through which
the celestial bodies — the moon, the stars, the planets — would pass to enter and exit the
skies. Although direct reference to these gates is scarce, textual mentions of the mechanisms
associated with physical gates are found as early as the Ur III period (ca. 2112–2004 B.C.E.).[3]
The eastern gate of heaven enables the entrance of the sun into the visible sky; through the
western gate, the sun sets and passes through the netherworld, realm of the dead, before
returning once again to the world above. Images of these gates are known from Old Akkadian
cylinder seals depicting the sun god stepping through a gateway.

Several Sumerian myths dealing with journeys to the netherworld from the surface of
the earth indicate that the entrance to the netherworld is marked by a gate or gatehouse.[4]
Most notably, the myth of Inana's Descent describes the journey of the goddess to the netherworld, in order, she claims, to witness the funerary rites of her sister's husband. After making
the decision to leave, the narrative first recounts how she abandoned each of her earthly
cult centers and gathered her divine powers and raiments before setting out. On the way,
she dismisses her vizier, Ninšubur, whom she has instructed to perform laments on Inana's
behalf. Then she approaches the gate of the netherworld and hails the gatekeeper (Inana's
Descent, lines 73–76; Sladek 1974).

The myth is normally understood to depict the movement of the goddess in her astral
form, the planet Venus, which, in the course of its natural orbit, dips below the horizon.[5] As
she encounters them, the gates of the netherworld, just like the cosmic gates of sunrise and
sunset, clearly mark the boundary between the earth's surface and the netherworld.

In Inana's Descent, the name given to the entrance to the netherworld is "palace Ganzer"
(*e₂-gal ganzer*).[6] This is also the name of the gate outside which Gilgameš sits and cries in the

---

possibility of innovation, motivated by social or political change between periods (most clearly marked
by the shift in the usage of Sumerian to Akkadian
for administrative documents between the Ur III to
the Old Babylonian periods) should be held in mind.
Contemporary material written in Akkadian, as well
as useful parallels from later eras of Mesopotamian
history, may also be drawn upon, should they serve
to illuminate the often opaque religious traditions.

[2] For detailed presentation of the evidence, see
Heimpel 1986; Horowitz 1998, pp. 266–67; Polonsky
2002, pp. 216ff.; Steinkeller 2005. On the horizon, see
Woods 2009.

[3] As in one Ur III personal name: **ur-si-gar-an-na-
ka** "The-one-of/Dog-of-the-bolt-of-heaven" (AUCT I
461 obv. 3). References to gods opening, or functioning as, the "bolt" (giš**sigar**) of these doors/gates are
more common than reference to the gate itself.

[4] In general, see Horowitz 1998, pp. 358–59; for the
Sumerian evidence, see Katz 2003, pp. 192–94.

[5] Alster 1974, pp. 28–29; Wilcke 1976; Heimpel 1982;
Katz 2003, pp. 95–98; Cooley 2008. Other interpretations are also offered, including that of Buccellati
(1982), for which see below.

[6] On the term "Ganzer," see Steinkeller, forthcoming;
Veldhuis 2003, p. 3; Katz 2003, pp. 85–91; Horowitz
1998, pp. 287–88.

myth of Gilgameš, Enkidu, and the Netherworld, where it again indicates the border between the worlds of the living and the dead.[7] The term also appears, although without clear reference to the netherworld, in the myth Inana and Enki, which describes the goddess's journey to Eridu, where she steals the divine powers (me) from her father, Enki. After she returns to Uruk, Inana grants several place names, one of which is "The house Ganzer was built."[8]

A comparable example appears in the myth of Enlil and Ninlil (Behrens 1978), which describes the banishment of the god Enlil to the netherworld following a sexual encounter with the goddess Ninlil. The goddess nevertheless follows him on his journey, continuing to have sex with him as he adopts different disguises, and after each encounter, giving birth to another deity. Their first meeting after his arrest takes place at the gate of the city of Nippur, where the goddess conceives Nergal, the male ruler of the netherworld (Enlil and Ninlil, lines 54–65).[9] Katz observes that this may imply "that the gate symbolized the dividing line between the Nippur of the living and the realm of the dead. Though Enlil and Ninlil does not name the city-gate ganzer, it provides a functional parallel."[10] This idea is supported by two further texts, which characterize the grave as the gate to the netherworld. The Death of Dumuzi describes the grave as "a great door" preventing ascension from the netherworld,[11] while another text, concerned with evil demons emerging from the same location, states that "in the grave the gate is open for them."[12] These examples, then, utilize the image of the gate as a symbol of the border between the worlds of the living and the dead.[13]

Although the myth of Inana and Enki does not describe a netherworld journey, despite the mention of the term ganzer, other elements may be relevant here. The final stop upon the goddess's return to Uruk is the gate of her Gipar-shrine, which is the entrance to her inner chamber (Inana and Enki II iv 56–57). The term used for the latter is agrun, which is most

---

[7] abul ganzer igi-kur-ra-ka dur$_2$ im-ma-ni-in-gar / ^{d}bil$_3$-ga-mes ir$_2$ im-ma-an-pa$_3$ sig$_7$-sig$_7$ im-ĝa$_2$-ĝa$_2$ "At the gate of Ganzer, in front of the netherworld, he sat down. Gilgameš wept, he was sobbing ..." (Gadotti 2005, p. 310, lines 167–68).

[8] e$_2$ ga-an-ze$_2$-er ba-du$_3$ mu-še$_3$ ba-an-sa$_4$ (Inana and Enki II vi 41 = Farber-Flügge 1973, p. 60). See also: ibid., pp. 92–94, 220; Alster 1974, pp. 25–26 and Katz 2003, pp. 85–86. It is uncertain that this toponym can be reasonably identified with the entrance of the netherworld, usually written ganzer(igi.kur.za) or ganzer$_3$(igi.kur), but in Inana and Enki spelled phonetically: ga-an-ze$_2$-er. Compare the spelling given in lexical lists, e.g., Diri Nippur 138: ga-an-ze$_2$-er = igi.kur.za = da-ni-n[a] (MSL 15, 16). This spelling could suggest a verbal form; Alster suggests "let me get away!" (1974, pp. 25–26), but it is worth noting that the verbal root ze$_2$-er or zi.r "destroy, tear out, remove" is the same used to describe how Inana is stripped of her accoutrements as she enters the gates of the netherworld.

[9] Ninlil's temple, where Enlil is arrested, is called ki-ur$_3$, which means "foundation." This title frequently appears in conjunction with the epithet ki-gal, also a term for "foundation," but literally, "great place," and another name for the netherworld (as in the

name of the ruler of the netherworld: Ereškigal (ereš-ki-gal). A lexical list gives the equation ki-ur$_3$-ra = ni-ri-ib KI-tim "entrance to the netherworld" (Antagal G: 19 + 22 = MSL 17).

[10] Katz 2003, p. 45, n. 114; see also, ibid., p. 38, and Selz 1995.

[11] urugal$_2$ ig gal-am$_3$ igi-ĝa$_2$ ba-an-gub ur$_5$ nu-mu-un-da-e$_{11}$ "The grave is a great door; it stands in front of me, it (the grave) does not let me ascend" (Death of Dumuzi, line 41).

[12] Udughul A vii 47–49: a-ra-li-a giri$_3$ [mu]-⌈un-ne⌉-e-gar / ⌈urugal-la⌉ ka$_2$ mu-⌈un⌉-ne-⌈e⌉-gal$_2$ / abul ^{d}utu šu$_2$-a-še$_3$ e$_3$-meš "In Arali (the netherworld) the path is laid out for them / In the grave the gate is open for them. (The demons) went out the main gate toward the sunset" (Geller 1985, p. 34, lines 250–52).

[13] This function is not reserved exclusively for gates, however, as other myths also have boundaries marked by natural features, particularly rivers, as in the myth of Ningišzida's Journey to the Netherworld (Jacobsen and Alster 2000). The myth Enlil and Ninlil also has Enlil cross a river as part of his journey after he has exited the gate of Nippur (Enlil and Ninlil, line 93).

often applied in myth to the inner sanctum of the sun god, Utu (Heimpel 1986, pp. 128–29). As the place where the sun spends the night, it could, by extension, allude to the nether-world (Caplice 1973).[14] The *agrun* also appears in yet another tale of Inana, that of Inana and Šukaletuda (Volk 1995), in which the goddess again leaves behind her cities to travel to the kur. This part of the myth is unfortunately quite poorly preserved, but it may be the location of the garden where Inana lies down to rest at the end of her journey (Alster 1974, p. 30).

In both Inana's Descent and Enlil and Ninlil the gate to the netherworld and the city gate of Nippur respectively are just one stop on a longer itinerary, in both cases destined for the netherworld. In Inana's Descent, the entrance to the netherworld is the final stop after Inana abandons her seven cult cities.[15] On her return journey in Inana and Enki, she travels from Eridu, stopping seven times, her journey then culminates in Uruk, where she goes first to the Gate of Joy (II iv 29–32) before proceeding to the gate of her shrine.[16]

In order to enter the netherworld, which is envisioned as a walled city, Inana must pass through a series of seven gates; at each gate she is required to give up an item of jewelry or clothing, in order to gain access. She is thus stripped of her powers until finally she is naked, vulnerable, and eventually lifeless. The text Ur-Namma A (Flückiger-Hawker 1999, pp. 93–182), a literary description of the death of the founder of the Ur III dynasty, also implies seven gates when he gives gifts to seven gatekeepers as part of the funeral.[17]

Two additional examples are not explicitly connected with the netherworld: the myth How Grain Came to Sumer recounts the decision of Ninazu to go to the netherworld/moun-tain (kur) and includes his idea to begin this journey by going to "Utu of the seventy doors."[18] This may indicate Utu's position at the gate of the netherworld, or at least the gate which the sun god passed through by night (Katz 2010, p. 112 n. 18). The roughly contemporary Old Babylonian epic of Etana, which recounts in Akkadian the mythical king's flight to heaven on the back of an eagle, mentions in its introductory lines that "full seven gates were bolted against the hero."[19]

It is possible that the Mesopotamian conception of the entrance to the netherworld as having seven gates is dependent mainly on the text of Inana's Descent.[20] This convention is certainly in evidence throughout the later Akkadian literature dealing with the netherworld

---

[14] The term is closely associated with *abzu*, the un-derground cosmic waters, domain of Enki and by-name for his temple in Eridu (Cunningham 1997, p. 12; Woods 2009, p. 200, n. 67).

[15] There is some variation among the manuscripts for these lines, with one adding seven extra cities, while two sources abbreviate the list to her main cult centers, Uruk and Zabalam (Sladek 1974, pp. 183–86). A parallel may be seen in the prologue to Inana and Šukaletuda, although the text following the mention of her temples in Uruk and Zabalam is lost and by the time we can resume the narrative, the story has moved on to describe an encounter between Enki and a raven. On this itinerary, see Buccellati 1982, pp. 3–5; Katz 2003, pp. 254–56.

[16] On the geographic setting of this route, see Jacob-sen 1960, p. 181.

[17] ⌈i₃-du₈⌉ g[al] ⌈kur⌉-ra imin-bi niĝ₂-ba ba-ab-šum₂-mu "He gives gifts to the seven great gate-keepers of the netherworld" (Ur-Namma A, line 76).

[18] How Grain Came to Sumer, line 31: ᵈutu ᵍⁱˢig 70-am₃.

[19] Translation after Foster 2005, p. 535 = Old Babylo-nian version, I/A 10. On the various interpretations of this line, see Foster 2005, p. 535 n. 3 and, earlier, Lambert 1980, pp. 81–82. Etana appears as a help-er (a₂-dah) and gatekeeper in the netherworld in Elegy on the Death of Nanaya, line 97 (Kramer 1960; Sjöberg 1983) and an Old Babylonian Hymn to Utu (Cohen 1977, p. 14, lines 78–79).

[20] The seven gatekeepers mentioned in Ur-Namma A here being derived from Inana's Descent; see Katz 2003, p. 124 n. 32; and Flückiger-Hawker 1999, p. 171: "This line appears to be a contamination of that ver-sion [of Inana's Descent], or another tradition."

— most obviously in the Akkadian counterpart to Inana's Descent, Ištar's Descent, and the myth Nergal and Ereškigal, the latter showing the strong influence of its predecessors.[21]

It is not clear whether the gate to the netherworld and the gates of heaven were identified, although they both fulfilled an equivalent function. In Nergal and Ereškigal, the entries to heaven and the netherworld are clearly separate, with movement between the two via the ascension of a staircase, which reached the Gate of Anu, Enlil, and Ea (Nergal and Ereškigal (late version), lines 13′–14′). The Nineveh version of the Etana myth does contain a numerical parallel, where the eagle relates passing through the gate of Anu, Enlil, and Ea, and then the gate of Sin, Šamaš, Adad, and Ištar (Etana [Nineveh version] III/B 3–6) — seven gods in total.[22]

The conception of a gatehouse with seven gates is inconsistent with the typical Mesopotamian city gate, which would feature only up to three (Katz 2003, p. 192). The famous Ištar gate of Babylon, for example, comprised two gateways, the outer gate smaller than the second, inner one. The thickness of most of these walls meant that monumental gateways did not allow simply a step or two to pass from one area to the next, but formed dark passageways, or were viewed as significant buildings in their own right, as in the case of E-dubla-mah at Ur, the gatehouse providing access to the ziggurat court.

Dina Katz has argued against any architectural significance for the number, asserting instead that the sequence held "an important literary function" allowing the gradual removal of Inana's powers and amplifying the narrative tension (Katz 2003, pp. 192–93; 2005, p. 82 n. 93).[23] The recurrence of the number seven as a typological feature explains the correlation between the number of stops Inana makes en route to Uruk in Inana and Enki, and the number of cities she abandons in Inana's Descent, as well as the number of gates at the entrance to the netherworld.[24] The seven stops do not represent a realistic itinerary, but hold further meaning.

It is worth emphasizing the plurality of gates in a Mesopotamian city. Within the bounds of the city wall lay another enclosed space: the sacred precinct, wherein the temples of the city stood. This area too was typically walled and accessed by numerous different gateways. The sacred precinct contained numerous buildings, including temples as well as other cultic facilities, but was typically dominated by the main shrine of the god of the city. This was his/

---

[21] The Akkadian myth Nergal and Ereškigal is known in its earliest version from the Middle Babylonian period (in general, see Pettinato 2000; for English translation, Foster 2005, pp. 506–24 with detailed bibliography and references there). In the course of the story, the god Nergal stations fourteen gods at gates (lines 66–73). Although the text clearly uses the term *bābu* "gate, entrance," it is possible that the number refers to the doors or door leaves, and each god is being stationed at either side of the gate, in the usual manner of the sculpted gateway guardians. Alternatively, each gateway, as noted earlier, contained an inner and outer gate, and both the whole and the parts could be defined in the same manner (Novotny 1999, esp. p. 28 n. 15, on the latter theory). In the late version, access is provided through seven gates clearly mentioned (i 20–26; iii 38′–44′).

For other Akkadian-language texts featuring, or implying, seven netherworld gates, see Horowitz 1998, pp. 358–59; note particularly: An Address of Marduk to the Demons (p. 356) and Utukku Lemnutu V 62–63 (Geller 2007); both texts are part of the magical literature dealing with exorcising demons.

[22] See Sanders 1999, pp. 81ff. and n. 58, where he observes that rather than "single gates devoted to multiple gods; we must have here an instance of a contextually plural *nomen regens* with singular morphology (cf. *GAG* §64l)."

[23] Also: Katz (1995) arguing that the need for Inana to undress in the myth is also a narrative device and does not represent the tradition of the dead being naked.

[24] Ferrara raised the question of a possible relationship, "apart from the obviously toponymic one," between these myths (1978, p. 354).

her house (Sumerian e₂), which was not just a single structure, but a walled estate, whose gateways typically led into an open court in which stood the main temple. The example of the Ištar gate, noted above, was just one of eight gates that enabled access to the inner city, raising the possibility that the sequence in Inana's Descent describes a circumambulation rite, or other type of ritual procession.[25]

The symbolism of the number seven in Near Eastern literature is widely attested (Reinhold 2008). In myth, it is often applied to groups of divine beings, typically those who assist or accompany major deities, as well as demons (CAD S s.v. *sibittu*; KAR 142).[26] These divine or demonic groups frequently occur in magical texts, especially incantations against demons. Several Sumerian examples of such incantations also utilize the number seven or sevenfold repetition to mark divisions of the cosmos, particularly seven heavens (an) and seven earths (ki) (Horowitz 1998, pp. 208–20). There is little evidence outside of the magical literature for the existence of seven heavens and earths,[27] although lexical texts do indicate the equation of the number seven with the Akkadian term *kiššatu* "all, totality,"[28] which may mean that it is a way to convey a large, complete, or innumerable unit. Sanders, however, suggests that "[t]his operation seems to be a device of ritual language whereby an anonymous cluster of objects is transformed into a sharply defined and unified group. This would explain why it is only in texts with strong ritual associations that parts of the cosmos are divided into seven" (Sanders 1999, p. 236). If the number seven is a feature of magical language, it may therefore have ritual or magical significance when it occurs in mythological texts. This value may be due to the lunar calendar, with the connection between seven-day periods and the performance of purification rituals and offerings (Cunningham 1997, p. 26).

As observed above, a common interpretation of the myths of Inana (Inana's Descent, Inana and Enki, Inana and Šukaletuda) has been that they depict the celestial movements of the planet Venus, and that any ritual journey associated with the myth was secondary: an earthly reflection of the goddess's cosmic travels. Nevertheless, it is clear that the texts incorporate some very strong ritual elements.

The most relevant passage in this context describes the lament that Inana's vizier, Ninšubur, is instructed to perform before the gods Enlil, Nanna, and Enki on behalf of her mistress:

> When I have gone to the netherworld,
> Perform the laments for me on the mounds,
> Play the šem₃-instrument for me in the assembly,
> Go around the temples of the gods for me!
> Scratch your eyes for me, scratch your nose for me!
> Scratch at your upper thighs, the secret place, for me!

---

[25] See further below and Gabbay, this volume.

[26] These groupings appear in several of the myths previously discussed: the gods who seize Enlil in Enlil and Ninlil are "the fifty great gods and the seven gods who decree the destinies" (lines 56–57: dingir-gal-gal ninnu-ne-ne / dingir nam-tar-ra imin-na-ne-ne); the Anunakene, who pass judgment on Inana in the netherworld, are its "seven judges" (Inana's Descent, line 167); the demons who seize Dumuzi as a substitute for Inana in the netherworld (Inana's

Descent, lines 351–52). Groups of seven appear in the earliest literature, both Sumerian and Semitic, from the Early Dynastic III (ca. 2500 B.C.E.) (Cunningham 1997, pp. 20, 25–26).

[27] Horowitz points to much later Hebrew and Arabic traditions that seem to echo this formulation, but finds no direct evidence in the Mesopotamian material (1998, pp. 216–18).

[28] Nabnitu XIV 32–36 (= MSL 16 135); *RA* 16, 166 ii 24 and dupl. CT 18 29 ii 19 (after CAD K s.v. *kiššatu* A).

Like one who has nothing, dress in a single garment for me,
Alone [set] your foot in the Ekur, the temple of Enlil!

When you have entered the Ekur, the temple of Enlil,
Make a lament before Enlil:
"[Father] Enlil, don't let anyone subdue your child in the netherworld,
Don't let your precious metal be mixed in the dirt of the netherworld
Don't let your precious lapis lazuli be split with the mason's stone
Don't let your boxwood be chopped up there with the carpenter's lumber."
(Inana's Descent, lines 33–46)

The first part of Ninšubur's instructions correlates to known ritual practices, specifically, lamentation rites associated with both funerary and divine cults. Both the playing of the šem₃-instrument and the circumambulation (niĝin) of temples are well attested in connection with the performance of laments (er₂) (Heimpel 1998; Gabbay 2011; Gabbay, this volume).[29] The commands to mutilate her face and body and to dress in rags are common to other myths dealing with mourning (Alster 1983).

The lament that Ninšubur is to recite compares the killing of Inana to the destruction of precious metals, wood, and stone. These lines are clearly intended to describe the goddess, but mention materials used in the manufacture of divine statues (Buccellati 1982, p. 5; George 1985). Buccellati (1982) raised the possibility that Inana's Descent was inspired by ritual practice, specifically, the destruction and renewal of a cult statue. The earthly stops would then represent the progress of the statue prior to its destination, where the statue was ritually stripped and destroyed, just like the goddess as she passes through the gates of the netherworld. Although the evidence for such a ritual procession is limited,[30] it is feasible that, just as cult statues could be born, they could also die.[31]

Rather than as an account of destruction, it may be feasible to read the items of clothing and jewelry that Inana gives up at each gate in the context of funerary ritual.[32] The literary

---

[29] Indeed, the Eršema (er₂-šem₃-ma "laments of the šem₃-instrument") is a name given to a specific genre of prayer, which was written in a Sumerian dialect known as Emesal, which is closely associated with both lamentations and the goddess Inana (Cohen 1981; 1988, pp. 11–15).

[30] One issue with this proposal is the absence of any mention of Nergal or his cult center, Kutha, from the Sumerian text. In contrast, the Akkadian version equates the netherworld with the city of Kutha when the gatekeeper admits Ištar through the first gate (lines 40–41). Ereškigal, queen of the netherworld and sister of Inana, is the only one featured, and it is likely that Nergal did not supplant her until a later period (Katz 2003, pp. 385–89, 404–20). There is the possibility that the destination was Ereškigal's cult city, but her cult is scarcely attested. One example of offerings to her, alongside her son, Ninazu, is known from pre-Sargonic Lagaš (DP 51 obv. ii 6–iii 5) and just one reference to the construction of a temple for her is known from an inscription of Lu-UTU, ruler of Umma in the Old Akkadian period (RIME/2.11.6.2

and discussion in Katz 2003, pp. 352–55). She does receive gifts and offerings in a funerary context: a sacrificial sheep in the Ur III period occurs as part of the rites for the deceased Šu-Suen (YBC 4190 rev. i 21; see further below) and various items in the funeral of Ur-Namma, according to the literary description, at least (Ur-Namma A, lines 97–101).

[31] The usual verb in Sumerian for the production of a statue is tu.d "to give birth," e.g., Gudea Statue A iii 2–3: alan-na-ni-še₃ "he fashioned it [diorite] into his statue." On the fashioning and consecration of the divine cult statue, see in general Walker and Dick 2001 and especially ibid., pp. 5–6, for the early periods; on these rituals as analogy to birth, see Boden 1998, pp. 170ff.; for the repair of a damaged statue: TuL 27 (Walker and Dick 2001, pp. 228ff.). Note that the removal of a statue for repair was accompanied by ritual laments and mourning (Boden 1998, pp. 139–40); see also Hurowitz 2003, pp. 155–56.

[32] An alternative and much later parallel may be seen in the first-millennium Babylonian New Year's Festival, in the course of which the king is divested

account of the funerary of Ur-Namma (Ur-Namma A) describes the burial of the king and the accompanying rites, although in sometimes opaque literary language. Following the burial, the text recounts Ur-Namma's journey to the netherworld (Ur-Namma A, lines 72–75), his arrival, and welcome (lines 76–83) before the elaborate offerings to gods (lines 84–131), including both gifts of objects, food offerings, and animal sacrifices.[33] The deities who receive these offerings are specifically chthonic deities,[34] among them Ereškigal. Several of the items offered are also found among the articles relinquished by Inana, including garments, her pin, and her symbols of power (Katz 1995, p. 223). It is quite likely, however, that whoever wrote down Ur-Namma A was acquainted with the text of Inana's Descent, based on other allusions.[35] In addition, the items offered to Ereškigal are known from several other literary sources.[36]

Ur-Namma's arrival at the netherworld is not stated outright but is signaled in the text by his presentation of gifts to the seven gatekeepers (Ur-Namma A, line 76). The nature of these gifts is not explicit, but the use of the term nig$_2$-ba (Akkadian *qīštu*) "gift, votive offering" suggests that these are objects, rather than animal sacrifices or food offerings, consistent with Inana's Descent. It seems that these gifts, along with the subsequent offerings to particular chthonic gods, are the grave goods to be placed in the tomb of the deceased (Katz 2003, p. 334; George 2003, vol. 1, pp. 488–89). The implication, then, is that at the grave (which, according to some texts, is the gate of the netherworld), gifts are required to gain entry.

Gates in the Ur III Cult

The need for especial protection at gates and doors is evident from the practice of placing apotropaic figures, particularly lions and bulls, at entrances as freestanding statues, terra-cotta reliefs, and as decorations on or around the doors. Such sculpted guardians are well known from the royal palaces of the first millennium B.C.E., but the tradition is clearly a long-standing one (e.g., Huxley 2000, pp. 119–22).[37] Literary descriptions provide further attestations for the importance of these figures.[38] The hymn to the chthonic goddess Nungal,

---

of his insignia prior to spending the night in a ritual prison. On this rite and particularly this prison structure as representative of the netherworld, see Ambos 2010 and Ambos, this volume.

[33] Analysis of text follows Flückiger-Hawker 1999, p. 95.

[34] Ur-Namma A, lines 84–131, with specific mention of Nergal, Gilgameš, Ereškigal, Dumuzi, Namtar, Hušbisag (Namtar's wife), Ningišzida, Dimmekug, Ninazimua (wife of Ningišzida); compare also with the gods receiving offerings in other literary accounts of funerary proceedings: Death of Gilgameš, Elegy on the Death of Nanaya, and the Epic of Gilgameš (George 2003, vol. 1, pp. 487–90; Katz 2003, pp. 357 ff.; Wilcke 1970, pp. 82 ff.).

[35] E.g., Ur-Namma A, lines 76, 97, 151–52 (Flückiger-Hawker 1999, p. 172, note to lines 85–86).

[36] Flückiger-Hawker 1999, pp. 173–74, note to line 98.

[37] For the sculptural evidence from the third and second millennia B.C.E., see Braun-Holzinger 1999, pp. 154 ff.

[38] Rim-Sin F, lines 9–12, describes the design of the gate, with a sun-disc at the top and to the right and left a bison (Brisch 2007, p. 229); Keš Temple Hymn, line 92, places a recumbent lion at its gate, and line 95 has a bull on the bolt of the door (Wilcke 2006, p. 232); Ur-Namma B, line 24, describing the rebuilding of the Ekur, states that "the Anzû bird has spread its talons" over the gates of the temple complex (Flückiger-Hawker 1999, p. 191); Lament for Eridu, kirugu 3:1 refers to one of the city gates as "lion-faced" (Green 1978, pp. 134–35 and 148, esp. n. 24); snakes appear on the gate of the temple of Ištaran at Der (Temple Hymns, lines 417–18) and an Old Babylo-

for example, has a lengthy description of the fearsome gate of her temple, featuring mythical beasts, scorpions, lions, eagles, and snakes (Nungal A, lines 13–24).[39]

The rituals associated with the installation of these figures are not well documented for the earlier periods, but first-millennium texts do provide detailed instructions on the placement and type of various apotropaic figurines, as well as the appropriate accompanying incantations (Wiggermann 1992, pp. 58–64). Of interest here is the fact that the twin gods situated on either side of the gate, Meslamtaea and Lugalirra, are both chthonic deities (ibid., p. 59).[40] The tradition of gods associated with the netherworld standing guard at gateways is reflected in the myth of Adapa, which features Dumuzi and Gizzida as the doorkeepers of "Anu's gate."[41]

The need for such protection might be explained by the possibility of evil demons or other dangers lurking in doorways or sneaking into houses through unguarded doors and windows. This fear is widely attested in the Akkadian magical literature:[42] one incantation against the bite of a dog, for example, describes the animal as "crouched at the threshold."[43] Incantations against Lamaštu, a female demon linked to the death of infants, especially in childbirth, relate how she goes along or blocks "the gate of the child," here likely a reference to the vulva, or birth canal.[44] One incantation in particular describes the role of the twin gods driving her out through the window and past the door socket,[45] while another explicitly states that she enters through the "door of the house."[46]

Given the potential dangers lurking in gates and doors and the prophylactic measures taken against them, it is not surprising then that passage through gates also required special procedures. An extant Old Babylonian prayer indicates that it was intended to be recited for the well-being of the king as he entered the city gate of Ur.[47] The possibly third-millennium

nian Naram-Sin inscription describes the installation of inscribed snakes at the door to the court of the temple of Erra in Kutha (Erra and Naram-Sin, lines 48–49 = Westenholz 1997, pp. 198–99).

[39] The hymn Nungal A (Sjöberg 1973) describes the temple of the goddess as a prison — indeed, the name of her temple, E-kur, is a term for prison in a late text (Maul 1988, no. 57 rev. 6; after Civil 1993, p. 75 n. 6) — but the image that is presented is clearly very similar to that of the netherworld. In this case, at least, the entrance to the temple is the entrance to the netherworld. On the Nungal hymn, the E-kur, the prison, and the netherworld, see Sjöberg 1973; Frymer 1977; Hallo 1979, 1985; Civil 1993; and Heimpel 1996b.

[40] The pairing of these two gods can be dated at least to the early second millennium B.C.E. based on a hymn to the two together, Ibbi-Suen B (Sjöberg 1972; Katz 2003, p. 424). Tintir, the detailed topographical listing of the shrines and structures of Babylon, probably from the late second millennium, indicates the existence of 180 stations (*manzāzu*, standing places for divine statues) of the gods Lugalirra and Meslamtaea throughout Babylon (Tintir V 86). It is possible that many of these were situated at gateways across the city. A. R. George remarks on the often demonic character of the gods occupying the

city's large number of minor, but also most accessible, shrines. Despite the numbers, few locations are given, although one exception is the shrines of the Asakku demons, seven in number, and mostly situated at temple gates (George 1992, p. 369).

[41] Adapa Fragment B, lines 18–28 and repeated lines 37–55 = Izre'el 2001, pp. 18–19.

[42] Note in particular the first-millennium incantation en₂ ab.ta nam.mu.un.da.ku₄.e.ne ("Incantation: they shall not enter through the opening"), which specifies the gate, the threshold, and various parts of the door as the origin of various malevolent forces (Borger 1969).

[43] OECT 11 4: 5–6; see also YOS 11 20: 7 "[the ... of the thres]hold is [her] station" of the demoness Lamaštu, discussed below.

[44] Farber 1981, pp. 61–62, lines 4–6; YOS 11 19: 6; BIN 2 72.

[45] "Both the (two) gods saw her; they had her go out through the window, they made her slip out past the door socket" (YOS 11 19: 12–14).

[46] "She came in through the gate of the house; she was slipping past the door socket" (BIN 2 72: 6–7).

[47] Rim-Sîn D (Brisch 2007, pp. 203–09; see Brisch's discussion, pp. 62–64 and 208, note to line 7, on abul

literary prayer RBC 2000, which has been interpreted as a petition to enter the netherworld (Veldhuis 2003), reads in part: "may its door ... stand open; may its bolt ... turn around."[48]

Substantial evidence is available for gates both as recipients of offerings and as the focus of other ritual activities in the late third millennium B.C.E. There are several rituals that appear to be primarily associated with festivals involving entering and exiting the temple or city. At Girsu a ritual known as the "bringing out of the milk eaters" (ga-gu₇-e₃-a) featured provisions of oil and dates for the city gates (Sallaberger 1993, pp. 299–300).[49] While this may be a festival for the entry or exit of the young, still suckling flocks, we also find mention of the god Ningišzida, a chthonic god who took a boat ride to the netherworld (Jacobsen and Alster 2000), the shed (ga₂) of his barge, as well as offerings for deceased rulers of the city.[50] The use of oil to ritually anoint gates and door parts is known to have been a common practice (Zettler and Sallaberger 2011, p. 27), but the dates could have been food offerings for the gate itself. Provisions of dates for the temple of Nanna, specifying a gate, the goddess Haia, the "place of the throne," as well as the statue of a dead king (Amar-Suen) are also a feature of a group of texts from Ur.[51]

Also at Girsu, a festival for the goddess Bau features offerings to the city gate upon her return from a journey (Sallaberger 1993, pp. 292–93 on the u₂-šim "fragrant grass/herb" festival). Attestations of ritual journeys of divine statues, indicated by the phrase dingir [PLACE]-še₃ du "the god going to [PLACE]," do not necessarily specify offerings to gates.[52] The same may be said for most festivals for deities exiting and entering their shrines.

It is possible that these offerings in this context are linked to rituals known from later periods for the "Opening of the Gates" (Akkadian *pīt bābi*), which formed a part of the regular cult practice.[53] This ritual of opening was likely a necessary part of the daily cult, to enable its main practitioners to enter the temple first thing in the morning (Linssen 2004, p. 36). The ritual was also a key element in certain specific festivals; the Babylonian *kislimu*[54] ritual, for example, requires the opening of the gate alongside the recitation of a balag-lamentation (Çağirgan and Lambert 1991–1993, pp. 91, 100). From the periphery, Emar in the mid-second millennium B.C.E., we have detailed ritual texts describing the opening and closing of the cemetery gates during the month Abû (Emar 452 and 463; see Fleming 2000, discussion pp.

---

mah as the city-gate of Ur, rather than the gate to the temple complex, contra Charpin 1986, pp. 285ff.).

[48] The prayer has also been understood as a plea for release from prison (Hallo 1985) and even as a love charm (Katz 2004).

[49] The texts typically specify two, three, or four gates by name (abul barag ᵈutu "City Gate of the Chapel of Utu"; abul ᵈba-u₂ "City Gate of Bau"; abul e₂-gal "City Gate of the Palace"; abul ᵈnanše "City Gate of Nanše") or specify the location at the four gates (e.g., ITT 5 6925 obv. 2: abul-4-ba). For this rite as a circumambulation, see Gabbay, this volume.

[50] Ningišzida: Orient 16 103 159 rev. 1; the shed of his barge: ITT 5 6823 obv. 6; deceased rulers, Gudea and Ur-Namma: ITT 5 6823 rev. 1–2.

[51] MVN 13 129; UET 3 105, 111, 133, 139, 142; UET 3 147 has ki-a-nag "libation place" instead of statue;

UET 3 110, 232, and 257 are very similar but with no mention of Amar-Suen (UET 3 257 adds ma₂ šu-nir an-na-ka "the boat of the standard of heaven"); see further Sallaberger 1993, pp. 75ff. UET 3 201 and 218 also describe offerings for the temple of Nanna and its three gates as part of a monthly lunar festival.

[52] Zettler and Sallaberger 2011, esp. p. 3. See also SNAT 409 with offerings in Umma to the "great gate" (obv. i 12: ka₂ gu-la) and the "huge city-gate" (rev. i 22: abul mah) as the god Šara enters the city/temple (Sallaberger 1993, pp. 238 and 243).

[53] See Linssen 2004, pp. 36–39, on the rites in Hellenistic Babylonian, and especially p. 36 n. 79 for bibliography. See also Cohen 1993, pp. 138–40; see CAD B s.v. *bābu* b′ for other Old Babylonian and later rituals at gates.

[54] Named for the ninth month of the calendar; see Langdon 1980, pp. 135ff.

173–95 and edition pp. 280–93). Fleming observes that, "[t]he timing of these offerings alone suggests a focus on the underworld. The 25th to the 27th days cover the last stages of the moon's light and influence .... In Mesopotamian tradition, the 28th and 29th days of every month belong to Nergal and the underworld" (Fleming 2000, p. 186).

Gates do occur as recipients of sacrificial animals as part of long lists of offerings to every part of a temple.[55] By far the most frequent offerings of sacrificial animals for gates, however, are those for the "gate of the shrine" (ka$_2$ eš$_3$)[56] coupled with the gate of the Gipar (ka$_2$ gi$_6$-par$_4$) at Uruk. These offerings were closely associated with the cult of Inana, particularly in her aspect as Nanaya, the planet Venus and the visible manifestation of the goddess in the sky.[57] While this gate received regular offerings (sa-du$_{11}$) as part of the cult,[58] other specific offerings for the gate clearly had to do with disappearance of the goddess (nig$_2$-ki-zah$_3$ "offering for the place of disappearance"); that is, when the visible form of Inana disappeared, it meant the entrance of the goddess into the netherworld (Cohen 1993, pp. 475–76).

Perhaps also connected are certain offerings that were part of lamentation rites for various goddesses linked to netherworld journeys. These rites, known as gi-ra-num$_2$ (Akkadian *gerrānum*), were practiced in the cities of Ur and Uruk (Cohen 1993, pp. 472 ff.). In one instance, a lamentation offering for Inana is expressly said to be provided at the gate.[59] It is possible that this was the assumed location of many of the other offerings of this type, which detail was simply not provided as a matter of course in the often laconic receipts. Other offerings for pairs of goddesses (Annunitum and Ulmašitum; Belat-Suhner and Belat-darraban), who are likely also forms of Inana, also appear and are said to take place "at the gate of Geštinana."[60] Similarly, offerings for the gate of Ninsun, a goddess usually cast as the divine mother of the Ur III rulers, may also relate to the royal funerary cult.[61] These texts seem to deal with a procession from Ur to Ku'ara, and in both cases the gate of Ninsun is the first to receive a sacrifice after the offerings in Ur are completed, that is, the first stop upon reaching Ku'ara. Weiershäuser, however, has recently connected these offerings with the royal funerary cult, which concurs with Geštinana's role in myth as a mourning goddess (2012, pp. 347–56).

---

[55] The gate of Enlil in Nippur appears as a recipient of offerings for every part of the temple complex, but it is also the location of certain statues, particularly those associated with the royal family. See PDT 2 1173; TCL 2 5501; MVN 15 146 and Sallaberger 1993, pp. 98–99, on gate complex as location of statues, and especially BiOr 9 173. See also above, on food offerings of dates for the statue of Amar-Suen.

[56] Although the name of the shrine is not specified, it is most likely the temple of Inana (Sallaberger 1993, p. 212).

[57] For Nanaya as a form of Inana, see Heimpel 1982, pp. 15 ff. and Steinkeller, forthcoming. On these offerings, see Sallaberger 1993, pp. 212 ff.; on the offerings at the gate as part of the Queen's cult, see ibid., p. 220, and Weiershäuser 2008, p. 63–64. Westenholz notes an oracular text (W 19900: 1) that mentions the entrance of Nanaya, possibly into the Eanna temple,

and connects it to a royal hymn which positions Nanaya "at the liminal location of the doorway" (Westenholz 2007, p. 310).

[58] E.g., MVN 18 82.

[59] OIP 115 31 obv. 1–2 has the regular offering of 1 fattened sheep for the lamentation of Inana at the gate of ... .

[60] SAT 2 47 obv. 1–4 has 2 goats for Belat-suhner and Belat-darraban at the gate of Geštinana (for these two goddesses, see Cohen 1993, pp. 136 ff. and 252 ff.; as foreign imports and as the personal goddesses of the Ur III queen, Šulgi-simti, see Sallaberger 1993, p. 19); OIP 115 128 obv. 1–4 has 2 goats for Annunitum and Ulmašitum at the gate of Geštinana.

[61] TCL 2 5514 obv. 16; TCL 2 5482 rev. i 4. For the latter, see Sallaberger 1993, p. 107. AUCT I 488 is also related and all three may be connected to the cult of Geštinana (Weiershäuser 2012, p. 351).

We move now from the funerary cult to the actual burial proceedings. Thanks to detailed monthly expense records, we know a great deal about the funeral of Šu-Suen, one of the Ur III kings (ca. 2037–2029 B.C.E.).[62] As part of the preparations for his burial, a number of animals were offered first to several netherworld gods (Ninazu, Ereškigal, Ninšubur in Enegi, and Ningišzida in Gišbanda) in a boat and then to a series of gates: the great gate of the moon god Nanna; the great gate of the king; … ; the great gate of the throne; the gate of the throne of Šulgi; the gate of the throne of Amar-Suen[63] — the latter two being former kings of Ur. This sequence is part of the second of four rituals, focusing "on the residents of the netherworld and [preparing] for the coming event."[64] That is to say, the sacrifices for the gates prepared the way for the king's burial, his entrance into the netherworld.

Šu-Suen's journey did not end there. One month after his burial, further offerings were made by his successor to a group of netherworld gods including to "Šu-Suen at the gate of Šulgi" and "Šu-Suen at the gate of Utu" as well as to the deified entrance to the netherworld, Ganzer.[65] Steinkeller argues that, "the ritual behind this group of offerings symbolized Šu-Suen's journey through the netherworld to assume his … station in the sky."[66]

These texts show a disparity between the different groups of offerings: the sacrifices as part of the burial having the gates themselves as recipients, while the rites taking place after the funeral give the gates as the location of the offering, which is itself directed at the deceased king.[67] The idea that the gate itself was the intended recipient would not be exceptional; other inanimate objects that constitute focal points of the cult, such as thrones or beds, were also known to receive offerings. It is also feasible that these offerings were in fact directed at the gateway guardians, the sculpted animal, mythical, or divine figures described above, which decorated or were stationed by the gate.[68] Alternatively, the doorkeeper of Enlil, Kalkal,[69] received offerings separate from, although alongside, those for the gate of Enlil (e.g., PDT 2 1173 i 6–7; see Such-Gutiérrez 2003, vol. 1, p. 106).

Of the gates receiving sacrifices as part of the funeral, three are "of the throne," two of which belong to dead kings and one unspecified. These thrones are quite probably a reference to the cult of the dead: it seems that a throne or chair, or seated statue of the deceased, formed the focus of much of the post-burial cult (Katz 2010, pp. 111–12 n. 15; Katz 1999; Sallaberger 1993, pp. 147ff. esp. n. 696; Winter 1992), which included the transport of the throne as part of ritual processions to other cities (Jagersma 2007, p. 298). While these thrones may have been housed in their own building when not on the road (Sallaberger 1993, p. 147 n. 698), it is possible that they, like other statues, were sometimes situated in the gate complex of the temple (ibid., p. 99).

---

[62] YBC 4190+MVN 13 120 (Sigrist 1999; Katz 2007).

[63] YBC 4190 rev. i 20ff. and MVN 13 120 obv. 1′–rev. 2′: 1 sila₄ abul ᵈNanna / 1 maš₂ abul lugal! 1 sila₄ / ᵈNin-giš-zi-da / 1 sila₄ ᵈNin-a-zu / 1 sila₄ abul ᵍᶦˢgu-za / 1 sila₄ ka₂ gu-za ᵈŠul-gi / 1 sila₄ ka₂ gu-za ᵈAmar-ᵈSuen; see Katz 2007, p. 175.

[64] Katz 2007, p. 179.

[65] PDT 1 563 obv. i 9–16.

[66] Steinkeller, forthcoming, and bibliography there on the ascension of dead kings of the Ur III to heaven.

[67] A similar division may be seen between the offerings for goddesses at the gate of Geštinana and offerings for the gates of the Gipar themselves.

[68] Also suggested by Sigrist (1992, p. 176), citing part of Šu-Suen's funerary rites (MVN 13 120).

[69] For Kalkal as the doorkeeper in myth, see Nanna-Suen's Journey, lines 258ff. (Ferrara 1973). In somewhat similar fashion to Inana's Descent, when the moon god, Nanna-Suen, arrives at the gate of Nippur he hails the gatekeeper (lines 258–64), then provides a lengthy list of offerings that he is bringing for Enlil (lines 265–308). See also Sallaberger 1993, pp. 98–105.

The location of statues of dead rulers at gates may have something to do with the association between semi-mythical kings and the entrance of the netherworld.[70] Etana, Gilgameš, and Dumuzi are all semi-mythical kings of Sumer, and all take cosmic journeys. Etana appears in the Elegy to Nanaya alongside NEti, gatekeeper of the netherworld as part of a funerary ritual and as a steward (nu-banda₃) who opens to the door of the netherworld in an Old Babylonian Hymn to Utu (Cohen 1977). In the Hymn to Utu, Etana appears alongside Gilgameš, who is also in the Elegy to Nanaya, as well as among the gods receiving offering as part of Ur-Namma's funerary proceedings.[71] Dumuzi's chthonic associations are well documented, but his position in myth as a former king of Uruk should not be ignored in this regard.[72] "Famous kings who have died" are also recipients of offerings as part of Ur-Namma's funeral, and their attestation in the text immediately following the offerings to the seven nameless gatekeepers of the netherworld could be suggestive (Ur-Namma A, lines 76–77).

Conclusions

In mythology, gates are used to symbolize the boundary between worlds: the visible and the invisible; the human and divine; but most often the worlds of the living and the dead. In some instances, this access was not through a single gate, but through seven — a number with strong ritual and magical overtones. In incantations, seven is used to divide and inventory(?) the cosmos — a usage echoed in the literature for gates and divine itineraries. Other ritual elements in these myths suggest that they reflect, or are reflected in, actual ritual practice, raising a possible correlation between divine journeys and ritual offerings at gates. This is especially true for journeys to the netherworld and literary depictions of funerary practice.

A variety of sources indicate that gates of cities and temples were magically and ritually significant locations, demanding protection against evil influences and necessitating propitiatory measures to enable safe passage. Routine offerings to gates as part of the temple are definitely attested, but it is in specific contexts and part of certain festivals that they occur in larger numbers and as part of a sequence. City and temple gates are typically the focus of ritual activity in rites of entry and egress, but such rites are especially well known for the cults of the various manifestations of Inana, a goddesses whose mythology was concerned primarily with lamentation and journeys to the netherworld. Finally, the funerary rituals of Šu-Suen, king of Ur, demonstrate the importance of offerings to gates as preparation for his burial and entry into the netherworld.

If ritual, as I note in the introduction to this volume, is a performance intended to direct the gaze of its participants, then in this instance, I would argue that these sacrifices and offerings serve to underline the liminal status of the proceedings, emphasizing both movement (from one world to the next) and separation (by marking the boundary). This performance is both reflected and reciprocated in the multiplicity and shape of this particular architectural form, its monumentality (depth and dimension), sculptural decoration, as well as its

---

[70] Note also that the group of offerings from Ur mentioned earlier associate the goddess Haia, the place of the throne, and the statue of the deceased Amar-Suen with the gate of the temple of Nanna.

[71] For NEti, Gilgameš, and Etana in these texts, see now Katz 2003, pp. 376–77.

[72] This is not, however, to give credence to the idea that, after Šulgi ascended to heaven, he became a doorkeeper (i₃-du₈) of the netherworld (Steinkeller, forthcoming; cf. Hallo 1991, pp. 158–59).

attendant mythology. The evidence suggests that the symbolism of the gate as a cosmic boundary in mythology was acknowledged through ritual practice. Above all, sacrifices at gates were necessary for entry (human or divine) into the netherworld.

Abbreviations

AUCT I	Marcel Sigrist, *Neo-Sumerian Account Texts in the Horn Archaeological Museum*. Institute of Archaeology Publications, Assyriological Studies 4. Andrews University Cuneiform Texts I. Berrien Springs: Andrews University Press, 1984.
BIN 2	James B. Nies and Clarence E. Keiser, *Historical, Religious and Economic Texts and Antiquities*. Babylonian Inscriptions in the Collection of James B. Nies 2. New Haven: Yale University Press; Oxford: Oxford University Press, 1920.
BiOr 9	Jacobus Schoneveld, "Der Gott Ki-ZA." *Bibliotheca Orientalis* 9 (1952): 173–72
CAD	A. Leo Oppenheim et al., editors, *The Assyrian Dictionary of the Oriental Institute of the University of Chicago*. Chicago: The Oriental Institute, 1956–2010.
CT 18	E. A. Wallis Budge, *Cuneiform Texts from Babylonian Tablets in the British Museum*, Part 18. London: Trustees of the British Museum, 1964.
DP	M. Allotte de la Fuÿe, *Documents présargoniques*. Paris: E. Leroux, 1908–20.
ITT 5	Henri de Genouillac, *Inventaire des tablettes de Tello*, vol. 5. Paris: E. Leroux, 1921.
KAR	Erich Ebeling, *Keilschrifttexte aus Assur religiösen Inhalts*, Volume 1: *Autographien*. Wissenschaftliche Veröffentlichungen der Deutschen Orient-Gesellschaft 28/3. Leipzig: J. C. Hinrichs, 1919.
MSL 15	Miguel Civil, ed., *The Series DIRI = (w)atru*. Materials for the Sumerian Lexicon 15. Rome: Pontificium Institutum Biblicum, 2004.
MSL 16	Irving L. Finkel, *The Series SIG$_7$.ALAN = Nabnītu*. Materials for the Sumerian Lexicon 16. Rome: Pontificium Institutum Biblicum, 1982.
MSL 17	Antoine Cavigneaux, Hans G. Güterbock, and Martha Roth, *The Series Erim-ḫuš = anantu and An-ta-gál = šaqû*. Materials for the Sumerian Lexicon 17. Rome: Pontificium Istitutum biblicum, 1985.
MVN 13	Marcel Sigrist, David I. Owen, and Gordon D. Young, *The John Frederick Lewis Collection*, Part 2. Materiali per il Vocabolario Neosumerico 13. Rome: Multigrafica Editrice, 1984.
MVN 15	David I. Owen, *Neo-Sumerian Texts from American Collections*. Materiali per il vocabolario Neosumerico 15. Rome: Multigrafica Editrice, 1991.
OECT 11	O. R. Gurney, *Literary and Miscellaneous Texts in the Ashmolean Museum*. Oxford Editions of Cuneiform Texts 11. Oxford: Clarendon Press, 1989.
OIP 115	Marcus Hilgert, *Cuneiform Texts from the Ur III Period in the Oriental Institute 1. Drehem Administrative Documents from the Reign of Šulgi*. Oriental Institute Publications 115. Chicago: The Oriental Institute, 1998.
Orient 16	Tohru Gomi, "Administrative Texts of the Third Dynasty of Ur in the Merseyside County Museums, Liverpool." *Orient: Report of the Society for Near Eastern Studies in Japan* 16 (1980): 1–110.
PDT 1	M. Çığ, H. Kızılyay, and A. Salonen, *Die Puzriš-Dagan-Texte der Istanbuler Archäologischen Museen*, Part 1. Annales Academiae Scientiarum Fennicae 92. Helsinki: Suomalaisen Tiedeakatemia, 1954.
PDT 2	Fatma Yıldız and Tohru Gomi, *Die Puzriš-Dagan-Texte der Istanbuler Archäologischen Museen*, Part 2. Freiburger altorientalische Studien 16. Stuttgart: Franz Steiner Verlag Wiesbaden, 1988.

RA 16	F. Thureau-Dangin, "Un vocabulaire de Koujoundjik." *Revue d'Assyriologie et d'Archéologie Orientale* 16/2 (1919): 165–71.
RIME/2	Douglas Frayne, *Sargonic and Gutian Periods (2334–2113 B.C.)*. The Royal Inscriptions of Mesopotamia, Early Periods 2. Toronto: University of Toronto Press, 1993.
SAT 2	Marcel Sigrist, *Texts from the Yale Babylonian Collections*, Part 1. Sumerian Archival Texts 2. Bethesda: CDL Press, 2000.
SNAT	Tohru Gomi and Susumu Sato, *Selected Neo-Sumerian Administrative Texts from the British Museum*. Abiko: Research Institute Chuo-Gakuin University, 1990.
TCL 2	Henri de Genouillac, *Tablettes de Dréhem*. Texts cunéiformes du Louvre 2. Paris: Librairie Orientale Paul Geuthner, 1973.
UET 3	Léon Legrain, *Ur Excavations, Texts* 3: *Business Documents of the Third Dynasty of Ur.* Publications of the Joint Expedition of the British Museum and of the University Museum, University of Pennsylvania, Philadelphia, to Mesopotamia. London: Harrison & Sons, 1937–1947.
YBC	Tablets in the Babylonian Collection, Yale University Library
YOS 11	J. Van Dijk, A. Goetze, and M. I. Hussey, *Early Mesopotamian Incantations and Rituals*. Yale Oriental Series, Babylonian Texts 11. New Haven: Yale University Press, 1985.

Bibliography

Alster, Bendt

    1974   "On the Interpretation of the Sumerian Myth 'Inanna and Enki.'" *Zeitschrift für Assyriologie und vorderasiatische Archäologie* 64/1: 20–34.

    1983   "The Mythology of Mourning." *Acta Sumerologica* 5: 1–16.

Ambos, Claus

    2010   "Ritual Healing and the Investiture of the Babylonian King." In *The Problem of Ritual Efficacy*, edited by William S. Sax, Johannes Quack, and Jan Weinhold, pp. 17–44. Oxford: Oxford University Press.

Behrens, Hermann

    1978   *Enlil und Ninlil: Ein sumerischer Mythos aus Nippur*. Studia Pohl, Series maior 8. Rome: Biblical Institute Press.

Boden, Peggy Jean

    1998   The Mesopotamian Washing of the Mouth (*mis pi*) Ritual: An Examination of Some of the Social and Communication Strategies which guided the Development and Performance of the Ritual which Transferred the Essence of the Deity into its Temple Statue. Ph.D. dissertation, The Johns Hopkins University.

Borger, R.

    1969   "Die erste Teiltafel der *zi-pà*-Beschwörungen (ASKT 11)." In lišān mithurti: *Festschrift Wolfram Freiherr von Soden zum 19.4.1968 gewidmet von Schülern und Mitarbeitern*, edited by Wolfgang Röllig, pp. 1–23. Alter Orient und Altes Testament 1. Kevelaer: Butzon & Bercker; Neukirchen-Vluyn: Neukirchener Verlag.

Braun-Holzinger, Eva A.

    1999   "Apotropaic Figures at Mesopotamian Temples in the Third and Second Millennia." In *Mesopotamian Magic: Textual, Historical, and Interpretive Perspectives*, edited by Tzvi Abusch and Karel van der Toorn, pp. 149–72. Ancient Magic and Divination 1. Groningen: Styx.

Brisch, Nicole

2007   *Tradition and the Poetics of Innovation: Sumerian Court Literature of the Larsa Dynasty (c. 2003-1763 B.C.E.).* Alter Orient und Altes Testament 339. Münster: Ugarit-Verlag.

Bruschweiler, Françoise

1987   *Inanna: la déesse triomphante et vaincue dans la cosmologie sumérienne; recherche lexicographique.* Les Cahiers du CEPOA 4. Leuven: Peeters.

Buccellati, Giorgio

1982   "The Descent of Inanna as a Ritual Journey to Kutha?" *Syro-Mesopotamian Studies* 4/3: 3–7.

Çağirgan, Galip, and W. G. Lambert

1991–1993   "The Late Babylonian Kislīmu Ritual for Esagil." *Journal of Cuneiform Studies* 43/45: 89–106.

Caplice, Richard

1973   "É.NUN in Mesopotamian Literature." *Orientalia*, n.s., 42: 299–305.

Charpin, Dominique

1986   *Le clergé d'Ur au siècle d'Hammurabi: (XIXᵉ-XVIIIᵉ siècles av. J.-C.).* Paris: Librairie Droz.

Civil, Miguel

1993   "On Mesopotamian Jails and Their Lady Warden." In *The Tablet and the Scroll: Near Eastern Studies in Honor of William W. Hallo,* edited by Mark E. Cohen, Daniel C. Snell, and David B. Weisberg, pp 72–78. Bethesda: CDL Press.

Cohen, Mark E.

1977   "Another Utu Hymn." *Zeitschrift für Assyriologie und vorderasiatische Archäologie* 67/1: 1–19.

1981   *Sumerian Hymnology: The Eršemma.* Hebrew Union College Annual Supplements 2. Cincinnati: Hebrew Union College.

1988   *The Canonical Lamentations of Ancient Mesopotamia.* Potomac: Capital Decisions, Inc.

1993   *The Cultic Calendars of the Ancient Near East.* Bethesda: CDL Press.

Cooley, Jeffrey L.

2008   "Early Mesopotamian Astral Science and Divination in the Myth of Inana and Šukaletuda." *Journal of Ancient Near Eastern Religions* 8/1: 75–98.

Cunningham, Graham

1997   *Deliver Me from Evil: Mesopotamian Incantations, 2500-1500 B.C.* Studia Pohl, Series maior 17. Rome: Pontificio Instituto Biblico.

2007   "A Catalogue of Sumerian Literature." In *Analysing Literary Sumerian: Corpus-based Approaches,* edited by Jarle Ebeling and Graham Cunningham, pp. 351–412. London: Equinox.

Farber, Walter

1981   "Zur älteren akkadischen Beschwörungsliteratur." *Zeitschrift für Assyriologie und vorderasiatische Archäologie* 71: 51–72.

Farber-Flügge, Gertrud

1973   *Der Mythos Inanna und Enki unter besonderer Berücksichtigung der Liste der me.* Studia Pohl 10. Rome: Biblical Institute Press.

Ferrara, A. J.

1973   Nanna-Suen's Journey to Nippur. Studia Pohl, Series maior 2. Rome: Biblical
                Institute Press.

1978   Review of *Der Mythos "Inanna und Enki" unter besonderer Berücksichtigung der Liste
                der me*, by Gertrud Farber-Flügge. *Journal of Near Eastern Studies* 37/4: 350–54.

Fleming, Daniel E.

2000   *Time at Emar: The Cultic Calendar and the Rituals from the Diviner's Archive*. Meso-
                potamian Civilizations 11. Winona Lake: Eisenbrauns.

Flückiger-Hawker, Esther

1999   *Urnamma of Ur in Sumerian Literary Tradition*. Orbis biblicus et orientalis 166.
                Freiburg: University Fribourg Switzerland; Göttingen: Vandenhoeck & Ruprecht.

Foster, Benjamin R.

2005   *Before the Muses: An Anthology of Akkadian Literature*. 3rd edition. Bethesda: CDL
                Press.

Frymer, Tikva Simone

1977   "The Nungal-Hymn and the Ekur-Prison." *Journal of the Economic and Social History
                of the Orient* 20/1: 78–89.

Gabbay, Uri

2011   "Laments in Garšana." In *Garsana Studies*, edited by David I. Owen, pp. 67–74.
                Cornell University Studies in Assyriology and Sumerology. Bethesda: CDL Press.

Gadotti, Alhena

2005   "Gilgameš, Enkidu and the Netherworld" and the Sumerian Gilgameš Cycle.
                Ph.D. dissertation, Johns Hopkins University.

Geller, Markham J.

1985   *Forerunners to Udug-Hul: Sumerian Exorcistic Incantations*. Freiburger altorientali-
                sche Studien 12. Stuttgart: F. Steiner Verlag.

2007   *Evil Demons: Canonical* Utukku lemnutu *Incantations*. State Archives of Assyria
                Cuneiform Texts 5. Helsinki: Neo-Assyrian Text Corpus Project.

George, A. R.

1985   "Observations on a Passage of 'Inanna's Descent.'" *Journal of Cuneiform Studies*
                37/1: 109–13.

1992   *Babylonian Topographical Texts*. Orientalia Lovaniensia Analecta 40. Leuven: De-
                partement Orientalistiek und Uitgeverij Peeters.

2003   *The Babylonian Gilgamesh Epic: Introduction, Critical Edition and Cuneiform Texts*.
                2 volumes. Oxford: Oxford University Press.

Green, M. W.

1978   "The Eridu Lament." *Journal of Cuneiform Studies* 30/3: 127–67.

Hallo, William W.

1979   "Notes from the Babylonian Collection, I: Nungal in the Egal: An Introduction
                to Colloquial Sumerian?" *Journal of Cuneiform Studies* 31/3: 161–65.

1985   "Back to the Big House: Colloquial Sumerian Continued." *Orientalia*, n.s., 54:
                56–64.

1991   "The Death of Kings: Traditional Historiography in Contextual Perspective." In
                *Ah, Assyria ...: Studies in Assyrian History and Ancient Near Eastern Historiography
                Presented to Hayim Tadmor*, edited by Mordechai Cogan and Israel Eph'al, pp.
                148–65. Jerusalem: Magnes Press.

Heimpel, Wolfgang

    1982   "A Catalog of Near Eastern Venus Deities." *Syro-Mesopotamian Studies* 4/3: 10–22.

    1986   "The Sun at Night and the Doors of Heaven in Babylonian Texts." *Journal of Cuneiform Studies* 38/2: 127–51.

    1996a   "The Gates of the Eninnu." *Journal of Cuneiform Studies* 48: 17–29.

    1996b   "The Mountain Within." *Nouvelles Assyriologiques Brèves et Utilitaires* 1996/1: 19.

    1998   "A Circumambulation Rite." *Acta Sumerologica* 20: 13–16.

Horowitz, Wayne

    1998   *Mesopotamian Cosmic Geography.* Mesopotamian Civilizations 8. Winona Lake: Eisenbrauns.

Hurowitz, Victor Avigdor

    2003   "The Mesopotamian God Image, from Womb to Tomb." *Journal of the American Oriental Society* 123/1: 147–57.

Huxley, Margaret

    2000   "The Gates and Guardians in Sennacherib's Addition to the Temple of Assur." *Iraq* 62: 109–37.

Izre'el, Shlomo

    2001   *Adapa and the South Wind: Language Has the Power of Life and Death.* Mesopotamian Civilizations 10. Winona Lake: Eisenbrauns.

Jacobsen, Thorkild

    1960   "The Waters of Ur." *Iraq* 22: 174–85.

Jacobsen, Thorkild, and Bendt Alster

    2000   "Ningišzida's Boat-ride to Hades." In *Wisdom, Gods and Literature: Studies in Assyriology in Honour of W. G. Lambert,* edited by A. R. George and Irving L. Finkel, pp. 315–44. Winona Lake: Eisenbrauns.

Jagersma, Bram

    2007   "The Calendar of the Funerary Cult in Ancient Lagash." *Bibliotheca Orientalis* 64: 289–307.

Katz, Dina

    1995   "Inana's Descent and Undressing the Dead as a Divine Law." *Zeitschrift für Assyriologie und vorderasiatische Archäologie* 85: 221–33.

    1999   "The Messenger, Lulil and the Cult of the Dead." *Revue d'Assyriologie* 93: 107–18.

    2003   *The Image of the Netherworld in the Sumerian Sources.* Bethesda: CDL Press.

    2004   "RBC 2000: Out of Prison, into the Netherworld, or, Perhaps, a Love Charm?" *Jaarbericht van het Vooraziatisch-Egyptisch Genootschap "Ex Oriente Lux"* 38: 71–76.

    2005   "Death They Dispensed to Mankind: The Funerary World of Ancient Mesopotamia." *Historiae* 2: 55–90.

    2007   "Sumerian Funerary Rituals in Context." In *Performing Death: Social Analyses of Funerary Traditions in the Ancient Near East and Mediterranean,* edited by Nicola Laneri, pp. 167–88. Oriental Institute Seminars 3. Chicago: The Oriental Institute.

    2010   "The Naked Soul: Deliberations on a Popular Theme." In *Gazing on the Deep: Ancient Near Eastern and Other Studies in Honor of Tzvi Abusch,* edited by Jeffrey Stackert, Barbara Nevling Porter, and David P. Wright, pp. 107–20. Bethesda: CDL Press.

Kramer, Samuel Noah

    1960   "Death and the Nether World According to the Sumerian Literary Texts." *Iraq* 22: 59–68.

1991   "The Death of Ur-Nammu." In *Near Eastern Studies: Dedicated to H. I. H. Prince Takahito Mikasa on the Occasion of His Seventy-fifth Birthday,* edited by Masao Mori, Hideo Ogawa, and Mamoru Yoshikawa, pp. 193–214. Bulletin of the Middle Eastern Culture Center in Japan 5. Wiesbaden: Harrassowitz.

Lambert, W. G.
1980   "New Fragments of Babylonian Epics." *Archiv für Orientforschung* 27: 71–82.

Langdon, Stephen
1980   *Babylonian Menologies and the Semitic Calendars.* Reprint. The Schweich Lectures of the British Academy 1933. Munich: Kraus-Thomson Organization.

Linssen, Marc J. H.
2004   *The Cults of Uruk and Babylon: The Temple Ritual Texts as Evidence for Hellenistic Cult Practises.* Leiden: Brill; Boston: Styx.

Maul, Stefan M.
1988   *"Herzberuhigungsklagen": Die sumerisch-akkadischen Ersahunga-Gebete.* Wiesbaden: Harrassowitz.

Novotny, Jamie R.
1999   "Were there Seven or Fourteen Gates of the Netherworld?" *Zeitschrift für Assyriologie und vorderasiatische Archäologie* 89: 24–28.

Pettinato, Giovanni
2000   *Nergal ed Ereškigal: il poema assiro-babilonese degli inferi.* Rome: Accademia nazionale dei Lincei.

Polonsky, Janice
2002   The Rise of the Sun-God and the Determination of Destiny in Ancient Mesopotamia. Ph.D. dissertation, University of Pennsylvania.

Ragavan, Deena
2011   The Cosmic Imagery of the Temple in Sumerian Literature. Ph.D. dissertation, Harvard University.

Reinhold, Gotthard G. G., editor
2008   *Die Zahl Sieben im Alten Orient: Studien zur Zahlensymbolik in der Bibel und ihrer altorientalischen Umwelt / The Number Seven in the Ancient Near East: Studies on the Numerical Symbolism in the Bible and Its Ancient Near Eastern Environment.* Frankfurt am Main: Peter Lang.

Sallaberger, Walther
1993   *Der kultische Kalender der Ur III-Zeit.* Untersuchungen zur Assyriologie und vorderasiatischen Archäologie 7. Berlin: Walter de Gruyter.

Sanders, Seth L.
1999   Writing, Ritual and Apocalypse: Studies in the Theme of Ascent to Heaven in Ancient Mesopotamian and Second Temple Judaism. Ph.D. dissertation, Johns Hopkins University.

Selz, Gebhard J.
1995   *Untersuchungen zur Götterwelt des altsumerischen Stadtstaates von Lagash.* Occasional Publications of the Samuel Noah Kramer Fund 13. Philadelphia: University of Pennsylvania Museum.

Sigrist, Marcel
1992   *Drehem.* Bethesda: CDL Press.
1999   "Livraisons et dépenses royales durant la Troisième Dynastie d'Ur." In *Ki Baruch Hu: Ancient Near Eastern, Biblical, and Judaic Studies in Honor of Baruch A. Levine,*

edited by Robert Chazan, William W. Hallo, and Lawrence H. Schiffman, pp. 111–52. Winona Lake: Eisenbrauns.

Sjöberg, Ake W.

1972   "Hymns to Meslamtaea, Lugalgirra and Nanna-Suen in Honour of King Ibbisuen (Ibbisin) of Ur." *Orientalia Suecana* 19–20: 140–78.

1973   "Nungal in the Ekur." *Archiv für Orientforschung* 24: 19–46.

1983   "The First Pushkin Museum Elegy and New Texts." *Journal of the American Oriental Society* 103: 315–20.

2002   "Götterreisen." *Reallexikon der Assyriologie und vorderasiatischen Archäologie* 3: 480–83.

Sladek, William R.

1974   Inanna's Descent to the Netherworld. Ph.D. dissertation, Johns Hopkins University.

Steinkeller, Piotr

2005   "Of Stars and Men: The Conceptual and Mythological Setup of Babylonian Extispicy." In *Biblical and Oriental Essays in Memory of William L. Moran,* edited by Agustinus Gianto, pp. 11–47. Biblica et orientalia 48. Rome: Pontificio Instituto Biblico.

Forthcoming   "How Did Šulgi and Išbi-Erra Ascend to Heaven?"

Such-Gutiérrez, Marcos

2003   *Beiträge zum Pantheon von Nippur im 3. Jahrtausend.* 2 volumes. Materiali per il vocabolario sumerico 9. Rome: Università degli studi di Roma "La Sapienza."

van Gennep, Arnold

(1909) 1960   *Les rites de passage: étude systématique des rites de la porte et du seuil; de l'hospitalité; de l'adoption etc.* Paris: Émile Nourry, 1909. Published in English in 1960 as *The Rites of Passage,* translated by Monika B. Vizedom and Gabrielle L. Caffee. Chicago: University of Chicago Press.

Veldhuis, Niek

2003   "Entering the Netherworld." *Cuneiform Digital Library Bulletin* 2003/6. Available online at http://cdli.ucla.edu/pubs/cdlb/2003/cdlb2003_006.html

Volk, Konrad

1995   *Inanna und Šukaletuda: Zur historisch-politischen Deutung eines sumerischen Literaturwerkes.* SANTAG 3. Wiesbaden: Otto Harrassowitz.

Walker, Christopher B. F., and Michael B. Dick

2001   *The Induction of the Cult Image in Ancient Mesopotamia: The Mesopotamian* Miš Pî *Ritual.* State Archives of Assyria Literary Texts 1. Helsinki: Neo-Assyrian Text Corpus Project.

Weiershäuser, Frauke

2008   *Die königlichen Frauen der III. Dynastie von Ur.* Göttinger Beiträge zum Alten Orient 1. Göttingen: Universitätsverlag Göttingen.

2012   "Geštinanna und die Mutter des Šulgi." In *Organization, Representation, and Symbols of Power in the Ancient Near East* (Proceedings of the 54th Rencontre Assyriologique Internationale at Würzburg, 20–25 July 2008), edited by Gernot Wilhelm, pp. 347–56. Winona Lake: Eisenbrauns.

Westenholz, Joan Goodnick

1997   *Legends of the Kings of Akkade: The Texts.* Mesopotamian Civilizations 7. Winona Lake: Eisenbrauns.

2007   "The True Shepherd of Uruk." In *From the Workshop of the Chicago Assyrian Diction-ary 2: Studies Presented to Robert D. Biggs, June 4, 2004*, edited by Martha T. Roth, Walter Farber, Matthew W. Stolper, and Paula von Bechtolsheim, pp. 305–24. Assyriological Studies 27. Chicago: The Oriental Institute.

Wiggermann, F. A. M.

1992   *Mesopotamian Protective Spirits: The Ritual Texts.* Cuneiform Monographs 1. Gron-ingen: STYX & PP Publications.

Wilcke, Claus

1970   "Eine Schicksalsentscheidung für den toten Ur-Nammu." In *Actes de la XVIIe Ren-contre Assyriologique Internationale, Université libre de Bruxelles, 30 juin–4 juillet 1969*, edited by André Finet, pp. 81–92. Publications du Comité belge de recherches historiques, épigraphiques et archéologiques en Mésopotamie 1. Ham-sur-Heu-re: Comité belge de recherches en Mésopotamie.

1976   "Inana/Ištar." *Reallexikon der Assyriologie und vorderasiatischen Archäologie* 5: 74–87.

2006   "Die Hymne auf das Heiligtum Keš: Zu Struktur und 'Gattung' einer altsume-rischen Dichtung und zu ihrer Literaturtheorie." In *Approaches to Sumerian Lit-erature: Studies in Honour of Stip (H. L. J. Vanstiphout)*, edited by Piotr Michalowski and Niek Veldhuis, pp. 201–38. Leiden: Brill.

Winter, Irene

1992   "'Idols of the King': Royal Images as Recipients of Ritual Action in Ancient Meso-potamia." *Journal of Ritual Studies* 6: 13–42.

Woods, Christopher

2004   "The Sun-God Tablet of Nabû-apla-iddina Revisited." *Journal of Cuneiform Studies* 56: 23–103.

2009   "At the Edge of the World: Cosmological Conceptions of the Eastern Horizon in Mesopotamia." *Journal of Ancient Near Eastern Religions* 9: 183–239.

Zettler, Richard L., and Walther Sallaberger

2011   "Inana's Festival at Nippur under the Third Dynasty of Ur." *Zeitschrift für Assy-riologie und vorderasiatische Archäologie* 101: 1–71.

10

"WE ARE GOING TO THE HOUSE IN PRAYER": THEOLOGY, CULTIC TOPOGRAPHY, AND COSMOLOGY IN THE EMESAL PRAYERS OF ANCIENT MESOPOTAMIA

Uri Gabbay, Hebrew University, Jerusalem

I. Introduction

Balaĝ and Eršema prayers written in the Emesal register of Sumerian played an important role in the temple cult of ancient Mesopotamia, probably from as early as the third millennium B.C.E. and until the first century B.C.E.[1] They were sung by the gala (*kalû*) priest and were accompanied by musical instruments, some of which gave these genres their names: the balaĝ-instrument accompanied the Balaĝ prayers, and the šèm-instrument (Akkadian *ḫalḫallatu*) accompanied the Eršema prayers (literally, "laments of the šèm-instrument").[2] The content of these prayers is usually mournful, lamenting the destruction of cities and temples. There are many indications that Emesal prayers were not always sung statically, but were rather connected to processions and circumambulations. This is evident not only through ritual texts but also even in the wording of the prayers themselves, which uses a large range of verbs of motion, such as e₃ "to go out," di-di "to wander," niĝin "to circle," ul₄ "to hurry," te "to approach," and ku₄ "to enter." At times, the spatial aspects of the content of the prayers and the ritual instructions prescribing their performance (or a combination of both) appear to correspond to the general theological, and on occasion also cosmic, significance of the prayers. The following article investigates the theological and cosmic significance of cultic motion, especially with regard to the directions of these motions, using internal evidence from the prayers themselves, ritual texts, and administrative documents. These spatial aspects of motion will be connected with the literary content, structure, and theology of Balaĝ and Eršema prayers.

---

[1] In the following article, the first letter of genres of Emesal prayers is capitalized, hence Balaĝ, Eršema, Šuila, but non-capitalized balaĝ refers to the musical instrument. The article uses textual data from various periods and locations, even though at times this could admittedly be a risky task. In my opinion, the careful use and comparisons of these materials can reveal the religious and theological system in which the prayers were performed during the various periods. Once such a system is recognized and defined, it is possible to trace the continuity and changes that occurred within it, at times connected to historical developments and at times to internal religious developments. I would like to acknowledge the extensive use I made of the CDLI and ETCSL digital resources, and especially BDTNS, in the preparation of this article. I thank Professor Wolfgang Heimpel for reading and commenting on an earlier draft of this article.

[2] The problems related to the identification of these instruments will not be dealt with here; see Gabbay forthcoming a, VI.

II. Spatial Aspects in Emesal Prayers

According to the ancient Near Eastern religious perception, one of the most important things a person can ask from a god, under normal circumstances or in a normal state, is for this god to remain calm. Divine wrath is terrible and, if not calmed in time, can be directed toward the god's own city, temple, and people. To assure that the god remains calm, his statue is seated in his cella, where he receives supplications, offerings, and music. The physical resting of the god on his seat is connected to the mental and theological resting of the god's mind. The following paragraph examines how the content of some Balaĝ prayers, describing the divine wrath and asking for its appeasement, is related to the locations and directions of motion described in the Balaĝ.

II.1. *"Theological Topography"*

From a literary point of view, the content of Emesal prayers, especially Balaĝ compositions, is often arranged circularly, beginning and ending in the temple. The god is described as leaving his own city due to a catastrophe, or causing catastrophe by leaving his city. This catastrophe is the subject of the lament. At times the lamentation is uttered by the goddess of the city, the city's only survivor, roaming and circling the streets, witnessing all the destruction and death. At the end of the Balaĝs, the god is asked to return to his city, to sit on his throne, and to never leave it again. Therefore, almost all Balaĝs and Eršemas end with a section that asks the god to stay in his temple and remain calm. This theology varies slightly in different Balaĝs, depending on the god to whom they are directed. In Balaĝs to Enlil, Enlil is described as raging and thereby leaving his temple and city, causing destruction to his own city and the entire land. After lamentations, he is asked to return to his city and calm down. In Balaĝs to Enki, the situation is a bit more complex. Enki is described as leaving his city as a result of Enlil's rage, causing him to be plagued by a disturbed state of mind. After the destruction is over, and perhaps after Enlil himself has been pacified, Enki is asked to return to his city, sit in his temple, and be calm.[3] A lament about the abandoned and destroyed city and the goddess roaming its parts is nicely depicted in the Balaĝ abzu pe-el-la₂-am₃, "the Abzu is defiled," addressed to the god Enki. It is especially preserved in the first millennium B.C.E, but is also partially known from the Old Babylonian period.[4] The first section mourns the destruction of the temple:

line 1	The *abzu* is defiled! Eridu is plundered!
	The true House! The *abzu* is defiled! Eridu is plundered!
	The true House, the House of Enki,
	The true House, the House of Damgalnuna,
5	The true House, the House of Asarluḫi (= Marduk),
	The true House, the House of Panunanki (= Zarpanītu),
	The true House, the House of Sukkalmaḫa,
	The true House, the House of Muzebasa'a (= Nabû),
	The true House, the House of Nammu,
10	The true House, the House of Nanše,
	The true House, the House of Ara (= Usmû)!

---

[3] This literary structure is also found in the Sumerian Eridu Lament (ETCSL c.2.2.6).

[4] For this Balaĝ, see Cohen 1988, pp. 47–64; cf. Maul 2005, pp. 17–25, no. 2.

The Abzu, which was built in a pure place,
Eridu, which was built in a good place,
My still E-engur,
15 My purified standard,
My glorified standard,
The grand courtyard, my small *abzu*,
The grand courtyard, my large *abzu*,
[...], my perfect thing!
20 My holy dais, set up facing east,
Babylon, my city having sighs,
My open House into which gifts were brought in,
My chamber of cedar, by the edge of the sea,
The midst of the *šegbar* which no one can see.
25 Its front is in tears, its midst is in tears,
Its front, one enters it in tears!
Its midst, one exits it in sighs!

The *abzu* mentioned in the first line is the body of subterranean waters where the god Enki cosmically abides. But it is also the name of the temple of Enki, where his statue both mythologically and cultically abides. The implication of the *abzu* being defiled is that Enki, who should be sitting in the *abzu* both cosmically and mythologically, is not there. He left not only his abode in the cosmic *abzu*, but also his earthly temple. Therefore, the various parts of the abandoned temple, once glorious structures, are now described as defiled, leading to tears and sighs within them.

The next section contains a passage that describes the goddess of the city, Damgalnuna, and her entourage, rushing out of the temple complex to meet the god Enlil, who brought the destruction, in order to calm him down. On her way to him, she utters a lament over her destroyed city:

Because of the defiled *abzu* we are rushing to him,
40 And we, because of the defiled *abzu*, we are rushing to him,
The lord Enki, because of the defiled (*abzu*) we are rushing to him!
The lord, because of the defiled *abzu*, does not dwell in the *abzu*,
The lord Enki, because of the destruction, does not dwell in Eridu!
The lord does not dwell in the *abzu*, he is *silent*,
45 The lady Damgalnuna does not dwell in Eridu, the lady is is *silent*!
[That lady ...] is going to him because of her defiled House,
[...] is going to him because of her plundered assembly,
She is going to him because of her destroyed cattlepen (and) [...],
She is going to him because of her destroyed treasure house (and) slain people,
50 She is going to him because of her defiled funerary offerings,
She is going to him because of her outer House in which an enemy passed,
She is going to him because of her holy places which were *set aside*,
She is going to him because of her defiled banquet hall!
Day and night she cries out, she is going to him,
55 She cries out over her destroyed cattlepen; she is going to him,
She moans over her uprooted sheepfold; she is going to him!
On account of her House she walks about bending down, she cries bitterly,
On account of her defiled cella she walks about, she cries bitterly,
On account of her leveled treasure house she walks about, she cries bitterly!

60   "*Your storm!*[5] *... I sat down!*" she cries feverishly,
        My-Lady, "What will become of me?" cries feverishly,
        Lady of the House, "Enlil, how long?!" says prostrating.
        She is going to him because of her defiled House, her plundered city!

After this section, the goddess begins lamenting the temple. Later she begins wandering and circling the outskirts of the city in lamentations, passing alongside the canals and ditches and out to the fields and steppe outside the city, from where water and vegetation used to be brought to the city:

90   I am circling (àm-niĝin-e-en), I am circling the plundered place!
        I am circling! I am circling the plundered place, ...
        My one of the ditches lies in the ditches, ...
        My one of the canals lies in the canals! ...
        My one who went to the vegetation was carried off,
95   My one who went to the water was carried off,
        My one who carried vegetation does not carry vegetation for anyone, he was carried off,
        My one who carried water does not carry water for anyone, he was carried off!
        The dogs who know me made me known to the enemy,
        The dogs who do not know me follow the enemy!

The rest of the composition is not well preserved, but may have continued with a description of Enki and Damgalnuna returning to their shrines (and, cosmically, to the abzu), perhaps after Enlil was calmed, and then asked to stay in their cellas. In compositions addressed to Enlil, there is added emphasis on heart pacification, since the entire catastrophe was caused by his raging heart.

Indeed, such descriptions are found in Balaĝs to Enlil, for example, in a section found toward the end of several such compositions in the Old Babylonian period and in the first millennium B.C.E.[6] The opening lines of this section describe the god returning to his city, accompanied by his entourage and his balaĝ-instrument:

    We are going to the House in prayer, in prayer!
    We are going in prayer (with)? the balaĝ-instrument *fit* for the House!
    We are going to Enlil in prayer (with)? the circumambulating balaĝ (balaĝ niĝin-na)!
    We, god and man, are going to Enlil in prayer (with)? the balaĝ!
    We, god and man, who were circumambulating, are going in prayer!
    We are going to that House in supplication!
    We are going to that Place in supplication! We are going to Enlil!
    We are going to calm the heart of the lord! We are going to Enlil!
    We are going to calm the heart, to pacify the mind! We are going to Enlil!
    We will calm the heart of the lord! We are going to Enlil!

This section continues with a very long list of gods who are invoked to help calm the god. At the end of the list, and prior to the supplication of the mother goddess, a general

---

[5] Cohen 1988, p. 52, line 60: u₄-da? // u₄-ma!, but BM 54745 on which this line is preserved seems to have: u₄-zu // ᵁ₄-ki (collated).

[6] See Cohen 1988, pp. 234–42: c+239–383, 279–91: e+263–92, 302–10: c+113–256, 355–66: a+177–285.

reference to the gods is made, followed by mention of the city to which Enlil is now return-ing, namely, his city of Nippur:[7]

> The gods of heaven, the gods of earth,
> The Anuna-gods standing in heaven,
> The Anuna-gods standing on earth!
> The bar of Nippur! The bolt of Nippur!

Then another section follows, either of the Balaĝ prayer itself, or in the first millennium especially in the Eršema prayer that is appended to it, with a concluding plea or supplication asking Enlil not to abandon his city, not to bring destruction again, and to calm his heart from now on. An example is the first-millennium Eršema alim-ma umun ĝir₃-ra, which is appended to the Enlil Balaĝ am-e bara₂ an-na-ra:[8]

> May your heart be calmed! May your mind be pacified!
> Alas, lord! May An calm you!
> Lord, Great Mountain, Enlil! May your heart be calmed!
> In the shrine Ekur, may I calm his heart! May I pacify his mind!
> Lord of the lands! May I calm his heart!
> How long? Great Mountain Enlil! May your heart be calmed! May your mind be pacified!

After the lamenting and mourning and when the god is present in his dwelling, the heart pacification is meant to ensure that calamities and misfortunes will not recur.

II.2. Cultic Topography

Although this may seem entirely hypothetical, I would like to offer a cultic topographical analysis of the content of the sections cited above, beginning with the Balaĝ abzu pe-el-la₂-am₃. The original topographical context of this Balaĝ was most probably Enki's temple in the city of Eridu, the E-abzu. Later, it was also performed in other temples, especially the Esaĝil of Babylon, and indeed the name of this temple was added to the litanies of this Balaĝ, as in other compositions.

In the discussion above, I related to Enki leaving his city in the theological, as well as cosmic, levels. But there is also a cultic and very concrete level to this. Cultically, in a calen-drical or other cultic occasion, Enki's representation, as a statue or symbol, leaves his abode, the abzu, and is directed in procession out of the temple. Returning to the first section of the Balaĝ cited above, it is evident that the sequence of localities enumerated in this liter-ary description reflects a movement from the inner cella of the temple outward. The section begins with a general introduction, mourning the destruction of the entire temple complex and city, syncretizing it, in the usual way known in Emesal litanies, also with the temples of Marduk and Nabû. Then, the text becomes more specific, beginning with the mention of E-engur (line 14), another name for the subterranean body of water, here probably referring not to the whole temple but to the main cella within it. It is possible that in the context of

---

[7] See CT 42, 3 v 40–43 (Cohen 1988, p. 290: e+269–72). In the first millennium B.C.E., the address to the gods of heaven and earth is slightly different, and after the mention of the bolt of Nippur, bolts of other cit-ies are added, see, e.g., Cohen 1988, p. 310: c+225–32.

[8] *SBH* 22: 29′–38′ // BaM Beih. 2, 19 r. 1′–5′ // *BL* 163+ r. iv 11–21; see Gabbay forthcoming b, no. 14.

a procession leaving the temple with the image of Enki, this is the starting point. The cultic personnel that will begin the process are in the cella and are removing the statue of Enki, or another of his representations, from his seat. The text continues with a mention of the cultic standards (lines 15–16), probably referring to standards in the cella or at its entrance, through which the procession is leaving. The text continues with a mention of the court-yards (lines 17–18), known to be situated outside the inner cellas of Mesopotamian temples, implying the movement of the procession through these courtyards. The mention of the dais facing east (line 20) refers to another cult room located at the eastern part of the temple, probably close to the east gate,[9] implying perhaps that the procession was leaving the temple through this gate. From there the procession may have reached the external parts of the temple, the place where offerings were normally brought as greetings to the god (line 22) by those persons who could not enter the actual temple. Then, it may have proceeded to a cedar porch or chamber (line 23: ma ^{ĝiš}erin-a), located near the gate,[10] perhaps containing in its inner part an image of a wild goat or ram, associated with Enki and the abzu, and now not seen by the procession leaving the gate (line 24).[11] Finally, the procession is standing outside the temple, facing its front for the last time (lines 25–26), before proceeding on its journey away from the temple (line 27).

The next section cited above (lines 39–63) contains a passage that explicitly describes the utterance of the participants of a procession (either the same procession leaving the temple earlier or an additional one that joined it) in the first-person plural, rushing out of the temple with the images of the god Enki and his consort Damgalnuna. The procession in this passage seems to pass by cultic areas outside the main cellas of Enki and Damgalnuna, such as the treasure house, the place for funerary offerings, the "outer House," and the banquet

---

[9] The east shrine of Mesopotamian temples was considered a place of divine judgment and divine assemblies. In the third millennium B.C.E., for example, the Šugalam gate, identified by Heimpel (1996, pp. 20–21) as the east gate of the Eninnu temple in Ĝirsu (see below, section IV), is considered a place of divine judgment (Gudea cylinder A viii: 6; see Edzard 1997, p. 74; cf. Heimpel 1996, pp. 20, 25), and a dais (bara$_2$) located at the area of the gate, where the procession route Ĝirnun ended, is likewise considered a place of divine judgment (Gudea cylinder A xxii: 20–22; see Edzard 1997, p. 83; cf. Heimpel 1996, pp. 20–21, 25–26). The dais at the Ĝirnun procession route is also clearly associated with the rising sun in a different passage, where it is mentioned just before the gu$_2$-en-na assembly and throne hall, probably indicating that they were situated close to each other (Gudea cylinder B xvi: 7–18; see Edzard 1997, p. 97). As pointed out to me by Professor Andrew George in a remark following a lecture on this topic in the annual conference of the Israel Society for Assyriology and Ancient Near Eastern Studies in Beer-Sheva (February 2012), the eastern annex of Marduk's Esaĝil temple in Babylon in the first millennium B.C.E. (as well as the eastern annexes of Aššur's Eršara temple in Assur and Anu's Rēš temple in Seleucid Uruk,

built on the model of the Esaĝil) was probably the location of the Ubšu-ukkina and the Du$_6$-ku$_3$, where the divine assembly met to pronounce destinies; see George 1999 (differently: Pongratz-Leisten 1994, pp. 47–64). The connection of the east part of temples to divine judgment and decisions on destinies is of course connected to the image of the sun god Utu/Šamaš as the divine judge.

[10] Note that a cedar porch or chamber (a-ga erin) is considered the place of judgment in an inscription of Gudea found on a few bricks and thus may be associated with the place of judgment applied to the eastern gate and dais (see n. 9 above); see Edzard 1997, pp. 141–42, no. 44 (cf. Heimpel 1996, pp. 19–20, 24); and cf. Gudea cylinder A xxii: 3–4 (Edzard 1997, p. 83; cf. Heimpel 1996, pp. 19–20, 25). Note that ma ^{ĝiš}erin-a in the Balaĝ is the Emesal equivalent of a-ga erin in the Gudea inscription, as in another case where Emesal ma corresponds to a-ga: a-ga balaĝ-a-bi gu$_4$ gu$_3$ nun di (Gudea cylinder A xxviii 17; see Edzard 1997, p. 87), and ma balaĝ-ĝa$_2$ gu$_4$ gu$_3$ di nun-n[a$^?$] (*SBH* 50a: 18).

[11] "The midst of the *šegbar* which no one can see" occurs also in the myth Enki's Journey to Nippur, line 47 (ETCSL c.1.1.4).

hall (lines 49–53), implying perhaps that the procession is still in the temple complex, but not in its main shrine.

According to one of the following passages in the composition, the procession now begins a mournful circumambulation (niĝin) of the temple and city (lines 90–91), passing alongside the canals and ditches (lines 92–93). From there it turned to the fields outside the city, from where water and vegetation used to be brought to the city (lines 94–97), at the border of the steppe lying outside the city, where dogs dwell and wander (lines 98–99).

After the circumambulation of the city, passing through the steppe outside the city, the procession heads back to the city and temple. This image is found in the passage from the Enlil Balaĝ cited above, which again describes the utterance of the participants of the procession in the first-person plural that they are going to the city where they will calm the heart of Enlil ("We are going to calm the heart of the lord!"). The participants are carrying the image of the god, as well as the balaĝ-instrument that participated in the circumambulation of the city (balaĝ niĝin-na). After naming the long list of gods while making their way into the city, the procession arrives at the city gates, addressing their bars and bolts ("The bar of Nippur! The bolt of Nippur!").

Finally, when the procession arrives at the temple, they seat the image of Enlil in his cella and complete the prayer with a section asking Enlil to remain calm and not to abandon his city again. In the cited passage from the Eršema, this is explicitly said to take place in the temple ("In the shrine Ekur, may I calm his heart! May I pacify his mind!"). As noted, pleas for the pacification of the heart of the deity are appropriate at the end of a ritual, when the god is re-seated on his throne. The address to the deity in the second person may indeed imply that the gala priest is addressing the statue of the god in front of him, seated back in his cella.

III. Cultic Topography in Rituals versus Spatial Aspects in Emesal Prayers

I assume that the reconstruction according to content proposed in the previous section of the article reflects the earlier performances of the Balaĝ prayers. However, in the first millennium B.C.E., the traditional Balaĝ and Eršema prayers were more and more associated with the cella of the god. At times, they were performed before or after a procession but, unlike in earlier periods, were usually not part of it.[12] What was sung, then, during the procession? On festive occasions, in which the king also participated, especially the Akitu festival, Šuila prayers were recited (Shibata forthcoming).[13] In other cases, a specific form of Eršema prayers was used, natively called Ritual (kidudû) Eršemas, as opposed to the Eršemas that were appended to Balaĝs and actually served as their final section. The difference between the Ritual Eršemas and those appended to Balaĝs is that while the latter compositions end with a supplication for the appeasement of the god's heart, which is appropriate for their performance in front of the god in his cella, the Ritual Eršemas do not normally contain such sections. Indeed, these Ritual Eršemas, which do not contain a supplication for calming the god, are not usually performed before the sitting god in his cella (but see section III.3 below).

---

[12] E.g., various Emesal prayers are performed before and after procession in the spring festivals in Assur; see Maul 2000, pp. 402–06. See Gabbay forthcoming a, VII.4.2.

[13] For an analysis of Šuila prayers in their topographical context, see Shibata forthcoming, I.5.1.

III.1. Procession from the Temple: Cult and Prayer

A first-millennium B.C.E. ritual text describes the cultic acts to be performed when a divine statue has to be repaired and is removed from its throne to be taken to the workshop (Farber 2003, p. 209, lines 1–10):

> If a divine statue falls into a critical state of disrepair and the god has the desire to be renovated ... you enter the presence of this god ... at night, when there is no one around, and cover him with a cloth. You leave and light a pile of wood. You perform a Balaĝ (*takribtu*).[14] You make this god rise from his pedestal, and the *kalû*-priest uncovers his head. He beats his chest and says "Woe!" He sings (the Ritual Eršema) uru₂ a-še-er-ra ("The city is in sighs"). He takes the god by the hand. Until the god enters the workshop and takes his seat, he must not cease singing.

The Ritual Eršema uru₂ a-še-er-ra, "The city is in sighs," is sung, probably over and over again, in a procession leaving the cella of the god, and heading toward the workshop. The cultic activity is not over yet. It will take a while until the statue, and consequently the god himself, will be seated back in his temple. Meanwhile the god spends his time outside his temple, a liminal and awesome state, which may be explained as a sign of divine wrath. It is no coincidence that the procession occurs at night, before the sun has risen. The absence of celestial light is an image of the absence of the divine presence, both theologically, as the god leaving his city in rage, and concretely, as the statue of the god leaving its cella. It is not yet the time to calm the divine anger. This will be done when the god is headed back to his seat after the repair, and the entire ritual is over. Indeed, the Ritual Eršema uru₂ a-še-er-ra, "The city is in sighs," does not contain a supplication for calming the angry god, but only describes the divine abandonment caused by divine wrath.[15] The prayer begins with a lament over the destroyed city and temple (lines 1–3):

> The city is in sighs! How long will it *stay destroyed*?
> My city, Nippur, is in sighs! How long will it *stay destroyed*?
> The brickwork of Ekur is in sighs! How long will it *stay destroyed*?

These lines describe the lament over the city and temple, evidently caused by the god abandoning it, and cultically mirrored by the damaged image of the god leaving his shrine in procession. As noted above, in addition to the theological and cultic abandonment, this situation is also evident cosmically, as the sun concealing itself from mankind at night, when the ritual is performed.

The next lines describe the goddess of the city lamenting her city. A few lines in her lament relate to the coming out of the "Word" of the god, that is, the god's destructive decision to leave the city by commanding its destruction (lines 24–27):

> It is overwhelming! It is overwhelming! It comes out from the city!
> The Word of great An is overwhelming! It comes out from the city!
> The Word of Enlil is overwhelming! It comes out from the city!
> He made my city cry out in bitter misery! Its people were heaped up!

---

[14] See Gabbay 2011, pp. 70–73.

[15] For this Eršema, see Cohen 1981, pp. 117–21, no. 35; Gabbay forthcoming b, no. 50.

The lament describes the destructive Word of the god as leaving the city. This destructive divine Word is a common motif in Emesal prayers and is often described as its result: the destruction itself. The Word leaving the city in the passage above is not only the command to destroy the city, but also its actual destruction. And this destruction is the consequence of the god leaving his city. This is true theologically, as the absence of the god from his city enables its destruction, but is also reflected cultically in the concrete ritual act of the procession leaving the temple toward the workshop.

The end of the composition is still mournful and contains no supplication or wish for the end of the destruction or for the god's pacification. As mentioned, this absence of supplication is in agreement with the cultic setting of the prayer during the procession of the statue leaving his shrine, a ritual enactment of the divine abandonment, which is not the time for supplications. The time for this will only be when the god returns to his seat in his temple.

III.2. Procession to the Temple: Cult and Prayer

A ritual text, known from Seleucid Uruk, describes the cultic acts that should be performed when the restoration of the image of the god in the workshop is completed and it undergoes purifying rituals on the riverbank (Mayer 1978, pp. 444–58). The ritual begins at night (line 3), when offerings are made to various gods, mostly nocturnal, including stars, and Nuska, the lamp god (lines 3–5). During this period, two Balaĝs, including their accompanying Eršemas, are performed (lines 9–12), one of which is the Balaĝ u_4-dam ki am_3-us_2, "It reaches earth like Day" (line 9), known from other sources to be performed at the end of the night before dawn.[16] Then, at dawn (line 13), offerings and libations are performed, including another Balaĝ and Eršema (lines 13–28), after which the text describes the return of the statue of the god from the river to his cella (lines 28–32):[17]

> The god will head to the temple from the river bank. The king will hold the hand of the god and will recite ....[18] The *kalû*-priest (singing the Ritual Eršema) nir-ĝal$_2$ lu$_2$ e$_3$-NE ("Prince, appearing!") will hold the hand of the god .... When he arrives in the main gate of the temple (the *kalû*-priest shall sing the Ritual Eršema) e$_2$ ša$_3$-ab ḫuĝ-ĝe$_{26}$-ta ("House, so that the heart be calmed!") ... until the god sits in his seat, the [recitati]ons(?) and prayers will be performed ...

The Ritual Eršema nir-ĝal$_2$ lu$_2$ e$_3$-ne, "Prince, appearing!," which includes about a hundred lines, is one of the longest known Eršemas in the first millennium B.C.E.[19] What is unusual about this Ritual Eršema is that it ends with a supplication, a very rare phenomenon in Ritual Eršemas. The composition begins with a description of the appearance of the god (lines 1–2):

> Prince, appearing — who can fathom you? Honored one, prince, appearing — who can fathom you?

---

[16] For ritual attestations prescribing the singing of the Balaĝ u_4-dam ki am_3-us_2, and other Balaĝs, to a cultic performance just before dawn, see Gabbay forthcoming a, VII.6.1.

[17] The translation of this passage is based on Mayer's (1978, p. 446) transliteration and on the copy in BaM Beih. 2, 1.

[18] Perhaps restore: [g]a$^{!?}$-n[a]$^{!?}$ [umun-e]$^?$, referring to the recitation given in full in lines 31ff.

[19] See Gabbay forthcoming b, no. 54. The Eršema is preserved on *BL* 9a+*BL* 73.

The god is described as appearing, using the verb e₃ which is also used for "going out." Here the verb is used in its known nuanced meaning of "appearance" and in a non-finite construction, indicating the presence of the god who is already outside his shrine, both in the divine and cultic realms.

But since the god is now heading back to his temple and will soon be seated in his seat, supplications can begin. And indeed, the Eršema ends with a long supplication. It first begins with a litany asking various gods to make a supplication to the god heading back to his temple, in his different names (lines a+39–51):

> May he who knows what is in his heart say a prayer to you, lord!
> May he who knows what is in the heart of An say a prayer to you, lord!
> May he who knows what is in the heart of the honored one say a prayer to you, lord!
> May he who knows what is in the heart of great An say a prayer to you, lord!
> May he who knows what is in the heart of the Great Mountain, father Enlil, say a prayer to you, lord!
> May he who knows what is in the heart of Enki say a prayer to you, lord!
> May he who knows what is in the heart of Asarluḫi (= Marduk) say a prayer to you, lord!
> May he who knows what is in the heart of Enbilulu say a prayer to you, lord!
> May he who knows what is in the heart of Muzebasa'a (= Nabû) say a prayer to you, lord!
> May he who knows what is in the heart of Dikumaḫa say a prayer to you, lord!
> May he who knows what is in the heart of the great hero say a prayer to you, lord!
> May he who knows what is in the heart of Nuska say a prayer to you, lord!
> This day, oh god, balaĝ-instrument of laments, this day has risen! May he say a prayer to you, lord!

The list of gods enumerated in this passage, beginning with An and ending with Dikumaḫa, is a standard sequence of gods in first-millennium B.C.E. litanies in Emesal prayers.[20] But the addition of Nuska at its end (line a+50) is very rare.[21] This alludes to the time of day in which the Eršema was performed. According to the ritual text, the performance occurred just after sunrise. Nuska is the lamp god, associated in the first millennium B.C.E. especially with the very last stage of the night, just before dawn. Indeed, he participated in this cult before the final stage of the ritual (see above). Now that the sun is rising, Nuska is mentioned for the last time, since there is no more need for the use of the lamp, and it can be blown out. Once the lamp is off, and the sun has fully risen bringing daylight, the supplication turns to address this (line a+51): "This day, oh god, balaĝ-instrument of laments, this day has risen!" The image of the rising sun is linked to the favorable appearance of the god, soon to be seated on his throne, at the end of the procession. The supplication continues, addressing various gods,[22] ending with a litany mentioning Kalkal, the doorkeeper, Enlilazi, the

---

[20] See Gabbay forthcoming a, IV.5.1 with table 2.

[21] For the litany "May he who know what is in the heart," addressed to various gods (Marduk, Ninurta, Utu), using fixed sequences of divine names, but add-

ing Nuska to them at the end, see Gabbay forthcoming a, IV.5.1 with table 3.

[22] Note that Nuska is mentioned here too, but as a god in the sanctuary of Nippur, and not as the lamp god connected to the night performance.

overseer, and Ur-Suena, the herald of the temple (lines a+62–64), all standing at the temple's gate, alluding to the procession approaching the temple:[23]

> May Kalkal, the great doorkeeper of Ekur say a prayer to you, lord!
> May the lofty overseer Enlilazi say a prayer to you, lord!
> May Ur-Suena, the herald of the outer shrine say a prayer to you, lord!

Now that the procession is almost at the temple, the supplication can be more explicit, asking the gods to plea to the main god directly, in the second person, not to abandon his city and temple again (lines a+65–82):

> "Do not abandon your city!" may they each say to you, may they each say a prayer
> to you!
> ...
> "You are its lord! Do not abandon it!" may they each say to you, may they each say
> a prayer to you!
> "You are its shepherd! Do not abandon it!" may they each say to you, may they
> each say a prayer to you!

The supplication ends by asking the god, again perceived as the sun or day that has already risen, to return and remain in his temple (a+83):

> "Day, return to that House! Do not abandon it!" may they each say to you! may
> they each say a prayer to you!

By now, the procession probably passed through the gate of the temple, and according to the ritual text, another Eršema is now to be sung until the god takes his seat: "House, so that the heart be calmed!" (see above). Unfortunately, the content of this prayer is not known since no manuscript of it could be identified. But another ritual text also prescribes this prayer to the very end of a procession, just before the god is seated on his seat.[24] It is obvious according to the incipit that the prayer dealt with the pacification of the heart in relation to the entrance into the temple.

After the procession is over and the restored god is reseated, the ritual text prescribes offerings, and an unspecified Balaĝ prayer is sung (lines 32–34), obviously including an Eršema ending with a plea for the pacification of the god's heart, recalling the destruction, and asking for the future appeasement of the god.

III.3. Performance in the Temple: Cult and Prayer

Lastly, I would like to address three short Ritual Eršemas that actually contain "heart pacification units" per se. These are the Eršemas ur-saĝ ^{d}ut-u$_{18}$-lu "Hero Utulu," kur-gal a-a ^{d}mu-ul-lil$_2$ "Great Mountain, father Enlil," and i-lu-ke$_4$ i-lu-ke$_4$ "She of 'alas!,' she of 'alas!,'" directed to Ninurta, Enlil, and Inana, respectively, all ending with similar heart

---

[23] Note the mention of the gods Kalkal, Ur-Suen, and Enlilazi in Ur III documents listing offerings in the context of entering (ku$_4$) into the temples of Enlil and Ninlil in Nippur, at times involving the balaĝ- instrument as well (Sallaberger 1993, part 1, pp. 98–105).

[24] See Maul 2000, p. 402: 5', 7'–8'; p. 405: 24'; p. 406: 6–7, 16–17, 23–24$^!$.

pacifications.[25] Cohen (1981, p. 27 n. 136) noted the exceptional nature of these Ritual Eršemas and concluded that the heart pacification unit that appears at their end is due to their poor scribal craftsmanship. However, I do not agree that these Eršemas are poorly composed, and I believe that the solution to the inclusion of three heart pacification units, unlike other Ritual Eršemas, is found in the ritual setting of their performance. Following is the heart pacification unit of the Eršema ur-saĝ ^{d}ut-u$_{18}$-lu in one of its versions (lines 12–23):[26]

> Day! So that the heart be pacified! Storm! So that the mind be pacified!
> Heart of the great hero! So that the heart be pacified!
> Heart of Utulu! So that the heart be pacified!
> Heart of the lord Dikumaḫa! So that the heart be pacified!
> Heart of the beautiful woman Baba! So that the heart be pacified!
> Heart of Nintinuga! So that the heart be pacified!
> Heart of the Lady-of-Isin! So that the heart be pacified!
> Heart of Gašan-gutešasiga (= Tašmētu)! So that the heart be pacified!
> Heart of My-Lady Nanaya! So that the heart be pacified!
> Heart of (variant: Princess) the lady of Ḫursaĝkalama! So that the heart be pacified!
> Heart of (variant: Princess) the lady of Eturkalama! So that the heart be pacified!
> Heart of (variant: Princess) the lady of Babylon! So that the heart be pacified!

According to my proposed classification, such prayers should be sung in front of the sitting statue of the god in his or her cella, the appropriate place for the god to be pacified. Indeed, short ritual instructions appended to two of these Eršemas (ur-saĝ ^{d}ut-u$_{18}$-lu and i-lu-ke$_4$ i-lu-ke$_4$) prescribe these compositions to the cella. Thus, the composition cited above is to be sung before the statue of the goddess in her cella on the third day of each month according to a Late Babylonian tablet:[27]

> During (each) month, on the third day, before the evening meal, in the shrine of
> Tašmētum (this composition) shall be sung

The performance of this Eršema in the evening may imply that the goddess will soon have the opportunity to pacify the god intimately when they go to sleep together.[28]

IV. Cultic Topography in Ur III Administrative Documents

Although no tablets containing Balaĝ prayers have survived from the third millennium B.C.E., it is most likely that Emesal prayers already existed in this period (Cooper 2006). Many tablets dating to the Ur III period mention administrative transactions involving the gala priest, laments (er$_2$), and the balaĝ-instrument, at times all in the same context, and it

---

[25] See Cohen 1981, pp. 143–49, nos. 45, 53, 49; Gabbay forthcoming b, nos. 60, 71, 78.

[26] This version is found in CT 42, 12: 12–23 and CTMMA 2, 14 (Maul 2005, pp. 95–96): 12–23. Another version is found in MLC 382: 2′–19′. See Gabbay forthcoming b, no. 60.

[27] See CT 42, 12: 26; cf. Cohen 1981, p. 41. A slightly different version of the same Eršema, found on MLC 382, has a similar instruction (lines 21′–22′): "Month-

ly, on the third day, accompanied by a ḫalḫallatu-instrument, in the shrine of Nanaya, before Nanaya (this composition) shall be sung" (cf. Cohen 1981, p. 41). The same tablet has a similar instruction for the Eršema i-lu-ke$_4$ i-lu-ke$_4$ (r. 14–15). See Gabbay forthcoming b, nos. 60, 78.

[28] For this motif, cf., e.g., the concluding line of the Šamaš Hymn (Lambert 1960, p. 138, line 200).

is probable that such attestations refer to a performance of Emesal prayers ("laments" er$_2$) by the gala, to the accompaniment of the balaĝ-instrument.[29] In addition, many documents mentioning the gala, the balaĝ, or laments (or the combination of these elements) often imply a cultic movement. Thus, processions may be referred to when gates are mentioned in such documents, implying a cultic movement through them (see Ragavan, this volume).[30]

IV.1. The Circumambulating balaĝ in Ĝirsu

The most instructive evidence from Ur III documents involves circumambulations. The following section focuses on Ur III documents from Ĝirsu that record provisions of flour and beer for rituals involving the "balaĝ of the day circumambulating the city" (balaĝ u$_4$-da iri niĝin-na).[31] Of special interest are three documents[32] that list provisions in relation to various topographical designations, indicating cultic "stops" in which offerings and other ritual acts were performed.[33]

The following table summarizes the various topographical stops.[34]

---

[29] See Gabbay forthcoming a, III.2.

[30] Cf. gates enumerated in the same context as laments and the gala priest (e.g., CUSAS 3, 1035, mentioning a ritual involving a gate, the gala, and a *takribtum*, the Akkadian equivalent of er$_2$, i.e., an Emesal prayer; cf. Gabbay 2011, pp. 70–73), or the balaĝ-instrument (e.g., SET 88, PTS 400). Of special interest are two documents from Drehem (AnOr 7, 58 and CTNMC 9) that list animals for offerings at Uruk (Sallaberger 1993, part 1, p. 221; part 2, p. 127, table 74). The first tablet lists animals for the shrine (eš$_3$-še$_3$), the god ^{d}muš-a-igi-ĝal$_2$, Ninigizibara (the balaĝ-instrument of Inana), laments of circumambulation at the gate of the Ĝipar (er$_2$ niĝin-na / ka ĝi$_6$-par$_4$-a), an offering for the "day of 'rise up, you all!'" (sizkur$_2$ u$_4$ zi-ga-ze-na-a), and then materials for the disappearing place (niĝ$_2$ ki-zaḫ$_3$) of Nanaya (i.e., the place temporarily left by Nanaya when going out in procession elsewhere; Sallaberger 1993, part 1, p. 190). The second tablet lists similar cultic acts in lines r. 11–20, naming animals for the gate of the shrine (ka eš$_3$), the disappearing place of Nanaya, the "day of 'rise up, you all!,'" the gate of the Ĝipar (ka ĝi$_6$-par$_4$-ra), and the House of Nanaya.

[31] Variants: balaĝ u$_4$-da and balaĝ u$_4$-da e$_2$ iri niĝin (see below); cf. Gabbay 2011, p. 70, with references in n. 22.

[32] TCTI 1, 796 (see Heimpel 1998); MVN 2, 143 (see WMAH 143); HLC 2, 23.

[33] Note that both the first tablet (TCTI 1, 796) and the third tablet (HLC 2, 23) mention the gala(-maḫ),

making it very probable that these rituals indeed included Emesal prayers (and note that TCTI 1, 796, also includes "laments" er$_2$). The gala-maḫ Utubara, acting as mediator (ĝir$_3$) of the provisions involving the balaĝ u$_4$-da iri niĝin-na and ab$_2$-be$_2$-ra in HLC 2, 23, is also the mediator for the provisions of the balaĝ u$_4$-da iri niĝin-na in OBTR 92 (month 7), and for the ab$_2$-er$_2$ Antasura in ABTR 1 (month 12; this document has the exact amounts of provisions for this instrument as in HLC 2, 23, both stemming from month 12 of an undated year, and may actually be records of the same transaction, the latter collecting several transactions which were recorded individually). A third tablet (Amherst 65; month 6) records provisions for the balaĝ u$_4$-da iri niĝin$_2$-na supervised by a different gala-maḫ, Lu-kirizal.

[34] It is difficult to date TCTI 1, 796 because it contains only one personal name, which is quite common. Among the personal names in HLC 2, 23, three, including titles, can safely be identified elsewhere. These are: A-gu-a lu$_2$-^{ĝiš}tukul (i: 17), SIG$_4$-de$_3$-li lu$_2$-šud$_3$-šud$_3$ (i: 22), and Ur-ab-ba lu$_2$-DU (probably for lu$_2$-kaš$_4$; r. i: 10), who according to other documents can be dated to a period of seventeen years between the years Amar-Suen 2 and Šu-Suen 9, which includes the time of the second tablet MVN 2, 143 (Šu-Suen 1). As to the month, although rituals involving the balaĝ iri niĝin-na are known from various months, the tablet shares many similarities with other tablets dating to month 12 (MVN 2, 143 and HLC 2, 23, discussed below, as well as OBTR 27).

	TCTI 1, 796 (No Date)	*MVN 2, 143* (month 12, year Šu-Suen 1)	*HLC 2, 23 iii: 4–r. ii: 14* (month 12)
1	For the Houses of the gods	For the Piriĝ-gin$_7$-DU canal	The runners
2	For the lament of offering	For the House of Antasura	Offering materials at the meadow of the bank of the Piriĝ-gin$_7$-DU canal and the bank of the Tigris
3	Offering of the royal ša$_3$-ge-guru$_7$ rite	For the U$_3$-sur canal	The ga-gu$_7$ e$_3$-a rite
4	Offering materials for Šugalam and Uruk-House	For the NINA-DU canal	The balaĝ of the day circum-ambulating the city
5	Divine balaĝ of the day circumambulating the House and city	Offering materials for the garden at Kisura	Magan-boat
6	Offering materials for the Cow-of-laments instrument at Antasura	Divine balaĝ of the day cir-cumambulating the city	Offering materials for the mouth/gate of the Ĝir(?) canal
7	[Offering materials] for the Piriĝ-[gin$_7$-DU canal] (?)	—	For the Cow-of-laments in-strument at Antasura
8	—	—	Meal of the king at the Holy-City
9	—	—	Offering at the Bird-House

The picture that arises when taking these documents into account, and with due caution that they do not all necessarily refer to the same rite, is that a procession with the circumam-bulating balaĝ headed northwestward and probably returned circularly southeastward. The first document (TCTI 1, 796) records rituals in the temple complex, including offerings, la-ments, and a royal prayer, then moving outside through the Eninnu's east gate (šu-ga-lam),[35] and turning westward to a stop at what is probably the west gate (e$_2$-unu^{ki} "House-Uruk," that is, the house facing Uruk at the southwest),[36] creating a course of at least a semicircle around the temple from east to west. The procession then begins a circumambulation with the balaĝ-instrument.[37] Following this, the procession arrives in Antasura, where a performance with

[35] For the identification of Šugalam as the Eninnu's east gate, see Heimpel 1996, pp. 20–21.

[36] The names e$_2$-unu^{ki} and igi e$_2$-unu^{ki} were the sub-ject of some discussion. Sallaberger (1993, part 1, p. 298) understood (igi) e$_2$-unu^{ki} as a place outside of Ĝirsu, and Heimpel (1996, pp. 20, 23) noted that it may also refer to a gate, the west gate according to his reconstruction. It seems to me that e$_2$-unu^{ki} and igi e$_2$-unu^{ki} should be distinguished in Ur III docu-ments, the former being the name of the gate, as in our document and in ITT 5, 6823 (mentioned in the context of other gates), and the latter referring to an area outside the city facing (igi) this gate (i.e., located to the west of the city), as in the documents

RTC 311, MCS 8, 65, MVN 2, 149 (all with the provi-sions for balaĝ u$_4$-da igi e$_2$-unu$^{(ki)}$še$_3$).

[37] It should be noted that this is the only occurrence where the circumambulating balaĝ-instrument is mentioned in connection to a circumambulation around the temple and not only in connection to other locations in and out of the city, and indeed the phrase balaĝ u$_4$-da e$_2$ iri niĝin is mentioned here rather than the regular phrase, which omits e$_2$ "House" (I follow Heimpel 1998, p. 13, in understand-ing the phrase as balaĝ u$_4$-da e$_2$ iri niĝin, rather than balaĝ u$_4$-da-ke$_4$ iri niĝin as understood by Sal-laberger 1993, part 1, p. 297).

the "Cow of laments" instrument occurs.[38] Antasura was located outside the city, close to the western border (sur) between the regions of Lagaš and Umma, probably northwest of Ĝirsu.[39] From there the procession may have proceeded to the Pirig̃-gin₇-DU canal (if restored correctly),[40] perhaps in the northern area as well, since it is associated with the Tigris, which flows north of Ĝirsu (see below).

The second document (MVN 2, 143) may describe the continuation of the procession and part of its way back to the city. It begins with rations for the "runners," here referring to participants in the hurrying procession.[41] It then mentions the Pirig̃-gin₇-DU canal and proceeds to the House of Antasura, the reverse order of localities that appeared in the previous document (if restored correctly). From there it turned to the U₃-sur canal, associated with the Pirig̃-gin₇-DU canal in other documents as well,[42] and according to its name, probably situated in the border area too (sur). From there the procession must have proceeded southward to the NINA(-še₃)-DU canal (which also ran through Ĝirsu), here probably referring to the northwestern part of the canal,[43] and arrived at the gardens of Kisura, which was probably situated upstream on this canal, northwest of Ĝirsu.[44] Then the document mentions the balag̃ circumambulating the city, perhaps implying that the procession was about to return to Ĝirsu, probably circumambulating it while doing so (cf. below), although this final destination is not documented in the text.

Some detailed information is derived from the third document (HLC 2, 23), probably referring to the procession headed eastward back to Ĝirsu, giving more details for the way between the Pirig̃-gin₇-DU canal and Antasura, although these details do not entirely agree with the previous tablet, and may indicate a different course. It first mentions the meadow between the Pirig̃-gin₇-DU canal and the Tigris, implying a northern location.[45] Then the ga-gu₇-e₃-a rite is mentioned, which is known to have taken place outside the city, circumambulating its gates,[46] after which the circumambulating balag̃-instrument is mentioned, implying

---

[38] For the understanding of ab₂-bi₂-ra as a syllabic writing for *ab₂-er₂-ra (see OBTR 27: r. 1: ab₂-er₂ an-ta-sur-ra), see Heimpel 1998, p. 15 (but I do not agree with Heimpel that it refers to the šem₃-instrument; for a discussion of "cow instruments," see Gabbay forthcoming a, VI.4.8.7).

[39] See Falkenstein 1966, pp. 164–65; Heimpel 1998, p. 15. Since Umma lies northwest of the Lagaš region, I understand Antasura to lie in the northwestern area of the border (and not only west as described by Heimpel). Note that the element an-ta "upper" may point at this (i.e., an-ta-sur-ra, "upper border"); cf. also Selz 1995, p. 24 n. 63, and 227 n. 1103.

[40] Only the sign PIRIG is preserved, but the restoration is likely, especially since this canal is also associated with Antasura in the next tablet MVN 2, 143.

[41] Cf. the reference to a procession as *lismu* "running," in Old Babylonian Mari (Durand and Guichard 1997, p. 55, iii: 6–13), and the speech uttered by the participants of the procession in the Balag̃ abzu pe-el-la₂-am₃, cited above (section II.1): "We are rushing to him."

[42] See n. 44 below.

[43] For the i₇-NINA^{ki}-še₃-DU canal, see Carroué 1986; Heimpel 1994, p. 31; de Maaijer 1998, p. 64.

[44] See Heimpel 1994, pp. 18, 27. Note that Kisura is associated with the two canals listed earlier in the text, the Pirig̃-gin₇-DU canal and U₃-sur canal in MVN 22, 113 (listing men from Kisura for work), the former also associated with Kisura in TCS 1, 185.

[45] The Pirig̃-gin₇-DU canal is also associated with the Tigris in BPOA 1, 1569.

[46] See Sallaberger 1993, part 1, pp. 299–300. Note that earlier in the same document (HLC 2, 23 ii: 21), in the listings for the eleventh month, the same rite is associated with the four gates (KA₂^{!}.GAL-4-ba; collated from a photograph in CDLI). Note also ITT 5, 6780, where the ga-gu₇-e₃ rite of the four gates is listed before the balag̃ of the day circumambulating the city (balag̃ u₄-d[a] / ⌈iri⌉ ni[g̃in]). Note especially RTC 312 (month 2, Šu-Suen 1), where the ga-gu₇-e₃-a rite is associated with the four gates (abul-4-ba) and is listed after an offering for the Cow-of-Laments at Antasura. Similarly, OBTR 88 (= CUSAS 16, 116) (month 12) associates the ga-gu₇-e₃-a-rite with Antasura. The ga-gu₇-e₃-a-rite is also associated with four gates elsewhere; see Sallaberger 1993, part 2, pp. 175–76, table 106a (note ITT 5, 6925, which also lists beer to be given in fields, rivers, and in Kisura). It is also associated with two gates in TCTI

that the circumambulation of the gates of the city also involved the balaĝ-instrument. Then
a Magan-boat is mentioned, perhaps implying that at least part of the journey was made by
boat. Following this, another canal is mentioned,[47] perhaps where the boat passed. Then the
procession probably headed back to the (north)western area right outside the city, where
Antasura was situated, as the Cow-of-Laments instrument in Antasura is mentioned in the
text.[48] The text then mentions royal rituals in the Holy City, the temple area of Ĝirsu, where
the Eninnu was located, implying perhaps that the procession has already left Antasura and
headed back into the city. Later the unidentified Bird-House (e₂-mušen) is mentioned.[49]

The course from and to the Eninnu with the circumambulating balaĝ is not entirely
clear since not all locations can be identified, but it is quite evident that the course began
westward and returned eastward, circumambulating the city at its outskirts in the steppe
(and perhaps involving also a circumambulation, or partial circumambulation, of the temple
within the city wall before leaving the city). This of course resembles the daily course of the
sun as perceived in ancient Mesopotamian thought, rising in the east and reaching the west
in the evening, and then at night making its journey in the netherworld from west to east,
rising again at the east on the next morning. If this resemblance is correct and not coincidental, the course of the circumambulation had a cosmic aspect to it, the god leaving and
returning to his temple mirroring the setting and rising of the sun.

Could this course be connected to the procession described in the Balaĝs themselves and
in ritual texts, as discussed in sections II and III above? It should be noted that the phrase
balaĝ niĝin-na, which occurs at the concluding section of many Enlil Balaĝs in the description
of the procession returning to the city, is very similar to the phrase balaĝ u₄-da iri niĝin-na
in the Ur III documents from Ĝirsu. It should also be noted that the procession in the Balaĝ
abzu pe-el-la₂-am₃ is described as leaving through the east gate of the temple, as in the
Ur III document, where its first stop is at Šugalam, the east gate of the Eninnu temple. Not
much is known about the geography and cultic topography of Eridu, but taking into account
the re-orientation of the Balaĝ abzu pe-el-la₂-am₃ into the context of the city of Babylon,
whose temple complex was located on the east side of the Euphrates (cf. maps in George 1992,

1, 819 (month 10), and with three gates in TÉL 61
(month 10, Šu-Suen 1) and SAT 1, 191 (month 11).
The references to two and three gates may imply a
semi-circular course rather than a full circumambulation of the four gates.

[47] The text has ka i₇-ĝir₂ (r. i: 15), an unknown canal.
Maeda (1980, p. 206) notes that it is either ĝir₂ (for
ĝir₂-nun; not known as a canal), or muš (but colla-
tion from the photograph in CDLI shows that it is
ĝir₂).

[48] See line r. i: 21: ab₂-bi₂-ra! an!-ta-sur!-ʳra!ⁿ-šè!
(collated from a photograph in CDLI); cf. Maeda 1980,
p. 206; Sallaberger 1993, part 1, p. 297 n. 1378.

[49] Some information on the way back to Ĝirsu may
also be derived from another document (DAS 240),
which, although not mentioning the circumambulating balaĝ, lists some localities at the western
outskirts of the city and perhaps implies a procession returning to the city. It begins with the gar-

dens of Kisura, which was already mentioned as
the final destination in the second document (MVN
2, 143), and then proceeds to igi e₂-unuᵏⁱ-še₃, the
area outside the city that faced the western gate
of the Eninnu (see n. 36 above). The reverse of the
tablet may describe the procession headed toward a
water outlet in the area of Ĝirnun, another locality
at the west of the district (probably not related to
the Ĝirnun processional way; see Falkenstein 1966,
p. 28. Ĝirnun is associated in ASJ 2, p. 31, no. 87, and
CT 7, no. 27, with the Nun canal, which flowed in
the border between the Lagaš district and Umma
and then through Umma; see de Maaijer 1998, p. 64;
Steinkeller 2001, p. 55). Then, offerings at a "small-
vine (orchard?)" (niĝ-siskur₂-ra ĝⁱˢĝeštin-ban₃-
da) are mentioned, followed by a water outlet of the
Ninĝirsu canal, which is also not located (cf. Carroué
1997, pp. 37–38).

pp. 20, 24), it is possible that mention of the canal and rivers later in the text could imply a cultic movement westward in the initial part of the procession, as in the case of Ur III Ĝirsu.

As demonstrated above (sections II and III), the procession out of the temple involved laments over the god leaving his temple, both physically, as an image in the procession, and theologically, as abandoning his city in rage.[50] This would correspond to a westward direction, where the sun, an image of the divine favorable manifestation, leaves the world westward toward the netherworld. The arrival of the procession at the western outskirts of the district, outside the city, passing by canals and meadows, imitates the goddess wandering in the outskirts of the city and in the steppe adjacent to it, lamenting her destroyed city. The use of the Cow-of-Laments instrument at this point may be connected to the common image of the goddess as a cow crying over her destroyed cattle pen in Emesal prayers.[51] Cosmically, this western location in the fields and steppe outside the city may be mirrored by the sun's setting and journey into the netherworld, which was associated with the western steppe. Although there is no indication for this in the Ur III documents discussed above, it is possible that the procession westward outside the city took place in the evening and the return to the city eastward occurred at sunrise, as in ritual texts of the first millennium B.C.E. (see section III.2 above), thereby mirroring the cosmic journey of the sun not only geographically but temporally as well.

V. Conclusion

In conclusion, the cultic topography and directions described in Emesal prayers and in texts relating to their cultic performance are connected to the theological notions of divine wrath and abandonment, as well as divine conciliation and return to the temple. These notions could also be cosmically connected, both spatially and temporally, to the course of the sun, or sun god, the divine judge and the most prominent divine cosmic manifestation, abandoning the upper world every evening and returning to it at sunrise. But what appears to us as different categories relating to literary content, mythology, ritual action, and time of day were in fact four angles of one religious perception in ancient Mesopotamia. The processions from and to the temple were actually conceived theologically as the god abandoning his temple and then returning to it, since the Mesopotamian god was real and concrete and not only metaphysical. And this concrete and theological divine abandonment and return were also part of the daily cosmic abandonment and return of the celestial bodies, especially the sun. The image of the rising sun was not just a literary simile for the divine appearance; it was an actual manifestation of it. And finally, the prayers that were performed within these ritual, theological, and cosmic contexts were not just recitations loosely connected to them, but were the way in which the concrete ritual enactment in the temple's surroundings was connected and identified with the theological and cosmic perceptions.

Lastly, I would like to address the issue of continuity and change that Emesal prayers underwent regarding their topographical context, from the third millennium to the first millennium B.C.E. The Balaĝ prayers were originally performed as part of processions and

---

[50] Note Heimpel's (1998, p. 16) mention of the biblical circumambulation of the walls of Jericho, but unlike the Mesopotamian case, where the god returns to the temple after the circumambulation to sit calmly on his throne, there is no appeasement in the biblical story, and Jericho is indeed destroyed.

[51] Cf. Gabbay forthcoming a, IV.2.4.

circumambulation, as indicated by their content and Ur III administrative references. The conclusion of the performance was in the cella, in front of the seated god, asking for his appeasement. In the first millennium B.C.E., the entire Balaĝs were usually performed in the cella and were hardly connected to processions and circumambulations anymore. In the rare cases in which they were connected to such acts, they were usually performed just before or after them and not during their course. But while there was a change in the topographical context of this specific genre of prayers, the general religious and systematic perception regarding the location of the prayers was still maintained. Emesal prayers were still performed during processions, but these were not Balaĝs, but Šuilas and Ritual Eršemas. The connection of these prayers to the direction of the processions during which they were performed maintained the theology of the Balaĝs: the god leaving his city and consequently bringing destruction upon it is cultically mirrored by the statue of the god leaving the temple in procession; and the god returning to his city to sit in his cosmic abode is mirrored by the statue of the god returning to the temple in procession and then being asked in supplication to stay calm after sitting on his throne, the most natural and normal location for such a supplication.

Abbreviations

ABTR	William R. Arnold, *Ancient-Babylonian Temple Records in the Columbia University Library*. New York: Columbia University Press, 1896.
Amherst	Theophilius G. Pinches, *The Amherst Tablets,* Part 1. London: B. Quaritch, 1908.
AnOr 7	Nikolaus Schneider, *Die Drehem- und Djoḫa-texte im Kloster Montserrat (Barcelona) in Autographie und mit systematischen Wörterverzeichnissen*. Analecta Orientalia 7. Rome: Pontificio Istituto Biblico, 1932.
ASJ 2	Tohru Gomi, "Neo-Sumerian Administrative Tablets in the British Museum, I.' *Acta Sumerologica* 2 (1980): 1–36.
BaM Beih.	Baghdader Mitteilungen Beiheft
BDTNS	Database of Neo-Sumerian Texts: http://bdtns.filol.csic.es/
BL	Stephen Langdon, *Babylonian Liturgies*. Paris: Paul Geuthner, 1913.
BM	Tablet siglum of the collection of the British Museum
BPOA 1	Tohru Ozaki and Marcel Sigrist, *Ur III Administrative Tablets from the British Museum*, Part One. Biblioteca del Próximo Oriente Antiguo 1. Madrid: Consejo Superior de Investigaciones Científicas, 2006.
CDLI	Cuneiform Digital Library Initiative: http://www.cdli.ucla.edu/
CT 7	Leonard W. King, *Cuneiform Texts from Babylonian Tablets, &c., in the British Museum*, Part 7. London: Trustees of the British Museum, 1899.
CT 42	Hugo H. Figulla, *Cuneiform Texts from Babylonian Tablets in the British Museum*, Part 42. London: Trustees of the British Museum, 1959.
CTNMC	Thorkild Jacobsen, *Cuneiform Texts in the National Museum, Copenhagen*. Leiden: C. T. Thomsen, 1939.
CUSAS 3	David I. Owen and Rudolf H. Mayr, *The Garšana Archives*. Cornell University Studies in Assyriology and Sumerology 3. Bethesda: CDL Press, 2007.
CUSAS 16	Steven Garfinkle, Herbert Sauren, and Marc Van De Mieroop, *Ur III Tablets from the Columbia University Library*. Cornell University Studies in Assyriology and Sumerology 16. Bethesda: CDL Press, 2010.

DAS	Bertrand Lafont, *Documents administratifs sumériens provenant du site de Tello et conservés au Musée du Louvre*. Paris: Editions Recherche sur les civilisations, 1985.
ETCSL	Electronic Text Corpus of Sumerian Literature: http://etcsl.orinst.ox.ac.uk/
HLC	George A. Barton, *Haverford Library Collection of Cuneiform Tablets or Documents from the Temple Archives of Telloh*, Volumes 1–3. Philadelphia: John C. Winston, 1905–14.
ITT 5	Henri de Genouillac, *Inventaire des Tablettes de Tello conservées au Musée Impérial Ottoman 5: Époque Présargonique, Époque d'Agadé, Époque d'Ur*. Paris: Geuthner, 1921.
MCS	Manchester Cuneiform Studies
MLC	Tablet siglum of the collections of the J. Pierpont Morgan Library
MVN	Materiali per il vocabolario neo-sumerico
OBTR	Robert J. Lau, *Old Babylonian Temple Records*. Columbia University Oriental Studies 3. New York: Columbia University Press, 1966.
PTS	Tablet siglum of the collection of the Princeton Theological Seminary
RTC	François Thureau-Dangin, *Recueil de Tablettes Chaldéennes*. Paris: E. Leroux, 1903.
SAT 1	Marcel Sigrist. *Texts from the British Museum*. Sumerian Archival Texts 1. Bethesda: CDL Press, 1993.
SBH	George A. Reisner, *Sumerisch-babylonische Hymnen nach Thontafeln griechischer Zeit*. Berlin: W. Spemann, 1896.
SET	Tom B. Jones and John W. Snyder, *Sumerian Economic Texts from the Third Ur Dynasty*. Minneapolis: University of Minnesota Press, 1961.
TCS 1	Edmond Sollberger, *The Business and Administrative Correspondence under the Kings of Ur*. Texts from Cuneiform Sources 1. Locust Valley: Augustin, 1966.
TCTI 1	Bertrand Lafont and Fatma Yıldız, *Tablettes cunéiformes de Tello au Musée d'Istanbul datant de l'époque de la IIIᵉ Dynastie d'Ur*, Volume 1 (ITT II/1, 1617–1038). Uitgaven van het Nederlands Historisch-Archaeologisch Instituut te İstanbul 65. Brill: Leiden, 1989.
TÉL	Charles Virolleaud, *Tablettes économiques de Lagash (époque de la IIIᵉ dynastie d'Ur) copiées en 1900 au Musée Impérial Ottoman*. Cahiers de la Société asiatique 19. Paris: Société asiatique, 1968.
WMAH	Herbert Sauren, *Wirtschaftsurkunden aus der Zeit der III. Dynastie von Ur im Besitz des Musée d'Art et d'Histoire in Genf*. 2 volumes. Pubblicazioni del Seminario di semitistica. Ricerche 6; Materiali per il vocabolario neosumerico 2. Naples: Musée d'art et d'histoire, 1969–1974.

Bibliography

Carroué, François
1986   "Le 'Cours-d'eau-allant-à-NINAᵏⁱ.'" *Acta Sumerologica* 8: 13–57.
1997   "La chronologie interne du règne de Gudea, Partie I." *Acta Sumerologica* 19: 19–51.
Cohen, Mark E.
1981   *Sumerian Hymnology: The Eršemma*. Hebrew Union College Annual, Supplement 2. Cincinnati: Hebrew Union College.
1988   *The Canonical Lamentations of Ancient Mesopotamia*. Bethesda: Capital Decisions Limited.

Cooper, Jerrold S.

2006   "Genre, Gender and the Sumerian Lamentation." *Journal of Cuneiform Studies* 58: 39–47.

de Maaijer, Remco

1998   "Land Tenure in Ur III Lagaš." In *Landless and Hungry? Access to Land in Early and Traditional Societies*, edited by Bernard Häring and R. de Maaijer, pp. 50–57. Center of Non-Western Studies Publications 67. Leiden: Research School CNWS, School of Asian, African, and Amerindian Studies

Durand, Jean-Marie, and Michael Guichard

1997   "Les Rituels de Mari." In *Recueil d'études à la mémoire de Marie-Thérèse Barrelet: Mémoires de N.A.B.U. 4*, edited by Dominique Charpin and Jean-Marie Durand, pp. 19–78. Florilegium marianum 3. Paris: SEPOA.

Edzard, Dietz Otto

1997   *Gudea and His Dynasty*. The Royal Inscriptions of Mesopotamia, Early Periods 3/1. Toronto: University of Toronto Press.

Falkenstein, Adam

1966   *Die Inschriften Gudeas von Lagaš*, Volume 1: *Einleitung*. Analecta Orientalia 30. Rome: Pontificium Institutum Biblicum.

Farber, Walter

2003   "Singing an *eršemma* for the Damaged Statue of a God." *Zeitschrift für Assyriologie* 93: 208–13.

Gabbay, Uri

2011   "Laments in Garšana." In *Garšana Studies*, edited by D. I. Owen, pp. 67–74. Cornell University Studies in Assyriology and Sumerology 6. Bethesda: CDL Press.

Forthcoming a   *Pacifying the Hearts of the Gods: Sumerian Emesal Prayers of the First Millennium B.C.E.* Heidelberger Emesal Studien 1. Wiesbaden: Harrassowitz.

Forthcoming b   *The Eršema Prayers of the First Millennium B.C.E.* Heidelberger Emesal Studien 2. Wiesbaden: Harrassowitz.

George, Andrew R.

1992   *Babylonian Topographical Texts*. Orientalia Lovaniensia Analecta 40. Leuven: Departement Oriëntalistiek.

1999   "E-sangil and E-temen-anki, the Archetypal Cult-Center." In *Babylon: Focus mesopotamischer Geschichte, Wiege früher Gelehrsamkeit, Mythos in der Moderne*, edited by Johannes Renger, pp. 67–86. Colloquien der Deutschen Orient-Gesellschaft 2. Saarbrücken: Saarbrücker Druckerei und Verlag

Heimpel, Wolfgang

1994   "Towards an Understanding of the Term siKKum." *Revue d'Assyriologie et d'Archeologie Orientale* 88/1: 5–31.

1996   "The Gates of Eninnu." *Journal of Cuneiform Studies* 48: 17–29.

1998   "A Circumambulation Rite." *Acta Sumerologica* 20: 13–16.

Lambert, Wilfred G.

1960   *Babylonian Wisdom Literature*. Oxford: Clarendon Press.

Maeda, Tohru

1980   "Collations of G. A. Barton, Haverford Library Collection of Cuneiform Tablets and Documents." *Acta Sumerologica* 2: 197–224.

Maul, Stefan M.

2000   "Die Frühjahrsfeierlichkeiten in Aššur." In *Wisdom, Gods and Literature: Studies in Assyriology in Honour of W. G. Lambert*, edited by Andrew R. George and Irving L. Finkel, pp. 389–420. Winona Lake: Eisenbrauns.

2005   "Bilingual (Sumero-Akkadian) Hymns from the Seleucid-Arsacid Period." In *Literary and Scholastic Texts of the First Millennium B.C.*, edited by Ira Spar and Wilfred G. Lambert, pp. 11–116. Cuneiform Texts in the Metropolitan Museum of Art 2. New York: The Metropolitan Museum of Art.

Mayer, Werner R.

1978   "Seleukidische Rituale aus Warka mit Emesal-Gebeten." *Orientalia* 47: 431–58.

Pongratz-Leisten, Beate

1994   Ina šulmi īrub: *Die Kulttopographische und ideologische Programmatik der* akītu-*Prozession in Babylonien und Assyrien im I. Jahrtausend v. Chr.* Baghdader Forschungen 16. Mainz: Philipp von Zabern.

Sallaberger, Walther

1993   *Der kultische Kalender der Ur III-Zeit.* Untersuchungen zur Assyriologie und Vorderasiatischen Archäologie 7/I–II. Berlin: De Gruyter.

Selz, Gebhard

1995   *Untersuchungen zur Götterwelt des altsumerischen Stadtstaates von Lagaš.* Philadelphia: University of Pennsylvania Museum.

Shibata, Daisuke

Forthcoming   *Die Šu'ila-Gebete im Emesal.* Heidelberger Emesal Studien 3. Wiesbaden: Harrassowitz.

Steinkeller, Piotr

2001   "New Light on the Hydrology and Topography of Southern Babylonia in the Third Millennium." *Zeitschrift für Assyriologie* 91: 22–84.

11

TEMPORARY RITUAL STRUCTURES AND THEIR COSMOLOGICAL SYMBOLISM IN ANCIENT MESOPOTAMIA

*Claus Ambos, Heidelberg University**

Introduction

The issue of the seminar and the resulting volume *Heaven on Earth: Temples, Ritual, and Cosmic Symbolism in the Ancient World* deals with the important topic of sacred space. I approach this matter from my field of study, Assyriology, which is dedicated to the study of the cuneiform cultures of the ancient Near East.

There are various ways of approaching the topic in question. It would be of course quite obvious to deal with permanent religious architecture such as temples and sanctuaries that could reach monumental dimensions. A temple was believed to be the house of a deity who lived there in the shape of his or her cult statue and was taken care of and fed by humans. By their layout and architectural features, the sanctuaries of the ancient Near East expressed in many respects cosmic symbolism.

Beyond that, symbolism was also expressed by movement through ritual and religious space, for example, during the processions of the gods during the festivals of the cultic calendar. During the New Year's festivals, the deities left their sanctuaries in the city and went in a solemn procession, accompanied by the king, to their so-called *akītu*-houses outside the city in the steppe.[1]

These ritual and religious spaces are created by permanent and even monumental architecture. But in ancient Near Eastern rituals, temporary ephemeral structures and installations that existed only for the duration of the respective ritual performance also played an important role. Such ritual space was composed of buildings or structures made of perishable materials such as, for example, reed, flour or dust, and (loose) earth.

The ritual structures made of these materials could be of a vast variety. Our sources mention huts, prisons, wells, roads, watercourses, and mountains. Thus on the one hand, these structures were reproductions of man-made buildings that existed in a permanent form also independently of any ritual performance, and on the other hand, these structures were reproductions of elements of the natural landscape. Both by their architectural design

* Research for this article was conducted in the framework of the Collaborative Research Center 619 "The Dynamics of Ritual," supported by the German Research Council (DFG). I am grateful to Christopher Frechette SJ (Boston College) for correcting my English and commenting upon an earlier draft of this article

[1] Farber 1987, pp. 212–27; Pongratz-Leisten 1994, 1998–2001, 2006–2008; Sallaberger 1998–2001; Zgoll 2006.

as well as by the movement and actions of the ritual's participants performed in them, these temporary structures and buildings expressed essential features of Mesopotamian worldview and cosmic geography.

The pertinent rituals were not rituals of the temple cult but rather rituals to dispose of evil and impurity. For the people of the ancient Near East, impurity was a physical thing that could be removed from a person or an object in a physical way. It could, however, not be annihilated — thus, once removed it had to be stored or deposited securely at some uninhabited place. Therefore rituals that served to get rid of impurity were as a rule performed in uninhabited wastelands such as the steppe or desert, where evil and impurity could remain without causing further harm, or they were performed at a secluded place at the riverside, where impurity could be disposed of in the watercourse. These rituals could be performed in the case of actual need, when some evil had occured to a person; it is, however, also attested that such rites were carried out at fixed dates of the cultic calendar.

It is the setting and layout of such rituals that I discuss in this paper. At least the more complex rituals had their own characteristic setting and layout. This ritual space, however, was seen and perceived only by the ritual experts and their client(s), since these rituals were never performed in public. The focus of this article is on the written sources, since pictorial representations of the rituals discussed here are not extant.

The rituals are mainly known from ritual handbooks that served for the requirements of the experts performing these rites. These texts were transmitted over generations in the so-called stream of tradition (Oppenheim 1977, p. 13) until the end of the traditional Mesopotamian culture. Comprehensive and detailed handbooks are generally from the first millennium B.C.E., but they certainly belong to a much older tradition reaching back into the second and even third millennium B.C.E.

Another source for our knowledge of ritual in the cultures of the ancient Near East are numerous texts from the daily life of the ritual experts. Of enormous importance for the study of ancient Near Eastern ritual and religion is the correspondence of the Assyrian kings Esarhaddon and Ashurbanipal with ritual experts and scholars at their court at Nineveh in the seventh century B.C.E. Through these letters and reports, we can obtain a rather vivid picture of ritual and religious life in the ancient Near East (Parpola 1993).

The Ritual *bīt salāʾ mê*: The King Performing the Nocturnal Path of the Sun by Passing through a Prison of Reeds

The Ritual Setting

As a first example, I present a ritual of the re-investiture of the Babylonian king, which was called *bīt salāʾ mê* "House of sprinkling water." *bīt salāʾ mê* formed part of a larger cluster of rituals that were performed for the Babylonian ruler during the New Year's festival in autumn at the equinox. For reasons of space, I focus on *bīt salāʾ mê*.[2]

---

[2] For the cluster of rituals and the New Year's festival in autumn, see Ambos 2008, 2010, and 2012. A monographic study with an edition of the pertinent cuneiform texts is forthcoming (Ambos, forthcoming a). The following presentation of the ritual *bīt salāʾ mê* is a condensed and slightly modified version of Ambos 2010.

For the performance of the ritual, the king traveled to a specially arranged space in the steppe where he stayed for one night and the following morning. This ritual space was a complex of buildings made of reeds. It consisted of a so-called prison made of reeds and of a reed hut that served as a temporary shrine. These two buildings were situated in a courtyard that was surrounded by a reed fence. The prison was very small, measuring only three cubits in length and width. The whole complex measured about 13 × 13 cubits — this is at least the measure given for the surrounding reed fence.

The king passed through this ritual space from west to east during the night and morning. In the evening, at sunset, the king and the ritual experts entered this reed building by the western door. The king was not wearing his royal insignia. During the night, he stayed in the prison made of reeds and recited prayers to various heavenly bodies and to the gods of the cities Nippur and Babylon, the two cities of Babylonian kingship. These were the very gods who had granted rulership to him. The king presented himself to these gods as a miserable and guilty individual and asked them to intercede on his behalf with his personal tutelary gods, who had turned away from him. As a result, the king was prone to physical and mental illness, social exclusion, and financial disaster — in short, the foundations of his rulership were threatened. Consequently, it was the intention of the king to restore harmony between him and the divine sphere in order to strengthen his endangered rulership.[3]

In the morning at sunrise, the king left the prison and entered the reed hut. This building was a temporary shrine where many gods had assembled to decide the request of the king. There were present the gods Ea, Šamaš, and Asalluḫi, the divine board whose favorable decision ensured the success of a ritual performance. Also present were the personal tutelary gods of the king. All these deities were addressed by the king with prayers and sacrifices. Thanks to divine intercession, the angry gods became reconciled, and thus harmony between the king and the divine sphere was restored.

It seems that in the reed hut the king also underwent an ablution, stripped off the clothes he had worn in prison, and put on his royal garment. Then he placed himself before the rising sun in the eastern door of the complex of reed buildings. Two exorcists stood to his left and right, and by means of conifer cones they sprinkled him with holy water. The royal insignia were also sprinkled with water, and finally the king was invested with his regalia in front of the rising sun. Immediately afterward, the king returned to the city from the reed building in the steppe. After some concluding rites there, the king was now able to take part in the events of the New Year's festival.

The Prison of Reeds and Its Inherent Meaning

A cosmic symbolism was expressed both by an inherent deeper meaning that was peculiar to the reed buildings as well by the movement that the king performed during the ritual performance. It was no accident that the person — in this case the king — who suffered from the anger of the gods stayed during a ritual performance in a prison. It is a topos in the so-called wisdom literature that for the person who had been forsaken by his or her tutelary gods the familiar social environment became a prison. In the so-called Poem of the Righteous

---

[3] These prayers belong to the genre of "Akkadian" *šu-il₂-la₂* "hand-lifting." For this genre, see now the study by Frechette (2012), specifically pp. 166–76 for the nocturnal cycle of prayers in *bīt salāʾ mê*.

Sufferer, the protagonist, who is subject to the anger of his gods, describes his situation in the following words:[4]

> I take to a bed of bondage; going out is a pain;
> My house has become my prison.
> My arms are stricken — which shackles my flesh;
> My feet are limp — which fetters my person.

Clearly, a person alienated from his or her gods had become inert, had lost his or her agency and his or her ability to act. During the ritual performance, the king experienced this god-forsaken state physically by staying in a prison.

In addition, the prison evidently was a representation of the netherworld. The goddess of prison, Nungal or Manungal, belonged to the circle of netherworld deities, and the temple of the deity bore the Sumerian name Ekur, which is also attested as a designation of the netherworld and was translated by the Babylonians as "prison" (Cavigneaux and Krebernik 1998–2001; Maul 1988, pp. 263–66).

Interestingly, the king moved through the ritual space from west to east. He entered the complex of reed buildings in the evening by the western door. During the night he stayed in the prison of reeds, which he left in the morning in order to enter the reed hut and finally to receive his regalia in the eastern door of the complex of reed buildings in front of the rising sun. By moving from west to east, the king followed the path of the sun during the night. And according to Mesopotamian ideology, the king *was* the likeness of the sun on earth among the people. During the night, the sun passed through the netherworld. So the king's nocturnal stay in prison should be seen as analogous to the stay of the sun in the netherworld during the night. It was certainly no accident that the king embodied the sun directly before the important astronomical event of the fall equinox, when the New Year's festival in autumn took place.

Excursus: A Prison Made of Flour

A ritual space arranged in a comparable way is attested in another ritual as well. This ritual served to reconcile the angry tutelary gods of a private person and thus may be considered a private version of the royal ritual *bīt salāʾ mê*.[5]

Here, however, the prison was not made of reeds but of flour. The layout of the structure is as follows: A ritual space had been fenced off against the outside world with a circle of reed standards. Inside the space thus created, a reed hut was erected that served as a temporary shrine for the gods participating in the ritual. Then, also within the circle of reed standards, the so-called prison was drawn with flour. And finally, into the prison of flour, a mudbrick was placed. The person affected by the anger of his or her gods, while sitting on the brick in the prison, recited prayers to bring about reconciliation with the divine sphere. At the conclusion of the ritual, the exorcist grasped the hand of his or her client and led him/her out of the prison and out of his/her miserable state.

---

[4] Lambert 1996, pp. 44f., tablet II, lines 95–98.

[5] KAR 90; Ebeling 1931, pp. 114–20; Lambert 1974, pp. 269f.

Shrines Made of Reeds as Places of Life and Well-being

After his nocturnal stay in the prison, the king moved to a reed hut, which served as a temporary shrine. This reed shrine was in its inherent qualities totally different from the prison. Sanctuaries made of reeds are attested in many ancient Near Eastern rituals (Taracha 2001; Seidl and Sallaberger 2005/2006). Here the gods participating in a ritual assembled.

Reed was considered a pure and apotropaic building material, connected to the cosmic subterranean ocean, the *apsû*. The reed's place of origin, the reed bed, was the epitome of life and well-being, because — in marked contrast to the desert — it was a place abundant in water, teeming with fish, birds, and other animals. In a shrine made of reeds, a person could thus meet the gods in a pure, apotropaic, and vitalizing environment. A reed shrine had a marked juridical aspect as a place where divine judgment was pronounced: In many rituals, the divine board Ea, Šamaš, and Asalluḫi stays there in order to decide the request of the person who had addressed the gods by performing the ritual. In addition, many other gods who were connected to the building material and its provenance, that is, the reed and the reed bed, stayed in the reed shrine. To illustrate the characteristics of a reed shrine, I cite a passage from a prayer from the ritual *bīt rimki* "Bath-house" (which I discuss in more detail below). The text quoted features the king in the reed shrine meeting the gods (Watanabe 1991, pp. 372–78, lines 69–104; this English translation is my own):

> When you (the king) are stepping to the reed shrine of the Bath-house,
> may Nunurra/Ea, the lord of the craft of the purification priest, whose ingenuity is perfect,
> stand by you with his incantation of life!
> When fish and bird, the characteristic (animals) of the reed bed, are brought to your fore-
>   head,
> may Nammu, the lady who rides(?) in the great and high sea,
> cause to drift away like clouds the *mangu-* and *luʾtu*-illness of your forehead!
> May Ningirim, the daughter of Enki/Ea,
> recite for you the incantation of life!
> When you approach the pedestal of "The Seven of Them" in order to prostrate yourself,
> may the gods who dwell on the pedestal calm their hearts toward you!
> May Nammu, the mother of the house, say to you: "Stay well!"
> Like an ewe which keeps turning around to its lamb, so may life keep turning around to
>   you!
> When you are prostrating yourself before Enki/Ea,
> may king Enki/Ea lift up your head!
> When you are prostrating yourself before Utu/Šamaš,
> may Utu/Šamaš, the great lord of heaven and earth, [grant you] a life of good health!
> By the commands of Asari/Marduk,
> may a happy life be bestowed on you as a gift!

The reed shrine is a place that gives life. Here the angry hearts of the gods are calmed. The goddesses Nammu and Ningirim are associated with reed and the reed bed and the animals living there, and they exercise their purifying power in the shrine. The shrine is also the setting for rites of separation from evil: The king's impurity is transmitted to the characteristic inhabitants of the reed bed, fish and birds, which serve as carriers to take it away. In marked contrast to the prison as a representation of divine anger and the netherworld, the reed shrine is a place of life and harmony with the divine sphere.

Moving through Ritual Space as a Rite of Passage

It is useful for our further understanding of the layout of the aforementioned ritual space to apply the scheme of the rites of passage, as developed by Arnold van Gennep, to the sequence of ritual events.[6] According to van Gennep, an ideal rite of passage can be divided into three phases: rites de séparation (rites of separation), rites de marge (rites during a marginal state), and rites d'agrégation (rites of aggregation). Rites of separation serve to separate a person (or a group) from his or her older state or position. The person is then in a liminal or marginal state between the old and the new state or position. This liminal or marginal state is characterized by ambiguity, indeterminacy, and even reversal of status. Rites of aggregation serve to introduce the person to his or her new position or state.[7]

In the ritual *bīt salāʾ mê* there is a close interrelation between space and status — space and status in fact reflect each other. The prison where the king stays for one night represents a liminal state: the king suffers from the anger of the gods and its consequences. For the king, this marginal state is in fact a state of status reversal: while staying in the prison, he has temporarily lost his royal status and is no longer a king — and in fact he is not wearing his royal insignia. But he regains his kingship in the morning when leaving the prison — and consequently the liminal state — by moving through the reed hut to the eastern gate to undergo his re-investiture.

Various rites of separation from the status of suffering from the anger of the gods and rites of aggregation to the status of a king were employed, which cannot be discussed here in detail. For the rites of separation, I refer only to the ablution of the king and the change of clothes in the reed hut, as well as to his being sprinkled with water during the investiture. Stripping off old clothes and rinsing the body are well-attested rites for physical separation from evil, which was in fact considered a physical thing clinging to a person and his or her body. An obvious rite of aggregation to kingship was of course the investiture.

As was observed by van Gennep, the liminal phase of a rite of passage may often feature ritual death and rebirth of the person undergoing the rite. If the prison of reeds in the steppe had a netherworld aspect, we may ask whether the king actually "died" during the ritual performance when entering the prison in the evening and was "reborn" when leaving it in the morning at sunrise. Although this notion is never explicitly alluded to in the pertinent text, there are indications that this conception indeed existed.

The king re-enacted the nocturnal path of the sun by moving through the prison-netherworld from west to east — and like the rising sun, he left the prison-netherworld in the morning. In ancient Mesopotamia, the emergence of a baby from the womb of the mother was seen as analogous to the sun's emergence from the dark netherworld, that is, its rising in the morning (see in general Polonsky 2000 and 2006; Woods 2009, pp. 219–25). As the sun rises at the horizon to continue its journey across the sky, so is the birth of a child described as a journey starting at the horizon in the mother's womb. The sun god is one of the gods assisting the woman in labor. Both birth (or the cutting of the umbilical cord) and sunrise were the characteristic dates when destiny was ordained: at birth or the cutting the umbilical cord, the fate of the newborn child was decreed by the gods; at sunrise, the gods assembled around the sun god to decide the destiny of the day.

---

[6] See van Gennep 1909. For writing this article I used the German translation (van Gennep 1999).

[7] Drawing on van Gennep, Victor Turner (e.g., 1969; German edition 2000) focused in his works intensively on the liminal phase of the tripartite scheme.

Interestingly, in the ancient Near East, the concept of a birth hut made of reeds is attested. This structure was intended for the mother animals of a herd. The name of the mother-goddess Nin-tu contains the word tur₅ which means "birth hut" and serves also as a metaphor for the womb (Jacobsen 1973). Whether the prison of reeds had the connotation of a birth hut is not brought up in the ritual handbook. It is of interest, however, that prison in the ancient Near East was connected to death and rebirth. One of the gods assisting the mother goddess Nintu during childbirth was the goddess of prison, Nungal, who was also involved in cutting the umbilical cord and decreeing the fate of the newborn (Attinger 2003, pp. 18 and 24, lines 71 f.). Nungal resided in the netherworld at that very place where the sun god rose in the morning leaving the netherworld (Attinger 2003, pp. 18 and 24, line 68). In addition to the netherworld and the womb, the prison was also an archetypical place of darkness. The Akkadian terms *nūra kullumu* "to show the light" and *nūra/šamaš amāru* "to see the light/the sun" can refer both to the disimprisonment of a detainee from the dark and obscure prison as well as to the emergence of a baby from the dark and obscure womb at birth.[8]

So the king passes through the space — and thus moving passes from an old position to a new one.[9] It is a rite of passage, however, in the sense that the king does not lose an old status to gain a new status, but rather he regains a desirable lost or at least endangered old status, that is, kingship and harmony with the divine sphere. It is, in other words, a rite of return to an old position.[10]

The Ritual *bīt rimki* — "Bath House"

The incantation cited above to illustrate the characteristics of a reed shrine was from the ritual *bīt rimki* — "bath house."[11] This ritual served for the purification of the king, and as the ritual *bīt salāʾ mê* "house of sprinkling water," it was thus named after the structure in which this purification took place. Likewise, *bīt rimki* was performed in a temporary complex made of reeds in the steppe. The layout, however, was different.

Bīt rimki "bath house" was the name of the ritual setting. This bath house consisted of a sacred space that was fenced off from the outside world by a circle of reed standards. Inside this secluded area, a reed hut or several reed huts were constructed that served as temporary shrines (Seidl and Sallaberger 2005/2006, pp. 62 f.). During the night, the ritual expert made the king recite a long cycle of prayers to the major gods of the pantheon and to the stars and planets. The king asked the gods for their support, mercy, and favor as well as for their intercession with his personal gods on his behalf.[12]

In the morning at sunrise, after having bathed himself and put on a clean garment, the king passed through seven "houses," as they are called in the text. These houses must have

---

[8] Many attestations are given in CAD A/2 s.v. *amāru* A 5 (pp. 21 f.); CAD K s.v. *kullumu* 5 c (pp. 524 f.); and CAD N/2 s.v. *nūru* A 1 d) 1′–2′ (p. 349); see also Farber 1989, pp. 149–52.

[9] That rites for the passage from one (social) state to a new (social) state can involve a corresponding passage through space was in fact already observed by van Gennep (1909).

[10] The term "rites of return" was coined by anthropologist Crapanzano (1992, pp. 260–80). On the use-

fulness of this notion for ancient Near Eastern studies, see Ambos, forthcoming b.

[11] On *bīt rimki*, see Læssøe 1955 and Farber 1987, pp. 245–55, and 1997.

[12] These prayers belong to the genre of "Akkadian" *šu-il₂-la₂* "hand-lifting." For this genre, see Frechette 2012, specifically pp. 176–80 and 201–08 regarding the nocturnal cycle of prayers.

been seven structures connected to the bath house. Perhaps they were rooms, stations, or sections that formed part of it. In every single house he performed rites of purification and recited prayers to the sun god Šamaš.

However, since the ritual *bīt rimki* has never been adequately published, it remains difficult to reconstruct the layout of the structure in the steppe in greater detail. Therefore I leave my discussion at these few words, even though this extensive and complex ritual deserves a greater appreciation. In the next paragraph, however, I discuss in greater detail a fragmentarily preserved ritual sequence that might in fact belong to *bīt rimki*.

Arranging Miniature Landscapes: The Boundaries of the Civilized World

I now present rituals that feature arrangements made of reproductions of important elements of the physical space of the ancient Near Eastern landscape. I also deal with arrangements that have reproductions of elements of landscape as well as of man-made buildings. I cite one example from a ritual to purify the king:[13]

> With a peg of tamarisk wood you dig seven watercourses, you heap up seven mountains of loose earth, ⌜you draw⌝ seven roads of fl[our]. The ruler crosses the watercourses, mountains, and roads [and recites in front of the sungod Šamaš]:
> "Šamaš, lord of the upper and lower world, the one who releases heaven and earth [...]! (...). You (the various evils) will [by the command] of the gods Šamaš, Adad, and Ma[rduk ... cross the seven watercourses], cross [the seven mountains, and go away on the seven roads to] remote(?!) [regions]!"

It is a well-known ritual technique that one made the evil pass over mountains and watercourses. In many if not all Mesopotamian rituals for removing evil, the formula *lībir nāra libbalkit šadâ* "may it cross the river and may it cross the mountain" is attested.[14]

For the Mesopotamians, mountains and watercourses were the natural boundaries of the civilized world. Alongside the rivers and irrigation canals in the alluvial plain of the Euphrates and the Tigris Rivers lay the cultivated land that was confined in the east by the Zagros Mountains and in the north by the Taurus Mountains. In the west, the land beyond the watercourses was steppe and desert. Both the mountains and the steppe and desert beyond the cultivated land were considered strange and hostile regions, haunted by demons and home of the forces of chaos. The roads mentioned above in the royal ritual also refer to distant regions. The term employed here, *ḫarrānu*, does not mean streets within the town or city, but rather long-distance roads and trading routes; the word can also denote the activities practiced on it as, for example, long-distance trading and military campaigns to foreign countries.

---

[13] Ebeling 1954, pp. 80–83; Maul 1994, pp. 91f.; Ambos, forthcoming a, §II.3.3.3. The ritual sequence is extant on the three fragments K 3231, K 7978, and K 10547 and has hitherto not been assigned to a known ritual. In one of the fragments (K 10547), a bath house (*bīt rimki*) is mentioned in destroyed context. So this rite might have been a part of the *bīt rimki* ritual discussed above. K 10547 has hitherto been only partially published as an autograph in Bezold 1889–99, III 1096: 6′–9′); a complete copy is given below. Text K 3231 has been published as an autograph in Bezold 1889–99, II 515: 1–4 only) and in Langdon 1927, pl. 23. Collations are published below. K 7978 is published as a hand copy in King 1896, no. 59.

[14] Mayer 1976, p. 268; Maul 1994, pp. 91f.

Since there existed a large net of watercourses, it was possible to cross a river or irrigation canal during the performance of a ritual without difficulty. In fact, it is well attested that rituals, or at least sequences of them, were performed at the riverbank. The crossing of roads also would have been within the realm of possibility during a ritual performance. Crossing a mountain, however, would have been hardly feasible while performing a ritual. Therefore it is well attested in rituals that one worked with miniature representations of those physical or other spaces to be crossed.

Interesting in this context is an instruction given in another ritual handbook:[15]

> You lay out two drawings with pebbles, crosswise. With a peg of tamarisk wood you open seven watercourses, you dig seven wells [...]. You heap up oil and syrup, and behind him/it [...] he (the ritual expert?) makes ... cross over it ... [...].[16]

Wells, like other subterranean structures such as, for example, the foundations of a building, reached toward the netherworld. It is attested that when digging a real well (not for use in a ritual), prayers and sacrifes were directed to the gods of the netherworld, whose sphere one intruded (Ambos 2004, pp. 70f.). When a person crossed over several miniature wells, this very connection to the netherworld plays a role. While crossing these wells, the person could purify him/herself by washing him/herself with the water of these wells and sending all the impurity down to the netherworld.

A similar setting is alluded to in a prayer from a ritual against the evil eye:[17] "Make the eye cross the seven watercourses, make the eye cross the seven irrigation canals, make the eye cross the seven mountains." A ritual instruction is not extant, but we may assume that in fact seven watercourses, canals, and mountains were arranged at the ritual setting.

Interestingly, the rite of crossing could be performed by different persons. A person affected by impurity could transmit it to a carrier who then had to cross the boundaries of the civilized world in order to carry the evil to distant regions. This rite was performed not necessarily only with the help of miniature representations but if possible also with the help of the real physical space. In a ritual that served to ward off the evil announced by an inauspicious omen, a stranger — an "unknown man" as he is called in the ritual instruction— is used as a carrier (Maul 1994, pp. 484–94). In the house of the affected person the carrier had to absorb the evil, and then he was bound, had to cross the river, and had to travel to an unknown place.

The affected person could, however, also perform the crossing rite himself, as, for example, the king crossing the miniature watercourses, mountains, and roads in the example cited above. This ritual technique is not only attested for crossing miniature representations of physical and other space, but also could, if possible, be performed with the real objects. According to a ritual handbook, a person suffering from the anger of his tutelary gods had to cross a watercourse. Then he had to perform ritual actions at the other side of the watercourse for Ea. Thus he would get rid of impurity and achieve reconciliation with the divine sphere (Ebeling 1956, pp. 22f.).

---

[15] LKA 139 rev. 32–35; the first sentence of the passage quoted here is cited in CAD I/J s.v. *išqillatu.*

[16] CAD N/1 s.v. *nabalkutu* 5b (p. 19) suggests a translation "he overturns his h[and]," but considers the passage "difficult." This passage from LKA 139 is also discussed in Ambos, forthcoming a, §II.3.3.3.

[17] Ebeling 1949, pp. 204f., lines 17f.

For the efficacy of this rite, two explanations are possible. Crossing the boundaries of the civilized world, one could carry his or her impurity to a far-away place, get rid of it and leave it there, and return purified to the civilized world. Especially when crossing a watercourse or well, the affected person also had the opportunity to wash him/herself in order to be cleansed of impurity.

Seen from another point of view, watercourses and mountains were obstacles for evil forces and could be arranged in the course of a ritual performance to impede demons in their attempts to assail their victim. From an incantation directed against the demon Lamaštu, we learn how humans could defend themselves against her machinations. Lamaštu is given her travel supplies and is made to withdraw herself. Then mountains and watercourses, which cannot be crossed, are arranged so that she can never return (Farber 1987, pp. 257f., lines 32f.).

In conclusion, it can be stated that ephemeral temporary structures made of perishable materials played an important role in ancient Near Eastern rituals. Structures of this kind were employed to create miniaturized representations of the various regions of the cosmos that then served as setting for the ritual performance. The different regions of the cosmos possessed particular inherent qualities on which the ritual expert wanted to draw on in order to enhance the efficacy of the performance of the respective ritual. As shown by various examples in this article, such settings were used in many different rituals with purposes such as expressing aspects of royal ideology or bringing about reconciliation with the alienated gods, purification, and control of evil.

Appendix: The Royal Ritual of Crossing Watercourses, Mountains, and Roads

Above I cite a passage from a royal ritual in the course of which the king must cross miniature watercourses, mountains, and roads. This passage is extant on the fragments K 3231, K 7978, and K 10547. In Ambos, forthcoming a, §II.3.3.3, I give a score transliteration and translation of these texts. Of the three fragments, only K 10547 has never been published completely as autograph. I take the opportunity to publish here a hand-copy of this fragment (fig. 11.1).

Likewise I was able to make some collations of K 3231, which I also publish here in handcopy (fig. 11.2). Publication of these autographs is made with the kind permission of the Trustees of the British Museum.

K 10547 obv. col. I (?)   **K 10547 rev. col. IV (?)**

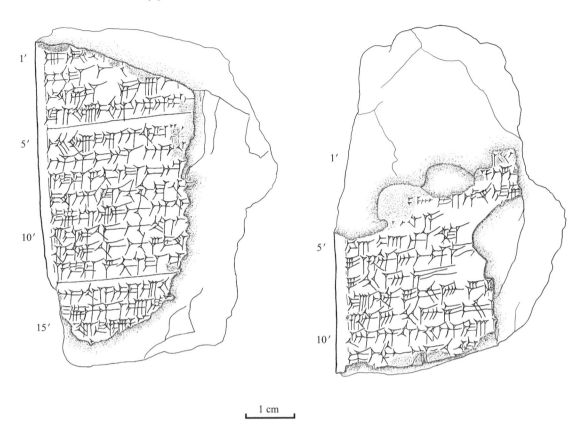

1 cm

Figure 11.1. K 10547, obverse and reverse

K 3231 obv. 1-2 (last preserved signs before break)

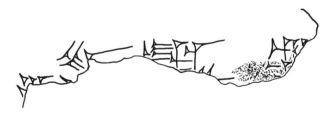

Figure 11.2. K 3231, obverse

Abbreviations

CAD   A. Leo Oppenheim et al., editors, *The Assyrian Dictionary of the Oriental Institute of the University of Chicago*. Chicago: The Oriental Institute, 1956–2010.

KAR   Erich Ebeling, *Keilschrifttexte aus Assur religiösen Inhalts*. Wissenschaftliche Veröffentlichungen der Deutschen Orient-Gesellschaft 28 and 34. Leipzig: J. C. Hinrichs, 1919/1923.

LKA   Erich Ebeling, *Literarische Keilschrifttexte aus Assur*. Berlin: Akademie-Verlag, 1953.

Bibliography

Ambos, Claus

2004   *Mesopotamische Baurituale aus dem 1. Jahrtausend v. Chr*. Dresden: ISLET.

2008   "Das 'Neujahrs'-Fest zur Jahresmitte und die Investitur des Königs im Gefängnis." In *Fest und Eid: Instrumente der Herrschaftssicherung im Alten Orient*, edited by Doris Prechel, pp. 1–12. Kulturelle und sprachliche Kontakte 3. Würzburg: Ergon.

2010   "Ritual Healing and the Investiture of the Babylonian King." In *The Problem of Ritual Efficacy*, edited by William Sax, Johannes Quack, and Jan Weinhold, pp. 17–44. New York: Oxford University Press.

2012   "Rituelle Wege an babylonischen Königssitzen." In *Orte der Herrschaft: Charakteristika von antiken Machtzentren*, edited by Felix Arnold, Alexandra W. Busch, Rudolf Haensch, and Ulrike Wulf-Rheidt, pp. 139–47. Menschen, Kulturen, Traditionen 3. Rahden: Verlag Marie Leidorf.

Forthcoming a   *Der König im Gefängnis und das Neujahrsfest im Herbst: Mechanismen der Legitimation des babylonischen Herrschers im 1. Jahrtausend v. Chr. und ihre Geschichte*. Dresden: ISLET.

Forthcoming b   "'Rites of Passage' or, Rites of Return'? Some Remarks on the Classification of Mesopotamian Rituals." In volume edited by Alice Mouton.

Attinger, Pascal

2003   "L'Hymne à Nungal." In *Literatur, Politik und Recht in Mesopotamien: Festschrift für Claus Wilcke*, edited by Walther Sallaberger, Konrad Volk, and Annette Zgoll, pp. 15–34. Orientalia Biblica et Christiana 14. Wiesbaden: Harrassowitz.

Bezold, Carl

1889–1899   *Catalogue of the Cuneiform Tablets in the Kouyunjik Collection*, Volumes 1–5. London: British Museum Press.

Cavigneaux, Antoine, and Manfred Krebernik

1998–2001   "Nungal." *Reallexikon der Assyriologie und vorderasiatischen Archäologie* 9: 615–18. Berlin: De Gruyter.

Crapanzano, Vincent

1992   *Hermes' Dilemma and Hamlet's Desire: On the Epistemology of Interpretation*. Cambridge: Harvard University Press.

Ebeling, Erich

1931   *Tod und Leben nach den Vorstellungen der Babylonier*. Berlin: Walter de Gruyter.

1949   "Beschwörungen gegen den Feind und den bösen Blick aus dem Zweistromlande." *Archiv Orientální* 17/1: 172–211.

1954	"Beiträge zur Kenntnis der Beschwörungsserie Namburbi." *Revue d'Assyriologie* 48: 1–15, 76–85.
1956	"Beiträge zur Kenntnis der Beschwörungsserie Namburbi." *Revue d'Assyriologie* 50: 22–33, 86–94.

Farber, Walter

1987	"Rituale und Beschwörungen in akkadischer Sprache." In *Rituale und Beschwörungen* I, edited by Otto Kaiser, pp. 212–81. Texte aus der Umwelt des Alten Testaments II/2. Gütersloh: Gütersloher Verlagshaus Gerd Mohn.
1989	*Schlaf, Kindchen, schlaf! Mesopotamische Baby-Beschwörungen und -Rituale*. Mesopotamian Civilizations 2. Winona Lake: Eisenbrauns.
1997	"*Bīt rimki* - ein assyrisches Ritual?" In *Assyrien im Wandel der Zeiten* (XXXIXe Rencontre Assyriologique Internationale, Heidelberg 6.–10. Juli 1992), edited by Hartmut Waetzoldt and Harald Hauptmann, pp. 41–46. Heidelberger Studien zum Alten Orient 6. Heidelberg: Heidelberger Orientverlag,

Frechette, Christopher G.

2012	*Mesopotamian Ritual-prayers of "Hand-lifting" (Akkadian Šuillas): An Investigation of Function in Light of the Idiomatic Meaning of the Rubric*. Alter Orient und Altes Testament 379. Münster: Ugarit-Verlag.

Jacobsen, Thorkild

1973	"Notes on Nintur." *Orientalia*, n.s., 42: 274–98.

King, Leonard W.

1896	*Babylonian Magic and Sorcery: Being "The Prayers of the Lifting of the Hand."* London: Luzac.

Læssøe, Jørgen

1955	*Studies on the Assyrian Ritual and Series* bît rimki. Copenhagen: Ejnar Munksgaard.

Lambert, W. G.

1996	*Babylonian Wisdom Literature*. Winona Lake: Eisenbrauns. Originally published Oxford: Oxford University Press, 1960.
1974	"Dingir.šà.dib.ba Incantations." *Journal of Near Eastern Studies* 33/3: 267–322.

Langdon, Stephen

1927	*Babylonian Penitential Psalms*. Oxford Editions of Cuneiform Texts 6. Paris: Librairie Orientaliste Paul Geuthner.

Maul, Stefan M.

1988	*"Herzberuhigungsklagen": Die sumerisch-akkadischen Eršahunga-Gebete*. Wiesbaden: Harrassowitz.
1994	*Zukunftsbewältigung: Eine Untersuchung altorientalischen Denkens anhand der babylonisch-assyrischen Löserituale (Namburbi)*. Baghdader Forschungen 18. Mainz am Rhein: Philipp von Zabern.

Mayer, Werner

1976	*Untersuchungen zur Formensprache der babylonischen "Gebetsbeschwörungen"*. Studia Pohl Series Maior 5. Rome: Biblical Institute Press.

Oppenheim, A. Leo

1977	*Ancient Mesopotamia: Portrait of a Dead Civilization*. Revised edition, completed by Erica Reiner. Chicago: University of Chicago Press. Originally published 1964.

Parpola, Simo

1993	*Letters from Assyrian and Babylonian Scholars*. State Archives of Assyria 10. Helsinki: Helsinki University Press.

Polonsky, Janice

2000 "ki-^dutu-è-a: Where Destiny is Determined." In *Landscapes: Territories, Frontiers and Horizons in the Ancient Near East*, Part 3: *Landscape in Ideology, Religion, Literature and Art*, edited by Lucio Milano et al., pp. 89–100. History of the Ancient Near East, Monographs III/3. Padua: Sargon.

2006 "The Mesopotamian Conceptualization of Birth and the Determination of Destiny at Sunrise." In *If a Man Builds a Joyful House: Assyriological Studies in Honor of Erle Verdun Leichty*, edited by Ann K. Guinan et al., pp. 297–311. Cuneiform Monographs 31. Leiden: Brill.

Pongratz-Leisten, Beate

1994 Ina šulmi īrub. *Die kulttopographische und ideologische Programmatik der* akītu-*Prozession in Babylonien und Assyrien im 1. Jahrtausend v. Chr.* Baghdader Forschungen 16. Mainz am Rhein: Philipp von Zabern.

1998–2001 "Neujahr(sfest). B. Nach akkadischen Quellen." *Reallexikon der Assyriologie* 9: 294–98.

2006–2008 "Prozession(sstraße). A. In den schriftlichen Quellen." *Reallexikon der Assyriologie* 11: 98–103.

Sallaberger, Walther

1998–2001 "Neujahr(sfest). A. Nach sumerischen Quellen." *Reallexikon der Assyriologie* 9: 291–94.

Seidl, Ursula, and Walther Sallaberger

2005/2006 "Der 'Heilige Baum.'" *Archiv für Orientforschung* 51: 54–74.

Taracha, Piotr

2001 "Hethitisch ^f*kippa*- und das Sumerogramm (É.)GI.PAD mesopotamischer Texte." *Altorientalische Forschungen* 28: 132–46.

Turner, Victor W.

1969 *The Ritual Process: Structure and Anti-Structure*. The Lewis Henry Morgan Lectures 1966. New York: Aldine.

2000 *Das Ritual: Struktur und Anti-Struktur*. Frankfurt: Campus Verlag.

van Gennep, Arnold

1909 *Les rites de passage: étude systématique des rites de la porte et du seuil; de l'hospitalité; de l'adoption etc.* Paris: Émile Nourry, 1909. Published in English in 1960 as *The Rites of Passage*, translated by Monika B. Vizedom and Gabrielle L. Caffee. Chicago: University of Chicago Press.

1999 *Übergangsriten (Les rites de passage).* Frankfurt: Campus Verlag.

Watanabe, Kazuko

1991 "Segenswünsche für den assyrischen König in der 2. Person Sg." *Acta Sumerologica* 13: 347–87.

Woods, Christopher

2009 "At the Edge of the World: Cosmological Conceptions of the Eastern Horizon in Mesopotamia." *Journal of Ancient Near Eastern Religions* 9: 183–239.

Zgoll, Annette

2006 "Königslauf und Götterrat: Struktur und Deutung des babylonischen Neujahrsfestes." In *Festtraditionen in Israel und im Alten Orient*, edited by Erhard Blum and Rüdiger Lux, pp. 11–80. Veröffentlichungen der Wissenschaftlichen Gesellschaft für Theologie 28. Gütersloh: Gütersloher Verlagshaus.

12

SACRED SPACE AND RITUAL PRACTICE AT THE END OF PREHISTORY IN THE SOUTHERN LEVANT

*Yorke M. Rowan, The Oriental Institute**

*Dynamic and continuously reformulated, religion is often expressed through ritual perfor-
mance. Ritual paraphernalia, iconography, and sacred built or natural space provide tangible
evidence to understand the human need to materialize the ethereal nature of religious belief.
During the late prehistoric periods in the southern Levant, an apparent increase in ritual
practice suggests a dramatic change during a time of demographic expansion and economic
intensification. In this paper, the spaces for ritual practice are examined in relationship to
the larger community and society, concentrating on the Chalcolithic period (ca. 4500–3600
B.C.). Specifically, the identification of sacred ceremonies and the built or natural space for
their performance is contrasted to earlier Neolithic practices. Comparative analysis allows
for some insights into continuity and changes during this period of high ritual density, and
some possible reasons for this intensification.*

Introduction

In the absence of texts, how might archaeology reveal the spiritual world of ancient
people? Can we presume to shed light on the structure of the immaterial? One factor working
in favor of using archaeological evidence to understand ancient religious belief and practice
is a human desire to materialize the numinous, to provide physical substance to the spiritual,
and to establish the sensual as part of practice. Ritual practice is a key aspect of religion,
but performance continuously changes as it is challenged, corrected, reconfigured, and repeated — in short, it is dynamic. Although many aspects of ritual performance will not be
found in the material remains, the archaeological record will sometimes include the ritual
paraphernalia, iconographic representation, or sacred natural and built space and landscapes
of ritual performative space. The notion that religious belief and practice may be studied,
even in prehistoric society, has gained increasing acceptance in recent years (Barrowclough
and Malone 2007; Fogelin 2007; Insoll 2004a, 2004b; Kyriakidis 2007; Rowan 2012; Whitley
and Hays-Gilpin 2008) although no consensus on definitive terms and methodology is near.

Fogelin (2007) recently reviewed approaches to the archaeological investigation of religion. In some instances, archaeologists identify and interpret data related to ritual practice
based on evidence originating in the archaeological record, leading to an understanding of

* These interpretations about the evidence for ritual
practice during the Chalcolithic were greatly influenced by years of debate and collaboration with
David Ilan. I would also like to take this opportunity
to thank Morag Kersel for reading and commenting on an earlier draft of this paper. In addition,
my thanks to Deena Ragavan for organizing such a
stimulating and rewarding conference.

the manner and structure that form the framework for an ancient religion. Others start with religion as known through text and mythologies and use this knowledge to reconstruct ritual practice and belief. Ideally, these options would function in a dialectic and complementary fashion, but without texts or oral traditions, the archaeologist of prehistory is left with only the first approach — the archaeological record.

My primary goal in this paper is the identification in the archaeological record of ritual spaces and some insights into how those spaces changed during later prehistory prior to the emergence of Early Bronze Age towns in the southern Levant. I am particularly interested in tracing changes over the course of several millennia, from the Pre-Pottery Neolithic (PPN) to the Chalcolithic period. The PPN (ca. 11,700–8400 BP) is generally subdivided into the PPNA and PPNB; a more recent addition of the PPNC or final PPNB is increasingly accepted (Kuijt and Goring Morris 2002). In order to consider such a long period of time, this discussion is limited to the southern Levant (fig. 12.1), providing only summaries of the PPN and Late Neolithic.

Neolithic Antecedents: Pre-Pottery Neolithic

Considerable research has explored Pre-Pottery Neolithic (8500–6250 B.C.) ritual practices across southwestern Asia. Most studies focus on either descriptions of material evidence for rituals, or the ways in which these ceremonial rites may indicate belief in the afterlife and/or ancestor worship. More broadly, Verhoeven (2002) examines Neolithic ideology and beliefs through the contextual examination of symbols, art, and burial rites. Alternatively, Kuijt (2000b) examines how ritual practices may have served to integrate communities and act as a leveling mechanism to counter growing inequality.

Many of these ritual practices apparently became more pronounced during the PPNB, with a particular florescence during the Middle PPNB (8100–7250 B.C.). Skull removal, already evident during the Natufian and continuing into the PPNA (9700–8500 B.C.), expands, with skull plastering, painting, and modification across a range of communities (Kuijt and Goring-Morris 2002; Twiss 2007). Cranial deformation also seems to occur (Kuijt and Goring-Morris 2002). In the southern Levant, skulls from ʿAin Ghazal and Jericho both exhibit cranial manipulation and plastering during the PPN. Both sites recovered large statues and busts, presumably for community rituals, as they were created for display through placement in upright positions in public space (Schmandt-Besserat 1998). The two caches of statues from ʿAin Ghazal, better preserved than those discovered at Jericho in the 1930s, contain approximately thirty-two figurines (Rollefson and Kafafi 2007). At ʿAin Ghazal, modeled skulls include eyeliner and irises made of asphalt (Rollefson 1983, 1986), closely resembling these statues. Some suggest that the statues represent divinities (Schmandt-Besserat 1998), while others propose ancestors (Kenyon 1957), although they are more likely to represent people connected to the ancestral line rather than ancestors, since some statues are adolescents (Rollefson 2004; Rollefson and Kafafi 2007).

According to Kuijt and Goring-Morris (2002, p. 419), special purpose or communal architecture, although appearing earlier, during the PPNA, increases during the Middle PPNB and into the Late PPNB. These structures seem to be situated in highly visible locations (Kuijt 2000a), such as a physically separated area (e.g., Beidha; see Kirkbride 1966, 1968). Perhaps the clearest examples in the southern Levant are known from ʿAin Ghazal, dated to the Late PPNB (Rollefson 1983, 1986, 1998a, 1998b, 2001). At ʿAin Ghazal, where broad exposures allowed the excavators to distinguish between residential and community space, both circular buildings and rectangular buildings were interpreted to be ritual structures ("cultic shrines and temples," Rollefson 2001, pp. 82–85) primarily based on architectural style, spatial layout, and details (e.g., orthostats, plaster, furniture). Two partially preserved round structures, situated between rectangular buildings, were interpreted as cult buildings (fig. 12.2). One, with four building phases, was reorganized in the final phase when a space enclosed by a circular wall (ca. 2.5 m diameter) with eight red-painted lime plaster surfaces accumulated (Rollefson 2001, p. 82, fig. 3.7). A pit (ca. 60 cm diameter, ca. 40 cm depth) was centered in the room as part of an installation; a pair of channels radiating below the floor have been interpreted as ducts to draw in air to feed a raised hearth (Rollefson 2001, p. 82; Rollefson and Kafafi 1994, fig. 10). Based on the unusual interior, small size, and constricted access, the ritual function of the structure was considered relatively clear. Approximately five meters to the south a very similar building, less carefully constructed, functioned in an apparently similar manner, possibly after the more carefully constructed version fell out of use (Rollefson 1998b, 2001).

Elsewhere at ʿAin Ghazal, two Late PPNB rectangular structures strongly indicate specialized function (fig. 12.3). One, measuring 4 × 5 m, was built with care using rectangular stone slabs; near the center of the southern wall, two limestone blocks outline a patch of burned clay, with two large amorphous stones delineating one end of the "altar-like platform" (Rollefson 2001, p. 83). North of this altar, three orthostats stand approximately 70 cm high; midway between the standing stones and the eastern wall is a red-painted lime plaster hearth (ca. 50 cm) set off by small limestone slabs. In the center of the eastern wall, another orthostat of bright white limestone was incorporated into the wall, possibly with an anthropomorphic quality (ibid., p. 84). The other rectilinear structure, about 100 m downhill, was clearly larger despite destruction from erosion. Several rooms were still evident, with walls standing over 1 m in places. Inside, the floor was made of clay, and against the middle of the eastern wall, an altar comprised of two large limestone slabs set atop three pairs of orthostats was nearly two meters long. In front of the altar, a hearth of white plaster surrounded by slabs was approximately 1 m in diameter. A small square cubicle of limestone slabs set into the clay floor had no artifacts in direct association (Rollefson 1998a, 2001). In the room, Rollefson (2001, p. 84) suggests that a "holy of holies" is created by a screen of stones, blocking viewing into the east room.

Interior constructions in the rectangular "temples" distinguish them on a functional level from the circular plastered shrines. Rollefson (2001) notes that the orthostats incorporated into walls are similar to the shrine identified by Kenyon at Jericho (Kenyon 1981, pp. 306–07, pls. 172–73); orthostats, monoliths, and stelae are also known from Kfar Hahoresh and Beidha, often occurring in threes (Kuijt and Goring-Morris 2002, p. 420). Without artifacts associated with these structures, the nature of ritual practices is impossible to know, but the absence of any human remains — including plastered or modified skulls — suggests that perhaps they functioned differently.

Other PPNB sites also exhibit strong ritual components. One that was clearly the focal point of ritual practice in the southern Levant is the Judean Desert cave site of Nahal Hemar, where masks and other ritual paraphernalia suggest a place of ritual practice or deposition, perhaps exclusively (Bar-Yosef and Alon 1988). Kfar Hahoresh also appears to have a major ritual function, with both plastered skulls and skeletal remains of animals and humans purposively arranged (Goring-Morris 2000).

By the PPNC (8600–8250 cal. BP) (Rollefson and Simmons 1986), the agglomerative process leading to sometimes massive settlements of the PPNB on the eastern side of the Jordan River abates, and some sites are entirely abandoned. Concomitant with the disaggregation of population, architecture, art, and mortuary practices shifted dramatically; lithic production is less standardized (Byrd 1994; Rollefson 2001; Rollefson and Köhler-Rollefson 1993; Twiss 2007). Causes for this break in cultural continuity, or "collapse," probably reflect a combination of environmental and social factors; some scholars stress the effects of environmental degradation resulting from climactic or anthropogenic forces (Bar-Yosef 2001; Köhler-Rollefson 1988; Rollefson and Köhler-Rollefson 1989), while others emphasize social stress induced by population growth or a combination of these factors (Kuijt 2004; Banning 2004, Simmons 2000). Whatever the cause, population dispersal is widely accepted as a reason for the change in settlement size and location.

Neolithic Antecedents: Late (Pottery) Neolithic

The Neolithic to Chalcolithic transition includes a variety of terms used to describe and classify late sixth- to early fifth-millennium entities. Our poor understanding of the Late Neolithic to Chalcolithic transition has improved dramatically in recent years, and the continuity of people and their traditions is well documented (Banning 1998, 2002, 2010; Lovell 2001; Banning et al. 2004). Population disaggregation apparently continued into the Late Neolithic (6250–4700[?] B.C.). Although there are exceptions, most Late Neolithic sites are small villages or farmsteads in the arable zones, with relatively basic, coarse pottery, expedient chipped stone tools, and relatively insubstantial architecture. Alongside this general dispersal, the broad similarity of PPNB sites throughout the Levant disappeared; in their place, localized entities arose. The earliest of these, the Yarmukian, is the best known, while the attributes of later Wadi Rabah, Jericho IX, and Qatifian phases continue to be debated. Nonetheless, abandonment of the region, proposed by Kenyon (1979), no longer seems tenable (Rollefson 2001).

Circular and rectilinear buildings are found during the Yarmukian phase (Garfinkel 1993; Gopher and Gophna 1993; Kafafi 1985, 1988, 2001; Twiss 2007), the latter sometimes found with a curvilinear end (an "apse"); additional building variants are more fragile (Gopher and Gophna 1993; Twiss 2007). Substantial architecture and organized sites were recovered at ʿAin Ghazal and Shaʾar Hagolan. Multicellular courtyards at Shaʾar Hagolan certainly demonstrate continuity with the sophistication of earlier building techniques, but the general impression of expedient or flimsy structures holds for many sites.

In contrast to earlier PPN traditions, evidence for ritual practices is notably rare or absent; the few burials indicate various intramural and extramural interments, primary and secondary practices (under floors, in cists) that rarely include grave goods. Skull removal, apparently absent by the PPNC, is also absent (Rollefson 2001). At some sites, figurines are abundant (e.g., Shaʾar Hagolan; Garfinkel, Korn, and Miller 2002, including both the anthropomorphic figurines with cowrie shell-shaped eyes and the much more schematic engraved river pebbles; figurines were absent from other sites (Garfinkel 1993; Garfinkel, Korn, and Miller 2002; Gopher and Gophna 1993). Clearly demarcated ritual spaces are also difficult to identify, although recent research in the eastern desert regions of Jordan are identifying likely ritual areas (Rowan, Rollefson, and Kersel 2011; Wasse, Rollefson, and Rowan forthcoming).

Chalcolithic

Major cultural transformations took place in the southern Levant during the Chalcolithic period (4500–3600 B.C.), but within this long period, no internal chronology is agreed upon. Expansion of agro-pastoralist communities in number and size led to increased occupation of regions such as the Golan Heights and the Beersheba Valley, where few Neolithic settlements are attested. Secondary animal products may have played an increasingly important role in the economy (Evershed et al. 2008), although the impact of horticulture, particularly the domesticated olive, is poorly understood and under-examined (but see Lovell 2008). Craft production exhibits greater technological expertise, raw materials from medium- and long-range distances, and innovative changes in form and decoration. Secondary mortuary treatment of the body is increasingly attested, and the attendant equipment becomes vastly more diversified than in previous eras. Status goods, too, are more prominently evident, frequently in mortuary contexts.

Chalcolithic socioeconomic organization appears dissimilar when comparing regions, although to what degree this might reflect chronological differences is unclear. In some regions, such as the Golan, there are few attributes of ranked, hierarchical status, while in other regions, particularly the large northern Negev villages (e.g., Abu Matar, Bir es-Safadi, and Shiqmim); there are weak indicators of non-egalitarian structure, such as larger buildings and prestige objects (Rowan and Golden 2009). Although some scholars would propose that ranked, hierarchical societies — chiefdoms — dominate Chalcolithic society (e.g., Gal, Smithline, and Shalem 2007; Gopher and Tsuk 1996; Levy 1986, 1995), others tend toward more egalitarian interpretations (Gilead 1988, 2002; Joffe 2003; Joffe, Dessel, and Hallote 2001). These points are relevant to the present discussion because interpretations of evidence for ritual praxis and practitioners seem to reflect a scholar's preferred model of social complexity; where scholars see chiefdoms, interpretations of "priests" and "sanctuaries" are dominant, whereas those who see less hierarchical organization view shamans as the ritual leaders. Yet the mutual exclusivity of these two positions should be demonstrated rather than assumed; there is no reason that both forms of ritual leaders could not have existed concurrently (Rowan and Ilan 2007).

Although the Chalcolithic period is relatively rich in iconography and imagery, interpretation of the meaning behind these images is difficult given the lack of texts. For this reason, many scholars rely on cosmologies and mythologies of neighboring regions (i.e., Egypt and Mesopotamia) and inferences from later periods (Amiran 1981; Merhav 1993; Gal, Smithline, and Shalem 2011). This approach has value, but in order to understand ritual practice and sacred space we must privilege material culture evidence for ritual action. Rather than rely on retrodictive interpretations focused on iconography and symbolism from later, state societies, this discussion focuses on evidence for recurrent ritual practice as a lens on the structure of religious belief. I argue that Chalcolithic ritual practice existed in diverse contexts, and the similarities are not always immediately apparent. Across the landscape, both above ground and below, sanctuaries, caches, subterranean chambers, and burial deposits are interconnected, and the ties that bind them enable us to reconstruct fragments of Chalcolithic practices, and belief.

Such a study is much too ambitious for the present discussion, and will be treated more fully elsewhere (see Rowan and Ilan 2012). For the prehistoric context of this study I limit myself to three examples. For the Chalcolithic of Palestine, the identification of ritual practice and sacred space is typically relegated to only a few sites. One site in particular, En Gedi, will serve as a starting point for an examination of ritual space during the Chalcolithic — both the identification of ritual space and the interpretation of the rites performed there.

En Gedi

The small complex at En Gedi, excavated from 1961 to 1964 (Ussishkin 1980), is situated near two springs on a remote promontory overlooking the Dead Sea to the east. Four primary components constitute the known architecture (fig. 12.4): a courtyard, two rectilinear broad rooms, and a gatehouse (Ussishkin 1980). A shallow circular feature lined with large flat stones, possibly a pit, is situated in the center of the courtyard. Mazar (2000) proposed that it marks the location of a sacred tree, a phenomenon known from later temples, but the stone lining makes this supposition unlikely. A stone bench abuts the interior of each long wall in the main broad room, while a semi-circular stone feature is built into the bench along the northern long wall and was interpreted as an "altar." Placed inside this semicircle was a white, crystalline, limestone drum. On either end of the broad room, a series of small shallow pits contained ashes and charcoal. A ceramic quadruped (bull?) carrying two churns was recovered in the ashy matrix near the semicircle. One of the few complete vessels found was a fenestrated pedestal bowl, upside down atop two ibex or gazelle horns. Many such horns were recovered in this room. Other cultural material found during excavation included mollusca, animal bones, two pendants, and two beads. An alabaster jar fragment found near the central courtyard basin is Egyptian in origin or inspiration (Ussishkin 1980, pp. 21, 24–25). Pedestaled, fenestrated bowls and the pointed bases of "cornets" (see fig. 12.10) make up the majority of the ceramic assemblage, in contrast to the standard assemblage found at traditional Chalcolithic settlements (e.g., Abu Matar, Bir es-Safadi, or Shiqmim; see Levy and Menahem 1987; Commenge-Pellerin 1987, 1990). The high number of cornets recovered at En Gedi was unparalleled until the excavations at Gilat (see below). Without domestic items such as cooking and storage vessels, flint tools, hearths, or pits, most archaeologists agree that the En Gedi complex served as a ritual structure, whether termed a "temple" (e.g., Gilead 2002; Ottoson 1980), "sanctuary" (e.g., Levy 1995, 2006), or "shrine" (e.g., Mazar 2000; Ussishkin 1980). Three elements are highlighted by this small assemblage: ceramic fenestrated stands, ceramic cornets, and ruminant horns. These elements are further indication that the En Gedi sanctuary was indeed a ritual structure.

Architectural similarities of the En Gedi complex to later Early Bronze examples fostered widespread acceptance among archaeologists that this represents a locus of ritual practice. Yet this has inspired little methodical examination of ritual praxis in broader contexts, with the exception of the mortuary realm (Rowan and Ilan 2012). Turning from the En Gedi complex to the wider Chalcolithic society, a few examples of non-residential, non-domestic structures with associated deposits suggest intramural ritual areas at other sites. Our next example draws from the type site of the period, Tulaylat al-Ghassul.

Tulaylat al-Ghassul

Excavations began at Tulaylat al-Ghassul in 1929, motivated in part by the possibility that the ruins represented biblical Sodom and Gomorrah (North 1982, p. 59). Eight seasons of excavation (1929–1938) by the Pontifical Biblical Institute revealed a 20 hectare village with rooms, courtyards, pits, and alleys (Bourke 1997, p. 395; Mallon, Koeppel, and Neuville 1934) to a depth of five meters. The early campaign exposed three wall murals, called Les Personnages, L'Oiseau, and L'Etoile of Ghassul; two more murals were found during North's excavations in the winter of 1959/60, the Geometric and the Tiger (Cameron 1981). Two more paintings, the Procession and the zigzag fragment, were found during the excavations led by Hennessy (Bourke 2001). A final mural fragment, the Garlanded Sickle, was recovered by the University of Sydney team (Bourke et al. 2000, fig. 18). The polychrome murals of black, yellow, red, white, and brown include motifs that appear to represent architectural features, tools, anthropomorphic and zoomorphic figures, and geometrical designs. Scenes such as Les Personnages appear to include figures wearing masks. The best known, most complex, and most colorful fragment includes representations of animals, structural elements (possibly architecture), and a large geometric eight-point star. Outside of one small fragment from Tell Abu Hamid, these eight murals from Ghassul remain the sole known examples of Chalcolithic mural art in the southern Levant.

Without parallels or comparison, the discovery of Ghassul led to the recognition of a new chronological period, and new cultural entity, the Ghassulian. Although there was little context for the finds, and no comparative imagery, investigations at Ghassul provided the first evidence for symbolic practices and abstract representation for the period. Despite the remarkable discoveries at Ghassul, our knowledge of the larger context for these finds has been dramatically limited for many years due to different standards of publication in the early twentieth century. This only recently changed with some publications by the current director Stephen Bourke and his students at the University of Sydney.

Peta Seaton's dissertation (2008) recounts the previously unpublished material from J. B. Hennessy's excavations from the mid-1970s and more recent investigations led by Bourke from 1994 to the present. Focused on one section of Ghassul, Seaton summarizes the stratigraphy, architecture, and material culture that constitutes the evidence for a "sanctuary precinct" in Area E. In this detailed study of the material and architecture in this area, Seaton then examines the justification for the "cultic" attribution of the precinct, and whether or not extrapolation to broader concerns about cult expression, individual aggrandizing, and risk management is warranted.

For brevity I can only summarize the major attributes that set this complex apart from other sections of the site. Area E (fig. 12.5) includes two rectilinear buildings, perpendicular to each other; one linked to a stone arc by a paved path, or "avenue." To the north and west are two long "temenos" walls. Two pits are noted to the north of the temenos wall, while another pit is enclosed by the western temenos wall. These structures co-existed contemporaneously in the Classic Courtyard phase, although Seaton (2008, pp. 25–32) notes several building phases.

Sanctuary A

This is a large (exterior dimensions: 9.75 × 4.75 m; interior dimensions 7.9 × 2.6 m) paved long room oriented north–south, constructed predominantly of medium-size cobbles, with mudbrick superstructure. A possible internal mudbrick bench construction is set along the eastern long wall. The paving stones include at least two floor replasterings. The door, set in the long east wall, includes three parallel lines of river stones as steps into the interior, with decayed food still preserved against the lower step. In places, silting and weather-hardened flooring was covered with reed matting; a destruction level is associated with the reed mats and includes burned mudbrick, ash, and collapsed wall and ceiling material. One, and possibly both long wall interiors and the short northern wall had painted plaster; two patches of plaster lay on a burned wooden beam in the center of the room. Objects from this destruction level included fenestrated pedestaled stands, open form vessels, one cornet base, a footed vessel with possible horn, a ceramic figurine limb fragment, a ceramic spoon, a painted ceramic "bracelet" and a painted double kernos (fig. 12.6). This is oriented perpendicular to Sanctuary B.

Sanctuary B

Oriented east–west along the long axis, this structure is smaller, with internal dimensions of 2.56 × 4.60 m. A central door in the southern wall opens facing the Dead Sea. Rim and body sherds of the double kernos from Sanctuary A were found in this phase of Sanctuary B, confirming contemporaneity of the two structures. Three cornet bases and fragments of anthropomorphic figurines were found directly at the entrance to Sanctuary B.

Altar Arc ("Semi-circular Installation")

A paved "avenue" links a semi-circular installation — the Altar Arc — to the east, perpendicular to Sanctuary A and roughly parallel to Sanctuary B, which is north of the avenue. This avenue, a triple row of flat paving stones, links the central doorway on the east side of Sanctuary A to the semi-circular structure. The semi-circular altar structure was made of two rows of large river stones. At the center of the semi-circular feature, a natural, roughly circular (ca. 70 cm) sandstone cobble is installed above the paved avenue, steadied by smaller stones. Two parallel grinding depressions are visible on top of this sandstone. Within the Altar Arc, a dark burned ashy layer extended to within 10 cm inside of the wall face, where a large basalt pillar or stand (Seaton 2008, pl. 93) was lying against the inside of the wall.

Temenos Courtyard

In addition to the unusual hollow, pierced limbed vessel, the area bound by the long temenos walls on the north and west included familiar ritual items: fragments of large numbers of cornets, fenestrated stands, fine and deep bowls, and a footed goblet.

In terms of architecture, there are a few parallels between this area of Ghassul and En Gedi. Although Ghassul is not fully enclosed like En Gedi, Sanctuary A is similar in size and shape to the En Gedi broad room; the mudbrick bench along the interior of one long wall echoes those at En Gedi. An important difference is the placement of what possibly served as the "altar"; at En Gedi the non-local stone was found inside the broad room, whereas the comparable stone at Ghassul was found in the courtyard. In both cases, however, the stone was placed on or near the stone-built arc, located in the broad room at En Gedi but in the center of the courtyard at Ghassul. Artifact assemblages from both exhibit strong parallels, particularly the strong presence of cornets, fenestrated stands, and footed vessels. The presence of figurines at both sites, although anthropomorphic at Ghassul and zoomorphic at En Gedi, is evocative given their rarity at Chalcolithic sites in general. Finally, the painted double painted kernos from Ghassul is a vessel type unique to the period.

Unlike En Gedi, Tulaylat al-Ghassul is a large complex site with domestic occupation and specialized intramural areas, including some dedicated to ceremonial purposes. For this reason, these two sites appear dissimilar in many respects, yet parallels exist between the spaces designated for ritual practice. In many ways, our third example, Gilat, is more complicated because of the lack of clearly delineated spatial boundaries.

Gilat

Similar to Tulaylat al-Ghassul, a rich assemblage of artifacts was recovered during the seven seasons of excavation at Gilat, a 12-hectare site located approximately 20 kilometers northeast of Beersheba. Unlike Ghassul, however, multiple occupations and rebuilding episodes created complex stratigraphy and fragmentary mudbrick architecture buildings, rendering coherent plans elusive (Levy et al. 2006). Despite the chaotic nature of the architectural remains, the remarkable artifacts, deposited primarily in fills and pits, attest to a site dissimilar to any others except perhaps Ghassul.

The best known finds are the evocative vessels, the Gilat Lady (fig. 12.7) and the Ram with Cornets (fig. 12.8) (Alon 1976; Commenge et al. 2006a; Ilan and Rowan 2012, figs. 7.10–11), but these iconic anthropomorphic and zoomorphic vessels are only one aspect of this copious and diverse assemblage, much of it apparently related to ceremonial rites. The unique Gilat Lady figurine, in particular, was the subject of multiple interpretations, many perceiving her as a goddess (Alon 1976, 1977; Amiran 1976, 1989; Amiran and Tadmor 1980; Epstein 1978, 1982; Fox 1995; Joffe, Dessel, and Hallote 2001; Merhav 1993; Tadmor 1986). Holding a churn on her head, a fenestrated stand under her arm, and seated on a ring-shaped object, the Gilat Lady is intriguing. The exact archaeological context of both vessels, however, is not entirely clear, and the broader context of the site paints a much more complex picture than could possibly be derived from one or two elaborate vessels.

In addition to standard Chalcolithic ceramic vessel forms, miniature versions of standard Chalcolithic vessels, such as stemmed chalices, tubular beakers, and churns are found in the assemblage. Others, such as the large, thick cylindrical vessels — torpedo jars — are unusual or unknown forms at other sites (see Commenge et al. 2006a). Some vessels, particularly churns and holemouth jars, include numerous examples manufactured of non-local clays (Goren 1995, p. 295; Goren 2006, p. 371). This is true of some torpedo jars as well, which may have been used for transport and storage of oil, based on the gas chromatography identification of lipids consistent with olives (Burton and Levy 2006), a newly domesticated fruit during the Chalcolithic (Bourke et al. 2007; Neef 1990; Zohary and Spiegel-Roy 1975). Ceramic fenestrated, pedestaled stands were commonly found (fig. 12.9). Finally, a large number of cornets were recovered (fig. 12.10). This is a rare or non-existent vessel type at most sites, but occurs in substantial numbers at other ritual sites such as Ghassul and En Gedi, as noted above.

Rare and unusual forms of material culture are not limited to ceramic vessels. Basalt fenestrated stand fragments, analogous to the ceramic form, were found in the hundreds. Created of basalt originating either in the Golan/Galilee or central Jordan, a two- or three-day journey (Rowan et al. 2006), the vessels were labor intensive, difficult to manufacture, and possibly broken intentionally. Other non-local materials include rocks (e.g., granite, scoria, chlorite schist, carnelian, amazonite, and hematite) for the manufacture of palettes, spindle whorls, mace-heads, beads (Rowan et al. 2006), and violin-shaped figurines (Commenge et al. 2006b). A few of the mace-heads exhibit morphology more similar to those from early predynastic Egyptian forms (Rowan et al. 2006). Approximately seventy-six violin-shaped figurine fragments represent a minimum of fifty-three figurines, some with breasts (figs. 12.11–12), more than the sum of all others recovered from southern Levantine sites (Commenge et al. 2006b, fig. 15.20). Also non-local were the mollusk species from the Nile, the Red Sea, and the Mediterranean, more frequent than at other Chalcolithic sites (Bar-Yosef Mayer 2006). Even farther afield, the six pieces of obsidian recovered at Gilat were traced to different sources in Anatolia (Yellin, Levy, and Rowan 1996). Although probably available locally, hundreds of ostrich eggshell fragments were found, and a cache of four whole ostrich eggs grouped together in a shallow pit were buried in an open plaza area (Levy et al. 2006, p. 110, pl. 4.35).

Alon and Levy (1989) interpret Gilat as a center for regional pilgrimage. Utilizing Renfrew's criteria outlined for identifying cultic activity at the Cycladic Bronze Age site of Phylakopi (Renfrew 1985), Alon and Levy categorize eighteen attributes as indicative of ritual activity, including much of the material culture discussed above. Their interpretation is convincing, although the reasons for a ritual sanctuary are not elaborated.

Human burial was apparently a key aspect of the ritual process at Gilat. Burial density at Gilat is much higher than at typical (non-ritual) Chalcolithic settlements. An estimated ninety individuals (Smith et al. 2006) were found, most in primary burials. Many were placed in shallow pits, but scattered bones and disturbed disarticulated skeletal elements were common. In one mudbrick-lined pit, possibly the secondary usage of a silo, nine individuals were recovered: three adults, three adolescents, and three children (Levy et al. 2006, pl. 5.19). Nearby, a mud-plastered pit contained a complete basalt fenestrated stand, bone tools, and burned gazelle horn cores. Horn cores were also evident at En Gedi and may be indicative of some ritual function. Mortuary practices extended even to a canine; the interment of an aged dog, articulated, with a complete and unusual vessel, is perhaps the earliest known canine with a burial offering discovered in the Levant (Grigson 2006, pp. 237–38; pl. 6.3b).

If pilgrimage is part of the process that led to this ritual site, mortuary activity must have been a central experience at Gilat (Ilan and Rowan 2012). Central elements of the material culture assemblage found at Gilat — such as fenestrated stands, cornets, and ruminant horns — parallel those of En Gedi, yet there are clearly profound differences. If Gilat is a pilgrimage site with an integral mortuary component, it probably also served other needs. The presence of non-local materials, some rare and atypical to other sites, distinguish it from En Gedi. Despite the lack of coherent architecture, the large assemblage of pottery, chipped stone, and ground stone implements suggest a domestic component, with long-term occupation.

Final Remarks

The present examination focuses on just a few cases of evidence for ritual practices, particularly during the Chalcolithic period. Despite the brevity of our review for the later southern Levantine Neolithic phases, the contrast to ritual activity during the Chalcolithic is striking. This is perhaps unsurprising given the length of time examined. The addition of tactile and visual objects during the Chalcolithic that appear within ritual spaces contrasts to that of the Neolithic, where few ritual objects can be directly associated with the buildings considered "shrines" and "temples." Clearly, Neolithic people in the southern Levant had ritual equipment too; the modified skulls, statuettes, and possibly animal figurines were often recovered from "structured deposits"(Bradley 1990). Unlike the Chalcolithic, however, these ritual items were generally not found with the formalized space built for rites.

In contrast to the Late Neolithic, a renewal of ritual space, architecture, and equipment is evident for the Chalcolithic, but this is far from codified. Architecturally, the Area E sanctuary at Tulaylat al-Ghassul bears little resemblance to that at Gilat, but there are similarities to the En Gedi complex. Both Ghassul and En Gedi have large open space bound by an enclosure wall that includes two rectilinear rooms, although their relationship to each other seems dissimilar. Associated pits are found at both sites. Bearing in mind that the scale of these two sites is dissimilar, the presence of any similarities is notable. Moreover, the presence of more than eight plaster painted murals across Tulaylat al-Ghassul suggests other areas of the site had additional ritual areas.

Although no "altar" similar to those found at Ghassul or En Gedi was found at Gilat, other enigmatic stone constructions were noted in the excavation report. In places, stone "platforms" were preserved, but how they functioned is obscure (Levy et al. 2006).

Despite the diverse components of the respective material culture assemblage of each site, common elements are detectable. Most notable, the prominence of ceramic cornets and pedestaled, fenestrated stands (both in basalt and ceramic) at Gilat and En Gedi, and in Area E of Tulaylat al-Ghassul, are strikingly similar and otherwise uncommon at settlement sites. The unusual vessels from Ghassul (the double kernos, in particular) and Gilat (torpedoes, miniature forms, tubular vessels) are conspicuous too. Finally, the presence of horn cores at Gilat and En Gedi, found in caches or offering pits at both sites, are atypical of standard domestic deposits or rubbish. And if I was to indulge in speculation, the possible similarity of animal horns to the cornets, which may have been a ceremonial drinking vessel, seems a key symbol.

I have explored the ritual contexts occurring within a settlement, such as Tulaylat al-Ghassul, those consigned to special, extramural places on the landscape, as at En Gedi, and those with a complex of ritual purposes, such as Gilat. For the Chalcolithic, a reliance on specially constructed monuments is insufficient to determine the function, or functions, of an area. Thus the site of En Gedi may represent a sanctuary placed within a ritual landscape. Yet other sites such as Gilat, unremarkable in their architecture (or at least the preservation) or the location on an undefined landscape, nonetheless evoke a richness in ritual practice, and elaborate objects employed in those rites.

At this point in prehistory, the sphere of ritual praxis is identifiable, both within the domestic context of habitation sites or extramurally, particularly through the secondary mortuary treatment of burials held at cemeteries and caves established away from settlements. At the same time, this separation is far from codified and large settlement sites such as Tulaylat al-Ghassul, for example, include areas delineated for ritual practice for some segment of the community.

This cursory exploration of identifying ritual through the archaeological record comments on the complicated relationship between extramural formal ritual spaces and the places where people lived, which contained active, even elaborate ritual areas in domestic settlements. A key component to our understanding of this complex relationship was barely touched upon, however, yet it was central to Chalcolithic life — the process of death. Although Chalcolithic burial included primary and secondary treatments of the body, most secondary burial occurs outside of settlements, in burial caves, dolmens, and tumuli. The diverse mortuary processes of the Chalcolithic include some of the most elaborate iconography on the ossuaries, and some of the richest burial goods (Ilan and Rowan 2012; Rowan and Ilan, in press; Gal, Smithline, and Shalem 1997, 1999). But the most common burial goods include open-form vessels, and the pedestaled fenestrated bowls similar to those recovered from En Gedi, Gilat, and Tulaylat al-Ghassul. Mortuary assemblages thus support recognition of redundant elements in the ritual repertoire.

Archaeologists frequently tend to view ritual and religion as conservative and unchanging, the product of long-lived traditions. But at times ritual also acts as a dynamic force for change, and a change in ritual may instigate modification of religious belief itself (Fogelin 2007, pp. 58–59). Ritual practice underwent a crucial change in the Chalcolithic. Formal shrines or sanctuaries, distinct from domestic settlements, were established. The newly introduced, clearly defined functional spaces of the sanctuaries at En Gedi, Ghassul, and perhaps Gilat echo the importance given to formalized space at some PPN sites, such as ʿAin Ghazal, Beidha, and Jericho. Unlike the Neolithic, however, material culture in the Chalcolithic exhibits some redundancy of symbols and equipment that indicates ritual praxis included a standardized repertoire of material culture for performance in designated places. These dramatic changes, with parallels to mortuary practices, highlight the radical departure of ritual praxis from those of the earlier Neolithic phases. There is no need to ignore the long period of time during which these fundamental changes occurred, but the emergence of rich Chalcolithic ritual practices and beliefs hints at new concerns and preoccupations, sharply contrasting to those of earlier prehistory.

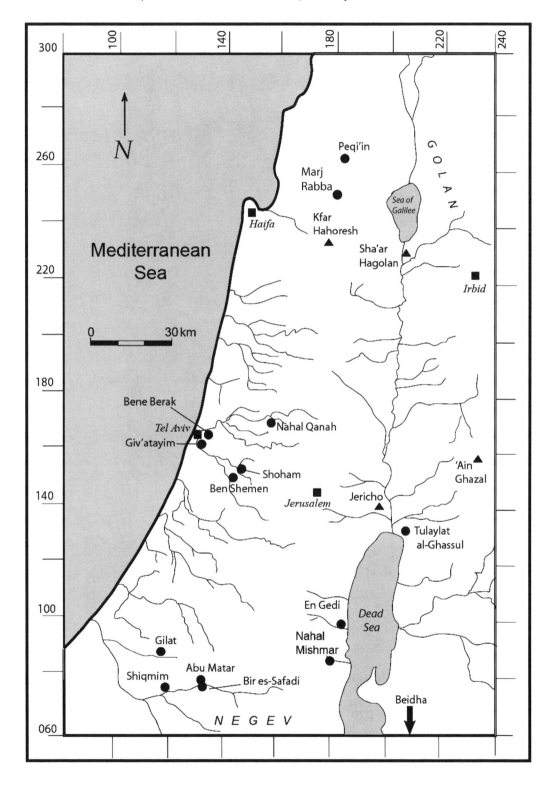

Figure 12.1. Map of selected Neolithic and Chalcolithic sites in the southern Levant

Figure 12.2. Cult shrine at ʿAin Ghazal
(photo by Yusif Zoʼbi, courtesy the ʿAin Ghazal Project)

Figure 12.3. Ritual structure at ʿAin Ghazal
(photo by B. Degedeh, courtesy the ʿAin Ghazal Project)

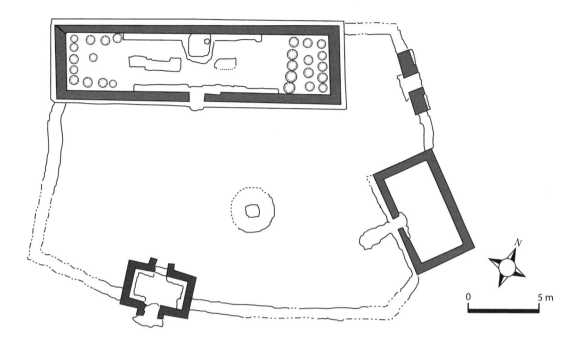

Figure 12.4. Schematic plan of En Gedi ritual complex (after Ussishkin 1980, fig. 3)

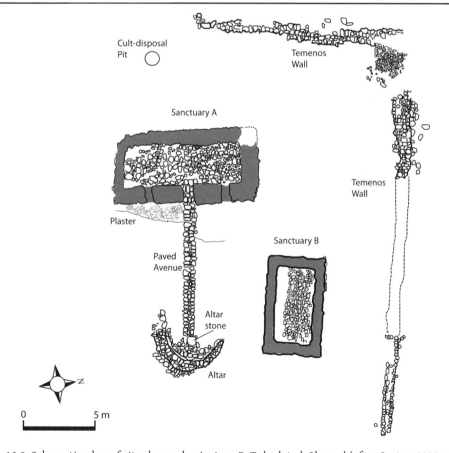

Figure 12.5. Schematic plan of ritual complex in Area E, Tulaylat al-Ghassul (after Seaton 2008, pl. 8)

Figure 12.6. Double cornet vessel from Area E, Tulaylat al-Ghassul
(image courtesy of the University of Sydney Teleilat Ghassul Excavation Project)

Figure 12.7. The Gilat Lady, an
anthropomorphic ceramic vessel from Gilat
(photo by Clara Amit, courtesy of the Israel
Antiquities Authority)

Figure 12.8. The Ram with Cornets, a zoomorphic ceramic
vessel from Gilat (photo by Clara Amit, courtesy of the Israel
Antiquities Authority)

Figure 12.9. Ceramic fenestrated stand from Gilat (image courtesy of Thomas E. Levy, the UCSD Levantine Archaeology Laboratory)

Figure 12.10. Ceramic cornet from Gilat (photograph by Clara Amit, courtesy of the Israel Antiquities Authority)

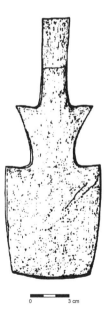

Figure 12.11. Stone violin-shaped figurine from Gilat (image courtesy of Equinox Publishing, Ltd.)

Figure 12.12. Incomplete stone violin-shaped figurine from Gilat (photo by Clara Amit, courtesy of the Israel Antiquities Authority)

Bibliography

Alon, David

1976   "Two Cult Vessels from Gilat." *ᶜAtiqot* 11 (English series): 116–18.

1977   "A Chalcolithic Temple at Gilath." *Biblical Archaeologist* 40/2: 63–65.

Alon, David, and Thomas E. Levy

1989   "The Archeology of Cult and Chalcolithic Sanctuary at Gilat." *Journal of Mediterranean Archeology* 2: 163–221.

Amiran, Ruth

1976   "Note on the Gilat Vessels." *ᶜAtiqot* 11 (English series): 119–20.

1981   "Some Observations on Chalcolithic and Early Bronze Sanctuaries and Religion." In *Temples and High Places in Biblical Times* (proceedings of the colloquium in honor of the centennial of Hebrew Union College-Jewish Institute of Religion, Jerusalem, 14–16 March 1977), edited by Avraham Biran, pp. 47–53. Jerusalem: Nelson Glueck School of Biblical Archaeology.

1989   "The Gilat Goddess and the Temples of Gilat, En-Gedi and Ai." In *L'Urbanisation de la Palestine à l'âge du Bronze ancien: bilan et perspectives des recherches actuelles*, edited by Pierre de Miroschedji, pp. 53–60. British Archaeological Reports, International Series 527. Oxford: Archeopress.

Amiran, Ruth, and Miriam Tadmor

1980   "A Female Cult Statuette from Chalcolithic Beer-sheba." *Israel Exploration Journal* 30: 137–39.

Banning, Edward B.

1998   "The Neolithic Period: Triumphs of Architecture, Agriculture, and Art." *Near Eastern Archaeology* 61/4: 188–237.

2002   "Consensus and Debate on the Late Neolithic and Chalcolithic of the Southern Levant." *Paléorient* 28/2: 148–55.

2004   "Changes in the Spatial Organization of Transjordanian Settlements from Middle PPNB to Late Neolithic." In *Central Settlements in Neolithic Jordan* (proceedings of a symposium held in Wadi Musa, Jordan, 21–25 July 1997), edited by Hans-Dieter Bienert, Hans Georg K. Gebel, and Reinder Neef, pp. 215–32. Studies in Early Near Eastern Production, Subsistence, and Environment 5. Berlin: Ex oriente.

2010   "Houses, Households, and Changing Society in the Late Neolithic and Chalcolithic of the Southern Levant." *Paléorient* 36/1: 49–87.

Banning, Edward B.; Kevin Gibbs; Michael Gregg; Seiji Kadowaki; and Lisa Maher

2004   "Excavations at a Late Neolithic Site in Wadi Ziqlab, Northern Jordan." *Antiquity* 78 (302). Available online at http://www.antiquity.ac.uk/projgall/banning302/

Bar-Adon, Pesah

1980   *The Cave of the Treasure: The Finds from the Caves in Nahal Mishmar.* Judean Desert Studies. Jerusalem: Israel Exploration Society.

Bar-Yosef Mayer, Daniella E.

2006   "Marine and Riverine Shells from Gilat." In *Archaeology, Anthropology and Cult: The Sanctuary at Gilat, Israel*, edited by Thomas E. Levy, pp. 320–26. London: Equinox.

Bar-Yosef, Ofer

2001   "From Sedentary Foragers to Village Hierarchies: The Emergence of Social Institutions." In *The Origin of Human Social Institutions*, edited by W. G. Runciman, pp. 1–38. Proceedings of the British Academy 110. Oxford: Oxford University Press.

Bar-Yosef, Ofer, and David Alon
  1988   "Naḥal Ḥemar Cave." *ʿAtiqot* 18 (English series).

Barrowclough, David A., and Caroline Malone, editors
  2007   *Cult in Context: Reconsidering Ritual in Archaeology*. Oxford: Oxbow.

Bonogofsky, Michelle
  2003   "Neolithic Plastered Skulls and Railroading Epistemologies." *Bulletin of the American Schools of Oriental Research* 331: 1–10.

Bourke, Stephen J.
  1997   "The 'Pre-Ghassulian' Sequence at Teleilat Ghassul: Sydney University Excavations 1975–1995." In *The Prehistory of Jordan*, II: *Perspectives from 1997*, edited by Hans Georg K. Gebel, Zeiden Abdel-Kafi Kafafi, and Gary O. Rollefson, pp. 395–417. Studies in Early Near Eastern Production, Subsistence, and Environment 4. Berlin: Ex oriente.
  2001   "The Chalcolithic Period." In *The Archaeology of Jordan*, edited by Burton MacDonald, Russell Adams, and Piotr Bienkowski, 107–62. Levantine Archaeology 1. Sheffield: Sheffield Academic Press.

Bourke, Stephen J.; Jaimie L. Lovell; Rachel Sparks; Peta Seaton; L. Mairs; and J. Meadows
  2000   "A Second and Third Season of Renewed Excavation by the University of Sydney at Tulaylat al-Ghassul (1995–1997)." *Annual of the Department of Antiquities of Jordan* 44: 37–89.
  2007   "A Fourth Season of Renewed Excavation by the University of Sydney Tulaylat al-Ghassul (1999)." *Annual of the Department of Antiquities of Jordan* 51: 35–80.

Bradley, Richard
  1990   *The Passage of Arms: An Archaeological Analysis of Prehistoric Hoards and Votive Deposits*. Cambridge: Cambridge University Press.
  2005   *Ritual and Domestic Life in Prehistoric Europe*. New York: Routledge.

Burton, M., and Thomas E. Levy
  2006   "Organic Residue Analysis of Selected Vessels from Gilat: Gilat Torpedo Jars." In *Archaeology, Anthropology and Cult: The Sanctuary at Gilat, Israel*, edited by Thomas E. Levy, pp. 849–62. London: Equinox.

Byrd, Brian F.
  1994   "Public and Private, Domestic and Corporate: The Emergence of the Southwest Asian Village." *American Antiquity* 59/4: 639–66.

Cameron, D. O.
  1981   *The Ghassulian Wall Paintings*. London: Kenyon-Deane.

Commenge, Catherine; Thomas E. Levy; David Alon; and Eric Kansa
  2006a   "Gilat's Ceramics: Cognitive Dimensions of Pottery Production." In *Archaeology, Anthropology and Cult: The Sanctuary at Gilat, Israel*, edited by Thomas E. Levy, 394–506. London: Equinox.
  2006b   "Gilat's Figurines: Exploring the Social and Symbolic Dimensions of Representation." In *Archaeology, Anthropology and Cult: The Sanctuary at Gilat, Israel*, edited by Thomas E. Levy, pp. 739–830. London: Equinox.

Commenge-Pellerin, Catherine
  1987   *La poterie d'Abou Matar et de l'Ouadi Zoumeili (Beershéva) au IVᵉ millénaire avant l'ère chrétienne*. Cahiers du Centre de recherche français de Jérusalem 3. Paris: Association Paléorient.
  1990   *La poterie de Safadi (Beershéva) au IVᵉ millénaire avant l'ère chrétienne*. Cahiers du Centre de recherche français de Jérusalem 5. Paris: Association Paléorient.

Epstein, Claire

  1978   "Aspects of Symbolism in Chalcolithic Palestine." In *Archaeology in the Levant:*
                Essays for Kathleen Kenyon, edited by P. R. S. Moorey and Peter Parr, pp. 23–35.
                Warminster: Aris & Phillips.

  1982   "Cult Symbols in Chalcolithic Palestine." *Bollettino del Centro Camuno di Studi*
                Preistorici 19: 63–81.

Evershed, Richard P., et al.

  2008   "Earliest Date for Milk Use in the Near East and Southeastern Europe Linked to
                Cattle Herding." *Nature* 455: 528–31.

Fogelin, Lars

  2007   "The Archaeology of Religious Ritual." *Annual Review of Anthropology* 36: 55–71.

Fox, Nili Sacher

  1995   "The Striped Goddess from Gilat: Implications for the Chalcolithic Cult." *Israel*
                Exploration Journal 45/4: 212–25.

Gal, Zvi; Howard Smithline; and Dina Shalem

  1997   "A Chalcolithic Burial Cave in Peqi'in, Upper Galilee." *Israel Exploration Journal*
                47: 145–54.

  1999   "New Iconographic Aspects of Chalcolithic Art: Preliminary Observations on
                Finds from the Peqi'in Cave." *ʿAtiqot* 37: 1–16.

  2007   "Gender and Social Hierarchy in the Chalcolithic Period in the Light of the
                Peqi'in Cave, Israel." In *The Archaeology of Difference: Gender, Ethnicity, Class and*
                the "Other" in Antiquity; Studies in Honor of Eric M. Meyers, edited by Douglas R.
                Edwards and C. Thomas McCollough, pp. 41–48. Annual of the American Schools
                of Oriental Research 60/61. Boston: American Schools of Oriental Research.

  2011   "The Peqi'in Cave: A Chalcolithic Cemetery in Upper Galilee, Israel." *Near Eastern*
                Archaeology 74/4: 196–206.

Garfinkel, Yosef

  1993   "The Yarmukian Culture in Israel." *Paléorient* 19/1: 115–34.

Garfinkel, Yosef; N. Korn; and Michele A. Miller

  2002   "Art from Shaʿar Hagolan." In *Shaʿar Hagolan 1: Neolithic Art in Context*, edited by
                Yosef Garfinkel and Michele A. Miller, pp. 188–208. Oxford: Oxbow.

Gilead, Isaac

  1988   "The Chalcolithic Period in the Levant." *Journal of World Prehistory* 2/4: 397–443.

  2002   "Religio-magic Behavior in the Chalcolithic Period of Palestine." In *Aharon Kem-*
                pinski Memorial Volume: Studies in Archaeology and Related Disciplines, edited by
                Shmuel Ahituv and Eliezer D. Oren, pp. 103–28. Beersheva: Ben-Gurion Univer-
                sity of the Negev.

Gopher, Avi, and Ram Gophna

  1993   "Cultures of the Eighth and Seventh Millennia BP in the Southern Levant: A
                Review for the 1990s." *Journal of World Prehistory* 7/3: 297–353.

Gopher, Avi, and Tsvika Tsuk

  1996   "The Chalcolithic Assemblages." In *The Naḥal Qanah Cave: Earliest Gold in the South-*
                ern Levant, edited by Avi Gopher and Tsvika Tsuḳ, pp. 91–138. Monograph series
                of Tel Aviv University, Sonia and Marco Nadler Institute of Archaeology 12. Tel
                Aviv: Institute of Archaeology of Tel Aviv University.

Goren, Yuval

  1995   "Shrines and Ceramics in Chalcolithic Israel: The View Through the Petrographic
                Microscope." *Archaeometry* 37: 287–305.

2006   "The Technology of the Gilat Pottery Assemblage: A Reassessment." In *Archaeology, Anthropology and Cult: The Sanctuary at Gilat, Israel*, edited by Thomas E. Levy, 369–39. London: Equinox.

Goring-Morris, Nigel

2000   "The Quick and the Dead: The Social Context of Aceramic Neolithic Mortuary Practices as Seen from Kfar Hahoresh." In *Life in Neolithic Farming Communities: Social Organization, Identity, and Differentiation*, edited by Ian Kuijt, pp. 103–36. Fundamental Issues in Archaeology. New York: Kluwer Academic/Plenum Press.

Grigson, Caroline

2006   "Farming? Feasting? Herding? Large Mammals from the Chalcolithic of Gilat." In *Archaeology, Anthropology and Cult: The Sanctuary at Gilat, Israel*, edited by Thomas E. Levy, pp. 215–319. London: Equinox.

Ilan, David, and Yorke M. Rowan

2012   "Deconstructing and Recomposing the Narrative of Spiritual Life in the Chalcolithic of the Southern Levant (4500–3600 BCE)." In *Beyond Belief: The Archaeology of Religion and Ritual*, edited by Yorke M. Rowan, pp. 89–113. Archaeological Papers of the American Anthropological Association 21. Hoboken: Wiley-Blackwell.

Insoll, Timothy

2004a   *Archaeology, Ritual, Religion*. London: Routledge.

2004b   *Belief in the Past: Proceedings of the 2002 Manchester Conference on Archaeology and Religion*, editor. British Archaeological Reports, International Series 1212. Oxford: Archaeopress.

Joffe, Alexander H.

2003   "Slouching Toward Beersheva: Chalcolithic Mortuary Practices in Local and Regional Context." In *The Near East in the Southwest: Essays in Honor of William G. Dever*, edited by Beth Alpert Nakhai, pp. 45–67. Annual of the American Schools of Oriental Research 58. Boston: American Schools of Oriental Research.

Joffe, Alexander H.; J. P. Dessel; and Rachel S. Hallote

2001   "The 'Gilat Woman': Female Iconography, Chalcolithic Cult, and the End of Southern Levantine Prehistory." *Near Eastern Archaeology* 64: 8–23.

Kafafi, Zeidan

1985   "Late Neolithic Architecture from Jebel Abu Thawwab, Jordan." *Paléorient* 11: 125–27.

1988   "Jebel Abu Thawwab: A Pottery Neolithic Village in North Jordan." In *The Prehistory of Jordan: The State of Research in 1986*, edited by Andrew N. Garrard and Hans Georg K. Gebel, pp. 451–71. British Archaeological Reports, International Series 396. Oxford: British Archaeological Reports.

2001   *Jebel Abu Thawwab (Er-Rumman), Central Jordan: The Late Neolithic and Early Bronze Age I Occupations*. Monographs of the Institute of Archaeology and Anthropology 3. Berlin: Ex oriente.

Kenyon, Kathleen M.

1957   *Digging Up Jericho*. London: E. Benn.

1979   *Archaeology in the Holy Land*. 4th edition. London: E. Benn.

1981   *Excavations at Jericho*, Volume 3: *The Architecture and Stratigraphy of the Tell*. London: British School of Archaeology in Jerusalem.

Kirkbride, Diana

1966   "Five Seasons at the Pre-pottery Neolithic Village of Beidha in Jordan." *Palestine Exploration Quarterly* 98: 8–72.

1968   "Beidha: Early Neolithic Village Life South of the Dead Sea." *Antiquity* 42/4:
                       263–74.

Köhler-Rollefson, I.
    1988   "The Aftermath of the Levantine Neolithic Revolution in the Light of Ecological
                       and Ethnographic Evidence." *Paléorient* 14/1: 87–93.

Kuijt, Ian
    2000a   "People and Space in Early Agricultural Villages: Exploring Daily Lives, Com-
                       munity Size, and Architecture in the Late Pre-Pottery Neolithic." *Journal of An-
                       thropological Archaeology* 19/1: 75–102.

    2000b   "Keeping the Peace: Ritual, Skull Caching, and Community Integration in the
                       Levantine Neolithic." In *Life in Neolithic Farming Communities: Social Organization,
                       Identity, and Differentiation*, edited by Ian Kuijt, pp. 137–62. Fundamental Issues
                       in Archaeology. New York: Kluwer Academic/Plenum Press.

    2004   "When the Walls Came Down: Social Organization, Ideology, and the 'Collapse'
                       of the Pre-Pottery Neolithic." In *Central Settlements in Neolithic Jordan* (proceed-
                       ings of a symposium held in Wadi Musa, Jordan, 21–25 July 1997), edited by
                       Hans-Dieter Bienert, Hans Georg K. Gebel, and Reinder Neef, pp. 183–99. Studies
                       in Early Near Eastern Production, Subsistence, and Environment 5. Berlin: Ex
                       oriente.

Kuijt, Ian, and Nigel Goring-Morris
    2002   "Foraging, Farming, and Social Complexity in the Pre-Pottery Neolithic of the
                       Southern Levant: A Review and Synthesis." *Journal of World Prehistory* 16/4: 361–
                       440.

Kyriakidis, Evangelos, editor
    2007   *The Archaeology of Ritual*. Cotsen Advanced Seminars 3. Los Angeles: Cotsen In-
                       stitute of Archaeology.

Levy, Thomas E.
    1986   "Social Archaeology and the Chalcolithic Period: Explaining Social Organiza-
                       tional Change During the 4th Millennium in Israel." *Michmanim* 3: 5–20.

    1995   "Cult, Metallurgy and Rank Societies — Chalcolithic Period (ca. 4500–3500 BCE)."
                       In *The Archaeology of Society in the Holy Land*, edited by Thomas E. Levy, pp. 226–
                       44. London: Leicester University Press.

    2006   *Archaeology, Anthropology and Cult: The Sanctuary at Gilat, Israel*, editor. London:
                       Equinox.

Levy, Thomas E., and N. Menahem
    1987   "The Ceramic Industry at Shiqmim: Typological and Spatial Considerations."
                       In *Shiqmim* I: *Studies Concerning Chalcolithic Societies in the Northern Negev Desert,
                       Israel (1982-1984)*, edited by Thomas E. Levy and David Alon, pp. 313–32. British
                       Archaeological Reports, International Series 356. Oxford: British Archaeological
                       Reports.

Levy, Thomas E.; David Alon; J. Anderson; Yorke M. Rowan; and Morag Kersel
    2006   "The Sanctuary Sequence: Excavations at Gilat: 1975–77, 1989, 1990–1992." In
                       Archaeology, Anthropology and Cult: The Sanctuary at Gilat, edited by Thomas E.
                       Levy, pp. 95–212. London: Equinox.

Lovell, Jaimie L.
    2001   *The Late Neolithic and Chalcolithic Periods in the Southern Levant: New Data from the
                       Site of Teleilat Ghassul, Jordan*. British Archaeological Reports, International Series
                       974 / Monographs of the Sydney University Teleilat Ghassul Project 1. Oxford:
                       Archaeopress.

2008 "Horticulture, Status and Long-range Trade in Chalcolithic Southern Levant: Early Connections with Egypt." In *Egypt at Its Origins* 2 (proceedings of the international conference "Origin of the State. Predynastic and Early Dynastic Egypt," Toulouse, France, 5–8 September 2005), edited by Béatrix Midant-Reynes and Yann Tristant, pp. 741–62. Orientalia Lovaniensia Analecta 172. Leuven: Peeters.

Mallon, Alexis; Robert Koeppel; and René Neuville

1934 *Teleilat Ghassul* I: *compte rendu des fouilles de l'Institut biblique pontifical, 1929-1932.* Rome: Pontifical Biblical Institute.

Mazar, A.

2000 "A Sacred Tree in the Chalcolithic Shrine at En-Gedi: A Suggestion." *Bulletin of the Anglo-Israel Archaeological Society* 18: 31–36.

Merhav, R.

1993 "Sceptres of the Divine from the Cave of the Treasure at Nahal Mishmar." In *Studies in the Archaeology and History of Ancient Israel in Honour of Moshe Dothan*, edited by Michael Heltzer, Arthur Segal, and Daniel Kaufman, pp. 21–42. Haifa: Haifa University Press. [In Hebrew]

Neef, Reinder

1990 "Introduction, Development and Environmental Implications of Olive Culture: The Evidence from Jordan." In *Man's Role in the Shaping of the Eastern Mediterranean Landscape*, edited by Sytze Bottema, G. Entjes-Nieborg, and Willem van Zeist, pp. 295–306. Rotterdam: A. A. Balkema.

North, R.

1982 "The Ghassulian Lacuna at Jericho." In *Studies in the History and Archaeology of Jordan* I, edited by Adnan Hadidi, pp. 59–66. Amman: Department of Antiquities, Hashemite Kingdom of Jordan.

Ottoson, Magnus

1980 *Temples and Cult Places in Palestine.* Acta Universitatis Upsaliensis, Boreas 12. Uppsala: Uppsala University.

Renfrew, Colin

1985 *The Archaeology of Cult: The Sanctuary at Phylakopi.* Supplementary Volume 18. London: The British School of Archaeology at Athens.

Rollefson, Gary O.

1983 "Ritual and Ceremony at Neolithic Ain Ghazal (Jordan)." *Paléorient* 9/2: 29–38.
1986 "Neolithic ʿAin Ghazal (Jordan): Ritual and Ceremony II." *Paléorient* 12: 45–52.
1998a "'Ain Ghazal (Jordan): Ritual and Ceremony III." *Paléorient* 24: 43–58.
1998b "The Aceramic Neolithic." In *The Prehistoric Archaeology of Jordan*, edited by Donald O. Henry, pp. 102–26. British Archaeology Reports, International Series 705. Oxford: Archaeopress.
2001 "The Neolithic Period." In *The Archaeology of Jordan*, edited by Burton MacDonald, Russell Adams, and Piotr Bienkowski, pp. 67–105. Levantine Archaeology 1. Sheffield: Sheffield Academic Press.
2004 "Where are the Dead? Some Points to Consider." In *Central Settlements in Neolithic Jordan* (proceedings of a symposium held in Wadi Musa, Jordan, 21–25 July 1997), edited by Hans-Dieter Bienert, Hans Georg K. Gebel, and Reinder Neef, pp. 169–75. Studies in Early Near Eastern Production, Subsistence, and Environment 5. Berlin: Ex oriente.

Rollefson, Gary O., and I. Köhler-Rollefson

1989   "The Collapse of Early Neolithic Settlements in the Southern Levant." In *People and Culture Change* (proceedings of the Second Symposium on Upper Palaeolithic, Mesolithic, and Neolithic Populations of Europe and the Mediterranean Basin), edited by Israel Hershkovitz, pp. 73–90. Biblical Archaeology Reports, International Series 508. Oxford: British Archaeological Reports.

1993   "PPNC Adaptations in the First Half of the 6th Millennium B.C." *Paléorient* 19/1: 33–42.

Rollefson, Gary O., and Zeidan Kafafi

1994   "The 1993 Season at ʿAin Ghazal: Preliminary Report." *Annual of the Department of Antiquities of Jordan* 38: 11–32.

2007   "The Rediscovery of the Neolithic Period in Jordan." In *Crossing Jordan: North American Contributions to the Archaeology of Jordan*, edited by Thomas E. Levy, P. M. Michèle Daviau, Randall W. Younker, and May Shaer, pp. 211–18. London: Equinox.

Rollefson, Gary O., and Alan H. Simmons

1986   "The Neolithic Village of ʿAin Ghazal, Jordan: Preliminary Report on the 1984 Season." *Bulletin of the American Schools of Oriental Research Supplement* 24: 145–64.

Rowan, Yorke M.

2012   "Beyond Belief: The Archaeology of Religion and Ritual." In *Beyond Belief: The Archaeology of Religion and Ritual*, edited by Yorke M. Rowan, pp. 1–10. Archaeological Papers of the American Anthropological Association 21. Hoboken: Wiley-Blackwell.

Rowan, Yorke M., and Jonathan Golden

2009   "The Chalcolithic Period of the Southern Levant: A Synthetic Review." *Journal of World Prehistory* 22/1: 1–92.

Rowan, Yorke M., and David Ilan

2007   "The Meaning of Ritual Diversity in the Chalcolithic of the Southern Levant." In *Cult in Context: Reconsidering Ritual in Archaeology*, edited by David A. Barrowclough and Caroline Malone, pp. 249–56. Oxford: Oxbow.

2012   "The Subterranean Landscape of the Southern Levant During the Chalcolithic Period." In *Sacred Darkness: A Global Perspective on the Ritual Use of Caves*, edited by Holley Moyes. Boulder: University Press of Colorado.

Rowan, Yorke M.; Thomas E. Levy; David Alon; and Yuval Goren

2006   "The Ground Stone Industry: Stone Bowls, Grinding Slabs, Palettes, Spindle Whorls, Maceheads and Related Finds." In *Archaeology, Anthropology and Cult: The Sanctuary at Gilat,* edited by Thomas E. Levy, pp. 575–684. London: Equinox.

Rowan, Yorke M.; Gary O. Rollefson; and Morag Kersel

2011   "Maitland's 'Mesa' Reassessed: A Late Prehistoric Cemetery in the Eastern Badia, Jordan." *Antiquity* 85/327, March. Online at http://www.antiquity.ac.uk/projgall/rowan327/

Schmandt-Besserat, Denise

1998   "ʿAin Ghazal 'Monumental' Figures." *Bulletin of the American Schools of Oriental Research* 310: 1–17.

Seaton, Peta

2008   *Chalcolithic Cult and Risk Management at Teleilat Ghassul: The Area E Sanctuary.* Monographs of the Sydney University Teleilat Ghassul Project 2 / British Archaeology Reports, International Series 1864. Oxford: Archaeopress.

Simmons, Alan H.

2000 "Villages on the Edge: Regional Settlement Change and the End of the Levantine Pre-Pottery Neolithic." In *Life in Neolithic Farming Communities: Social Organization, Identity, and Differentiation*, edited by Ian Kuijt, pp. 211–30. New York: Kluwer Academic/Plenum.

Smith, Patricia; Tania Zagerson; Pamela Sabari; Jonathan Golden; Thomas E. Levy; and Leslie Dawson

2006 "Death and the Sanctuary: The Human Remains from Gilat." In *Archaeology, Anthropology and Cult: The Sanctuary at Gilat*, edited by Thomas E. Levy, pp. 327–66. London: Equinox.

Tadmor, Miriam

1986 "Naturalistic Depictions in the Gilat Sculptured Vessels." *Israel Museum Journal* 5: 7–12.

Twiss, Katheryn C.

2007 "The Neolithic of the Southern Levant." *Evolutionary Anthropology* 16/1: 24–35.

Ussishkin, David

1980 "The Ghassulian Shrine at En-Gedi." *Tel Aviv* 7: 1–44.

Verhoeven, Marc

2002 "Ritual and Ideology in the Pre-Pottery Neolithic B of the Levant and Southeast Anatolia." *Cambridge Archaeological Journal* 12/2: 233–58.

Wasse, A.; Gary O. Rollefson; and Yorke M. Rowan

Forthcoming "In Loving Memory: The Late Prehistoric Necropolis at Wisad Pools, Eastern Badia, Jordan." In *Prehistoric Jordan: Past and Future Research*, edited by Gary O. Rollefson and B. Finlayson. Amman: Department of Antiquities.

Whitley, David S., and Kelley Hays-Gilpin

2008 *Belief in the Past: Theoretical Approaches to the Archaeology of Religion*. Walnut Creek: Left Coast Press.

Yellin, Joseph; Thomas E. Levy; and Yorke M. Rowan

1996 "New Evidence on Prehistoric Trade Routes: The Obsidian Evidence from Gilat, Israel." *Journal of Field Archaeology* 23/3: 361–68.

Zohary, Daniel, and Pinhas Spiegel-Roy

1975 "Beginnings of Fruit Growing in the Old World." *Science* 187/4174: 319–27.

13

EGYPTIAN TEMPLE GRAFFITI AND THE GODS: APPROPRIATION AND RITUALIZATION IN KARNAK AND LUXOR

Elizabeth Frood, University of Oxford*

In this chapter, I consider how clusters of graffiti in particular areas of Egyptian temples offer a relational and performative perspective on the creation, organization, and meaning of sacred space, and attempt to integrate this micro-view with wider architectural contexts and primary decorative programs that are the more common focus of study. Temple graffiti are often interpreted as evidence for "popular religion" and non-elite involvement in temples, particularly major ones. However, restricted access to temple spaces and the diversity of graffiti indicate that their creation was one of a range of internally focused forms of practice and display relating to temple personnel, especially in outer areas such as exterior walls and open courts. My principal aims are to rethink the institutional practice of graffiti and, more broadly, to assess distinctions between interior and exterior in temples. Interpreting graffiti as socially embedded acts or events (Baird and Taylor 2011b, p. 6) highlights the dynamism of temples, which were repeatedly renegotiated and reconfigured by individuals and institutions. This renegotiation is visible in the appropriation and intensified significance of specific exterior and secondary spaces.

I focus on formal graffiti that include images of gods, building on distinctions made by Claude Traunecker (1991) in his survey of divine images in temples. He integrates discussion of formal graffiti with cult statues and reliefs that show the king performing rituals for gods, the latter being the primary form of temple decoration (fig. 13.1). This detailed analysis situates graffiti within a broad spectrum of divine representation, emphasizing its diversity and plurality. Discussing the status of these "images détournées," Traunecker suggests that "leur caractère hiérophanique n'est pas consécutif à un acte [rituel] mais à la révélation de leur statut dans l'esprit de ceux qui les côtoyaient quotidiennement pour des raisons de service" (1991, p. 89). I consider both possibilities, not only that graffiti are connected with the articulation of places by temple personnel (also Traunecker 1979, pp. 27–30; 1982) but that their creation can be understood as a ritual act, a performance. Some graffiti mobilize

* Many thanks to Deena Ragavan for the invitation to her inspiring seminar in Chicago. I am grateful to all participants for discussion, as well as Deena, John Baines, Christoph Bachhuber, and Chloé Ragazzoli for reading and commenting on drafts. The project on which this paper is based would be impossible without the archive of Claude Traunecker, and all his encouragement and advice. I would also like to thank

Ibrahim Soliman, Director of the Temples of Karnak, and everyone at the Centre Franco-Égyptien d'Étude des Temples de Karnak for their support, especially Christophe Thiers, Sébastien Biston-Moulin, Pierre Zignani, Jean-François Gout, and Awad Abdel Radi Mohamed. Christophe and Sébastien kindly supplied the plans of the Amun complex and the temple of Ptah, and Ray Johnson the plan of Luxor temple.

performance explicitly, for example, by evoking speeches. Evidence such as this opens a window onto practice, especially the ritualization of specific actions and places. This process, in Catherine Bell's formulation, is "a way of doing things to trigger the perception that these practices are distinct and the associations they engender are special" (Bell 1992, p. 220). Bell's analysis examines the connection between strategies of ritualization and the negotiation of power relationships; graffiti in many modern urban environments are acts of appropriation, as they are in the ancient Egyptian contexts that I treat (cf. Mairs 2011, p. 157; Plesch 2002a, p. 143). In this, graffiti may complement, but are not identical with, other, more traditional forms of nonroyal self-presentation such as statues and stelae.

I begin with a definition of the types of graffiti that are treated in this chapter, as well as their contexts in temple complexes. I then examine three categories of graffiti: 1) scenes of deities that relate to human, nonroyal worshipers, on a traditional or semi-traditional model; 2) single figures of deities in previously undecorated spaces; and 3) the adaptation and transformation of primary decoration through graffiti. These categories are exemplified by groups of graffiti in temples in Thebes (modern Luxor) in Upper Egypt: Luxor temple and two temples within the complex of Amun at Karnak. Each case-study involves more than one of these categories. The secondary inscriptions that constitute graffiti in these contexts are clearly marked as different from related primary decoration and this difference is essential to their status.

This discussion develops out of my project to record, edit, and publish hieroglyphic, hieratic, and figural graffiti from Karnak, in collaboration with the Centre Franco-Égyptien d'Étude des Temples de Karnak. Much of this corpus is derived from the comprehensive archive of graffiti at the site gathered and analyzed by Traunecker in the 1960s and 1970s (see Traunecker 1979) and now held in the Griffith Institute, Oxford.[1] I have begun with graffiti in the Ptah temple, a small structure in the northern part of the precinct; I present aspects of these graffiti as my third case-study (cf. Ragazzoli and Frood 2013). The approach outlined here is preliminary and based on a relatively early stage of research.

Definitions

In this article, "graffiti" designates a text and/or image inscribed or inked on a surface, here a temple wall, that was not originally intended to receive it. This definition differs from many modern western perceptions of graffiti as illicit, counter-cultural, and often subversive, but agrees with research on graffiti from cultural contexts ranging from the classical world (e.g., Baird and Taylor 2011a) to early modern Europe (e.g., Fleming 2001; Plesch 2010, pp. 142–47). Textual graffiti, often integrated with pictures, are attested for almost all periods of ancient Egypt and are part of scribal self-presentation, and so an elite institution.[2] Purely pictorial graffiti can be more difficult to relate to institutions (Cruz-Uribe 2008a). In the temple environments I study, pictures and texts are closely interrelated and probably derive from similar practices.

---

[1] This project relates closely to those developed by Helen Jacquet-Gordon (2004) and Jean-Claude Degardin (2009, 2010) for graffiti in the temple of Khonsu in Karnak. The material I treat here is generally more formal than the graffiti they present, although my approach overall is complementary.

[2] E.g., Parkinson 1999, p. 92; Ragazzoli 2011. A. J. Peden (2001) and Hana Navrátilová (2010) provide surveys of the range of graffiti from ancient Egypt. Navrátilová in particular usefully focuses on implications of context.

This definition is not without problems. One is how far we can distinguish primary and secondary inscription, especially in temples that were in use over centuries or millennia, accumulating decoration in areas perhaps not originally intended to receive it or not executed after their initial construction (e.g., Brand 2007, pp. 52–59). Traditional Egyptian temple decoration, visual and textual, centered almost exclusively on presenting the relationship between the king and the gods, and material with this content and focus is primary in most contexts. Separating the royal and primary from nonroyal and secondary is productive for an initial categorization of graffiti (Cruz-Uribe 2008b, pp. 200–02). This distinction, however, breaks down to some extent in late second- and early first-millennium Thebes, when kings were not commissioning decoration and members of the ruling priestly families were taking on royal features of display. Nonetheless, a distinction between a royal style of self-presentation in special contexts and something more typically nonroyal in others seems to be maintained.[3]

It is also difficult to distinguish between the "formal" and the "informal." Even in discussions of graffiti as an institutional practice, they are normally considered to be informal, spontaneous products of individuals, rather than something that might be a group commission. This distinction is especially problematic in temples where graffiti were sometimes modeled on traditional, formal forms of display. Many of the inscriptions I discuss, especially the images of gods, are very formal: beautifully carved, painted, and sometimes associated with formal hieroglyphic texts. It is location, features of content and presentation (such as isolated figures of gods without a ritual performer) and, occasionally, association with less formal hieroglyphic and hieratic inscriptions which point toward considering these compositions as graffiti.

Thus, graffiti constitutes a diverse and varied practice, with temple graffiti holding a distinctive position. Graffiti practices vary from temple to temple in relation to access, style, and content. Patterns of survival complicate the picture. Recent discussions have centered on demotic, Greek, and Coptic graffiti as indicators of change in the meaning of sacred spaces in the late first millennium B.C.E. and early centuries C.E., including the final closure of temples with the spread of Christianity.[4] This work has enormous potential for understanding social contexts of script selection and use (e.g., Mairs 2011), as well as how temples and parts of temples were re-imagined by different religious communities.[5] These issues are relevant for Karnak and Luxor temples, which bear many demotic, Greek, and Coptic graffiti. I attempt to use this work on later periods to illuminate patterns from many centuries earlier.

---

[3] Mark Ciccarello (1979) distinguishes between "kingship documents" and "priesthood documents," as well as a special "Karnak style," for Pinudjem I, a priest-king of the Twenty-first Dynasty (ca. 1075–945 B.C.E.; inscriptions of Pinudjem are discussed further below). For broader analysis of the self-presentation of Theban priest-kings from this period, especially through the formulation of their titles, see Römer 1994, pp. 1–131.

[4] E.g., Cruz-Uribe 2008b, pp. 218–24; Dijkstra 2008, pp. 97–102, 175–218; 2012, pp. 22–26. For an overview of temple graffiti, especially from the Graeco-Roman period, see Dijkstra 2012, pp. 19–22.

[5] E.g., Rutherford 2003. A related example from much earlier is the dipinti hieratic prayers on walls and columns in the hypostyle hall of the temple of the Eighteenth Dynasty king Thutmose III (ca. 1479–1425 B.C.E.) at Deir el-Bahri on the Theban west bank (Marciniak 1974). These were largely written in the late New Kingdom (ca. 1290–1075 B.C.E.) and indicate that during this time the temple was a more accessible votive environment dedicated to the goddess Hathor (Dolińska 2007, pp. 78–81).

Graffiti Showing Deities in Luxor and Karnak:
Space, Time, and Popular Religion

Temple graffiti in Luxor temple and in the Amun precinct in Karnak range from roughly scrawled names and titles to carefully carved relief scenes incorporating complex hiero-glyphic and/or hieratic texts and figures. Hieroglyphic is the pictorial form of the script associated with monumental display. Hieratic is its cursive form, used for manuscript and documentary purposes, that was also developed for more formal, monumental contexts in the first millennium (e.g., Frood 2010, pp. 112–13). Almost all identifiable graffiti in the two complexes were incised into walls rather than executed in ink, but some bear traces of paint. Ink graffiti may have been more widespread than now appears to be the case.[6]

The temple complex at Karnak is a sprawling set of interconnected structures dedicated to the state god Amun-Re on the east bank of the Nile in Thebes (fig. 13.2). Karnak was prob-ably founded around 2000 B.C.E., developing into a vast complex from the New Kingdom (ca. 1500 B.C.E.) onward. Temples for members of his group, the goddess Mut, the child god Khonsu, and the war god Montu, lie immediately to the south and north. The temple of Amun was the preeminent state temple in southern Egypt from the mid-second millennium B.C.E. As a prime focus of royal investment, it was constantly reworked throughout its history: buildings were dismantled, added to, rearranged; decorative programs were erased, recarved, and elaborated (overview: Blyth 2006). These processes complicate the analysis of graffiti.

In contrast, the temple of Luxor is smaller and more unitary (fig. 13.3). I treat this seem-ingly more straightforward case first. Graffiti practices in the temple are quite distinctive, perhaps relating to specific aspects of the temple's function (brief survey: Jasnow 1994). It lies about 2.5 kilometers south of Karnak and may have been founded rather later. The temple was dedicated to an ithyphallic form of Amun, Amenemope, and functioned in some way as a secondary location for the cult of Amun-Re. However it also had special status, at least in part through association with the royal *ka*, a principle that transmitted kingship through generations (Bell 1985).

Even when context is well understood, graffiti can be difficult to date. Dating often relies on combined analysis of context, content, orthography, prosopography, and paleog-raphy. It seems that graffiti-writing in Theban temples intensified as a practice from the late New Kingdom (Dynasties 19–20; ca. 1290–1075 B.C.E.) onward, although there are earlier examples.[7] One of these is a figure of a priest with hieroglyphic caption that was inked in red on the north side of the altar in the solar complex of the Eighteenth Dynasty female king Hatshepsut (ca. 1473–1458 B.C.E.) at Deir el-Bahri on the Theban west bank (Karkowski 2003, p. 255, pl. 53A). This graffito was whitewashed soon after execution and therefore probably dates to the original decoration of this suite under Hatshepsut. It is of a very different char-acter to the material I treat here, especially as presence rather than visibility seems to have been the central concern of its creator.

---

[6] A rare example of a surviving ink graffito from Luxor temple is the sign for "scribe" on a fragment of the Ramessid gateway built into the gateway of Philip Arrhidaeus (Epigraphic Survey 1998, p. 56, pl. 205, Gr. 16).

[7] Crudely incised figural graffiti and a very small amount of textual graffiti on blocks from the temple of Medamud, about 8 kilometers northeast of Luxor, have been dated to the Middle Kingdom (ca. 1975–1640 B.C.E.; Cottevieille-Giraudet 1931, pp. 36–37); these warrant a new study to secure this dating.

Graffiti of a formal type — lengthy hieroglyphic texts and images of priests and gods — first appear in the late New Kingdom in Karnak (Frood 2010, pp. 116–22) and are attested sporadically at Karnak and Luxor throughout the first millennium. In particular, finely carved graffiti of individual gods and groups of gods that are found in both temples seem to date across this period. At Luxor, an ithyphallic Amun-Re carved in raised relief on the west exterior wall between side doors leading into the hypostyle hall and the court of Amenhotep III bears traces of recarving as well as an inscription claiming its restoration under the Twenty-first Dynasty priest-king, Menkheperre (ca. 1045–989 B.C.E.; Brand 2004). A cluster of images of deities, including large ithyphallic and seated figures of Amun, is located at another side entrance into the forecourt (fig. 13.3A) (Porter and Moss 1972, pp. 335 [219–220]). Two long inscriptions detailing the restoration of temple structures and cult equipment were carved among these figures, one dated to Alexander the Great and Philip Arrhidaeus (332–316 B.C.E.)[8] and the other belonging to a later Ptolemaic priestly family (Jansen-Winkeln 2005). Both are addressed to the priests who would have used this doorway. The later text refers to divine processional images (*sšmw*) and it is tempting to suggest that these are evoked by the nearby pictures, at least some of which may have been carved at the same time. At Karnak, a broadly datable example is a sunk relief ithyphallic god carved on the exterior jamb of a side door leading into the temple of Montu from the neighboring temple of the god Harpre. Its inscription probably dates to the creation of this doorway during repair and remodeling in the Twenty-fifth Dynasty (ca. 715–657 B.C.E.; Gabolde and Rondot 1993, pp. 258–60, fig. 4, pl. 6B).

The examples I treat in this paper can mostly be ascribed to the early to mid-first millennium (Dynasties 21–25) and their appearance relates in part to the political fragmentation and decentralization which characterizes the first half of this period. The Theban area was under the control of high priests who held quasi royal authority, a new political context that had a broad impact on developments in self-presentation. Localism is certainly a significant factor, as is the displacement of the symbolic figure of the king. Nonetheless, long-standing traditions of nonroyal self-presentation were maintained. For Theban elites, temple statues were a primary means of asserting claims to temple space, although it is seldom known where they were originally set up (e.g., Brandl 2008; Price 2010). Alongside this traditional medium, others emerged or intensified, including graffiti. I return to relationships between these strategies in my conclusion.

Graffiti of divine images have often been interpreted as objects of popular devotion and worship and connected with the "rise of personal piety" from the mid–late second millennium onward, rather than being related to elite modes of self-presentation.[9] This interpretation depends on features of content and style, but most especially on their location in areas thought to be accessible to ordinary people. As such they are understood to delineate "contact zones" (Ashley and Plesch 2002, pp. 4–6; with Plesch 2002b, p. 181), points of interface and perhaps tension, between the restricted temple cult and the wider populace. Peter Brand (2004; 2007, pp. 64–65) in particular argues that graffiti of gods on some exterior walls in Karnak and Luxor were set up by priesthoods of the late second and early first millennium

---

[8] For translation of sections of the text and references, see Gorre 2009, pp. 53–57. He dates the inscription to Alexander IV rather than Alexander the Great (2009, pp. 53–54), but this is almost certainly incorrect. I am grateful to Francisco Bosch Puche, who is re-editing this text, for discussion.

[9] E.g., Dils 1995; and compare Luiselli 2011, pp. 58–59 with references. Agnès Cabrol's account (2001, pp. 720–31) of "popular" religious practices in Theban temples, especially in connection with processional routes, gives a sense of the range of evidence, including some graffiti.

in order to provide places of worship for non-elites who could enter the temple enclosures but not the temple proper.

Central to Brand's argument is the veiling of some graffiti alongside images of gods in interior primary decoration. Building on earlier discussions (e.g., Dils 1995), he argues (2004, pp. 263–64; 2007, pp. 59–65) that holes piercing the stone around many of these images supported frames for fabric coverings which could reveal the image to ordinary people at particular times. I consider the notion of veiling as anachronistic. Moreover, as Brand acknowledges (2007, p. 61), it does not fully account for the variety in the patterning of holes around scenes and figures. The holes, which have not been studied in detail, more probably point to different types of "enrichment" of images (Traunecker 1991, pp. 88–89), sometimes through gilding (Borchardt 1933; Fischer 1959, pp. 196–98) or embellishments with wood, fabric, or other materials. These may have been temporary. On the exterior of the rear wall of the Graeco-Roman temple of the goddess Hathor at Dendara is a large carving of her head which bears traces of gilding and the fixings for a wooden canopy (Cauville 1990, p. 86). This example, though much later than many discussed by Brand, shows how primary images could be elaborated in ways that almost certainly related to central cult performances (cf. Laroche and Traunecker 1973–1977, pp. 194–95).

Pictorial graffiti of gods often show them alone, or in somewhat disparate, seemingly jumbled groups, rather than interacting in ritual scenes as is common in traditional primary decoration (Brand 2007, p. 64). They mostly lack offering tables or other ritual parapher-nalia. The fact that some figures are solitary may make them more directly involving and participatory. I argue here that the exterior spaces on which they were carved were prob-ably not widely accessible. Rather, the images would have participated in and ritualized the movements of priests and temple staff, as is suggested particularly by their typical location near side doors. Temple personnel would have entered by these side doors from service and administrative areas. Once inside the temple, they were no longer performing for themselves but for the gods in an official capacity. If the graffiti mark internally oriented, secondary places of piety, veneration, and ritual action by these people (e.g., Traunecker 1979; Guglielmi 1994, pp. 58–59; Cabrol 2001, pp. 721–22) rather than being the sites for popular worship as Brand proposes, the mechanisms for their development and use need to be considered fur-ther, as well as what they imply about the meanings of areas of temples.

Graffiti in Luxor Temple: Priestly Families and Divine Utterance

Exterior sectors of Luxor temple bear some of the most extensive groupings of second-ary divine figures, with a number at a very large scale and concentrated near side doors, as with the two examples noted above. An exterior section of wall, beside a side entrance leading into inner areas of the temple, is carved with a vast array of secondary divine figures and non-divine emblems, such as fecundity figures, in complex and diverse groupings (fig. 13.3B) (Brand 2004, pp. 261–62; 2007, p. 64; with Porter and Moss 1972, p. 335 [221]; Schwaller de Lubicz 1958, vol. 2, pl. 33). Some deities are captioned, including seated figures of Amun, standing ones of Mut, and squatting ones of Khonsu. These images are usually understood as practice models for carving or focal points for popular religion (Brand 2004, pp. 261–62 with n. 17), but were carefully carved, and some required scaffolding for their execution and were painted. Therefore they represent a large investment connected with temple activities and performances, although of a different character to traditional temple decoration. Their location relates to priestly movement in and out of inner temple areas, as is also the case with comparable images elsewhere in the temple and at Karnak.

A valuable example is a large group of graffiti on the facade of the east gate leading into the long colonnaded hall between the court of Ramesses II and the forecourt of Amenhotep III (fig. 13.3C). Graffiti of various types are distributed across the wall surface, in the previously uninscribed space below the main area of decoration as well as integrated into primary scenes of royal ritual before gods. The most visible are two scenes belonging to the Twenty-first Dynasty high priest, later king Pinudjem I, which were inscribed just below head height underneath the primary scenes and over erased royal texts. Both are modeled on traditional monumental styles of display. One, at a very large scale, shows Pinudjem as high priest, followed by women of his family, censing and libating before two forms of Amun, Mut, and Khonsu (fig. 13.4) (Porter and Moss 1972, pp. 307 [27]; Epigraphic Survey 1998, pp. 52–54, pls. 199–200, Gr. 1; Jansen-Winkeln 2007a, p. 17, no. 22a). This mixed presentation integrates royal elements — the ritual gestures and the cartouche of one of the women in the caption — with others that are characteristically nonroyal or priestly (e.g., Pinudjem's accoutrements).

Only the upper part of the second scene survives (fig. 13.5). It was carved in raised relief farther to the east, on the rear wall of the Ramessid court, immediately below a row of personified foreign places bearing offerings. It shows an erased figure of Pinudjem's father Payankh, with his four sons behind him, their arms raised in adoration before an ithyphallic figure of Amun-Re. A woman called Nodjmet, probably Pinudjem's mother, stands behind the god in a place normally reserved for goddesses. This exceptional position suggests that she is being honored posthumously. A prayer that she may have "a [long] lifetime in [...] within Thebes (*ꜥḥꜥw [qꜣ] m [...?] m-ẖnw wꜣst*)" is given in the caption above (Jansen-Winkeln 2007a, p. 17, no. 22b; Haring 2012, p. 149, pl. 16). Although the word for "lifetime" is usually used of this world, occasionally it can refer to the afterlife (e.g., Barta 1968, p. 126). Here it could reflect Nodjmet's semi-deified status. The caption also states that Pinudjem dedicated the scene for his father, probably deceased (Taylor 1998, pp. 1151–52). The area separating the two scenes is largely lost, but traces of a possibly contemporaneous figure worshiping a god suggest that this space could have been filled with other graffiti (Epigraphic Survey 1998, pp. 55–56, pl. 204, Gr. 9).

The group of secondary inscriptions asserts the importance of the priestly group, among whom female kin are prominent. Their position close to the processional axis, with one of them below offering bearers, binds them to core rituals of procession and provision. The use of raised relief for the second scene is striking because even very formal graffiti are usually incised or carved in sunk relief. Raised relief is associated with interiors, and hence spaces with a heightened sanctity. Here the choice of raised relief grants a generalized prestige to the scene, as is also the case for the raised relief ithyphallic Amun carved on the temple's west exterior wall (Brand 2004). The court of Ramesses II, open to the sky and behind the entrance pylon, includes a barque shrine, indicating that it could serve as a temporary and transitional resting point for the barque in festivals and procession.[10] The court was probably understood as an exterior space (although not generally accessible), thus appropriate for the display of power and authority — partly via affirmation of lineage — by and to the priesthood.

---

[10] For discussion of the relationship of the barque, a "mobile temple," to earlier architecture and decorative programmes in Luxor temple, including analysis of the creation and delineation of "interior" and "exterior" spaces, see Baines 2006, pp. 277–82.

On the east jamb of the doorway, close to the scene of Pinudjem before the triad and directly below the primary scenes, are two figures of deities: a small standing figure of Mut (Epigraphic Survey 1998, p. 55, pl. 203, Gr. 4) and a very large ithyphallic figure of Amun, the eye, eyebrow, and chin-strap of which once bore inlay (height ca. 2 m; fig. 13.6; with Epigraphic Survey 1998, p. 55, Gr. 5). The latter bears a hieroglyphic caption that mobilizes human need and potential response; he is "[Amun-Re]-Kamutef, mighty [god], the one who protects (or: 'advocate for') the wretched ([jmn-rˁ]-kȝ-mwt.f [nt̠r] nˁš pȝ wšb jȝd)," the latter being a somewhat rare epithet newly attested at the end of the New Kingdom (Leclant 1955; Leitz 2002, vol. 2, p. 592).[11] Both images may "emulate" divine figures in the nearby primary decoration (Cruz-Uribe 2008a, p. 2), and the use of these models may itself have been a ritual/devotional act. This form of Amun "who protects the wretched" is also present in the elaborate grouping of gods on the temple's exterior wall discussed above (Schwaller de Lubicz 1958, vol. 2, pl. 33C). The two graffiti may have been carved at the same time or perhaps reference one another in some way.

Other graffiti on the facade of the gateway are fully integrated into the primary decoration. A scene of Amenhotep III offering incense to Amun and Mut (later recarved for Ramesses II), which is directly above some priestly graffiti, incorporates a hieroglyphic caption in five columns before Mut's face (fig. 13.7; with Epigraphic Survey 1998, pl. 202, p. 54, Gr. 2). The text begins with a dedicatory formula on behalf of its commissioner, the high priest of Amun Shoshenq, son of a king Osorkon.[12] The following three damaged columns are spoken by the goddess, granting benefactions to a woman in the high priest's household: "I (fem.) have given to the songstress of the residence of the high priest, Djedbastetesankh, daughter of Padi[... ...] life, prosperity, and health ... [love, before?] Shoshenq, true of voice, [the ...?] high priest of Amun (dj.n.j n ḥst nt ḥnw n ḥm-nt̠r-tpy d̠d-bȝst-jw.s-ˁnḫ sȝt [pȝ-dj-... ...] ˁnḫ wd̠ȝ snb ... [mrwt m-bȝḥ] šsnq mȝˁ-ḥrw [pȝ..?] ḥm-nt̠r-tpy n jmn)." By placing a speech in the mouth of the goddess, the dedicator reoriented the already ancient ritual scene to a personal context, while positioning Shoshenq as the mediator for this divine beneficence. It is suggestive that this graffito, like Pinudjem's about a century earlier, relates to a woman in the family. This is a likely instance of graffiti generating dialogues; "'speaking' to each other and their surroundings, as well as to a viewer" (Baird and Taylor 2011b, p. 7). In this particular case, the height of the graffito on the wall and lightness of the carving mean that, unless painted, it may hardly have been visible. Nonetheless, the act of inscription in this potent space may have been enough to invoke the benefits which are enumerated and to relate their bestowal to the family context. Probably hundreds of years later, a figure of the child-god Khonsu was added in front of the body of the goddess (fig. 13.7; with Epigraphic Survey 1998, pl. 202, pp. 54–55, Gr. 3). The damaged accompanying text begins with Khonsu's speech — "words spoken by" (d̠d mdw jn) — which seems to offer protection to a particular person: "[that the] perfect [name] of the servant of Amen[... ...-?]khonsuiy,[13] true of voice, [remain] in the presence of

---

[11] The epithet nt̠r nˁš "mighty god"is only known from the Third Intermediate and Graeco-Roman periods (Leitz 2002, vol. 4, p. 427), pointing to a late date for the whole.

[12] Shoshenq is probably the later king or "co-regent" Shoshenq II (ca. 890 B.C.E.), son of Osorkon I

(Epigraphic Survey 1998, p. 54, n. b; Jansen-Winkeln 2007b, p. 56, no. 28).

[13] The Epigraphic Survey (1998, pp. 54–55 with n. e) suggests restoring "servant of Amenhotep," the deified Eighteenth Dynasty official Amenhotep son of Hapu, followed by the personal name "[Padi]khonsuiy."

Amun, Mut, and Khonsu, that he may beg for himself favor, power, a long lifetime, and a great and good old age as a gift, his body whole with health and life (... [*mn rn?*] *nfr bȝk n jmn* [... ...-?]*ḫnsw-jy mȝꜥ-ḫrw m-bȝḥ jmn mwt ḫnsw r dbḥ n.f ḥswt wsr ꜥḥꜥw qȝ jȝw ꜥȝ nfr m ḥnk jw ḥꜥ.f tm m snb ꜥnḫ*)." These two "speaking" graffiti in front of Mut seem to activate and enliven the primary decoration. The addition of Khonsu, who was third in the Theban triad with Amun and Mut, "completes" the original ritual scene (Epigraphic Survey 1998, p. 55, n. f), so his location was carefully selected and perhaps heightened the potency of the whole.

The entire wall bears a multi-layered set of additive transformations, accumulations of meaning that relate to and make play with the primary decoration. These meanings are specific and individual, as well as being self-evidently secondary and mostly highly visible, especially through the use of inlay as well as the sheer scale of Pinudjem's scenes. The process of addition is therefore central to their function. These acts of dedication, addition, and enrichment through graffiti appropriate and re-fashion divine images for the individual and the priestly group. They probably relate directly to priestly activities connected with the court and the primary axis through the temple; more broadly, they ritualize, and perhaps renew, this contact zone between outer and inner areas.[14]

The Temple of Ramesses III in Karnak: Addition and Circulation

Groups of graffiti with the mixed contexts and content of the wall at Luxor, combining new inscriptions in previously uninscribed areas with subtle addition to and transformation of primary decoration, are relatively rare in both Karnak and Luxor (Traunecker 1991, p. 89, with n. 65). My second case-study is a similar set of interconnected and personal dedications on an exterior wall of a barque shrine of Ramesses III (ca. 1187–1156 B.C.E.), which was constructed in the court in front of what was then the first entrance pylon, standing perpendicular to the main temple axis (figs. 13.2, 13.8). In the Third Intermediate Period, Shoshenq I (ca. 945–925 B.C.E.) enclosed the area in front of the pylon with massive walls and gateways, incorporating the front part of the Ramesses III temple and monumentalizing the court. On the east side an elaborate gate, the "Bubastite portal," was constructed between the side of the temple and the pylon, next to a side entrance into Ramesses III's temple.

Running along the east exterior wall are two registers of scenes of Ramesses III offering to various deities (indicated in the caption to fig. 13.8). Toward the center of the lower register, two scenes of the king bear small hieroglyphic graffiti in single columns in front of the bodies of the goddesses Nekhbet and Tefnut (Epigraphic Survey 1936b, pls. 104, 105f, h). Both are dedicatory formulas of members of temple staff; differences in orthography indicate that they were carved at different times. The likely first was carved before the face of Nekhbet, who stands in a shrine (figs. 13.1, 13.9): "dedicated by (or: 'made by') the chief servant of the domain of Amun Iuuenamun (*jr.n ḥry sḏm(w)-ꜥš n pr jmn jw.w-n-jmn*)."[15] The shrine's frame bears six deep, regular piercings, suggesting that it was enriched by gilding or some sort of structure or frame (some smaller holes are also visible within the shrine).

[14] Susanne Bickel (2009, p. 52) makes a similar suggestion for a royal inscription carved in monumental hieratic, thus a "secondary" style, at the point of transition between the court of Amenhotep III and the hypostyle hall in Luxor temple.

[15] My thanks to Mark Smith for the reading of the name.

The use of the hieroglyphic script and framing lines for the graffito show that it was modeled on primary scene captions and that the text was intended to be integrated with the primary decoration, although distinct from it. The second inscription carved before the figure of Tefnut in the nearby scene lacks the framing lines: "dedicated by the overseer of brewers of the domain of Amun [...?]enamun (*jr.n ḥry ʿtḥw n pr jmn* [...?]-*n-jmn*)." The scene itself does not bear traces of additional enrichment. As with the group in Luxor, this points to the extent to which graffiti generate graffiti, producing "graffiti spaces" that are often quite contained and distinct (Navrátilová 2010); in temples this seems also to ritualize place, through marking these areas as different and special.[16] Iuuenamun's graffito may also assert his involvement in the enriching of the image of the goddess. His name is well attested from the New Kingdom (Ranke 1935–1977, vol. 1, p. 14, no. 1) so his text may have been carved relatively soon after the temple was built, perhaps as a way of delineating and redefining the activities and movements of temple staff in relation to the building.

Personal contexts of dedication extend farther along this side of the temple and onto its front through the carving of two new secondary divine images: a figure of Ptah in a niche-like area created by the "lip" at the rear of the temple pylon and a seated figure of Amun-Re on the eastern corner of the pylon's facade (figs. 13.10–11). There is now no obvious visual relationship between the two, but because they are so close to each other, they are likely to be connected to common practices. The damaged figure of Amun, which includes holes for enrichment, would have been the more visually prominent (fig. 13.10). A damaged hieroglyphic caption in a column before the god's face gives a divine speech on the model of primary temple scenes: "Words spoken by Amun-Re, lord of the thrones of the Two Lands ... (*ḏd mdw jn jmn-rʿ nb njsw tꜣwy* ...)." On a block to the right, level with Amun's head, are traces of a small standing figure with arms raised in adoration.

The figure of Ptah is partly incised and partly rendered in raised relief (fig. 13.11; cf. Epigraphic Survey 1936b, pl. 112k). The god is almost a meter high and stands on a beveled plinth, in his usual effigy-form. His eye was deeply carved for inlay (now lost). In front of his face are six damaged columns of a hieroglyphic caption in raised relief. Traces of an incised baldachin that would have enclosed his figure are visible above his head. The caption includes a wish characteristic of nonroyal self-presentations — "that he (Ptah) may give life, prosperity, health, a perfect lifetime in his domain, bearing joy ... (*dj.f ʿnḫ wḏꜣ snb ʿḥʿw nfr m pr.f ḥr ršwt* ...)." A dedicatory text of a priest was carved in raised relief below the scene, appearing to form part of a unitary composition, although both texts may have been added later. As with the Pinudjem scene in Luxor, the use of raised relief is notable. Alongside the prestige associated with this technique, here it may also evoke an interior context. This sense is heightened architecturally by the location, which creates a semi-enclosed, almost niche-like space. Nine piercings surrounding the figure may have supported a structure. The shiny flicker of the inlaid eye in this shady area would have contributed to the image's visual impact.

Some graffiti along the eastern side of the Ramesses III temple were meant to be highly visible, perhaps focal points for viewing and action. They can perhaps be imagined as clearly delineated, brightly decorated "shrines" or "stations" marking out the daily movements of priests and other temple staff through the new side doors and courts. They are not only pious

---

[16] The *jr.n* dedicatory formula, which is a very common way of claiming responsibility for a monument, indicates that incising the text into the wall could be a dedicatory or votive act in itself (compare Plesch 2002a; 2002b, esp. pp. 182–86, on early modern graffiti as dedicatory acts in some Italian churches).

interventions but seem also to govern and ritualize these regular activities. The court they lead to was a central performative space for festivals and other cultic activities, although by no means a generally accessible area. Such additions and reworking create "contact zones" between the central rituals of temples, which are manifested in the primary decoration and realize core cosmologies, and daily, ephemeral but vital practices, activities, and performances. The personal dedications which lay claim to their creation, both here and at Luxor, also bind the scenes to the performance of their re-creation, enrichment, and renewal, as well as to particular people.

The Temple of Ptah in Karnak: More Marks = More Sacred = More Marks?

The final groups of graffiti I discuss are on the walls of the temple of Ptah. These constitute one of the most concentrated clusters at Karnak (Traunecker 1979, p. 24). The material is comparable to the examples from Ramesses III and Luxor in its association with side doors and movement, however here clear distinctions are made between the images of gods and personal inscriptions.

The Ptah temple lies in the northern part of the later Amun precinct (figs. 13.2, 13.12). For most of its history, it was independent from the precinct proper, lying outside the second-millennium enclosure wall. It may therefore have functioned as a barque shrine for the god on procession from the main temple. The second-millennium core of the temple was considerably reworked from the early first millennium onward, especially its access routes and entrance. Five gateways leading into the temple were successively added from ca. 715 B.C.E. onward, the final being that of Ptolemy XII Auletes. In the 370s (Thirtieth Dynasty) the temple was incorporated into the precinct behind a massive mudbrick enclosure wall which comes very close to its north side (Thiers and Zignani 2011b, p. 21). Ongoing investigation by the Centre Franco-Égyptien d'Étude des Temples de Karnak is transforming understanding of the temple's position, function, and relationship to other structures in the area (e.g., Thiers and Zignani 2011a). This work will have a significant impact on the interpretation of the graffiti, especially those on exterior walls. Here I present some preliminary thoughts on just a few examples.

The majority of the graffiti in the Ptah temple cluster along the south exterior wall of the main building, although a number of individual graffiti and groups of graffiti are located on the north exterior wall and the gateways, while a scene on the rear exterior wall may indicate that there was a contra-temple constructed there and integrated with the temple cult (cf. Laroche and Traunecker 1973–1977, pp. 194–95). I focus here on the figural and textual graffiti on the otherwise uninscribed north and south exterior walls, since these seem to relate to patterns of movement and circulation comparable to those discussed for Luxor temple and the temple of Ramesses III.

On the north side, near a side door, two graffiti of deities were carefully and precisely carved approximately midway between the side entrance and the rear of the temple: a large standing figure of Ptah facing west toward the door (fig. 13.13), and a smaller standing figure of an effigy-form Osiris facing east toward the rear. The only other graffito on this wall is a small, roughly carved divine barque nearby. Although the two figures of gods are relatively close together, they differ in scale and position and do not relate to each other in any straightforward way: Osiris is half the size of Ptah and higher up the wall. Upper sections of their figures were carved on infill blocks that are now partly or entirely lost; the face, hands, and accoutrements of Ptah are missing, as is the head of Osiris.

There are no accompanying inscriptions, and features of iconography are not distinctive, so dating is problematic. I suggest that the figures were carved before the enclosure wall was constructed in the 370s B.C.E. This wall constrained entry and exit, which were the regular activities in the temple to which these figures probably relate.[17] The relationship of these images to the movements and practices of temple staff is supported by comparison with the previous examples. Both figures also bear holes, indicating that they were enriched. As at the temple of Ramesses III, these embellishments will have heightened the impact of the images, and distinguished their role in delineating and ritualizing circulation.

On the south exterior wall are more extensive clusters of graffiti of varied type, formality, and content. Some areas are so densely inscribed with layered hieratic graffiti that many are almost illegible. These graffiti seem to consist mainly of the names and titles of priests and scribes. The most visually prominent elements are two scenes of gods on neighboring blocks near the middle of the wall (figs. 13.14–15). The blocks are palimpsest — the scenes were inscribed over graffiti, traces of which remain visible — and more graffiti of names and titles in hieratic and hieroglyphic scripts were written below and around the scenes. One of the scenes was recarved, and both are surrounded by piercings, some of which are filled in with plaster. Thus a zone of graffiti was perhaps formalized and ritualized through the addition of scenes and subsequently by ongoing inscription in relation to the scenes. Additionally, some of the graffiti were almost certainly plastered over during stages of reworking, with the plaster then falling away, while others seem to have been erased.[18] All these interventions complicate the understanding of the wall as a graffiti zone, although the close spatial relationship between the two modes is clear.

The likely earlier of the two scenes shows the ibis-headed god Thoth on the left, with a lunar disc on his head and in a striding pose, before standing figures of Ptah and Hathor, both of whom face toward the main temple axis. All three are depicted in conventional poses and costume. An offering table bearing a vessel for libations and a lotus bloom that stands in front of Hathor was probably added when the scene was recarved. A caption in six short columns above the scene gives the deities' names and epithets. Thoth's pose before the other two deities, as well as the epithet "true scribe of the Ennead" included in his caption, asserts his mediating capacity in the divine world, a role in which he is well attested in royal and nonroyal contexts (e.g., Stadler 2009). He may also act as an intermediary for the individuals in the surrounding graffiti. Overall, the scene's composition is more traditional than the graffiti of gods discussed above for Luxor temple and the Ramesses III temple. Compositions that show gods facing one another and interacting are typical of nonroyal contexts, and they increase and diversify from the late second millennium onward. An example is the lunette of a Nineteenth Dynasty non-royal stela in the British Museum that shows Thoth addressing Osiris, Isis, and Horus; the stela's owner and his wife are depicted below (EA 74847:

---

[17] Constraint became closure in the Ptolemaic period, when an internal staircase was built that blocked the north side entrance, and a new side entrance was created on the south (Thiers and Zignani 2011b, p. 21).

[18] Compare the evidence for the whitewashing of graffiti in temples at Deir el-Bahari in the later New Kingdom, perhaps in connection with restoration of the reliefs (Dolińska 2007, p. 78).

Malek 2012, p. 310, no. 803-056-750).[19] A wall in the hall of a nonroyal tomb on the Theban west bank, dating to the reign of Ramesses II (ca. 1279–1213 B.C.E.), displays a row of stelae showing goddesses interceding with other deities on the owner's behalf (Seyfried 1995, pl. 30), while related scenes in the hall show Thoth and the deified Eighteenth Dynasty king Amenhotep I acting as mediators (Seyfried 1995, pls. 30, 32). The overall effect is that of a processional route, perhaps mimicking the environment of a temple court (Seyfried 1995, p. 113). Something comparable may be alluded to on the south wall of the Ptah temple, but is more generalized and, perhaps, inclusive.

At some point, perhaps centuries, later, the figures of all three gods in the graffito were recarved. This recarving is particularly visible in the new outlines of their bodies. The scene was vividly painted or repainted; traces of bright yellows, blues, and reds remain throughout. The second scene may have been carved at the same time as the restyling of this one. It shows Thoth with an undifferentiated, effigy-form body, standing behind a figure of Ptah, who is also in effigy-form. Both gods face right, toward the rear of the temple. This distinctive iconography for Thoth seems unattested before the first millennium (Leitz 2002, vol. 7, p. 640 with references; e.g., Munro 1973, pl. 19, figs. 67–68). A Late Period, perhaps Twenty-fifth Dynasty date, seems likely stylistically, and accords well with the extensive reworking of the temple and surrounding area attested during this time.[20] Thoth's effigy-form body aligns him visually with Ptah, and perhaps also asserts his syncretism with Khonsu, another lunar god who was often depicted in effigy-form. Such iconography relates to Thoth's complex roles and associations (overview: Stadler 2012), especially his lunar aspect, which are visible in later primary decoration elsewhere in Karnak (e.g., Graindorge 2002).

Although the figures of the two gods are carved within a delineating frame, the latter's base extends to the right, where a further column for text was marked out but not inscribed, suggesting that more elements were planned than executed. These could have included a worshiping human figure, or perhaps another god as in the first scene. The caption that was carved evokes the presence and participation of worshipers in a column which addresses Ptah: "praise to your *ka*, O lord of the gods (*jꜣw n kꜣ.k pꜣ nb nṯrw*)." The extent to which these imagined worshipers encompass the individuals whose names surround the scene remains an open question, as some or all of these graffiti may have been covered by plaster, at least for a while.

Monumental environments often appear to collapse time, and seem distant from human actors. Areas like this, however, make it possible to plot long, probably punctuated, processes of addition, formalizing, and re-formalizing of sacred areas. These processes almost certainly relate to wider developments in this part of the temple complex. Excavation has revealed Twenty-fifth Dynasty monumental gates close to the south side of the Ptah temple, delineating an east–west processional axis, and indicating the extent to which this area was a focal point during this period alone.[21] The graffiti therefore offer a way to circumscribe the practice of particular groups in relation to these sacred spaces and routes, including their movements around temple complexes, where they pause, and where they focus attention

[19] Photographs are available via the British Museum Collection Database: http://www.britishmuseum.org/research/search_the_collection_database.aspx.

[20] My thanks to Martin Stadler for discussion of the iconography of this scene and for references.

[21] This axis was blocked by the last Ptolemaic enclosure wall (Thiers and Zignani 2011a, p. 15).

outside the interior primary spaces. Movements, gestures, and relations are solemnized and ritualized, reorganized and structured in a new way. These ways of selecting areas, then commissioning and/or creating graffiti have wider implications for changing meanings of places within temples.

Discussion

In bringing together these various styles of secondary inscription, I am working toward a re-examination of contrasts between formal and informal, institutional and personal, in sacred space. This material foregrounds the presence, movements, and activities of the people who managed temples in the first millennium. The inscription of graffiti was their practice, so it has wide-ranging political, religious, and spatial implications. As a strategy to assert the legitimacy and authority of priestly groups, seen here particularly with Pinudjem's inscriptions in Luxor, some graffiti appear closely comparable to more traditional forms of self-presentation, especially statues and stelae, which can similarly appropriate parts of temples, especially outer areas such as open courts.[22] However, formal graffiti are never very widespread, so this is not a replacement of traditional forms with something that was perhaps cheaper and easier to commission. Formal graffiti incorporate distinctive features, and are a new form of display whose development seems closely connected with changing power structures in Thebes in the early first millennium.

The distinctiveness of these graffiti lies partly in their tendency to focus on pictures of gods, and the re-working and presentation of these images in seemingly non-traditional ways. In this these graffiti can be distinguished from, for example, inscriptions of high priests of the late New Kingdom that were inscribed on exterior walls of the southern processional route at Karnak. These scenes and texts prioritized individual status in their appropriation of temple areas associated with service and administration (Traunecker 1979, pp. 27–30; Frood 2007, pp. 54–83), although principles of decorum restricting the representation of gods during this earlier period may have also placed constraints on display within such personal contexts in temples. The later graffiti of gods, while often citing individual acts of dedication, attest to and mobilize wider group practices. The scenes on the exterior of the Ptah temple seem to be an explicit instance of this, especially as the surrounding graffiti of scribes and priests may not have always been visible. However, these practices remain very much bound up with the display of status and prestige, for example, through the fine carving and painting of some graffiti that indicate the commissioning of artists, as well as various strategies of enrichment.

Graffiti as acts of place-making (Fisher 2009, pp. 184–85) formalize areas that were almost certainly sites for other ritual, devotional, and votive activities of personnel (e.g., offering, libation, prayer) that are now largely irretrievable archaeologically. An exception may be a graffito of a vessel inscribed on one of the two gates built by the Twenty-fifth Dynasty king

---

[22] A biographical text inscribed on a late New Kingdom stela of a high priest reports finding statues of ancestors and nobles "cast down and scattered" in areas of the open courts (wbꜣw) at Karnak, including "the great outer court of the temple (wsḫt ꜥt n bnr n ḥwt-nṯr)" (Boraik 2007). His description of their restoration follows: "He had them lifted up and re-established in the great stone festival court (wsḫt ꜥt ḥbyt n jnr) in which the offerings of Amun were laid." It is likely that the priest's stela, which was discovered at a site of secondary deposition, was set up with the statues in this outer court.

Shabaka (ca. 715–700 B.C.E.) at the entrance to the Ptah temple (fig. 13.12). Traunecker ob-serves (1982, p. 58) that an emplacement for a large vessel on the ground nearby suggests that the graffito marked a place for purification or libation before entering the temple proper. It is likely that other graffiti "sign-post" practice in comparable ways. Repeated activities may be indicated by the "dialogues" of graffiti that develop, as well as by the piercings that surround many of the images, some of which were later plastered over, pointing to different elaborations at different times. Ongoing investment is further demonstrated by the recarving of graffiti, including ithyphallic figures of Amun in Luxor temple and the temple of Montu at Karnak (Brand 2004, pp. 259–60) and one of the scenes on the south wall of the Ptah temple. Even the possible erasures near this scene attest to the potential salience and potency of graffiti and the areas in which they are inscribed.

Thus graffiti not only delineate places of devotion for temple staff, they ritualize their regular activities and movements in association with central cult rituals and performances. The gods depicted are mostly major deities and this strengthens the connection with pri-mary cult;[23] although their forms, such as Amun's ithyphallic iconography (see Baines, this volume), are often specifically intercessory and outward looking, so appropriate to more visible contexts. This activity and visibility has specific implications for distinctions between interior and exterior, normally so sharply distinguished in architecture and decoration. Graffiti of both formal and informal types tend not to occur in interiors (cf. Frood 2010), but rather suggest a complex reconfiguring of exterior parts of sacred precincts which ren-ders their meaning more explicit and expansive. This could be seen as a reconfiguring of traditional hierarchical ordering of cult places, and the articulation of secondary (exterior) places and practices into central activities and cosmologies. Much in this material is personal and individual, which forms part of its reorientation and meaning. The inscriptions are, in some sense, institutional, but the "institutional" context was diversifying and transform-ing. Graffiti-inscription is a conscious and selective act of appropriation and ritualization of exterior areas and doorways, not only because space was available for inscription, but also because it was highly visible to the people who mattered, other temple personnel. Graffiti relate directly to their active involvement in the creation and re-creation of places, and inform their patterns of movement, pausing, gaze, and action.

---

[23] This contrasts with some formal late New King-dom graffiti in Karnak that show individuals before minor and/or specialized deities such as Horus-Shed, Taweret, and the deified Eighteenth Dynasty king Amenhotep I and his mother Ahmose Nefertari (Traunecker 1979, pp. 26–30, figs. 1–2).

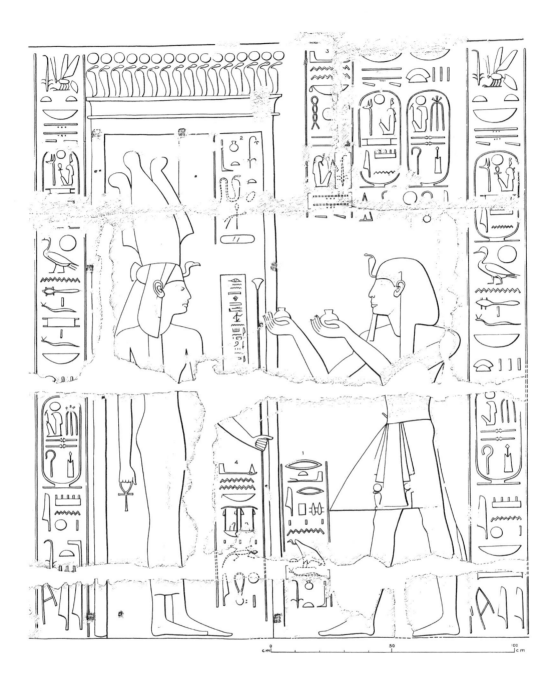

Figure 13.1. Scene of Ramesses III offering wine to the goddess Nekhbet; east exterior wall of the temple of Ramesses III, Karnak (Epigraphic Survey 1936b, pl. 105h)

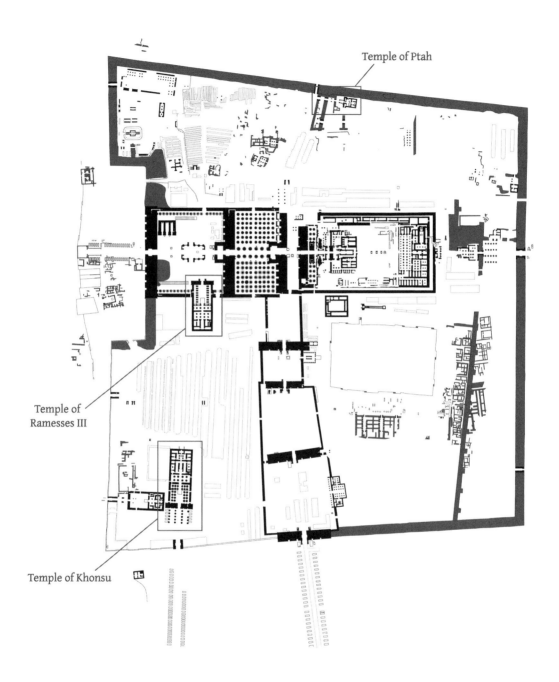

Temple of Ptah

Temple of
Ramesses III

Temple of Khonsu

Figure 13.2. Plan of the temple complex of Amun at Karnak (© CNRS-CFEETK)

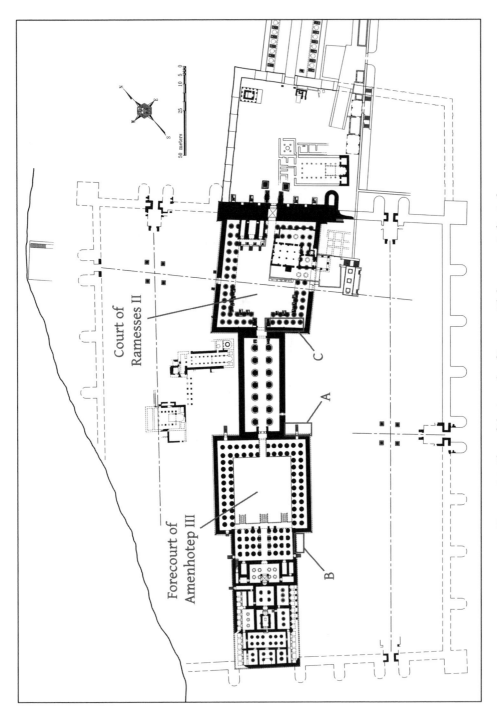

Figure 13.3. Plan of the temple of Luxor, with key areas indicated
(courtesy of the Epigraphic Survey and Jay Heidel)

Figure 13.4. Graffito scene of Pinudjem and female kin before two forms of Amun, Mut, and Khonsu; east facade of the colonnade of Amenhotep III, Luxor temple (Epigraphic Survey 1998, pl. 199)

Figure 13.5. Graffito scene of Pinudjem and male kin before Amun-Re and his mother Nodjmet; east side of the rear wall of the court of Ramesses II, Luxor temple (photograph by E. Frood)

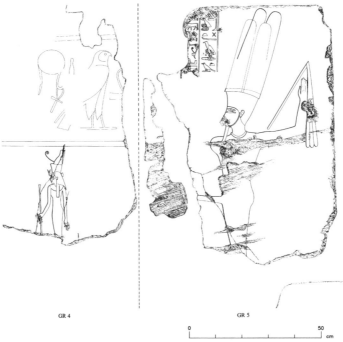

Figure 13.6. Graffito of Amun-Re-Kamutef "who protects the wretched;" east facade of the colonnade of Amenhotep III, Luxor temple (Epigraphic Survey 1998, pl. 203)

Figure 13.7. Graffiti before the face of Mut, whose nose, breast, and arm are visible in the photograph; east facade of the colonnade of Amenhotep III, Luxor temple (Epigraphic Survey 1998, pl. 201)

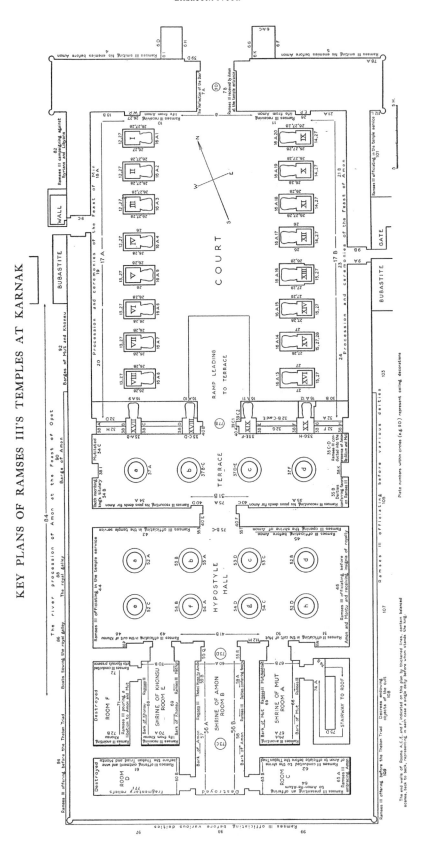

Figure 13.8. Plan of the temple of Ramesses III, Karnak (Epigraphic Survey 1936a, fig. 1)

Figure 13.9. Detail of the graffito of Iuuenamun before the goddess Nekhbet; east exterior wall of the temple of Ramesses III, Karnak (cf. fig. 13.1; Epigraphic Survey 1936b, pl. 105h)

Figure 13.10. Graffito of Amun-Re; east corner of the facade of the pylon of the temple of Ramesses III, Karnak (Epigraphic Survey 1936a, pl. 78a)

Figure 13.11. Graffito of Ptah; rear of the pylon of the temple of Ramesses III, Karnak
(Epigraphic Survey 1936b, 112l)

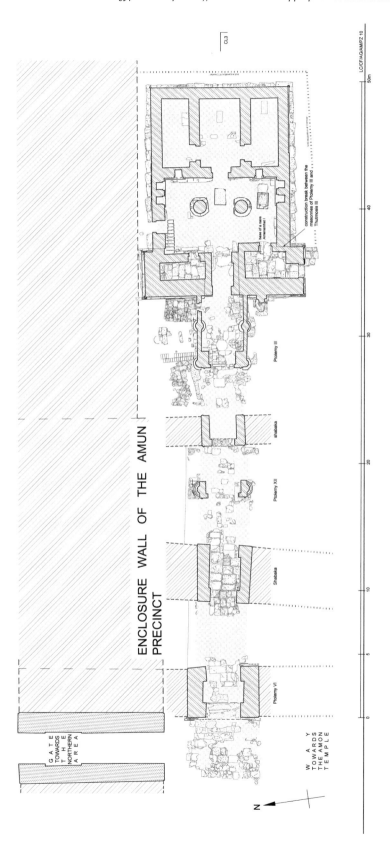

Figure 13.12. General plan of the temple of Ptah, Karnak (© CNRS-CFEETK)

Figure 13.13. Graffito of Ptah; north exterior wall of the temple of Ptah (© CNRS-CFEETK/P. Batard)

Figure 13.14. Graffito scene of Thoth before Ptah and Hathor, with other hieratic and hieroglyphic graffiti; south exterior wall of the temple of Ptah (© CNRS-CFEETK/P. Batard)

Figure 13.15. Graffito scene of Thoth and Ptah, with other hieratic and hieroglyphic graffiti;
south exterior wall of the temple of Ptah (© CNRS-CFEETK/P. Batard)

Bibliography

Ashley, Kathleen, and Véronique Plesch

2002   "The Cultural Processes of Appropriation." *Journal of Medieval and Early Modern Studies* 32/1: 1–15.

Baines, John

2006   "Public Ceremonial Performance in Ancient Egypt: Exclusion and Integration." In *Archaeology of Performance: Theaters of Power, Community, and Politics*, edited by Takeshi Inomata and Lawrence S. Coben, pp. 261–302. Lanham: AltaMira.

Baird, J. A., and Claire Taylor, editors

2011a   *Ancient Graffiti in Context*. Routledge Studies in Ancient History 2. London and New York: Routledge.

2011b   "Ancient Graffiti in Context: Introduction." In *Ancient Graffiti in Context*, edited by J. A. Baird and Claire Taylor, pp. 1–19. Routledge Studies in Ancient History 2. London and New York: Routledge.

Barta, Winfried

1968   *Aufbau und Bedeutung der altägyptischen Opferformel*. Ägyptologische Forschungen 24. Glückstadt: Augustin.

Bell, Catherine M.

1992   *Ritual Theory, Ritual Practice*. Oxford: Oxford University Press.

Bell, Lanny

1985   "Luxor Temple and the Cult of the Royal Ka." *Journal of Near Eastern Studies* 44: 251–94.

Bickel, Susanne

2009   "The Inundation Inscription in Luxor Temple." In *The Libyan Period in Egypt: Historical and Cultural Studies into the 21st-24th Dynasties* (Proceedings of a conference at Leiden University, 25–27 October 2007), edited by G. P. F. Broekman, R. J. Demarée, and O. E. Kaper, pp. 51–55. Egyptologische Uitgaven 23. Leiden: Nederlands Instituut voor het Nabije Oosten; Leuven: Peeters.

Blyth, Elizabeth

2006   *Karnak: Evolution of a Temple*. London and New York: Routledge.

Boraik, Mansour

2007   "Stela of Bakenkhonsu, High Priest of Amun-Re." *Memnonia* 18: 119–26.

Borchardt, Ludwig

1933   "Metallbelag an Steinbauten." In *Allerhand Kleinigkeiten*, edited by Ludwig Borchardt, pp. 1–11. Leipzig: Pries.

Brand, Peter J.

2004   "A Graffito of Amen-Re in Luxor Temple Restored by the High Priest Menkhepere." In *Egypt, Israel, and the Mediterranean World: Studies in Honor of Donald B. Redford*, edited by Gary N. Knoppers and Antoine Hirsch, pp. 257–66. Probleme der Ägyptologie 20. Leiden and Boston: Brill.

2007   "Veils, Votives, and Marginalia: The Use of Sacred Space at Karnak and Luxor." In *Sacred Space and Sacred Function in Ancient Thebes*, edited by Peter F. Dorman and Betsy M. Bryan, pp. 51–83. Studies in Ancient Oriental Civilization 61. Chicago: The Oriental Institute.

Brandl, Helmut

2008   *Untersuchungen zur steinernen Privatplastik der dritten Zwischenzeit: Typologie, Ikonographie, Stilistik.* 2 volumes. Berlin: MBV.

Cabrol, Agnès

2001   *Les voies processionnelles de Thèbes.* Orientalia Lovaniensia Analecta 97. Leuven: Peeters.

Cauville, Sylvie

1990   *Le temple de Dendera: guide archéologique.* Bibliothèque Générale 12. Cairo: Institut français d'archéologie orientale.

Ciccarello, Mark

1979   *The Graffito of Pinutem I in the Tomb of Ramesses XI.* Theban Royal Tomb Project. New York: The Brooklyn Museum Theban Expedition.

Cottevieille-Giraudet, Rémy

1931   *Rapport sur les fouilles de Médamoud (1930): la verrerie - les graffiti.* Fouilles de l'Institut français d'archéologie orientale du Caire. Rapports préliminaire 8. Cairo: Institut français d'archéologie orientale.

Cruz-Uribe, Eugene

2008a   "Graffiti (Figural)." In *UCLA Encyclopedia of Egyptology*, edited by Willeke Wendrich. Los Angeles. Available online at http://escholarship.org/uc/item/7v92z43m

2008b   *The Graffiti from the Temple Precinct.* Hibis Temple Project 3. San Antonio: Tambopata Partners – Van Siclen.

Degardin, Jean-Claude

2009   "Pérennité d'accès au toit du temple de Khonsou: pourquoi?" In *Elkab and Beyond: Studies in Honour of Luc Limme*, edited by Wouter Claes, Herman de Meulenaere, and Stan Hendrickx, pp. 233–43. Orientalia Lovaniensia Analecta 191. Leuven: Peeters.

2010   "Le fonctionnement du toit du temple de Khonsou à Karnak." *Cahiers de Karnak* 13: 227–41.

Dijkstra, Jitze H. F.

2008   *Philae and the End of Ancient Egyptian Religion: A Regional Study of Religious Transformation (298-642 CE).* Orientalia Lovaniensia Analecta 173. Leuven: Peeters.

2012   *The Figural and Textual Graffiti from the Temple of Isis at Aswan.* Beitrage zur Ägyptischen Bauforschung und Altertumskunde 18; Syene 1. Mainz: Philipp von Zabern.

Dils, Peter

1995   "'Ptah-de-la-grande-porte': un aspect du fonctionnement du temple de Medinet Habu." *Scriba* 4: 65–80.

Dolińska, Monika

2007   "Temples at Deir el-Bahari in the New Kingdom." In *6. Ägyptologische Tempeltagung, Leiden, 4.-7. September 2002: Funktion und Gebrauch altägyptischer Tempelräume*, edited by Ben J. J. Haring and Andrea Klug, pp. 67–82. Akten der Ägyptologischen Tempeltagungen 1; Ägypten und Altes Testament 33; Königtum, Staat und Gesellschaft früher Hochkulturen 3. Wiesbaden: Harrassowitz.

Epigraphic Survey

1936a   Reliefs and Inscriptions at Karnak, Volume 1. *Ramses III's Temple within the Great Inclosure of Amon,* Part 1. Oriental Institute Publications 25. Chicago: The University of Chicago Press.

| 1936b | Reliefs and Inscriptions at Karnak, Volume 2. *Ramses III's Temple within the Great Inclosure of Amon,* Part 2; *and Ramses III's Temple in the Precinct of Mut.* Oriental Institute Publications 35. Chicago: The University of Chicago Press. |
| 1998 | Reliefs and Inscriptions at Luxor Temple, Volume 2. *The Facade, Portals, Upper Register Scenes, Columns, Marginalia, and Statuary in the Colonnade Hall.* Oriental Institute Publications 116. Chicago: The Oriental Institute. |

Fischer, Henry George

| 1959 | "Review of Medinet Habu V: The Temple Proper I." *American Journal of Archaeology* 63/2: 195–98. |

Fisher, Kevin D.

| 2009 | "Elite Place-making and Social Interaction in the Late Cypriot Bronze Age." *Journal of Mediterranean Archaeology* 22/2: 183–209. |

Fleming, Juliet

| 2001 | *Graffiti and the Writing Arts of Early Modern England.* London: Reaktion Books. |

Frood, Elizabeth

| 2007 | *Biographical Texts from Ramessid Egypt.* SBL Writings from the Ancient World 26. Atlanta: Society of Biblical Literature. |
| 2010 | "Horkhebi's Decree and the Development of Priestly Inscriptional Practices in Karnak." In *Egypt in Transition: Social and Religious Development of Egypt in the First Millennium B.C.E.* (Proceedings of an International Conference, Prague, September 1–4, 2009), edited by Ladislav Bareš, Filip Coppens, and Květa Smoláriková, pp. 103–28. Prague: Czech Institute of Egyptology, Charles University in Prague/Agama. |

Gabolde, Luc, and Vincent Rondot

| 1993 | "Une catastrophe antique dans le temple de Montou à Karnak-Nord." *Bulletin de l'Institut français d'archéologie orientale* 93: 245–64. |

Gorre, Gilles

| 2009 | *Les relations du clergé égyptien et des lagides d'après les sources privées.* Studia Hellenistica 45. Turnout: Peeters. |

Graindorge, Catherine

| 2002 | "Les théologies lunaires à Karnak à l'époque ptolémaïque." *Göttinger Miszellen* 191: 53–58. |

Guglielmi, Waltraud

| 1994 | "Die Funktion von Tempeleingang und Gegentempel als Gebetsort: zur Deutung einiger Widder- und Gansstelen des Amun." In *Ägyptische Tempel: Struktur, Funktion und Programm* (Akten der Ägyptologischen Tempeltagungen in Gosen 1990 und in Mainz 1992), edited by Rolf Gundlach and Matthias Rochholz, pp. 55–68. Hildesheimer Ägyptologische Beiträge 37. Hildesheim: Gerstenberg. |

Haring, Ben

| 2012 | "Stela Leiden V 65 and Herihor's Damnatio Memoriae." *Studien zur altägyptischen Kultur* 41: 139–52. |

Jacquet-Gordon, Helen

| 2004 | Temple of Khonsu, Volume 3. *The Graffiti on the Khonsu Temple Roof at Karnak: A Manifestation of Personal Piety.* Chicago: The Oriental Institute. |

Jansen-Winkeln, Karl

| 2005 | "Ein Priester als Restaurator: zu einer ptolemäischen Inschrift am Luxortempel." *Zeitschrift für ägyptische Sprache und Altertumskunde* 132: 35–39. |
| 2007a | *Inschriften der Spätzeit* I: *Die 21. Dynastie.* Wiesbaden: Harrassowitz. |

2007b   *Inschriften der Spätzeit* II: *Die 22.–24. Dynastie.* Wiesbaden: Harrassowitz.

Jasnow, Richard
1994   "The Graffiti of Luxor Temple." *Chicago House Bulletin* 5/2. Available online at:
                      http://oi.uchicago.edu/research/projects/epi/chb5-2.html

Karkowski, Janusz
2003   *The Temple of Hatshepsut: The Solar Complex.* Varsovie: Éditions Neriton.

Laroche, Françoise, and Claude Traunecker
1973–1977   "La chapelle adossée au temple de Khonsou." *Cahiers de Karnak* 6: 167–96.

Leclant, Jean
1955   "Osiris *p3-wšb-i3d.*" In *Ägyptologische Studien*, edited by Otto Firchow, pp. 197–204.
                      Deutsche Akademie der Wissenschaften zu Berlin, Institut für Orientforschung,
                      Veröffentlichung 29. Berlin: Akademie-Verlag.

Leitz, Christian, editor
2002   *Lexikon der ägyptischen Götter und Götterbezeichnungen.* 8 volumes. Orientalia
                      Lovaniensia Analecta 110–16, 129. Leuven: Peeters.

Luiselli, Maria Michela
2011   *Die Suche nach Gottesnähe: Untersuchungen zur persönlichen Frömmigkeit in Ägypten
                      von der 1. Zwischenzeit bis zum Ende des Neuen Reiches.* Ägypten und Altes Testa-
                      ment 73. Wiesbaden: Harrassowitz.

Mairs, Rachel
2011   "Egyptian 'Inscriptions' and Greek 'Graffiti' at El Kanais in the Egyptian Eastern
                      Desert." In *Ancient Graffiti in Context*, edited by Jennifer A. Baird and Claire Tay-
                      lor, pp. 153–64. Routledge Studies in Ancient History 2. New York and London:
                      Routledge.

Malek, Jaromir, editor
2012   *Topographical Bibliography of Ancient Egyptian Hieroglyphic Texts, Statues, Reliefs and
                      Paintings* 8: *Objects of Provenance Not Known* 4: *Stelae (Dynasty XVIII to the Roman
                      Period).* Oxford: Griffith Institute.

Marciniak, Marek
1974   *Deir el-Bahari* I: *les inscriptions hiératiques du temple de Thoutmosis III.* Varsovie,
                      PWN: Éditions Scientifiques en Pologne.

Munro, Peter
1973   *Die spätägyptischen Totenstelen.* Ägyptologische Forschungen 25. Glückstadt: Au-
                      gustin.

Navrátilová, Hana
2010   "Graffiti Spaces." In *Egypt in Transition: Social and Religious Development of Egypt in
                      the First Millennium B.C.E.* (Proceedings of an International Conference, Prague,
                      September 1–4, 2009), edited by Ladislav Bareš, Filip Coppens, and Květa Smo-
                      láriková, pp. 305–32. Prague: Czech Institute of Egyptology, Charles University
                      in Prague/Agama.

Parkinson, Richard
1999   *Cracking Codes: The Rosetta Stone and Decipherment.* London: British Museum Press.

Peden, A. J.
2001   *The Graffiti of Pharaonic Egypt: Scope and Roles of Informal Writings (c. 3100–332 B.C.).*
                      Probleme der Ägyptologie 17. Leiden and Boston: Brill.

Plesch, Véronique

2002a   "Graffiti and Ritualization: San Sebastiano at Arborio." In *Medieval and Early Modern Rituals: Formalized Behavior in Europe, China and Japan*, edited by Joélle Rollo-Koster, pp. 127–46. Leiden: Brill.

2002b   "Memory on the Wall: Graffiti on Religious Wall Paintings." *Journal of Medieval and Early Modern Studies* 32/1: 167–97.

2010   "Destruction or Preservation? The Meaning of Graffiti at Religious Sites." In *Art, Piety and Destruction in European Religion, 1500–1700*, edited by Virginia Raguin, pp. 137–72. Visual Culture in Early Modernity. Aldershot: Ashgate.

Porter, Bertha, and Rosalind L. B. Moss

1972   *Topographical Bibliography of Ancient Egyptian Hieroglyphic Texts, Reliefs, and Paintings* 2: *Theban Temples*. 2nd edition. Oxford: Griffith Institute and Oxford University Press.

Price, Campbell

2010   Nonroyal Late Period Statuary from the Karnak Cachette. Ph.D. dissertation. Liverpool: University of Liverpool.

Ragazzoli, Chloé

2011   "Lire, écrire, survivre: les graffiti de scribes au Nouvel Empire." In *Lieux de savoir 2: les mains de l'intellect*, edited by Christian Jacob, pp. 290–311. Paris: Albin Michel.

Ragazzoli, Chloé, and Elizabeth Frood

2013   "Writing on the Wall: Two Graffiti Projects in Luxor." *Egyptian Archaeology* 42: 30–33.

Ranke, Hermann

1935–1977 *Die ägyptischen Personennamen*. 3 volumes. Glückstadt: Augustin.

Römer, Malte

1994   *Gottes- und Priesterherrschaft in Ägypten am Ende des Neuen Reiches: ein religionsgeschichtliches Phänomen und seine Grundlagen*. Ägypten und Altes Testament 21. Wiesbaden: Harrassowitz.

Rutherford, Ian

2003   "Pilgrimage in Greco-Roman Egypt: New Perspectives on Graffiti from the Memnonion at Abydos." In *Ancient Perspectives on Egypt*, edited by Roger Matthews and Cornelia Roemer, pp. 171–90. Encounters with Ancient Egypt. London: University College London Press.

Schwaller de Lubicz, R. A.

1958   *Le temple de l'homme: Apet du sud à Louqsor*. 3 volumes. Paris: Caractères.

Seyfried, Karl-Joachem

1995   *Das Grab des Djehutiemhab (TT 194)*. Theben 7. Mainz: Philipp von Zabern.

Stadler, Martin A.

2009   *Weiser und Wesir: Studien zu Vorkommen, Rolle und Wesen des Gottes Thot im ägyptischen Totenbuch*. Orientalische Religionen in der Antike 1. Tübingen: Mohr Siebeck.

2012   "Thoth." In *UCLA Encyclopedia of Egyptology*, edited by Jacco Dieleman and Willeke Wendrich. Los Angeles. Available online at http://escholarship.org/uc/item/2xj8c3qg.

Taylor, John H.

    1998   "Nodjmet, Payankh and Herihor: The End of the New Kingdom Reconsidered." In *Proceedings of the Seventh International Congress of Egyptologists, Cambridge, 3-9 September 1995*, edited by Christopher J. Eyre, pp. 1143–55. Orientalia Lovaniensia Analecta 82. Leuven: Peeters

Thiers, Christophe, and Pierre Zignani

    2011a   "The Temple of Ptah." In *French-Egyptian Center for the Study of the Temples of Karnak: Activity Report 2011*, edited by Mansour Boraik and Christophe Thiers, pp. 15–29. Luxor: CFEETK (http://www.cfeetk.cnrs.fr/).

    2011b   "The Temple of Ptah at Karnak." *Egyptian Archaeology* 38: 20–24.

Traunecker, Claude

    1979   "Manifestations de piété personnelle à Karnak." *Bulletin de la Société française d'égyptologie* 85: 22–31.

    1982   "Le peuple de Karnak." *Histoire et archéologie: les dossiers* 61: 55–59.

    1991   "Observations sur le décor des temples égyptiens." In *L'image et la production du sacré: actes du colloque de Strasbourg, 20-21 janvier 1988*, edited by Françoise Dunand, Jean-Michel Spieser, and Jean Wirth, pp. 77–101. Paris: Méridiens Klincksieck.

14

THE TRANSFORMATION OF SACRED SPACE, TOPOGRAPHY, AND ROYAL RITUAL IN PERSIA AND THE ANCIENT IRANIAN WORLD

Matthew P. Canepa, University of Minnesota, Twin Cities

The Problem of an Iranian Temple Tradition

In contrast to the other ancient Western Asian cultures treated in this volume, the ancient Iranian world did not develop a unified tradition of temple architecture that evolved continuously through all periods.[1] It is important to assert this at the outset because throughout the last century scholars have repeatedly posited, and often attempted to reconstruct, a trans-millennial tradition of Iranian temple architecture, that is, a tradition of architecture built to house a cult image in the manner of a Babylonian, Elamite, or Greek temple, or a sacred, ever-burning fire in the manner of a late antique or medieval Zoroastrian fire temple. Scholarship from the last century either imposed reconstructed visions of a primordial "Aryan" temple, or took late antique or even modern Zoroastrian fire temples and fire cult as normative and vainly sought these imagined or anachronistic architectural or ritual forms in the archaeological evidence. A rotating cast of structures were enlisted as potential Achaemenid fire temples, including the so-called *āyadana* at Susa, the Kaʿba-ye Zardošt at Naqš-e Rostam, the Zendān-e Solaymān and the mudbrick terrace of the "Sacred Precinct" at Pasargadae, various structures at Persepolis including Xerxes I's "Gate of Nations," the courtyard of the *hadiš*, Kuh-e Ḵʷāja in Sīstān, and Taḵt-e Solaymān in Iranian Azerbaijan. Scholarship often tried to explain the sites' divergent heterogeneity of architectural forms through multiple social, functional, or, in the cases of Nazi-era scholarship, racial categories.[2]

---

[1] This divergence is manifest in the catalog of sites collected by Shenkar 2007 and 2011. While some archaeological literature restricts "Iran" or "Iranian" to sites within the Islamic Republic of Iran or the geographical expanse of the Iranian plateau, in the field of ancient Iranian studies and this paper, "Iranian" also includes the overlapping Iranian linguistic and cultural spheres that extended beyond the borders of the modern nation-state or geographical region. This encompasses peoples who spoke an Iranian language (Av. *airiia-*/OPers. *airiya-*/MPers. *ēr*/ Bactrian *airia*), and often designated their homelands as an "Iranian Land" (e.g., Av. *Airyanəm vaēĵō*, MPers. *Ērānwēz*). These Iranian peoples or their rulers further identified themselves according to the region they inhabited (Persian, Parthian), or their dynasty

(Achaemenid, Arsacid, Kushan, Sasanian, etc.). In addition, large parts of the former Achaemenid empire were ruled by former satrapal dynasties who cultivated their Iranian roots and culture, though the majority of the peoples they ruled were not (e.g., Orontid Armenia).

[2] For example, Erdmann argued the *āyadana* at Susa represented a "popular" tradition of architecture and fire cult (*Stadtheiligtum*) while the Kaʿba-ye Zardošt and Zendān-e Solaymān represented "courtly" fire temples (*Hofheiligtum*) of the Persian elite (Erdmann 1941, p. 22). Boyce posited the existence of a discrete split between "fire temples" and "image temples," and that creedal differences lay behind them (Boyce 1975b, p. 456; 1982, pp. 216–31; Boyce and Grenet 1991, p. 74). Strzygowski sought

Although they might have disagreed on finer points, various strains of scholarship wove these disparate structures together into a linear, developmental architectural and religious tradition and traced its influence thence into non-Iranian architectural and religion.[3]

All the sites cited as the earliest Persian fire temples by these earlier strains of scholarship have since proven to have served something other than a fire cult, to have been built well after the Achaemenid era, or both. Of these, scholarship depended particularly heavily on the so-called āyadana at Susa, as it was the only site thought to be from the Achaemenid era that presented a structure that appeared to match later, post-Achaemenid ground plans.[4] It served as the lynchpin. The late nineteenth-century explorer and self-taught archaeologist Marcel-Auguste Dieulafoy explored this structure using primitive methodologies.[5] Dieulafoy arrived at an Achaemenid date primarily because the structure incorporated Achaemenid column bases and rested on a gravel foundation, a building technique now known to have persisted in the region through well into the Parthian era.[6] Later analysis of the site's ceramics and architectural members by more competent archaeologists revealed that the structure in fact dates to the late Seleukid or early Parthian period (ca. second century B.C.E.) and merely incorporated mismatched Achaemenid bases spoliated from nearby Susa.[7] Although this evidentiary cornerstone has long since been removed, the scholarly edifice built on it has only recently fully collapsed.

Paralleling this largely Western European debate and later spliced with it, mid- to late twentieth-century Soviet archaeology put forth a heterogeneous grouping of sites and structures as contenders for the title of earliest Iranian fire temple. These include the mid-second- to early first-millennium sites of Jarkutan in northern Bactria (Uzbekistan); Togolok-1, Togolok-21, and Gonur in Margiania (Turkmenistan); and a structure from an earlier level of Kazakl'i-yatkan, all associated with the Bactria Margiana Archaeological Complex (BMAC).[8] Just as contemporary scholarly consensus has rejected the excavators' attempts to connect the BMAC with early Iranian or Indo-Iranian culture, none of the early "fire temples" from Bactria, Margiana, and Chorasmia show evidence of Iranians or Iranian cults.[9] Needless to say, these sites have nothing to do with "Zoroastrian" cult.

---

an essential "Aryan" architectural form in Iranian fire temples, a centralized structure built on a "radiating" plan (strahlenförmige Grundriss) that could be discerned in the architecture of any "Aryan" people, from Armenians to Germans (Strzygowski 1927, 1935; Maranci 1998).

[3] Oelmann 1921; Strzygowski 1927, 1935; Godard 1938; Wachsmuth 1938; Erdmann 1941, pp. 11–22; Hinz 1942; Wikander 1946, pp. 58–71; Gullini 1964; Schippmann 1971; Boyce 1975a–b (among others); Yamamoto 1979, 1981; Azarnoush 1987; Choksy 2007. Eventually allied with similar endeavors in the Third Reich, some of these early scholars, such as Strzygowski, Hinz, and Wikander, studied Iranian religion and architecture as part of reconstructing a quintessential "Aryan" architecture. See Arvidsson 2006 and Maranci 1998 for historiographical context. Although he later indulged in the same sort of speculation, Herzfeld's early assessment in Iranische Felsreliefs is the only one that has stood the test of time:

"Schon für die sasanidische Zeit bleibt das Problem der Feuertempel sehr dunkel. Für die ältere Zeit, die achaemenidische, ist es völlig unlösbar" (Sarre and Herzfeld 1910, p. 239; cf. Herzfeld 1935, pp. 28, 44; Herzfeld 1941, pp. 215, 230, 301–06).

[4] Oelmann 1921, pp. 278–79; Strzygowski 1927, p. 7; 1930, p. 455; Godard 1938, pp. 12–13; Wachsmuth 1938; Erdmann 1941, pp. 15–18, 75; Wikander 1946, pp. 70–71; Gullini 1964, pp. 264–68; Schippmann 1971, pp. 466–515.

[5] Amiet 1995.

[6] Dieulafoy 1890–1892, vol. 4, pp. 411–19.

[7] Ghirshman 1976, vol. 1, pp. 197–200; Stronach 1985, pp. 619–21.

[8] Reviewed most recently in Shenkar 2007.

[9] Anthony 2007, pp. 421–37 and p. 505 n. 42; Bakels 2003. In general, the methods by which these sites were excavated and interpreted were primitive and proceeded without regard for stratigraphy or recording (Salvatori 2003, 2007, 2008).

Without clear archaeological evidence, a variety of textual sources were then enlisted to reconstruct an Iranian temple tradition, despite internal contradictions, anachronism, and lack of specificity.[10] These textual sources have often overshadowed the authentic archaeological and epigraphic evidence. The various components of the Avesta contain no mention of temples, fire or otherwise, even in its youngest sections. A variety of conflicting classical sources have commonly been cited as proof that early Iranian religions did not use temples, or dismissed as uninformed by those who sought an ancient tradition. Neither approach, it turns out, is entirely true. The first, and most influential for both ancient and modern authors, is Herodotus. In a short excursus, Herodotus describes "Persian" religion, by which he means the religious customs of several Iranian peoples. He famously states: "It is not [the Persians'] custom to set up statues, temples (*nēous*) or altars, but consider those who do to be foolish" (*Histories* 1.131–40). A handful of later classical authors, some writing before the fall of the Achaemenids, show the influence of, or at least do not contradict, Herodotus, stressing that the Persians sacrifice in open air.[11]

While it neither mentions "temples" (*naos*) nor "sanctuaries" (*hieron*), a fragment of the *Babyloniaka* of Berossos, a Babylonian priest who wrote a history of Babylon in Greek for Antiochos I (281–61 B.C.E.), has been especially important for scholarly debate on Persian religion.[12] The passage states:

> [The Persians, the Medes and the Magi] did not believe in wooden or stone images of the gods but in fire and water like the philosophers. Later, however, after many years they began to worship statues in human form as Berossus reports in the third book of his Chaldaean history. Artaxerxes, the son of Darius, the son of Ochus, introduced this practice. He was the first to set up an image of Aphrodite Anaitis [Anāhitā] in Babylon and to require such worship from the Susians, Ecbatanians, Persians and Bactrians and from Damascus and Sardis.[13]

Berossos only mentions that Artaxerxes II introduced the veneration of statues (*agalmata*) of the goddess Anāhitā, not temples. Nevertheless, scholars repeatedly used this passage as the basis for arguing that: 1) Artaxerxes II introduced temples into Persian religion and, occasionally, that 2) these temples housed a fire cult along with a cult statue.

The dominant interpretation of these texts that continues to affect scholarship arises from the arguments of Stig Wikander and Mary Boyce. They, and those who followed them, generally accepted Herodotus and held that the Persians did not use temples until the time of Artaxerxes II. Wikander argued that a cult of fire "must have" joined Artaxerxes II's image cult of Anāhitā in a temple since he believed this to be the primordial Iranian cult.[14] According to Wikander this combination thus created the first "fire temples." Building on earlier scholarship, most notably that of Kurt Erdmann (1941), he assumed that this late Achaemenid temple architecture established a pan-Iranian tradition that evolved continuously through

[10] Reviewed critically in de Jong 1997, pp. 343–52.

[11] Dino of Kolophon, FrGrH 690 F 28 (Clement of Alexandria, *Protrepticus* 5.65.1). Xenophon, *Cyropaedia* 8.7.3. Influence of Herodotus noted in, among others, Cicero, *De Republica* 3.9.14 and *De Legibus* 2.10.26, and Strabo, *Geographia* 15.3.13. See below for further discussion of the Roman sources.

[12] Wikander 1946, p. 61.

[13] Burstein 1978, p. 29, 5.2. In addition, some have argued that Yašt 5 lines 126–29 appears to contain an inserted section written in the Achaemenid era that describes the iconography of a cult statue of Anāhitā; see de Jong 1997, p. 272.

[14] Wikander 1946, p. 60. On the context of his scholarship, see Arvidsson 2006, p. 234.

the Sasanian era. While generally accepting Wikander's interpretation of Berossos, in the late twentieth century Mary Boyce, the influential scholar of the history of Zoroastrianism, hypothesized that a rival temple cult of fire that excluded images "must have" emerged from an offended orthodox Zoroastrian community to counter Artaxerxes II's introduction of statues and, presumably, temples.[15] This, she argued, was the genesis of the true Zoroastrian fire temple, a tradition that she argued persisted in purity alongside the heterodox "image temples" until the Sasanians suppressed the worship of cult statues in late antiquity. Despite the persistent influence of Wikander and, especially, Boyce, no archaeological or indigenous textual evidence of any kind corroborates their claims that grand, officially sponsored Achaemenid Zoroastrian fire temples were the genesis of a pan-Iranian tradition of temple architecture. In addition, while the Achaemenid royal inscriptions show the prominence of the god Auramazdā and impact of Avestan concepts, it is abundantly clear that the Achaemenids did not adhere to anything approaching orthodox Zoroastrianism, which is a late antique and early medieval phenomenon. While the Achaemenids themselves would not have necessarily used either term, it makes more sense to speak of Achaemenid "Mazdaism" instead of Achaemenid "Zoroastrianism," which would be an overt anachronism.

A much different pattern emerges when one applies a more disciplined approach with emphasis on credible archaeological evidence and indigenous textual and epigraphic sources. The recent revolution in Achaemenid studies made possible by the study of the Persepolis Fortification Archive has greatly augmented the body of authentic, indigenous evidence available and has provided a salutary correction and reorientation to the field.[16] This paper explores the development of Iranian sacred space, topography, architecture, and royal ritual. It focuses primarily on the Achaemenid period and examines continuities and, just as importantly, new developments and changes in Seleukid Iran (310–141 B.C.E.) and the Arsacid empire (ca. 238 B.C.E.–ca. 224 C.E.) until the Sasanian era (224–642 C.E.). In doing so, it reorients debate away from reconstructing a continuous, linked architectural and ritual tradition, which is not indicated in the evidence. Instead this paper calls attention to the abundant evidence we do have of Iranian sacred spaces and ritual and the constant, creative tension between continuity, massive ruptures, and innovation that characterize it.

Religious Architecture in Iran and Iranian Religions before the Achaemenids

The first temples that appear in a region and in a time period securely inhabited by Iranians, and thus likely built and used by Iranians, were excavated at the site of Tepe Nuš-e Jān in Media. The site yielded evidence of two temples, the "Central Temple" and "Western Temple," which were in use sometime during the seventh century B.C.E. (fig. 14.1).[17] The exterior of the Central Temple presented an elaborate, roughly symmetrical cruciform shape, while the Western Temple had an irregular ground plan formed from two rectangular sections of different size joined together. Although the ground plans of the two structures diverge, they

---

[15] Boyce 1975b, p. 456; 1982, pp. 216–31; Boyce and Grenet 1991, p. 74.

[16] It is not too strong to say that Henkelman (2008) is in a large part responsible for this correction. Garrison (forthcoming) provides a similar valuable

reorientation with regards to Achaemenid visual culture. Shenkar's recent recataloging (2007, 2011) of temples provides a very important reassessment of the archaeological evidence.

[17] Stronach and Roaf 2007, pp. 213–17.

shared a number of internal features that indicate their architects and patrons intended them to serve a similar cultic tradition. Both temples have a single entrance, an entrance corridor, an antechamber with a spiral ramp leading to a second story above the antechamber, a large central sanctuary decorated with niches, a lockable door to the sanctuary, and a single freestanding fire holder located to the left of the entrance to the sanctuary.[18] The excavators recovered no evidence of the deity or deities honored at the temples. Only the altar might suggest a relationship with ancient Iranian religious traditions, although this is far from conclusive.[19] While the shape of the altar, roughly square with a stepped fire capital, evokes later Achaemenid fire altars, the Central Temple's fire holder was made of plastered mudbrick versus stone. In contrast to remains and sculptural portrayals of Achaemenid fire holders, the shaft of that of Tepe Nuš-e Jān was very short, raising the top of the altar only .85 meters from floor level. At the end of its life, the Central Temple was decommissioned and carefully sealed up by filling it with shale and immuring the top of the walls with brick, a procedure that recalls Mesopotamian decommissioning practices.[20] The altar was given special attention to ensure that it was protected. A small .80-meter-high mudbrick wall was built around it and the space between the altar and the protecting wall was carefully filled with shale fragments.[21]

The external features of these temples recall aspects of Urartian temples, and their offset sanctuary entrances evoke the Elamite temples from Čoḡā Zanbīl, which are among the few Elamite temples that have been excavated. While certain features, such as a divided inner sanctuary and niches, vaguely parallel those features in Mesopotamian temples, neither presents the typical Mesopotamian straight-axis *Langraum* ground plan, nor did their cultic furniture recall Mesopotamian temple furnishings.[22] The exterior plan and tower-like appearance of the Central Temple vaguely evoke Urartian temples, but the overall design of the temples finds no ready parallel at any other site.[23] Their architectural traditions grew from ancient Western Asian architectural traditions generally but were not rooted in any one exclusively.

While Boyce dismissed them entirely, preferring to explain them away as foreign temples introduced by a Median king's non-Iranian queen, others have proclaimed the temples the first unquestionably orthodox Zoroastrian fire temples.[24] Neither of these absolutist pronouncements were based on the archaeological evidence, but were arrived at by comparing the structures positively or negatively to late antique and medieval Zoroastrianism.[25] Though

---

[18] Ibid., p. 197.

[19] Ibid., pp. 82–83 and 210–11.

[20] Ibid., pp. 88–91.

[21] Ibid., pp. 88–89.

[22] In contrast, the temple at Hasanlu, built ca. 1250 B.C.E. at a site south of Lake Orumiyeh, responded to this Mesopotamian/Syrian tradition. Unlike Tepe Nuš-e Jān, the city's inhabitants were not Iranians and the cult does not appear to have been an Iranian cult (Dyson and Voigt 2003).

[23] Stronach and Roaf 2007, pp. 198, 211–12; Tourovets 2005.

[24] Boyce largely downplayed or ignored this scholarship as it emerged in the later part of her career. She strenuously argued that the temples served

non-Iranian gods, largely since they did not fit into her chronology, not because of the archaeological evidence (Boyce 1982, pp. 36–37).

[25] See Shenkar's assessment of Azarnoush 1987 and Choksy 2007 (Shenkar 2007, p. 173). In addition to being methodologically unsound considering we have very little primary source evidence on early Zoroastrian practice, retrojecting late antique Zoroastrianism does not make sense in light of scholarship's growing consensus that Zoroaster indeed flourished in the late seventh to early sixth century B.C.E., after the construction of these structures (Gnoli 2000, p. 165; 2003). Azarnoush (1987) argued that the roughly cruciform shape of the Central Temple matched that of the palace at Bīšāpūr and, because of this alone, they shared the same function.

they did not provide sufficient evidence to identify the exact nature of the cults they hosted, the temples at Tepe Nuš-e Jān clearly show that some Medes adopted architecture for cultic purposes and this may have had some relationship to Iranian religiosity. They are important insofar as they force scholars to nuance and reconsider the scope and accuracy of the claims of Herodotus and other classical sources. Most significantly, the architectural and cultic designs of the temples do not reappear in the Achaemenid era and did not ultimately contribute to a larger, continuous tradition of Iranian or Persian sacred architecture.[26]

Achaemenid Ritual Practice and Sacred Architecture in Persia and the Iranian Plateau

Within the wider province of Pārsa, no evidence has emerged of a structure that was used as a Zoroastrian fire temple or a "house of a god" in the architectural and ritual tradition of a Mesopotamian or Elamite temple.[27] Similarly, past and current excavations around Susa, Ecbatana, Persepolis, and Pasargadae have not produced evidence of anything that resembles a temple dating to the Achaemenid era. The archaeological evidence suggests that the Achaemenid kings did not build temples in Iran. This contrasts sharply with royal traditions of patronage in Babylon, Assyria, and Elam as well as with evidence of the Achaemenids' own patronage of non-Persian temples and cults in Mesopotamia, Anatolia, and Egypt. Temple building and restoration were important royal practices in ancient Western Asia, especially prominent in Elam, the region whose people and culture most profoundly impacted and guided the genesis and development of the early Persian empire.[28] A wide variety of sacred structures flourished in Elamite religion and the pre-Achaemenid Elamite language contained a rich and nuanced vocabulary for various types of temples, shrines, and chapels.[29] The vast majority of these Elamite sacred structures are known only by the inscriptions on the bricks that once constituted them. While most Elamite temples are lost, the Middle Elamite site of Čogā Zanbīl preserves the actual ground plans of a number of temples, which, by and large, relate to Mesopotamian architectural traditions.[30] This once widespread and important institution all but disappears after the rise of the Achaemenids. Indicative of this precipitous decline, no archaeological evidence of an Achaemenid-era, Elamite-style temple has yet emerged in Elam or Pārsa, be it an actual site or even just a few inscribed bricks.

Turning to the epigraphic sources, careful observers of Achaemenid sources have pointed out that Darius I never boasts of building or restoring temples in his royal inscriptions.[31] The only mention of temples arises in a passage in the Elamite and Akkadian versions of his Bīsotūn inscription, which was written for the whole empire and disseminated widely. Here Darius I states that he rebuilt the sacred sites that Gaumata destroyed.[32] The Elamite version calls these sites "temples," as does the Akkadian version (Achaemenid Elamite ᴬᴺ*zí-ia-an*ᴬᴺ: *ziyan*, lit., "places of seeing [the gods]," "temples"; Babylonian *É.* ⌜ᴹᴱˢ⌝ *šá* DINGIR. ᴹᴱˢ "houses of the gods"). While the Elamite and Akkadian versions agree, the Old Persian

[26] Boucharlat 1984, pp. 122–24. Contra Azarnoush 1987.

[27] Root 2010, p. 171; Boucharlat 2005.

[28] Henkelman 2008.

[29] Potts 2010; 2011, p. 815.

[30] Ghirshman 1968, pp. 9–41.

[31] Calmeyer 1992, p. 107; Potts 1999, p. 325; Root 2010, p. 171.

[32] DBp 1.63–4.

version, instead, chooses a more open-ended term from root *yad-* "to sacrifice": *āyadanā* ("places of sacrifice," "cult sites").

Darius I does not distinguish these sacred sites ritually, geographically, or architecturally, despite the fact that he carefully recorded all other details of the rebellious lands elsewhere in his inscriptions. The mention of "temple restorations" joins a list of other wrongs that Darius I made right and like them was intended to be a generic and programmatic demonstration of good kingship rather than a specific record of individual restorations. Darius I disseminated the text of the inscription throughout the empire, with a fragmentary Aramaic version appearing in Egypt.[33] Old Persian, Elamite, and Akkadian versions of the text appear as monumental inscriptions alongside figural sculpture in a monument that was carved into the living rock at the site of Bīsotūn in Media and installed along the sacred way of Babylon.[34] Darius I continued the Persian policy of subsidizing various cults throughout the empire after the re-conquest, many no doubt including temples. As a programmatic statement of good, divinely inspired kingship, this passage was adapted to the cultural idioms of the regions where it was sent.[35] Readers of the text would expect that the king would restore or purify a temple if he would act in accordance with the actions of ancient Elamite, Babylonian, or Egyptian royal precedent, while an open-air cult site would make sense within Iranian religious experience and landscape.

Taken altogether, the archaeological, archival, and epigraphic evidence presents one very important fact: while temples might have existed on the Iranian plateau, extensive temple building in the manner of the kings of Elam was one aspect of Elamite culture that the Achaemenids evidently did not apply in their home province of Pārsa.[36] Given the profound impact of Elamite culture on other aspects of Persian culture, this state of affairs might seem anomalous, but only if one assumes absolute continuity between Persian religion and pre-Achaemenid Elamite religion and with highland Elamo-Persian practices and those of the lowlands. While the Persian empire in general cultivated and reinvigorated many aspects of the previous eras' religious practices, we have no evidence that the new Teispid and Achaemenid royal families of Pārsa continued the traditions of temple building and restoration that marked Elamite royal patronage practices in the Early and Middle Elamite era. We can only speculate whether this was because temples were never prominent in Pārsa in the Middle or Neo-Elamite periods, or if this change arose from a cultural shift.[37] The fact that we have no evidence of pre-Achaemenid Elamite temples in the core of Pārsa compared to the lowlands would suggest that this was the normal state of affairs in the highlands before the rise of the Persian empire.

While not involving fire or image temples, the available archaeological and archival evidence of Persian religious activity and patronage does present a coherent picture of Persian sacred architecture and ritual in their homeland of Pārsa and a few of their provincial

---

[33] The Aramaic version, which is very close to the Akkadian version and reflects later changes and refinements to Darius I's message, also calls them "houses of the gods" (Schmitt 1990).

[34] Schmitt 1990; Seidl 1999.

[35] Tuplin 2005, pp. 227–35.

[36] There are a handful of mentions of *ziyan* in the Persepolis archive; see below. It is possible that the mentions of sanctuaries (*hiera*) in Elymais and Media

in the post-Achaemenid classical sources were ancient temples (*ziyan*) that survived from the Achaemenid era. However, without further evidence it is equally likely the temples were built in the Seleukid era or were simply open-air sanctuaries.

[37] I would hesitate from trying to connect it to an inter-Iranian religious conflict with one side supporting Elamite religions and the other promoting Iranian or Zoroastrian cult; DB 1.63–4.

centers. The Persepolis Fortification Archive tablets allude to a rich repertoire of Persian rituals performed at sites within Pārsa. These include daily offerings, huge sacrifices, and funerary cults. In a few instances the tablets provide clues as to the topographical context of the rituals. The most commonly occurring ritual is the *lan*, or "offering" ritual, which was performed with bread, beer or wine, and occasionally sheep or goats.[38] The *lan* was a common sacrifice that individual cultic personnel supported by the state performed monthly or even daily for a diverse assortment of Elamo-Persian gods.[39] The offering (*daušiyam* or *gal*) allocated for these sacrifices served as allowances for the priests performing it. Although some erroneously argued that the *lan* was a "Zoroastrian state ritual" celebrated for Auramazdā, the Persians performed the *lan* for a wide variety of gods, the vast majority of whom were non-Iranian.[40] Furthermore, unlike other rituals, the *lan* is not mentioned in the Old Persian royal inscriptions when the king sacrifices to Auramazdā, which one would expect if it were the chief state ritual.[41]

In addition to the *lan*, the Persepolis Fortification Archive records provisions given for sacrifices offered for the benefit of deceased kings at an offering table (*bašur*) at their tomb monument (*šumar*).[42] Like the *lan*, the *šumar/bašur* sacrifices occurred daily and the commodities offered also functioned as rations for the responsible ritual specialists. Like the *lan*, grain or bread along with beer or wine formed the core of the commodities offered at the funerary monuments. The *šumar/bašur* officiants also received livestock to sacrifice for the benefit of the kings and, of course, consume afterwards.[43]

The sacrifices at the royal tomb monuments took place in the open air. The main feature of these precincts was the tomb monument itself (*šumar*), offering tables (*bašur*), and associated support buildings. These monuments could either be freestanding ashlar masonry tombs such as that of Cyrus the Great, or rock-cut tombs of the sort favored by Darius I and his successors (figs. 14.2–3). Textual and archaeological evidence indicates that the tomb monuments had buildings for the tomb guardians and officiants, however, these were staging and storage areas. We have no evidence that the tomb monument or tables were connected with some sort of enclosed *naos*-like space that functioned as a "house for a god" as was the case for cult rendered for the Seleukid kings. The Chicago expedition never excavated the areas before the tombs cut into the Kuh-e Raḥmat. However, between 1955 and 1957 the Archaeological Institute of Persepolis under the direction of ʿAlī Sāmī did explore this area.[44] In front of the tomb attributed to Artaxerxes II the excavators discovered a 20-meter-square platform that supported a hall with two columns in the center with narrow rooms on two sides and porch in the front. A similar platform 32 meters long preceded the tomb attributed to Artaxerxes III (fig. 14.4). This supported a complex of sun-dried brick buildings with stone column bases and thresholds, which unfortunately the author does not describe in further

---

[38] Henkelman 2011, p. 93; cf. Abdi 2006–2007.

[39] Henkelman 2008, pp. 281–304.

[40] It should also be noted that the Persepolis Fortification Archive regularly records priests called "magi" (*makuš*) sacrificing to non-Iranian gods and priests with an Elamite title (*šatin*) sacrificing to Iranian gods (Henkelman 2008, pp. 215–53).

[41] Henkelman 2011, pp. 96–98; 2008, pp. 206–07, 232–36. Contra Razmjou (2004, 2010), who speculated that rituals took place in the *tačara* of Darius I, no textual

or archaeological evidence exists that ritual activity took place there. The *tačara* reliefs portray the provisions of the royal table, a constant preoccupation in the Persepolis archive (Henkelman 2010).

[42] The texts can use these words interchangeably (Henkelman 2003; 2008, pp. 287–91; Canepa 2010a).

[43] Arrian, *Anabasis* 29.1–11; Henkelman 2003, pp. 137–40; Canepa 2010a.

[44] Sāmī 1958, pp. 58–60.

detail. The excavations discovered broken sections of the door's tomb: a double-leaved door with a sliding latch on the inner side turned by a key, opening inward.[45] Also recovered in this area was a stone slab 1.03 meters square, which had a raised smaller square surrounded on all sides by a recessed channel with an opening to drain anything poured onto the raised section. The excavator related it to two stone troughs discovered nearby and it is tempting to see this as a *bašur*. A bronze trumpet 1.20 meters long with a 60 centimeter diameter bell was discovered near this tomb and could have been a part of the cultic paraphernalia.[46]

Fragmentary relief sculptures found at the satrapal capital of Daskyleion in Western Anatolia could relate to this institution. One relief portrays male figures in profile wearing long tunics drawn together with belts, robes over their shoulders and each with a *kyrbasia* on his head, drawn over the mouth (fig. 14.5).[47] The figures hold *barsoms* in their left hands and raise their right hands while intently looking at a structure before them crowned with Achaemenid-style *kyma rerversa* that rises to eye level. This example portrays sacrificial activity that roughly corresponds to the Persepolis Fortification Archive and other evidence of Mazdaean sacrifice, with the heads of a sacrificed ram and bull lying at the officiants' feet on bundles of grass or twigs, which themselves rest on a platform or table attached to the structure before them. The other example portrays a structure with prominent coffers or a coffered door crowned by moldings that recall molding on the Tomb of Cyrus (fig. 14.6). This structure should be eye level to the figure in profile as the other one, however, it was imaginatively and incorrectly restored as a tower. The officiant holds a *barsom* in his right hand and staff in his left. Recalling Strabo, who mentions that the magi point to the focus of their sacrifice with a staff, the figure carefully places his staff at the bottom edge of the structure (Strabo, *Geographia* 15.3.14). We do not know what the roofs of the structures looked like because the top portions of the reliefs are missing, cutting them off. Some of the closest parallels come from Achaemenid tombs stemming from the Persian presence in Anatolia, such as Taş Kule, though the heartland tombs such as Pasargadae or Bozpār provide parallels.[48]

Though performed less frequently, the Persepolis Fortification Archive indicates that the Achaemenids' most important, prestigious, not to mention expensive, religious rituals were large-scale royal sacrifices followed by massive feasts. These include the *šip* sacrifice and the *bakadaušiyam* (Old Persian **bagadauçiyam*), if indeed these are not references to one and the same type of ritual.[49] Like the *lan*, the Persians performed these rituals for a variety of gods beyond Auramazdā, who plays a relatively minor role compared to Elamite gods. Auramazdā was not the only god to receive such an elaborate sacrifice in the records of the Persepolis archive, yet it is significant that the *šip* is the only type of ritual that Achaemenid royal inscriptions mention when a king specifically names the type of sacrifice he performed for Auramazdā. The religious terminology used in the Elamite translations of the royal inscriptions coheres with the Elamite ritual terminology used in the Persepolis archive. While the Old Persian versions of Achaemenid royal inscriptions simply say that kings of kings generically "sacrificed" (*yad-*) to Auramazdā, the Elamite translations often provide more nuance. For example, in the Old Persian version of Darius I's famous inscription from Susa (DSf), the king simply states he sacrificed to Auramazdā (*yad-*).[50] The Elamite version of this inscription provides an equally

---

[45] Ibid., pp. 59–60.

[46] Ibid., p. 60.

[47] Borchhardt 1968, pp. 201–03.

[48] Cahill 1988; Vanden Berghe 1989; Canepa 2010a.

[49] The Persepolis archive records five locations that accommodated *šip* feasts: Tikranuš, Appištapdan (twice), Batrakataš/Pasargadae (three times), Išgi, and Pumu (Henkelman 2011, p. 109).

[50] DSfp 18.

generic wording. Darius I states, "I gave 'offerings' [*gal*] to Auramazdā," without specifying the type of ritual(s) in which offerings were consumed.[51] In contrast, in an inscription preserved in many copies, Xerxes I boasts that he destroyed a *daivadāna* ("place [for the worship] of the demons"), purified the site, and sacrificed there to Auramazdā.[52] While the Old Persian version again simply uses the generic verb "to sacrifice" (*yad-*), the Elamite version specifies the type of ritual used to worship both the *daivas* and Auramazdā: it calls them a *šip*, the grand feast celebrated for many people, which seamlessly connects to other mentions of this supreme example of Elamo-Persian religiosity as witnessed in the Persepolis archive. It claims that at the *daivadāna* a *šip* feast was performed for the *daivas* and after purifying it, Xerxes I "performed for Auramazdā his [appropriate] *šip*" (Elamite *šibbe hudda*).[53]

While they offer detailed accounts of the commodities needed to perform them, the Persepolis Fortification Tablets do not contain direct descriptions of the ritual protocol of these sacrifices. They do, however, often record the names of the sites where the rituals were staged and some of the features of those sites. Internal evidence in the Persepolis Fortification Archive, related archaeological sites, and classical sources that reflect these institutions flesh out these crucial yet terse indigenous records and all place them in open-air settings.[54] This combined evidentiary stream presents the *šip*, and likely the *bakadaušiyam*, as an elaborate open-air sacrificial feast presented for a large assembly of people arranged in concentric rings with the most important individuals at the center with altars standing at the center of the assembled crowd. Out of the hundreds of archival records extant, not a single tablet mentions that the *lan, šip, bakadaušiyam*, or *šumar/bašur* sacrifices ever took place at, in, or near a temple (*ziyan*).

While temples did not play a big part in their official architectonic vocabulary, the Persians did indeed develop a repertoire of sacred spaces that imprinted the natural and built environment with Persian imperial power. Achaemenid open-air sanctuaries form the most well-documented archaeological and textual evidence of unquestionably Persian sacred spaces. They consist of open-air spaces surrounded by some sort of precinct barrier and subsidiary buildings and often incorporate altars or some other special structure, such as a tomb monument or a tower, as an important focus.

The sites that host the *šip* and *bakadaušiyam* sacrifices most often in the Persepolis tablets, such as Tikranuš, Appištapdan, and Batrakataš (Pasargadae), were sites provisioned with either a palace, paradise (Elamite *parētaš*, Old Iranian *pairi.daiza*), or both.[55] The presence of paradises or royal palaces underscores the supremely royal nature of both the sites and the sacrifice no matter if it was officiated by the king of kings himself or one of his proxies, such as the chief official overseeing Pārsa, Pharnakes (Parnakka). Of the *šip* sites recorded in the Persepolis Fortification Archive, Pasargadae is the only one that has been localized and excavated. First explored by Herzfeld in the early twentieth century, and excavated by David Stronach between 1961 and 1963, Pasargadae preserves a large enclosure that accommodated

---

[51] DSfe 16–17. Similarly DSze 15, though it is missing the corresponding Old Persian passage.

[52] XPhp 37–38. Whether such a *daivadāna* ever existed is irrelevant to these discussions, though it would be severe anachronism to try read late antique/medieval "Zoroastrian" purity strictures into the texts (Sancisi-Weerdenburg 1989; Abdi 2010).

[53] XPhe 30, 32, 33, 34, 41, 44 corresponding to Old Persian *yad-*. The Akkadian version is closer to the Elamite describing the activity as a "religious festival" (*isinnu*) (Henkelman 2008, pp. 102–04).

[54] Xenophon, *Cyropaedia* 8.3.33–34; Appian, *Mithradates* 12.66; Diodorus, *Bibliothēkē* 19.22.2–3; Arrian, *Anabasis* 6.29.4–7; Strabo, *Geographia* 15.3.7.

[55] Henkelman 2008, pp. 427–52.

these activities and incorporated ritual furniture stemming from Iranian religious sensibilities not directly mentioned in the Elamite texts. The sacred precinct at Pasargadae consisted of a large open plain surrounded by low mud walls (fig. 14.7) and two, 2-meter limestone plinths set 9 meters apart and both supported by foundations.[56] One of these plinths had stairs leading up to it and together they evoke the image of the Achaemenid king standing on a platform worshipping a raised altar carrying a blazing fire. At the western end of the precinct rose a terrace measuring 74.85 × 50.40–46.65 meters, whose five levels were constructed out of dry-stone masonry with a mudbrick level on top.[57] Herzfeld, and many following him, wished to reconstruct the terrace as supporting a stone structure mirroring the Tomb of Cyrus thus providing an architectural reflection of the tomb on the opposite end of the complex. The mudbrick upper terrace, however, bore no evidence of foundations of such a structure, either of stone or mudbrick. Needless to say, the design of the terrace does not resemble the stereobate of the tomb. The size of the mudbricks from the upper terrace indicate only that it could have been built any time within the Achaemenid or Seleukid period, though more likely in the Seleukid era. No matter when it was constructed, the design of the terrace related to the layout and, thus, activities, of the enclosed precinct below, providing either a raised focal point or elevated viewing area for proceedings.

A number of other Achaemenid sites have been described as open-air ritual centers, though no archaeological, archival, or textual evidence directly documents the type of ritual practices performed there in the Achaemenid era. It is likely that the Median site of Bīsotūn (Old Persian *Bagastāna) was already sacred in the Achaemenid era and this contributed to Darius I's desire to carve his monumental rock relief there (fig. 14.8). The Achaemenid court physician Ctesias describes the mountain as "sacred to Zeus," and the site of a *paradeisos*.[58] The sanctuary precinct walls are still visible from aerial imagery and ran from one cliff spur to another, enclosing an area approximately 180 meters.[59] Within the precinct a sloping hillside leads up to a rubble field, which, in turn, abuts the cliffs. Two artificial terraces mark the hillside with evidence of cult activity on the southern ledge of the upper terrace. A rock-cut stair leads from the rubble field to a third zone that looked down upon Darius I's rock relief and preserves evidence of cult activity. The only evidence of cult are the natural, open-air cliff-side terraces, which have "fire bowls" or foundation holes carved into them, though these could just as well date from a later period.[60] The site of Ganj-nāma, also in Media, was a site of two rock-cut royal inscriptions carved by Darius I and Xerxes.[61] The inscriptions marked the site of a waterfall on a mountain pass and rock-cut holes in the natural open-air terrace above the site have been associated with ritual activity.[62]

The only sacred structure securely attached to an official Achaemenid context for which we have direct archaeological evidence of sacrifice is the site of Dahan-e Gōlāmān, a pre-planned Achaemenid city in Zranka (Hāmūn-e Helmand, eastern Iran), likely the provincial capital.[63] A large square structure (QN3), which measured 53.2 × 54.3 meters, contained a

[56] Stronach 1978, p. 138. Subsequent excavations on the Toll-e Takt has proven the elevated site was a treasury and fortress, not a sacred precinct (Chaverdi and Callieri 2010).

[57] Stronach 1978, pp. 142–45.

[58] Ctesias in Diodorus, *Bibliothēkē* 2.13.1–2. Reflecting the Iranian name, Diodorus (17.110.5) calls the site *theoprepestatē* "fitting for the gods" (Schmitt 1990).

Bernard (1980, p. 322) links the site with the toponym "Kampanda" (DB 2.27).

[59] Kleiss 1970; Bernard 1980, p. 319.

[60] Luschey 1989.

[61] Brown 2000.

[62] Schippmann 1971, pp. 380–88.

[63] Scerrato 1979.

square central courtyard containing three altars surrounded by four non-communicating porticos (fig. 14.9). The porticos hosted ovens and large-scale cooking facilities that could accommodate the type of feasts associated with Persian (though not necessarily Zoroastrian) religion as described in the fortification tablets. The north, east, and west porticos sheltered a number of clay ovens for baking bread. In the structure's second phase, the west portico contained large tanks used as large cooking pits, which were covered with greasy ashes mixed with crushed animal bones. The three central altars originally stood 7 meters high and were likely added in the second phase. In contrast to the Achaemenid fire holders found at Pasargadae, or the ones portrayed on the royal tombs, these altars were hollow and contained the fire inside them in a manner not dissimilar from the smaller installations under the porticos. The ritual activity generated a great deal of cooking detritus. The courtyard contained large quantities of ash mixed with burnt animal flesh and bones. This was plastered over in the refurbishment and accumulated again in later cultic activity. As the excavator stressed, these cultic installations used the same basic design as domestic kitchens in the city. As various authors have mentioned time and time again, the cultic activity that the site hosted contrasts with "orthodox" Zoroastrianism, which would not admit to the flames of a sacred fire anything but incense and a small portion of fat.[64] This structure hosted something quite different from an "orthodox" Zoroastrian cult of fire and this has often been cited to stress that the cult it hosted was non-Persian. Although it has traditionally been interpreted as a "non-Persian" cult site, it should be stressed that the sanctuary of Dahan-e Ḡolāmān presents nothing that disagrees with the view of Persian religiosity provided in our most abundant and indigenous evidence, the Persepolis Fortification Tablets, which do not cohere with Boyce's definition of orthodox Zoroastrianism either. The fact that the majority of the religious rituals mentioned in the Persepolis archive involved sacrifices of, and subsequent feasting on, bread, animals, and alcoholic beverages, suggests that the activities that took place in the structure would not have been foreign to *Persian* religiosity. It would not be surprising if such ritual provisions were to be discovered among the ruins at another major Achaemenid site.[65]

The satrapies of Anatolia were among the most important of the empire and here too the Achaemenid religious building centered on open-air cult sites. Satrapal seats received a sizable influx of Iranian settlers as well as official patronage of both Iranian and local gods. The introduction of the cult of Iranian gods, especially that of Anāhitā and to a lesser extent Mithra, made a deep impact on the religions of Anatolia. As the imperial center, Anatolia has not yielded any Achaemenid-era archaeological evidence of specifically Persian fire or image temples, though the Achaemenids contributed to temples of local gods.[66] Those constructions that the Persians built involve open-air sanctuaries and altars. The Persians were likely involved in the construction of a monumental altar with Persian stepped features built in a sanctuary of Artemis.[67] An altar dedicated to Cybele was rebuilt and converted to a different cultic use in the Achamenid era.[68] In addition to these sites that bear archaeological

[64] Boyce 1982, pp. 128–29; Genito 2010; de Jong 2002 shows that animal sacrifice is standard in the Avesta.

[65] Evoking, but not replicating, the ground plan of QN3 and not sharing its function, Soviet excavations of the late fifth-century B.C.E. site of Altin-10 near Balkh uncovered a square structure (36 × 36 m) with a central courtyard that the excavator termed a "pal-

ace." Sarianidi claimed to have found a "fire altar" made of unbaked bricks and plaster in one of the corner rooms, though nothing corresponding to the character of QN3 (Houtkamp 1991, p. 34).

[66] Dusinberre 2003, pp. 68–69.

[67] Ibid., pp. 60–64.

[68] Ibid., pp. 64–68.

evidence, classical textual sources describe a few other Achaemenid open-air sanctuaries located on elevated locales. Among these, Strabo relates that the Persians created a sanctuary at Zela, the site of a surprise victory over a band of Scythians. According to the author, the Persians raised a mound of earth over a rock in the plain, fortified it, and created a sanctuary to the gods "Anaitis, Omanus, and Anadatus" (his rendition of the Persians' chief gods) who share an altar (*Geographia* 11.8.4). The cult of Zeus Asbameios, reportedly of Persian origin, was connected with the city of Tyana and centered around a sacred volcanic spring in the mountains.[69]

In addition to sites securely attached to official patronage, or at least a Persian context, a few sites in Central Asia dating to the Achaemenid era, though not securely attached to Achaemenid patronage or Persian occupation, show evidence of cult activity and some even contained evidence of fire cult reminiscent of late antique Zoroastrianism. Most of these were excavated by the Soviets, then re-excavated after 1990. Köktepe in the Kashka Darya plain, near Shahr-e Sabz, Uzbekistan, showed evidence of a masonry platform built on the site of a courtyard from a previous period.[70] The excavators associated this platform with the incorporation of the region into the Achaemenid empire. The largely unpublished Uzbek and French re-excavation of Sangyrtepa has brought attention to a rectangular space, which may or may not have been enclosed, that appears to have hosted some sort of cult activity.[71] Sangyrtepa was a square mudbrick structure with evidence of four wooden posts set in the main room, which showed evidence of burning at a later stage. Some sort of portico likely fronted the structure and several steps led up to at least one side. Sangyrtepa showed evidence of libation pits, which might hint at continuities of ritual practice with later evidence at Ai Khanum, even if the architecture of the two sites does not directly relate.[72] It was not built on a platform but on level earth which had several pits filled with sand, pebbles, ash, or bones, which the excavators compared to Vedic purification rituals. In the past, scholars have been tempted to connect these sites linearly to the earlier (non-Iranian) BMAC sites and thence to Boyce's imagined Zoroastrian temple tradition. However, the wide divergence in design, materials, and cultic activity among them indicates that we are looking at diverse and unconnected architectural and religious traditions.

The fortress site of Cheshme Shafa (Češmeh-ye Šafā), located near Bactra (Balḵẖ), yielded a massive piece of roughly hewn limestone that measured ca. 2.10 meters high and 2.70 × 1.55 across on its top. It was obviously of local manufacture and craftsmanship, having been rolled down from a quarry up above the site. The rectangular dimensions and conical shape of the monolith's shaft do not closely correspond to known Achaemenid altars, although a hole on the top and evidence of burning on the lower section where it had not been exposed to the elements in later periods suggested to the excavators that it was an altar. Despite this, it is possible the stone was worked to present a rough profile, albeit two-stepped, that evoked but did not replicate the three-stepped Achaemenid altars known from Pasargadae and portrayed on the Achaemenid tombs. If it did function as an altar, as the evidence of burning on its lower section suggests, such discrepancies might have arisen because this royally charged

---

[69] Philostratus, *Vita Apollonii* 1.6; Ammianus Marcellinus, *Res Gestae* 23.6.19; Mitchell 2007, pp. 167–69.

[70] Rapin 2007, pp. 39–44.

[71] Archéologies d'Orient et d'Occident et textes anciens (AOROC), "Sangyr-tepe (Kashka-darya),"

http://www.archeo.ens.fr/spip.php?article505 [accessed Sept. 10, 2011].

[72] Discussed below; Grenet 1991; idem 2008 [2012], p. 30.

sculpture from the imperial center was likely transmitted to Bactria primarily through seal images. Some have speculated it might have been housed in some sort of structure, but the site's disturbed stratigraphy presents no clear evidence to support this or what went on around the object.[73]

The mound of Kindyktepa near the larger complex of Majdatepa (also called Bandyxon/Bandykhan I) presents compelling evidence of cultic activity. Previously explored by E. Rtveladze in the 1970s and more recently by a German-Uzbek expedition, the site is located in southern Uzbekistan on the right bank of the Urgul-Saj River, which eventually connects to the Surkhandarya valley. It yielded a small mud structure dated to the fourth century B.C.E. built on a platform with an irregular ground plan roughly 14.0 × 8.5 meters. Four irregularly placed mudbrick pillars were placed near the middle of the room, where the floor appears to have been repeatedly exposed to fire and deposits of pure ashes were found in the northern and eastern corners. A roughly 12 × 2 meter chamber lay to the northeast of the main chamber which contained pits filled with sand, mud, and ashes. The structure went out of use at the time of Alexander's conquest and was filled up with packed dirt.[74]

The architectural and cultic remains from Cheshme Shafa, Sangyrtepa, and Kindyktepa in no way present evidence of a unified architectural tradition and certainly not evidence of Zoroastrian temples inserted into the region by Persian official architecture. Rather, they resulted from the combination of regional cultic and architectural traditions with isolated and mediated influence from the imperial center. While Sangyrtepa's portico might evoke some Persian architecture, only the massive fire altar from Cheshme Shafa can be securely said to derive from official Persian forms. The altar itself, of course, does not indicate Zoroastrian practice. The altar retained evidence of burning, but no ash was excavated from it or around it. However, the abundant Persepolis Fortification Archive seal images indicate that if the altar hosted cult that conformed to Persian official cult, it certainly would not have conformed to Zoroastrian strictures. To judge by the Persepolis Fortification Archive sealings, the altar would have burned sacrificial animals and libations rather than holding a pure fire. The structures, on the other hand, reflect regional cultic traditions rather than the emplacement of an official, empire-wide Achaemenid system (see below). The evidence of pure ashes and the basic layout of the cultic space in the small structure at Kindyktepa does indeed correspond to other known cultic spaces. Significantly, clear comparanda do not come from Achaemenid Persia, Media, or Mesopotamia, but rather sites in the eastern Iranian world that have yielded the first clear and securely dated evidence of a structure hosting a fire cult. Kindyktepa's basic conformation of a main cultic space, including a main room, a single side chamber, and evidence of pure ash, corresponds to the size and layout of cultic spaces that hosted fire cults at the site of Tash-kʾirman Tepe in Uzbekistan (ancient Chorasmia), and the site of Mele Hairam in Turmenistan (ancient Parthia). Tash-kʾirman Tepe is dated to the fourth century B.C.E. by radiocarbon analysis while Mele Hairam dates to the second century C.E. They represent the earliest securely dated temples that unquestionably held fire cult.[75] Sangyrtepa did not preserve clear evidence of cultic activity involving a pure fire, though it shows some evidence of burning. This might relate to the clearer evidence

---

[73] Bensenval and Marquis 2008 [2010], pp. 987–88, fig. 9; Grenet 2008 [2012], pp. 30–31.

[74] Sverchkov and Boroffka 2009, p. 87; Boroffka and Sverchkov 2007.

[75] Betts and Yagodin 2007; Kaim 2004.

at Kindyktepe and Tash-k'irman Tepe, though the question should remain open, given San-gyrtepa's state of preservation and disturbed stratigraphy.

Thus, rather than representing the impact of official Persian fire-temple architecture, the evidence suggests that Kindyktepa and Tash-k'irman Tepe participated in an eastern Iranian cultic tradition that continued to develop through the period of Achaemenid domination and, as evidenced by Mele Hairam, into the Seleukid and Parthian periods. Only in the late Sasanian era do we have archaeological evidence of similar cultic spaces in the western Iranian world. Though intriguing, these temples' relationship to later Sasanian practices is, at this point, unclear, and should remain open until new evidence comes to light that can clarify whether and in what way these developments are linked.

The corpus of ritual scenes from the Persepolis Fortification seal impressions provides another important body of primary evidence. These have been made accessible through the pioneering work of Mark Garrison.[76] The seal imprints largely cohere with the indigenous archival and textual evidence: they do not portray fire or image temples conforming to Elamite, Mesopotamian, or late antique Zoroastrianism, but rather depict open-air sacrifice focused on various types of altars. The glyptic evidence portrays two general groups of scenes: rituals performed by figures in crowns and royal Persian robes, and rituals conducted by individuals in normal Iranian trouser suits (figs. 14.10–11). The rarer, more elaborate representations of royal individuals portray them standing before a coffered structure with two crenellations ending in finials. PFS 11* (see fig. 14.10) and PTS 22 are the only scenes where the crenellated tower structure has a spherical device in the central space. In three other examples a vegetal motif rises from the center, but never fire.[77] Those that portray scenes of non-royal officiants show individuals in procession to or standing before a blazing altar. Rather than holding a fire for veneration, these altars were clearly meant for immolating sacrificial offerings. In eleven particularly fine seals the fire altar appears before a taller, coffered structure or "tower" (e.g., fig. 14.11). About half of these seals pairing the blazing altars and towers portray the towers with crenellations, while the other half show two triangular masses that form a V-shape. There is no distinction in scene type between the crenellated and V-shaped tower types, but no fire on top. A fire always appears on the stepped altars, but a fire never appears on the taller coffered "towers." The officiants often carry libation vessels, pour offerings into the fire, drink ritual offerings themselves, and lead sacrificial animals to the altar. Although it runs counter to older assumptions that the Achaemenids followed the same sort of Zoroastrian prohibitions as medieval Zoroastrians, such seals portray the officiants killing the animals with knifes and some even feature a fire consuming an entire animal.[78]

Fire altars play a prominent role in many of the Persian seals and seal impressions.[79] A number of seal impressions portray images of male figures standing to the left facing a fire

---

[76] Garrison 2000 and forthcoming. I thank Mark Garrison for sharing with me ideas from his forthcoming book. Any misrepresentation here is my responsibility. While Prof. Garrison is cautious about referring to the stepped structures as "altars," so as not to confuse them with contemporary Parsi Zoroastrian altars, I do so here in the sense that these altars appear to have functioned as altars commonly did in the ancient world: they burned sacrificial offerings.

[77] Garrison forthcoming.

[78] Garrison forthcoming; seal PFUTS 33 on anepigraphic tablet PFUT 845-101; seal PFS 75 on anepigraphic tablet PFUT 2146-104; seal PFUTS 91 on anepigraphic tablet PFUT 691-103; seal PFUTS 111 on anepigraphic tablet PFUT 698-102; seal PFUTS 147 on anepigraphic tablet PFUT 547-201. Moorey 1979, p. 222, fig. 3B; Henkelman 2005, 2008, pp. 424–25.

[79] Garrison forthcoming.

altar with an upward-tapering "stepped" bowl that holds a fire altar. The stepped altar appears at the end of a procession or receives the sacrifices of a single individual. Fire, signified by shapes such as inverted cones or semi-circles marked with vertical lines or a small, interior cone, blazes forth from the top of these altars. The fire altars portrayed on the sealings are similar to fragments of altars found at various sites in Pārsa, including, most significantly, Pasargadae.[80] The stereotyped image of the king of kings standing on a plinth before a blazing stepped altar on the rock-cut royal tombs underscores centrality of fire altars in official Achaemenid ritual practice and religious visual vocabulary. Representatives of all of the lands effortlessly and willingly support the throne that supports the king of kings. Taken together with the archival, archaeological, and textual evidence, it is very likely that Darius I and his successors understood this iconic scene not simply as a symbolic representation but as a composite portrayal of the king's place as the central officiant in a major sacrificial feast such as the *šip* or *bakadaušiyam*. It is not inconsequential that later classical sources which mention the *šip* or mention sacrifices intended to evoke the *šip*, specify that a fire or fire altars lay at the center of the ritual assembly. This implies that the image of the Persian king before a fire altar portrays the central climactic event of the *šip*, rather than a separate "pure" Iranian fire cult.

While altars holding blazing fires were very important, the Achaemenid seals attest to a wider repertoire of Achaemenid sacred architecture and ritual furnishing associated particularly with the court. When the crenellated tower appears alone, it does so strictly in scenes replete with royal iconography such as date palms, paneled inscriptions, winged symbols, and attended by figures in royal dress (e.g., fig. 14.10).[81] The figures that stand before the towers always treat them with reverence. The figures in Persian courtly robes raise their right forearms and assume a pose that is similar to the kings on the royal tombs, often holding a flower similar to those held by Achaemenid kings elsewhere in Persepolis sculpture. The "stepped fire altars" and "towers" appear by themselves, however, they accompany each other where the figures perform ritual actions at a stepped altar that stands next to the tower. The Persian glyptic evidence does not show the officiants placing or pouring any of their offerings between the towers' crenellations. If shown, such activity takes place at a fire altar in front of the tower. This might indicate that the tower altars functioned simply as a focus for the ritual or a sacred object in and of themselves. While these seal images immediately bring to mind a range of representations of offering tables or altars from across ancient Western Asia and the eastern Mediterranean, horned crenellation along the southeast edge of the Persepolis platform provide some of the closest parallels both in terms of design and chronology.[82] As Margaret Cool Root pointed out, Persian palaces were treated, in effect, as sacred spaces and it is not outside the realm of possibility that such daily or festive offerings took place within the palace precincts in addition to those we know that took place in their proximity.[83]

---

[80] Stronach 1978, pp. 141–42; Garrison 1999.

[81] Garrison forthcoming.

[82] Galling 1925; Tilia 1977, p. 77. Though separated by about four centuries, a variety of Nabataean rock-cut tombs bear features, like towers with double crenellations, that evoke, but do not replicate, these Achaemenid images. Certain Nabataean temples also evoke the post-Seleukid temples (Anderson 2002). While older strains of scholarship saw these as directly participating in a co-temporal architectural tradition, it would be the work of a future study to explore the actual relationship among these various Persian, Middle Iranian, and Levantine forms.

[83] Root 2010. I would agree with this aspect of Razmjou 2010.

The appearance of "towers" or "tower altars" on the seals brings to mind two Achaemenid towers in Pārsa: the Zendān-e Solaymān and the Kaʿba-ye Zardošt (figs. 14.12–13). The Achaemenid towers contrast with the seal images with regards to their size relative to human scale and exterior features like stereobates and stairs leading to doorways. Neither tower bears evidence that they bore such crenellations in antiquity, marking a clear contrast with the structures portrayed on the seals. The images on the seals certainly are not meant to be portraits of the Zendān or Kaʿba, however, they did participate generally in the same wider architectural vocabulary of Persian royal and sacred power. The two towers were unique, set within the Persian heartland, and their patrons built them at two sites they intended to be deeply significant for the genesis and continuity of Persian kingship: Cyrus the Great's palace complex at Pasargadae and the Achaemenid necropolis begun by Darius I at Naqš-e Rostam near Persepolis.

Darius I constructed the Kaʿba-ye Zardošt in careful imitation of the Zendān-e Solaymān, though using more advanced masonry techniques, which have contributed to its superior state of preservation.[84] The ashlar masonry towers, whose faces measured 12.60 meters high × 7.25 meters wide, rest on a triple-stone plinth. They give the impression of having three stories, but the lower half of the tower is solid, while the upper half accommodates a single chamber measuring, in the case of the Kaʿba, 3.74 × 3.72 meters in area and 5.58 meters high.[85] An imposing flight of steps on the north of the structures leads to the elevated chamber. The lintel over the entrance with swooping "horns" perhaps recalls the crenellations on the seals as well as the wider visual vocabulary of sacred structures in Elamite culture. The doorways of the structures contained insets for double-leaved stone doors similar to those on the Achaemenid rock-cut tombs. As suggested by the door fragment found at Pasargadae and the missing sill and door jambs of the Kaʿba, once these doors were closed locked in place, they likely would have been broken open or had elements of the doorframe removed to gain access.[86]

Neither the Zendān nor Kaʿba stood alone. Both structures lay at the core of an ensemble of buildings, suggesting that they formed the focal point of a larger architectonic and ritual complex. Schmidt's test trenches revealed a dense concentration of buildings around the Kaʿba-ye Zardošt, which he dated variously to the Achaemenid, Hellenistic, and Sasanian eras.[87] Geomagnetic prospecting at Pasargadae indicates that the Zendān was the centerpiece of a larger complex.[88] A 45 meter wide stone structure that appears to contain a series of parallel rectangular chambers similar to Persian treasuries, archives, or internal storage areas of the Persepolis fortifications was oriented on the same axis as the tower and rose about 30 meters from the rear of the Zendān. To the southeast, a rectangular enclosure with subsidiary structures flanked the Zendān and the stone structure. Excavations in the vicinity of Naqš-e Rostam have revealed an early royal pavilion constructed about 500 meters from the Kaʿba-ye Zardošt, recalling Pasargadae.[89] This could indicate that the towers at Naqš-e Rostam and Pasargadae hosted activities that the king of kings could participate in or

---

[84] Nylander (1966) concluded that the Zendān was constructed before the Kaʿba, since the Kaʿba made use of iron clamps to join its blocks and the Zendān did not. The Zendān was likely built during the same period as the palaces of Pasargadae (ca. 540 B.C.E.), and the Kaʿba, during the reign of Darius I, sometime after 520 B.C.E. (Gropp 2004).

[85] Stronach 1967, pp. 287–88; Schmidt 1970, pp. 34–49.
[86] Stronach 1978, pp. 125–27, figs. 64, 131, and pl. 101a–b.
[87] Stronach 1967; Schmidt 1970, pp. 53–58, fig. 23.
[88] Boucharlat and Benech 2002; Boucharlat 2003, 2007; Benech, Boucharlat, and Gondet 2012.
[89] Tilia 1974.

publicly view, either from a distance or in short procession from these palaces or pavilions. The Kaʿba stood among dense complex of structures and rituals at Naqš-e Rostam relating to the site's rock-cut tombs. From excavations of the platforms in front of the rock-cut tombs behind Persepolis and the evidence in the Persepolis Fortification Archive, we can safely infer that structures meant to accommodate the tombs' guardians lay before each of the tombs at Naqš-e Rostam. This complex would have grown denser as each new tomb monument appeared along with its associated subsidiary structures.

Although theories abound, the exact functions of the Kaʿba-ye Zardošt and Zendān-e Solaymān remain unknown. While a number of scholars from the nineteenth and twentieth centuries assumed they were fire temples, a consensus has held for several decades that the towers' patrons did not build them to contain an ever-burning fire.[90] Considering the fact that the stone doors did not allow easy access, it seems logical that the towers' primary function was to contain or protect something admitting access to their interior chambers only seldomly. No matter what function scholars ascribe to them, most generally accept that they shared a similar purpose. If this is true, Darius I likely built the Kaʿba to allow Naqš-e Rostam to accommodate the same activities that the Zendān hosted at Pasargadae. If one accepts that the towers on the seals relate in some way to the Zendān and Kaʿba, the seals might provide evidence that broadly relates to Persian ritual practice involving such structures.[91] The sealings in the Persepolis Fortification corpus invariably portray the towers closed if indeed their artisans intended to represent them with doors at all. It seems that manifesting their contents, if there were any, was not important. In the seal images, individuals or groups process to the towers, stand or are seated in front of them. There they make offerings at a fire altar located in close proximity to the structures. The figures appear directly before the towers or at a stepped fire altar, and there raise their hands in reverence, pour or consume libations, or present or even kill a sacrificial animal. When the participants perform a ritual action they always do so before the tower, never inside or on top. While an officiant might have entered the Zendān and Kaʿba for other purposes, the seals suggest that their exterior facades were the main focal point of routine ritual activity, rather than their interior chambers.

It is indeed tempting to view the Zendān as belonging in some way to the "sanctuary" (*heiron*) that Plutarch's *Life of Artaxerxes* places at Pasargadae, though not necessarily functioning as a "temple" or *the hieron*.

> A little after Darius had died, [Artaxerxes] set out for Pasargadae so that the royal initiation might be completed by the Persian priests. There, there is a sanctuary of a warlike goddess, who might be compared to Athena. The initiate, passing into it, must take off his own robe and put on the one which Cyrus wore before he became king, and after eating a cake of preserved figs, chew some terebinth and drink cup of sour milk. If they do anything else in addition to these things, it is unknown to others. (Plutarch, *Life of Artaxerxes* 2.3.1–3)

---

[90] One of the older traditions of scholarship assumed the towers served the Achaemenids as fire altars or fire temples (theories reviewed in Schippmann 1971, pp. 194–95; Potts 2007, pp. 282–85). Several scholars, including Herzfeld (1908), Demandt (1968), and Boyce (1975b, pp. 457–58), argued that the Zendān and Kaʿba were tombs, despite the fact that all tombs of the Persian kings are accounted for. Frye (1974, p. 386) and Sancisi-Weerdenburg (1983) viewed the towers as treasuries for royal paraphernalia or as "coronation towers." For useful reviews of the literature and the various interpretations of the structure, see Gropp 2004 and Potts 2007.

[91] Garrison forthcoming.

The word *hieron* could refer either to a sanctuary precinct or perhaps a specific structure, though in a vaguer sense than *naos*. Providing a little more context, the text goes on to relate that a courtier accused Artaxerxes II's brother, Cyrus the Younger, of plotting to sneak into the sanctuary to assassinate the king during his initiation. Cyrus was accused of "planning to lie in wait in the sanctuary (*en tōi hierōi*) and, when the king removed his robe, attack and kill him." The vague wording of the passage makes it possible that he simply entered the precinct, the Zendān itself, if indeed it was a part of this sanctuary, or another structure (*Life of Artaxerxes* 2.3.3–5). Be that as it may, it is highly unlikely that Cyrus or his accusers would have thought it possible for someone to hide their incongruous presence even for an instant in a 3.7-meter-square chamber.

No archaeological or textual evidence securely attests to what the chambers of these towers held. While they clearly were not built to contain a fire, most of the other suggestions that scholarship has put forward are indeed tenable and should be kept as possibilities. The towers could have held some important object or set of objects, including royal initiation paraphernalia, a cult object or, at a later date, even a figural statue of the type introduced by Artaxerxes II, even if they were not originally constructed for that purpose. In fact, none of these conjectures are mutually exclusive, but any attempt to defend one single interpretation should be reserved until the areas around the towers have been fully excavated, even though the present generation might not live to witness it. Whatever their exact function, it is clear that the Kaʿba and Zendān were unique. Though Persian towers have generated several reconstructive fictions, no structure like the Zendān or Kaʿba has been discovered at any of the other Achaemenid royal residences or provincial capitals.[92] And while a handful of structures evoke them, such as the Persepolis Fortification Archive sealing and Anatolian tombs, we cannot securely speak of a widespread tradition of sacred tower architecture outside of Pārsa.[93]

Although temples (*ziyan*) did not play a prominent role in Persian religion as documented in the Persepolis archive, a few tantalizing hints suggest that Pārsa might not have been

[92] No Achaemenid-era structure that decisively functioned as a temple has been excavated in the Caucasus. In contrast, Urartian temples with similar ground plans but much different elevations and functions were widespread in the region in the Urartian period and these appear to have inspired cult activity and construction *after* the Achaemenid era (Gagošidze 1983, 1992; Knauss 2005, p. 202). After a period of neglect in the Achaemenid period, an Urartian temple at Armavir was reoccupied in the Orontid period along with other structures on the citadel. It must be stressed that this was a regional architectural tradition with Urartian roots and not evidence of the spread of structures similar to the two Achaemenid towers from Persia (Tirats'yan 1988, pp. 82–83; 2003a, pp. 98–99; 2003b, pp. 130–31). Soviet archaeologists excavated the partial foundations of a fifth- or early fourth-century B.C.E. ashlar structure at the Georgian site of Samadlo, which stood on top of the hill situated on the banks of the River Kura. The excavators only excavated a single side but nevertheless reconstructed it as supporting a tower similar to the Kaʿba and Zendān (Gagošidze 1996; Tsetskhladze 2001). Soviet archaeologists also reconstructed a structure at Uplistsikhe to resemble the Achaemenid towers in Pārsa, with only scanty evidence, while an Urartian-inspired temple would make equal sense.

[93] While it did not necessarily retain their original Achaemenid significance, this visual culture of reverence continued after their fall. The reverses of most of the *Fratarakid* coins portray a worshipper venerating a coffered tower with crenellations. These numismatic representations evoke the representations on the Persepolis Fortification sealings and Daskyleion reliefs, and many have likened them to the Kaʿba and Zendān (Potts 2007, pp. 296–97). The Sasanians, however, built tower monuments at Paikuli and Dum-e Mil that evoked these Achaemenid towers (Canepa 2010b, pp. 588–89). The Kaʿba in particular served an especially important role in the Sasanians' efforts to negotiate a meaningful relationship with the half-understood Achaemenids and the remnants of their empire.

entirely devoid of temples. Three tablets from the Persepolis Fortification Archive use the word *ziyan*, though none document that ritual occurred at them and only one connects the word with a toponym. Unfortunately, this place name, Harkurtiš, is not otherwise attested in the archive or located.[94] If they did not arise from a scribe's idiosyncratic desire to use a specifically Elamite cultural reference to refer to different type of sacred site or structure (e.g., the Persian word *bagina), these rare appearances of the word *ziyan* could perhaps attest to early Elamite temples that remained in service or a temple of an expatriate community. In this regard, a handful of temples to Mesopotamian gods seem to have existed on the Iranian plateau in the Median periods.[95] In the Achaemenid empire, expatriate communities, including Babylonians, Assyrians, and Greeks, brought their own religious traditions to Pārsa and constructed their own places of worship. It is clear that foreign gods were present in Iran but considered to be the internal affairs of expatriate communities. For the sixteen years of Darius I's reign that the Persepolis archive covers, we have no explicit record that these cults were integrated into or supported by the official state distribution system.[96] Eventually these gods began to receive some sort of patronage on the Iranian plateau, even just as a function of assimilation with Iranian gods such as Anāhitā and Auramazdā. A recently published Aramaic document mentioning an "offering for the sanctuary/altar (*bagina) of Bel" (*zwtrˀ ˁl bgnˀ lbyl*) might attest to the worship of this god in late Achaemenid Bactria and possibly, though not necessarily, a temple, as other references using the Iranian word *bagina describe open-air sanctuaries.[97]

In this light it is perhaps worthwhile to return to Xerxes I's "Daiva Inscription." Scholarship has often sought to attach various archaeological sites to Xerxes I's *daivadāna* passage, from the temple of Marduk in Babylon to the Parthenon in Athens.[98] However, the inscription itself describes the site and ritual in characteristically Elamo-Persian terms. The Babylonian version essentially calques it indicating it was a Persian concept. In describing the place, the Old Persian and Elamite versions both use the word *daivadāna* "place of the *daivas*," which the Elamite incorporates un-translated as *da-a-ma-da-na*, while the Babylonian version translates the term as *bīt lemnūti* "house of evil (creatures)."[99] According to the inscription, the *daivas* and Auramazdā were worshipped at exactly the same location, with exactly the same type of ritual: a *šip*, the specifically Elamo-Persian cultural and ritual idiom recognizable from the Persepolis archive.[100] In order to accommodate a *šip*, this site would most likely have been a sacred site of the type that we know accommodated other *šips*: an open-air sanctuary.[101]

In stressing that the sacred site and the ritual were Persian, this is not to say that *daiva*-worship or such actual site need ever existed or such an event ever took place, though it could have.[102] As with Darius I's restoration of temples, such a localized rebellion might have

---

[94] NN 2240, NN 1670, NN 0486 in Henkelman 2008, pp. 121, 469–73, 547–48. Viewed optimistically, these few mentions of temples could perhaps attest to parallel temple economies that the Persepolis archive only peripherally perceived.

[95] Radner 2003a, 2003b.

[96] Henkelmann 2011.

[97] C1: 37–39; see Shaked 2004, pp. 16–18, 45–46; Henkelman 2008, p. 212. Alternatively, if it was not merely a convention of imperial Aramaic to refer to Auramazdā as Bel, this could have arisen from Bel's assimilation with Auramazdā in the late Achaeme-

nid period, anticipating Hellenistic developments (Grenet 1991).

[98] See Duchesne-Guillemin 1987 and Gnoli 1993b for the various sites attached to these inscriptions.

[99] XPe 30, XPa 30; Herzfeld 1938, p. 33; CAD L s.v. *limnu*.

[100] Duchesne-Guillemin 1987; Gnoli 1993b; Henkelman 2008, p. 473.

[101] XPhe 30, 32, 33, 34, 41, 44. See below on evidence of the *šip*.

[102] Sancisi-Weerdenburg 1989.

taken place; however, it could be more useful and appropriate in such an inscription to present it as an open-ended statement of good, divinely inspired kingship. Like Darius I's *āyadana* passage, if he wished to, Xerxes clearly would have named the land of the quashed rebellion with the same level of specificity as that with which he named all the lands that bore him tribute at the inscription's start. The fundamental goal of the *daivadāna* passage was not to record events but to impose a religious duality on political activity in the realm: the king worshipped Auramazdā and the Great God guided his actions. Any rebellious person or province worshipped the *daivas* and the *daivas* were behind any rebellion against the imperial order.

The Achaemenid archaeological, archival, sigillographical, and textual evidence details a coherent repertoire of official Persian cult activities and sacred spaces. The most important and widespread of these were open-air sanctuaries. Paradises and palatial grounds accommodated cultic activity and fire altars, tombs, and sacred towers also served as ritual focuses. No evidence at all attests to Achaemenid fire temples. While we have vivid evidence of a repertoire of Achaemenid cult activities performed at a variety of sacred spaces, at this point we cannot speak of a widespread, unified, and replicated tradition of official Persian temple architecture implanted throughout the Achaemenid empire. This, of course, may change if further excavations yield more structures that correspond to known official sacred architecture, such as the towers or QN3. But rather than trying to fill the void with late antique forms or single examples, we should concentrate on the considerable evidence we do have.

New Traditions of Iranian Sacred Architecture in the Middle Iranian Era

Despite certain continuities, the Seleukid era oversaw massive changes across Iran and Western Asia and this holds true for sacred spaces as well. A widespread tradition of temple architecture only appears across the Iranian world with the rise of the Seleukid empire.[103] These architectural forms were not exclusive to Iranian cults, but appear in temples dedicated to a variety of deities throughout the Seleukid empire. What is significant, however, is that this is the first time we have substantial evidence for temples in the Iranian world. After a hiatus stretching from the fall of the Achaemenids through the early wars of the Successors, under Seleukos I (310–281 B.C.E.) Western Asia again experienced a fluorescence of building and city foundation. Seleukos I and his successors undertook an ambitious and successful program of city foundation that integrated new Seleukid traditions into the urban and religious life their vast empire.[104] With metropolises like Seleukeia-Tigris, the Syrian Tetrapolis, important satrapal capitals like Dura Europos in Syria and Ai Khanum (Āy Ḵānom) in Bactria, temple complexes like Takht-e Sangin (Taḵt-e Sangīn) on the Oxos, and re-founded Achaemenid cities like Seleukeia-Eulaios (Susa), the early Seleukids created a new metropolitan and provincial topography of power that integrated yet ultimately superseded that of the Achaemenids.[105]

Seleukid architectural forms transcended all previous and contemporary traditions, be they Babylonian, Persian, or Macedonian. In cities that had a long tradition of sacred

---

[103] Canepa forthcoming c.

[104] Mairs 2007, 2008; Leriche 2007a, 2007b; Held 2002; Briant 1978; Cohen 1978.

[105] Canepa forthcoming c.

architecture, for example, at Athens or at Uruk in Mesopotamia, the Seleukids built or rebuilt important sanctuaries engaging indigenous forms (fig. 14.14g).[106] In regions that did not have a well-established temple tradition, like the Iranian plateau, or in newly founded cities, like Dura Europos, the Seleukids introduced new forms that had a long and lasting impact (fig. 14.14c–d). Founded by Seleukos I about the same time as Seleukeia-Pieria and Antioch-Orontes (ca. 300 B.C.E.), Ai Khanum is particularly important for the study of Seleukid Asia. It remains the most thoroughly excavated Seleukid foundation from the Upper Satrapies and has yielded the best-preserved Seleukid sacred architecture from the Iranian lands.[107]

In the early Seleukid era several monumental temples with a number of shared characteristics appeared at roughly the same time in Syria, Mesopotamia, and along the Oxos River valley in Bactria. This is the first time where a unified, empire-wide tradition of sacred architecture encompassed the Iranian lands. For many years archaeologists and historians of art and religion have debated the origin and relationship of temples with similar features excavated at sites across Western and South Asia. The original excavators and later students of these sites in Bactria recognized that the basic ground plans of these temples resembled those of Seleukid-era temples from Mesopotamia and Syria.[108] As new archaeological discoveries have been integrated into scholarship, a clearer view of the relationship between these structures has emerged.

In the Persian Gulf, Iran, and Bactria, a few smaller structures appear using traditional Greek architecture with Persian architectural elements integrated into the structure's architectural members or ornament. The Ionic temple with Achaemenid-style bases on the island of Ikaros provides a good example of this phenomenon.[109] Traditional Greek temple architecture only appears in two structures dedicated to the cults of heroized or divinized dead: the heroön of the city founder, Kineas, and that of another unknown individual and his relatives (*mausolée au caveau de pierre*), possibly that of a post-Seleukid, Greco-Bactrian ruler.[110] The fact that these structures were built or rebuilt at roughly the same time as the city's temples indicates that all architectural options were open to the builders. For whatever reason, patrons or the citizens of Ai Khanum deemed traditional Greek temple architecture appropriate for the funerary *temenoi*, and the "mixed" Seleukid official architecture appropriate for structures dedicated to the worship of gods. Much like major Seleukid palaces, the largest and most important structures utilized an official architecture that deliberately and harmoniously incorporated Greek, Babylonian, and Persian architectural features to create something quite new.[111]

The temples of Zeus and Artemis at Dura Europos, the temple dedicated to the River Oxos excavated at Takht-e Sangin, the Temple with Niches and the Temple Outside the Walls at Ai Khanum all contain monumental architecture combining elements of these architectural traditions (fig. 14.14a–e).[112] The rectangular shape of their sanctuaries with antechambers (*pronaos*), a cult chamber (*naos*) often divided into multiple units or flanked with "sacristies,"

---

[106] S. Downey 1988, pp. 7–50.

[107] Bernard 2008; Coloru 2009, p. 149.

[108] Bernard 1976a, 1981, 1990; Schippmann 1971; Stronach 1985; S. Downey 1988; Hannestad and Potts 1990; Rapin 1992; Lindström 2009; Mairs, in press; Leriche 2010; Shenkar 2011.

[109] Jeppesen 1989. On the mausoleums, see Canepa 2010b.

[110] Bernard, ed., 1973, pp. 85–102 and 115; see the chronological chart p. 104. Bernard et al. 1976, pp. 25–39.

[111] Kopasacheili 2011; Canepa forthcoming c.

[112] Lindström 2009, pp. 129–31; Rapin 1992, p. 118.

reflect, but do not fully replicate, the internal features of varieties of Babylonian temple architecture. Babylonian temples normally contained these cultic spaces within larger complexes rather than centralized, freestanding structures. The exterior walls of these Seleukid temples often incorporated decorative niches, reflecting Babylonian treatments, combined with Greek architectural ornament. Their columns, bases, and capitals could incorporate both Persian and Greek forms. These structures put a Seleukid royal imprint on the civic cults of many regions' metropolises and several satrapies most important provincial cults.

Only a few clues exist regarding the nature of the cult or cults practiced in the Bactrian temples, and none of them conform strictly to any single religious tradition. For example, the colossal cult statue that appeared in a later phase of Ai Khanum's Temple with Niches (Phase II) had the iconography of Zeus.[113] While the statue received Greek cult, the sanctuary integrated a water channel and a series of libation jars buried in the crepis behind the temple suggesting Iranian religious practices.[114] This suggests that there was nothing contradictory about using Greco-Macedonian forms for venerating gods associated with an originally non-Greek cult.[115] Bernard discovered no evidence associated with the Temple Outside the Walls that provides a clue as to the nature of the deity or deities worshipped in the temple. Despite recent assertions, the Oxos Temple at Takht-e Sangin clearly did not host anything resembling a Zoroastrian, ever-burning fire cult in the Seleukid era. Altars excavated in the front of the temple resembled Greek altars.[116] Overall, the dedications correspond to Greek cultic practices, though names associated with them are just as often Iranian as Greek.[117]

Although the archaeological and textual evidence is fragmentary, a number of open-air cult sites that were important in the Achaemenid era received temples in the Seleukid and Parthian era, even post-Achaemenid Persepolis (fig. 14.14i). We have hints of these sites in classical textual sources, including Polybius, who describes the current condition of Hellenistic Iran; Arrian, who describes events during Alexander's campaigns; and Plutarch, who purports to describe events in the Persian empire or conquest of Alexander, though writing in the Roman period.[118] This body of textual sources comes from the early Roman period, well after the fall of the Achaemenid empire. It is only at this point that we begin to hear mention of "sanctuaries" (*hiera*), or, more rarely, a temple (*naos*). In Media, textual sources suggest that the Seleukids maintained (and periodically plundered) a temple to Artemis/Anāhitā near Ecbatana.[119] Unfortunately, no archaeological evidence of this structure has been discovered to corroborate the textual evidence. It is significant, however, that sources mention a temple

---

[113] Only fragments of the cult statue survive, including a left foot measuring 27 cm in length, indicating the statue was seated. The sandal on the foot carries a thunderbolt (Bernard 1969, pp. 313–55, esp. 338–41, figs. 15 and 1).

[114] Bernard 1970, pp. 300–49, esp. pp. 327–39; Bernard 1974, pp. 280–308, esp. 294–98; Francfort, Ligeron, and Valence 1984, pp. 81–84.

[115] Mairs, in press.

[116] Litvinskij and Pičikjan 2002, p. 90.

[117] Lindström 2009.

[118] For example, Antiochos III despoiled silver tiles and the gilded column revetment from the peristyle of the "Anais" temple (*naos*) at Ecbatana (Polybius, *Histories* 10.27.2). Macedonians encountered a sanctuary (*hieron*) to "Artemis" on Ikaros, which contained wild goats (Arrian, *Anabasis* 7.20.3–4). Artaxerxes II makes Aspasia a priestess of "Artemis of Ecbatana, whom they call Anaitis" (no direct mention of a temple or reference to a "sanctuary") (Plutarch, *Artaxerxes* 27.4). Sanctuary (*hieron*) of Anaitis (Isidore of Charax, *Parthian Stations* 6).

[119] Strabo, *Geographia* 11.13.5. Seleukos I: Pliny, *Natural History* 6.17.

in this region only from the Seleukid era on.[120] Bard-e Nešānda and Masjed-e Solaymān, two sites that both featured stone terraces, flourished well into the Seleukid and Parthian eras (fig. 14.14j–k).[121] Although the terraces might have originated in the Achaemenid era, temples appeared on them only in the Seleukid and Parthian eras. They have often been associated with the temples whose treasure Antiochos III and Antiochos IV tried to expropriate. If one day new archaeological explorations could provide more conclusive archaeological evidence, we might then be able speak more conclusively about whether such highland Elamite *hiera* incorporated temples in the Achaemenid era.

Seleukid architecture offered a challenging departure point for early Arsacid and Kushan official architecture.[122] Nisa, in present-day Turkmenistan, was the first imperial capital of the Arsacid dynasty of Iran (ca. 250 B.C.E.–ca. 226 C.E.). While "New Nisa" refers to the actual city on the plain below, "Old Nisa" refers to the city's fortified hilltop complex that hosted several monumental structures created in a succession of phases.[123] Old Nisa likely began as a fortress, though later the Arsacid king of kings Mithradates I (reigned 171–138 B.C.E.) re-founded it and converted the site to a ceremonial center that honored the memory of the Arsacid kings.[124] While their exact function is still debated, several structures at Nisa clearly departed from Seleukid sacred and palatial architecture.[125] They incorporate porticos, niched wall treatments, and central halls with four columns all decorated with Hellenistic architectural ornament and statuary. Beyond the imperial capital, a number of provincial sacred structures featuring a four-columned hall, central entrance portico surrounded by sacristies or ambulatories appear in the Parthian period at Susa, and Fratarakid Persepolis, among other sites.[126]

Seleukid architectural forms had a long history in Bactria after the province became independent and informed those of the Kushans. The original temples of Ai Khanum were rebuilt several times on similar ground plans after the city became the capital of the independent Kingdom of Bactria. Newly built temples that emerged during this period, such as that of Delberjin (fig. 14.14h), reflect the basic forms of those at Ai Khanum and Takht-e Sangin. This ground plan reappears in the first-century B.C.E. temple of Mohra Maliaran at Taxila, in present-day Pakistan.[127] After the fall of the Greco-Bactrian kingdom, the life of Ai Khanum and its temples came to an end when the city was destroyed around 145 B.C.E. However, the temples of Takht-e Sangin and Delberjin were rebuilt several times under the Kushans on similar plans.[128]

---

[120] Stronach 1985, pp. 619–22; Rapin 1992; Brown 1998. The standing remains of Kangavar, once thought to be those of the Seleukid temple, have been securely dated to the Sasanian era. It is questionable whether the site supported a temple at all and if this was the site of the temple mentioned by Isidore (Azarnoush 2009; Kleiss 2010).

[121] Potts 1999, pp. 371–73.

[122] Michels 2010; Dąbrowa 2010; Invernizzi 1994 [1996], 2001, 2005.

[123] Final publication: Invernizzi 2009; Invernizzi and Lippolis 2008.

[124] Invernizzi 2001, p. 134; Lippolis 2009.

[125] Invernizzi and Lippolis 2008, pp. 83–166, 265–82, 374–75 (though with caution with reference to the temple at Kuh-e Ḵᵂāja). Reflecting Parthian innovations, a 17-meter-diameter mudbrick structure, "The Round Hall," belonged to a later phase. It was linked to the Red Building by corridors and three passages (Invernizzi and Lippolis 2008, pp. 7–81).

[126] Shenkar 2011, p. 132; Rapin 1992, pp. 122–23.

[127] Rapin 1995.

[128] Delberjin's ceramics and the iconography of the Dioskouri painting associated with its earliest layer cohere better with a Greco-Bactrian versus a Kushan date; see Shenkar 2011, pp. 120 and 124–25; Bernard 1994, 1990.

The Kushan sanctuary at Surkh Kotal, built between 128 and 132 C.E., contained at its core a temple that departed from the architectural tradition begun by Seleukids and mediated by the Greco-Bactrian kingdom. Called by its creator *Kaneško-oanindo-bagolaggo* "the Sanctuary of Victorious Kaniška," Surkh Kotal consisted of an artificial terraced mountain ridgeline with a multi-level stairway leading up the mountain's eastern side.[129] The main temple ("Temple A") was a centralized, peripteral mudbrick and timber structure that rose in the center of the courtyard on a 47 × 40-meter brick podium (fig. 14.6). Although the site's excavator sought to find an example of a pre-Sasanian fire temple in the main temple at Surkh Kotal, he found no evidence of a Kushan fire cult.[130] This central cult room contained a .90-meter-high stone plinth that measured 4.25 × 4.25 meters and whose corners each carried large column bases. The ground plan corresponds closely to previous Bactrian temples, though here the "sacristies" have been converted to a continuous ambulatory corridor, a hallmark of later Iranian architecture. This ambulatory surrounds the *naos*, which housed a cult statue or statues, the likely purpose of the central plinth at its center. Like the Oxos Temple of Takht-e Sangin, the *naos* featured four columns.

The Achaemenid tradition of open-air sanctuaries did not disappear after the fall of that empire. Indeed, many of the sites that were important in the Achaemenid era continued to be places of cult in the Seleukid era and beyond, and new open-air enclosures or hilltop sanctuaries continued to be built. On the southwest edge of Ai Khanum's acropolis excavators discovered a large stepped podium located in the center of a sanctuary courtyard. This platform has been linked with similar structures discovered in Bactria and Iran and associated with open-air worship as described in classical authors.[131] The site of Bīsotūn continued to host cult activity and royal rock reliefs and inscriptions attest to its importance into the Seleukid, Parthian, and Sasanian eras.[132] At a certain point in the Seleukid era the sanctuary became associated with Herakles-Wahrām. According to Tacitus, writing about the cult in the Parthian era, the priests, once bidden by the god through a dream, would release a riderless horse with a quiver full of arrows into the surrounding mountains.[133] The horse would return exhausted and without the arrows and the god then would reveal the location of his slain quarry through another dream. At the southern entrance to the precinct, where the wall met the cliff, a Seleukid official created a high relief of a reclining Herakles. An inscription in Greek and Aramaic accompanied this relief indicating that the intended audience was not just the Macedonian elite.[134] In this same area Arsacid kings of kings carved several of their own rock reliefs, marking and claiming the sanctuary.

Strabo and Pausanius describe sanctuaries (*hiera*) of the Persian gods in Anatolia drawing in part from their firsthand experiences of local "Persian" cults in Cappadocia and Lydia, respectively.[135] In these passages, which provide evidence for the later development of Iranian cults in Roman Anatolia, Strabo describes "the tribe of the Magi called 'Fire Kindlers' (*Pyraithroi*), who are numerous in Cappodocia," while Pausanias mentions "Lydians called

---

[129] SK 4 in Schlumberger, Le Berre, and Fussman 1983–1990, vol. 1, pp. 11–20, 31–48, 49–62, 63–65 107–132.

[130] Fussman 1989, pp. 197–98. The later temples housed fire cults, but were built in the ruins of the sanctuary after its original cult had ceased to function (Schlumberger, Le Berre, and Fussman 1983–1990, vol. 1, pp. 28–29).

[131] Bernard 1976b, p. 307; S. Downey 1988, p. 75.

[132] Diodorus, *Bibliothēkē* 17.110.5; Isidore of Charax, *Parthian Stations* 5; Bernard 1980; Tubach 1995.

[133] Tacitus, *Annals* 12.13.

[134] Kleiss 1970; Luschey 1974, 1989.

[135] Mitchell 2007, p. 160.

Persians." Throughout his histories Strabo uses the word *heiron* to refer to all manner of sacred sites, but in this passage he specifies these as "fire sanctuaries" (*pyraithea*), which he describes as open-air enclosures (*sēkoi*). Strabo states: "[...] in the midst of these there is an altar, on which there is a large quantity of ashes and where the Magi keep the fire ever burning." Although he opens the section by paraphrasing Herodotus, and states that Persians do not use altars or statues (but omits "temples"), he goes on to say that:

> These same things are observed in the sanctuaries (*hiera*) of Anaïtis and Omanos; and these have sacred enclosures (*sēkoi*), and people process a wooden statue (*xoanon*) of Omanus. I have seen these things myself, but those other things and what comes next are mentioned in the histories. (Strabo 15.3.13–20)

Instead of mentioning a temple or a building when reporting about Achaemenid-founded sacred sites, Strabo speaks only of open-air sanctuaries, for example, the hilltop sanctuary at Zela (Strabo 11.8.4). He emphasizes that the most significant features of these sacred precincts were their enclosures that contained an altar in the middle. The only source that mentions, albeit cursorily, some sort of structure used in an Iranian cult is Pausanias:

> [...] the Lydians, who are called Persians, have sanctuaries (*heira*) in the city of Hiero-kaisareia and in Hypaipa. In each of the sanctuaries (*heira*) there is a shrine (*oikēma*), and in the shrine there is an altar with ashes on top. But the color is not like ashes, but something different. A magus, having entered the shrine and piled dry wood on the altar, first puts a tiara on his head and then sings an invocation to some god in a barbarous language completely incomprehensible in Greek. He sings while reciting from a book. It is necessary that the wood is kindled without fire and that brilliant flame blazes forth from the wood. (Pausanias 5.27.5–6)

Earlier interpretations of this passage have interpreted the *oikēma* as a small structure or room contained *inside* a larger enclosed temple like a *cella* in a Greek or Roman temple. This is not indicated in the text and without any archaeological evidence whatsoever of such larger "fire temples," it is safer to assume that Pausanias describes precincts containing altars like Strabo but with a small structure containing or acting as a covering for the altar. The unresolved dissonance between Strabo's summary of Herodotus and his own observations points to changes in Iranian religion between the Achaemenid empire and the Middle Iranian era. It also alludes to the fact that Iranian religious practices diverged markedly over the former lands of the Persian empire, with influences from dominant or neighboring cultures contributing to the process. In fact, some have argued the cults of "Persian Artemis" and "Artemis Anaitis" very likely did not originate from Iranian cults at all, but were rather the result of persianization of pre-existing Greek cults adding some Iranian cultic activities and titles to Greek cults of Artemis.[136]

No temple ground plan has been discovered or excavated at Hypaipa or Heirocaesarea from any period. The few fragments of architectural ornament are entirely from the Roman era.[137] The only explicit evidence of temples (though *not* fire temples) built for these "Persian" goddesses, "Persian Artemis" and "Artemis Anaitis," appears in the Roman period on coins. Generic representations of a tetra- or hexastyle, gabled Greco-Roman temples appear

---

[136] Brosius 1998.   [137] Reinach 1886, pp. 16–18; Weber 1892, p. 8.

on early imperial coins similar to other stereotyped numismatic representations of a temple.[138] An earthquake devastated this region in 17 C.E. and it was heavily rebuilt through the munificence of the emperor Tiberius, for which reason the city changed its name from Hiera Komē to Hierokaisareia (Hierocaesarea).[139] It is not too much of a stretch to see the cult statues of the Persian Artemis given new, standard Roman temples and cult statues of the sort reflected in the coins. But without archaeological evidence we must not close off the possibility that these were simply stereotyped numismatic symbols of some other cult site, not "portraits" of actual structures.

Like the Orontids of Armenia and Commagene, the kingdom of Pontos had its roots in the Persian satrapies of Cappadoccia and Phrygia and its dynasty claimed both Achaemenid and Seleukid descent.[140] Their kings were more Hellenized than the early Orontids and adopted aspects of contemporary Macedonian kingship. Later, the most important Pontic king, Mithradates VI (reigned 120–63 B.C.E.), incorporated and foregrounded Iranian kingship. After driving out the forces of Lucius Licinius Murena,

> [Mithradates VI] offered sacrifice to Zeus Stratius on a lofty pile of wood on a high hill, according to the fashion of his country, which is as follows. First, the kings themselves carry wood to the heap. Then they make a smaller pile encircling the other one, on which they pour milk, honey, wine, oil, and various kinds of incense. A banquet is spread on the ground for those present (as at the sacrifices of the Persian kings at Pasargadae) and then they set fire to the wood. The height of the flame is such that it can be seen at a distance of 180 kilometers from the sea, and they say that nobody can come near it for several days on account of the heat. Mithridates performed a sacrifice of this kind according to the custom of his country. (Appian, *The Mithridatic Wars* 66.83; trans. Horace White)

Several scholars have noted the parallels with the *šip* sacrifices at Pasargadae.[141] Whether this was the result of direct continuity, vague cultural memory, or creative reinvention is not clear, but the overall effect and significance makes perfect sense within Mithradates VI's ideological program of championing both the Hellenic and Persian traditions against the Romans.

The Seleukids introduced a tradition of dynastic cult where the Macedonian elite venerated the king, his family, and ancestors along with dynastic gods.[142] Nisa was important to the development of the Arsacid dynasty's experiments with dynastic cult partially inspired by Seleukid royal cult.[143] A domed structure at Nisa (the Round Hall) contained a portrait of Mithradates II and, along with other structures at the site, hosted some sort of cult activities connected to the memory of the kings of kings. Documents from the site indicate that the names of a number of estates and vineyards were named after living and deceased kings.[144]

---

[138] Imhoof-Blumer 1895, pp. 309–26; Mitchell 2007, pp. 159–60.

[139] Boyce and Grenet 1991, p. 225; Mitchell 2007, pp. 159–60.

[140] Mithradates VI boasted equally of his royal Persian and Macedonian descent, counting as ancestors Cyrus, Darius, Alexander, and Seleukos I (Justinus, *Epitome* 38.7.1; Mitchell 2005). On Pontic religion and temples, see Saprykin 2009.

[141] Henkelman 2012.

[142] Canepa forthcoming b.

[143] Dąbrowa 2011.

[144] The economic documents from Nisa record deliveries from estates dedicated to the kings Priapatius (ca. 191–76 B.C.E.), Mithradates I (ca. 171–38 B.C.E.), Artabanus I (ca. 127–24/3 B.C.E.), and Gotarzes I (ca. 90–78 B.C.E.), who appear to have been alive when the endowments were created and perhaps founded them during their lifetimes (Canepa forthcoming b).

Ostraka from Nisa document delivery of goods from these estates and it has been argued that they supported some sort of cult for the memory and the benefit of the king's soul.[145] Without any other information, we can only speculate on the presence of cult activities in the various structures of Old Nisa. In the same region, at the village of Asaak, Isidore of Charax reports that a perpetual fire was kept burning to commemorate the site where Arsakes was first recognized as king, thus creating a larger topography of memory celebrating the dynasty (Isidore of Charax, *Parthian Stations* 11). Like Parthian Nisa, Surkh Kotal was one of several Kushan dynastic sanctuaries that responded to the new, Seleukid-inspired Middle Iranian tradition of honoring kings and dynastic gods.[146]

The Persian tradition of sacrifices offered at funerary monuments or memorials continued in the Middle Iranian era, though reinvented and dramatically changed through an integration of Hellenistic cult and artistic elements. Interestingly, many of these, especially in the west, were variations of open-air sanctuaries. The Seleukid and Arsacid precedents inspired a variety of dynastic sanctuaries across the Parthian world including that of Shami in Elymaïs, Armenia, Pontos, and the *hierothēsia* of the border kingdom of Commagene.[147] Intriguingly, the new Arsacid practices appear to have augmented indigenous Persian traditions that stemmed from the Achaemenid satrapal roots of many of these dynasties. While we do not have corroborating archaeological evidence, textual evidence suggests that the Iranian kings of Armenia incorporated these newly emerging Iranian royal cultic practices by at least the end of the Arsacid era. The basic elements of the dynastic sanctuary of the Armenian kings, consisting of an open-air sanctuary, statues of the king, the king's ancestors, and the gods, and cultic activity.[148] Only under Arsacid influence does the additional element of the "ever-burning fire," appear at Armenian sanctuaries.

Like Armenia, the kingdom of Commagene (162 B.C.E.–17 C.E.) stood in a precarious place between the Roman and the Arsacid empires. It was one of the last Persian-Macedonian courts of this region to survive the coming of the Romans. The royal dynasty of Commagene had its roots in the Persian Orontid dynasty; however, as a Seleukid province, Commagene became heavily Hellenized. Iranian cultural forms regained prominence in the first century B.C.E. as part of a deliberate policy of on the part of the central court to underscore the kingdom's ancient roots that transcended Seleukid, Arsacid, or Roman claims in the region. Antiochus I (69–34 B.C.E.), the kingdom's main innovator in cult and artistic activity, established open-air dynastic sanctuaries called *hierothēsia* at a number of important sites within his kingdom, including the citadel of Arsameia-on-the-Euphrates (Gerger, Adiyaman province, Turkey) and Arsameia-on-the-Nymphaios.[149] The supreme site was the *hierothēsion* at Nemrud Dağı, situated on the most prominent mountain in Commagene. In addition to more frequent, small-scale sacrifices, these sites hosted colossal communal feasts funded by the king recalling (though not replicating) the *šip*.

---

[145] Boyce implies that the Nisa documents specifically refer to fires dedicated for the soul of the king, but ostraka contain no such mention of either (Boyce 1986; Canepa forthcoming b).

[146] Canepa 2010a, forthcoming b.

[147] Canepa 2010a, 2010b, forthcoming b.

[148] Movses Khorenats'i, 2.12 (trans. Thomson 2006, p. 146); 2.40 (trans. Thomson 2006, p. 179); 2.49 (trans.

Thomson 2006, p. 187). Compare Agathangelos 817–18 (trans. Thomson 1976, p. 355, and p. 491 n. 1); Canepa forthcoming b.

[149] For an overview of the dynasty, see Facella 2006, pp. 250–97; Canepa 2007. For an introduction to the archaeology and religion, see Jacobs 2011; Mittag 2011; Wagner 2000; Sanders 1996; Waldmann 1991.

Conclusion

While many of the sites and structures dealt with in this study have, in the past, been called fire temples, archaeological evidence of monumental Zoroastrian fire temples only appears unproblematically and in abundance in the Sasanian era (224–642 C.E.). The ranks of pre-Sasanian fire temples have thinned considerably as old sites have been subject to new dating technologies and more critical analyses.[150] Although scholars have attempted to do so before, it is still too early to write definitively about the early development of the pre-Sasanian Zoroastrian fire temple. Of the temples mentioned in this study, none originally were created as fire temples although a few were adapted to this function at a later date with the Sasanians' influence or compulsion. Those pre-Sasanian structures that have been reliably dated and show secure evidence of a fire cult follow a different architectural tradition unrelated to that of Achaemenid or Seleukid sacred architecture.[151]

While it likely had roots in late Parthian architecture, the Sasanians were responsible for the ultimate spread of a different type of sacred architecture that became closely associated with the new fire cult: the centralized, domed *čāhār ṭāq*. The *čāhār ṭāq* appears in grand palatial architecture under Ardashir I and was likely employed as a new, standard type of fire temple during the early Sasanian empire as well. These are ubiquitous throughout the province of Pārs (Pārsa), appearing in both big and small structures. Several grand, monumental sanctuaries that the Sasanians sponsored outside of Pārs incorporate this new style of temple architecture for the new orthodox Sasanian fire cult.[152] This new type of fire temple architecture and fire cult imprinted a variety of sanctuaries as the Sasanians systematically seized or destroyed all sites and traditions that could buttress a claim to royal power.[153] These included sites with connections to the Achaemenids, like Persepolis and Naqš-e Rostam, new royal cities such as Ardaxšīr-Xwarrah and Bay-Šābuhr, and sites outside of their Persian homeland built to embody the mythological locations and traditions of the Avesta. All are characterized by an incredible juxtaposition of continuity and innovation. For example, the Sasanians' memorial cults in their homeland show incredible continuity with the *šumar/bašur* cults of the Achaemenids, though the Sasanians put a sacred fire at their center.[154] Their radically new architectural and ritual forms made primordial Iranian epic and religious traditions tangible at sites such as Lake Kayānsīh at Kuh-e K̲ʷāja and Ādur Gušnasp at Takt-e Solaymān.[155] Some of these, like Kuh-e K̲ʷāja, show signs of an effaced Parthian (though not Achaemenid) presence. Others, such as the sanctuary of Ādur Gušnasp at Takt-e Solaymān, the Sasanians built at sites with no previous cultic or monumental activity. Although these sanctuaries were all newly built, they provided the Sasanians a no less powerful experience of the primordial pan-Iranian past and their place in it. This paper certainly does not present the final word on the development of Iranian temples, and new archaeological discoveries will surely enhance, if not transform, our understanding of the problem. However, it is my hope that if and when new evidence comes to light, such a re-evaluation can proceed unencumbered by earlier historiographical and theoretical burdens.

---

[150] Radiocarbon dating has proven that the complex at Kuh-e K̲ʷāja dates to the late Parthian or early Sasanian period. The architectural and sculptural features of the standing remains cohere better with Sasanian art (Ghanimati 2000; Canepa forthcoming a).

[151] Betts and Yagodin 2007; Kaim 2004.

[152] Canepa forthcoming a.

[153] Canepa 2010b; Huff 2008.

[154] Canepa 2010a.

[155] Canepa 2010b; forthcoming a.

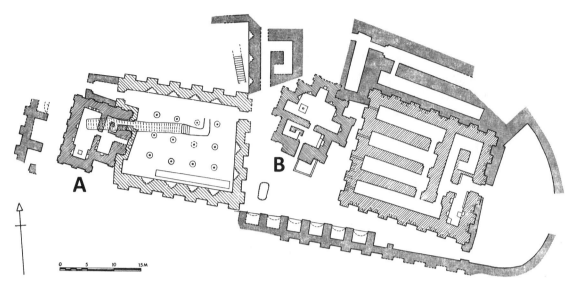

Figure 14.1. Plan of Tepe Nuš-e Jān. A: "Western Temple"; B: "Central Temple"
(after Stronach and Roaf 2007, fig. 1.9)

Figure 14.2. Tomb of Cyrus, Pasargadae

Figure 14.3. Rock-cut tombs at Naqš-e Rostam. Right to left: tomb of Darius I,
tombs attributed to Artaxerxes I and Darius II

Figure 14.4. Persepolis. Rock platform and foundations in front of the
tomb attributed to Artaxerxes III

Figure 14.5. Relief from Daskyleion portraying sacrificial scene
(Istanbul Archaeological Museum inv. no. 2361)

Figure 14.6. Relief from Daskyleion portraying male figure with *barsom*
(Istanbul Archaeological Museum inv. no. 5391)

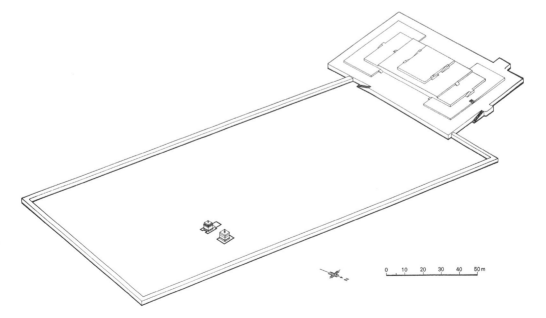

Figure 14.7. Plan of the sacred precinct at Pasargadae (after Stronach 1978, fig. 74)

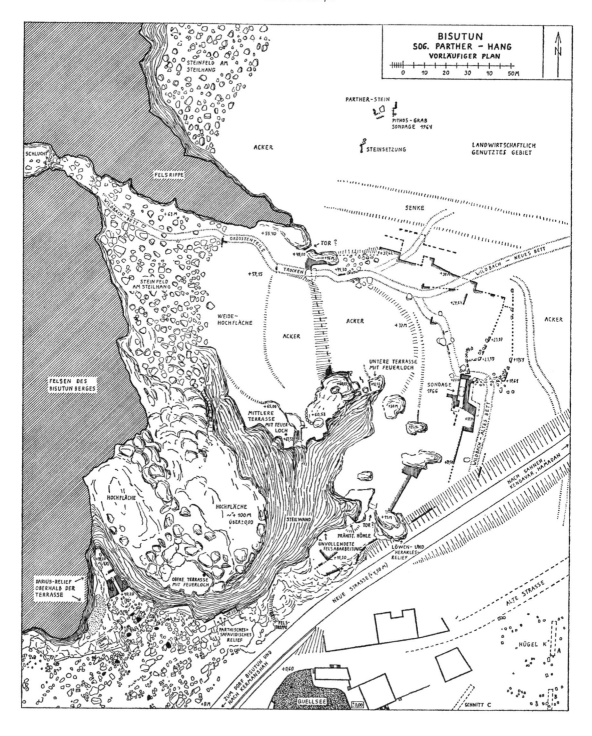

Figure 14.8. Plan of Bīsotūn (after Kleiss 1970, fig. 2)

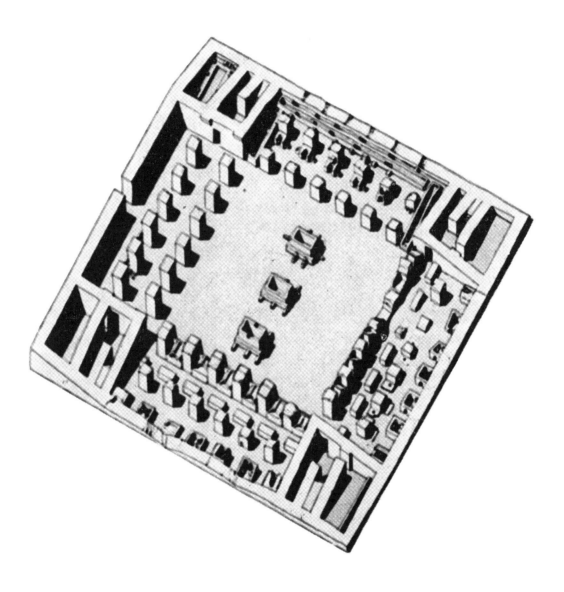

Figure 14.9. Isometric plan of QN3 Dahan-e Ḡolāmān (after Scerrato 1979, fig. 9)

Figure 14.10. PFS 11* (courtesy of the Persepolis Fortification Archive Seal Project
and the Persepolis Fortification Archive Project)

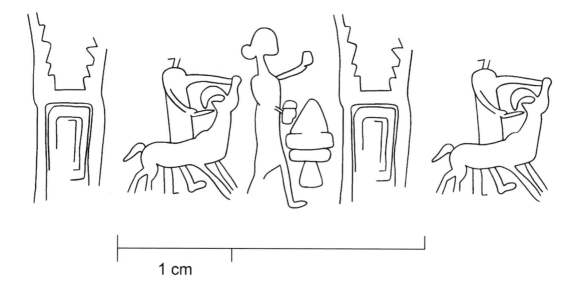

Figure 14.11. PFUTS 147 (courtesy of the Persepolis Fortification Archive Project)

Figure 14.12. View of Pasargadae with the remains of the Zendān-e Solaymān (lower right), the palatial district and garden of Cyrus (middle), and the tomb of Cyrus (upper left)

Figure 14.13. Naqš-e Rostam. View of the Kaʿba-ye Zardošt from above

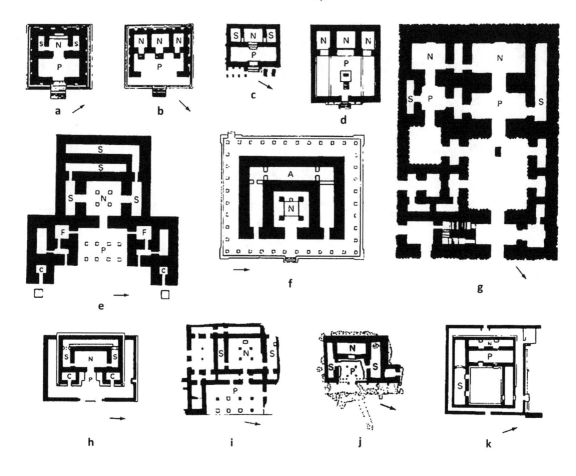

Legend

A   Ambulatory
C   Chapel
F   Later fire emplacement (not part of original construction)
N   Naos
P   Pronaos / Antechamber
S   "Sacristy"

Figure 14.14. Temple ground plans (adapted from Rapin 1992)

a.   Temple with Niches, Ai Khanum
b.   Temple Outside the Walls, Ai Khanum
c.   Temple of Artemis, Dura Europos
d.   Temple of Zeus Megistos Dura Europos
      (rebuilt on the Seleukid plans)
e.   Temple of the Oxos, Takht-e Sangin

f.   Main Temple, Surkh Kotal
g.   Seleukid Anu Temple, Bit Reš, Uruk
h.   Delberjin
i.   "Fratarakid Temple," Persepolis
j.   Bard-e Nešānda
k.   Masjed-e Solaymān

Abbreviations

CAD	*The Assyrian Dictionary of the Oriental Institute of the University of Chicago,* A. Leo Oppenheim et al., eds. Chicago: The Oriental Institute, 1956–2010.
FrGrH	*Die Fragmente der griechischen Historiker,* Felix Jacoby, ed. Leiden: Brill, 1923–1958.
PFA	Persepolis Fortification Archive

Achaemenid Inscriptions

The general system to refer to Achaemenid inscriptions consists of three letters. The first indicates the king (e.g., X = Xerxes); the second the site (e.g., S = Susa); the third is added to distinguish inscriptions of the same ruler at the same site.

DB	Darius I, Bīsotūn ("Bīsotūn Inscription")
DS	Darius I, Susa
XP	Xerxes I, Persepolis

Bibliography

Abdi, Kamyar

2006–2007   "The 'Daiva' Inscription Revisited." *International Journal of Ancient Iranian Studies* 6/1–2: 45–73.

2010   "The Passing of the Throne from Xerxes to Artaxerxes I." In *The World of Achaemenid Persia: History, Art and Society in Iran and the Ancient Near East,* edited by John Curtis and St. John Simpson, pp. 275–86. New York: I. B. Tauris.

Amiet, Pierre

1995   "Dieulafoy, Marcel-Auguste." In *Encyclopædia Iranica,* online edition, New York. www.iranica.com

Anderson, B.

2002   "Imperial Legacies, Local Identities: References to Achaemenid Persian Iconography on Crenelated Nabataean Tombs." *Ars Orientalis* 32: 163–207.

Anthony, David W.

2007   *The Horse, the Wheel, and Language: How Bronze-Age Riders from the Eurasian Steppes Shaped the Modern World.* Princeton: Princeton University Press.

Arvidsson, Stefan

2006   *Aryan Idols: Indo-European Mythology as Ideology and Science.* Chicago: University of Chicago Press.

Azarnoush, Massoud

1987   "Fire Temple and Anahita Temple: A Discussion on Some Iranian Places of Worship." *Mesopotamia* 22: 391–401.

2009   "New Evidence on the Chronology of the 'Anahita Temple.'" *Iranica antiqua* 44: 393–402.

Bakels, Corrie C.

2003   "The Contents of Ceramic Vessels in the Bactria-Margiana Archaeological
                Complex, Turkmenistan." *Electronic Journal of Vedic Studies* 9/1, article 3.
                http://www.ejvs.laurasianacademy.com/

Benech, Christophe; Rémy Boucharlat; and Sébastien Gondet

2012   "Organisation et aménagement de l'espace à Pasargades: reconnaissances ar-
                chéologiques de surface, 2003–2008." *Arta* 2012.003: 1–37.

Bensenval, Roland, and P. Marquis

2008 [2010]   "Les travaux de la Délégation Archéologique Française en Afghanistan (DAFA):
                résultats des campagnes de l'automne 2007 e Printemps 2008 en Bactriane et à
                Kaboul." *Comptes-Rendus de l'Académie des Inscriptions et Belles-Lettres*: 973–95

Bernard, Paul

1969   "Quatrième campagne de fouilles à Aï Khanoum (Bactriane)." *Comptes-rendus des
                séances de l'Académie des Inscriptions et Belles-Lettres* 113/3: 313–55.

1970   "Campagne de fouilles 1969 à Aï Khanoum en Afghanistan." *Comptes-rendus des
                séances de l'Académie des Inscriptions et Belles-Lettres* 114/2: 300–49.

1974   "Fouilles de Aï Khanoum (Afghanistan), campagnes de 1972 et 1973." *Comptes-
                rendus des séances de l'Académie des Inscriptions et Belles-Lettres* 118/2: 280–308.

1976a   "Les traditions orientales dans l'architecture gréco-bactrienne." *Journal asiatique*
                264: 245–75.

1976b   "Campagne de fouilles 1975 à Aï Khanoum (Afghanistan)." *Comptes-rendus des
                séances de l'Académie des Inscriptions et Belles-Lettres* 120/2: 287–322.

1980   "Héraclès, les grottes de Karafto et le sanctuaire du mont Sambulos en Iran."
                Studia iranica 9: 301–24.

1981   *"Problèmes d'histoire coloniale grecque à travers l'urbanisme d'une cité hellénistique
                d'Asie Centrale."* In *150 Jahre Deutsches archäologisches Institut, 1829–1979*, pp. 108–20.
                Mainz: Philipp von Zabern.

1990   "L'architecture religieuse de l'Asie centrale a l'époque hellénistique." In *Akten
                des XIII. Internationalen Kongresses für Klassische Archäologie, Berlin 1988*, pp. 51–59.
                Mainz: Philipp von Zabern.

1994   "Le temple du dieu Oxus a Takht-i Sangin en Bactriane: temple du feu ou pas?"
                Studia Iranica 23: 80–121.

2008   "The Greek Colony at Aï Khanum and Hellenism in Central Asia." In *Afghanistan:
                Hidden Treasures from the National Museum, Kabul* edited by edited by Fredrik T.
                Hiebert and Pierre Cambon, pp. 81–106. Washington, D.C.: National Geographic
                Society.

Bernard, Paul, editor

1973   *Fouilles d'Aï Khanoum 1. Campagnes 1965, 1966, 1967, 1968: rapport préliminaire publié
                sous la direction de Paul Bernard.* Mémoires de la Délégation archéologique fran-
                çaise en Afghanistan 21. Paris: Klincksieck.

Bernard, Paul; Henri-Paul Francfort; Jean-Claude Gardin; Jean-Claude Liger; Bertille Lyonnet; and
Serge Veuve

1976   "Fouilles d'Aï Khanoum (Afghanistan): campagne de 1974." *Bulletin de l'École
                française d'Extrême-Orient* 63: 5–58.

Betts, Alison V. G., and Vadim N. Yagodin

2007   "The Fire Temple at Tash-k'irman Tepe, Chorasmia." In *After Alexander: Central
                Asia Before Islam,* edited by Joe Cribb and Georgina Herrmann, pp. 435–53. Ox-
                ford: Published for the British Academy by Oxford University Press.

Borchhardt, Jürgen
  1968   "Epichorische, gräko-persisch beeinflußte Reliefs in Kilikien." *Istanbuler Mittei-lungen* 18: 161–211.

Boroffka, N., and L. Sverchkov
  2007   "Ýaz medeniýeti/Kultura Yaz /The Jaz Culture." *Miras* 1: 86–96.

Boucharlat, Rémy
  1984   "Monuments religieux de la Perse achéménide, état des questions." In *Temples et sanctuaires: séminaire de recherche 1981-1983*, edited by Georges Roux, pp. 119–35. Travaux de la Maison de l'Orient 7. Lyon: Maison de l'Orient et de la Méditer-ranée Jean Pouilloux.

  2003   "Le Zendan de Pasargades: de la tour 'solitaire' à un ensemble architectural données archéologiques récentes." In *A Persian Perspective: Essays in Memory of Heleen Sancisi-Weerdenburg*, edited by Wouter F. M. Henkelman and Amélie Kuhrt, pp. 79–99. Achaemenid History 13. Leiden: Nederlands Instituut voor het Nabije Oosten.

  2005   "Iran." In *L'archéologie de l'empire achéménide: nouvelles recherches*, edited by Pierre Briant and Rémy Boucharlat, pp. 221–92. Persika 6. Paris: De Boccard.

  2006   "Les destin des résidences et sites perses d'Iran dans la seconde moitie du IVᵉ siècle avant J.-C." In *La transition entre l'empire achéménide et les royaumes hellé-nistiques, vers 350-300 av. J.-C.*, edited by Pierre Briant and Francis Joannès, pp. 443–70. Persika 9. Paris: De Boccard.

  2007   "Achaemenid Residences and Elusive Imperial Cities." In *Getrennte Wege? Kom-munikation, Raum und Wahrnehmung in der alten Welt*, edited by Robert Rollinger, Andreas Luther, and Josef Wiesehöfer, pp. 454–71. Frankfurt am Main: Verlag Antike.

Boucharlat, Rémy, and Christophe Benech
  2002   "Organisation et aménagement de l'espace à Pasargades: reconnaissances ar-chéologiques de surface, 1999-2002." *Arta* 2002.001: 1–41.

Boyce, Mary
  1975a   *A History of Zoroastrianism,* Volume 1: *The Early Period.* Leiden: Brill.
  1975b   "On the Zoroastrian Temple Cult of Fire." *Journal of the American Oriental Society* 95/3: 454–65.
  1982   *A History of Zoroastrianism*, Volume 2: *Under the Achaemenids.* Leiden: Brill.
  1986   "Arsacids iv. Arsacid Religion." In *Encyclopædia Iranica* online edition, New York. www.iranica.com

Boyce, Mary, and Frantz Grenet
  1991   *A History of Zoroastrianism*, Volume 3: *Zoroastrianism under Macedonian and Roman Rule.* Leiden: Brill.

Briant, Pierre
  1978   "Colonisation hellénistique et populations indigènes. la phase d'installation." *Klio. Beiträge zur alten Geschichte* 60/1: 57–92.

Briant, Pierre; Wouter F. M. Henkelman; and Matthew W. Stolper, editors
  2008   *L'Archive des fortifications de Persépolis: état des questions et perspectives de recherches.* Paris: De Boccard.

Brosius, Maria
  1998   "Artemis Persike and Artemis Anaitis." In *Studies in Persian History: Essays in Memory of David M. Lewis,* edited by Maria Brosius and Amélie Kuhrt, pp. 226–38. Achaemenid History 11. Leiden: Nederlands Instituut voor het Nabije Oosten.

Brown, Stuart C.
    1998   "Ecbatana." In *Encyclopædia Iranica* online edition, New York. www.iranica.com
    2000   "Ganj-nāma." In *Encyclopædia Iranica* online edition, New York. www.iranica.com

Burstein, Stanley Mayer, editor and translator
    1978   *The Babyloniaca of Berossus.* 2nd edition. Sources from the Ancient Near East 1/5.
                    Malibu: Undena Publications.

Cahill, Nicholas
    1988   "Taş Kule: A Persian-period Tomb near Phokaia." *American Journal of Archaeology*
                    92/4: 481–501.

Calmeyer, Peter
    1979   "Fortuna-Tyche-Khvarnah." *Jahrbuch des Deutschen Archäologischen Instituts* 94:
                    347–65.
    1992   "Zur Genese altiranischer Motive. XI. 'Eingewebte Bildchen' von Städten." *Ar-
                    chäologische Mitteilungen aus Iran und Turan* 25: 95–124.

Canepa, Matthew P.
    2007   Review of *La dinastia degli Orontidi nella Commagene ellenistico-romana*, by Mar-
                    gherita Facella. *The Bryn Mawr Classical Review* 2007.01.21.
    2010a   "Achaemenid and Seleucid Royal Funerary Practices and Middle Iranian King-
                    ship." In *Commutatio et Contentio: Studies in the Late Roman, Sasanian, and Early
                    Islamic Near East,* edited by Henning Börm and Josef Wiesehöfer, pp. 1–21. Reihe
                    Geschichte 3. Düsseldorf: Wellem.
    2010b   "Technologies of Memory in Early Sasanian Iran: Achaemenid Sites and Sasanian
                    Memory." *American Journal of Archaeology* 114/4: 563–96.
    Forthcoming a   "Building a New Vision of the Past in the Sasanian Empire: The Sanctuary of
                    Lake Kayansih and the Great Fires of Iran." *Journal of Persianate Studies* 5.
    Forthcoming b   "Dynastic Sanctuaries and the Transformation of Iranian Kingship between Al-
                    exander and Islam." In *Persian Kingship and Architecture: Strategies of Power in Iran
                    from the Achaemenids to the Pahlavis,* edited by Talinn Grigor and Sussan Babaie.
                    London: I. B. Tauris.
    Forthcoming c   "Seleukid Sacred Architecture, Royal Cult and the Transformation of Iranian
                    Culture in the Middle Iranian Period." *Journal of the International Society for Iranian
                    Studies.*

Capdetrey, Laurent
    2007   *Le pouvoir séleucide: territoire, administration, finances d'un royaume hellénistique,
                    312-129 avant J.-C.* Rennes: Presses Universitaires de Rennes.

Carter, Martha L.
    1994   "Coins and Kingship: Kanishka and the Kushana Dynasty." In *A Treasury of Indian
                    Coins,* edited by Martha L. Carter, pp. 29–38. Bombay: Marg Publications.

Chaverdi, Alireza A., and Pierfrancesco Callieri
    2010   "Preliminary Report on the Irano-Italian Stratigraphic Study of the Toll-e Takht,
                    Pasargad: Investigations on the Material Culture of the Achamenid and Post-
                    Achaemenid Period in Fars." In *Ancient and Middle Iranian Studies* (proceedings
                    of the 6th European Conference of Iranian Studies, held in Vienna, 18–22 Sep-
                    tember 2007), edited by Maria Macuch, Dieter Weber, and Desmond Durkin, pp.
                    11–28. Wiesbaden: Harrassowitz.

Choksy, Jamsheed K.
    2007   "Reassessing the Material Contexts of Ritual Fires in Ancient Iran." *Iranica an-
                    tiqua* 42: 229–71.

Cohen, Getzel M.

  1978   *The Seleucid Colonies: Studies in Founding, Administration and Organization.* Wiesbaden: Franz Steiner.

Coloru, Omar

  2009   *Da Alessandro a Menandro: Il Regno greco di Battriana.* Studi ellenistic 21. Pisa: Fabrizio Serra.

Curtis, Vesta S.

  2007   "Religious Iconography on Ancient Iranian Coins." In *After Alexander: Central Asia Before Islam,* edited by Joe Cribb and Georgina Herrmann, pp. 413–34. Oxford: Published for the British Academy by Oxford University Press.

Dąbrowa, Edward

  2010   "The Parthians and the Seleucid Legacy." In *Interkulturalität in der Alten Welt: Vorderasien, Hellas, Ägypten und die vielfältigen Ebenen des Kontakts,* edited by Robert Rollinger, Birgit Gufler, Martin Lang, and Irene Madreiter, pp. 583–89. Wiesbaden: Harrassowitz.

  2011   ΑΡΣΑΚΕΣ ΘΕΟΣ. "Observations on the Nature of the Parthian Ruler-cult." In *Un impaziente desiderio di scorrere il mondo: Studi in onore di Antonio Invernizzi per il suo settantesimo compleanno,* edited by Carlo Lippolis and Stefano De Martino, pp. 247–54. Monografie di Mesopotamia 14. Florence: Le Lettere.

Debord, Pierre

  2003   "Le culte royal chez les Séleucides." In *L'Orient méditerréen: de la mort d'Alexandre aux campagnes de Pompée; cités et royaumes à l'époque hellénistique* (actes du colloque international de la SOPHAU, Rennes, 4–6 avril 2003), edited by Francis Prost, pp. 281–308. Toulouse: Presses Universitaires du Mirail.

de Jong, Albert

  1997   *Traditions of the Magi: Zoroastrianism in Greek and Latin Literature.* Religions in the Graeco-Roman World 133. Leiden: Brill.

  2002   "Animal Sacrifice in Ancient Zoroastrianism: A Ritual and Its Interpretations." In *Sacrifice in Religious Experience,* edited by A. I. Baumgarten, pp. 127–48. Studies in the History of Religions 93. Leiden: Brill.

Demandt, Alexander

  1968   "Studien zur Kaaba-i-Zerdoscht." *Archäologischer Anzeiger* 3: 520–40.

Dieulafoy, Marcel-Auguste

  1884–1889   *L'art antique de la Perse: Achéménides, Parthes, Sassanides.* 5 volumes. Paris: Librairie centrale d'architecture.

  1890–1892   *L'acropole de Suse, d'après les fouilles exécutées en 1884, 1885, 1886, sous les auspices du Musée du Louvre.* 4 volumes. Paris: Hachette.

Downey, Glanville

  1961   *A History of Antioch in Syria: From Seleucus to the Arab Conquest.* Princeton: Princeton University Press.

Downey, Susan B.

  1988   *Mesopotamian Religious Architecture: Alexander through the Parthians.* Princeton: Princeton University Press.

Duchesne-Guillemin, Jacques

  1987   "Āyadana." In *Encyclopædia Iranica* online edition, New York. www.iranica.com

Dusinberre, Elspeth R. M.

  2003   *Aspects of Empire in Achaemenid Sardis.* Cambridge: Cambridge University Press.

Dyson, Robert H., Jr., and Mary M. Voigt
　2003　　　　　　　 "A Temple at Hasanlu." In *Yeki Bud, Yeki Nabud: Essays on the Archaeology of Iran in Honor of William M. Sumner*, edited by Naomi F. Miller and Kamyar Abdi, pp. 219–42. Los Angeles: Cotsen Institute of Archaeology.

Erdmann, Kurt
　1941　　　　　　　 *Das iranische Feuerheiligtum.* Sendschrift der Deutschen Orient-Gesellschaft 11. Leipzig: J. C. Hinrichs.

Facella, Margherita
　2006　　　　　　　 *La dinastia degli Orontidi nella Commagene ellenistico-romana.* Studi ellenistici 17. Pisa: Giardini.

Francfort, Henri-Paul; Jean-Claude Ligeron; and Regis de Valence
　1984　　　　　　　 *Fouilles d'Aï Khanoum 3/2. le sanctuaire du temple à niches indentées: les trouvailles.* Mémoires de la Délégation archéologique française en Afghanistan 27. Paris: De Boccard.

Frye, Richard N.
　1974　　　　　　　 "Persepolis Again." *Journal of Near Eastern Studies* 33/4: 383–86.

Fussman, Gerard
　1989　　　　　　　 "The Māṭ devakula: A New Approach to Its Understanding." In *Mathurā: The Cultural Heritage,* edited by Doris M. Srinivasan, pp. 193–99. New Delhi: Manohar Publications for American Institute of Indian Studies.

Gagošidze, Julon M.
　1983　　　　　　　 "Le temples de l'époque préchrétienne en Géorgie." In *IV Symposium International sur l'Art Géorgien,* pp. 1–12. Tbilisi: "Mecniereba."
　1992　　　　　　　 "The Temples at Dedoplis Mindori." *East and West* 42: 27–48.
　1996　　　　　　　 "The Achaemenid Influence in Iberia." *Boreas* 19: 125–36.

Galling, Kurt
　1925　　　　　　　 *Der Altar in den Kulturen des alten Orients: Eine archäologische Studie.* Berlin: Karl Curtius.

Garrison, Mark B.
　1999　　　　　　　 "Fire Altars." In *Encyclopædia Iranica* online edition, New York. www.iranica.com
　2000　　　　　　　 "Achaemenid Iconography as Evidenced by Glyptic Art: Subject Matter, Social Function, Audience and Diffusion." In *Images as Media: Sources for the Cultural History of the Near East and the Eastern Mediterranean; 1st Millennium B.C.E.,* edited by Christoph Uehlinger, pp. 115–63. Orbis biblicus et orientalis 175. Fribourg: University Press; Göttingen: Vandenhoeck & Ruprecht.
　Forthcoming　　　 *The Religious Landscape at Persepolis: Altars, Fires, and Towers as Represented in the Glyptic from the Persepolis Fortification and Treasury Archives.* Paris: De Boccard.

Garrison, Mark B., and Margaret Cool Root
　1998　　　　　　　 *Persepolis Seal Studies: An Introduction with Provisional Concordances of Seal Numbers and Associated Documents on Fortification Tablets 1–2087.* 2nd edition. Achaemenid History 9. Leiden: Nederlands Instituut voor het Nabije Oosten.
　2001　　　　　　　 *Seals on the Persepolis Fortification Tablets 1. Images of Heroic Encounter.* 2 volumes. Oriental Institute Publications 117. Chicago: The Oriental Institute.

Geller, Mark J.
　1991　　　　　　　 "New Information on Antiochus IV from Babylonian Astronomical Diaries." *Bulletin of the School of Oriental and African Studies* 54/1: 1–4.

Genito, Bruno
  2010   "The Achaemenid Empire as Seen from Its Eastern Periphery: The Case of Dahan-i Ghulaman in Sistan." In *Proceedings of the 6th International Congress of the Archaeology of the Ancient Near East, 5-10 May 2009, "Sapienza", Università di Roma*, edited by Paolo Matthiae and Licia Romano, pp. 77–92. Wiesbaden: Harrassowitz.

Gera, Dov, and Wayne Horowitz
  1997   "Antiochus IV in Life and Death: Evidence from the Babylonian Astronomical Diaries." *Journal of the American Oriental Society* 117/2: 240–52.

Ghanimati, Soroor
  2000   "New Perspectives on the Chronological and Functional Horizons of Kuh-e Khwaja in Sistan." *Iran* 38: 137–50.

Ghirshman, Roman
  1968   *Tchoga Zanbil (Dur-Untash) 2. Téménos, temples, palais, tombes.* Mémoires de la Délégation archéologique en Iran 40. Paris: Paul Geuthner.
  1976   *Terrasses sacrées de Bard-è Néchandeh et Masjid-i Solaiman: l'Iran du sud-ouest du VIIIᵉ s. av. n. ère au Vᵉ s. de n. ère.* 2 volumes. Mémoires de la Délégation archéologique en Iran 45. Leiden: Brill.

Gnoli, Gherardo
  1993a   "Dahan-e Ḡolāmān." In *Encyclopædia Iranica* online edition, New York. www.iranica.com
  1993b   "Daivadāna." In *Encyclopædia Iranica* online edition, New York. www.iranica.com
  2000   *Zoroaster in History.* Biennial Yarshater Lecture Series 2. New York: Bibliotheca Persica Press.
  2003   "Agathias and the Date of Zoroaster." In *Studies Presented to Boris Ilich Marshak on the Occasion of His 70th Birthday*, edited by Matteo Compareti, Paola Raffetta, and Gianroberto Scarcia, http://www.transoxiana.org/Eran/. Venice: Transoxiana. Updated 2006.

Godard, André
  1938   "Les monuments du feu." *Athār-e Īrān* 3: 7–82.

Grenet, Frantz
  1991   "Mithra au temple principal d'Aï Khanoum?" In *Histoire et cultes de l'Asie centrale préislamique*, edited by Paul Bernard and Frantz Grenet, pp. 147–51. Paris: Éditions du Centre National de la Recherche Scientifique.
  2008 [2012] "Mary Boyce's Legacy for Archaeologists." *Bulletin of the Asia Institute* n.s. 22: 29–46.

Gropp, Gerd
  2004   "Kaʿba-ye Zardošt." In *Encyclopædia Iranica* online edition, New York. www.iranica.com

Gullini, Giorgio
  1964   *Architettura iranica dagli Achemenidi ai Sasanidi: Il "palazzo" di Kuh-i Khwagia (Seistan).* Turin: G. Einaudi.

Haider, Peter W.
  2008   "Tradition and Change at Assur, Nineveh and Nisibis between 300 B.C. and A.D. 300." In *The Variety of Local Religious Life in the Near East in the Hellenistic and Roman Periods*, edited by Ted Kaizer, pp. 194-207. Religions in the Graeco-Roman World 164. Leiden and Boston: Brill.

Hannestad, Lise, and Daniel T. Potts

1990   "Temple Architecture in the Seleucid Kingdom." In *Religion and Religious Practice in the Seleucid Kingdom,* edited by Per Bilde, pp. 91–123. Studies in Hellinistic Civilization 1. Aarhus: Aarhus University Press.

Held, Winfried

2002   "Die Residenzstädte der Seleukiden: Babylon, Seleukeia am Tigris, Ai Khanum, Seleukeia in Pieria, Antiocheia am Orontes." *Jahrbuch des Deutschen Archäologischen Instituts* 117: 217–49.

Henkelman, Wouter F. M.

2003   "An Elamite Memorial: the šumar of Cambyses and Hystaspes." In *A Persian Perspective: Essays in Memory of Heleen Sancisi-Weerdenburg,* edited by Wouter F. M. Henkelman and Amélie Kuhrt, pp. 101–72. Achaemenid History 13. Leiden: Nederlands Instituut voor het Nabije Oosten.

2005   "Animal Sacrifice and 'External' Exchange in the Persepolis Fortification Tablets." In *Approaching the Babylonian Economy* (Proceedings of the START Project Symposium held in Vienna, 1–3 July 2004), edited by Heather D. Baker and Michael Jursa, pp. 137–65. Alter Orient und Altes Testament 330. Münster: Ugarit-Verlag.

2008   *The Other Gods Who Are: Studies in Elamite-Iranian Acculturation Based on the Persepolis Fortification Texts.* Achaemenid History 14. Leiden: Nederlands Instituut voor het Nabije Oosten.

2010   "'Consumed before the King': The Table of Darius, that of Irdabama and Irtaštuna, and that of His Satrap, Karkiš." In *Der Achämenidenhof/The Achaemenid Court (Akten des 2. Internationalen Kolloquiums zum Thema "Vorderasien im Spannungsfeld klassischer und altorientalischer Überlieferungen"; Landgut Castelen bei Basel, 23.–25. Mai 2007,* edited by Bruno Jacobs and Robert Rollinger, pp. 667–775. Wiesbaden: Harrassowitz.

2011   "Parnakka's Feast: šip in Pārsa and Elam." In *Elam and Persia,* edited by Javier Álvarez-Mon and Mark B. Garrison, pp. 89–166. Winona Lake: Eisenbrauns.

2012   "The Achaemenid Heartland: An Archaeological-Historical Perspective." In *A Companion to the Archaeology of the Ancient Near East,* edited by Daniel T. Potts, vol. 2, pp. 931–62. Blackwell Companions to the Ancient World; Literature and Culture. Chichester and Malden: Wiley-Blackwell.

Herzfeld, Ernst E.

1908   *Pasargadae: Untersuchungen zur persischen Archäologie.* Leipzig: Dieterich Verlag.
1935   *Archaeological History of Iran.* The Schweich Lectures 1934. London: H. Milford and Oxford University Press.

1938   *Altpersische Inschriften.* Berlin: Dietrich Riemer.

1941   *Iran in the Ancient East: Archaeological Studies Presented in the Lowell Lectures at Boston.* London and New York: Oxford University Press.

Hinz, Walther

1942   "Altpersische Feuerheiligtümer." *Geistige Arbeit* 9/2: 1–2.

Houtkamp, Joske

1991   "Some Remarks on Fire Altars of the Achaemenid Period." In *La religion iranienne à l'époque achéménide* (actes du colloque de Liège, 11 décembre 1987), edited by Jean Kellens, pp. 23–48. Iranica antiqua, supplément 5. Gent: Iranica Antiqua.

Huff, Dietrich

2004   "Archaeological Evidence of Zoroastrian Funerary Practices." In *Zoroastrian Rituals in Context*, edited by Michael Stausberg, pp. 593–630. Numen Book Series; Studies in the History of Religions 102. Leiden and Boston: Brill.

2008   "Formation and Ideology of the Sasanian State in the Context of Archaeological Evidence." In *The Sasanian Era*, edited by Vesta Sarkhosh Curtis and Sarah Stewart, pp. 31–59. London and New York: I. B. Tauris.

Imhoof-Blumer, Friedrich

1895   *Zur Münzkunde Kleinasiens*. Bern: Société suisse de numismatique.

Invernizzi, Antonio

1990   "Arte seleucide in Mesopotamia." *Akten des XIII. Internationalen Kongresses für Klassische Archäologie, Berlin 1988*, pp. 19–23. Mainz: Philipp von Zabern.

1994 [1996]   "Die hellenistischen Grundlagen der frühparthischen Kunst." *Archäologische Mitteilungen aus Iran* 27: 191–203.

2001   "Arsacid Dynastic Art." *Parthica* 3: 133–57.

2004   *Seleucia al Tigri: Le impronte di sigillo dagli Archivi*. Missione in Iraq 2; Mnème 3. Alexandria: Edizioni dell'Orso.

2005   "Representations of Gods in Parthian Nisa." *Parthica* 7: 71–79.

2009   *Nisa Partica: Le sculture ellenistiche*. Florence: Le Lettere.

Invernizzi, Antonio, and Carlo Lippolis

2008   *Nisa Partica: Ricerche nel complesso monumentale arsacide, 1990-2006*. Florence: Le Lettere.

Jacobs, Bruno

2011   "Nemrud Dağı." In *Encyclopædia Iranica* online edition, New York. www.iranica.com

Jeppesen, Kristian

1989   *Ikaros: The Hellenistic Settlements*, Volume 3: *The Sacred Enclosure in the Early Hellenistic Period*. Danish Archaeological Investigations on Failaka, Kuwait 3. Copenhagen: Gyldendalske boghandel,

Kaim, Barbara

2004   "Ancient Fire Temples in Light of the Discovery at Mele Hairam." *Iranica antiqua* 39: 323–37.

Kaizer, Ted

2000   "The 'Heracles Figure' at Hatra and Palmyra: Problems of Interpretation." *Iraq* 62: 219–32.

Kleiss, Wolfram

1970   "Zur Topographie des Partherhangs in Bisotun." *Archäologische Mitteilungen aus Iran* 3: 133–68.

2010   "Kangavar." In *Encyclopædia Iranica* online edition, New York. www.iranica.com

Knauss, Florian S.

2005   "Caucasus." In *L'archéologie de l'empire achéménide: nouvelles recherches*, edited by Pierre Briant and Rémy Boucharlat, pp. 197–220. Paris: De Boccard.

Kopasacheili, Maria

2011   "Hybridization of Palatial Architecture: Hellenistic Royal Palaces and Governors' Seats." In *From Pella to Gandhāra: Hybridisation and Identity in the Art and Architecture of the Hellenistic East*, edited by Anna Kouremenos, Sujatha Chandrasekaran, and Roberto Rossi, pp. 17–34. British Archaeological Reports, International Series 2221. Oxford: Archaeopress.

Kuhrt, Amélie

1996   "The Seleucid Kings and Babylonia." In *Aspects of Hellenistic Kingship*, edited by Per Bilde, Troels Engberg-Pedersen, Lise Hannestad, and Jan Zahle pp. 41–54. Studies in Hellenistic Civilization 7. Aarhus: Aarhus University Press.

Leriche, Pierre

2007a   "Bactria, Land of a Thousand Cities." In *After Alexander: Central Asia before Islam*, edited by Joe Cribb and Georgina Herrmann, pp. 121–53. Oxford: Oxford University Press for the British Academy.

2007b   "Le città dell'oriente ellenistico." In *Sulla via di Alessandro: Da Seleucia al Gandhāra*, edited by Vito Messina, pp. 83–91. Milan: Silvana Editoriale.

2010   "Europos-Doura séleucide." *Electrum* 1: 23–44.

Lindström, Gunvor

2009   "Heiligtümer und Kulte im hellenistischen Baktrien und Babylonien – ein Vergleich." In *Alexander der Grosse und die Öffnung der Welt: Asiens Kulturen im Wandel*, edited by Sven Hansen, Alfried Wieczorek, and Michael Tellenbach, pp. 127–34. Publikationen der Reiss-Engelhorn-Museen 36. Mannheim: Schnell und Steiner.

Linssen, Marc J. H.

2004   *The Cults of Uruk and Babylon: The Temple Ritual Texts as Evidence for Hellenistic Cult Practice*. Leiden and Boston: Brill.

Lippolis, Carlo

2009   "Notes on the Iranian Traditions in the Architecture of Old Nisa." *Electrum* 15: 53–72.

Litvinskij, Boris Anatol'evich, and I. R. Pičikjan

2002   *Taxt-i Sangīn der Oxus-Tempel: Grabungsbefund, Stratigraphie und Architektur*. Archäologie in Iran und Turan 4. Mainz: Philipp von Zabern.

Luschey, Heinz

1974   "Bisutun. Geschichte und Forschungsgeschichte." *Archäologischer Anzeiger* 1974: 114–49.

1989   "Bīsotūn ii. Archaeology." In *Encyclopædia Iranica* online edition, New York. www.iranica.com

Mairs, Rachel R.

2006   Ethnic Identity in the Hellenistic Far East. Ph.D. dissertation, Cambridge University.

2007   "Ethnicity and Funerary Practice in Hellenistic Bactria." In *Crossing Frontiers: The Opportunities and Challenges of Interdisciplinary Approaches to Archaeology*, edited by Hannes Schroeder, Peter J. Bray, and P. Gardner, pp. 111–23. Oxford University School of Archaeology Monograph 66. Oxford: Oxford University School of Archaeology.

2008   "Greek Identity and the Settler Community in Hellenistic Bactria and Arachosia." *Migrations and Identities* 1/1: 19–43.

In press   "The 'Temple with Indented Niches' at Ai Khanoum: Ethnic and Civic Identity in Hellenistic Bactria." In *Cults, Creeds and Contests in the Post-Classical City*, edited by Richard Alston and Onno M. van Nijf. Groningen-Royal Holloway Studies on the Greek City after the Classical Age 3. Leuven: Peeters.

Maranci, Christina
  1998   "Armenian Architecture as Aryan Architecture: The Role of Indo-European
                  Studies in the Theories of Josef Strzygowski." *Visual Resources* 13: 363–80.

Messina, Vito
  2006   *Seleucia al Tigri: L'edificio degli archivi; Lo scavo e le fasi architettoniche.* Monografie
                  di Mesopotamia 8. Florence: Le Lettere.
  2007   "Seleucia al Tigri." In *Sulla via di Alessandro: Da Seleucia al Gandhāra*, edited by
                  Vito Messina, pp. 107–15. Milan: Silvana Editoriale.

Michels, Christoph
  2010   "Zum 'Philhellenismus' der Könige con Bithynien, Pontos und Kappadokien."
                  In *Interkulturalität in der Alten Welt: Vorderasien, Hellas, Ägypten und die vielfältigen
                  Ebenen des Kontakts*, edited by Robert Rollinger, Birgit Gufler, Martin Lang, and
                  Irene Madreiter, pp. 561–89. Wiesbaden: Harrassowitz.

Mitchell, Stephen
  2005   "In Search of the Pontic Community in Antiquity." In *Representations of Empire:
                  Rome and the Mediterranean World*, edited by Alan K. Bowman, Hannah M. Cot-
                  ton, Martin Goodman, and Simon Price, pp. 35–64. Proceedings of the British
                  Academy 114. Oxford: Oxford University Press for the British Academy.
  2007   "Iranian Names and the Presence of Persians in the Religious Sanctuaries of Asia
                  Minor." In *Old and New Worlds in Greek Onomastics*, edited by Elaine Matthews, pp.
                  151–71. Proceedings of the British Academy 148. Oxford: Oxford University Press
                  for the British Academy.

Mittag, Franz Peter
  2011   "Zur Entwicklung des 'Herrscher-' und 'Dynastiekultes' in Kommagene." In
                  *Studien zum vorhellenistischen und hellenistischen Herrscherkult: Verdichtung und
                  Erweiterung von Traditionsgeflechten*, edited by Linda-Marie Günther and Sonja
                  Plischke, pp. 141–60. Oikumene 9. Berlin: Verlag Antike.

Moorey, P. R. S.
  1979   "Aspects of Worship and Ritual on Achaemenid Seals." In *Akten des VII. Interna-
                  tionalen Kongresses für Iranische Kunst und Archäologie, München 7.-10. September
                  1976*, pp. 218–26. Berlin: Dietrich Reimer.

Nylander, Carl
  1966   "Clamps and Chronology (Achaemenid Problems II)." *Iranica antiqua* 6: 130–46.

Oelmann, Franz
  1921   "Persische Temple." *Jahrbuch des Deutschen Archäologischen Instituts/Archäologi-
                  scher Anzeiger* 1921: 273–88.

Pirngruber, Reinhard
  2010   "Seleukidischer Herrscherkult in Babylon?" In *Interkulturalität in der Alten Welt:
                  Vorderasien, Hellas, Ägypten und die vielfältigen Ebenen des Kontakts*, edited by Rob-
                  ert Rollinger, Birgit Gufler, Martin Lang, and Irene Madreiter, pp. 533–49. Wies-
                  baden: Harrassowitz.

Potts, Daniel T.
  1999   *The Archaeology of Elam: Formation and Transformation of an Ancient Iranian State.*
                  New York: Cambridge University Press.
  2007   "Foundation House, Fire Altars and the Frataraka: Interpreting the Iconography
                  of Some Post-Achaemenid Persian Coins." *Iranica antiqua* 47: 271–300.

2010   "Elamite Temple-building." In *From the Foundations to the Crenellations: Essays on Temple Building in the Ancient Near East and Hebrew Bible*, edited by Mark J. Boda and Jamie R. Novotny, pp. 49–70. Münster: Ugarit-Verlag.

2011   "Iran." In *The Oxford Handbook of the Archaeology of Ritual and Religion*, edited by Timothy Insoll, pp. 811–25. Oxford: Oxford University Press.

Radner, Karen

2003a   "An Assyrian View on the Medes." In *Continuity of Empire (?): Assyria, Media, Persia*, edited by Giovanni B. Lanfranchi, Michael Roaf, Robert Rollinger, pp. 37–64. Padua: Sargon.

2003b   "A Median Sanctuary at Bīt-Ištar." In *Continuity of Empire (?): Assyria, Media, Persia*, edited by Giovanni B. Lanfranchi, Michael Roaf, Robert Rollinger, pp. 119–30. Padua: Sargon.

Rapin, Claude

1992   "Les sanctuaires de l'Asie Centrale à l'époque hellénistique." *Études de Lettres* 4: 101–24.

1995   "Indo-Greeks and Vishnuism: On an Indian Object From the Sanctuary of the Oxus and Two Temples in Taxila." In *In the Land of the Gryphons: Papers on Central Asian Archaeology in Antiquity*, edited by Antonio Invernizzi, pp. 275–91. Florence: Le Lettere.

2007   "Nomads and the Shaping of Central Asia." In *After Alexander: Central Asia Before Islam Themes in the History and Archaeology of Western Central Asia*, edited by Joe Cribb and Georgina Herrmann, pp. 29–72. Oxford and New York: Oxford University Press for the British Academy.

Razmjou, Shahrokh

2004   "The *Lan* Ceremony and Other Ritual Ceremonies in the Achaemenid Period: The Persepolis Fortification Tablets." *American Journal of Archaeology. The Journal of the Archaeological Institute of America* 42: 103–17.

2010   "Persepolis: A Reinterpretation of the Palaces and their Function." In *The World of Achaemenid Persia: History, Art and Society in Iran and the Ancient Near East*, edited by John Curtis, St. John Simpson, and the British Museum pp. 231–53. New York: I. B. Tauris.

Reinach, Salomon

1886   *Chroniques d'Orient 3/4: Fouilles et découvertes a Chypre depuis l'occupation anglaise*. Paris: Ernest Leroux.

Root, Margaret Cool

2010   "Temple to Palace-King to Cosmos: Achaemenid Foundation Texts in Iran." In *From the Foundations to the Crenellations: Essays on Temple Building in the Ancient Near East and Hebrew Bible*, edited by Mark J. Boda and Jamie Novotny, pp. 165–219. Münster: Ugarit-Verlag.

Sachs, Abraham J., and Hermann Hunger.

1996   *Astronomical Diaries and Related Texts from Babylonia*. Vienna: Verlag der Österreichischen Akademie der Wissenschaften.

Salvatori, Sandro

2003   "Pots and Peoples: The 'Pandora's Jar' of Central Asia Archaeological Research." *Rivista di Archeologia* 27: 5–20.

2007   "About Recent Excavations at a Bronze Age Site in Margiana (Turkmenistan)." *Rivista di Archeologia* 31: 11–28.

2008   "The Margiana Settlement Pattern from the Middle Bronze Age to the Parthian-Sasanian: A Contribution to the Study of Complexity." In *The Bronze Age and*

Early Iron Age in the Margiana Lowlands: Facts and Methodological Proposals for a Redefinition of the Research Strategies, edited by Sandro Salvatori, Maurizio Tosi, and Barbara Cerasetti, pp. 57–74. Oxford: Archaeopress.

Sāmī, ʿAlī

1958   *Persepolis (Takht-i-Jamshid)*. Third edition. Shiraz: Musavi Printing Office.

Sancisi-Weerdenburg, H. W. A. M.

1983   "The Zendan and the Kaʾbah." In *Kunst und Kultur der Achämenidenzeit und ihr Fortleben*, edited by Heidemarie Koch and D. N. McKenzie, pp. 145–51. Berlin: D. Reimer.

1989   "The Personality of Xerxes, King of Kings." In *Archaeologia Iranica et Orientalis: miscellanea in honorem Louis Vanden Berghe*, edited by Léon De Meyer and Ernie Haerinck, pp. 549–61. Ghent: Peeters.

Sanders, Donald H., editor

1996   *Nemrud Dağı: The Hierothesion of Antiochus I of Commagene; Results of the American Excavations Directed by Theresa B. Goell*. 2 volumes. Winona Lake: Eisenbrauns.

Saprykin, Sergej

2009   "The Religion and Cults of the Pontic Kingdom: Political Aspects." In *Mithridates VI and the Pontic Kingdom*, edited by Jakob Munk Højte, pp. 249–76. Aarhus: Aarhus University Press.

Sarkissian, G. K.

1968   "On the Problem of the Cults of the Hellenistic World: The Cult of the Royal Dynasty in Ancient Armenia." In *Studien zur Geschichte und Philosophie des Altertums*, edited by János Harmatta, pp. 283–92. Budapest: Akadémiai Kiadó.

Sarre, Friedrich, and Ernst E. Herzfeld

1910   *Iranische Felsreliefs: Aufnahmen und Untersuchungen von Denkmälern aus alt- und mittelpersischer Zeit*. Berlin: E. Wasmuth.

Scerrato, Umberto

1979   "Evidence of Religious Life at Dahan-e Ghulaman, Sistan." In *South Asian Archaeology 1977: Papers from the Fourth International Conference of the Association of South Asian Archaeologists in Western Europe, Held in the Istituto Universitario Orientale, Naples*, edited by Maurizio Taddei, vol. 2, pp. 709–35. Istituto Universitario Orientale, Seminario di studi asiatici 6. Naples: Istituto Universitario Orientale.

Schippmann, Klaus

1971   *Die iranischen Feuerheiligtümer*. Berlin: Walter de Gruyter.

Schlumberger, Daniel; Marc Le Berre; and Gérard Fussman

1983–1990   *Surkh Kotal en Bactriane*. 2 volumes. Mémoires de la Délégation archéologique française en Afghanistan 25. Paris: De Boccard.

Schmidt, Erich F.

1970   *Persepolis 3. The Royal Tombs and Other Monuments*. Oriental Institute Publications 70. Chicago: University of Chicago Press.

Schmitt, Rüdiger

1990   "Bīsotūn iii. Darius's Inscriptions." In *Encyclopædia Iranica* online edition, New York. www.iranica.com

Seidl, Ursula

1999   "Ein Monument Darius' I. aus Babylon." *Zeitschrift für Assyriologie und vorderasiatische Archäologie* 89: 101–14.

Shaked, Shaul

2004			*Le satrape de Bactriane et son gouverneur: documents araméens du IVe s. avant notre ère provenant de Bactriane*. Paris: De Boccard.

Shenkar, Michael

2007			"Temple Architecture in the Iranian World before the Macedonian Conquest." *Iran and the Caucasus* 11: 169–94.

2011			"Temple Architecture in the Iranian World in the Hellenistic Period." In *From Pella to Gandhāra: Hybridisation and Identity in the Art and Architecture of the Hellenistic East*, edited by Anna Kouremenos, Sujatha Chandrasekaran, and Roberto Rossi,, pp. 117–39. British Archaeological Reports, International Series 2221. Oxford: Archaeopress.

Sinisi, Fabrizio

2008			"Tyche in Parthia: The Image of the Goddess on Arsacid Tetradrachms." *Numismatische Zeitschrift* 116/117: 231–48.

Stronach, David

1967			"Urartian and Achaemenian Tower Temples." *Journal of Near Eastern Studies* 26: 278–88.

1978			*Pasargadae: A Report of the Excavations Conducted by the British Institute of Persian Studies from 1961 to 1963*. Oxford: Clarendon Press.

1985			"On the Evolution of the Early Iranian Fire Temple." In *Papers in Honour of Professor Mary Boyce*, edited by Jacques Duchesne-Guillemin and Pierre Lecoq, vol. 2, pp. 605–27. Acta Iranica 25. Leiden: Brill.

Stronach, David, and Michael Roaf

2007			*Nush-i Jan 1. The Major Buildings of the Median Settlement*. London: British Institute of Persian Studies; Leuven: Peeters.

Strzygowski, Josef

1927			"Le temple du feu." *Revue des Arts Asiatiques* 4: 1–14.

1930			"Feuertempel." In *Wasmuths Lexikon der Baukunst*, edited by Günther Wasmuth, vol. 2, pp. 444–55. Berlin: E. Wasmuth.

1935			"Die seelische Gehalt der iranischen Kunst – Feuertempel und Avesta." *Ars Islamica* 2/2: 189–97.

Sverchkov, L. M., and N. Boroffka

2009			"Arkheologicheskie raboty v Bandykhane v 2006–2007 gody." *Arkheologicheskie issledovaniia v Uzbekistane 2006-2007* 6: 224–34. Tashkent: "FAN" Nashrieti.

Thomson, Robert W., translator

1976			*Agathangelos: History of the Armenians*. Albany: State University of New York Press.

2006			*Movses Khorenats'i: History of the Armenians*. Revised edition. Ann Arbor: Caravan Books.

Tilia, Ann B.

1974			"Discovery of an Achaemenian Palace near Takht-i Rustam to the North of the Terrace of Persepolis." *Iran* 12: 200–04.

1977			"Discoveries at Persepolis." *American Journal of Archaeology* 81/1: 67–77.

Tirats'yan, Gevork A.

1988			Культура Древней Армении: VI. ДО Н.Э. – III. В.Н.Э. (По Архэологитсеским Данным). Yerevan: Издательство АН Армянской С.С.П. (Armenian S. S. R. Academy of Sciences Publishing House).

| 2003a | "Armenian Towns of Hellenistic Times in Light of Archaeological Research." In *From Urartu to Armenia: Florilegium Gevork A. Tirats'yan in Memoriam*, edited by Ṛouben Vardanyan, pp. 127–38. Neuchâtel: Recherches et publications. |
| 2003b | "The Tower-shaped Sepulchre of P'arak'ar and Similar Monuments in Armenia and Western Asia." In *From Urartu to Armenia: Florilegium Gevork A. Tirats'yan in Memoriam*, edited by Ṛouben Vardanyan, pp. 95–103. Neuchâtel: Recherches et publications. |

Tourovets, Alexandre

| 2005 | "Some Reflexions about the Relation between the Architecture of the Northwestern Iran and Urartu. The Layout of the Central Temple of Nush-i Djan." *Iranica antiqua* 40: 359–71. |

Tsetskhladze, Gocha R.

| 2001 | "Georgia iii. Iranian Elements in Georgian Art and Archeology." In *Encyclopædia Iranica* online edition, New York. www.iranica.com |

Tubach, Jean-Pierre

| 1995 | "Herakles vom Berge Sanbulos." *Ancient Society* 1995: 241–71. |

Tuplin, Christopher

| 2005 | "Darius' Accession in (the) Media." In *Writing and Ancient Near Eastern Society: Papers in Honour of Alan R. Millard*, edited by Piotr Bienkowski, Christopher Mee, and Elizabeth Slater, pp. 217–44. Library of Hebrew Bible/Old Testament Studies 426. New York: T & T Clark International. |

Vanden Berghe, Louis

| 1989 | "Bozpār." In *Encyclopædia Iranica* online edition, New York. www.iranica.com |

van der Spek, Robartus J.

| 1985 | "The Babylonian Temple during the Macedonian and Parthian Domination." *Biblioteca Orientalis* 42: 541–62. |
| 2006 | "The Size and Significance of the Babylonian Temples under the Successors." In *La transition: entre l'empire achéménide et les royaumes hellénistiques; vers 350–300 av. J.-C.* (actes du colloque organisé au collège de France par la chaire d'histoire et civilisation du monde achéménide et de l'empire d'Alexandre et le réseau international d'études et de recherches achéménides, 22–23 novembre 2004), edited by Pierre Briant and Francis Joannès, pp. 261–307. Paris: De Boccard. |

Virgilio, Biagio

| 2003 | *Lancia, diadema e porpora: Il re e la regalità ellenistica.* 2nd edition. Studi ellenistici 11. Pisa: Giardini. |

Wachsmuth, F.

| 1938 | "The Principal Monuments. Achaemenid Architecture" In *A Survey of Persian Art from Prehistoric Times to the Present*, edited by Arthur Upham Pope, vol. 1, pp. 309–20. London and New York: Oxford University Press. |

Wagner, Jörg

| 2000 | *Gottkönige am Euphrat: Neue Ausgrabungen und Forschungen in Kommagene.* Mainz: Philipp von Zabern. |

Waldmann, Helmut

| 1991 | *Der kommagenische Mazdaismus.* Tübingen: Wasmuth. |

Weber, Georg

| 1892 | "Hypaepa, le kaleh d'Aiasourat: Birghi-Oedémich." *Revue des études grecques* 5: 7–21. |

White, Horace, translator

1912   *Appian's Roman History* II, *Books 8.2–12.* Cambridge: Harvard University Press.

Wiesehöfer, Josef

1994   "Discordia et Defectio - Dynamis kai Pithanourgia. Die frühen Seleukiden und
                       Iran." In *Hellenismus: Beiträge zur Erforschung von Akkulturation und politischer
                       Ordnung in den Staaten des hellenistischen Zeitalters* (Akten des Internationalen
                       Hellenismus-Kolloquiums, 9.–14. März 1994 in Berlin), edited by Bernd Funck,
                       pp. 29–56. Tübingen: J. C. B. Mohr.

Wikander, Stig

1946   *Feuerpriester in Kleinasien und Iran.* Lund: C. W. K. Gleerup.

Yamamoto, Yumiko

1979   "The Zoroastrian Temple Cult of Fire in Archaeology and Literature (I)." *Orient*
                       15: 19–53.

1981   "The Zoroastrian Temple Cult of Fire in Archaeology and Literature (II)." *Orient*
                       17: 67–104.

THE CATTLEPEN AND THE SHEEPFOLD: CITIES, TEMPLES, AND PASTORAL POWER IN ANCIENT MESOPOTAMIA

*Ömür Harmanşah, Brown University**

> Enlil, when you marked out the holy settlements, you also built Nibru, your own city. You (?) ... the Ki-ur, the mountain, your pure place. You founded it in the Dur-an-ki, in the middle of the four quarters of the earth. Its soil is the life of the Land, and the life of all the foreign countries. Its brickwork is red gold; its foundation is lapis lazuli. You made it glisten on high in Sumer as if it were the horns of a wild bull. It makes all the foreign countries tremble with fear. At its great festivals, the people pass their time in abundance.
>
> (Enlil in the E-Kur [Enlil A], lines 65–73; translation from Black et al. 2004, p. 323)

Introduction: Cities, Imagination, Pastoral Power

The construction of cities with their monumental structures, ceremonial spaces, and the cultural life of urban spaces occupy a considerable amount of space in the literary compositions of the southern alluvium during the early second millennium B.C.E. In the Sumerian literary composition Enlil in the E-Kur, quoted above, the city Nibru (Nippur) is described as the precious design and sacred foundation of its patron deity Enlil. Situated in the center of the cosmos, the city and its temples constitute the civilized social space where people congregate for benevolent festivals and take refuge in times of disorder. It is quite striking how the built structure of the city (its soil, its brickwork, and its foundations) is described as a physically powerful place and how the city's architectonic brilliance derives directly from its holiness, its mythologies, and its social significance.

The scholarship on Mesopotamian cities has largely focused on a series of standard anthropological questions concerning the emergence of urbanism in the contexts of development of social complexity, state formation, labor organization, craft specialization, population estimates, and settlement hierarchies during the Late Chalcolithic and Early Bronze

* This article developed out of a very brief but densely and painfully written section in my dissertation (Harmanşah 2005), a paper read at Penn's Graduate Humanities Forum in the session "Suspending (Dis) Belief" (2004) and presented to the Cultures and Religions of the Ancient Mediterranean (CRAM) workshop at Brown University (2007). I am grateful to Matthew Rutz, Jeremiah Peterson, Naomi Miller, and the participants of the CRAM workshop for reading various versions of this manuscript and providing generous criticism and serious help. Irene J. Winter has shown extraordinary support for the present ideas in several of our conversations.

Ages.[1] In response to such well-defined research priorities, archaeological work on fourth- and third-millennium urbanization concentrated on identifying the networks of settlement and irrigation systems (Stone 2005, p. 144), while discussions of urban space have been restricted to building projects of the royal patrons with little consideration of the complexity of social relations behind the production of urban space. The spatial configuration of urban landscapes and the history of specific cities have rarely been addressed from a historically informed and spatially grounded perspective.[2] Spatial configuration in this context cannot be reduced to the physical layout of urban spaces, location of this temple and that palace, alignment of streets and watercourses, where the markets and craft quarters are located, and how wealth is distributed across residential neighborhoods, etc., but I attend to political discourses, social practice, and everyday cultural processes through which the built environment is produced, maintained, and made meaningful in the social imagination.

Recent critical studies of urban space demonstrate that, beyond settlement layouts and population statistics, cities are layered topographies of cultural histories, sites of active place-making events, and public spaces of collective action, as well as platforms for cultural imagination and political discourse.[3] Alev Çınar and Thomas Bender (2007, p. xii) have succinctly put it: "the city is located and continually reproduced through ... orienting acts of imagination, acts grounded in material space and social practice." In this article I propose that such a complex understanding of the city as a layered set of spatial practices and cultural representations is possible through an archaeological approach to urban space. Here I use archaeology in two senses of the word, both in reference to the actual disciplinary methodologies of archaeology with its thorough understanding the long-term histories of settlement, and in reference to a Foucaultian definition of archaeology as a metaphor in seeking the genealogy of institutions and geographies of power. It is therefore possible to make the case for archaeology of the city to involve the incorporation of literary representations of the built environment in order to excavate the layered meanings of urban spaces and their politics.

In this paper, I intend to contribute to the archaeological discussions of what we know about the Mesopotamian city of the second (and to a certain extent third) millennium B.C.E., by investigating the concepts of the city and urban forms of life as they were represented in the corpus of poetry in Sumerian, which largely dates to the first half of the second millennium B.C.E. On one hand, this is an attempt to bridge the gap between archaeology and text, specifically archaeological accounts of the city in the ancient Near East and the literary representations of cities. On the other hand, it also stems from my desire to arrive at an understanding of the city from a cultural studies perspective in contrast to the quantification-based discussions of urbanism and urbanization of the southern alluvium. What I wish to accomplish is to understand the poetics of urban space in the ancient Near East, and to read cities as places of human experience, everyday practice, and cultural representation. The

---

[1] For recent reviews of early Mesopotamian cities and the emergence of urbanism, see, e.g., Algaze 2008, pp. 40–92; Ur 2007; Stone 1991, 2005, and 2007; Yoffee 2005, pp. 42–90; Van De Mieroop 1997.

[2] Although see now Baker 2011 for Iron Age cities of Babylonia.

[3] I borrow the concept of "cultural imagination" from Paul Ricoeur's phenomenological theory, and his particular discussion of ideology and utopia as two forms emerging from a common, creative domain of cultural imagination, represented in the cultural forms of the everyday world such as symbols, myths, poems, ideologies, and narratives (Ricoeur 1986 and 1991; see also Kaplan 2008, pp. 205–07).

arguments presented below are not philological ones but they should be understood as a contribution to architectural history in the ancient Near East.

"City laments" are a series of texts from the Sumerian literary corpus known primarily from copies produced in the Old Babylonian curricula of scribal schools (Black et al. 2004, pp. 127–28; Cooper 2006). These long compositions involve epic narratives of the destruction or decline of particular cities such as Nippur, Eridu, Ur, and Uruk, and, most crucially, glorify the subsequent restoring of these cities and their temples and their social life by the benevolent kings of the Middle Bronze Age, especially the rulers of the First Dynasty of Isin (Tinney 1996).[4] It is part of the argument here that the particular rhetoric of the moral/ritual decline and physical destruction of cities and their restoration by devoted kings is a phenomenon specific to the southern Mesopotamian dynasties of the early second millennium B.C.E., following the wide-scale collapse at the end of the third millennium (Cooper 2006, p. 40; Michalowski 1989, pp. 1–3). These early second-millennium texts mainly come from archaeological contexts of Mesopotamian cities, which at the time were undergoing an intensive episode of re-urbanization, as is well known from the archaeological work at places such as Nippur, Ebla, Mari, and others (Harmanşah 2007). Several of the texts are known primarily from copies produced in the Old Babylonian curricula of scribal schools, which were already ideologically charged places.[5] The scribes of the various urban institutions were influential on the survival and the state of preservation of certain literary compositions by means of their "process of sifting through and selecting materials" for their school curriculum, and their editing practices were often driven by ideological motivations of their royal patrons, particularly in the case of the so-called royal hymns and other court literature (Michalowski 1995, p. 2284; see also Brisch 2007). The construction and appropriation of a mythical-ancestral past, especially linking existing structures of rulership with the mythical heroes of Uruk, and the divine legitimation of the ruler were a major part of the intellectual exercises in the scholarly production of literary works in the courts of late third- and early second-millennium kings (Visicato 2000). As has been pointed out by various scholars previously, this intensive production of literary and other texts lead to the construction of an extremely rich body of pan-Mesopotamian heritage of oral history, and articulated a collective understanding of a "Mesopotamian" past, distilled in the mythologies, histories, and cultures of storytelling (Veldhuis 2004, pp. 66–80; Michalowski 1983).

This paper discusses two important metaphors one finds in early Mesopotamian poetry concerning the city: the cattlepen and the sheepfold (Sumerian **tur** and **amaš**), which derive from the Mesopotamian conceptualization of the king as shepherd and the society as his flock on the move. I suggest that this Mesopotamian political imagination of the late second millennium B.C.E. presents us not simply the case for the usually assumed role of such metaphors as "topoi" or "stock-strophes" associated fertility and prosperity (e.g., Ferrara 1995,

---

[4] Among the city laments, most prominently known are the Nippur Lament (Tinney 1996), Eridu Lament (Green 1978), Uruk Lament (Green 1984), Lament for Sumer and Urim (Michalowski 1989), Lamentation over the Destruction of Ur, the fragmentary text Ekimar Lament, and finally but a bit marginally the Curse of Agade (Cooper 1983, pp. 20–28; more recently, Cooper 2006). However, it is crucial to note that this grouping of the concerned texts under the definition of a textual genre is essentially a modern philological construct. See Tinney 1996, pp. 11–25, for a critical dicussion of genres, critical and ethnic genres, and city laments in Sumerian literature. On the city laments, see also Michalowski 1989, pp. 8–9.

[5] On the scribal school curricula, see Delnero 2010 with previous literature; also Black et al. 2004, p. xl.

pp. 87–95) but, more significantly, an informative case of what Michel Foucault has termed "pastoral power" as expressed in the literary texts (Foucault 2007, pp. 123–34; Golder 2007). Considering Foucault's notion of pastoral power as a royal rhetoric and a form of governmentality, I discuss the cattlepen and sheepfold as historically charged spatial metaphors used by the Isin-Larsa elites of the early second millennium B.C.E. that characterize the Mesopotamian city in between economies of pasturage and agriculture, between movement and settlement, between regimes of care and exercise of power, and, perhaps most significantly, between the local political discourse and an idealized pan-Mesopotamian past. In this context the city appears as a site where the king's ideals of beneficence and pastoral power finds expression, while royal power and notions of governmentality are presented not so much as absolute rule over a territory based on violence and terror (as often assumed in current scholarly literature), but over a "multiplicity" (the society, the "flock") based on beneficence and care. Using a powerful narrative of a romanticized urban past followed by catastrophe and destruction and the subsequent restoration of social order, the pastoral discourse derives its strength from the fact that it implicitly claims a shared Mesopotamian heritage of urban and rural prosperity while promoting Isin-Larsa kings for returning that prosperity to the people by rebuilding their cities and temples, restoring their rituals and festivals, reprovisioning the everyday life. The archetypal image Mesopotamian city and its sanctuaries as cattlepen and sheepfold portrayed as archetypal enclosures of agro-pastoral life in the southern alluvium is effectively entangled with symbolisms of animal husbandry as well as suggesting a unique relationship of care between the king and his subjects.

Inspired by the ancient Near Eastern history and the Christian West, Michel Foucault proposed that early forms of governmentality depended on the idea and organization of a pastoral type of social power. This idea is perhaps best articulated in his Collège de France lecture of 8 February 1978 on "governmentality," posthumously published in the volume *Security, Territory, Population*, a collection of his 1977–1978 lectures at the Collège.[6] In this memorable lecture, Foucault traces the origins of governmentality through a discussion of two forms, "the idea and organization of a pastoral type of power ... and ... the practice of spiritual direction, the direction of souls" (Foucault 2007, p. 123). Foucault takes his audience to the pre-Christian East in order to trace the genealogy of pastoral power as a prelude to Christian pastorate: "the theme of the king, god, or chief as shepherd (*berger*) of men, who are like his flock." This state discourse of domination and technology of governmentality is well attested in the Eastern Mediterranean world, as Foucault notes, and especially well documented in ancient Mesopotamian texts, which would have been available to Foucault through monographs such as Ilse Seibert's *Hirt, Herde, König: Zur Herausbildung des Königtums in Mesopotamien* (1969). Foucault argued that the shepherd's power manifests itself in a duty, a task to be undertaken. The form it takes is not the striking display of strength and superiority, but suggests zeal, devotion, and endless application. The shepherd is someone who keeps watch, developing a sense of vigilance and a regime of care (Pandian 2008).

---

[6] Michel Foucault lectured at the Collège de France from 1971 until his death in 1984, when he held the prestigious chair the History of Systems of Thought. These lectures have been reconstructed from sound recordings of a collection of his auditors and edited by Michel Senellart and translated by Graham Burchell for publication by Éditions de Seuil/Gallimard and Picador. Very different from his densely written work, these lectures present Foucault's thought process in his later life in the form of a powerful narrative.

Lamenting the City, the Cattlepen, the Sheepfold

The distinctive group of literary compositions called city laments, where the spatial metaphors of the cattlepen and the sheepfold are particularly prominent, portray a world in distress: the socio-cultural decline and physical destruction of prominent southern Mesopotamian cities. The city laments are in general terms associated with the highly performative eršemma and balag cult songs performed by the professional lamentation (gala) priests, often in the emesal register of Sumerian (Black 1991). City lamentations from southern Mesopotamia focus on human suffering and attempt to persuade the gods to restore social order. Near Eastern lamentations in general are considered effective in restoring the fertility of the land and the prosperity of societies (Bachvarova 2008, p. 18). As lengthy epic poems, the city laments portray the destruction of the cities of the southern alluvium along with their abandonment by their patron deities, while they "glorify royal reconstruction works in order to persuade the cities' patron deities to return home and to bless, and thereby legitimate, the current king" — that is, the king who has sponsored the literary composition (Green 1984, p. 253). These texts testify to the turbulent political landscape of the end of the third millennium in Mesopotamia and the subsequent decline of its major urban centers. They also need to be considered within their very specific sociopolitical context of the early second millennium, a time when energetic rulers sponsored building activities and the composition of such literary compositions in their royal cities. It is within these texts that historically conscious official discourses are presented linking the Isin-Larsa kings and their cities to their glorious predecessors of the Mesopotamian past. The cattlepen and sheepfold metaphors emerge in this context as a nostalgic imagination of urban economic prosperity of the third millennium B.C.E. while the character of southern Mesopotamian kingship shifts toward an ideology of pastoral power. It is true that cattlepens and sheepfolds also appear in late third-millennium texts such as the hymns sponsored by the kings of the Third Dynasty of Ur or cylinders of Gudea of Lagaš (see discussion below), those rulers of the third millennium B.C.E. who were ambitious builders of cities and temples. However, these terms become truly established and effective in the context of the city laments, linking Old Babylonian ideologies of kingship that were grounded in the idea of restoring urban spaces from the widespread destruction and collapse at the end of the third millennium B.C.E.

Cities such as Nippur, Eridu, Ur, and Uruk, for which lamentations have been composed, are all urban centers deeply rooted in the history of urbanization in the southern alluvium and prominent in the social memory of the Near Eastern societies of the second and first millennia. The prominent role of urban centers in the beginnings of civilized life is perhaps best expressed in the so-called flood story, a fragmentary late Old Babylonian text known mostly from a tablet now at the University of Pennsylvania Museum (CBS 10673+10867). Here the main plot is the creation and civilization of mankind ("black-headed people"), the institution of kingship, the founding of the five mythical cities, and a subsequent "flood" (Black et al. 2004, pp. 212–15).[7] In the poem, each of the five newly founded cities — Eridug, Bad-tibira,

---

[7] The tablet was excavated at Nippur in the third season of the expedition (1893–96) and is now in the University of Pennsylvania Museum of Archaeology and Anthropology. Unfortunately, only the lower third of the tablet is preserved. The cuneiform text was published by Arno Poebel (1914). Bottéro and Kramer (1989, p. 564) point to two pieces of possible duplicates, one from Ur, the other from an unknown provenience.

Larag, Zimbir (Sippar), and Šuruppag — are allocated to a major divinity of the Sumerian pantheon. Furthermore, these cities were endowed, on the one hand, with divine powers and the rituals and the social order that maintain the well-being of the society, the so-called mes (see discussion below), and, on the other hand, with kab₂-dug-ga, a legal status of sorts that most probably had something to do with irrigation rights (Civil 1994, pp. 153–63, esp. p. 160):

> After the ... of kingship had descended from heaven, after the exalted crown and throne of kingship had descended from heaven, the divine rites and the exalted powers were perfected, the bricks of the cities were laid in holy places, their names were announced and the [kab₂-dug-ga] were distributed. The first of the cities, Eridug, was given to Nudimmud the leader. The second, Bad-tibira, was given to the Mistress. The third, Larag, was given to Pabilsaĝ. The fourth, Zimbir, was given to hero Utu. The fifth, Šuruppag, was given to Sud. And after the names of these cities had been announced and the [kab₂-dug-ga] had been distributed, the river ..., ... was watered, and with the cleansing of the small canals ... were established. (Black et al. 2004, pp. 213–14)

The civilized world is described here in the form of a series of newly founded urban centers as seats of specific divinities, while their rights to water for irrigated agriculture and their herds, and the establishment of their cult practices seem to be significant for the maintenance of the social order. Similar to this narrative of the divine foundations of cities, in the hymn Enlil in the E-kur, the foundation of the city of Nippur and its main sanctuary complex were attributed to the god Enlil, while Nippur is conceptualized as being located at the center of the universe. The city is presented as monumental in a horizontal, earthly, human domain ("as if it were the horns of a wild bull"), which "makes all the foreign countries tremble with fear" and people congregate for benevolent festivals.[8] However, Nippur is also referred as dur-an-ki "Bond-of-Upper-and-Lower-Worlds," set on the human-divine vertical axis acting as a mediatory space (Westenholz 1998, p. 46). Nippur was considered as the meeting place of the divine assembly (ukkin), therefore it held the "shrine where destinies are decreed" (eš₃ nam tar.ra), it was "the city of decisions."[9] This religious prestige bestowed a fundamental ideological significance to Nippur among the early Mesopotamian dynasties. While no political entity ever had the prestige of holding Nippur as the capital city of its dynasty, every Mesopotamian king who had a territorial claim on a regional scale in the southern alluvium had to be legitimized by the divine assembly at Nippur and had to contribute to its prosperity, the building and restoration of its temples, the celebration of its festivals (Postgate 1992, p. 33). Although Nippur is a unique example among the cities of the southern alluvium in the fourth through second millennia B.C.E., the literary representations of this city are informative in discussing the cultural significance of urban space and urban life, out of which political discourses such as pastoral power were derived.

However, the central place of cities in the political imagination finds its best expression in the city laments, as discussed above. The Nippur Lament, most probably composed at the time of Išme-Dagan of the Isin dynasty (1953–1935 B.C.E.), as convincingly argued by Steve Tinney, "formed part of the contemporary presentation of the king as a friend of Nippur and

---

[8] Enlil in the E-Kur, lines 69–73; see epigraph at the beginning of this chapter.

[9] On Nippur's religious aspects as a city, see, e.g., Sallaberger 1997 and Lieberman 1992.

a favourite of its gods." (Tinney 1996, p. 1). The poem starts with an intriguing line, essential for the present discussion:[10]

line 1	After the cattle-pen had been built for the foremost rituals—
2	How did it become haunted? When will it be restored?
3	(Where) once the brick of fate had been laid—
4	Who scattered its rituals? The lamentation is reprised:
5	The *storeroom* of Nippur, shrine Duranki,
6	How did it become haunted? When will it be restored?
7	After Kiʾur, the cult-place, had been built,
8	After the brickwork of Ekur had been built,
9	After Ubšuʾukkina had been built,
10	After shrine Egalmaḫ had been built—
11	How did they become haunted? When will they be restored?
12	How did the true city become empty?
13	Its precious designs have been defiled!
14	How were the city's festivals neglected?
15	Its magnificent rites have been overturned!

The text offers a vivid image of Nippur in decline, with its urban landscape fully endowed with several sanctuaries, each invoked by name. The city is presented as an archetypal place where the decision for monumental construction was "divinely inspired" through the laying of "the brick of fate" or alternatively "decreed brickwork" (Tinney 1996, p. 130 n. 3). A contrasting *ekphrasis* of the city's desolate landscape with respect to its urban history tells us that such powerful, originary status of the urban landscape have now lost its meaning with the falling apart of its cult practices and subsequent abandonment. According to Steve Tinney's commentary, the two words that are invoked at the very beginning of the passage tur$_3$ ("cattlepen") and me ("divine ordinances/decrees" translated here as "foremost rituals") both carry symbolic references to "well-being, … collective safety, protection and agricultural prosperity of *the cattle-pen* on the one hand, and the orderliness of the natural and social worlds, as well as the rituals needed to maintain this order, on the other" (Tinney 1996, p. 127, emphasis mine). As Tinney (ibid., p. 125) points out, the cattlepen is used as a metaphor for the city of Nippur itself. It is the sacred space *par excellence*, built in accordance with the divinely ordained precious designs (giš-hur) and for the practicing of the ritual activity — precisely in the way it should take place — which were the essential conditions for the well-being of the world order. Then what is referred in the first line is actually the original construction as well as the raison-d'être of the city Nippur-qua-the cattle pen (tur$_3$) that holds the divine essences (me).

A conspicuous idea that one finds extensively in the literary compositions is that as the gods took residence at particular cities, they also brought their divine *decorum*, their divine essences (Sumerian me) for the architectural shaping of their earthly domains: their *temples* were described as embedded in the *urban fabric of the cities* (literally, "brickwork") and confined within the monumental *city walls*. Though risking a serious anachronism here, I use the word *decorum* in the original Latin sense "literary and dramatic propriety," that is, "befitting" in general terms. The term is useful, since in the Sumerian language there seems

---

[10] The transliterations and translations are from the scholarly edition of the text, Tinney 1996. For the history of research on the text, cf. Tinney 1996, pp. 6–8.

to be much concern toward the appropriateness, fitting-character of practices in accordance with social and religious norms, especially a great concern in defining aspects of craftsmanship. Winter's argument (2000, p. 33) on the "fitting/suitable" character of Mesopotamian temples, abundantly expressed in ancient texts as the positive visual quality of the buildings that provoked admiration, neatly confirms with this idea. *Decorum* is also used in antiquity as an architectural term, to denote, the way buildings should look like in accordance with certain social/cultural norms (see, e.g., Vitruvius, *On architecture* 1.2.5–7).

In the Nippur Lament, the thorough *ekphrastic* description of the urban landscape evokes many architectural metaphors. The common poetical expression "brickwork" (sig$_4$), for example, seems to refer to the physical corpus of the urban built environment. Similarly, in the Lament for Sumer and Urim, Umma is referred as "the brickwork in the midst of the highlands" (Michalowski 1989, p. 45; Black et al. 2004, p. 132, line 155). I interpret the expression as a visual metaphor for the architectural corpus of the city itself or its large complexes (such as sanctuaries), most likely from the visual dominance of sun-dried or kiln-fired mudbricks in the structural fabric of buildings. This formed the outstanding architectonic aesthetics of early Mesopotamian architecture (Moorey 1994, pp. 302–22). It is important to see the metaphorical aspect of the expression as a cumulative architectural corpus with a distinct tectonic quality.

The word me in Sumerian represents an abstract concept that refers to an extremely loaded semantic domain. In very simplified terms, it is translated as "essence," "a thing's divinely ordained essence," or "what a thing should be" (Klein 1997, p. 211; Glassner 1992). The *Reallexikon der Assyriologie* gives the traditional meaning as "göttliche Kräfte" (in reference to A. Falkenstein) or "divine ordinances," while it is also variously translated as "[divine or princely] office" (Jacobsen 1987, p. 378) or "prescriptions" (Rosengarten 1977).[11] The me appears to be intrinsic powers or characteristics of divine beings that make the essential activities within the natural and civilized worlds exist and function properly, and manifests itself in the human world as various forms of cultural institutions, social practices, or craftly representations of the divine.[12] In this way, it is almost consistently associated in the texts with ğiš-hur that denotes "(divine) plan, (precious) design." Both can be understood as divine powers that in one way or another become materially manifest in the real world, in the objects, spaces, and bodies that are touched or infused by such supernatural agencies.

Jacob Klein argued that me often stood for "a two-dimensional symbol or image, engraved or painted on a sign, banner or standard, representing the underlying abstract concept" (Klein 1997, p. 212). This intriguing idea may suggest that there is a seamless continuity

---

[11] *RlA* s.v. me (ğarza, *parṣu*). Yvonne Rosengarten (1977, p. 2) classified the various forms of translations that appear in Sumerological literature: a) those who understand me as "divine decrees, as orders issued by divine decisions," b) those who see it as "determined destinies imposed by the gods to the humans," c) those who believe that me refers to "sorts of models, archetypes, comparable to Platonic idea," and d) those who adopted more dynamic terms as "divine powers or crafts." One should refer to the Inanna and Enki myth, where an incredible list of the 94 me are listed as Inanna steals them from Enki and transfers them to humanity. Innana's list includes an assortment of social and cultural institutions, human and divine assets. For a translation and detailed study of this text, see Farber-Flügge 1973. See also Kramer and Maier 1989, pp. 57–68; Glassner 1992; Cavigneaux 1978.

[12] One of the most comprehensive definitions of me that I have come across is that of Kramer and Maier (1989, p. 57); "fundamental, unalterable, comprehensive assortment of powers and duties, norms and standards, rules and regulations ... relating to the cosmos and its components, to gods and humans, to cities and countries, and to the varied aspects of civilized life."

between the abstract concept and its material manifestation/visual representation in the Sumerian worldview. What is crucial for the present discussion is Klein's suggestion that the divinely bestowed me become manifest in objects of divine creation within the material world, including (but not restricted to) landscapes, countries, cities, temples, objects of exquisite craftsmanship, and the body-image of the king.[13] They derive their agency from the gods and these divine powers are visually expressed in their very materiality, while the mes of the universe may become obsolete, if they are not sustained by means of decorous, (re)productive social practices, as illustrated by the Nippur Lament (above). Therefore, the habituated rituals and recurrent building activities must have been very much part of this human anxiety for sustaining the effectiveness of mes.

The Lament for Sumer and Urim starts by evoking our four parallel concepts, the divine powers, precious designs, the cattlepen, and the sheepfold:[14]

lines 1–2   To overturn the appointed times, to obliterate the divine plans [ĝiš-hur], the storms gather to strike like a flood.

3–11   An, Enlil, Enki, and Ninḫursaĝa have decided its fate—to overturn the divine powers [me] of Sumer, to lock up the favourable reign in its home, to destroy the city, to destroy the house, to destroy the cattle-pen [tur₃], to level the sheepfold [amaš]; that the cattle should not stand in the pen, that the sheep should not multiply in the fold, that watercourses should carry brackish water, that weeds should grow in the fertile fields, that mourning plants should grow in the open country ...

The pairing of the cattlepen metaphor with the city seems even more obvious in this context, with a further possibility to associate the *sheepfold* with the temple complex.[15] The destruction of the city is associated with the abandonment of the ĝiš-hur and the disruption of the me. Such relationship between the cattlepen [tur₃] and the sheepfold [amaš], concerning their appearance together in the texts was already pointed out by Tinney (1996, p. 127). Later in the Nippur Lament, the day of restoration of Sumer and Akkad, brought in by Enlil in the personality of Išme Dagan, is celebrated as "the day for building the cattle pens and founding sheepfolds." A line in a different hymn to Išme Dagan (B 49) confirms the idea that the construction of cities and temples was a primary manifestation of the prosperity of the land: "May he [Enlil] build cattle-pens for you, may he enlarge sheepfolds" (Tinney 1996, p. 176 n. 254). Furthermore, Steinkeller (1999, p. 109 and n. 19) points out that the "cattle pen"

---

[13] This very point also explains the general confusion in the attempts to translate the word me; the ambiguity between the inherently possessed me and its representational manifestations in the human world. From the very different texts, in particular within the context of city laments, one gets the impression that mes of temples, cities, countries, etc., may become obsolete if they do not receive maintenance and utmost care, from the side of the human practices. It is exactly at this point that the idea of "foremost rituals" comes into play, since it is believed that the repeated and continuous cultic activity keeps the mes of the country alive and functioning, in such a way that the world is in order.

[14] Transliterations and translations are from Black et al. 2004, pp. 128–29; see also Michalowski 1989.

[15] Similarly, in the composition Enmerkar and Ensuhkešdanna, the city Ereš of the god Nisaba is also metaphorically referred as "the cattlepen, the house where the cows live" (line 172) and its sanctuary as "the holy sheepfold, the sheepfold of Nisaba" (line 185); Berlin 1979, pp. 50–53. In the Lament for Sumer and Urim (line 186), "the settlements of the E-danna of Nanna, like substantial cattle-pens, were destroyed" and so was Ki-abrig "which used to be filled with numerous cows and numerous calves" (line 200) (Black et al. 2004, p. 133).

appears as one of the recipients of beer in "two Uruk tablets dealing with the distribution of beer," along with "chief-administrators," "the festival of the Inana of the west (= evening)," and the "chief-supervisor of the gipar(?)."

It was also essential for the Mesopotamian kings to connect their political realm with that of the divine. As I have tried to demonstrate above, the functioning of all the urban institutions and thus the well-being of the social order were made possible by the "(precious) designs" [giš-hur] and "(divine) ordinances" [me] which I would like to call "divine *decorum*" of kingship. These would then shape the cultural landscape of the city, from the way the ritual activity had to be carried out, to the manner in which the required cultic building projects had to be accomplished with appropriate architectural qualities that befitted the divine me. It is possible therefore to argue that the seemingly abstract concepts of giš-hur and me are understood to be materially manifest or visually expressed in the architectural corpus, the urban fabric of Mesopotamian cities, as a divine *decorum* that guides the shaping of built environments and maintained by ongoing social and spatial practices.

Visual Representations and the Architecture of the Cattlepen

As a major urban economic institution within the Mesopotamian city, the temple was the source of collective identity, not simply because it held a significant place in the everyday social life with its cult activities but also because it was the "wealthy neighbor," a redistributive institution that initiated extensive agricultural production, animal husbandry, long-distance trade, and craft production (Postgate 1992, pp. 135–36; Stone 2005). It is well documented that the specialized economy of the early Mesopotamian urban institutions heavily depended on animal husbandry, especially cattle and sheep herding (Zeder 1991; Greenfield 2010), and this must have had important implications for the configuration of fortified urban spaces in the southern alluvium as well as the pictorial representations of them. Likewise, the extraordinarily rich visual repertoire of the late Uruk-period seal impressions, monumental stone vases, and inlaid architectural decorations excavated from the contexts of early urbanization in southern Mesopotamia form a corpus of imagery that corresponds well with the literary evidence by presenting the spatial realm of the temple household with frequent representations of herds of cattle (Seibert 1969, pp. 23–35; see also discussion in Winter 2010). In several of the published seals and seal impressions of the Late Uruk period, one finds a rich iconography of cattle herds, related buildings, and a prominent kingly figure identified by his special garb and his caring for the flocks. The associated architectural structures in these scenes are usually elaborately depicted and interpreted as temples and storehouses (Kawami 2001). Irene Winter (2010, p. 121) has suggested that the mudhif-like reed structure depicted on the alabaster trough from Uruk/Warka can be interpreted as a "sheep-fold."[16] Similar representations of reed structures with calves, lambs, and ringed bundle "standards" of Inana emerging from them are frequently attested on Late Uruk cylinder seals (fig. 15.1) and Early Bronze Age carved stone bowls from Ur and Khafaje.[17] I suggest that these vernacular reed

---

[16] See Moortgat 1969, pls. 17–18. This trough, 10.8 cm high and 103.0 cm long, was excataed in the Eanna complex; see Andrae 1930.

[17] Kawami 2001, p. 40; Winter 2010. For an example of green stone vase with relief representations of

a reed structure with Inanna reed bundles, found in the Early Dynastic levels of small neighborhood shrine at Khafaje, see Frankfort 1936, p. 69, fig. 54.

structures of the southern Mesopotamian marshes already point to an idealized primordial architectural type associated with abundance and urban prosperity on the one hand, and the cult of Inanna on the other. It is possible to assume that this Mesopotamian heritage of Late Uruk urbanization may have continued to percolate in the urban and architectural cultures of the third millennium B.C.E. in southern Mesopotamia and have impacted the formation of the powerful symbolism of the pastoral during the Early and Middle Bronze Ages.

Later and more complex examples of this architectural narrative of abundance and prosperity are seen in the Early Bronze Age. One important architectural ensemble comes from a small but precious temple of Ninhursag in southern Mesopotamia at the small site of Tell al Ubaid, built or restored by a certain king named A'annepada, son of Mesannepada, kings known from the so-called First Dynasty of Ur (ca. 2400 B.C.E.). This Early Dynastic IIIA–IIIB temple was excavated by H. R. Hall in 1919 and followed up by Leonard Woolley in 1923–24 (figs. 15.2–6) (Hall and Woolley 1927). The temple, which was in continuous use from the Early Dynastic III to the Ur III period, stood on a high mudbrick platform and was surrounded by an oval enclosure wall (Collins 2003, p. 84). The building presents us a rich assemblage of architectural technologies of cladding and decoration at the time. Two beautifully constructed columns that flanked the entrance were built from palm logs covered with a coating of bitumen and inlaid with mother of pearl, pink limestone, and black shale (fig. 15.3). The copper alloy high relief figure of the famous lion-headed Imdugud bird clasping two stags topped the entrance to the temple while the facade was decorated with a row of copper bulls, shell-inlaid narrative friezes, and elaborate multi-colored clay nails (fig. 15.4). This iridescent and luminous quality of the materials used on the building (mother of pearl, shell, copper alloy, black shale, limestone, among other materials) perhaps speaks to the notion of me, as a craftly representation of the divine — divine power made visible through the tantalizing exotic materials of faraway lands, as illustrated in the famous passage in Enmerkar and the Lord of Aratta (lines 37–54), where Enmerkar, king of Uruk, asks Inana to have the lord of Aratta provide precious exotic materials ("stones of their hills and mountains") for the building of Inana's holy Gipar, and explicitly says that this construction would cause Enmerkar's mes "become evident in Kullab" (line 53) (Vanstiphout 2003, p. 58).

More interestingly, on the facade of the temple of Ninhursag at Tell al Ubaid, an inlaid narrative relief panel represents the temple as a cattlepen (figs. 15.5–6). The narrative sequence, made with inlaid *Tridacna* shells and limestone on a bitumen and black shale background, depicts a milking scene with the dominance of human figures on the left and cattle on the right, while the composition is centered on the image of the temple. The vertical linear features in the representation of the temple most likely allude to the reed construction (upright reed bundles fastened together with bands of rope). The scene of cattle emerging from a gate is also known from Late Uruk cylinder seal designs and low relief decoration on an alabaster troughs (see discussion in Hall and Woolley 1927, pp. 113–14; and Winter 2010, p. 203). The architecture of this temple may be considered as an archaizing representation of an archetypal enclosure of a reed structure as cattle pen, as one would associate with the long-term building practices in the marshy landscape of the south. In light of the above discussion of Mesopotamian cities and temples as cattlepen and sheepfold, this scene becomes not just symbolically linked to Ninhursag, "lady of the steppe," but evocative from a political point of view as well. The political discourse operates on multiple levels here, both through the exuberant use of precious materials and prestigious craft technologies in the decoration of the temple facade (power over exotic resources of exotic landscapes), and its adherence to the worldview associated with pastoral power. The deliberate contrast in materials and technologies between the representation of the temple on the inlaid panel as an archetypal reed construction versus the luxuriously clad architectonics of the actual temple itself is striking. In my view, it points to the idealization of the temple household as a site of production grounded in the traditions of animal husbandry (therefore prosperity and fecundity), all embodied in the visual and architectural metaphor of the cattlepen. Speaking from this example, then, the architectural metaphor plays with temporality, both with references to a prosperous distant past in the collective Mesopotamian memory and a promised future guaranteed by the builder-king, while the representations remain deeply embedded in the oral culture of mythological tales and political discourses. Furthermore, the architectural metaphor also plays with materiality, shifting our focus from vernacular reed constructions of deep antiquity to the current ruling power's luxuriously sponsored monuments. While the decorum is maintained, political messages are also delivered.

The Shepherd and the Pastoral Power

In line with the literary, spatial, and visual metaphors of cattlepen and sheepfold, Mesopotamian rulers of the late third and early second millennium used "shepherd" [sipa] as a royal title, as sponsors of the making of those places.[18] In a cone inscription from Ur, Rim Sîn I was credited to have built a temple at Ur, so that the god Dumuzi, "*shepherd* of the broad steppe," would "multiply cattle and sheep in the cattle pens and sheepfolds" (Frayne 1990, E4.2.14.4, lines 20–24). If the fecundity of the land depended on the maintenance of its cities and temples, it was the *shepherd* who took credit for "building cattle pens and founding sheepfolds." Gudea was the "true shepherd" of his people on the behalf of Ningirsu.[19] Ur Namma was called "the foremost shepherd of Enlil" while Šulgi took on the title of being "the shepherd of the black-headed-people" or "shepherd of the land," among others.[20] In the Hymn to Nisaba, Išbi-Erra is summoned to exercise "the shepherdship of all the people." Examples can be multiplied, especially for the late third and early second millennium B.C.E., but it is evident that the early Mesopotamian rulers seem to have chosen to be "shepherds" as "the benevolent guardian" of their people. The shepherdship is then demonstrated through the construction and maintanence of sheepfolds and cattlepens. In a hymn to Rim-Sîn, king of Larsa (1822–1763 B.C.E.), it is declared to him that at the city of his kingship, Larsa, "where the mes of rulership have been cast," he has rightly been "chosen for the shepherdship of Sumer and Akkad."[21]

---

[18] For a thorough survey of the occurrences of Sumerian sipa, see Westenholz 2004 and Seux 1967, pp. 441–46. For Akkadian *rē'û* (= sipa) in the literature, see Seux 1967, p. 244–50. It is clear that the royal epithet "shepherd" was a long-term aspect of Mesopotamian kingship, so much so that the Late Assyrian rulers, who had a keen interest in establishing their ties to the ancient heroes of Mesopotamia, used it in the Iron Ages as well. See also Selz 2010, p. 10.

[19] See, e.g., Gudea Cylinder A vii 9; A xi 5; A xiv 5; A xxiv 9; A xxv 22; B viii 17 and B ii 7; most recent editions of the texts are found in Edzard 1997, pp.

69–101 (texts: Gudea E3/1.1.7CylA and B), and Wilson 1996, pp. 129–96. The phrase is alternatively as "righteous shepherd" or "faithful shepherd."

[20] Reisman 1969, p. 17, no. 61. See also Šulgi X 40, where Šulgi is given "the shepherdship of all the lands" [sipa-kur-kur-ra]; Klein 1981, pp. 138–39.

[21] Postgate 1992, p. 261, text 14:1. In other texts, Rim-Sin is referred as the "true shepherd"; see Kuhrt 1995, vol. 1, p. 79. Compare the expression for Šulgi in Šulgi D, line 60: "Enlil, the king of all the lands, [gave] you the shepherdship of the land" (Klein 1981, pp. 74–75).

This correlation of metaphorical expressions in the mytho-poetic language of the Sumerian compositions suggests an illuminating semantic nexus between the architecture of the city and the temple complex as the cattlepen and the sheepfold, and the king as the shepherd, holding the main institutions of the Mesopotamian society. As Anand Pandian has recently argued, one could see this very relationship in the Foucaultian concept of "pastoral power" as a form of "biopolitics" of the state, referring to "the government of a population modeled on the relationship between a figurative shepherd and the individual members of a flock" (Pandian 2008, p. 86). However, it is important to note that these metaphors point, not necessarily to a de-humanizing, enslaving discourse of the state toward its people, but, on the contrary, to the intimate and very genuine care that a shepherd offers to the well-being of his flock, as Pandian elegantly argues. This is somewhat in contrast to modern Western conceptualizations of shepherding as a political metaphor. In the context of everyday practice in early Mesopotamian cities, cattlepen and sheepfold appear as the perfect spatial metaphors that speak of this very intimacy and care between the king and his subjects. The literary evidence suggests that this was a prominent political discourse used by several of the early Mesopotamian kings and explains the reasons why construction of cities and temples occupy such a large space in their public monuments.

Conclusions

What I aim to do in this paper is an attempt to capture the cultural imagination of the early Mesopotamian city in the city laments of the early second millennium B.C.E. with a focus on the spatial metaphors of tur₃ and amaš, cattlepen and sheepfold, which present a nostalgic understanding of the then-lost cities of the Mesopotamian past. The urban space is reconstructed as a sheltering enclosure for the primary animals of domestication, sheep and cattle, while pastoralism and animal husbandry are imagined as primordial occupation of the early urban life. The concepts of me and giš-hur support this mytho-poetic and utopic conceptualization of the origins of the city — as divinely sanctioned and constructed spaces that are then maintained by appropriate rituals and divine powers. Here, I borrow Paul Ricoeur's definition of cultural imagination as "a map of ideas, stories, and images a society has about itself that integrates human action through interpretative schemas" (Kaplan 2008, pp. 204–05). Three important concepts in understanding cultural imagination are ideology, utopia, and memory. Ideology is an exchange between makers of political discourse and the audience of that discourse, and it aims to consolidate social order for the good of a dominant class. Utopia is innovative thinking that shatters that social order for the sake of liberation, and project the society to an imagined ideal that is either located in the future or the past.[22] Memory is a collectively shared vision of the past, an aspect of identity and belonging; collectively produced and politically manipulated body of the knowledge of the past (embedded in orality, texts, monuments, and visual culture).

In the rapidly changing urban environment of the early second millennium B.C.E., we see the articulation of a vision of ancient cities as archetypal enclosures of cattlepen and sheepfold, which constituted the spatial components of pastoral power while evoking nostalgic

---

[22] See Pongratz-Leisten 2006 on a Mesopotamian example of an urban utopia constructed in the texts of Gudea of Lagaš.

notions of primordial pastoral life and its associations of prosperity and moral purity. In the context of the political rhetoric of the kings of First Dynasty of Isin, the benevolent and caring king appears as a builder of cities and by definition becomes the shepherd of his flock. This reflection on the early Mesopotamian past by the early second-millennium kings is a creative one that somehow establishes an evolutionary perspective from pastoral lifestyles to agricultural and mercantile urban economies.

The visual metaphors that were associated with the city, the temple and the urban architectural corpus, and the visual metaphors that glorified the corporeal image of the king, were derived from similar concepts. As it is evident in the long-term concept of the Mesopotamian king as a devoted builder, the "*roi-bâtisseur*," the king had to build cities, temples, and other monumental buildings not only for satisfying the spatial needs for the functioning of urban institutions, but also for the maintenance of a worldly order (Lackenbacher 1992). The spectacular layout of his cities, the perfection of his architectural projects and the performance of urban rituals, were intimately linked to the perfection of the bodily image of the king, which was always the focus of attention in the public sphere. This "corporeal integrity of the monarch," to use Michel Foucault's term (2006) was maintained through a set of practices, performances, and discourses ranging from building activities to state spectacles involving the king's own body; from the bringing of exotic raw materials and goods to state-sponsored literary compositions. The divine and politicized power of the Mesopotamian ruler became manifest in the king's own bodily image: while the urban image of his cities, both of which were endowed with divinely inspired qualities of craftsmanship. This ideological agenda of the perfection of the king's image then is used as a legitimation for the acquisition of exotic and precious raw materials and skilled craftsmanship from marginal landscapes.

Mesopotamian literary sources are rich for understanding the image of the city in the late third- and early second-millennium collective imagination. In the Mesopotamian poems of this time period, the image of the city was associated with metaphors of the *cattlepen* and *sheepfold* that were heavily charged with socio-symbolic representations of economic prosperity, civilization of the inhabited world, and its maintenance through cultural institutions. In the discursive structure of these texts, the body of the king, the rituals of his city, the craftly artifacts in the public sphere, as well as public monuments of the city, all derive their material power from the divine mes endowed to them, and by this means constitute coherent components of a utopic ideal of worldly order. We must, of course, situate this utopic ideal in the political context of such state-sponsored literature under the Ur III and Isin-Larsa kings. Equally important, however, is the task for us to trace the intimate dialogue between the social practices, particularly building practices at the time of the composition of these poems and the literary representations that emerge in them. The Mesopotamian city then can only be understood through the careful parsing of social imaginations, official ideologies, as well as material practices in the making of the social world.

Figure 15.1. Sealing with representations of reed structures with cows, calves, lambs, and ringed bundle "standards" of Inana (drawing by Diane Gurney. After Hamilton 1967, fig. 1)

Figure 15.2. Tell al Ubaid, Temple of Ninhursag. Isometric reconstruction. Early Dynastic period (ca. 2600 B.C.E.) (Hall and Woolley 1927)

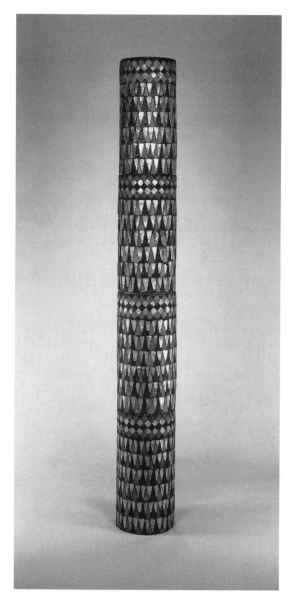
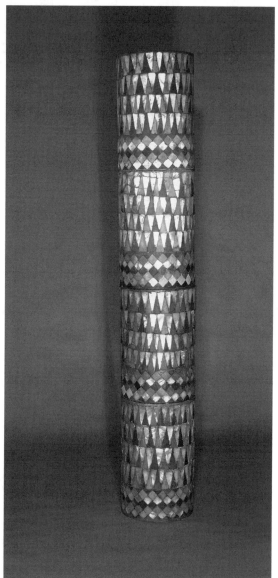

Figure 15.3. Tell al Ubaid, Temple of Ninhursag. Inlaid columns with red limestone, shell, and bitumen. Early Dynastic period (ca. 2600 B.C.E.) (© The Trustees of the British Museum)

Figure 15.4. Tell al Ubaid, Temple of Ninhursag. Copper bull sculpture from the frieze. Early Dynastic period (ca. 2600 B.C.E.) (© The Trustees of the British Museum)

Figure 15.5. Tell al Ubaid, Temple of Ninhursag. Tridacna shell-inlaid architectural frieze with bitumen and black shale. Early Dynastic period (ca. 2600 B.C.E.) (© The Trustees of the British Museum)

Figure 15.6. Tell al Ubaid, Temple of Ninhursag. Tridacna shell inlaid architectural frieze with bitumen and black shale. Early Dynastic period (ca. 2600 B.C.) (Hall and Woolley 1927)

Abbreviation

RlA   Erich Ebeling et al., eds, *Reallexikon der Assyriologie und vorderasiatischen Archäo-*
                        logie. Berlin: De Gruyter, 1928–

Bibliography

Algaze, Guillermo
    2008   *Ancient Mesopotamia at the Dawn of Civilization: The Evolution of an Urban Landscape*.
                        Chicago: University of Chicago Press

Andrae, Walter
    1930   "Steinbecher." *Amtliche Berichte Berliner Museen* 51/1: 2–4.

Bachvarova, Maria R.
    2008   "Sumerian Gala Priests and Eastern Mediterranean Returning Gods: Tragic Lamen-
                        tation in Cross-cultural Perspective." In *Lament: Studies in the Ancient Mediterranean
                        and Beyond*, edited by Ann Suter, pp. 18–52. Oxford: Oxford University Press.

Baker, Heather D.
    2011   "From Street Altar to Palace: Reading the Built Environment of Urban Baby-
                        lonia." In *The Oxford Handbook of Cuneiform Culture*, edited by Karen Radner and
                        Eleanor Robson, pp. 533–52. Oxford Handbooks. Oxford: Oxford University Press.

Berlin, Adele
    1979   *Enmerkar and Ensuhkešdanna: A Sumerian Narrative Poem*. Occasional Publications
                        of the Babylonian Fund 2. Philadelphia: The University Museum.

Black, Jeremy A.
    1991   "Eme-sal Cult Songs and Prayers." *Aula Orientalis* 9: 23–36.
    1998   *Reading Sumerian Poetry*. Ithaca: Cornell University Press.

Black, Jeremy A.; Graham Cunningham; Eleanor Robson; and Gábor Zólyomi
    2004   *The Literature of Ancient Sumer*. Oxford: Oxford University Press.

Bottéro, Jean, and Samuel Noah Kramer
    1989   *Lorsque les dieux faisaient l'homme: mythologie mésopotamienne*. Paris: Gallimard.

Brisch, Nicole M.
    2007   *Tradition and the Poetics of Innovation: Sumerian Court Literature of the Larsa Dynasty
                        (c. 2003–1763 B.C.E.)*. Alter Orient und Altes Testament 339. Münster: Ugarit-Verlag.

Cavigneaux, Antoine
    1978   "L'Essence divine." *Journal of Cuneiform Studies* 30/3: 177–85.

Çınar, Alev, and Thomas Bender, editors
    2007   "Introduction. The City: Experience, Imagination, and Place." In *Urban Imagi-
                        naries: Locating the Modern City*, edited by Alev Çınar and Thomas Bender, pp.
                        xi–xxvi. Minneapolis: University of Minnesota Press.

Civil, Miguel
    1994   *The Farmer's Instructions: A Sumerian Agricultural Manual*. Aula orientalis Supple-
                        menta 5. Barcelona: Editorial AUSA.

Collins, Paul

    2003   "Al Ubaid." In *Art of the First Cities: The Third Millennium B.C. from the Mediterranean to the Indus*, edited by Joan Aruz, pp. 84–88. New York: Metropolitan Museum of Art.

Cooper, Jerrold S.

    1983   *The Curse of Agade.* Johns Hopkins Near Eastern Studies. Baltimore: Johns Hopkins University Press.

    2006   "Genre, Gender and the Sumerian Lamentation." *Journal of Cuneiform Studies* 58: 39–47.

Delnero, Paul

    2010   "Sumerian Extract Tablets and Scribal Education." *Journal of Cuneiform Studies* 62: 53–69.

Edzard, Dietz Otto

    1997   *Gudea and His Dynasty.* The Royal Inscriptions of Mesopotamia, Early Periods 3/1. Toronto: University of Toronto Press.

Farber-Flügge, Gertrud

    1973   *Der Mythos "Inanna und Enki" unter besonderer Berücksichtigung der Liste der me.* Studia Pohl 10. Rome: Biblical Institute Press.

Ferrara, A. J.

    1995   "Topoi and Stock-strophes in Sumerian Literary Tradition: Some Observations, Part I." *Journal of Near Eastern Studies* 54: 81–117.

Foucault, Michel

    2006   *Psychiatric Power: Lectures at the Collège de France, 1973-1974*, edited by Jacques Lagrange and Arnold I. I. Davidson, translated by Graham Burchell. New York: Picador.

    2007   *Security, Territory, Population: Lectures at the Collège de France, 1977-1978*, edited by Michel Senellart. New York: Picador.

Frankfort, Henri

    1936   *Progress of the Work of the Oriental Institute in Iraq, 1934/35: Fifth Preliminary Report of the Iraq Expedition.* Oriental Institute Communication 20. Chicago: University of Chicago Press.

Frayne, Douglas R.

    1990   *Old Babylonian Period (2003-1595 B.C.).* The Royal Inscriptions of Mesopotamia, Early Periods, 4. Toronto: University of Toronto Press.

Glassner, Jean-Jacques

    1992   "Inanna et les me." *Nippur at the Centennial: Papers Read at the 35ᵉ Rencontre assyriologique internationale, Philadelphia, 1988*, edited by Maria deJong Ellis, pp. 55–86. Occasional Publications of the Samuel Noah Kramer Fund 14. Philadelphia: S. N. Kramer Fund, Babylonian Section, University Museum.

Golder, Ben

    2007   "Foucault and the Geneaology of Pastoral Power." *Radical Philosophy Review* 10: 157–76.

Green, M. W.

    1978   "The Eridu Lament." *Journal of Cuneiform Studies* 30/3: 127–67.

    1984   "The Uruk Lament." *Journal of the American Oriental Society* 104/2: 253–79.

Greenfield, Henri

    2010   "The Secondary Product Revolution: The Past, The Present and the Future." *World Archaeology* 42: 29–54.

Hall, H. R., and C. Leonard Woolley
  1927   *Al-'Ubaid: A Report on the Work Carried Out at Al-'Ubaid for the British Museum in 1919 and for the Joint Expedition in 1922-3*. Oxford: Oxford University Press.

Hamilton, R. W.
  1967   "A Sumerian Cylinder Seal with Handle in the Ashmolean Museum." *Iraq* 29/1: 34–41.

Harmanşah, Ömür
  2005   Spatial Narratives, Commemorative Practices and the Building Project: New Urban Foundations in Upper Syro-Mesopotamia During the Early Iron Age. Ph.D. dissertation, University of Pennsylvania.

  2007   "Upright Stones and Building Narratives: Formation of a Shared Architectural Practice in the Ancient Near East." In *Ancient Near Eastern Art in Context: Studies in Honor of Irene J. Winter by Her Students*, edited by Jack Cheng and Marian H. Feldman, pp. 69–99. Leiden: Brill.

Jacobsen, Thorkild
  1987   *The Harps that Once…: Sumerian Poetry in Translation*. Yale University Press: New Haven.

Kaplan, David M.
  2008   "Ricoeur's Critical Theory." In *Reading Ricoeur*, edited by David M. Kaplan, pp. 197–212. Albany: State University of New York Press.

Kawami, T. S.
  2001   "The Cattle of Uruk: Stamp Seals and Animal Husbandry in the Late Uruk/Jemdet Nasr Period." In *Proceedings of the XLVe Rencontre Assyriologique International*, Part 2: *Seals and Seal Impressions*, edited by William W. Hallo and Irene J. Winter, pp. 31–48. Bethesda: CDL Press.

Klein, Jacob
  1981   *Three Šulgi Hymns: Sumerian Royal Hymns Glorifying King Šulgi of Ur*. Ramat Gan: Bar-Ilan University Press.

  1997   "The Sumerian me as a Concrete Object." *Altorientalische Forschungen* 24: 211–18.

Kramer, Samuel Noah, and John R. Maier
  1989   *Myths of Enki, the Crafty God*. New York: Oxford University Press.

Kuhrt, Amélie
  1995   *The Ancient Near East, c. 3000-330 B.C.* 2 volumes. Routledge History of the Ancient World. London: Routledge.

Lackenbacher, Sylvie
  1982   *Le roi bâtisseur: le récits de construction assyriens des origines à Teglatphalasar III*. Études Assyriologique, Éditions Recherche sur les civilisations: Paris.

Lieberman, Stephen J.
  1992   "Nippur: City of Decisions." In *Nippur at the Centennial: Papers Read at the 35e Rencontre assyriologique internationale, Philadelphia, 1988*, edited by Maria deJong Ellis, pp. 127–36. Occasional Publications of the Samuel Noah Kramer Fund 14. Philadelphia: S. N. Kramer Fund, Babylonian Section, University Museum.

Michalowski, Piotr
  1983   "History as Charter: Some Observations on the Sumerian King List." *Journal of the American Oriental Society* 103: 237–48.

  1989   *The Lamentation Over the Destruction of Sumer and Ur*. Winona Lake: Eisenbrauns.

  1995   "Sumerian Literature: An Overview." In *Civilizations of the Ancient Near East*, edited by Jack M. Sasson, vol. 4, pp. 2279–91. New York: Simon & Schuster Macmillan.

Moorey, P. R. S.
    1994   *Ancient Mesopotamian Materials and Industries: The Archaeological Evidence*. Oxford: Oxford University Press.

Pandian, Anand
    2008   "Pastoral Power in the Postcolony: On the Biopolitics of the Criminal Animal in South India." *Cultural Anthropology* 23/1: 85–117.

Poebel, Arno
    1914   *Historical and Grammatical Texts*. Publications of the Babylonian Section 5. Philadelphia: University Museum.

Pongratz-Leisten, Beate
    2006   "Gudea and His Model of an Urban Utopia." *Baghdader Mitteilungen* 37: 45–59.

Postgate, J. Nicholas
    1992   *Early Mesopotamia: Society and Economy at the Dawn of History*. London: Routledge.

Reisman, Daniel
    1969   Two Neo-Sumerian Royal Hymns. Ph.D. dissertation, University of Pennsylvania.

Ricoeur, Paul
    1986   *Lectures on Ideology and Utopia*. Edited by George H. Taylor. New York: Columbia University Press.
    1991   *From Text to Action*. Translation of *Du texte à l'action*. Translated by Kathleen Blamey and John B. Thompson. Evanston: Northwestern University Press.

Rosengarten, Yvonne
    1977   *Sumer et le sacré: le jeu des prescriptions (me), des dieux, et des destins.* Paris: De Boccard.

Sallaberger, Walther
    1997   "Nippur als religiöses Zentrum Mesopotamiens im historischen Wandel." In *Die orientalische Stadt: Kontinuität, Wandel, Bruch*, edited by Gernot Wilhelm, pp. 147–68. Saarbrücken: Saarbrücker Druckerei und Verlag.

Seibert, Ilse
    1969   *Hirt, Herde, König: Zur Herausbildung des Königtums in Mesopotamien*. Deutsche Akademie der Wissenschaften zu Berlin, Schriften der Sektion für Altertumswissenschaft 53. Berlin: Akademie-Verlag.

Selz, Gebhard J.
    2010   "'The Poor Are the Silent Ones in the Country': On the Loss of Legitimacy; Challenging Power in Early Mesopotamia." In *Who Was King? Who Was Not King? The Rulers and the Ruled in the Ancient Near East*, edited by Petr Charvát and Petra Maříková Vlčková, pp. 1–15. Prague: Institute of Archaeology of the Academy of Sciences of the Czech Republic.

Seux, M.-J.
    1967   *Épithètes royales akkadiennes et sumériennes*. Paris: Letouzey et Ané.

Steinkeller, Piotr
    1999   "On Rulers, Priests and Sacred Marriage: Tracing the Evolution of Early Sumerian Kingship." In *Priests and Officials in the Ancient Near East* (papers of the Second Colloquium on the Ancient Near East, The City and Its Life, held at the Middle Eastern Culture Center in Japan, Mitaka, Tokyo, March 22–24, 1996), edited by Kazuko Watanabe, pp. 103–37. Heidelberg: Universitätsverlag C. Winter.

Stone, Elizabeth C.
    1991   "The Spatial Organization of Mesopotamian Cities." *Aula Orientalis* 9: 235–42.

2005   "Mesopotamian Cities and Countryside." In *A Companion to the Ancient Near East*, edited by Daniel C. Snell, pp. 141–54. Malden: Blackwell.

2007   "The Mesopotamian Urban Experience." In *Settlement and Society: Essays Dedicated to Robert McCormick Adams*, edited by Elizabeth C. Stone, pp. 213–34. Ideas, Debates, and Perspectives 3. Los Angeles: Cotsen Institute of Archaeology Press; Chicago: The Oriental Institute.

Tinney, Steve
1996   *The Nippur Lament: Royal Rhetoric and Divine Legitimation in the Reign of Išme-Dagan of Isin (1953-1935 B.C.)*. Occasional Publications of the Samuel Noah Kramer Fund 15. Philadelphia: University Museum.

Ur, Jason A.
2007   "Early Mesopotamian Urbanism: A New View from the North." *Antiquity* 81: 585–600

Van De Mieroop, Marc
1997   *The Ancient Mesopotamian City*. Oxford University Press: Oxford.

Vanstiphout, H. J. L
2003   *Epics of Sumerian Kings: The Matter of Aratta*. Writings from the Ancient World 20. Atlanta: Society of Biblical Literature.

Veldhuis, Niek
2004   *Religion, Literature, and Scholarship: The Sumerian Composition "Nanše and the Birds."* Cuneiform Monographs 22. Leiden: Brill.

Visicato, Giuseppe
2000   *The Power and the Writing: The Early Scribes of Mesopotamia*. Bethesda: CDL Press.

Westenholz, Joan Goodnick
1998   "The Theological Foundation of the City, the Capital City and Babylon," in *Capital Cities: Urban Planning and Spiritual Dimensions*, edited by Joan Goodnick Westenholz, pp. 43–54. Jerusalem: Bible Lands Museum.

2004   "The Good Shepherd." In *Schools of Oriental Studies and the Development of Modern Historiography*, edited by Antonio Panaino and Andrea Piras, pp. 281–310. Milan: Università di Bologna; Rome: IsIAO.

Wilson, E. Jan
1996   *The Cylinders of Gudea: Transliteration, Translation and Index*. Kevelaer: Verlag Butzon & Bercker; Neukirchener-Vluyn: Neukirchener Verlag.

Winter, Irene J.
2000   "The Eyes Have It: Votive Statuary, Gilgamesh's Axe, and Cathected Viewing in the Ancient Near East." In *Visuality Before and Beyond the Renaissance: Seeing as Others Saw*, edited by Robert S. Nelson, pp. 22–44. Cambridge: Cambridge University Press.

2010   "Representing Abundance: The Visual Dimension of the Agrarian State." In *On Art in the Ancient Near East*, Volume 2: *From the Third Millennium B.C.E.*, edited by Irene J. Winter, pp. 199–226. Leiden: Brill.

Yoffee, Norman
2005   *Myths of the Archaic State: Evolution of the Earliest Cities, States and Civilizations*. Cambridge: Cambridge University Press.

Zeder, Melinda A.
1991   *Feeding Cities: Specialized Animal Economy in the Ancient Near East*. Smithsonian Series in Archaeological Inquiry. Washington, D.C.: Smithsonian Institution Press.

16

SOURCES OF EGYPTIAN TEMPLE COSMOLOGY: DIVINE IMAGE, KING, AND RITUAL PERFORMER

*John Baines, University of Oxford**

Introduction

The late fourth millennium B.C.E. saw the rise of kingship in Egypt, alongside various fundamental developments that culminated in a single state, with a court hierarchy and some sort of administrative structure, controlling the entire Nile Valley north of the First Cataract as well as the Nile Delta (for the locations of places mentioned, see fig. 16.1). Examples of images that accompanied these developments, displaying and in part constituting them, can be seen as early as Tomb 100 at Hierakonpolis, which was probably the burial place of a local ruler around 3500 B.C.E. and is one of the oldest known mudbrick structures in Egypt (Naqada IIC; Quibell and Green 1902, pls. 75–78) (for chronology, see table 16.1). In the Naqada III period, a couple of centuries later, pictorial forms proliferated, with royal symbolism appearing in a variety of surviving media and contexts. Two- and three-dimensional works of art are the most approachable among sources relating to kingship, alongside the archaeology of royal necropolis sites. The world of living kings, their dwellings, and the ships in which they moved around their territory were surely more important than these inanimate carriers of symbolic meanings, but they are at best accessible at second hand in images, on which I concentrate.

The iconography of Egyptian kingship reached a lasting formulation that can be seen in the Narmer Palette (Dynasty 0, ca. 3000 B.C.E.), discussed below, which presents the king's centrality for the ordered world and his pivotal position in the cosmos.[1] The palette's design and iconography, which distilled and codified fundamental developments of the preceding period, may have been disseminated throughout the country. Its execution is not of the quality of such pieces as the slightly earlier Bull Palette (e.g., Malek 2003, pp. 26–27), and it may exhibit a more routine level of craftsmanship because it would have been produced in many exemplars for presentation in all the main temples and sacred sites of the country, which by Narmer's time was a cultural and political unity.

* I would like to thank Deena Ragavan very much for her invitation to the seminar in Chicago, which was an unusually stimulating and wide-ranging event, and for valuable comments on drafts of this chapter. I am very grateful to Gay Robins and Elizabeth Frood for criticisms of drafts, and to Christiana Köhler, Kathryn Piquette, and David Wengrow for references and comments.

[1] For a relatively traditional analysis of cosmological aspects, see Baines 1995, pp. 116–18; see also O'Connor 2011 and discussion below. Some overlap with those discussions is unavoidable.

Table 16.1. Chronological table: Naqada and dynastic periods in Egypt in
the fourth and third millennia B.C.E. (after Hendrickx 1996)

Periods	Dynasties	Rough Dates B.C.E.
Naqada IA–IIB	—	3900–3650
Naqada IC–IID	—	3650–3300
Naqada IIIA	—	3300–3150
Naqada IIIB	0	3150–3000
Early Dynastic	First–Third	3000–2600
Old Kingdom	Fourth–Eighth	2600–2150

The king dominates the composition of both sides of the Narmer Palette, while the gods and especially humanity are altogether less salient. Yet the king depended on the gods, as is shown in features of the scenes on the palette itself and on contemporary compositions, such as an ivory relief cylinder (fig. 16.2) on which he is depicted receiving life from the god Horus, who hovers as a hawk above and to the right of him while a vulture goddess spreads her wings in protection directly over him. By late in the following Early Dynastic period, an iconography of superficially equal interaction between the gods and the king had emerged in temple decoration on doorways, perhaps on small shrines, and in stone statuary, all of which were fixed, sacred contexts unlike the portable Narmer Palette. My aim in this chapter is to address the tension between the smaller-scale sacred forms of prehistory, which were presumably housed within structures that might have been made of perishable materials or of mudbrick, and the strict pictorial, compositional, and architectural conventions of later periods, which still looked to precedents in more evanescent models, if often only as fictions. Stone, while widely available and highly valued for vessels, statuary, and smaller objects, was not used in built structures until the Early Dynastic period.

Several identifications of possible ritual areas or temples of predynastic Egypt have been proposed, but none is completely secure, and their contexts are poorly understood (Anderson 2011, with references; Hikade 2011). The examples that have been suggested were perhaps places where rituals were performed rather than structures containing anything like cult images. These places, which are in the desert and are more accessible to archaeology than the Nile Delta, and especially than the floodplain of Upper Egypt, may have been untypical, because slightly elevated places on the floodplain, which were not too much at risk from the annual inundation, were probably the normal locations of settlements and their associated temples.

The exception to this pattern is the uncontexted find of three partly broken colossal statues of the god Min on the main later urban site at Koptos, together with some pieces of comparable date.[2] The statues, which are too large to have been concealed, for example

---

[2] Petrie 1896, pp. 7–9, pls. 3–5; Williams 1988 (in part problematic); Kemp, Boyce, and Harrell 2000; Adams and Jaeschke 1984.

behind an enclosure wall, bear secondary motifs and inscriptions probably of Naqada IIIA date, as well as exhibiting clear signs of later veneration by grinding out stone powder from them. They must therefore have been erected in an accessible setting, remaining there after they fell. In subsequent periods, Min, together with his cognate, the ithyphallic Amun, was the principal deity whose image was made fully visible in public processions. When almost all other deities were taken out, they were concealed in a shrine that was in its turn covered with cloth. This correlation between the form of the Min statues and later traditional practice, which is probably beyond coincidence, suggests by analogy that in early times most other deities would have been worshiped inside shrines and protected when brought out. Therefore we should not expect to find pictorial evidence of temple interiors and associated cult images of deities, because these were restricted, sacred contexts and images that would not be displayed.

By contrast with the dearth of available sites and our ignorance of their interiors, images of temples and ceremonial areas are relatively frequent in Naqada III and third-millennium sources, in both two and three dimensions (for the latter, see, e.g., Kemp 2006, p. 145, fig. 51; van Haarlem 1998). Tomb architecture that may have derived some features from buildings constructed for the living provides indirect evidence, both for religious practice and for visual forms.[3] The images display a world that remained crucial in Egyptian religion of later periods. In the transformations wrought by developments in mortuary monuments during the First through Third Dynasties, first in mudbrick and then in stone, forms and parts of temples and other structures used in the living context were depicted as three-dimensional dummy buildings. In the Fourth and Fifth Dynasties in particular, the forms were used as elements in an architectural vocabulary. At the same time, the reference of that vocabulary to specific structural features became weaker, being used rather as a source for decorative motifs or for symbolic associations. In much later revivals, however, some of the same motifs and forms recurred in images of the very ancient structures that they had originally depicted, or as emblems of their home cities (e.g., Kaiser 1987; Baines 1991, pp. 35–36). Thus, the tradition was multi-layered. Various modes of recourse to older sources were available, and the early motifs that I discuss here were returned to repeatedly.

For this chapter, the fact that structural elements of architecture and pictorial forms grew apart is crucial, because it parallels in part the move from an environment of ritual spaces and sacred buildings constructed in organic and perishable materials, in which the bodies and movements of cult images of deities, the king, and ritual performers were the central focus of value, to more exclusive sacred spaces constructed in solid materials, in which the interaction of king and deities was most powerfully depicted in images, as well as being enacted in lost performances. From the perspective of the archaeological record, this is a shift from action and material forms that are realized spatially to metaphor and representation that can be expressed in two-dimensional images with accompanying texts. While that change — which was surely less abstract than my formulation may suggest — probably constituted only part of the development, the increasing salience of representation among high-cultural forms has a later counterpart in changes in the funerary sphere, where around

---

[3] Compare Wengrow 2006, pp. 240–41; Wengrow 2007; Baines 2007, pp. 118–45 (related to the development of writing).

2000 B.C.E. modest burials, accompanied by often broken or worn personal possessions as grave goods, were superseded by more elaborate depositions that evoked the ritual and divine world through their arrangement and iconography (Seidlmayer 2001). Caches of artifacts from the Early Dynastic period, especially the Hierakonpolis Main Deposit (discussed below), which was associated with one of the most ancient cities, imply that changes of comparable character occurred then, accompanied by an increasing salience for fixed forms of prestigious objects and decoration.

Palettes as Indexes of Ritual Change and Continuity

The Narmer Palette (fig. 16.3) marks a radical change in another way. Its notional focus, and that of many other objects of its period, is on ritually applying paint, principally green and perhaps also black, to the area around the eyes. The circle at the palette's center, whose rim is formed by the necks of interlaced fantastic animals, is where the pigment would be ground and mixed, but, as on many examples, it shows no sign of use. The ritual application of pigment may also be evoked by the figure behind Narmer — who, Erich Winter (1994) suggests on the basis of the pot he carries and the enigmatic caption, may function both in his evident role as sandal bearer and as the person responsible for the oil binder for pigments. Such paints continued to be important in dynastic times, the most eloquent examples being the Third Dynasty statues of the couple Sepa and Nesa, which have wide bands of green paint beneath the eyes (Arnold and Ziegler 1999, nos. 11–13, not easily visible in photographs). These are most likely to have been applied as part of a vivification ritual performed on statues of deities as well as of human beings.

Cosmological features of the Narmer Palette's structure and decoration presumably enhanced the value of the ritual actions to which such objects traditionally related, investing the treated body — whether corporeal or a statue — with cosmic significance. When the palette, which encapsulated these ideas but was not itself used in rituals, was donated to an institution, its presence may have evoked and reinforced associated ideas, while also paving the way for the later increased use of complex, multi-register pictorial compositions as focuses of meaning and efficacy.

A different indication of the meaning of palettes is given by examples on which the grinding area is enveloped by arms forming the *ka* symbol, which is also a hieroglyphic sign; these show signs of use with green pigment.[4] The meaning of the *ka* as a dynamic principle and aspect of the person includes the transmission of vital force across the generations.[5] These palettes, which are rectangular rather than oval or heart-shaped in form, also have a rectangular rather than circular flat area, without a defined center for grinding, although traces of grinding are roughly circular. On an example from a tomb in the non-royal necropolis of Helwan, probably of the early First Dynasty, the hands of the *ka* sign come to just below

---

[4] Quibell 1905, p. 232, pl. 48:14234, 14235; Fischer 1980, p. 34, fig. 6. For an example of the same shape in the Oriental Institute Museum, with traces of pigment but without the *ka* design, see Teeter 2011, p. 199, no. 51, dated there to Naqada IIIA–B.

[5] The concept, which is notoriously difficult to define, is closely associated with the king, as well as being evoked in the presentation of offerings to tomb owners for their survival in the next world. See, e.g., Bolshakov 2001; for transmission down the generations as suggested by early personal names, see Helck 1954.

the top of the decorated area, while the hieroglyphs for "life, duration, power" fill the top at the center (fig. 16.4).[6] This trio of qualities was delegated from the gods to the king. The object, which is finely worked but not so elaborate or impressive as the Narmer Palette, was perhaps a royal gift to a privileged subordinate (compare the Brooklyn knife handle: Baines 2011, pp. 54–55, fig. 3.1). Real or symbolic use of the palette might impart those qualities to the recipient in the next life, and this may be the prime association of pigments such as those on the statues of Sepa and Nesa. In this life and within the hierarchies of the dynastic period, the qualities could only be fittingly given to the king by a deity. In the less hierarchical society of predynastic times, such prerogatives probably had a wider currency and application in this world.

The presence of the *ka* on the rectangular palettes has a different implication in relation to the king's own agency. From the First Dynasty onward, the king's Horus name, his fundamental title, was often shown as supported by the *ka* sign, notably in images of standards.[7] The royal *ka* was widely represented in scenes of the king offering to the gods (e.g., fig. 16.5) or, for example, smiting his enemies. Wolfgang Waitkus (2010), among others, has suggested that its presence or absence was determined by compositional constraints rather than theme, so that in principle it would be a constant feature of his presence in action before the gods. The *ka* was depicted in various emblematic forms and was probably not a visible presence except when displayed as a standard, in which form it could be related to the set of powerful emblems carried around the king in early reliefs (Beckerath 1956). Significantly, its location behind the king tends to alternate with a formula reading "the protection of all life and power around him for ever" (with variants), which partly overlaps in content with the group "life, duration, power" on the Helwan palette.[8] The *ka* perhaps both protects and enhances the king's power, while its divine associations can be compared remotely with the medieval European conception of the "king's two bodies" (Kantorowicz 1957).

One can distinguish implications of the oval and rectangular forms of palettes while assuming that both functioned to exchange qualities and enhance the agency of the person or image receiving the pigment. Both forms had probably accrued meaning over many centuries. In the new world of a state that depended symbolically on its dominant ruler, the rectangular palette would be a less prestigious form that inherited its function from earlier times while bearing a special meaning when donated by the king. The oval- or heart-shaped form was the

---

[6] Fischer 1980, p. 181, after Saad 1969, pl. 75. The original publication gives no details or indication of findspot. The grinding surface is unused. Christiana Köhler (personal communication) informs me that the object has not yet been identified among the stored finds from Helwan.

[7] Early examples and relevant discussion: Schweitzer 1956, p. 22, figs. 2–3, 52–62. Schweitzer and other scholars have termed the Horus name the *ka* name; Gardiner (1957, p. 72) was dismissive of the idea. Detailed examples with the *ka* element are present, for example, in the Fifth Dynasty mortuary temple of Sahure, including figure 16.12 here; see Borchardt et al. 1913, e.g., pls. 35, 46, two or more occurrences, implying an original presence of numerous figures.

The oldest probable representation of the royal *ka* as a personification, rather than a standard, dates to Khasekhemwy at the end of the Second Dynasty: Alexanian 1998, pl. 3:10.

[8] On the formula, see Winter 1968, p. 64; Blöbaum 2006, pp. 266–68: "Protektionsformel." Hermann Kees (1912, pp. 119–34) discussed a related set of symbols often shown behind the king in outdoor ritual contexts. One example (his fig. 14), a Late Period relief from Memphis that is based on early models, includes the symbols, the protection formula, and a man carrying an effigy of a scorpion, alluding to a procession of protective symbols. For reliefs from this monument, see Kaiser 1987, with pls. 42–48.

more important (collection: Petrie 1921). Of its many variants, some are clearly cosmological, notably the Narmer Palette. On a few examples, the grinding circle in the middle may symbolize the sun, notably where it is enveloped by snake-necked felids or a snake (e.g., Asselberghs 1961, pls. 70, 88, 95, 96). The Narmer Palette exhibits this feature, in addition to elements at the top that symbolize the sky and evoke the solar god Horus who would descend from there as a hawk, as in the design of the ivory cylinder (fig. 16.2). David O'Connor (2011) proposes that the register beneath the top on the other side presents sunrise through the scene of the king triumphing over his enemies, in a visual composition that can be compared with the elaborate description in the Cannibal Spell of the later Pyramid Texts (Goebs 2008, pp. 205–64). Whether or not all these interpretations can be reconciled, a powerful association is created between sustaining the cosmic order and painting the deity's cult image or the king's body with a material notionally prepared in the grinding area. Relevant cult actions would be performed with different equipment: the palette may have been an archaizing object at the time when it was created, while its dedication probably involved a ritual of its own.

The palette's cosmology is present as an architecture, represented by the paired bovid heads, the top of which signifies the cow of the sky and its four supports (e.g., Baines 1995, pp. 119–20). The motif in the middle between the bovid heads writes the king's Horus name (termed a *serekh*), but the hawk Horus himself, whose perch is suggested by the concave curve of the upper line, is absent.[9] This treatment may belong with the agency evoked by the grinding circle: the god Horus must be enjoined to descend onto his perch by the performances with which the palette is associated. At the same time, the scenes on both sides and the implied ritual show an active process that must be constantly repeated. The king may be visually dominant, but order depends on his coming together with the deity who descends from above. This focus on god and king and on divine status may be signified also by the oval shape, which appears to be confined to royal examples among the latest decorated examples. The rectangular form is perhaps a desacralized version suitable to those below the king in the state hierarchy. The Helwan Palette will then show that divine power could nonetheless be delegated to elite groups in humanity through the king.

The Narmer Palette's message is in a sense abstract: the object itself was an offering. This abstraction, which had probably been a norm for large decorated palettes for a couple of centuries, is essential in relation to later developments. What had become vital was not just the ritual action and material signified by palettes but the constructed and probably sacred environment in which rituals were set. The scale of the designs points toward the more expansive context of wall decoration; but from the next couple of centuries, very little such decoration has been discovered. A complementarity had developed between, on the one hand, the continuing focus on the cult of the gods and royal ceremonial and, on the other hand, the decorated spaces in which cult and ceremonial were performed. Moreover, all palettes, apart from scribal ones of a different form, disappear after Narmer. The associated conception of pigments and the transfer of agency may have become generalized in cult through the connection with the king's *ka*. Comparable ideas would then underlie temple and royal decoration as a whole. This hypothetical development would constitute a change in display rather than practice: the king was the sole protagonist of humanity shown in direct

---

[9] See Kaplony 1965, pp. 152–53. Narmer's successor Aha was the last king whose name form exhibited this feature, which was replaced by a straight top. The straight form probably represents a palace enclosure.

interaction with the gods, but priests, rather than he, were ritual performers. The treatment on the Narmer Palette implies that the king is as much the object of ritual performance as its protagonist. That status is probably valid for later periods too.[10]

The profound realignment of immovable structures and mobile artifacts around the beginning of the dynastic period is at most indirectly reflected in surviving buildings. The First and early Second Dynasties produce little evidence for a changing tradition of pictorial imagery, although significant amounts must have been created. Only from the late Second Dynasty onward are there clear examples of a developed style and repertory of forms. Although this pattern of attestation is probably due in part to chance, its implications should be examined for the period before strongly monumental forms are well attested, in the Third and Fourth Dynasties.

Sacred Forms and Practices of the Early Dynastic Period

The Early Dynastic period (First to Third Dynasties) is characterized by many changes in pictorial and compositional style, genres, and monumental forms. On a probably misleading retrospective view, those changes led to final definitions of style in the Old Kingdom, which supplies little evidence of comparably significant changes in convention or rejection of old practices during its course.

The principal sources for First Dynasty temple and palace structures and ritual practice are indirect, consisting of "tags" that were attached to royal grave goods and a fragmentary later annal stone,[11] inscribed stone vessels, and personal names. The tags, which were used only in the First Dynasty, bear year names, mostly of the kings in whose tombs they were deposited, as well as indications of the products with which they were associated.[12] The information in the year names can hardly be correlated with the Palermo Stone, either because known examples do not coincide or perhaps because different selections of information were made at different times. Among the events for which years were named were a biennial tour of the king through the country, manufacture of images of deities, performance of rituals, construction of buildings, and royal visits to temples. All but the first of these relate to the sacred domain, while the range as a whole highlights the mobility of Early Dynastic kingship, together with the tension between cult images and the locations where they were kept: at first the images seem to have possessed more material value than their physical settings. A division between the local and the central probably inhered in the images themselves, because the recently formed state overlaid cults that had emerged among particular communities with its strongly defined forms. Altogether later, in the Thirteenth Dynasty (ca. 1700 B.C.E.), the sole narrative of a priest's biographical inscription is his journey to the Memphite area to bring statues of Horus and Isis — presumably cult images — to his town of Hierakonpolis in the deep south (Hayes 1947; Kubisch 2008, pp. 310–14). This dependence on the temple workshops of the capital, the most important of which belonged to Ptah, the god of craftsmen (e.g., te Velde 1982, col. 1178; Helck 1991), may have been typical of most periods.

---

[10] I hope to address this issue with Elizabeth Frood in a future study.

[11] The Palermo Stone and related fragments. Best reproduction: Schäfer 1902; summary treatment: Wilkinson 2000.

[12] No convenient collection; many important examples are illustrated in a site report: Petrie 1901. Kathryn Piquette (2008) has studied the tags.

The year names on the earlier tags are pictorially organized, integrating writing into registers of images, partly as heraldic elements and partly as captions. Two principal methods of rendering buildings — with variants and overlaps — can be distinguished on the tags, both probably inherited from predynastic times (see Baines 2003). One shows in plan a rectangular, battlemented mudbrick enclosure that can contain one or more structures (e.g., fig. 16.6). The same basic treatment, fused with a schematic rendering of an elaborately patterned facade, forms the framework of the king's extremely common Horus name, the *serekh* (e.g., fig. 16.7). The other method shows buildings in profile, contributing to a scene-like treatment (e.g., fig. 16.8). This method was easily combined with representations of buildings in plan or in outline, as in figure 16.7 (right).

Two eloquent but enigmatic compositions of this latter type on tags, one of the reign of Aha, the probable first king of the First Dynasty, and the other of his successor Djer, show temple areas of the delta cities Sais (fig. 16.7) and Buto (fig. 16.8), the latter also rendering an enclosure in plan (possible archaeological correlate: Bietak 1994). The Aha tag indicates the king's visit by means of the two barques above the image of the temple. Both include a range of depictions of buildings, in addition to the most important one in the top register. The structure on the Aha tag appears to be made of perishable materials and defined by a fenced enclosure.[13] In the Djer design for Buto, an abstract sign for a rectilinear enclosure is complemented by something like a landscape. Even at this early date, the forms evoking these places are probably conventional, because contemporaneous buildings at Buto, among the very few such contexts that have been explored, were massive mudbrick structures (e.g., von der Way 1992). The perishable forms, however, retained their iconic status, continuing a tension between a partly imagined past of renewable and movable structures, on the one hand, and a more monumental present, on the other hand.

In their role as identifiers attached to grave goods, the tags were small but relatively public objects that must have been moved from one context to another. In keeping with conventions of decorum (Baines 2007, pp. 14–29), the images on them cannot depict what decorated the interiors of temples or the statues and equipment used there. The register compositions into which tags are organized, however, are designed for surfaces that would hardly be limited to the genre of which examples survive. Similar compositions could have been created in lost media, such as furniture in wood or other materials, paneling (known from false doors and a late Old Kingdom chapel at Elephantine: Kaiser et al. 1976, pp. 92–94), wall paintings on plaster, cloth hangings, or composite materials, of which suggestive fragments are known from Fifth Dynasty mortuary temples, including scenes of the king interacting with gods (Borchardt 1909, pp. 59–66; Landgráfová 2006). Those that were used inside temple complexes would have different content from that of the tags, because the context would be fitting for representations of deities in their full form, which was normally anthropomorphic with a human or animal head, not the images of images generally seen on the tags.

Here, it is almost necessary to posit an analogy with later conventions. Despite the emergence of normative pictorial frameworks such as strict registers in Dynasty 0, the scene types that become widespread in later times have few other known forerunners. In these types the king interacts directly with anthropomorphically rendered deities in an abstract but cosmologically defined and protected space. Early Dynastic examples show exterior scenes

---

[13] Other aspects: Baines 1991. I discuss landscape features of these designs in Baines, in press.

and are in iconographies that later counted as emblematic, being designed for less-than-sacred contexts or for the liminal surfaces of doorways (Baines 1985, pp. 277–305). These intermediate forms, notably where deities are depicted as images of statues, are relatively common on the tags, on seals, and as hieroglyphs (e.g., Kaplony 1963, vol. 3, passim; Lacau and Lauer 1959–1961, pls. 11, 16).

Two limestone reliefs from Gebelein, perhaps of the First Dynasty, exhibit highly developed forms (fig. 16.9; see also Morenz 1994). Gebelein is a provincial site, and the presence of this elaborate material suggests that comparable or superior works would have been widespread in more important locations. These reliefs again show exteriors, one register having clear affinities with the Narmer Palette, while another below, which is marked as sanctified by the demarcating sky sign with stars, evokes movement through an image of a boat as well as including a building made of perishable materials. The reliefs, which do not seem to come from stelae, were perhaps orthostats; their setting cannot be reconstructed. More generally, the character of third-millennium provincial temples for divine cult is uncertain (Dreyer 1986; Kemp 1989, pp. 53–107; 2006, pp. 101–60; Bussmann 2010). Those that are archaeologically attested were constructed in mudbrick and related materials and do not show evidence of painted wall decoration (but this is unlikely to survive); stone reliefs like those at Gebelein might have been grander alternatives to paintings. The principal divine cult temples of the period, which were probably in the Memphite area, at Heliopolis, and in the delta, remain out of reach of archaeology. Whether they were large stone structures cannot be known, but nothing points toward a more-than-occasional use of stone or of wall relief.[14]

Another index of change in styles of display and in the range of decorated artifacts is the Hierakonpolis Main Deposit, a vast body of objects that does not include anything definitely later than the First Dynasty.[15] The deposit, which was not a sealed or necessarily a single collection, was interred in a sacred location whose character is uncertain because no associated temple structure could be identified. The material presumably could not be destroyed or — except for decorated stone blocks — reused, but some pieces may have been rendered ineffective before deposition. The deposit included crucial pieces such as the Narmer Palette and the older Two Dog Palette (Whitehouse 2009, pp. 28–32), as well as stone mace-heads, fragments of temple furniture, and hundreds of anthropomorphic and animal statuettes in ivory and faience, many of types that have no later parallel. It is not known how the objects had been presented and displayed, but the absence of later parallels itself shows that associated forms, and perhaps practices, had been superseded. The most likely stimulus to deposition is a move toward more monumental settings, but that would not in itself explain changes in styles of object. Practices such as the use of oils and pigments to adorn and care for figures and statues evidently continued. The disappearance of ceremonial palettes therefore suggests that symbolic meanings associated with them, which possessed a general

---

[14] A possible exception is a stone structure reduced to foundations on the escarpment above Thebes: Vörös and Pudleiner 1998; Vörös 1998, pp. 55–63. The choice of stone may relate to the location, where it would have been laborious to use brick. The authors' dating is based on astronomical alignment and ceramics, but the latter are not illustrated or described. The structure is in any case impressive in scale for its context.

[15] For the setting, see McNamara 2008, with references. The initial publication left many questions unanswered: Quibell 1900; Quibell and Green 1902. See also, e.g., Adams 1974. David Wengrow (2006, pp. 178–87), for example, suggests a Fifth Dynasty date for the deposition, but the objects appear to be much older.

validity, may have been expressed on other media and in other contexts. The attestation of specific forms of fantastic animals on the Two Dog Palette and in the decoration of Twelfth Dynasty tombs, but not in the intervening 1,200 years, is just one pointer to the survival of significant motifs and ideas despite the impossibility of tracing the vehicles of transmission, which might have been through a mixture of material culture and surrounding narratives.[16]

Evidence for pictorial forms from the Second Dynasty is markedly different from that for the First Dynasty. After a hiatus in royal images and inscriptions from the earlier part of the dynasty, probably due to chances of preservation, the first known occurrence of a complete sentence in Egyptian is attested on a sealing from the reign of Peribsen (e.g., Baines 2007, p. 138, fig. 20), while the oldest significant pieces of temple relief are on granite and date to the following reign of Khasekhemwy, with one piece coming from the ceremonial area at Hierakonpolis (fig. 16.10; for another view of the piece, see Quibell 1900, pl. 1) and a group of fragments from the "Fort" (Alexanian 1998), a massive mudbrick enclosure probably prepared for the royal funeral ceremonies or mortuary cult. This material, particularly the scene of founding a temple where the king partners the goddess Seshat, is closer to later standard motifs than anything known from earlier, while continuing to display relatively public aspects of the king's role — such as rituals in which he would appear in the open or in a temporary building — rather than ones associated with temple interiors.

The most radical development in architectural and pictorial forms came under Djoser, Khasekhemwy's successor, for whom the first pyramid, the Step Pyramid at Saqqara, was constructed in stone (e.g., Firth, Quibell, and Lauer 1935; Lauer 1936). In its underground corridors were placed many thousands of First and Second Dynasty stone vessels presumably made for rituals, including festivals and the mortuary cult. The rituals probably ceased to be performed or used different equipment, so that the containers were no longer a leading focus of prestige (Baines 2007, pp. 184–86).

The pyramid complex commemorated the past in another way, with numerous dummy buildings whose forms evoked structures in perishable materials. Elements of their architectural vocabulary have later parallels, but comparable buildings did not continue to be constructed in stone. The Step Pyramid complex was a vital point of reference for subsequent periods, when people returned to it repeatedly for models (e.g., Dodson 1988; Baines and Riggs 2001). Relief decoration in the complex was sparse, but an uncontexted doorjamb evokes something like an esoteric board game that would aid access to the next world and is suggestive of how a wider cosmology may have been represented in some buildings.[17] In the underground areas close to the burial and in the complementary "South Tomb" are reliefs showing King Djoser performing the *sed*-festival that would ritually renew his rule after many years of reign, a core ritual toward which kings aspired from very early times. Djoser is presumably acting in the next world, but nothing in the reliefs is specifically mortuary, so that what they show might also occur in this world (Firth, Quibell, and Lauer 1935, pls. 15–17, 40–44).

---

[16] Newberry 1893b, pls. iv, xiii top right; less close: Newberry 1893a, pl. xiii top right; Shedid 1994, p. 26, fig. 31, p. 57, fig. 95; Wengrow (in press) suggests textiles as a possible medium of transmission of the motifs, some of which also occur on "ivory wands" of the same period: Altenmüller 1965. See also McDonald 2007, pp. 31–32.

[17] Arnold and Ziegler 1999, p. 171, no. 3. I owe the interpretation as evoking a board game to the BA dissertation of Natasha Jackson (University of Oxford, 2008).

An indication of the performative quality of images is provided by rough, irregularly shaped stelae of two types, very different from the dressed stone of completed work, that may have protected the monument during construction (fig. 16.11; further examples in Firth, Quibell, and Lauer 1935, pls. 86–87). These bore the king's titles and those of two of his daughters, facing images of the skin of a beheaded jackal suspended from a pole that are captioned with the name of Anubis, the god of the necropolis. The form of this object, for which the ancient word is *imiut*, probably derived from a fresh carcass used in a ritual (Köhler 1975). By the First Dynasty, it had become a piece of statuary that was commemorated as being "made (*msj*)" and was depicted on a tag as standing before the temple of the goddess Neith at Sais, where it may have been a protective emblem of sacred space (fig. 16.7).

The stelae in the Step Pyramid complex were discarded as construction progressed and had presumably served as temporary markers. Their stone material forms part of the shift toward using more durable materials that is seen much earlier in the tag with the *imiut* and exemplifies, in a different way from the dummy buildings, the paradox that impermanent forms retained their prestige in a monumental context that was intended to be permanent. The stone buildings transformed a temporary structure into something lasting, whereas the stelae bore reliefs in a pictorial mode that was used for lasting monuments but were nevertheless quickly discarded.

For this chapter, the most significant material from the reign of Djoser consists in a group of limestone relief fragments, probably from a miniature shrine, that were excavated at Heliopolis, the sacred city of the sun god Re.[18] The form of the complete object cannot be reconstructed, but it might have housed a small, portable divine image. The reliefs show deities next to quite extensive captions promising gifts to the king, a seated figure of the king with tiny profiles of the queen and two daughters, and part of the king's Horus name at a relatively larger scale (e.g., Arnold and Ziegler 1999, pp. 175–76, no. 7). These designs have a monumental quality that would suit far bigger compositions, such as those in the underground areas of the Step Pyramid. They do not, however, constitute normal temple relief of the king and deities in the style known from later periods, because the range of protagonists is different, and the deities are not in full anthropomorphic form with human-style clothing and direct interaction, even though the latter may be implied on one of the fragments by the phrase "exchange for this (*jsw nn*)" (fig. 16.13), a designation of royal–divine reciprocity that endured for millennia. While scenes of the king offering to a deity can be found in the mortuary temples of Old Kingdom kings, notably that of Sahure (fig. 16.12), they are a small minority, and the specialized context makes the status of such examples for the present argument uncertain.[19] Evidence for almost all later standard scene types remains elusive, although faience fragments from the Fifth Dynasty mortuary temple of Raneferef at Abusir that appear to fit scenes showing the king being introduced to a temple are very suggestive (Landgráfová 2006, esp. pp. 488–89, figs. 2.9:1–2).

The cosmological character of decoration presenting the king and deities is more clearly visible. The pattern of sky with stars above scenes (figs. 16.9, 16.12) demonstrates that an ideal, detemporalized world is being shown: the stars do not stand for night but rather for

---

[18] E.g., Donadoni Roveri and Tiradritti 1998, nos. 239–41; Morenz 2002, slightly problematic reconstruction. For "exchange," see Morenz 2002, pp. 148–49, 157, fig. 9; Baines 2007, p. 139, fig. 22.

[19] E.g., Fakhry 1961, fig. 18 (feet in upper register); Borchardt et al. 1913, pls. 35–38; Arnold and Ziegler 1999, no. 118.

an otherworldly setting, perhaps encompassing night and day, in which the king and deities interact. Some emblematic decoration renders this conception more immediate by showing human heads that stand for Aker, a god of the earth, emerging from the baseline on either side of a composition, as is known from the mortuary temple of Sahure (fig. 16.14). The same Aker head was even used in the framing of an ordinary vertical inscription on another column (Borchardt 1910, p. 64, fig. 81). The composition in figure 16.14 is almost fully equivalent to one that shows king and deity in human form, but it is in the emblematic mode appropriate to liminal and heraldic contexts. The absence of the Aker heads in scenes where anthropomorphic deities and kings are present might have been due in part to the incongruity of having a disembodied human head at ground level next to another figure's feet. A similar treatment is present on the Narmer Palette (fig. 16.3), but for an enemy and at a higher level in the composition.

Conclusion

The development I have sketched is toward increasing regularity in the composition and iconography of scenes showing the king and the gods. The final form of such scenes, however, is barely attested in available evidence and may not have crystallized fully until the second millennium. The regularity of the fully developed scenes has an abstract character: in temple reliefs of later periods, deities and the king interact in an imagined space that hardly relates spatially or temporally to this world. Features such as the significance of the royal *ka* for the king's role in temples are, if anything, less clear in later times than in the early evidence I have reviewed. The less regular early material seems to give a small window onto ritual performances that were not sited in inner areas of temples, whereas almost no direct evidence is available about the latter, either for which rituals were performed there or for how the spaces were decorated.

In the outer areas for which images and structures can be studied, there was a progressive transformation in materials, from the perishable buildings of Naqada II, through the mudbrick of Naqada III and the first two dynasties, to the stone of the Step Pyramid complex. The forms of buildings, however, looked back to the earlier materials, from which a sharp break was not made until the Fourth Dynasty. I have suggested that the focus on perishable structures was in some respects commemorated and consigned to the past in the Step Pyramid complex.

Developments in pictorial forms went through comparable transformations, but not in close parallel with changes in architecture. Perishable structures continued to be shown in later temple iconography and in tomb scenes of funeral rituals, but they are relatively uncommon in the core scenes of king and deity. Exceptions are scenes that depict deities whose images were not shrouded outside temples, with ephemeral-style buildings or other features acting as emblems of related aspects of their being, as with the lettuce patch of the ithyphallic Min/Amun-Re.[20] Rituals that would be performed in more public spaces could

---

[20] E.g., Petrie 1896, pl. 6, Seventeenth Dynasty, ca. 1650. The motif is attested from earlier, but scarcely in examples from an interior location.

be shown, and even cattle receive ceremonial eye paint (Borchardt et al. 1913, pl. 47, Fifth Dynasty). In such cases priests are sometimes included in scenes (e.g., Lacau and Chevrier 1956–1969, pl. 13, scene 4, Twelfth Dynasty).

Temple cult was maintained by priests and was carried out on cult statues or other material manifestations of gods. The priests deployed tangible substances — eye paint, unguents, perfumes — that are mentioned in texts but only sparingly indicated in images (incense is shown more clearly). Priests are not the people shown performing temple ritual; instead of them, we see the king. Cult images generally did not have the forms in which the gods are represented on temple walls (mostly of the mid-second millennium and later). Much later, compositions that may depict cult images presented a range of often exotic and archaic or archaizing forms, in a pattern known from many cultures.[21]

The development of monumental decorated stone temples for the cult of the gods, which are first securely attested from the second millennium, brought with it the very refined, rather abstract but cosmologically explicit relief compositions that are known in thousands of examples. In some respects these are uninformative, because they do not relate directly to the material world. Moreover, scarcely any temples have been recovered with an archaeological context that might show something about the less neat world of cult action in their interiors, for which the modes of agency I have mentioned would have been invoked and deployed.[22] The separation of temple decoration and cult performance appears almost total.

In dynastic times the decoration of relatively small, portable objects appears no longer to have driven development as it had in the preceding late predynastic period. While cult images retained their significance, as did the large and small statuary that was set up and subsequently deposited in temples, pictorial forms in two dimensions became the prime focus of religious imagery. For important works, that imagery was remarkably uniform throughout Egypt, and it may have contrasted in that respect with the variability of third-millennium temples and their contents (Bussmann 2010). The visual definition of the world of the gods and people was normative and probably controlled from the center.

In terms of content, perhaps we can do little more than map the decoration's increasing abstraction from the beginning of the dynastic period onward, while bearing in mind that it says little about how temples were made ritually into sites where human beings and deities encountered each other — in a sanctified microcosm that was not represented directly outside that context, and perhaps relatively little within it. Temples of the Graeco-Roman period bear extensive texts that go some way toward filling this gap by describing a deity's delight at the temple's perfection and joyful habitation of it, as well as much about the performance of rituals (e.g., Kurth 1994). For earlier times, pursuit of these questions is more difficult. I have attempted to indicate how one might address this lacuna in knowledge in other ways, by studying patterns of development of decoration in which meanings were transposed into pictorial forms in a somewhat fictionalized guise, and by pointing toward categories of material that do not survive.

---

[21] E.g., Eckmann and Shafik 2005, figs. 43–45 — either a standard or perhaps a cult image; Davies 1953, pls. 2–5; Roeder 1914; Spencer 2006; Chassinat 1947–1952; Chassinat and Daumas 1965.

[22] The Early Dynastic and Old Kingdom temple of Satet on Elephantine Island is a partial exception, but only offerings in hard materials such as faience survived from it; see Dreyer 1986. Another promising site is Tell Ibrahim Awad in the Delta; see, e.g., van Haarlem 2009.

I suggest that these changes were deliberate and self-conscious, being attested through events, of which examples are the discarding of the Hierakonpolis Main Deposit and the creation of the monuments of the Step Pyramid complex with the associated interment of stone vessels. The core underlying issues were probably sanctity and seclusion: what mattered most about statues of deities was that they be protected and attended to in a fitting manner within their cult places, so that the deities would inhabit them and impart their benefits to the king and humanity. The focus on deities, and on the king as the sole representative of humanity who could claim a similar status to them, marginalized the role of the normal ritual performer in the decoration and furnishing of temples. Titles of office holders and many texts show that priests were important in society, but they could not be celebrated in images alongside deities and the king. The slow development of idealized forms in which the king was depicted interacting with deities paralleled the separation between the content of temple decoration and the practices and personnel of cult. Not until the late second millennium was there an appreciable departure from this extreme idealization.

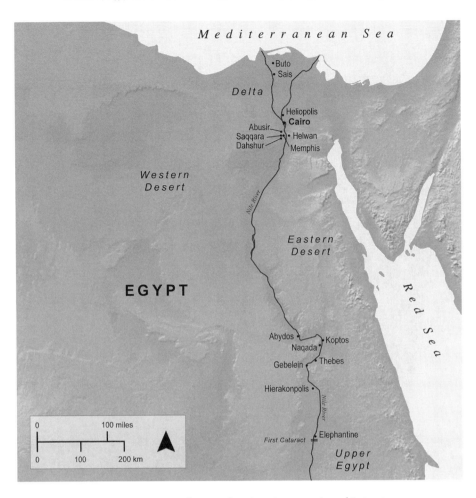

Figure 16.1. Map of Egypt showing sites mentioned in text

Figure 16.2. Cylinder of Narmer showing the king as the catfish of his name smiting Libyan enemies. Ivory, raised relief. Dynasty 0, ca. 3000 B.C.E. From the Hierakonpolis Main Deposit. Height ca. 5.7 cm. Oxford, Ashmolean Museum E.3915 (drawing courtesy of the Ashmolean Museum)

Figure 16.3. Narmer Palette. left: side with smiting scene. Siltstone, raised relief. Dynasty 0, ca. 3000 B.C.E. From the Hierakonpolis Main Deposit. Height 64 cm. Cairo, Egyptian Museum CG 14716 (photo by kind permission of Jürgen Liepe)

Figure 16.3 (*cont.*). Narmer Palette. right: side with grinding depression. Siltstone, raised relief. Dynasty 0, ca. 3000 B.C.E. From the Hierakonpolis Main Deposit. Height 64 cm. Cairo, Egyptian Museum CG 14716 (photo by kind permission of Jürgen Liepe)

Figure 16.4. Rectangular relief palette
from excavations of Zaki Saad at
Helwan. Siltstone. Naqada IIIB or First
Dynasty. Height ca. 18 cm. Present
location unknown (Saad 1969, pl. 75)

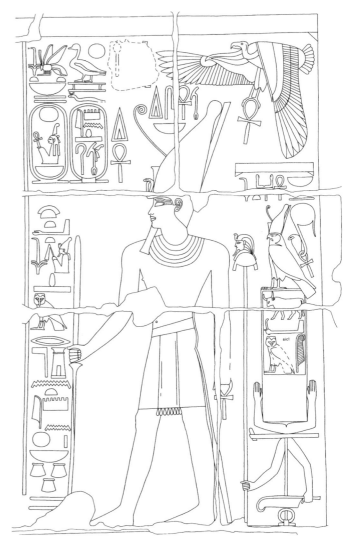

Figure 16.5. King Amenhotep III (ca. 1370 B.C.E.) standing with an
emblematic figure of his *ka* behind him. The *ka*, which is also a
writing of his Horus name, is surmounted by a sky sign indicating
its divinity and is captioned "the king's living *ka*." Sandstone relief.
Luxor Temple, room 18, west wall, lower register, rightmost scene
(Brunner 1977, pl. 153; wrongly numbered on plate, see key plate 23)

Figure 16.6. Two First Dynasty tags. Left, tag of the reign of Aha showing an enclosure within which is a figure of a cow goddess and a hieroglyph meaning "encircle." From Cemetery B at Abydos. Wood. Width 7.8 cm (Petrie 1901, pl. 11:1); Right, tag from the tomb of Den at Umm el-Qaʿab, Abydos. Ivory. Width ca. 4.5 cm. Cairo, Egyptian Museum JE 34905 (drawing by Marion Cox)

Figure 16.7. Tag with the name of Aha from his tomb complex in Cemetery B at Abydos, bearing three registers of pictorial materials and one of information about products. First Dynasty. Wood. Width ca. 10 cm. University of Pennsylvania Museum of Archaeology and Anthropology E9396 (Petrie 1901, pl. 3a:5)

Figure 16.8. Tag of the reign of Djer, probably from his tomb complex at Umm el-Qaʿab, Abydos. Ivory. First Dynasty. Width 4.8 cm. Berlin, Ägyptisches Museum 18026 (Scharff 1929–31, pp. 2, 171, fig. 92)

Figure 16.9. Royal relief fragment from Gebelein. Limestone. Height ca. 85 cm, width ca. 45 cm. Turin, Museo Egizio S. 12341 (Scamuzzi n.d.: pl. 8; copyright Fondazione Museo delle Antichità Egizie di Torino, used with permission)

Figure 16.10. Erased block of the reign of Khasekhemwy from Hierakonpolis, showing two scenes. Left, the king stands with before him a complex array of miniature figures of deities, perhaps signifying cult images; right, the foundation of a temple performed by the goddess Seshat and a second figure of the king, or possibly the god Thoth. Granite. Dimensions not stated. Cairo, Egyptian Museum JdE 33896 (Engelbach 1934, pl. 24)

Figure 16.11. Part of a rough, raised relief limestone stela showing an *imiut* offering life and power to the king's Horus name, with the names of two of his daughters behind. From the Step Pyramid complex of Djoser at Saqqara. Third Dynasty. Height 29.5 cm. Chicago, Oriental Institute Museum E13652

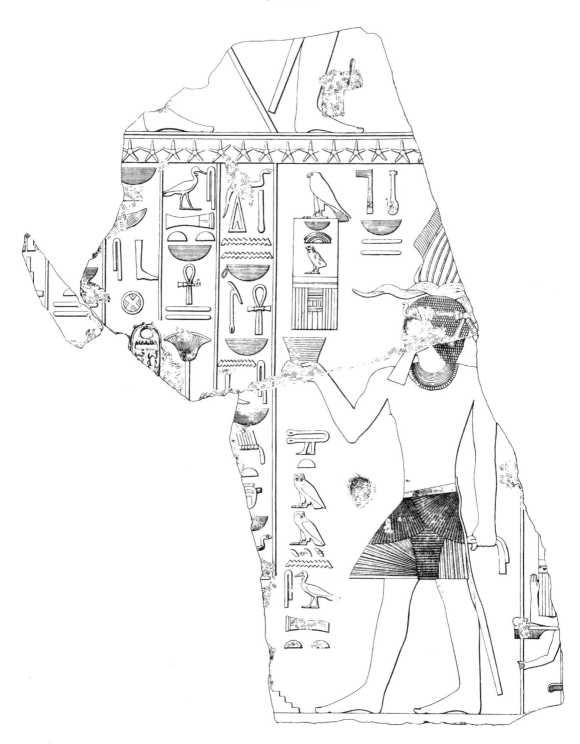

Figure 16.12. Scene of the king, with his *ka* behind him, offering to the goddess Bastet (figure lost), from the mortuary temple of Sahure at Abusir. Limestone, raised relief. Fifth Dynasty (with a secondary cartouche, probably of Thutmose IV of the Eighteenth Dynasty). Present location unknown.
Width of fragments ca. 130 cm (Borchardt et al. 1913, pl. 35)

Figure 16.13. Fragments from shrine of Djoser, from Heliopolis. Limestone, raised relief. Third Dynasty. Reconstructed width ca. 40 cm. Turin, Museo Egizio S. 2671/20, 2671/27, S. 2671/29 (Donadoni Roveri 1998, p. 55 fig. 2; copyright Fondazione Museo delle Antichità Egizie di Torino, used with permission)

Figure 16.14. Emblematic design showing king Sahure's Horus name receiving power and recurrence from Nekhbet, the goddess of Upper Egypt, who is shown as a vulture. One of two complementary versions carved in sunken outline (perhaps originally painted green) on granite columns from the king's mortuary temple at Abusir. Fifth Dynasty (Borchardt 1910, p. 45; see also figs. 44–45, 48, pl. 9)

Bibliography

Adams, Barbara

    1974   *Ancient Hierakonpolis* and *Ancient Hierakonpolis: Supplement.* Warminster: Aris & Phillips.

Adams, Barbara, and Richard Jaeschke

    1984   *The Koptos Lions.* Contributions in Anthropology and History Series 3. Milwaukee: Milwaukee Public Museum.

Alexanian, Nicole

    1998   "Die Reliefdekoration des Chasechemui aus dem sogenannten Fort in Hierakonpolis." In *Les critères de datation stylistiques à l'Ancien Empire,* edited by Nicolas-Christophe Grimal, pp. 1–29. Bibliothèque d'étude 120. Cairo: Institut français d'archéologie orientale.

Altenmüller, Hartwig

    1965   Die Apotropaia und die Götter Mittelägyptens. 2 volumes. Ph.D. dissertation, University of Munich.

Anderson, David A.

    2011   "Evidence for Early Ritual Activity in the Predynastic Settlement at El-Mahâsna." In *Egypt at Its Origins* 3 (Proceedings of the Third International Conference "Origin of the State: Predynastic and Early Dynastic Egypt," London, 27th July–1st August 2008), edited by Renée Friedman and Peter N. Fiske, pp. 3–29. Orientalia Lovaniensia Analecta 205. Leuven: Peeters.

Arnold, Dorothea, and Christiane Ziegler, editors

    1999   *Egyptian Art in the Age of the Pyramids.* Exhibition Catalogue, Metropolitan Museum of Art. New York: Metropolitan Museum of Art.

Asselberghs, Henri

    1961   *Chaos en beheersing: Documenten uit het Aeneolitisch Egypte.* Documenta et Monumenta Orientis Antiqui 8. Leiden: Brill.

Baines, John

    1985   *Fecundity Figures: Egyptian Personification and the Iconology of a Genre.* Warminster: Aris & Phillips; Chicago: Bolchazy-Carducci.

    1991   "On the Symbolic Context of the Principal Hieroglyph for 'God.'" In *Religion und Philosophie im alten Ägypten: Festgabe für Philippe Derchain zu seinem 65. Geburtstag,* edited by Ursula Verhoeven and Erhart Graefe, pp. 29–46. Orientalia Lovaniensia Analecta 39. Leuven: Peeters.

    1995   "Origins of Egyptian Kingship." In *Ancient Egyptian Kingship,* edited by David B. O'Connor and David P. Silverman, pp. 95–156. Probleme der Ägyptologie 9. Leiden: Brill.

    2003   "Early Definitions of the Egyptian World and Its Surroundings." In *Culture through Objects: Ancient Near Eastern Studies in Honour of P. R. S. Moorey,* edited by Timothy F. Potts, Michael Roaf, and Diana L. Stein, pp. 27–57. Oxford: Griffith Institute.

    2007   *Visual and Written Culture in Ancient Egypt.* Oxford: Oxford University Press.

    2011   "Ancient Egypt." In *The Oxford History of Historical Writing,* Volume 1: *Beginnings to A.D. 600,* edited by Andrew Feldherr and Grant Hardy, pp. 53–75. Oxford: Oxford University Press.

    In press   *High Culture and Experience in Ancient Egypt.* Studies in Egyptology and Ancient Near East. Sheffield: Equinox.

Baines, John, and Christina Riggs
    2001   "Archaism and Kingship: A Late Royal Statue and Its Early Dynastic Model." *Journal of Egyptian Archaeology* 87: 103–18.

Beckerath, Jürgen von
    1956   "Šmsj-Ḥrw in der ägyptischen Vor- und Frühzeit." *Mitteilungen des Deutschen Archäologischen Instituts, Abteilung Kairo* 14: 1–10.

Bietak, Manfred
    1994   "Zu den heiligen Bezirken mit Palmen in Buto und Sais: Ein archäologischer Befund aus dem Mittleren Reich." In *Zwischen den beiden Ewigkeiten: Festschrift Gertrud Thausing*, edited by Manfred Bietak, Johanna Holaubek, Hans Mukarovsky, and Helmut Satzinger, pp. 1–18. Vienna: Institut für Ägyptologie der Universität.

Blöbaum, Anke Ilona
    2006   *"Denn ich bin ein König, der die Maat liebt": Herrscherlegitimation im spätzeitlichen Ägypten; eine vergleichende Untersuchung der Phraseologie in den offiziellen Königsinschriften vom Beginn der 25. Dynastie bis zum Ende der makedonischen Herrschaft.* Aegyptiaca Monasteriensia 4. Aachen: Shaker.

Bolshakov, Andrey O.
    2001   "Ka, ka-chapel." In *The Oxford Encyclopedia of Ancient Egypt*, edited by Donald B. Redford, vol. 2, pp. 215–19. New York: Oxford University Press.

Borchardt, Ludwig
    1909   *Das Grabdenkmal des Königs Nefer-ir-keʒ-Reᶜ.* Ausgrabungen der Deutschen Orient-Gesellschaft in Abusir, 1902–1908, 5. Wissenschaftliche Veröffentlichung der deutschen Orient-Gesellschaft 11. Leipzig: Hinrichs.
    1910   *Das Grabdenkmal des Königs Šaʒḥu-Reᶜ*, Volume 1: *Der Bau.* Ausgrabungen der Deutschen Orient-Gesellschaft in Abusir, 1902–1908, 6. Wissenschaftliche Veröffentlichung der deutschen Orient-Gesellschaft 14. Leipzig: Hinrichs.

Borchardt, Ludwig; Ernst Assmann; Alfred Bollacher; Oskar Heinroth; Max Hilzheimer; and Kurt Sethe
    1913   *Das Grabdenkmal des Königs Šaʒḥu-Reᶜ*, Volume 2: *Die Wandbilder.* Ausgrabungen der Deutschen Orient-Gesellschaft in Abusir, 1902–1908, 7. Wissenschaftliche Veröffentlichung der deutschen Orient-Gesellschaft 26. Leipzig: Hinrichs.

Brunner, Hellmut
    1977   *Die südlichen Räume des Tempels von Luxor.* Archäologische Veröffentlichungen des Deutschen Archäologischen Instituts, Abteilung Kairo 18. Mainz: Philipp von Zabern.

Bussmann, Richard
    2010   *Die Provinztempel Ägyptens von der 0. bis zur 11. Dynastie: Archäologie und Geschichte einer gesellschaftlichen Institution zwischen Residenz und Provinz.* 2 volumes. Probleme der Ägyptologie 30. Leiden: Brill.

Chassinat, Emile
    1947–1952 *Le temple de Dendara* V. Cairo: Institut français d'archéologie orientale.

Chassinat, Emile; and François Daumas
    1965   *Le temple de Dendara* VI. Cairo: Institut français d'archéologie orientale.

Davies, Norman de Garis
    1953   *The Temple of Hibis in El Khargeh Oasis* III: *The Decoration.* The Metropolitan Museum of Art, Egyptian Expedition Publications 17. New York: Metropolitan Museum of Art.

Dodson, Aidan

    1988   "Egypt's First Antiquarians." *Antiquity* 62: 513–17.

Donadoni Roveri, Anna Maria, and Francesco Tiradritti

    1998   *Kemet: Alle sorgenti del tempo.* Exhibition Catalogue. Milan: Electa.

Dreyer, Günter

    1986   *Elephantine VIII: Der Tempel der Satet, die Funde der Frühzeit und des Alten Reiches.*
                            Deutsches Archäologisches Institut, Abteilung Kairo, Archäologische Veröffent-
                            lichungen 39. Mainz: Philipp von Zabern.

Eckmann, Christian, and Saher Shafik

    2005   *"Leben dem Horus Pepi": Restaurierung und technologische Untersuchung der Metall-*
                            skulpturen des Pharao Pepi I. aus Hierakonpolis. Römisch-Germanisches Zentralmu-
                            seum Mainz, Forschungsinstitut für Vor- und Frühgeschichte, Monographien
                            59. Mainz: Verlag des Römisch-Germanischen Zentralmuseums.

Engelbach, R.

    1934   "A Foundation Scene of the Second Dynasty." *Journal of Egyptian Archaeology* 20:
                            183–84.

Fakhry, Ahmed

    1961   *The Monuments of Sneferu at Dahshur* II: *The Valley Temple* I: *The Temple Reliefs.*
                            Ministry of Culture and National Orientation: Antiquities Department of Egypt.
                            Cairo: General Organization for Government Printing Offices.

Firth, Cecil M.; James Edward Quibell; and Jean-Philippe Lauer

    1935   *The Step Pyramid.* 2 volumes. Service des Antiquités de l'Egypte, Excavations at
                            Saqqara. Cairo: Institut français d'archéologie orientale.

Fischer, Henry George, editor

    1980   *Ancient Egypt in the Metropolitan Museum Journal.* New York: Metropolitan Museum
                            of Art.

Gardiner, Alan H.

    1957   *Egyptian Grammar, Being an Introduction to the Study of Hieroglyphs.* 3rd edition.
                            London: Oxford University Press for Griffith Institute.

Goebs, Katja

    2008   *Crowns in Egyptian Funerary Literature: Royalty, Rebirth, and Destruction.* Oxford:
                            Griffith Institute.

Hayes, William C.

    1947   "Ḥoremkhaʿuef of Nekhen and His Trip to It-Towe." *Journal of Egyptian Archaeol-*
                            ogy 33: 3–11.

Helck, Wolfgang

    1954   "Zu den theophoren Eigennamen des Alten Reiches." *Zeitschrift für ägyptische*
                            Sprache und Altertumskunde 79: 27–33.

    1991   "Zu Ptah und Sokar." In *Religion und Philosophie im alten Ägypten: Festgabe für*
                            Philippe Derchain zu seinem 65. Geburtstag, edited by Ursula Verhoeven and Erhart
                            Graefe, pp. 159–64. Orientalia Lovaniensia Analecta 39. Leuven: Peeters.

Hendrickx, Stan

    1996   "The Relative Chronology of the Naqada Culture: Problems and Possibilities."
                            In *Aspects of Early Egypt*, edited by A. Jeffrey Spencer, pp. 36–69, 159–74 (bibli-
                            ography). London: British Museum Press.

Hikade, Thomas

    2011   "Origins of Monumental Architecture: Recent Excavations at Hierakonpolis HK29b and HK25." In *Egypt at Its Origins 3* (Proceedings of the Third International Conference "Origin of the State: Predynastic and Early Dynastic Egypt," London, 27th July–1st August 2008), edited by Renée Friedman and Peter N. Fiske, pp. 81–107. Orientalia Lovaniensia Analecta 205. Leuven: Peeters.

Jackson, Natasha

    2008   Board Games as Symbols of Transition in Ancient Egypt. B.A. thesis, University of Oxford.

Kaiser, Werner

    1987   "Die dekorierte Torfassade des spätzeitlichen Palastbezirkes von Memphis." *Mitteilungen des Deutschen Archäologischen Instituts, Abteilung Kairo* 43: 123–54.

Kaiser, Werner; Günter Dreyer; Robert Gempeler; Peter Grossmann; Gerhard Haeny; Horst Jaritz; and Friedrich Junge

    1976   "Stadt und Tempel von Elephantine: Sechster Grabungsbericht." *Mitteilungen des Deutschen Archäologischen Instituts, Abteilung Kairo* 32: 67–112.

Kantorowicz, Ernst H.

    1957   *The King's Two Bodies: A Study in Mediaeval Political Theology.* Princeton: Princeton University Press.

Kaplony, Peter

    1963   *Die Inschriften der ägyptischen Frühzeit.* 3 volumes. Ägyptologische Abhandlungen 8. Wiesbaden: Harrassowitz.

    1965   "Eine Schminkpalette von König Skorpion aus Abu 'Umûri (Untersuchung zur ältesten Horustitulatur)." *Orientalia* 34: 132–67.

Kees, Hermann

    1912   Der Opfertanz des ägyptischen Königs. Doctoral dissertation, Ludwig-Maximilians-Universität, Munich.

Kemp, Barry J.

    1989   *Ancient Egypt: Anatomy of a Civilization.* London: Routledge.

    2006   *Ancient Egypt: Anatomy of a Civilization.* 2nd edition. London: Routledge.

Kemp, Barry J.; Andrew Boyce; and James Harrell

    2000   "The Colossi from the Early Shrine at Coptos in Egypt." *Cambridge Archaeological Journal* 10: 211–42.

Köhler, Ursula

    1975   *Das Imiut: Untersuchungen zur Darstellung und Bedeutung eines mit Anubis verbundenen religiösen Symbols.* 2 volumes. Göttenger Orientforschungen 4, Ägypten 4. Wiesbaden: Harrassowitz.

Kubisch, Sabine

    2008   *Lebensbilder der 2. Zwischenzeit: Biographische Inschriften der 13.-17. Dynastie.* Deutsches Archäologisches Institute, Abteilung Kairo, Sonderschrift 34. Berlin: De Gruyter.

Kurth, Dieter

    1994   *Treffpunkt der Götter: Inschriften aus dem Tempel des Horus von Edfu.* Zurich: Artemis.

Lacau, Pierre, and Henri Chevrier

    1956–1969   *Une chapelle de Sésostris Ier à Karnak.* 2 volumes. Service des antiquités de l'Egypte. Cairo: Institut français d'archéologie orientale.

Lacau, Pierre, and Jean Philippe Lauer

    1959–1961   *La pyramide à Degrés* IV: *Inscriptions gravées sur les vases*. Service des antiquités de l'Egypte, fouilles à Saqqarah. Cairo: Institut français d'archéologie orientale.

Landgráfová, Renata

    2006   "Faience Inlays and Tablets of Egyptian Blue." In *Abusir* IX: *The Pyramid Complex of Raneferef; The Archaeology*, edited by Miroslav Verner, pp. 451–92. Excavations of the Czech Institute of Egyptology. Prague: Czech Institute of Egyptology.

Lauer, Jean-Philippe

    1936   *La pyramide à Degrés: l'architecture*. 2 volumes. Service des antiquités de l'Egypte, fouilles à Saqqarah. Cairo: Institut français d'archéologie orientale.

Malek, Jaromir

    2003   *Egypt: 4,000 Years of Art*. London: Phaidon.

McDonald, Angela

    2007   "A Metaphor for Troubled Times: The Evolution of the Seth Deity Determinative in the First Intermediate Period." *Zeitschrift für ägyptische Sprache und Altertumskunde* 134: 26–39.

McNamara, Liam

    2008   "The Revetted Mound at Hierakonpolis and Early Kingship: A Reinterpretation." In *Egypt at Its Origins* 2 (Proceedings of the International Conference "Origin of the State: Predynastic and Early Dynastic Egypt," Toulouse, 5th–8th September 2005), edited by Béatrix Midant-Reynes and Yann Tristant, pp. 899–934. Orientalia Lovaniensia Analecta 172. Leuven: Peeters.

Morenz, Ludwig D.

    1994   "Zur Dekoration der frühzeitlichen Tempel am Beispiel zweier Fragmente des archaischen Tempels von Gebelein." In *Ägyptische Tempel – Struktur, Funktion und Programm* (Akten der ägyptologischen Tempeltagungen in Gosen 1990 und in Mainz 1992), edited by Rolf Gundlach and Matthias Rochholz, pp. 217–38. Hildesheimer Ägyptologische Beiträge 37. Hildesheim: Gerstenberg.

    2002   "Die Götter und ihr Redetext: Die ältestbelegte Sakral-Monumentalisierung von Textlichkeit auf Fragmenten der Zeit des Djoser aus Heliopolis." In *5. Ägyptologische Tempeltagung: Würzburg, 23.-26. September 1999*, edited by Horst Beinlich, pp. 137–58. Ägypten und Altes Testament 33: 3. Wiesbaden: Harrassowitz.

Newberry, Percy E.

    1893a   *Beni Hasan* I. Archaeological Survey of Egypt 1. London: Egypt Exploration Fund.

    1893b   *Beni Hasan* II. Archaeological Survey of Egypt 2. London: Egypt Exploration Fund.

O'Connor, David

    2011   "The Narmer Palette: A New Interpretation." In *Before the Pyramids: The Origins of Egyptian Civilization*, edited by Emily Teeter, pp. 149–52. Oriental Institute Museum Publications 33. Chicago: The Oriental Institute.

Petrie, W. M. Flinders

    1896   *Koptos*. London: Bernard Quaritch.

    1901   *The Royal Tombs of the Earliest Dynasties, 1901,* Part 2. Egypt Exploration Fund, Memoir 21. London: Egypt Exploration Fund.

    1921   *Corpus of Prehistoric Pottery and Palettes*. British School of Archaeology in Egypt and Egyptian Research Account, 23rd Year, 1917. London: British School of Archaeology in Egypt.

Piquette, Kathryn E.
    2008   Writing, Art and Society: A Contextual Archaeology of the Inscribed Labels of Late Predynastic–Early Dynastic Egypt. Doctoral dissertation, University College London.

Quibell, James Edward
    1900   *Hierakonpolis* I. Egyptian Research Account Memoir 4. London: Bernard Quaritch.
    1905   *Archaic Objects.* Catalogue Général des Antiquités Egyptiennes du Musée du Caire. Cairo: Institut français d'archéologie orientale.

Quibell, James Edward, and F. W. Green
    1902   *Hierakonpolis* II. Egyptian Research Account Memoir 5. London: Bernard Quaritch.

Roeder, Günther
    1914   *Naos.* Catalogue Général des Antiquités Egyptiennes du Musée du Caire. Leipzig: Breitkopf und Härtel.

Saad, Zaki Youssef
    1969   *The Excavations at Helwan: Art and Civilization in the First and Second Egyptian Dynasties.* Norman: University of Oklahoma Press.

Schäfer, Heinrich
    1902   *Ein Bruchstück altägyptischer Annalen.* Abhandlungen der Preussischen Akademie der Wissenschaften 1902, Anhang. Berlin: Georg Reimer.

Scharff, Alexander
    1929–1931   *Die Altertümer der Vor- und Frühzeit Ägyptens.* 2 volumes. Staatliche Museen zu Berlin, Mitteilungen aus der Ägyptischen Sammlung 4–5. Berlin: Curtius.

Schweitzer, Ursula
    1956   *Das Wesen des Ka in Diesseits und Jenseits der alten Ägypter.* Ägyptologische Forschungen 19. Glückstadt: J. J. Augustin.

Seidlmayer, Stephan Johannes
    2001   "Die Ikonographie des Todes." In *Social Aspects of Funerary Culture in the Egyptian Old and Middle Kingdoms* (Proceedings of the Symposium held at Leiden, 6–7 June 1996), edited by Harco Willems, pp. 205–53. Orientalia Lovaniensia Analecta 103. Leuven: Peeters.

Shedid, Abdel-Ghaffar
    1994   *Die Felsgräber von Beni Hassan in Mittelägypten.* Zaberns Bildbände zur Archäologie 16. Mainz: Philipp von Zabern.

Spencer, Neal
    2006   *A Naos of Nekhthorheb from Bubastis: Religious Iconography and Temple Building in the 30th Dynasty.* British Museum Research Publications 156. London: British Museum.

te Velde, Herman
    1982   "Ptah." In *Lexikon der Ägyptologie*, edited by Wolfgang Helck and Wolfhart Westendorf, vol. 4, cols. 1177–80. Wiesbaden: Harrassowitz.

Teeter, Emily, editor
    2011   *Before the Pyramids: The Origins of Egyptian Civilization.* Oriental Institute Museum Publications 33. Chicago: The Oriental Institute.

van Haarlem, Willem M.
    1998   "Archaic Shrine Models from Tell Ibrahim Awad." *Mitteilungen des Deutschen Archäologischen Instituts, Abteilung Kairo* 54: 183–85.

2009   *Temple Deposits at Tell Ibrahim Awad.* Amsterdam: [van Haarlem].

von der Way, Thomas

1992   "Indication of Architecture with Niches at Buto." In *The Followers of Horus, Studies Dedicated to Michael Allen Hoffman*, edited by Renée Friedman and Barbara Adams, pp. 217–26. Oxford: Oxbow Books.

Vörös, Győző

1998   *Temple on the Pyramid of Thebes: Hungarian Excavations on Thoth Hill at the Temple of Pharaoh Montuhotep Sankhkara, 1995-1998.* Budapest: Százszorszép Kiadó.

Vörös, Győző, and Rezsö Pudleiner

1998   "Preliminary Report of the Excavations at Thoth Hill, Thebes: The Pre-11th Dynasty Temple and the Western Building." *Mitteilungen des Deutschen Archäologischen Instituts, Abteilung Kairo* 54: 335–40.

Waitkus, Wolfgang

2010   "Die Verteilung der Darstellungen des königlichen Ka in der Tempeldekoration der griechisch-römischen Zeit." In *Edfu: Materialien und Studien*, edited by Dieter Kurth and Wolfgang Waitkus, pp. 115–30. Die Inschriften des Tempels von Edfu Begleithefte 6. Gladbeck: PeWe-Verlag.

Wengrow, David

2006   *The Archaeology of Early Egypt: Social Transformations in North-East Africa, 10,000 to 2650 B.C.* Cambridge World Archaeology. Cambridge: Cambridge University Press.

2007   "Enchantment and Sacrifice in Early Egypt." In *Art's Agency and Art History*, edited by Robin Osborne and Jeremy Tanner, pp. 28–41. New Interventions in Art History. Oxford: Blackwell.

In press   *The Origin of Monsters: Image and Cognition in the First Age of Mechanical Reproduction.* Princeton: Princeton University Press.

Whitehouse, Helen

2009   *Ancient Egypt and Nubia in the Ashmolean Museum.* Oxford: Ashmolean Museum.

Wilkinson, Toby A. H.

2000   *Royal Annals of Ancient Egypt: The Palermo Stone and Its Associated Fragments.* Studies in Egyptology. London: Kegan Paul International.

Williams, Bruce Beyer

1988   "Narmer and the Coptos Colossi." *Journal of the American Research Center in Egypt* 25: 35–59.

Winter, Erich

1968   *Untersuchungen zu den ägyptischen Tempelreliefs der griechisch-römischen Zeit.* Österreichische Akademie der Wissenschaften, philosophisch-historische Klasse, Denkschriften 98. Vienna: Hermann Böhlaus Nachfolger.

1994   "Wer steht hinter Narmer?" In *Zwischen den beiden Ewigkeiten: Festschrift Gertrud Thausing*, edited by Manfred Bietak, Johanna Holaubek, Hans Mukarovsky, and Helmut Satzinger, pp. 279–90. Vienna: Institut für Ägyptologie der Universität.

17

MIRROR AND MEMORY: IMAGES OF RITUAL ACTIONS IN GREEK TEMPLE DECORATION

Clemente Marconi, New York University

The purpose of this essay is to fill a gap in the scholarship on Greek temple decoration. It is generally agreed that the Parthenon frieze (fig. 17.1), which has as its subject the Panathenaic festival, represents the most significant document of Greek architectural sculpture, and there is a notable number of images of ritual actions attested for the decoration of Greek sacred architecture. Yet, in the field of Greek art, it is generally assumed that the representation of rituals did not have a part in the figural decoration of Greek temples, which would have largely been dedicated to gods, heroes, and monsters. The immediate goal of this contribution is to reassess the evidence for this thus far unrecognized category of images; its main ambition, however, is to address the significance of these representations from a larger, hermeneutic perspective, analyzing their role within the context of the interactive relationship between human ritual participants and built ritual contexts.[1]

Let me start, first, with the paradox that I point out above: the case of the Parthenon frieze. This carved band, which ran around the building's cella walls, has as its subject the Panathenaea, the major Athenian civic festival in honor of its patron goddess Athena, celebrated every year in midsummer.[2] The core of this festival was the great procession winding from the Kerameikos through the agora up to the Akropolis, and culminating in the presentation to the goddess of an elaborate robe, and in a large sacrifice at Athena's Great Altar.

Accordingly, on the Parthenon frieze, in following the interpretation by Jenifer Neils,[3] one sees in sequence, moving from west to east: the prelude to the procession, with the inspection of the horses; the procession itself, led by marshals and articulated into an equestrian parade and a pedestrian parade; and finally, receiving the procession, the eponymous heroes and the gods, the latter presumably gathered on the Akropolis ground, and framing the peplos ceremony.

The Parthenon frieze represents the best visualization of the Panathenaea, and yet, this interpretation of the monument as a depiction of the real festival has been quite controversial. I am referring to alternative interpretations of the frieze as a representation of the heroic past, generally based on the assumption that this would be the only known instance of the depiction of a historical, rather than mythological event in Greek temple decoration.[4] Often quoted, within this context, is the remark by Arnold Walter Lawrence, that "never before had a contemporary subject been treated on a religious building and no subsequent

---

[1] See especially Jones 2000.

[2] See more recently Sourvinou-Inwood 2011, pp. 263–311.

[3] Neils 2001, pp. 125–201.

[4] See, e.g., Connelly 1996, pp. 54–55.

instance is known ...."[5] This remark has served as the basis for the alternative, mythological readings of the Parthenon frieze, but it is in fact quite wrong.

The problem at stake here goes beyond the literature concerning the Parthenon frieze. One could mention the *Thesaurus Cultus et Rituum Antiquorum* (abbreviated *ThesCRA*), an encyclopedic project published since 2004 concerning the Greek, Etruscan, and Roman world, which systematically reviews the evidence concerning ritual actions, including their ancient representations, and in which images of ritual actions on Greek architecture are significantly underrepresented, in contrast with the Etruscan and Roman material. This is very much within the traditional paradigm of interpretation of Greek art, which emphasizes its idealism and lack of representation of historical events, in contrast with the drive toward realism and contemporary history of Etruscan and Roman art.[6]

Yet, the fact of the matter is that throughout the history of Greek sacred architecture over twenty buildings bore decoration which may well be interpreted as representations of ritual actions, often performed by mortals. By ritual actions I am referring to performances such as processions, dances, banquets, dedications, sacrifices, and libations. The evidence is uneven and fragmentary, as is usual for most Greek architectural sculpture. In addition, in some instances, an alternative, mythological interpretation has been posited for the scenes that may be considered ritual actions, although this is more the result of preconceived notions about what should be the subject of Greek temple decoration than of sound iconographical judgment. All in all, however, the extant evidence makes clear that we are dealing with a phenomenon of some significance, covering the full chronological spectrum, from the Orientalizing down to the Hellenistic period, with all the regions of the Greek world being represented, including Mainland Greece, the Aegean, Asia Minor, and the West.

The largest group of images of ritual actions in Greek temple decoration depicts processions. This is hardly a surprise, considering the importance of processions in Greek and Roman religious practice, which prompted the Christian admonition to "abjure the devil and his procession."[7] Processions were regularly included in the annual rituals and festivals in honor of the gods, and they played an important role in strengthening the sense of belonging to the same community of the participants, who at the same time, in marching along the processional route expressed their control of the urban and extraurban space.

The Parthenon frieze offers the best example of a procession in Greek sacred architecture, not least thanks to its remarkable state of preservation, which allows for the understanding of the complexity of such images, beginning with the division of the participants into subgroups. The same subject, however, is already met in association with sacred architecture as early as the seventh century, and it was featured on major buildings of the Archaic period, such as the Artemision at Ephesos (fig. 17.2). Interestingly, the Parthenon offers the only occurrence of this iconography on Greek sacred architecture after the close of the Archaic period.

The second largest group of images of ritual actions shows dances. Here again, the relevance of the subject goes along with its significance in Greek religious practice.[8] Not only was the choral performance an essential component of the spectacle of a religious festival but

---

[5] Lawrence 1972, p. 144.
[6] See especially Hölscher 1973.

[7] On processions in the Greek world, see *ThesCRA* I, pp. 1–20.
[8] On dances, see *ThesCRA* II, pp. 299–343.

part of that spectacle was also the multiplicity of choral performances, which usually found its expression in the competition between several choruses. The subject was of particular significance during the Archaic period: the best preserved instance is the Temple of Hera II at Foce del Sele (fig. 17.3); the most intriguing — unfortunately lost to us — was the Throne of Apollo at Amyklai, which featured, along with the dance of the Phaiakians at the song of Demodokos, the dance of the Magnesians who helped Bathykles to make this monument. As is the case of processions, we have only one instance of choral dancing after the close of the Archaic period: the frieze of the Hall of Choral Dancers at Samothrace (fig. 17.4).

Third, after processions and choral dances, come banquets, for which the best attestations in architectural decoration are offered by the contemporary Archaic temples of Athena at Assos (fig. 17.5) and at Larisa on the Hermos. With one exception, these scenes all come from Asia Minor, where banqueting played a significant role in the life and self-representation of the elites, and they all date to the Archaic period.[9]

With dedications, relating to the essential action of votive offering,[10] which could involve both individuals and entire communities, we come to the discussion of Archaic caryatids and their immediate sources of inspiration. The latter refers to the korai decorating the column drums of the Temple of Apollo at Didyma. These figures likely served as a model for the caryatids used on a series of treasuries at Delphi.[11] The rich attire and elaborate hairstyles of these caryatids, along with their gesture of extending one hand (documented for one of the caryatids of the Siphnian Treasury; fig. 17.6), makes them votaries of high status,[12] very appropriate for the buildings rich in decoration and offerings whose entablature they contributed to support.

In comparison with processions, dances, and dedications, other forms of ritual performances are less documented. There are only two attestations for sacrifices, although this was by far the most important form of ritual action in Greek religion,[13] and — coherent with the general tendency in Greek art to refrain from the representation of the killing of the sacrificial victim — they are both focused on the preparatory stage, of leading the animal to the altar. This, as the Parthenon frieze shows, could fall under the representation of processions, from which they appear to be divorced in the cases under consideration. I am referring to the column bases of the Artemision at Ephesos and to the parapet surrounding the Temple of Athena Nike on the Akropolis.

Last but not least, we have only one attestation for libations,[14] namely, the Caryatids of the Erechtheion (fig. 17.7) on the Akropolis, who originally held phialai in their right hands.

In consideration of the paradox mentioned at the outset, I thought it necessary to outline the various forms of ritual actions featured in the decoration of Greek sacred architecture. This review of the evidence has already pointed out some aspects of the phenomenon. In terms of geographical distribution, our scenes are quite evenly documented in the various

---

[9] On banquets, see *ThesCRA* II, pp. 218–50.

[10] On dedications, see *ThesCRA* I, pp. 269–318.

[11] As particularly argued by Mylonas Shear (1999).

[12] Cf. the Akropolis korai, and their analogous extended forearm gesture. The most plausible interpretation of these images of young women is as bearers of offerings: see Karakasi 2003, pp. 124, 135–39. Against the alternative identification of the Akropo-

lis korai as images of Athena (advocated, in particular, by B. S. Ridgway and C. M. Keesling), stretching out one or both hands toward the worshipper (Keesling 2003, pp. 144–61), see Meyer and Brüggeman 2007, pp. 19–25.

[13] On sacrifices, see *ThesCRA* I, pp. 59–134.

[14] On libations, *ThesCRA* I, pp. 269–318.

regions of the Greek world. Things are different, however, in chronological terms, given that the vast majority of our scenes date to the Archaic period. Looking at the phenomenon from this perspective, one may suggest that, taking inspiration from the Near Eastern neighbors, Archaic Greek sacred architecture offered a repertoire of images of ritual actions that occasionally provided the inspiration for builders of later periods. Indeed, consider the importance of some of the structures featuring these scenes, such as the Throne of Apollo at Amyklai, the treasuries at Delphi, the Temple of Hera at Samos, the Artemision at Ephesos, or, finally, the Temple of Hera at Foce del Sele.

In turning to the general interpretation of the phenomenon, a good place to start is the concept of *decorum/decor*, or appropriateness.[15] This idea plays an important role in Greek and Latin sources in relation to architecture and the visual arts (the main text being Vitruvius, *On architecture* 1.2.5–7), and until recently it has received surprisingly little attention in scholarship on Greek architectural sculpture.[16] Appropriateness, generally speaking, requires that works of art define and are defined by the nature of the space in which they appear. At the semantic level, as regards iconographical motifs, this means that the themes of decoration must be appropriate to the character of the building. When one considers that the primary experience of temples and treasuries was as monumental backdrops for ritual performances that generally took place in the open-air, along sacred paths and around altars, and that images of ritual actions are generally found on the exterior of these buildings, the correspondence of these images to the notion of *decorum/decor* is clear. Yet, precisely this correspondence between images of ritual actions and actual performances invites us to reconsider these representations in terms of their agency.

In order to explore this aspect, let me take a step back and point to the fact that these images of ritual actions generally appeared on the same buildings with the more common representations of gods, heroes, and monsters. For these representations, a larger anthropological interpretation is available.[17] A main tenet of religious belief is the existence of supernatural forces, and cult brings humans participating in ritual action closer to these forces. Given that the sense of the numinous is at the root of religious experience, one of the main features of many religious rituals is to induce this sense of awe and thus to make the participant feel closer to the transcendental forces than he or she might feel in everyday life. In doing so, sacred ritual bridges the gulf between this world and the world beyond. And, since ritual action usually takes place in a special location — the sanctuary — this sanctuary becomes the liminal zone between This World and the Other World, for it partakes in the qualities of both.[18]

Keeping this anthropological perspective in mind, it is possible to understand the status of images of gods, heroes, and monsters on Greek temples. With their subjects, these images contributed to the creation of the liminal nature of the sanctuary as a place closer to the Other World, a place distant from This World. In doing so, this figural decoration contributed to the effort of ritual performance, which would have included the various acts of worship in the sacred space, like processions, performances of hymns, dances, dramas, and sacrifices, to induce a sense of the numinous in the participants.

---

[15] Horn-Oncken 1967; Pollitt 1974, pp. 341–47; Perry 2005, pp. 28–77; Hölscher 2009, p. 62.

[16] But for Egyptian architecture, see Arnold 1962 and Baines 1990.

[17] For what follows, see Marconi 2007, p. 28, with references.

[18] Leach 1976.

With this, we are brought back to the images that form the subject of this essay. Unlike the images of gods, heroes, and monsters, that were supposed to enhance the sense of displacement and difference from the Other World, images of ritual actions referred to the liminal space of the sanctuary, and to the performances that unfolded in association with the very buildings that they decorated, along with their mortal performers.

Greek architects and sculptors were seemingly aware of this difference in subjects and actors in these scenes: it cannot be a coincidence that images of ritual actions on Greek sacred architecture were often featured on the lower parts of buildings, close to eye level. In such cases (as at Prinias, Ephesos, and Delphi), when images of ritual actions were combined with images of gods, heroes, and monsters, there is a clear difference in status between the mortals and immortals, reflected in their different positioning on the buildings: the mortals closer to the ground, the immortals closer to the heavens.

First and foremost, this positioning was about hierarchy; yet, at the same time, the location of mortals close to eye level reinforced the connection between the images of ritual actions and the worshippers actually performing such actions, prompting the public to interact with the images, and to realize not only their performativity, but also their function as a mirror.[19]

This mirror function was further enhanced, at the semiotic level, by the movement of the scenes of ritual actions, in relation to the buildings that they decorated. The Parthenon frieze, with its image of a procession around the cella, moving from west to east, in the same direction of the actual Panathenaic procession, is the best example of this phenomenon, but a similar treatment of the progress of processions and choral dancers revolving around buildings or their parts, such as columns, is documented in several other cases.

The mirror function of these images was further enhanced by their particular emphasis on the adornment of their participants, including their elaborate hairstyles, rich garments, and jewelry, almost a signature of images of ritual actions on Greek sacred architecture, which directly reflected the adornment of the participants in religious festivals, especially processions and choruses.[20]

In the experience of sacred architecture, and in the conversation between worshippers and buildings, images of ritual actions thus took a special prominence, within what has also been described as a general strategy of ritual-architectural allurement.[21] In this role, images of ritual actions on Greek sacred architecture are similar to the votive offerings featuring analogous scenes dedicated in Greek sanctuaries.[22]

For the interpretation of these images, a key text is Pausanias's (*Description of Greece* 10.18.5) discussion of a group of bronze statues in the Sanctuary of Apollo at Delphi featuring a sacrifice and a procession dedicated by the people of a small town in the northeastern Peloponnese, Orneai.[23] According to Pausanias, during a war, the people of Orneai vowed to Apollo that if they succeeded, they would institute a procession in his honor every day at Delphi, and sacrifice a number of animals. However, after defeating their enemies, the people of Orneai found that the expense and trouble of fulfilling their vow daily was too great and, instead, dedicated bronze figures representing a sacrifice and a procession. Pausanias's story

---

[19] Cf. the self-reflexive play of painted vases for the symposion: Lissarrague 1990, pp. 87–106.

[20] See, e.g., Calame 2001 and Jones Roccos 1995.

[21] Jones 2000.

[22] Rouse 1902; Keesling 2003; *ThesCRA* I, pp. 269–318.

[23] Ioakimidou 1997, pp. 29–34, 127–35.

has always fascinated those interested in the relationship between art and ritual.[24] This is because, according to that story, the sculptural group was not only a commemoration and product of ritual action — a votive offering — but was itself the enactment, through its figures, of a ritual action. More precisely, the sculpture was not just an enactment, but a reenactment of the ritual, each and every day, from the day of the dedication up to the time of Pausanias and beyond. Two aspects of this narrative are striking: one is the power of pre-sentification of the statues, which not only stand for, but also act for the people that they represent; the other is the temporal dimension of the monument. The group of statues is not the commemoration of a procession and sacrifice once performed in the honor of Apollo as an expression of thanks for a military victory. The monument represents the performance of a new procession and a new sacrifice each and every day.

Interestingly, the base of this monument described by Pausanias is partially preserved (fig. 17.8), and shows that the sculpture featured a solemn march, with several over life-size figures arranged in pairs, closely spaced, and preceded by a young assistant leading the sacrificial animals to the altar. Placed to the south of the Temple of Apollo, on the terrace that included several other offerings and the monumental altar of the god, these statues would have looked as if they were marching toward the altar of Apollo, the very place where the sacrifice was supposed to be performed. Thus, the sculptural group not only replicated the appearance of a sacrifice, it must have also appeared, to people entering the sanctuary and ascending through the processional route to the altar of Apollo to perform a sacrifice, to be a reflection of their own actions.

We are thus back to the correspondence between representation and performance noted in relation to images of ritual actions adorning sacred buildings, which in the case of the dedication at Delphi centuries later generated the story of a sacrifice performed by the statues each and every day, just as "the sense of a text in general reaches far beyond what its author originally intended" (Gadamer 2004, p. 365). This is the agency of the images I mentioned before. Inherent to these images, because of their subject and location, was their function as mirror and memory: mirror, at the time of the festival, for the community of worshippers celebrating the gods; and memory, for the rest of the time, until the next festival was performed, and beyond.

This commemorative power of sculpture, to last forever, and speak forever, provides a critical layer of meaning to the images of ritual actions on Greek sacred architecture.[25] Commemorating religious festivals was no minor task in a religious system like the Greek one, which laid particular emphasis on traditionalism as an important dimension of ritual. Hence the principle that sons must perpetuate the rituals of their fathers, and the definition of reverence toward the gods (*eusebeia*), according to Isokrates (7.30), as "to change nothing of what our forefathers have left behind."

With this we come to the social dimension of the images under consideration. I have already noted that the majority of them refer to processions and choral dances. In these images, therefore, the emphasis lies not just on festivals, but collective actions.

The anthropology of religion, in particular the work of Émile Durkheim, the functionalists, and the early structuralists, has taught us that the religious festival has the critical function in societies of bringing people together and of creating a strong bond among them.[26]

---

[24] Elsner 1996, pp. 526–27.

[25] Marconi 2009, p. 172.

[26] Bell 1992, pp. 171–81; Bell 1997, pp. 23–60.

This was particularly true for the Greek polis of the Archaic and Classical periods, where the religious festival was the main occasion for constructing and shaping group identities.[27] By ordering the social body into ranks and making it process toward the sanctuaries to participate in collective sacrifices, or by arranging particular groups in choruses, rituals enhanced the self-consciousness of the participant of her- or himself as a part of the community.

Greek festivals were, first and foremost, experiences of visual splendor, so much so that for the Greeks, the same term, *theoria*, meant both going to a sanctuary and beholding.[28] The *theoros* was the participant in a sacred embassy who entered the sanctuary and was captivated by the spectacle that surrounded him. It was a spectacle made of people, with their costumes, ornaments, and performances, but also of images, from votive offerings to architectural sculptures. Images of ritual actions on Greek sacred architecture were clearly meant to be part of such a spectacle, and I suggest that they were also meant to operate as an active agent in constructing and shaping the identity of the religious community.

Appendix:
Main Images of Ritual Actions in Greek Temple Decoration

Processions

- Athens, Old Athena Temple (?), frieze (?), procession of men and women at the presence of gods (?), 510 B.C.E.: Schrader 1939, pp. 387–99 nos. 474–79; Bookidis 1967, pp. 338–47 F 76; Floren 1987, p. 247 n. 13; Santi 2010, pp. 231–35; Despinis 2009, pp. 354–61.

- Athens, Parthenon, frieze, Panathenaic procession, 447–438 B.C.E. (fig. 17.1): Brommer 1977; Jenkins 1994; Berger and Gisler-Huwiler 1996; Neils 2001.

- Ephesos, Temple of Artemis, column drums, festive procession with men, women, and horses, 560–530 B.C.E. (fig. 17.2): Pryce 1928, pp. 47–63 B 86–B 138; Bookidis 1967, pp. 276–80 F61; Floren 1987, p. 392 n. 13; Muss 1994, pp. 43–56; Bammer and Muss 1996, pp. 49–51; Marconi 2007, pp. 21–23.

- Ephesos, Temple of Artemis, parapet sima, procession, 520–460 B.C.E.: Pryce 1928, pp. 68–76 B 147–B 170; Bookidis 1967, pp. 281–85 F62; Floren 1987, p. 393 n. 17; Muss 1994, pp. 79, 87; Bammer and Muss 1996, pp. 51–53; Marconi 2007, pp. 23–24.

- Francavilla Marittima, Building III, geison revetment, procession to a sanctuary, 580–570 B.C.E.: Mertens-Horn 1992, pp. 51–52; Marconi 2007, p. 15.

- Metapontion, Temple C, geison revetment, procession to a sanctuary, 580–570 B.C.: Floren 1987, p. 430 note 169; Mertens–Horn 1992, pp. 46–73, 110–17; Marconi 2007, p. 15.

---

[27] On festivals in the Greek world, see *ThesCRA* VII, pp. 3–172.

[28] On *theoria*, Gadamer 2004, pp. 119–25 remains fundamental; for the application of this concept to the study of Greek sculpture, in particular, temple decoration, see Marconi 2004, p. 224; see more recently Neer 2010, pp. 11–13.

- Prinias, Temple A, orthostate frieze, parade of armed riders, 630–620 B.C.E.: Pernier 1914, pp. 48–54, 93–98; Bookidis 1967, pp. 269–75 F 60; Floren 1987, p. 130 n. 51; D'Acunto 1995, pp. 44–50; Watrous 1998 (the suggested identification of the riders with the Kouretes is not particularly compelling, since the latter are generally represented as dancers, and only rarely as riders: see Lindner 1997).

- Samos, Temple of Hera IV or North Building, frieze ("Kleiner Tempelfries"), procession (?), 510–500 B.C.E.: Buschor 1933, pp. 12–13; Buschor 1957, pp. 30–31; Bookidis 1967, pp. 289–92 F 64; Freyer-Schauenburg 1974, pp. 195–97, 200–01, nos. 116–17, 119, 127 (identification with a procession questioned: but frag. no. 116, featuring the feet of three figures standing to the left, closely spaced, is strongly suggestive of this subject); Floren 1987, p. 357 n. 68; Furtwängler and Kienast 1989, pp. 55–56, 156–58 nos. 21–22, 24.

- Samos, Temple of Hera II, frieze, parade of warriors, 670–650 B.C.E.: Freyer-Schauenburg 1974, pp. 184–85 no. 103; Floren 1987, p. 356 n. 60; Kienast 2001 (unwarranted skepticism about the attribution to the Temple of Hera II); Marconi 2007, p. 4.

- Siris, unidentified building, geison revetment, procession to a sanctuary, 580–570 B.C.E.: Mertens-Horn 1992, p. 52; Marconi 2007, p. 15.

Dances

- Amyklai, Throne of Apollo, friezes, dance of the Phaiakians at the song of Demodokos and dance of the Magnesians who helped Bathycles to make the throne (Pausanias, *Description of Greece* 3.18.11, 14), 520–510 B.C.E.: Faustoferri 1996, pp. 100–01, 211, 264.

- Foce del Sele, Temple of Hera II, metopes, choros of young women, 510–500 B.C.E. (fig. 17.3): Zancani Montuoro and Zanotti-Bianco 1951–1954, vol. 1, pp. 123–61; Bookidis 1967, pp. 227–30 M 54; Simon 1967, pp. 294–95 (suggested identification of the scene with the abduction of Helen by Theseus and Peirithoos problematic in the absence of any indication of the two men; contra Kahil 1988, pp. 511–12 no. 54); Floren 1987, p. 433 n. 209.

- Karaköy, unattributed building, parapet sima, women and girls dancing, 540–530 B.C.E. (fig. 17.9): Pryce 1928, pp. 116–17 B 282; Bookidis 1967, pp. 304–08 F 68; Tuchelt 1970, pp. 111–14 K 86; Floren 1987, p. 387 n. 56.

- Kyzikos, unattributed building, column base, a girl and two youths holding hands and dancing in a circle, 540 B.C.E. (fig. 17.10): Bookidis 1967, pp. 313–15 F 70; Floren 1987, p. 405 n. 14.

- Samothrace, Hall of Choral Dancers, frieze, choroi of women, 350–325 B.C.E. (fig. 17.4): Lehmann and Spittle 1982, pp. 172–262; Marconi 2010.

- Sybaris, unattributed building, frieze, choros of women, 530 B.C.E.: Bookidis 1967, pp. 240–44 M 57; Zancani Montuoro 1972–1973, pp. 62–66; Floren 1987, p. 432 n. 198; Mertens 2006, pp. 135–36, fig. 230.

Banquets

- Assos, Temple of Athena, architrave, cultic banquet, 540–530 B.C.E. (fig. 17.5): Bookidis 1967, pp. 319–22 F 72; Dentzer 1982, pp. 235–37, 576 R 66; Finster-Hotz 1984, pp. 46–78; Floren 1987, p. 402 n. 4; Wescoat 1995; Baughan 2011, p. 29; Wescoat 2012.

- Çal Dağ (Kebren), unattributed building, geison revetment, reclining banquet, 540–530 B.C.E.: Åkerström 1966, p. 7; Dentzer 1982, pp. 234–35, 576 R 67; Baughan 2011, p. 29.

- Corcyra, unattributed building, pediment, Symposion of Dionysos, 510–500 B.C.E.: Cremer 1981; Dentzer 1982, pp. 248–50, 607 R 331; Gasparri 1986, p. 456 no. 370; Floren 1987, p. 196 n. 54; C. Maderna-Lauter in Bol 2002-, vol. 1, pp. 261–62, 323; Baughan 2011, p. 28.

- Ephesos, Temple of Artemis, parapet sima, reclining banquet, 520–460 B.C.E.: Pryce 1928, p. 84 B 203; Bookidis 1967, pp. 281–85 F62; Floren 1987, p. 393 n. 17; Muss 1994, pp. 81, 86; Bammer and Muss 1996, pp. 51–53; Marconi 2007, pp. 23–24; Baughan 2011, pp. 28–29.

- Samos, Temple of Hera IV or North Building, frieze ("Kleiner Tempelfries"), reclining banquet, 510–500 B.C.E.: Buschor 1933, pp. 14–16, 19; Bookidis 1967, pp. 289–92 F 64; Freyer-Schauenburg 1974, pp. 199–201 nos. 124–27; Dentzer 1982, pp. 237–38, 605 R 312; Floren 1987, p. 357 n. 68; Furtwängler and Kienast 1989, pp. 55–56, 156–58 nos. 29–32; Baughan 2011, p. 28.

- Larisa, Temple of Athena II (?), geison revetment, reclining banquet, 540–530 B.C.E.: Boehlau 1940–1942, vol. 2, pp. 64–80; Åkerström 1966, pp. 48–50, 54–61, Group 3; Bookidis 1967, pp. 365–72 F 83; Dentzer 1982, pp. 230–34, 575–76 R64; Floren 1987, p. 400 n. 1; Rolley 1994-1999, vol. 1, pp. 226–27; Baughan 2011, p. 29.

Dedications

- Delphi, Treasury of Siphnos, caryatids, 530–525 B.C.E. (fig. 17.6): Picard and de La Coste-M'esselière 1928, pp. 57–71; de La Coste-Messelière and Marcadé 1953, pp. 360–64; Schmidt-Colinet 1977, pp. 216–17 W3; Schmidt 1982, pp. 74–75, 232–33; Daux and Hansen 1987, pp. 147–53; Floren 1987, p. 173 n. 9; Rolley 1994–1999, vol. 1, p. 224, figs. 216, 277; Mylonas Shear 1999, p. 70; Neer 2001, pp. 315–18.

- Delphi, unattributed treasury (ex-Kindian head), caryatids, 530 B.C.E.: Picard and de La Coste-Messelière 1928, pp. 1–6, 9–18; de La Coste-Messelière and Marcadé 1953, pp. 354–60; Langlotz 1975, pp. 62–63; Schmidt-Colinet 1977, p. 216 W 2; Schmidt 1982, pp. 72–74, 232; Floren 1987, p. 338 n. 35, pl. 29:6; Rolley 1994–1999, vol. 1, pp. 223–24, fig. 276; Mylonas Shear 1999, p. 70.

- Delphi, unattributed treasury (ex-Knidian caryatids), caryatids, 510–500 B.C.E.: Picard and de La Coste-Messelière 1928, pp. 6–18; de La Coste-Messelière and Marcadé 1953, pp. 346–53; Langlotz 1975, pp. 59–61; Schmidt-Colinet 1977, p. 216 W 1; Schmidt 1982, pp. 72–74, 231–32; Floren 1987, p. 332 n. 35, pl. 29:1; Rolley 1994–1999, vol. 1, pp. 223–24, fig. 215; Mylonas Shear 1999, p. 70.

- Delphi, unattributed treasury (smaller caryatids), caryatids, 525–500 B.C.E.: de La Coste-Messelière and Marcadé 1953, pp. 364–68; Schmidt 1982, pp. 75–76, 233; Rolley 1994–1999, vol. 1, p. 224.

- Didyma, Temple of Apollo II, column drums, priestesses bearing offerings (?), 550–520 B.C.E.: Gruben 1963, pp. 106–12; Blümel 1963, pp. 57–58; Bookidis 1967, pp. 296–98 F 66; Floren 1987, p. 386 n. 52, pl. 33:3; Rolley 1994–1999, vol. 1, p. 221, fig. 271; Mylonas Shear 1999, p. 78.

Sacrifices

- Ephesos, Temple of Artemis, column bases, bulls led to the sacrifice, 560–530 B.C.E.: Pryce 1928, pp. 64–65 B 141–B 144; Bookidis 1967, pp. 276–80 F61; Floren 1987, p. 392 n. 16; Muss 1994, p. 44; Bammer and Muss 1996, pp. 49–51; Marconi 2007, pp. 21–23.

- Athens, Temple of Athena Nike, Parapet, Nikai leading bulls to the sacrifice, 430–420 B.C.E.: Carpenter 1929; Jameson 1994; Hölscher 1997; Simon 1997; Brouskari 1998; Kalogeropoulos 2003.

Libations

- Athens, Erechtheion, caryatids, 421–406 B.C.E. (figure 17.7): Lauter 1976; Schmidt-Colinet 1977, pp. 217–18 W 5; Schmidt 1982, pp. 79–84; Scholl 1995; Scholl 1998.

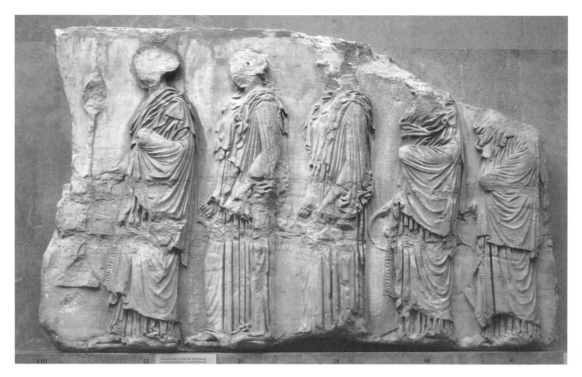

Figure 17.1. Parthenon, frieze, Panathenaic procession. British Museum E57–E61 (photo by the author)

Figure 17.2. Ephesos, Temple of Artemis, column base restored by A. S. Murray (Murray 1896)

Figure 17.3. Foce del Sele, Temple of Hera II, restored by F. Krauss
(Zancani Montuoro and Zanotti-Bianco 1951–1954, vol. 1, pl. 31)

Figure 17.4. Samothrace, Hall of Choral Dancers, frieze depicting a choros, F(S)1. Archaeological Museum of Samothrace (photo by the author)

Figure 17.5. Assos, Temple of Athena, architrave depicting a cultic banquet
(after Wescoat 2012, p. 165, fig. 81)

Figure 17.6. Delphi, caryatid from the Siphnian
Treasury. Delphi Archaeological Museum
(photo by the author)

Figure 17.7. Athens, caryatid from the
Erechtheion. British Museum
(photo by the author)

Figure 17.8. Delphi, base of the monument of the Orneatai (photo by the author)

Figure 17.9. Karaköy, parapet sima depicting a dance (Demangel 1932, fig. 54)

Figure 17.10. Kyzikos, column base depicting a dance. Istanbul Archaeological Museum (photo by the author)

Abbreviation

ThesCRA   *Thesaurus Cultus et Rituum Antiquorum.* Basel and Los Angeles: J. Paul Getty Museum, 2004– .

Bibliography

Åkerström, Åke

1966   *Die architektonischen Terrakotten Kleinasiens.* Skrifter utgivna av Svenska institutet i Athen 4/11. Lund: Gleerup.

Arnold, Dieter

1962   *Wandrelief und Raumfunktion in ägyptischen Tempeln des Neuen Reiches.* Münchner ägyptologische Studien 2. Berlin: Hessling.

Bacon, Francis H.; Joseph Thacher Clarke; Robert Koldewey; and Harold Wilmerding Bell

1902–1921   *Investigations at Assos: Drawings and Photographs of the Buildings and Objects Discovered during the Excavations of 1881-1882-1883.* Cambridge: Archaeological Institute of America.

Baines, John

1990   "Restricted Knowledge, Hierarchy, and Decorum: Modern Perceptions and Ancient Institutions." *Journal of the American Research Center in Egypt* 27: 1–23.

Bammer, Anton, and Ulrike Muss

1996   *Das Artemision von Ephesos: Das Weltwunder Ioniens in archaischer und klassischer Zeit.* Zaberns Bildbände zur Archäologie 20. Mainz: Philipp von Zabern.

Baughan, Elizabeth P.

2011   "Sculpted Symposiasts of Ionia." *American Journal of Archaeology* 115/1: 19–53.

Bell, Catherine M.

1992   *Ritual Theory, Ritual Practice.* Oxford and New York: Oxford University Press.

1997   *Ritual: Perspectives and Dimensions.* Oxford and New York: Oxford University Press.

Berger, Ernst, and Madeleine Gisler-Huwiler

1996   *Der Parthenon in Basel: Dokumentation zum Fries.* Studien der Skulpturhalle Basel 3. Mainz: Philipp von Zabern.

Blümel, Carl

1963   *Die archaisch griechischen Skulpturen der Staatlichen Museen zu Berlin.* Berlin: Akademie-Verlag.

Boehlau, Johannes; Lennart Kjellberg; and Åke Åkerström

1940–1942   *Larisa am Hermos: Die Ergebnisse der Ausgrabungen, 1902-1934.* Berlin: W. de Gruyter.

Bol, Peter C., editor

2002–   *Die Geschichte der antiken Bildhauerkunst.* Mainz: Philipp von Zabern.

Bookidis, Nancy

1967   A Study of the Use and Geographical Distribution of Architectural Sculpture in the Archaic Period: Greece, East Greece and Magna Graecia. Ph.D. dissertation, Bryn Mawr College.

Brommer, Frank

1977   *Der Parthenonfries: Katalog und Untersuchung.* Mainz: Philipp von Zabern.

Brouskari, M. S.

1998   "Τὸ θωράκιο τοῦ ναοῦ τῆς Ἀθηνᾶς Νίκης." *Archaiologikē ephēmeris* 137.

Buschor, Ernst

1933   "Heraion von Samos: Porosfriese." *Mitteilungen des Deutschen Archäologischen Instituts, Athenische Abteilung* 58: 1–21.

1957   "Altsamischer Bauschmuck." *Mitteilungen des Deutschen Archäologischen Instituts, Athenische Abteilung* 72: 1–34.

Calame, Claude

2001   *Choruses of Young Women in Ancient Greece: Their Morphology, Religious Role, and Social Functions.* Translated by Derek Collins and Janice Orion. Lanham: Rowman & Littlefield.

Carpenter, Rhys

1929   *The Sculpture of the Nike Temple Parapet.* Cambridge: Harvard University Press.

Connelly, Joan B.

1996   "Parthenon and *Parthenoi*: A Mythological Interpretation of the Parthenon Frieze." *American Journal of Archaeology* 100/1: 53–80.

Cremer, M.

1981   "Zur Deutung des jüngeren Korfu-Giebels." *Archäologischer Anzeiger* 96: 317–28.

D'Acunto, Matteo

1995   "I cavalieri di Priniàs ed il tempio A." *Annali del Seminario di studi del mondo classico: Sezione di archeologia e storia antica* 2: 15–55.

Daux, Georges, and Erik Hansen

1987   *Le trésor de Siphnos: Planches.* Fouilles de Delphes, École française d'Athènes 2. Paris: De Boccard.

de La Coste-Messelière, Pierre, and Jean Marcadé

1953   "Corés delphiques." *Bulletin de correspondance hellénique* 77: 346–76.

Demangel, Robert

1932   *La frise ionique.* Bibliothèque des écoles françaises d'Athènes et de Rome 136. Paris: De Boccard.

Dentzer, J.-M.

1982   *Le motif du banquet couché dans le Proche-Orient et le monde grec du VIIe au IVe siècle avant J.-C.* Bibliothèque des écoles françaises d'Athènes et de Rome 246. Paris: École française de Rome.

Despinis, G.

2009   "Αρχαϊκά ηρώα με ανάγλυφες ζωφόρους." *Annuario della Scuola archeologica di Atene e delle Missioni italiane in Oriente* 87: 349–66.

Elsner, John

1996   "Image and Ritual: Reflections on the Religious Appreciation of Classical Art." *Classical Quarterly* 46/2: 515–31.

Faustoferri, Amalia

1996   *Il trono di Amyklai e Sparta.* Aucnus 2. Naples: Edizioni scientifiche italiane.

Finster-Hotz, Ursula

1984   *Der Bauschmuck des Athenatempels von Assos: Studien zur Ikonographie.* Archaeologica 34. Rome: G. Bretschneider.

Floren, Josef

    1987   *Die griechische Plastik*, Volume 1: *Die geometrische und archaische Plastik*. Handbuch der Archäologie. Munich: Beck.

Freyer-Schauenburg, Brigitte

    1974   *Bildwerke der archaischen Zeit und des Strengen Stils*. Samos 11. Bonn: In Kommission bei R. Habelt.

Furtwängler, Andreas E., and Hermann Kienast

    1989   *Der Nordbau im Heraion von Samos*. Samos 3. Bonn: In Kommission bei R. Habelt.

Gadamer, Hans-Georg

    2004   *Truth and Method*. 2nd revised edition. Translation revised by Joel Weinsheimer and Donald G. Marshall. London and New York: Continuum.

Gasparri, Carlo

    1986   "Dionysos." *Lexicon iconographicum mythologiae classicae* 3: 414–514.

Gruben, Gottfried

    1963   "Das archaische Didymaion." *Jahrbuch des Deutschen Archäologischen Instituts* 78: 78–177.

Hölscher, Tonio

    1973   *Griechische Historienbilder des 5. und 4. Jahrhunderts v. Chr.* Beiträge zur Archäologie 6. Würzburg: K. Triltsch.

    1997   "Ritual und Bildsprache. Zur Deutung der Reliefs an der Brüstung um das Heiligtum der Athena Nike in Athen." *Mitteilungen des Deutschen Archäologischen Instituts, Athenische Abteilung* 112: 143–66.

    2009   "Architectural Sculpture: Message? Programs? Towards Rehabilitating the Notion of 'Decoration.'" In *Structure, Image, Ornament: Architectural Sculpture in the Greek World* (Proceedings of an International Conference held at the American School of Classical Studies, 27–28 November 2004), edited by Peter Schultz and Ralf von den Hoff, pp. 54–67. Oxford: Oxbow Books.

Horn-Oncken, Alste

    1967   *Über das Schickliche: Studien zur Geschichte der Architekturtheorie*. Abhandlungen der Akademie der Wissenschaften in Göttingen, Philosophisch-Historische Klasse 3/70. Göttingen: Vandenhoeck und Ruprecht.

Ioakimidou, Chrissula

    1997   *Die Statuenreihen griechischer Poleis und Bünde aus spätarchaischer und klassischer Zeit*. Quellen und Forschungen zur Antiken Welt 23. Munich: Tuduv-Verlagsgesellschaft.

Jameson, M. H.

    1994   "The Ritual of the Athena Nike Parapet." In *Ritual, Finance, Politics: Athenian Democratic Accounts Presented to David Lewis*, edited by Robin Osborne and Simon Hornblower, pp. 307–24. Oxford: Clarendon Press.

Jenkins, Ian

    1994   *The Parthenon Frieze*. Austin: University of Texas Press.

Jones, Lindsay

    2000   *The Hermeneutics of Sacred Architecture: Experience, Interpretation, Comparison*. 2 volumes. Cambridge: Harvard University Press for Harvard University Center for the Study of World Religions.

Jones Roccos, Linda
    1995   "The Kanephoros and Her Festival Mantle in Greek Art." *American Journal of Archaeology* 99/4: 641–66.

Kahil, Lilly
    1988   "Helene." *Lexicon iconographicum mythologiae classicae* 4: 498–563.

Kalogeropoulos, Konstantinos
    2003   "Die Botschaft der Nikebalustrade." *Mitteilungen des Deutschen Archäologischen Instituts, Athenische Abteilung* 118: 281–315.

Karakasi, Katerina
    2003   *Archaic Korai*. Los Angeles: The J. Paul Getty Museum.

Keesling, Catherine M.
    2003   *The Votive Statues of the Athenian Acropolis*. Cambridge: Cambridge University Press.

Kienast, H. J.
    2001   "Der Kriegerfries aus dem Heraion von Samos." In *Agalma: Meletes gia ten archaia plastike pros timen tu Giorgu Despine*, edited by Despoina Tsiaphake, pp. 13–20. Thessalonike: Ypurgeio Politismu.

Langlotz, Ernst
    1975   *Studien zur nordostgriechischen Kunst*. Mainz: Philipp von Zabern.

Lauter, H.
    1976   "Die Koren der Erechtheion." *Antike Plastik* 16: 7–54.

Lawrence, A. W.
    1972   *Greek and Roman Sculpture*. 2nd edition. London: Harper & Row.

Leach, Edmund R.
    1976   *Culture and Communication: The Logic by Which Symbols are Connected; An Introduction to the Use of Structuralist Analysis in Social Anthropology*. Themes in the Social Sciences. Cambridge and New York: Cambridge University Press.

Lehmann, Phyllis Williams, and Denys Spittle
    1982   *Samothrace: Excavations Conducted by the Institute of Fine Arts of New York University, Volume 5: The Temenos*. New York: Pantheon Books,.

Lindner, Ruth
    1997   "Kouretes, Korybantes." *Lexicon iconographicum mythologiae classicae* 8: 736–41.

Lissarrague, F.
    1990   *The Aesthetics of the Greek Banquet: Images of Wine and Ritual*. Translated by Andrew Szegedy-Maszak. Princeton: Princeton University Press.

Marconi, Clemente
    2004   "Kosmos: The Imagery of the Archaic Greek Temple." *Res: Anthropology and Aesthetics* 45: 209–24.

    2007   *Temple Decoration and Cultural Identity in the Archaic Greek World: The Metopes of Selinus*. Cambridge and New York: Cambridge University Press.

    2009   "The Parthenon Frieze: Degrees of Visibility." *Res: Anthropology and Aesthetics* 55/56: 156–73.

    2010   "Choroi, Theōriai and International Ambitions: The Hall of Choral Dancers and Its Frieze." In *Samothracian Connections: Essays in Honor of James R. McCredie*, edited by Olga Palagia and Bonna D. Wescoat, pp. 106–35. Oxford and Oakville: Oxbow Books.

Mertens, Dieter
    2006   *Städte und Bauten der Westgriechen: von der Kolonisationszeit bis zur Krise um 400 vor Christus.* Munich: Hirmer.

Mertens-Horn, Madeleine
    1992   "Die archaischen Baufriese aus Metapont." *Mitteilungen des Deutschen Archäologischen Instituts, Römische Abteilung* 99: 1–122.

Meyer, Marion, and Nora Brüggemann
    2007   *Kore und Kouros: Weihegaben für die Götter.* Wiener Forschungen zur Archäologie 10. Vienna: Phoibos.

Murray, A. S.
    1896   "The Sculptured Columns of the Temple of Diana at Ephesus." *Journal of the Royal Institute of British Architects* 3: 41–54.

Muss, Ulrike
    1994   *Die Bauplastik des archaischen Artemisions von Ephesos.* Sonderschriften des Österreichischen Archäologischen Institutes 25. Vienna: Eigenverlag des Österreichischen Archäologischen Instituts.

Mylonas Shear, Ione
    1999   "Maidens in Greek Architecture: The Origin of the 'Caryatids.'" *Bulletin de correspondance hellénique* 123: 65–85.

Neer, Richard T.
    2001   "Framing the Gift: The Politics of the Siphnian Treasury at Delphi." *Classical Antiquity* 20: 273–336.
    2010   *The Emergence of the Classical Style in Greek Sculpture.* Chicago: University of Chicago Press.

Neils, Jenifer
    2001   *The Parthenon Frieze.* Cambridge: Cambridge University Press.

Pernier, L.
    1914   "Templi arcaici sulla Patela di Prinias in Creta." *Annuario della Scuola archeologica di Atene e delle Missioni italiane in Oriente* 1: 18–111.

Perry, Ellen
    2005   *The Aesthetics of Emulation in the Visual Arts of Ancient Rome.* Cambridge: Cambridge University Press.

Picard, Charles, and Pierre de La Coste-Messelière
    1928   *Art archaïque: les Trésors "ioniques."* Fouilles de Delphes, École française d'Athènes 4/2. Paris: De Boccard.

Pollitt, J. J.
    1974   *The Ancient View of Greek Art: Criticism, History and Terminology.* Yale Publications in the History of Art 25. New Haven: Yale University Press.

Pryce, F. N.
    1928   *Catalogue of Sculpture in the Department of Greek and Roman Antiquities of the British Museum*, Volume 1, Part 1: *Prehellenic and early Greek.* London: Trustees of the British Museum.

Rolley, Claude
    1994–99   *La sculpture grecque.* 2 volumes. Les manuels d'art et d'archéologie antiques. Paris: Picard.

Rouse, W. H. D.

    1902   *Greek Votive Offerings: An Essay in the History of Greek Religion.* Cambridge: The University Press.

Santi, Fabrizio

    2010   *I frontoni arcaici dell'Acropoli di Atene.* Rome: "L'Erma" di Bretschneider.

Schmidt, Evamaria

    1982   *Geschichte der Karyatide: Funktion und Bedeutung Der Menschlichen Träger- und Stützfigur in der Baukunst.* Beiträge zur Archäologie 13. Würzburg: K. Triltsch.

Schmidt-Colinet, Andreas

    1977   *Antike Stützfiguren: Untersuchungen zu Typus und Bedeutung der menschengestaltigen Architekturstütze in der griechischen und römischen Kunst.* Frankfurt: Universität.

Scholl, Andreas

    1995   "Χοηφόροι: Zur Deutung der Korenhalle des Erechtheion." *Jahrbuch des Deutschen Archäologischen Instituts* 110: 179–212.

    1998   *Die Korenhalle des Erechtheion auf der Akropolis: Frauen für den Staat.* Frankfurt: Fischer Taschenbuch.

Schrader, Hans, editor

    1939   *Die archaischen Marmorbildwerke der Akropolis.* Frankfurt am Main: V. Klostermann.

Simon, Erika

    1967   "Die vier Büßer von Foce del Sele." *Jahrbuch des Deutschen Archäologischen Instituts* 82: 275–95.

    1997   "An Interpretation of the Nike Temple Parapet." In *The Interpretation of Architectural Sculpture in Greece and Rome*, edited by Diana Buitron-Oliver, pp. 127–43. Studies in the History of Art 49. Washington, D.C.: National Gallery of Art.

Sourvinou-Inwood, Christiane

    2011   *Athenian Myths and Festivals: Aglauros, Erechtheus, Plynteria, Panathenaia, Dionysia.* Oxford Oxford University Press.

Tuchelt, Klaus

    1970   *Die archaischen Skulpturen von Didyma: Beiträge zur frühgriechischen Plastik in Kleinasien.* Berlin: Gebr. Mann.

Watrous, L. Vance

    1998   "Crete and Egypt in the Seventh Century B.C.: Temple A at Prinias." In *Post-Minoan Crete* (Proceedings of the First Colloquium on Post-Minoan Crete, Held by the British School at Athens and the Insititute [sic] of Archaeology, University College London, 10–11 November 1995), edited by William G. Cavanagh, Mike Curtis, J. N. Coldstream, and A. W. Johnston, pp. 75–79. British School at Athens Studies 2. Athens and London: British School at Athens.

Wescoat, Bonna Daix

    1995   "Wining and Dining on the Temple of Athena at Assos." In *The Art of Interpreting*, edited by Susan C. Scott, pp. 292–320. Papers in Art History from the Pennsylvania State University 9. University Park: Pennsylvania State University.

    2012   *The Temple of Athena at Assos.* Oxford: Oxford University Press.

Zancani Montuoro, Paola

    1972–1973   "Divinità e templi di Sibari e Thurii." *Atti e memorie della Società Magna Grecia* 13/14: 57–68.

Zancani Montuoro, Paola, and Umberto Zanotti-Bianco

    1951–1954   *Heraion alla foce del Sele.* 2 volumes. Rome: Libreria dello Stato.

18

TEMPLES OF THE DEPTHS, PILLARS OF THE HEIGHTS, GATES IN BETWEEN

Davíd Carrasco, Harvard University

142. The "Construction" of the Sacred Space

The supremely sacred places — altars and sanctuaries — were, of course, constructed according to the traditional canons. But, in the last analysis this construction was based on a primeval revelation which disclosed the archetype of the sacred space *in illo tempore*, an archetype which was then indefinitely copied and copied again with the erection of every new altar, temple or sanctuary. We find examples everywhere of this construction of a sacred place following an archetypal pattern.

(Eliade 1996, pp. 371–72)

Approaching the Essays

In the Beginning was Place, said the philosopher. This mythic statement leads me as a historian of religions to ask two questions. Who or what created both the "beginning" and this "Place?" And, how did this primordial place come to be materialized, cared for, and made real in everyday life? According to Mircea Eliade, all sacred places discovered and made by humankind were dependent "on a primeval revelation which disclosed the archetype of the sacred space *in illo tempore.*" Then this model of the revelation was imitated and repeated in "the erection of every new altar, temple or sanctuary." And so it seems from reading the nine diverse and impressive essays in the first three parts of the book. The canonical traditions of the cultures examined here have, with one exception, answered these questions by reference to creation myths; all of them focus, in part, on the creative powers of divinities — both distant from and close to humankind.

In her cogent introduction to this volume, Deena Ragavan writes that "The fundamental basis of this volume is the interaction among three intertwining themes: sacred architecture (which by its nature shapes and delimits sacred space), ritual practice, and cosmology." She encourages readers interested in the various ways that temples and shrines were understood as reflections or embodiments of the cosmos to also pay attention to comparative examples. Her aim is that multiple methods and discoveries will shine light on specific cases as well as the myriad ways that human beings achieve orientation in the world through center-oriented structures and ritual practices. As a means of gaining historical and theoretical leverage for this book, Ragavan summarizes previous approaches to the theme of heaven and earth and gives emphasis to the contested place of Mircea Eliade's interpretive language found in *axis mundi* and *imago mundi* as used, misused, challenged, and rediscovered by subsequent scholars. A thorough application and interrogation of Eliade's lexicon must also include his *in illo tempore, coincidencia oppositorium, hierophany, kratophany,* and the central notion of "archetype and repetition," which was once the title of his most influential work, *The Myth of Eternal Return.*

Although Eliade is not referred to in most of these papers, his influence and conceptions are present in overt and subtle forms. Some readers will want to know that the best expression of Eliade's vision of *homo religiosus* regarding the tie between temple, cosmos, and ritual repetition appears in his larger work *Patterns in Comparative Religions*, where his chapters on the sky and sky gods, sacred trees, sun gods, the mystique of the moon, sacred places, and the "centre of the world" have both inspired and challenged readers seeking to understand the religious dimensions of place and time across time periods and geographies. In fact, paper after paper in this volume attests to the ancient practices of "archetypes" and "repetition" in the societies where temples, palaces, shrines, houses, miniatures, ritual, and literature were inspired by or modeled on storm gods, numinous mountains, water, seeds, trees, ancestral times, the union of sky and earth, and other potent elements of the cosmos. We learn herein that the intimacy of these links between heaven and earth were crucial to the orientation and longevity of cities, towns, temples, mountain landscapes, sculptures, and even literary traditions.

To more fully understand the interpretive significance of this volume, *Heaven On Earth: Temples, Ritual, and Cosmic Symbolism in the Ancient World*, it is important to refer to the writings of three other scholars whose work on this theme, in distinct cultural areas, have used and made innovations of the Eliade framework, thereby revitalizing the interpretive milieu which helped bring this collection of essays to life. The powerful role of ceremonial places and actions in the rise of urban life produced what the urban geographer Paul Wheatley called the "pivots of the four quarters." In his magisterial comparative study of primary urban generation, *The Pivot of the Four Quarters: A Preliminary Inquiry into the Origins and Nature of the Ancient Chinese City*, especially in the chapter "The Nature of the Ceremonial Center," Wheatley makes an exhaustive review of factors inducing the rise of urbanism organized around capital cities and then writes,

> the earliest foci of power and authority took the form of ceremonial centers, with religious symbolism imprinted deeply on their physiognomy and their operation in the hands of organized priesthoods. This itself is powerful testimony to the role of religion in the complex of interacting factors involved in the process of urban genesis. (Wheatley 1971, p. 304)

Wheatley makes clearer than anyone before or since how these urbanized ceremonial centers (in China, Mesopotamia, Egypt, Mesoamerica, and the Indus Valley and Peru) functioned to restructure society, advance technological innovation, articulate the basic values of a society and, through sensational ritual displays, and act

> as mirrors to society at large, as reflectors of a sacrally sanctioned social order, as inculcators of the attitudes and values appropriate to that order, and, not least, as symbolic statements about the nature of society, which could serve as guides to action for its constituent individuals and groups. (ibid., p. 305)

Wheatley worked with the definition of cities as the "effective organization of space" and he repeatedly stated that the combination of "cosmo-magical thought," ceremonial precincts, and ritual life was the social and symbolic source of this efficacy — whether it took economic, technological, religious, or political forms. What Wheatley did not show was *how these rituals* — or, in Ragavan's phrase, "a ritual landscape" — actually revitalized the ties between temples and cosmos.[1] Ragavan rightly credits Jonathan Z. Smith's multiple essays on the relationship between ritual and place as having provided cogent examples and new theoretical advantages to understand how rituals provide intense and illuminating focus for members of society, thereby strengthening the commitments to temple traditions. After some years of critiquing Eliade's ontological model (see Smith 1972), Smith wrote a new introduction to the 2005 re-release of *The Myth of the Eternal Return*, in which he concluded that Eliade's vision and approach was distinctly applicable to many traditional societies. He wrote,

> One simply cannot understand the great imperial cosmologies of Eurasia and Mesoamerica, which narrate complete histories of order, without understanding this sort of "ontology" that takes as its imperative the Hermetic maxim "as above, so below." (Smith 2005, p. xiii)

Smith sometimes calls for a reversal of the Eliadian model of "As Above, So Below" and urges scholars to examine the ritual *construction* of sacred space in ways that reflect Durkheimian insights that are akin to the maxim of "As Below, So Above." In his remarkable essay "To Put in Place," found in *To Take Place: Toward Theory in Ritual*, Smith challenges Wheatley's theory of central place while appreciating the "range of terminology and notions on which we will continue to draw: the city as a 'ceremonial center' with one of its chief crafts being the 'technology of ritual display'; the city as an 'organizing principle'; and urbanism as the 'hierarchical patterning of society in its totality'"(Smith 1997, p. 52).

This kind of dialogue between Wheatley and Smith had led, in part, to Smith's insistence on two visions of how human beings organize their homes, kingdoms, and cosmoi — what he calls "the locative view" (in which everything must be put in its proper place for social and sacred efficacy to abound) and "the utopian view," which gives emphasis and value to being in "no place" (in which possibility, openness, and a free range of space leads to creative relations and understandings). I attempted a modest correction of Smith's privileging of the "locative vision" of religion and society when, working with Aztec materials, I saw equal attention given, in myth and ritual, to what I call a "ceremonial landscape" linking specific buildings such as the Pyramid of the Sun in Teotihuacan, Mexico, or the Aztec Great Temple to a pulsating, experiential landscape that reached far beyond those buildings.

By ceremonial landscape I mean a territory including but also beyond the main ritual precinct, one that is marked, mapped, and rejuvenated by complex sets of performances that communicated knowledge about the social and symbolic order of the Aztec world and its wider sacred geography. This larger ritual landscape, consisting of specific geographical, social, and architectural terrains, was subjected to a conscious design, systematic pattern or cosmovision. The repeated constructions of these ceremonial landscapes showed[2] the practice and need for "changing places," which highlighted two kinds of transformations in ritual: 1) people are spiritually changed in these ritual/architectural locations and 2) people experience the radical difference between a sacred place and the outside world thereby grasping the fuller sense of what a cosmically imbued location is and means (Carrasco 1998).

---

[1] For an alternative view of ritual and landscape, see my introductory essay on "ceremonial landscapes" in Carrasco 1998.

[2] In ways similar to Deena Ragavan's work.

Still, Smith's locative vision of place is favored by a number of the papers in this volume, and although we seldom see writing that suggests or reverts to the radical reversal to "As Below, So Above," many of them refer to the role of rituals and ritual actors (more often by kings and queens) in regenerating cosmic forces whose presence in or around the temple thereby revitalizes rulers, shrines, and social solidarity. These interpretive efforts remind me of the special achievement of the historian of religions Lindsay Jones, whose examination of Mesoamerican polities known as Chichén Itzá and Tula led to the stimulating concept of "ritual-architectural events," a concept that is sometimes mirrored in some essays and which should be included in future studies. In a rare appeal to the hermeneutical approaches of Martin Heidegger, Hans Georg Gadamer, and Eliade, Jones focuses on the "superabundance of architecture" whose fulsome meanings reside in an active dialogue with the "autonomy, inexhaustibility, and superabundance of possibility that reside in every instance of sacred architecture" (Jones 1995, p. 193). This prodigious possibility of meaning (for the ritual actors and for scholars) emerges only when we acknowledge the

> intrinsically dialogical nature of the experience of art and architecture that makes it less appropriate to imagine a pre-Columbian pilgrim craning his neck for a better view of the Castillo — as though it were simply an inert, inanimate, mute structure — than to conceive of the pilgrim and pyramid as mutual partners in lively repartee or, better still, as withy players in a brisk game that will, before its end, transform them both. (ibid., p. 197)

While some papers may drift toward the craning necks of ritual observers, more often they strive to show some degree of active participation by members of society in building, visiting, and worshiping at shrines and temples. Every paper to a greater or lesser extent engages in four important issues: 1) the application or testing of theoretical approaches to the problem; 2) use of a method that focuses on cultural expressions of the ties between temple, ritual, and cosmos; and 3) comparison of cosmos and temple/shrine — either broadly, as between distant traditions that have been put in contact, or narrowly, as within a particular tradition itself where variations are evident in historical time and location. One of the most interesting topics within some essays is cultural encounters between diverse traditions and what happens in contact zones that mix one religious orientation to another. Finally, 4) the question of who is maintaining cosmic and social order is addressed with various answers. Although usually it is the elites or gods who are presented as putting the cosmos in order through ritual and power, a few papers give attention to the "everyday people."

The Essays

In "Naturalizing Buddhist Cosmology in the Temple Architecture of China: The Case of the Yicihui Pillar," Tracy Miller focuses intensely on a single, modest but complex, vertical structure made of limestone in order to understand how "cosmology embodied in the Buddhist monuments of South Asia was mapped onto the indigenous architectural traditions of the Yellow River Valley." Miller calls this mapping of a cultural encounter a "translation" and not "transplantation" of foreign cosmic notions into a visual language that local peoples could read and understand. Erected in central Hebei province, the Benevolent (Society's) Stone Pillar of Kindness and Compassion was actually a "memorial for the burial of rebels fighting against the Northern Wei government." The pillar was then carved with a lengthy text narrating both a story of origins and a list of the names of the devotional society that cared for the pillar.

As in almost all the papers in the first three parts, the pillar's tie between great and small, monumental and miniature, macro and micro is represented for didactic and performative purposes. What is outstanding is the emphasis on shapes, numbers, angles, and the pride of place given to the symbolism of the center throughout the history of cultural contact. To illustrate the crucial role of shapes and numbers in different traditions, Miller compares the pillar with several other texts and buildings including the *Mingtang* (明堂, Bright Hall or Hall of Light) located in the Western Han capital of Chang'an. The ritual efficacy of the building depends on the incorporation of the "circle and square, heaven and earth, monthly progression, and the cycle of the seasons ... into a single, multi-storied building organized around a central axis." What we see in both the monumental Mingtang and the modest Yicihui Pillar is the ways in which a visible archetype was created by consolidating "multiple systems of knowledge about the cosmos" in a mandala pattern. Miller's interpretation sets the stage for many elements in other papers in this section when she writes about the tie between the natural cosmology of the pillar and its ritual efficacy as a symbol of the journey toward reincarnation for individuals and society.

In "Images of the Cosmos: Sacred and Ritual Space in Jaina Temple Architecture in India," Julia A. B. Hegewald illuminates the exquisite cosmology of the Jaina, where we are surprised to read that "Jainism does not have a creation story or cosmogony" because the cosmos is thought to be eternal and self created. One question is how can people have a cosmos without a story of its origin or appearance? Hegewald introduces us to an elaborate relationship between the search for personal enlightenment and the didactic and representational powers of art and architecture. Readers unfamiliar with the Jains of India will be pleased to learn how the "highly intricate and convoluted textual descriptions of the Jaina universe have been translated into visual and concrete physical shape" and made easier to understand through the carvings, paintings, sculpture, and architectural models found in Jaina temples throughout South Asia. Two outstanding images that focus the seeker during the journey toward liberation are the outline of an hourglass and "the structure of the universe as a triangle topped by a diamond shape" — both of which symbolize, among other realities, the cosmic person. The illustrations in this essay show the fascinating tie between these designs and the images of cosmic mountains and cosmic islands. This monumental sense of the universe is miniaturized, as sculptures in metal and larger ones in stone are revered inside the Jaina temples all over India.

Hegewald emphasizes that the Jainas were deeply committed to filling their ritual spaces with mythical and cosmic symbolism in order not only to transform places into cosmic space and time but also to enable individuals to "anticipate their own enlightenment" by giving the human soul a landscape in which to take a pilgrimage through the universe. These images that appear in miniature reproductions often represent holy pilgrimage sites along the path of pilgrims' progress and usually on mountains. In this context, the persistent notion of archetype and repetition also appears in Jaina writings, which reveal a tight relationship between cosmic and mythical structures and events that then serve as models for the individual seeker of liberation. In Jaina mythology, the twenty-four omniscient Jinas are the model travelers who have made the journey to Mount Meru for blessings and instructions which they pass on in open-air theatres or "assemblages," thereby communicating the importance of both individual search and community awareness of mythical teachings. Hegewald's elegant essay shows how embedded these ideas and patterns are in every society when we learn that the temple structures provided the devotees and especially the laity "with a stage for the re-enactment of mythical proceedings to allow human beings to participate in divine and cosmic events and to anticipate their own enlightenment." In other words, cosmology becomes theater in the service of human salvation.

Karl Taube's highly detailed "The Classic Maya Temple: Centrality, Cosmology, and Sacred Geography in Ancient Mesoamerica" carries on his tour de force style of using an ensemble approach, that is, combining his formidable knowledge of pictorial, architectural, and ritual practices to clarify the central archetypes and patterns of Maya and Mesoamerican religions. Taube shows how the emphasis on centrality in Maya cosmology is reiterated at all levels and locations of the Mesoamerican world. From the maize fields to the local four-cornered house dwelling to the flowering mountains and architectural structures — a sacred geography of center, cardinal, and intercardinal directions and periphery permeates — even to the miniature world of ear spools, jades, and bowls.

Of particular interest to those looking for innovations in how we understand temple and cosmos is the longevity and persistence of this model in this part of the Americas. Taube documents and interprets how this cosmology with its manifestation in temple architecture continues on from the Pre-Classic period down to the present peoples of Mesoamerica and contemporary Maya houses. Taube tells us of the mythic episode of creation when three stones were used to lift the sky from the earth and open the space in which all life could then prosper. This widespread mythic episode was also symbolized in "the humble three-stone hearth of Maya households," which is used today in many Maya communities.[3]

Taube's work reveals, in ways that a previous generation of writers could not, the spatial drama of Maya rituals when he elaborates how ritual life was carried out on stairways, plazas, mountains, and even cornfields. The impression is that rituals modeled on cosmic stories and images were a way of life for the Maya and not just what they did on specific ritual days. This pervasive cosmos and ritual pattern was extended, in some cases, to the ways smoke was directed to emerge from ritual vessels — toward the four quarters of the universe.

Betsey A. Robinson, in "On the Rocks: Greek Mountains and Sacred Conversations," moves the story to the Mediterranean and uses a narrow comparative method for a fresh look at a literary and sculptural tradition in relation to the sacred landscapes of the mountains of Helicon and Parnassus in what was Greek cultural territory. As in Tracy Miller's paper, cultural negotiations by communities in conflict are of interest, for by "31 B.C.E., Roman political hold was complete, but cultural and religious negotiations still continued" and numerous sanctuaries upheld Greek traditions well into the Roman period. We learn that among a variety of classical Greek mountain sanctuaries, reflecting a "divine predilection for heights," Helicon and Parnassus were not just distant peaks where one imagined the Muses, but rather nearby valleys and the peaks themselves were beckoning centers where poets, musicians, and others went to make direct contact with inspiring forces and, for the fortunate who reached the summit, "actually see tablets of Hesiod's *Works and Days* ..., which strengthened claims of Hesiod's historicity and the charisma of the place."

---

[3] And for those of us reflecting on the recent cultural fashion of worrying about the end of the world according to the Maya calendar we learn that the "three-stone sign" (also associated with some Maya kings) was found in inscriptions describing the mythic event of origin in 3114 B.C.E., when time first began.

Several new insights about exempla in nature and cultural activity appear, as in one poetic document by Corinna, wherein two mountains are posed as contestants *in a singing duel* that is watched over by the Muses! In this case, the mountains are archetypes for human singers — or as Johathan Z. Smith would have it, the singers were models for the mountains and their sounds of wind and thunder. Robinson says it more simply, observing that "Greek art buried the distinction between men, gods, and mountains."[4]

In "Seeds and Mountains: The Cosmogony of Temples in South Asia" Michael W. Meister seeks to "question and problematize South Asia's material remains" through an examination of the typology of the temple-mountain as "both a source and model of the ordered world." What Meister shows in his historically deep analysis, however, is the dynamic meaning of natural symbols, in particular what he calls "seeds." The seed symbol which appears at first glance to signify center, place, and stasis between earth and sky, upon further reflection also emphasizes, in the form and decorations of caves, shrines, and temples, the direction of "opening out" and spreading sacred energies into personal and social worlds. The dynamic symbol of this centripetal pattern for Meister is the "seed of the *amala* fruit ... as an emblem of cosmic parturition."

These symbols of giving birth took material form in *āmalaka*-crowned temples in the fourth–fifth centuries C.E., which carry an abundance of foliage and "multiplying *āmalakas*" on the temples. What is crucial to understanding the influence of these symbols is that while the *amala* fruit provides the essential "seed" of life, during the evolution of temple architecture it becomes capable of pouring its radiance outwardly, down mountains, across natural landscapes, into ancient chapels, caves, flat-roofed lineage temples, and more.[5] This expansion outward from the *amala* fruit takes its form in temples that are also likened to mountains showing a great spectrum of cosmic meanings stretching from the tiny seed to the mountain ranges that raise the view of horizons upward toward heaven.

In Gary Beckman's "Intrinsic and Constructed Sacred Space in Hittite Anatolia," we read of the variety of acts of devotion at two types of sacred places — in nature and in buildings. He writes about not only the worshiping of gods at temples and sites in urban spaces but also "the modification of peaks and springs, both within and outside of settlements." Unlike the other papers, Beckman begins with a cosmic crisis caused with the abandonment by the deity of his worshipers resulting in a devastating drought. Water, vital to the success of humanity, was associated with storm gods who resided on the many mountain peaks of the region — showing the closeness, in Hittite thought, of god and topography and local communities. We learn just how local and intimate these gods could be, for among the "Thousand Gods of Hatti," many local avatars were identified with particular towns or mountains, and in a few cases the name of the city could be identified in the script as either god or mountain. Thus, mountains are "numinous" for the Hittites and this numinosity spreads to any particular feature in the landscape that is associated with water, including "mountains, rivers, springs, the great sea, heaven and earth, winds, and clouds." We read that this prolific pattern of

---

[4] One wonders when reading this essay to what extent cosmos, temple, and human relations inspired artists in other societies to develop multimedia displays at cultural and religious sanctuaries — as did the Greeks.

[5] This dynamism is seen clearly in Meister's discussion of the Nagari gateway (gateways are central to Ragavan's paper) and other sites where we read, "If a stone or rock-cut temple's sanctum was meant to be an opening in the cosmic strata ... acting as a 'womb' or *garbha-gṛha* (womb-house) for creation, the icon made visible within proliferates into the expanding world."

sacred associations reached into key political events, such as when a ruler summoned not only the lords of other communities *but the mountains themselves*, as gods, to witness treaties between warring rivals.

One outstanding example was when distant mountains could be summoned to Hattusa to participate in the ceremonies. For instance, note this invocation:

> Hey, Mt. Šarišša, get up! Hasten back to His Mighty Majesty and the Mighty Queen (Tawananna), the watchmen (of the land of Ḥatti), for the fattened oxen and rams!
> ... Let good news always find them, His Mighty Majesty and the Queen, on the throne of iron!

As in many papers, rulers are strongly associated with these places of sacred fertility and they sometimes rule over the enormous human effort, through physical labor, to construct symbolic places in their entirety and not just reshape or decorate a natural landscape.

In Deena Ragavan's "Entering Other Worlds: Gates, Rituals, and Cosmic Journeys in Sumerian Sources," we encounter a particular emphasis on a theme modestly touched upon in other papers, namely, a series of ritual practices which are 1) directed intensely toward places of transition and 2) especially, in the materials she looks at, between the world of the living and that of the dead. This essay uses an interpretive approach close to my work on "changing places" through its emphasis on the tie between gift giving and sacred itineraries that affect and reflect profound social and spiritual changes. Again we see the presence of the archetype and repetition model, only now with a stronger sense of the dialectics between ritual and myth.

Ragavan gives ample attention to multiple kinds of gates in the Sumerian textual tradition — gates of heaven, gates into the underworld, gates of sunrise and sunset, graves as gates, the Gate of Joy, "full seven gates ... bolted against the hero," the Ishtar gate of Babylon, fearsome gates, and more.[6] The importance of ritual at gates is evident in the myths and accounts where gifts are presented (or jewels and clothes are taken off) at gates and to gatekeepers. Ragavan argues that the sequence of the goddess Inana giving up clothes and jewelry is the model *of or for* a funerary ritual and the arrival into the underworld. This pattern of gifts and gates is seen most elaborately in the funeral of one of the Ur III kings, where animal offerings are made to a series of gates including the "great gate of the king, the great gate of the throne of Shulgi," which Ragavan suggests prepares the king's entry into the netherworld.[7] The prodigious importance of these gates for rulers is clear when we realize that thrones are also gates, and that gates themselves and the guardians of gates all receive ritual sacrifices.

In Susanne Görke's "Hints at Temple Topography and Cosmic Geography from Hittite Sources," we meet a problematic archaeological record that challenges the author (thus the notion of "hints"). She asks, "what can we really know about the ways temples and festival were thought of and built as 'cosmic concepts'?" As in several other papers, the archaeological record shows cultural encounters that mattered and changed art and ideology — in this

---

[6] One begins to think that a future conference should be organized around the theme of "Gates, Rituals, and Cosmos."

[7] With regard to movements to and through gates, Ragavan invokes the work of Victor Turner on the second, that is, threshold, phase of the ritual process. Perhaps more use of Turner's insightful language, especially where he invokes the symbolism of caves, ambivalence, and potentiality, would illuminate these passageways even more.

case, the "influences of Mesopotamian, South Anatolian, and Northern Syrian ideas that came to Central Anatolia due to political and territorial changes." Throughout these changes, however, one institution stands firm — kingship.

Görke is able to tease out some of the ritual sequence for worshipping gods including the postures and numbers of times the rulers drink to the gods. She also provides "rudimentary hints" about the temples themselves — courtyards, inner chambers, pillars, kitchens, and statues peek at us through the fragmented evidence.[8] Further, we learn that in some cases at least, "the temple is built for a god *by the gods*" (italics mine) and sometimes the foundations are known to be the opening to the underworld. The suggestion is, as in the case of a mythological text telling that the "goddess Inara built herself a house on a rock" that one of Eliade's *hierophanies* or manifestations of sacred power occurred there.

Görke shows how scholars have reached a consensus after analyzing key texts about various festivals and the kings, servants, bodyguards, singers, dancers, shepherds, warriors, and more who celebrate in palaces, temples, gates, and sacred stones. It appears that two different cosmologies are at work in this society: one divided the world into heaven-earth/netherworld "without strict borders and with the possibility for gods to move back and forth between the realms." This flexibility, closer to J. Z. Smith's utopian model, suggests temples "without strict rules of access, and no barring of the public." But the other model seems to be a locative division of the cosmos into heaven, earth, and underworld divided by strict borders, all replicated in the temples where the public is forbidden for inner sanctums and only the privileged cultic leaders may enter. One hopes for the day when these hints can be put on firmer ground, archaeologically and in interpretive style.

Each of these essays forming part of *Heaven on Earth: Temples, Ritual, and Cosmic Symbolism in the Ancient World* makes its own creative play, reminiscent of Lindsay Jones's notion of dialogue, between author and place. Some lean more strongly toward Eliade's appreciation of ontology while others favor Wheatley's pivot of the world and still a few like Smith's notion of ritual work. A few mix the approaches. Given the state of play and reflection on "heaven on earth" or "earth up in heaven," it is best to give my final word to Italo Calvino, who writes about invisible cities in many ways. In a chapter called "Thin Cities," we read,

> The city's gods, according to some people, live in the depths, in the black lake that feeds the underground streams. According to others, the gods live in the buckets that rise, suspended from a cable, as they appear over the edge of the wells, in the revolving pulleys, in the pump handles, ... in the blades of the windmills that draw the water up from the drillings ... all the way up to the weathercocks that surmount the airy scaffoldings of Isaura, a city that moves entirely upward. (Calvino 1972, p. 20)

---

[8] We are reminded of Ragavan's paper when we read that when the king "reaches the gate in town, the ALAM.ZU₉-man shouts *aḫa* in front of the door."

Bibliography

Calvino, Italo

    1972   *Invisible Cities.* Translated from the Italian by William Weaver. San Diego: Harcourt Brace.

Carrasco, Davíd, editor

    1998   *Aztec Ceremonial Landscapes: To Change Place.* Niwot: University Press of Colorado.

Eliade, Mircea

    1996   *Patterns in Comparative Religion.* Reprint edition. Translated by Rosemary Sheed. Lincoln: University of Nebraska Press.

Jones, Lindsay

    1995   *Twin City Tales: A Hermeneutical Reassessment of Tula and Chichén Itzá.* Niwot: University Press of Colorado.

Smith, Jonathan Z.

    1972   "The Wobbling Pivot." *The Journal of Religion* 52/2: 134–49.

    1997   *To Take Place: Toward Theory in Ritual.* Chicago: University of Chicago Press.

    2005   "Introduction to the 2005 Edition." In *The Myth of the Eternal Return: Cosmos and History.* 2nd edition, by Mircea Eliade, pp. ix–xxii. Princeton: Princeton University Press.

Wheatley, Paul

    1971   *The Pivot of the Four Quarters: A Preliminary Enquiry into the Origins and Character of the Ancient Chinese City.* Edinburgh: Edinburgh University Press.

19

COSMOS AND DISCIPLINE

Richard Neer, University of Chicago

It is an irony of the respondent's lot that, often as not, the more a paper prompts sustained engagement, the less feasible it is to do justice to its complexities — such are the exigencies of time and space. With eight very substantial papers in Parts 4–6 to discuss, and limited space in which to do it, I am not able to address each contribution in detail. I hope merely to pull out some generalities and point to some larger conceptual questions that the papers raise in aggregate, and I beg the pardon of those colleagues whose works I do not address with the fullness they deserve. I would, however, like to underscore what a pleasure it has been both to hear and to read such a rich and broad array of work — and to be reminded, again, of how much one does not know, and how much remains to be done.

Turning to business, the basic terms under discussion in these sessions were *architecture, ritual practice,* and *cosmic symbolism.* To each term there corresponds an academic discipline — archaeology, the history of religion, and philology — each with its own particular methods for producing and classifying knowledge. It is one of the points of a conference such as this one to juxtapose these methods and, in so doing, to reveal incompatibilities, blind spots, or tacit assumptions. My brief is to juxtapose the *ancient, cosmic* orders that have constituted the content of these papers, with the *modern, disciplinary* orders — the ways of ordering evidence — that have determined their form.

Architecture and *kosmos*

To begin with the notion of cosmic symbolism — the idea that, to quote the conference program, "ritual practice and temple topography provide evidence for the conception of the temple as a *reflection*, or *embodiment*, of the cosmos" (italics added). So we have the cosmos and we have the temple, and we use ritual and topography to show how the temple is a reflex or incarnation — what idealist historiography would have called "the sensuous presentation" — of the larger abstract conceptualization. The cardinal question here is, how do we order these concepts and these pieces of evidence in chains of inference?

I start with the Greek situation, not just because I know it best but because it is rather straightforward. In the Greek context, a tempting way to think about cosmic symbolism in the context of temple architecture is, literally, as the creation of the *kosmos*, that is, of the upper portion of a temple. As Clemente Marconi reminded us a few years back, everything above the architrave of a Greek temple could be called the *kosmos* in Greece, and this applied particularly to the décor.[1] To speak of cosmic symbolism in this context involves putting two kinds of evidence, the philological and the archaeological, words and temples, into some

---

[1] Marconi 2004, pp. 211–24.

kind of productive relation. Which term will have logical priority? One arrangement of the evidence will see the temple as a reflection or embodiment the cosmos. But one might also urge the opposite view: that orderly architecture might provide a *model* for at least some Greek conceptions of a cosmically ordered universe. In other words, it may not be that architecture symbolizes, reflects, embodies the *kosmos*, so much as that the *kosmos* is like architecture, perhaps an extrapolation from, or a mystification of, an untheorized practice. In the Greek case, at any rate, there is some justification for this suggestion. Aryeh Finkelberg has argued convincingly that the use of the Greek word *kosmos* in an abstract and speculative sense, as a universal system or theodicy, is a late Classical and Hellenistic development, only anachronistically retrojected onto earlier periods.[2] Down to Xenophon's time, on this view, *kosmos* primarily meant any orderly arrangement or adornment, anything *kata kosmon*, like a well-laid table or a well-appointed coiffure. There simply was no Greek *kosmos* in the sixth century B.C. But there was architecture.

The example that immediately comes to mind is the Presocratic philosopher Anaximander, who modeled the earth in the image of a column drum, with a diameter three times its height.[3] We do not know enough about Anaximander to speak very intelligently about him, but one thing we can say is that architecture seems to have provided at least some of the terminology in which he thought his *kosmos* — and that is enough for my purposes. For Anaximander, the *kosmos* is like architecture, not the other way around; the column is not the symbol of some antecedent notion of the cosmic, so much as the paradigm from which the *kosmos* is theorized *ex post facto*.

The Builder or Demiurge of Plato's *Timaeus* might be thought to represent both the climax and the final defeat of this tradition — defeat, in that least part of Plato's point was to abstract philosophical knowledge from the worldly know-how of the builder. But the larger point is that we need to be careful about simply assuming that cosmic symbolism will run from base material culture to abstract ideas, like a sort of anagogical progression. Maybe religion is the epiphenomenal category. At an extreme, as the case of Anaximander might suggest, perhaps the cosmic symbolism is itself a reflex of architectural practice, not the other way around.

This raises my first pair of questions: to what extent can we see temples producing a *kosmos*, as opposed to reflecting one? And, by what specific strategies might a material or ritual generalize itself into something of universal or "cosmic" significance?

It is at this point, obviously, that ritual comes in, but once again the problem consists in how to prioritize the evidence. The Parthenon frieze is as good an example as any (leaving aside the whole question of whether the Parthenon functioned as a temple or a treasury). I was especially glad that Clemente Marconi put paid to the old canard that the iconography of the frieze is somehow unique or unprecedented. I am also happy to go along, broadly speaking, with his idea that "inherent to these images, because of their subject and location, was their function as mirror and memory: mirror, at the time of the festival, for the community of worshippers celebrating the gods; and memory, for the rest of the time, until the next festival was performed, and beyond." But the Parthenon frieze presents at least two specific problems, both germane. First, the ritual procession on the frieze does not correspond in many of its details to the written accounts; notoriously, it shows men carrying a type of

---

[2] Finkelberg 1998, pp. 103–36.

[3] Texts conveniently available in Graham 2010, pp. 56–59, frags. 19–20.

vessel that we are told was carried by a special class of women, it gives the cavalry a wildly exaggerated role, and in general it seems to do its best to give the iconographers headaches.[4] Second, the frieze is a continuous band that shows the beginning of a procession in one part of the city and the end of the procession in another part. That is to say, it shows multiple moments and multiple spaces along its length. So if it is a mirror, then there is no one place or time that the frieze as a whole may be said to reflect or represent; if it is a memory, then we have to come to grips with it as a memory of something that never happened. Marconi's remarks about the construction of the sanctuary as a liminal space, a sort of non-site, seem quite apt to this curious artifact — for the time and space of the Parthenon frieze are themselves non-times and non-spaces.

What all this points to, for present purposes, is the *constitutive* role of the frieze in the manufacture of both *kosmos* and ritual. The Parthenon frieze is not quite a reflection of ritual practice, not quite a symbol of some antecedent set of beliefs, so much as it is generative of both.

Plan and Elevation

More generally, architecture, *kosmos,* and ritual coincide in the notion of space. So how are we to think of archaeological space? This question seemed to motivate many of the papers, in one way or another, and rather than proposing an answer of my own, I merely suggest a way to think of the various responses.

I feel that our authors might be divided into two camps depending on the conception of space — ritual, architectural, political — that subtends their research. One model of space takes it to be an abstract metric for establishing mathematically determinate relations between points. Think of a map or a site plan. Within this demarcated space we can, by means of grids, specify sacred and non-sacred "zones," or points, the criteria of which are first and foremost architectural, that is, archaeologically visible in the form of artifacts such as walls and foundations that articulate and divide space on site plans (Yorke Rowan's paper shows this beautifully). This conception seems closely aligned to surveying practices — specifically, practices like gridding out sites preparatory to excavation and the subsequent production of site plans. If our fundamental model is the grid and our fundamental technologies are the surveyor's transit and the site plan, then we might be apt to think of space in terms of exactly these articulating features and to emphasize relations *between* these determinate zones in our research programs.

For example, Matt Canepa's magisterial survey of a thousand-plus years of sacred architecture across tens of thousands of square miles of real estate would be literally inconceivable without this conception of space and its attendant technologies, from transits and tripods to GPS. Here we have discrete cultural and political units (Greek, Achaemenid, Sasanian, and so on) articulated spatially into territories, and temporally in chronological succession, that are immediately "visualizable" in the familiar format of a historical atlas. These units provide what I am calling articulating features — within which there are determinate types of architecture, like the fire temple — and the daunting task of the scholar is to show how these units and types relate to one another within a larger cultural history. An example is when Canepa observes that "the largest and most important structures [at Ai Khanum] utilized an

---

[4] On these issues, see Neils 2001.

official architecture that deliberately and harmoniously incorporated Greek, Babylonian, and Persian architectural features to create something quite new."

Zooming in from macro to micro, there is something similar on offer, I feel, in Uri Gabbay's account of propitiatory ritual. Here the operative terms are inside versus outside, and east versus west: exactly the terms for which a site plan is particularly apt. Orientation, here, is to the cardinal points and to the passage of the sun across the sky; within this system, instead of tracking the peregrinations of motifs, styles, and architectural types, we track the peregrinations of a statue from one zone to another. Yorke Rowan, similarly, performs something close to a miracle in employing minimal criteria for the identification of what he calls "clearly defined" ritual spaces, which in turn cashes out to mean clearly defined *in plan*.

This way of approaching space has obvious benefits, above and beyond the production of site plans that help us to keep track of our finds. In each of these cases, the specific conception of space enables a research agenda. That conception of space is one that I am associating — speculatively but not, I hope, implausibly — with technologies of mapping and survey, and ultimately with the gridded site plan. This is, I emphasize, no bad thing, nor is it even particularly surprising that something like this approach should loom so large in our disiciplines. In observing, for instance, that Matt Canepa's paper involves a particular conception of space and particular technological infrastructure, I do not mean to suggest that it is anything less than dazzling. My goal is to defamiliarize something, which is not to criticize it; I want to be very clear on this score. The only thing I would want to resist is the idea that there is only *one* right way to talk about space.

Because of course there are other ways to think about it, and this takes me to my second group of papers. In these cases, space is not locatory but body-based. Instead of mapping space cartographically, or orienting it to fixed compass points or celestial bodies, one might, for instance, orient it relationally, to entities — in front, behind, underneath, and so on. When it comes to architecture, plans of course are important, but elevations are surely important as well, certainly if what we are interested in is anything to do with actual lived experience: users of buildings come to know plans (if they do) through elevations both interior and exterior. Examples of a more bodily, "elevation-friendly" approach would include Elizabeth Frood's fascinating study of the ways in which Egyptian temple personnel gave meaning to the spaces through which they passed, Ömür Harmanşah's account of the metaphorics of space and power in Mesopotamia, and John Baines's description of the production of non-existent spaces for the gods in Egyptian architecture. Of course, some papers in other sessions also exemplified this tendency, like Betsey Robinson's wonderful discussion of Parnassus, but these are beyond the scope of the present discussion.

At the risk of oversimplification, then, one might contrast a mode of research based on plans to a mode based on elevations. The one will define space absolutely, as a grid, and track movements or events within that space. The other will be inclined to define it relationally and — this is important — to show how practices or events *constitute* or *posit* sites, locations, or places. In the one case, the space is a given, and the scholar's job is to track movements in it and to describe the meanings — symbolic, historical, or otherwise — of those movements. In the other, space not a given. It is a function of ritual, or of politics, and the scholar's job is to track the process of its emergence, of spatialization or localization or what Edward Casey rather barbarously calls "placialization," the constitution of meaningful places.[5]

---

[5] See, for instance, Casey 2001, pp. 683–93.

There is a reason, of course, why archaeologists tend not to talk about elevations: they rarely survive intact. We deal with foundations, which cry out to be seen in plan. But that fact only proves my point, which is that the material constraints of our discipline determine our conception of space, which in turn determines our research agendas and what counts as serious scholarship. The result is a fine example of our old friend the "hermeneutic circle." Yet this formulation is too simple, for the circle does not remain unbroken. Elizabeth Frood's paper demonstrates as much. Talking about writing on the vertical plane of walls — elevation — she argues that the graffiti "delineate places of devotion for temple staff" and "ritualize their regular activities and movements in association with central cult rituals and performances," thereby "reconfiguring ... traditional hierarchical ordering of cult places." Here the temple area is taken as given — a more or less neutral spatial array — and Frood documents a process of manipulation and transformation effected through secondary inscription on the interior elevations.

Or take Ömür Harmanşah's fascinating piece on spatial metaphors in Mesopotamia. The real topic here is the mapping of a lived, politico-religious geography — the way in which power does not merely articulate space, as it were, by surveying it, but actually constitutes locations, sites, and spaces as they are lived and experienced in an "everyday practice" that need not entail any synoptic or cartographic schematization. "In the context of everyday practice in early Mesopotamian cities, cattlepen and sheepfold appear as the perfect spatial metaphors that speak of this very intimacy and care between the king and his subjects." The shift from a synoptic plan to something like the phenomenology of the everyday, hence of politics, seems to me very important, and it exemplifies the second conception of space as I have described it.

Having said as much, I am not sure why Harmanşah characterizes giš-hur and me as "abstract concepts ... materially *manifest* or visually *expressed* in the architectural corpus, the urban fabric of Mesopotamian cities" (italics added). Once again we are back to the question of ordering evidence. This idealization of the discursive, as that which precedes material manifestation in architecture, rather as the spirit precedes its *Darstellung*, is exactly the sort of thing I hoped to put at issue with the example of Anaximander. Why not say the opposite: that the "abstract concepts" were extrapolated from the "everyday practice" of shepherding and city life, indeed, that they order and rationalize everyday practice according to an expressly political logic? Especially given that the overall thrust of Harmanşah's paper leads us, very engagingly, away from transcendental concepts and toward a pragmatics of everyday space.

There is, of course, an answer to this question as well. It is that we, as historians, tend to use the texts to make sense of the artifacts, so it is the most natural thing in the world to give logical priority to those texts. The result is a view of architecture and space as the symbolization of a discursive content extracted from texts, which makes archaeology and art history into the handmaidens of philology. But the path of our inferences need not correspond to the actual order, or *kosmos*, of the historical situation. We need the texts to make sense of the ruins, but that does not mean that the ruins were, historically, symbols of the "cosmic" ideas found in those texts. I cannot help feeling that in some cases the purely forensic ordering of the evidence may have taken on a life of its own, that the *kosmos* being symbolized is that of the scholarly disciplines and a well-ordered argument.

So this leads to my second question or proposition: if, inspired by Anaximander, we try the experiment of flipping our hierarchy and take "cosmic symbolism" to imply a *kosmos* reflecting architecture, and not architecture reflecting a *kosmos*, then what happens to the notion of architecture and ritual space? The seminar broached this question, and I certainly am not in a position to answer it; but I suggest that we will tend to move from plans to elevations in our agendas of research, and from assuming architecture to be a function of belief and liturgy to at least taking seriously the possibility that belief and liturgy are functions of architecture, or at any rate stand in a dynamic and reciprocal relation to same.

Other Senses

If all this seems rather too schematic, then that may be because we have reduced the number of variables in play perhaps a bit too much. Plan versus elevation, locatory space versus bodily space, this is all a bit Manichean. With this thought in mind, I have one more question, which I can state more succinctly. Ömür Harmanşah's emphasis on what he calls "visual metaphors" seems extremely promising, but it raises a point that may be a bit odd to hear from a historian of art. It is simply this: whether interested in tracing cartographies or in mapping metaphors, all these papers have strongly emphasized *vision* as the prime means of access to ancient spatialities and also as the prime means by which the ancients themselves articulated space. Space is now, and was in antiquity, something to *see* or *read*. This special place for vision holds true even when discussing ritual practices that were extremely rich sensorially, involving song and food and smoke and drums and lowing beasts and drinks and sweaty crowds. I do not mean to suggest that there is anything particularly wrong with this emphasis on the visual, but it is worth noting that there are at least four other senses, and we probably should not assume that vision was the most important — certainly when it comes to ritual space, and at least potentially in the case of temple architecture as well. In the case of, say, a nocturnal procession accompanied by song and fire, smell and hearing may be equally if not more important in spatial orientation.

Recalling the other four senses can suggest potentially fruitful lines for future research: what happens if we think of a ritual landscape as something experienced other than visually? This question is not necessarily any more challenging than the more familiar visual ones. We extrapolate visual experience from site plans, and there is no reason in principle why we could not extrapolate other sensoria as well. Ritual landscapes are a fascinating topic, but what about ritual soundscapes and "smellscapes"?[6] Anybody who has ever heard the muezzin's call as the sun goes down, or been woken by it at the crack of dawn — or, for that matter, anybody who has even heard a churchbell ring on Sunday morning — knows the importance of sound in establishing a ritual topography. Smell, touch, and taste have their places as well. A sweaty, jostling crowd; the sound of a victim's demise; the stink of its blood, or of incense or smoke; a thirsty procession ending in a drink — these too are integral to the spatialization of ritual. To be sure, there are significant practical difficulties to mounting arguments about the full range of the ancient sensorium. Yet it may be helpful merely to raise the question, if only because it is a reminder of how incomplete our evidence is, hence how theory-laden our conclusions are. Even to talk about space in bodily terms, near and far, before and behind, will be reductive and impoverished if we conceive those spatial relations exclusively in visual terms.

---

[6] See, e.g., Hung 2005, ch. 4; Drobnick 2006.

We need the transit and the grid, and we need the ancient texts. Yet if we do not attend to the phenomenology of sacred space, but constitute it from the outset in the absolute terms of the measured site plan, then we risk begging the question of cosmic symbolism. Exactly because we will have based our research from the outset on an abstract structuring principle — will have made it *cosmic*, so to speak — the results will inevitably be the symbol of our own disciplinary *kosmos*.

Bibliography

Casey, Edward S.
  2001   "Between Geography and Philosophy: What Does It Mean to Be in the Place-world?" *Annals of the Association of American Geographers* 91: 683–93.

Drobnick, Jim, editor
  2006   *The Smell Culture Reader.* New York: Berg.

Finkelberg, Aryeh
  1998   "On the History of the Greek ΚΟΣΜΟΣ." *Harvard Studies in Classical Philology* 98: 103–36.

Graham, Daniel W.
  2010   *The Texts of Early Greek Philosophy: The Complete Fragments and Selected Testimonies of the Major Presocratics.* Cambridge: Cambridge University Press.

Hung, Wu
  2006   *Remaking Beijing.* Chicago: University of Chicago Press.

Neils, Jennifer
  2001   *The Parthenon Frieze.* New York: Cambridge University Press.

Marconi, Clemente
  2004   "Kosmos: The Imagery of the Archaic Greek Temple." *Res: Anthropology and Aesthetics* 45: 209–24.